Child Welfare Law and Practice

Representing Children, Parents, and State Agencies in Abuse, Neglect, and Dependency Cases

Marvin Ventrell & Donald N. Duquette

General Editors

Angela McAdory

BRADFORD PUBLISHING COMPANY
Denver, Colorado

DISCLAIMER

This book is intended to provide general information with regard to the subject matter covered. It is not meant to provide legal opinions or to offer advice, nor to serve as a substitute for advice by licensed, legal, or other professionals. This book is sold with the understanding that Bradford Publishing Company and the author(s), by virtue of its publication, are not engaged in rendering legal or other professional services to the reader.

Bradford Publishing Company and the author(s) do not warrant that the information contained in this book is complete or accurate, and do not assume and hereby disclaim any liability to any person for any loss or damage caused by errors, inaccuracies, omissions, or usage of this book.

Laws, and interpretations of those laws, change frequently, and the subject matter of this book can have important legal consequences that may vary from one individual to the next. It is therefore the responsibility of the reader to know whether, and to what extent, this information is applicable to his or her situation, and if necessary, to consult legal, tax, or other counsel.

Library of Congress Cataloging-in-Publication Data

Child welfare law and practice : representing children, parents, and state agencies in abuse, neglect, and dependency cases / Marvin Ventrell & Donald N. Duquette, general editors.
    p. cm.
Includes bibliographical references and index.
ISBN 1-932779-14-0
1. Children—Legal status, laws, etc.—United States. I. Ventrell, Marvin R., 1959- II. Duquette, Donald N. III. Title.

KF3735.Z9C47 2005
344.7303'27--dc22

                                 2005010085

Second Printing

Published 2005 by Bradford Publishing Company
1743 Wazee Street, Denver, Colorado 80202
www.bradfordpublishing.com

ABOUT THE EDITORS

Marvin Ventrell, J.D.

Marvin Ventrell has been the chief executive officer of the National Association of Counsel for Children (NACC) since January, 1994. From 1985 to 1994 he was in private practice, where he represented hundreds of children in both delinquency and dependency cases. He is the recipient of the ABA National Child Advocacy Award and the Kempe Award. He is a member of the Colorado and Montana Bar Associations, a Fellow of the Colorado Bar Foundation, and has served as a juvenile law consultant to numerous organizations including the U.S. Department of Health and Human Services, the National Council of Juvenile and Family Court Judges, the American Bar Association, and the Kempe Children's Center. He serves on the editorial staff of the *Children's Legal Rights Journal* and as reviewer for *Child Abuse & Neglect, the International Journal*. He is editor of the NACC's *Guardian* and annual *Children's Law Manual*. He is a trial skills trainer for the National Institute of Trial Advocacy and a lecturer in child welfare and juvenile justice trainings. He is the author of numerous articles and book chapters regarding children and the law. He co-authored the *ABA (NACC Revised) Standards of Practice for Lawyers Who Represent Children in Abuse and Neglect Cases* and the *NACC Recommendations for Representation of Children in Abuse and Neglect Cases.*

Donald N. Duquette, J.D.

Donald Duquette is Clinical Professor of Law and Director of the Child Advocacy Law Clinic at the University of Michigan Law School, where he has taught since 1976. In 1997-98, Professor Duquette spent a sabbatical year in Washington, D.C., at the U.S. Children's Bureau, where he drafted *Permanency for Children: Guidelines for Public Policy and State Legislation*, as part of President Clinton's Adoption 2002 Initiative on Adoption and Foster Care. He has written and taught extensively on interdisciplinary approaches to child welfare law and has published over 40 articles and book chapters on the subjects of child protection, foster care, and child advocacy. Professor Duquette has received many awards, including the NACC Outstanding Legal Advocacy Award, the North American Council on Adoptable Children Adoption Activist Award, and the Gerald G. Hicks Child Welfare Leadership Award from the Michigan Federation of Private Child and Family Agencies. He serves as a member of the NACC Board of Directors.

CONTRIBUTING AUTHORS

Sue Badeau, B.A., is the Deputy Director of the Pew Commission on Children in Foster Care. She has been a child welfare professional for over 22 years and was a Public Policy Fellow in the U.S. Senate in 1999.

Katherine Brady, J.D., is a staff attorney at the Immigration Legal Resource Center in San Francisco, California and the author of several manuals and articles about immigration law. She is the director of the ILRC National Project on Immigrant Children.

Donald C. Bross, J.D., Ph.D., is Legal Counsel and Education Director of the Kempe Children's Center in Denver, Colorado.

Amanda George Donnelly, J.D., is a Staff Attorney at the National Association of Counsel for Children (NACC).

Donald N. Duquette, J.D., is Clinical Professor of Law and Director of the Child Advocacy Law Clinic of the University of Michigan Law School. He is also a member of the National Association of Counsel for Children (NACC) Board of Directors.

Donna Furth, J.D., is a member of the Board of Directors of the National Association of Counsel for Children (NACC), a member of the NACC Certification Project Advisory Board, and an officer of the Northern California Association of Counsel for Children. She practices child welfare law, with an emphasis on appellate matters, and teaches at the University of San Francisco School of Law.

Sarah Gesiriech is the Special Assistant to the Deputy Director of the U.S. Department of Health and Human Services. Previously she worked as the Associate Director at the Domestic Policy Council for the White House.

Lisa A. Granik, J.D., was a staff attorney at the ABA Center on Children and the Law and author of the First Edition of *Representing Parents in Child Welfare Cases: A Basic Introduction for Attorneys.*

Ann M. Haralambie, J.D., is a certified family law specialist practicing in Tucson, Arizona. She is also an author and speaker in the fields of family and children's law.

Karen Aileen Howze, J.D., is a Magistrate Judge, Superior Court of the District of Columbia.

Terri James-Banks, M.S.W., L.C.S.W., is Director of the Community Caring Program at the Kempe Children's Center in Denver, Colorado.

Stacy A. Klapper, Psy.D., is a licensed clinical psychologist, specializing in infant mental health. Dr. Klapper is on the faculty of the Irving Harris Program in Child Development and Infant Mental Heath at the University of Colorado Health Sciences Center. She is the team psychologist for the Infant Program at the Kempe Children's Center/Children's Hospital in Denver, Colorado, and she maintains a small private practice.

Mimi Laver, J.D., is Assistant Director of Child Welfare at the ABA Center on Children and the Law, Washington, D.C. She previously was a Deputy City Solicitor representing the Department of Human Services and the Department of Health in Philadelphia, Pennsylvania.

Christina Little, Ph.D., is a licensed psychologist and the Director of Research and Evaluation for the Infants in Foster & Kinship Care Program at the Kempe Children's Center, Department of Pediatrics, University of Colorado School of Medicine.

Steven Lubet, J.D., is Professor of Law at Northwestern University School of Law in Chicago, Illinois.

Kathleen McNaught, J.D., is a staff attorney at the ABA Center on Children and the Law in Washington D.C.

John E.B. Myers, J.D., is Professor of Law at University of the Pacific, McGeorge School of Law.

Bernard P. Perlmutter, J.D., is Director and Clinical Instructor of Law at the Children & Youth Law Clinic, an in-house legal clinic at the University of Miami School of Law. He is also a Clinical Fellow at the law school's Center for Ethics and Public Service.

Diane Boyd Rauber, M.Ed., J.D., has co-authored or edited several ABA Center on Children and the Law publications, including the COURT IMPROVEMENT PROGRESS REPORTS, A JUDGE'S GUIDE: MAKING CHILD-CENTERED DECISIONS IN CUSTODY CASES, and REPRESENTING PARENTS IN CHILD WELFARE CASES.

Jennifer Renne, J.D., is Assistant Director of Child Welfare at the ABA Center on Children and the Law in Washington, D.C.

Colene Flynn Robinson, J.D., is a private practitioner representing children in Dependency Court in Denver, Colorado. From 2001 to 2004 she was Senior Staff Attorney at the National Association of Counsel for Children.

Miriam Rollin, J.D., is the Policy Representative for the National Association of Counsel for Children in Washington, D.C.

Carolyn S. Salisbury, J.D., is Associate Director and Instructor of Law at the Law School's Children & Youth Law Clinic. She teaches classes in Children and the Law, Public Interest Advocacy and Ethics, Community Justice and Ethics, and Legal Research and Writing. She also serves as Co-Director of the law school's Public Interest Law Summer Program.

Frank Vandervort, J.D., is Clinical Assistant Professor of Law at the Child Advocacy Law Clinic of the University of Michigan Law School.

Marvin Ventrell, J.D., is the President/CEO of the National Association of Counsel for Children (NACC).

TABLE OF CONTENTS

About the Editors iii

Contributing Authors v

Foreword. xxix

Introduction xxxiii

I. THE CONTEXT OF CHILD WELFARE LAW

Chapter 1   AMERICA'S CHILDREN 1
  § 1.1 Who Are America's Children and How Are They Doing? 1
    § 1.1.1 Indicators of Well-Being 2
      Living Arrangements 2
      Educational Attainment of Parents 3
      Poverty 4
      Health Insurance 4
  § 1.2 Child Maltreatment 4
    § 1.2.1 Poverty, Race, and Child Maltreatment 6
    § 1.2.2 America's Children in Foster Care 7
      The Current System 8
      Challenges Faced by Foster Children 9
      Improving the System 11
    § 1.2.3 The Impact of Child Maltreatment on America 12
      Crime 12
      Economic Impact 13
      The Advocate's Role in Promoting Systemic Improvement 13

Chapter 2   PHYSICAL, SEXUAL, AND EMOTIONAL CHILD
      ABUSE AND NEGLECT 15
  § 2.1 Physical Abuse 15
    § 2.1.1 Fractures 16
    § 2.1.2 Bruises 17
    § 2.1.3 Lacerations 19
    § 2.1.4 Burns 19
    § 2.1.5 Internal (Abdominal and Thoracic) Injuries 21
    § 2.1.6 Abusive Head Trauma 22
    § 2.1.7 Munchausen by Proxy Syndrome 23
    § 2.1.8 Medical Ramifications 24
  § 2.2 Sexual Abuse 24
    § 2.2.1 Intrafamilial Child Sexual Abuse 24
    § 2.2.2 Pedophilia 25
    § 2.2.3 Diagnosing Sexual Abuse 27
  § 2.3 Emotional Abuse 28
  § 2.4 Neglect 30
    § 2.4.1 Emotional Neglect 30
    § 2.4.2 Physical Neglect 30
    § 2.4.3 Medical Neglect 31

§ 2.4.4 Failure to Thrive 32
§ 2.4.5 Educational Neglect 33

**Chapter 3 MENTAL HEALTH AND RELATED PROFESSIONAL
EVALUATIONS IN CHILD WELFARE PROCEEDINGS** 35
§ 3.1 Introduction 35
§ 3.2 Mental Health Professionals 36
§ 3.2.1 Psychiatrists 37
§ 3.2.2 Psychologists 37
§ 3.2.3 Social Workers 38
§ 3.2.4 Evidentiary Privilege and Confidentiality 38
§ 3.3 Evaluations 38
§ 3.3.1 Evaluating the Evaluation 39
§ 3.3.2 Mental Health Evaluations 40
§ 3.3.3 Parent-Child Relationship Evaluations 41
§ 3.4 Psychological Tests 43
§ 3.4.1 Psychometric Tests 44
§ 3.4.2 Personality Tests 45
§ 3.4.3 Projective Tests 45
§ 3.4.4 Developmental and Intelligence Tests 46
§ 3.4.5 Neuropsychological Tests 47
§ 3.4.6 Achievement Tests 47
§ 3.4.7 Checklists and Inventories 48
§ 3.4.8 Scoring and Interpreting Test Results 48
§ 3.5 Child Sexual Abuse Evaluations 49
§ 3.6 Conclusion 51

**Chapter 4 THE IMPACT OF MALTREATMENT ON CHILD
DEVELOPMENT** 53
§ 4.1 Child Development 53
§ 4.1.1 Physical Development 56
§ 4.1.2 Cognitive Development 57
§ 4.1.3 Language Development 60
§ 4.1.4 Social and Emotional Child Development 61
Stage 1 – Basic Trust vs. Mistrust 62
Stage 2 – Autonomy vs. Shame and Guilt 63
Stage 3 – Initiative vs. Self-Doubt 65
Stage 4 – Industry vs. Inferiority 67
Stage 5 – Identity vs. Role Confusion 68
§ 4.1.5 Attachment, Separation, and Loss 70
§ 4.2 Long-term Effects of Maltreatment 73
§ 4.3 Importance of Developmental Level for Child Abuse/Neglect Issues . . . 74
§ 4.3.1 Communicating with the Child 75
§ 4.4 Conclusion 76

Chapter 5 FAMILY DYNAMICS IN CHILD MALTREATMENT 79
§ 5.1 Introduction 79
§ 5.2 Circumstances in Which Child Maltreatment Occurs 79
§ 5.2.1 Lack of Empathy 80
§ 5.2.2 "Trigger" Behaviors 81

§ 5.2.3 Domestic Violence 81
§ 5.2.4 Substance Abuse. 82
§ 5.2.5 Mental Conditions; Postnatal Depression 82
§ 5.2.6 Isolation 82
§ 5.3 Perspectives for Understanding Abusive or Neglectful Parenting 83
§ 5.3.1 Psychodynamic Theory and Practice. 83
§ 5.3.2 Social and Economic Ecology 83
§ 5.3.3 Biology 84
§ 5.3.4 Developmental Psychopathology. 84
§ 5.3.5 Conclusions 84
§ 5.4 Consequences of Maltreatment. 85
§ 5.5 Treatment for Abused and Neglected Children 86
§ 5.6 Treatment for Parents. 88
§ 5.6.1 Treatment Goals 88
§ 5.6.2 Effectiveness of Voluntary and Court-Ordered Treatment. 88
§ 5.6.3 Measuring Change in Parenting Capacity 90
§ 5.6.4 Parents Who Are the Most Difficult to Treat 91
§ 5.7 Decisions Regarding Placement, Reunification, and Termination 93
§ 5.8 Summary 93

**Chapter 6   CULTURAL CONTEXT IN ABUSE AND NEGLECT
PRACTICE: TIPS FOR ATTORNEYS** 95
§ 6.1 Introduction 95
§ 6.2 Defining Cultural and Subcultural Context. 95
§ 6.3 The Players 97
§ 6.3.1 Parents' Attorney 97
§ 6.3.2 Guardians Ad Litem 97
§ 6.4 Beginning the Process. 98
§ 6.4.1 Begin at the Commencement of the Case 99
§ 6.4.2 Beginning the Questioning Process. 99
§ 6.5 At the Initial Hearing 100
§ 6.6 Between Disposition and the First Permanency Hearing. 102
§ 6.7 From the First Permanency Hearing through Case Resolution 104
§ 6.8 APPLA is the Final Option. 108
§ 6.9 Conclusion. 110

II. THE LEGAL FRAMEWORK OF CHILD WELFARE LAW

Chapter 7   THE HISTORY OF CHILD WELFARE LAW 113
§ 7.1 Introduction 113
§ 7.2 Dependency Court Jurisdiction. 113
§ 7.3 Origins of Child Maltreatment and Protection. 115
§ 7.3.1 Maltreatment. 115
§ 7.3.2 Child Protection 116
§ 7.3.3 Sixteenth- and Seventeenth-Century England: Creation of
a System of Family Law. 117
Family Law for the Wealthy 118
Family Law for the Poor 118
§ 7.3.4 Colonial America: Transplanting and Developing the
English System 120

§ 7.3.5 Nineteenth-Century America: The Rise of the
Parens Patriae System 123
The House of Refuge Movement. 124
Ex parte Crouse and *Parens Patriae*. 126
Special Cases of Child Abuse 128
A Scientific Development 132
§ 7.3.6 The Juvenile Court: Institutionalizing and Developing the
Parens Patriae System 132
Founding and Dependency Philosophy 132
Gault and the Transformation of Delinquency out from
Parens Patriae 135
"The Battered Child," CAPTA, and the Evolution of Dependency
Within *Parens Patriae* 135
The Dependency Court at the Beginning of the
Twenty-First Century 139
§ 7.4 Conclusion. 142

Chapter 8 FEDERAL CHILD WELFARE LAW AND POLICY:
UNDERSTANDING THE FEDERAL LAW AND FUNDING
PROCESS 143
§ 8.1 Introduction to Federal Child Welfare Funding Legislation 143
§ 8.2 Timeline of Major Federal Child Welfare Legislation. 145
§ 8.3 Summary of Federal Funding Sources for Child Abuse and Neglect. . . . 146
§ 8.3.1 Foster Care Reimbursements to States. 146
§ 8.3.2 Adoption Assistance Reimbursements to States 147
§ 8.3.3 Promoting Safe and Stable Families Program (PSSF) 147
§ 8.3.4 Child Welfare Services Program 147
§ 8.3.5 Chafee Foster Care Independence Program 147
§ 8.3.6 Child Abuse Prevention and Treatment Act Programs (CAPTA) . . 148
§ 8.3.7 Other Smaller Federal Funding Sources. 148
§ 8.4 Key Federal Statutory Requirements. 149
§ 8.4.1 The Child Abuse Prevention and Treatment Act 149
§ 8.4.2 Titles IV-B and IV-E of the Social Security Act 151
Adoption Assistance and Child Welfare Act of 1980. 152
§ 8.4.3 The Indian Child Welfare Act 157
Jurisdiction and Standing 157
Application 158
Notice 158
Higher Standards of Evidence 159
Placement. 160
Failure to Comply. 160
Inapplicable to Some Native American Children 160
§ 8.4.4 The Multi-Ethnic Placement Act. 161
Application 161
Enforcement 162
§ 8.4.5 Special Immigrant Juvenile Status. 163
§ 8.4.6 The Foster Care Independence Act (Chafee) 164
§ 8.5 Other Relevant Federal and Uniform Statutes 166
§ 8.5.1 The Uniform Child Custody Jurisdiction and Enforcement Act . . . 166

§ 8.5.2 The Parental Kidnapping Prevention Act 167
§ 8.5.3 Accessing Substance Abuse Treatment Records 168
§ 8.5.4 Health Insurance Portability and Accountability Act of 1996
    (HIPAA) 169
§ 8.5.5 Americans with Disabilities Act of 1990 (ADA) 170
§ 8.5.6 Individuals with Disabilities Education Act (IDEA)............. 171
§ 8.5.7 Education for Homeless Children and Youths Act 172
§ 8.5.8 Children's Health Act of 2000 173
§ 8.5.9 Family Education Rights and Privacy Act of 1974 (FERPA)...... 173
§ 8.6 Current Federal Funding for Other Supports for Children and
Families.. 174
§ 8.6.1 Temporary Assistance for Needy Families (TANF).............. 175
§ 8.6.2 Medicaid.. 175
    Eligibility 176
    Benefits.. 176
§ 8.6.3 State Children's Health Insurance Program (SCHIP) 176
§ 8.6.4 Supplemental Security Income (SSI) 177
    Eligibility 177
§ 8.6.5 Other Federally Sponsored Assistance........................ 177
    Nutrition Assistance Programs.................................... 178
    Section 8 Housing Assistance 178
    Child Care and Development Block Grant (CCDBG) 178
    Head Start 178
    Post-Secondary Education Loans, Grants, and Work-Study.......... 179
    Block Grants to States and Localities 179
    Other Federal Laws 180
§ 8.7 Sally's Case: Applying Selected Federal Funding Streams and
Statutory Requirements.. 181

Chapter 9   CHILD WELFARE CONSTITUTIONAL CASE LAW 185
§ 9.1 Parent's Rights 185
§ 9.1.1 *Meyer v. Nebraska*.. 185
§ 9.1.2 *Pierce v. Society of Sisters* 186
§ 9.1.3 *Prince v. Massachusetts* 186
§ 9.1.4 *Troxel v. Granville*.. 187
§ 9.2 Constitutional Rights of Children and Youth 188
§ 9.2.1 *In re Gault* 188
§ 9.2.2 *Tinker v. Des Moines Independent Community School Dist.*........ 190
§ 9.2.3 *Bellotti v. Baird* 190
§ 9.2.4 *Wisconsin v. Yoder* 191
§ 9.2.5 *Parham v. J.R.* 192
§ 9.3 Children Born out of Wedlock / Right of Putative Fathers 192
§ 9.3.1 *Stanley v. Illinois* 192
§ 9.3.2 *Quilloin v. Walcott*.. 193
§ 9.3.3 *Caban v. Mohammed* 194
§ 9.3.4 *Lehr v. Robertson* 195
§ 9.3.5 *Michael H. v. Gerald D.*.. 196
§ 9.4 Termination of Parental Rights................................... 197
§ 9.4.1 *Lassiter v. Dept. of Social Services* 197

§ 9.4.2 *Santosky v. Kramer* 198
§ 9.4.3 *M.L.B. v. S.L.J.* 198
§ 9.5 Foster Parent Relationships 199
§ 9.5.1 *Smith v. Org. of Foster Families for Equality & Reform* 199
§ 9.6 State Agency Duties 201
§ 9.6.1 *DeShaney v. Winnebago County Dept. of Social Services* 201
§ 9.6.2 *Youngberg v. Romeo* 202
§ 9.6.3 *Suter v. Artist M.* 203
§ 9.7 Access to Child Protective Service's Records 204
§ 9.7.1 *Pennsylvania v. Ritchie* 204
§ 9.8 Social Security Benefits for Children in Foster Care 205
§ 9.8.1 *Washington State Dept. of Social and Health Services v.*
Guardianship Estate of Keffeler 205
§ 9.9 Indian Child Welfare Act 205
§ 9.9.1 *Mississippi Band of Choctaw Indians v. Holyfield* 205
§ 9.10 Children's Statements and Testimony 206
§ 9.10.1 *Crawford v. Washington* 207
§ 9.10.2 *Coy v. Iowa* 207
§ 9.10.3 *White v. Illinois* 208
§ 9.10.4 *Maryland v. Craig* 208
§ 9.10.5 *Idaho v. Wright* 209
§ 9.11 Parent's Right against Self-incrimination in Child Protection Cases . . . 210
§ 9.11.1 *Baltimore City Dept. of Social Services v. Bouknight* 210

III. THE CHILD WELFARE LEGAL PROCESS

Chapter 10   A CHILD'S JOURNEY THROUGH THE CHILD
WELFARE SYSTEM 213
§ 10.1 Introduction 213
§ 10.2 Reporting Child Maltreatment 216
§ 10.3 Reporting by Professionals 217
§ 10.4 Reporting by Nonprofessionals 218
§ 10.4.1 Good Faith: Immunity from Civil Liability 218
§ 10.4.2 Liability for Making False or Malicious Report 219
§ 10.5 Investigating Child Maltreatment 219
§ 10.5.1 Time Frame 219
§ 10.5.2 Risk Assessment 220
§ 10.5.3 Safety Assessment 221
§ 10.5.4 Investigating Evidence of Child Maltreatment 221
§ 10.5.5 Interpreting Labels of "Founded" or "Unfounded" on
Agency Reports 222
§ 10.5.6 Emergency Protective Custody 222
§ 10.6 Initiating Court Action 223
§ 10.7 Emergency Removal/Detention 224
§ 10.8 Pretrial Discovery and Motion Practice 225
§ 10.9 Adjudication 225
§ 10.10 Disposition 226
§ 10.11 Case Plans 228

§ 10.12 Review Hearings 229
§ 10.13 Permanency Hearings. 230
§ 10.14 Termination of Parental Rights. 232
§ 10.15 Post-Termination Review Hearings 233
§ 10.16 Achieving Permanence for the Child. 233

Chapter 11   DEPENDENCY COURT JURISDICTION AND INTERSTATE
        AND INTERNATIONAL PROCEEDINGS. 235
§ 11.1 Jurisdiction of the Dependency Court and Collateral Courts 235
§ 11.2 Causes of Action 235
§ 11.3 Party Status and Standing 236
§ 11.4 Interstate Proceedings. 237
    § 11.4.1 Interstate Compact on the Placement of Children (ICPC). 237
    § 11.4.2 Interstate Compact on Adoption and Medical Assistance
        (ICAMA). 237
    § 11.4.3 Interstate Compact on Mental Health (ICMH) 237
    § 11.4.4 Uniform Child Custody Jurisdiction Act (UCCJA). 238
    § 11.4.5 Uniform Child Custody Jurisdiction and Enforcement Act
        (UCCJEA). 238
    § 11.4.6 Uniform Child Witness Testimony by Alternative Methods
        Act (UCWTAMA). 240
§ 11.5 International Proceedings 242
    § 11.5.1 Hague Convention on the International Aspects of Civil Child
        Abduction (Hague Convention on Child Abduction) 242
    § 11.5.2 Hague Convention on Protection of Children and Co-operation
        in Respect of Intercountry Adoption (Hague Convention on
        Intercountry Adoption). 244
    § 11.5.3 United Nations Protocol to Prevent, Suppress and Punish
        Trafficking in Persons, Especially Women and Children,
        supplementing the United Nations Convention against
        Transnational Organized Crime. 245

Chapter 12   COLLATERAL PROCEEDINGS. 247
Part 12A: Delinquency. 247
    § 12A.1 Delinquency and Status Offenses 247

Part 12B: Criminal Proceedings 248
    § 12B.1 Interface Between Civil Child Protection and Criminal
        Prosecution 248
    § 12B.2 The Child's Attorney or Guardian Ad Litem in the
        Criminal Case 251
    § 12B.3 Protective Orders 252

Part 12C: Divorce, Child Custody, and Visitation Proceedings. 252
    § 12C.1 Staying Together or Divorcing 252
    § 12C.2 Child Welfare and Family Court Interaction 255
    § 12C.3 Coordinating Legal Proceedings 256

Part 12D: Domestic Violence 257
    § 12D.1 Domestic Violence 257

Part 12E: Guardianships 259
   § 12E.1 Guardianships 259

Part 12F: Immigration—Representing Children Who Are Not
   United States Citizens. 260
   § 12F.1 Introduction 260
   § 12F.1.1 What is Special Immigrant Juvenile Status? 261
   § 12F.1.2 What are the Benefits and Risks of Applying? 261
   § 12F.1.3 What are the Requirements for Special Immigrant
      Juvenile Status? 261
   § 12F.1.4 What is the Procedure for Applying? 261
   § 12F.1.5 When Must the Child Apply and How Long Does the
      Process Take? 262
   § 12F.1.6 What Cases Carry a Risk of Being Denied? 262
   § 12F.1.7 Technical Assistance for SIJS 262

Part 12G: Advocacy for Foster Youth in Mental Health Commitment
   Proceedings 263
   § 12G.1 Introduction. 263
   § 12G.2 Background 264
   § 12G.3 The Legal Framework 265
      § 12G.3.1 *Parham v. J.R.* 265
      § 12G.3.2 State Laws 269
      § 12G.3.3 Provisions Governing Psychiatric Commitment of Foster
         Children 270
   § 12G.4 Therapeutic Jurisprudence Considerations 271
   § 12G.5 Ethical Role and Responsibilities of the Child's Attorney 274
      § 12G.5.1 Lawyer as Counselor 275
      § 12G.5.2 Lawyer as Negotiator and Mediator 276
      § 12G.5.3 Lawyer as Zealous Advocate 277
   § 12G.6 Protection of Children's Rights Within Residential Treatment
      Centers and Hospitals 278
   § 12G.7 Advocacy for Other Legal Entitlements and Services for the Child . . 280
   § 12G.8 Conclusion 282

Part 12H: Educational Advocacy 283
   § 12H.1 Introduction. 283
   § 12H.2 Preliminary Steps 284
      § 12H.2.1 What Signs Should I Look for That a Child Needs Special
         Education Services? 284
      § 12H.2.2 What Do I Do if I Suspect a Child Needs Special Education
         Services, But is Not Yet Identified? 284
   § 12H.3 Education Decision Makers 286
      § 12H.3.1 How Do I Determine Who Can Act as the Parent or if a
         Surrogate Parent is Needed? 286
      § 12H.3.2 Who Can Be Appointed as a Surrogate for a Child in
         Foster Care? 287
      § 12H.3.3 How Can a Foster Parent Be the Education Decision Maker? . . 288

§ 12H.4 Special Education Process 289
§ 12H.4.1 When Should an Eligibility Meeting Occur and What
Should Happen at the Meeting to Determine Eligibility for
Special Education Services? 289
§ 12H.4.2 Who is Part of the Individualized Education Program
(IEP) Team? 291
§ 12H.4.3 What is an Individualized Education Program (IEP) and
How Should it Be Developed?.................................. 292
§ 12H.4.4 How Should I Prepare for an IEP Meeting? 294
Before the Meeting... 294
At the Meeting 294
§ 12H.5 Monitoring and Implementation 295
§ 12H.5.1 What Do I Do if I Suspect a Child is Identified with the
Wrong Disability?.. 295
§ 12H.5.2 How Should I Monitor the Student's Progress and the
Implementation of the IEP?.................................. 296
§ 12H.5.3 What If I Do Not Agree with the Decision Reached by the
IEP Team?.. 296
§ 12H.6 Conclusion 297

**Chapter 13 CONFIDENTIALITY OF JUVENILE COURT
PROCEEDINGS AND RECORDS** 299
§ 13.1 Introduction 299
§ 13.2 Historical Background 299
§ 13.3 Benefits of Open Court Proceedings 300
§ 13.4 Arguments Against Open Court Proceedings 302
§ 13.5 The NACC's Position 303

Chapter 14 SPECIAL EVIDENTIARY ISSUES 305
§ 14.1 Selected Evidence Issues 305
§ 14.2 Expert Testimony.. 305
§ 14.2.1 Qualifications to Testify as Expert Witness 305
§ 14.2.2 Bases for Expert Opinion 306
§ 14.3 Syndrome Evidence.. 307
§ 14.3.1 Battered Child Syndrome 309
§ 14.3.2 Battering Parent Syndrome 311
§ 14.3.3 Munchausen Syndrome by Proxy 311
§ 14.3.4 Shaken Baby Syndrome 313
§ 14.3.5 Posttraumatic Stress Disorder 314
§ 14.3.6 Posttraumatic Stress Disorder in Litigation................... 315
§ 14.3.7 Acute Distress Disorder 317
§ 14.3.8 Child Sexual Abuse Accommodation Syndrome 318
§ 14.3.9 Parental Alienation Syndrome............................. 318
§ 14.4 Evidentiary Privileges and Confidentiality 320

Chapter 15 CHILDREN IN COURT 323
§ 15.1 Introduction 323
§ 15.2 Suggestibility... 323
§ 15.2.1 Age and Suggestibility.................................... 323

§ 15.2.2 Questioning by Authority Figures; The Social Demands
of Interviews 325
§ 15.2.3 Central Details vs. Peripheral Details...................... 325
§ 15.2.4 Ambiguous Body Touch 326
§ 15.2.5 Participant vs. Bystander................................ 326
§ 15.2.6 Negative Stereotypes and Accusatory Atmosphere 326
§ 15.2.7 Lowering Suggestibility 328
§ 15.3 Testimonial Competence 329
§ 15.3.1 Capacity to Observe.................................... 330
§ 15.3.2 Memory 330
§ 15.3.3 Capacity to Communicate............................... 330
§ 15.3.4 Intelligence... 330
§ 15.3.5 Understanding the Difference Between Truth and Falsehood.... 330
§ 15.3.6 Duty to Testify Truthfully 331
§ 15.3.7 Burden of Proof Regarding Testimonial Competence.......... 332
§ 15.3.8 Oath or Affirmation.................................... 332
§ 15.4 The Effects of Testifying on Children: Psychological Research 333
§ 15.5 While Children are on the Witness Stand 333
§ 15.5.1 Emotional Support..................................... 334
§ 15.5.2 Preparing Children to Testify............................ 334
§ 15.5.3 Scheduling a Young Child's Testimony 334
§ 15.5.4 Leading on Direct...................................... 334
§ 15.5.5 Testimonial Aids....................................... 335
§ 15.5.6 Allowing a Child Witness a Comfort Item.................. 335
§ 15.5.7 Recesses During Child's Testimony....................... 335
§ 15.6 Hearsay 335
§ 15.6.1 Hearsay Defined....................................... 336
§ 15.6.2 Exceptions to the Hearsay Rule........................... 336
Prior Inconsistent Statements............................. 337
Prior Consistent Statements 337
Charge of Fabrication 338
Impeachment by Contradiction 338
Impeachment by Evidence of Untruthful Character 338
Impeachment with Prior Inconsistent Statements............. 339
Impeachment Charging Lapse of Memory.................... 339
Present Sense Impressions 339
Excited Utterances....................................... 340
Fresh Complaint of Rape or Sexual Abuse 341
Diagnosis or Treatment Exception 342
Residual and Child Hearsay Exceptions..................... 342
§ 15.6.3 Hearsay and the Confrontation Clause..................... 344
§ 15.7 Should Children Attend Court Hearings?..................... 345
§ 15.7.1 Children's Presence in their Court Proceedings: NACC Policy ... 346

Chapter 16   NON-ADVERSARIAL CASE RESOLUTION 349
§ 16.1 Introduction 349
§ 16.2 Mediation 350
§ 16.2.1 Definition... 350
§ 16.2.2 Philosophy and Principles............................... 351

§ 16.2.3 The Mediation Process 352
    Opening Statement.. 352
    Uninterrupted Time 352
    The Exchange 353
    Separate Meetings 353
    Setting the Agenda.. 353
    Building the Agreement 353
    Writing the Agreement and Closing 353
§ 16.3 Family Group Conferencing 354
    § 16.3.1 Philosophy and Principles............................ 354
    § 16.3.2 Structure of Family Group Conferencing............... 354
§ 16.4 Voluntary Relinquishment Counseling 355
§ 16.5 Uses of NACR in Child Welfare Cases 356
§ 16.6 Effectiveness of NACR 359
§ 16.7 Compromising Child Safety or Well-Being 361
§ 16.8 Conclusion.. 362

Chapter 17   ESTABLISHING LEGAL PERMANENCE FOR THE CHILD.. 363
§ 17.1 Introduction 363
§ 17.2 Principles for Permanency Options 364
§ 17.3 Adoption.. 365
    § 17.3.1 Adoption Subsidies 365
    § 17.3.2 Post-Adoption Contact 367
    State Laws 367
    Benefits and Pitfalls 368
    Elements of a Successful Post-Adoption Contact Agreement 369
    Determining Whether Post-Adoption Contact is Appropriate 369
    Enforcing the Agreement 370
§ 17.4 Permanent Guardianship 371
§ 17.5 Standby Guardianship.................................... 375
§ 17.6 Another Planned Permanent Living Arrangement.............. 376
§ 17.7 Re-establishing Parental Rights After Termination 378

Chapter 18   CHILD WELFARE APPELLATE LAW AND PRACTICE ... 381
§ 18.1 Introduction 381
§ 18.2 Initial Considerations 382
    § 18.2.1 Is the Order Appealable? 382
    The Final Judgment Rule 382
    Collateral Final Orders 382
    Interlocutory Orders Appealable by Statute 382
    Interlocutory Orders Reviewable as a Matter of Discretion......... 383
    § 18.2.2 What are the Time Limits? 384
    Time Limit for Filing Notice of Appeal 384
    Notice of Appeal Vests Jurisdiction in Appellate Court 384
    § 18.2.3 Does Your Client Have Standing?....................... 384
    § 18.2.4 Was the Error Preserved? 385
    § 18.2.5 What is the Standard of Review? 386
    Findings of Fact.. 386
    Discretionary Decisions...................................... 387

Issues of Law 387
Mixed Questions of Law and Fact 388
§ 18.2.6 Was the Error Prejudicial? 388
The Test of Prejudice 388
Federal Constitutional Errors 388
Errors that are Reversible Per Se 388
Factors in Evaluating Prejudice 389
§ 18.3 Stay Requests 389
§ 18.3.1 Effect of Filing an Appeal—Execution of the Judgment
Not Always Stayed 389
§ 18.3.2 Making the Request for a Stay 390
§ 18.3.3 Factors Considered in Ruling on a Stay Request 390
§ 18.4 Procedural Sequence on Appeal 391
§ 18.4.1 In General 391
§ 18.4.2 Appeals of Right 391
Notice of Appeal 391
The Appellate Record 391
Appellant's Opening Brief 392
Appellee's Brief 393
Appellant's Reply 393
Oral Argument 393
§ 18.4.3 Discretionary Appeals 394
§ 18.5 The Problem of Post-Judgment Events 394
§ 18.5.1 Judicial Notice 395
§ 18.5.2 Request that Additional Evidence Be Taken 396
§ 18.6 Extraordinary Writs 397
§ 18.6.1 Appellate vs. Original Jurisdiction 397
§ 18.6.2 How Writs are Different from Appeals 397
Extraordinary Nature of Writ Relief 397
Writ Review May Supplement, But Not Substitute for, an Appeal 398
Parties in a Writ Proceeding 398
Types of Traditional Writs 399
Writs Abolished in Some States 400
Statutory Writs Distinguished from Traditional Writs 400
§ 18.6.3 Procedure in Traditional Writ Proceeding 401
The Petition 401
The Reviewing Court's Alternatives 401
§ 18.7 Conclusion 402

IV. THE ROLE AND DUTIES OF LEGAL COUNSEL
IN CHILD WELFARE PROCEEDINGS

**Chapter 19 REPRESENTING THE STATE OR WELFARE AGENCY:
THE ROLE AND DUTIES OF AGENCY COUNSEL** 403
Part 19A: ABA Agency Attorney Standards 403
Introduction 403
A. Definitions 404
B. Role 405
C. Fulfillment of Obligations 408

D. Ethical and Practice Considerations 419
E. Administrative Responsibilities 421

Part 19B: Agency Attorneys and Caseworkers: Working Well Together 431
§ 19B.1 Introduction 431
§ 19B.2 Roles of Attorneys and Social Workers 432
  § 19B.2.1 Defining the Client 432
  § 19B.2.2 Remember Your Obligations 433
  § 19B.2.3 Define Responsibilities 433
  § 19B.2.4 Decide Who Calls the Shots 434
§ 19B.3 Need for Collaboration 434
  § 19B.3.1 Communication 435
  § 19B.3.2 Mutual Respect 435
  § 19B.3.3 Trust 435
  § 19B.3.4 Teamwork 436
§ 19B.4 Strengthening the Relationship 436
  § 19B.4.1 Informal Sessions 436
    Find Shared Beliefs 436
    Facilitate in Comfort 437
    Be Concrete 437
    Understand Each Others' Languages 437
    Share Basic Information 438
    Reach Outcomes 438
  § 19B.4.2 Interdisciplinary Training 438
  § 19B.4.3 Multidisciplinary Teams 439
§ 19B.5 Conclusion 439
§ 19B.6 Sample Protocol for Termination Petitions 440
**§ 19B.7 Sample Protocol for Dispute Resolution Between Agency
Attorney and Caseworker** 441
§ 19B.8 Attorney – Social Worker Responsibilities 442

**Chapter 20   REPRESENTING PARENTS: THE ROLE AND DUTIES
OF RESPONDENTS' COUNSEL** 443

**Part 20A: Representing Parents in Child Welfare Cases: A Basic
Introduction for Attorneys** 443
§ 20A.1 Introduction 443
§ 20A.2 The Role of Parents' Counsel in Child Protection Proceedings 444
  § 20A.2.1 General Responsibilities of Parents' Attorneys 444
  § 20A.2.2 The Effect of the Adoption and Safe Families Act 446
  § 20A.2.3 Pre-Trial Independent Investigation 451
  § 20A.2.4 Emergency Removal Hearing 452
  § 20A.2.5 Mediation and Alternative Dispute Resolution 454
  § 20A.2.6 Adjudication 456
  § 20A.2.7 Disposition 457
  § 20A.2.8 Review Hearings 460
  § 20A.2.9 Permanency Hearings 462
  § 20A.2.10 Termination of Parental Rights 463
  § 20A.2.11 Appeal 466

Part 20B: Incarcerated Parents 467
  § 20B.1 Right to Participate 467
    § 20B.1.1 Practice Tips 469
      Judges: 469
      Parents' Attorneys: 470
      Agency Attorneys: 470
      Children's Representatives: 470
  § 20B.2 Reasonable Efforts 471
    § 20B.2.1 Practice Tips 472
      Judges: 472
      Parents' Attorneys: 472
      Agency Attorneys: 472
      Children's Representatives: 473
  § 20B.3 Reasonable Efforts Not Required 473
    § 20B.3.1 Practice Tips 474
      Judges: 474
      Parents' Attorneys: 474
      Agency Attorneys: 475
      Children's Representatives: 475
  § 20B.4 Termination of Parental Rights 475
    § 20B.4.1 Incarceration as a Ground or Factor in TPR 475
    § 20B.4.2 Length of Incarceration 476
    § 20B.4.3 Nature of Crime 477
    § 20B.4.4 Practice Tips 478
      Judges: 478
      Parent's Attorneys: 478
      Agency Attorneys: 478
      Children's Representatives: 478
  § 20B.5 Conclusion 479
  § 20B.6 Programs 479
  § 20B.7 Literature 480

Part 20C: Representing a Parent with Diminished Capacity 481
  § 20C.1 Introduction 481
  § 20C.2 The Mason Case 481
  § 20C.3 Model Rule 1.14: Representing a Client with Diminished Capacity . . 483
    § 20C.3.1 Maintaining a Normal Client-Lawyer Relationship 483
    § 20C.3.2 Assessing Client Capacity 484
    § 20C.3.3 Viewing Capacity as a Continuum 486
    § 20C.3.4 Taking Protective Action 487
    § 20C.3.5 Appointing a Guardian 488
    § 20C.3.6 Maintaining Client Confidentiality 489
    § 20C.3.7 Eliciting the Client's Position 489
    § 20C.3.8 Advocating in and out of Court 490
  § 20C.4 Conclusion 491

Chapter 21   REPRESENTING CHILDREN AND YOUTH. 493
Part 21A: The Role and Duties of the Child's Lawyer 493
  § 21A.1 Introduction to the Representation of Children 493

§ 21A.2 Basic Lawyer Ethics: The Model Code and Model Rules. 496
§ 21A.3 The Best Interests vs. Expressed Wishes Conundrum 498
§ 21A.4 The "Child's Attorney" Response. 500
   § 21A.4.1 The ABA Standards of Practice for Lawyers Who Represent
     Children in Abuse and Neglect Cases. 501
   § 21A.4.2 The ABA (NACC Revised) Standards of Practice. 501
§ 21A.5 The "Two Distinct Roles" Response 502
§ 21A.6 The "Duties" Response 502
   § 21A.6.1 NACC Recommendation for Representation of Children in
     Abuse and Neglect Cases 502
   § 21A.6.2 The ABA Standards and NACC Revised ABA Standards
     Focus on Duties. 505
§ 21A.7 The Child's Wishes Are Always Relevant 511
§ 21A.8 Conclusion 513

Part 21B: Developmentally Appropriate Lawyering 514
§ 21B.1 Introduction. 514
§ 21B.2 Meeting With Your Child Client 514
   § 21B.2.1 Choosing a Location 515
   § 21B.2.2 Communicating at the Child's Level 515
   § 21B.2.3 Establishing Rapport and Asking Questions 517
   § 21B.2.4 Helping the Child Feel Comfortable 517
   § 21B.2.5 Being Aware of Your Own Responses. 517
   § 21B.2.6 Explaining Your Role as Attorney 518
   § 21B.2.7 Keeping Your Client Informed About the Case 518
§ 21B.3 Determining the Child's Capacity 518
§ 21B.4 The Lawyer's Duties. 519
   § 21B.4.1 Identifying Permanency Needs and Protecting Important
     Affiliations 519
   § 21B.4.2 Maintaining the Child's, Property, Records, and Social History. . 520
   § 21B.4.3 Advocating for Appropriate Closure After Termination 521

Part 21C: Special Challenges for the Child's Lawyer: Conflict of Interest,
  Attorney-Client Privilege, Waiver of Rights, and Sibling Association. 521
§ 21C.1 Conflict of Interest 521
   § 21C.1.1 Representation of Siblings 521
   Confidentiality. 523
   Waiver. 524
   § 21C.1.2 Payment of Attorney Fees by a Third Party 524
§ 21C.2 Attorney-Client Privilege 526
§ 21C.3 Waiver of Rights 527
§ 21C.4 Sibling Association 529

Part 21D: Case Assessment and Planning. 530
§ 21D.1 Introduction. 530
§ 21D.2 Investigate the Facts. 531
§ 21D.3 Develop a Theory of the Case 531
   § 21D.3.1 Preliminary Facts—A Sample Case. 532
   § 21D.3.2 Focus Questions 532
   The Role of the Child's Advocate 532

Determining the Child's Position   533
Permanency Goal   534
Stage of the Litigation   534
Cause of Action   535
The Characteristics of the Individual Child   535
The Child's Safety and Well-being.   535
Fact Analysis   535
Subjective Bias   536
§ 21D.4 Litigation Strategy   537
§ 21D.5 Conclusion   537
§ 21D.6 Child Welfare Case Checklist   538

Chapter 22   TRIAL ADVOCACY   545
Part 22A: Case Analysis   545
§ 22A.1 The Idea of a Persuasive Story   545
§ 22A.1.1 Trials as Stories   545
§ 22A.1.2 Planning a Sample Story   546
§ 22A.2 The Ethics of Persuasive Storytelling   548
§ 22A.2.1 Assuming That You "Know" the Truth.   548
§ 22A.2.2 Assuming That You Do Not Know the Truth   548
§ 22A.2.3 The Special Case of the Criminal Law   550
§ 22A.3 Preparing a Persuasive Trial Story   550
§ 22A.3.1 Developing Your Theory and Your Theme   551
Theory.   551
Theme.   551
§ 22A.3.2 Planning Your Final Argument.   552
§ 22A.3.3 Planning Your Case in Chief   552
Consider Your Potential Witnesses and Exhibits   552
Evaluate Each Witness Individually   553
Decide Which Witness to Call   553
§ 22A.3.4 Planning Your Cross Examinations   554
§ 22A.3.5 Reevaluating Everything That You Have Done   555
§ 22A.4 Conclusion   555

Part 22B: Evidentiary Foundations   556
§ 22B.1 The Requirement of Foundation   556
§ 22B.2 Components of Foundation   557
§ 22B.2.1 Relevance   557
§ 22B.2.2 Authenticity   558
§ 22B.2.3 Specific Admissibility   558
§ 22B.3 Establishing Foundations.   559
§ 22B.3.1 Using a Single Witness   559
§ 22B.3.2 Using Multiple Witnesses.   559
§ 22B.3.3 Conditional Admissibility.   560
§ 22B.3.4 Using Adverse Witnesses.   561
§ 22B.3.5 Cross Examination   562

Part 22C: Direct Examination   563
§ 22C.1 The Role of Direct Examination   563

§ 22C.1.1 Introduce Undisputed Facts. 563
§ 22C.1.2 Enhance the Likelihood of Disputed Facts. 564
§ 22C.1.3 Lay Foundations for the Introduction of Exhibits. 564
§ 22C.1.4 Reflect Upon the Credibility of Witnesses 564
§ 22C.1.5 Hold the Attention of the Trier of Fact. 565
§ 22C.2 The Law of Direct Examination. 565
§ 22C.2.1 Competence of Witnesses. 565
§ 22C.2.2 Non-leading Questions 565
§ 22C.2.3 Narratives 566
§ 22C.2.4 The Non-opinion Rule 567
§ 22C.2.5 Refreshing Recollection 567
§ 22C.3 Planning Direct Examinations 567
§ 22C.3.1 Content 568
What to Include. 568
What to Exclude 570
§ 22C.3.2 Organization and Structure 572
Start Strong and End Strong: The Overall Examination. 574
Start Strong and End Strong: The Sub-examinations. 574
Use Topical Organization 575
Do Not Interrupt the Action 576
Give Separate Attention to the Details 577
Try Not to Scatter Circumstantial Evidence 578
Defensive Direct Examination. 579
Affirmation Before Refutation. 579
Get to the Point. 580
End with a Clincher 580
Ignore Any Rule When Necessary 580
§ 22C.4 Questioning Technique 581
§ 22C.4.1 Use Short, Open Questions. 581
§ 22C.4.2 Use Directive and Transitional Questions. 581
§ 22C.4.3 Reinitiate Primacy. 583
Use General Headline Questions 583
Explain Where You Are Going 584
Use Body Movement 584
§ 22C.4.4 Use Incremental Questions 584
§ 22C.4.5 Reflect Time, Distance, Intensity 587
§ 22C.4.6 Repeat Important Points 590
§ 22C.4.7 Use Visual Aids 591
§ 22C.4.8 Avoid Negative, Lawyerly, and Complex Questions 591

Part 22D: Cross Examination 593
§ 22D.1 The Role of Cross Examination. 593
§ 22D.2 The Law of Cross Examination 594
§ 22D.2.1 Leading Questions Permitted 594
§ 22D.2.2 Limitations on Scope 594
§ 22D.2.3 Other Restrictions. 595
Argumentative Questions 595
Intimidating Behavior 595
Unfair Characterizations 595

Assuming Facts 596
Compound and Other Defective Questions. 596
§ 22D.3 The Content of Cross Examination. 596
§ 22D.3.1 Consider the Purposes of Cross Examination 597
§ 22D.3.2 Arrive at the "Usable Universe" of Cross Examination 598
The Entire Universe. 598
The Usable Universe 598
§ 22D.3.3 Risk Averse Preparation 599
§ 22D.4 The Organization of Cross Examination 601
§ 22D.4.1 Organizing Principles 601
§ 22D.4.2 Guidelines for Organization 603
Do Not Worry About Starting Strong. 604
Use Topical Organization 604
Give the Details First. 605
Scatter the Circumstantial Evidence 606
Save a Zinger for the End. 606
§ 22D.4.3 A Classic Format for Cross Examination 608
Friendly Information 608
Affirmative Information 608
Uncontrovertible Information 609
Challenging Information 609
Hostile Information 609
Zinger 609
§ 22D.5 Questioning Technique 609

Part 22E: Expert Testimony 610
§ 22E.1 Introduction 610
§ 22E.2 Standards for Expert Testimony. 611
§ 22E.2.1 Areas of Expertise. 611
§ 22E.2.2 Scope of Opinion. 612
§ 22E.2.3 Bases for Opinion 612
§ 22E.3 The Expert's Overview. 613
§ 22E.4 Offering Expert Testimony 615
§ 22E.4.1 Introduction and Foreshadowing 615
§ 22E.4.2 Qualification. 616
Technical Requirements 616
Persuasive Qualification 617
Tender of the Witness 618
§ 22E.4.3 Opinion and Theory 618
Statement of Opinion. 619
Statement of Theory. 620
§ 22E.4.4 Explanation and Support 621
Data 621
Assumptions 622
§ 22E.4.5 Theory Differentiation 622
§ 22E.4.6 Conclusion 624

Part 22F: Exhibits 625
§ 22F.1 The Role of Exhibits 625

§ 22F.2 Types of Exhibits 626
   § 22F.2.1 Real Evidence 626
   § 22F.2.2 Demonstrative Evidence 626
   § 22F.2.3 Documentary Evidence 627
§ 22F.3 Pretrial Procedures for the Admission of Exhibits 628
   § 22F.3.1 Pretrial Conferences and Orders 628
   § 22F.3.2 Motions in Limine 629
   § 22F.3.3 Stipulations 629
   § 22F.3.4 Requests to Admit 630
§ 22F.4 Offering Exhibits at Trial 630
   § 22F.4.1 Mark the Exhibit for Identification 630
   § 22F.4.2 Identify the Exhibit for Opposing Counsel 631
   § 22F.4.3 Examine the Witness on the Foundation for the Exhibit 632
      Show the Exhibit to the Witness 632
      Identify the Exhibit 632
      Complete the Foundation for the Exhibit 633
   § 22F.4.4 Offer the Exhibit Into Evidence 633
   § 22F.4.5 Publish and Use the Exhibit 634
      Publication 634
      Using the Exhibit 634

Part 22G: Making and Meeting Objections in Child Welfare Cases 636
§ 22G.1 Introduction 636
§ 22G.2 Whether to Object 637
§ 22G.3 Protocol for Objecting 637
   § 22G.3.1 Making the Objection 637
   § 22G.3.2 Meeting the Objection 638
   § 22G.3.3 Conditional Offers (FRE 104) 638
   § 22G.3.4 Offers of Proof (FRE 103) 638
§ 22G.4 Preservation of the Record for Appeal (FRE 103) 638
§ 22G.5 Objecting Before Trial: Motion in Limine 639
§ 22G.6 Making and Meeting the Objections 639
   § 22G.6.1 The General Rule 639
   § 22G.6.2 Objections as to Form 639
   § 22G.6.3 Evidentiary Objections 640

APPENDICES

**Appendix A-1: NACC Recommendations for Representation of Children
in Abuse and Neglect Cases** 647

**Appendix A-2: American Bar Association Standards of Practice
for Lawyers Who Represent Children in Abuse and Neglect Cases
(NACC Revised Version)** 667

Appendix B: Recommended Reading 711

Appendix C: Child Welfare Organizational Resources 717

FOREWORD

The Practice of Child Welfare Law: From Child Saving to Empowerment, From Cause to Profession*

by Marvin Ventrell[1]

"Child saving" is a term used to describe the work of late nineteenth-century social reformers who sought to "save" neglected, abandoned, and abused children from the effects of poverty largely brought on by the industrialization and urbanization of America.[2] The "saving" typically took the form of removal of poor children from their families and placement in Reformatories where, through an inculcation of white, protestant, middle class values, children, the child savers believed, could become proper citizens. Some of these children avoided lives of destitution because of the child savers, but there is also evidence that many children grew up without family in harsh environments that provided little respect for the individual or opportunity for quality of life.

The child savers' paternalistic and authoritarian methods do not necessarily withstand the scrutiny of modern progressive thought. While well intentioned, the child savers often exercised unbridled discretion over the lives of children and families. Due process of law was ignored and seen as an impediment to producing good outcomes. The child savers believed they knew what was best for children and had the right to implement it.

Given the benefit of historical hindsight, it is easy to criticize the child savers as self-important and misguided. Yet their sympathy for the plight of children was real and formed the basis for the child advocacy movement of the twentieth century. They were the early child advocates from which current child welfare practice has grown. They identified a cause that has now become a profession.

As we work to improve the practice of child welfare law in the twenty-first century, we should be both students and critics of the child savers. We are moved to action by the same sympathy for the plight of children in need of care, yet the experience of over a century has taught us that children deserve more than sympathy. Children also deserve fair processes that respect their autonomy and dignity as individuals, family members, and rights-based American citizens. The

---

* This work has been adapted from its original form as published in The Colorado Lawyer at: Vol 32, No. 1 (January 2003). *See* Marvin Ventrell, *From Cause to Profession: The Development of Children's Law and Practice*, 32 COLO. LAW., Vol. No. 1, p. 65 (2003).

[1] Marvin Ventrell, J.D., is President/CEO of the National Association of Counsel for Children, Denver, CO.

[2] ANTHONY M. PLATT, THE CHILD SAVERS: THE INVENTION OF DELINQUENCY (Chicago: University of Chicago Press 1969, 1977).

lesson of *In re Gault*[3] in the development of juvenile delinquency law is that due process, more than benevolent intentions, produces fair outcomes. The *Gault* decision exposed the myth of child saving and the inherent abuses of a system without due process, which ignores the rights of the individual for the pro-claimed "good of the individual."

The development of the practice of law for children is very much about the development of children from a sympathetic underclass worthy of welfare to a rights-based citizenry, capable of demanding justice through due process.[4] Children at the opening of the twenty-first century certainly do not, and most would agree should not, hold all of the rights of adults. But children have become something they were not in the nineteenth and much of the twentieth centuries—persons under the law who may demand certain things, including due process of law. This is important because the development of these rights gives rise to a legal profession to protect those rights. The historical development of children's rights teaches us a great deal about the relationship between our view of children and the quantity and quality of services we provide. Children's status can be viewed as a movement from children as property, to children as welfare recipients, to children as rights-based citizens. The degree of legal services available to children corresponds to these stages. Children viewed as property receive no legal services since property holders may do essentially as they wish with their property. Children as a welfare class will receive the services that the state chooses to grant. These services promote the state's interest or, at best, what the state views as the child's interest. But children as rights-based citizens are situated to receive the full benefit of independent legal counsel as they demand the enforcement of their rights.[5]

Although children have been occasionally represented by legal counsel throughout American history, it was not until the 1960s and 1970s that we began to see a practice of law for children. A legal specialty requires a body of law at its base, and until society and the law began to view children as having protectable legal interests, there was not much for lawyers to do.[6]

But as this body of law developed, a corresponding practice of law developed around it. The early child representatives were the lay advocates of the child saving movement. They were passionate advocates driven by a single-minded vision of what was best for children. They functioned without legal process or professional standards. While they undoubtedly helped many children, their service

---

[3] 387 U.S. 1 (1967).

[4] Marvin Ventrell, *Preface, in* ROBERT C. FELLMETH, CHILD RIGHTS & REMEDIES: HOW THE US LEGAL SYSTEM EFFECTS CHILDREN (Atlanta, GA: Clarity Press 2002).

[5] This analysis appears in Marvin Ventrell, *The Practice of Law for Children*, 66 MONT. L. REV. 1 (forthcoming Spring 2005).

[6] For a more detailed coverage of the history of the development of child welfare law, *see* Chapter 7, The History of Child Welfare Law.

was limited. That changed with the development of proceedings based on due process, and federal and state child protection law. While it is true that there has been no *Gault* decision in the federal dependency context giving children a constitutional right to legal counsel,[7] the dependency system has become a process-based system that creates important work for the lawyers representing children, parents, and state agencies.

Child protection cases are now handled in a rights-based legal process where unrepresented parties do not fair well. Ours is a system premised on the notion that competing independent advocacy produces just results. Courts' decisions are only as good as the information on which they are based. Information comes to the court through the presentation of evidence by trained legal advocates. Litigants are not qualified to "speak for themselves" in this complex arena. Children in particular are unable to speak for themselves in court. They require legal counsel, particularly when one considers that the outcomes of these proceedings involve basic human needs, family relationships, and safety decisions that can be a matter of life and death.

The challenge to provide quality legal representation for children, parents, and agencies is enormous. The most recent federal statistics show 2.6 million reports of child maltreatment involving 4.5 million children in 2002.[8] CAPTA mandates a representative for these children,[9] and many state laws require the child's representative to be an attorney.[10]

At the same time, child welfare law has become an increasingly complex area of practice that requires lawyers to not only understand complex federal and state law and procedure, but also detailed institutional information regarding child welfare funding streams, treatment and placement options, medicine, mental health, and child development. And all of this takes place in a context of devastating abuse, neglect, and poverty, which makes the work emotionally taxing.

What was once a cause has become a profession for highly trained and skilled attorneys. Child welfare law has arrived as a distinct legal specialty, as evidenced by the extensive body of state and federal law and procedure, law school curriculum, scholarship, continuing legal education, and national and state standards of practice for attorneys.

---

[7] *But see Kenny A. ex rel. Winn v. Perdue*, 218 F.R.D. 277 (N.D. Ga. 2003), a class action suit brought by foster children in DeKalb and Fulton Counties in Georgia for the counties' failure to provide adequate and effective legal representation to children in their care. The federal district court of Georgia issued an order denying the defendants' motions for summary judgment on the grounds that dependent children in Georgia have both a statutory and constitutional right to counsel.

[8] CHILDREN'S BUREAU, U.S. DEP'T OF HEALTH AND HUMAN SERVS., CHILD MALTREATMENT 2002, at iii (2004), *available at* http://www.acf.hhs.gov/programs/cb/publications/cm02/cm02.pdf.

[9] 42 U.S.C. § 5106a(b)(A)(xiii).

[10] *See* Colorado example at COLO. REV. STAT. §§ 19-1-111, 19-1-103(59).

Yet the profession is still young and underdeveloped. Children are not simply small adults, and our assumptions and rules of lawyering are not automatically transferable to the child law context. The role and duties of the child's attorney are still developing. Likewise, the nuances of representing parents and state agencies present special challenges for the child welfare attorney.

The result is that, while the practice of child welfare law has arrived as a professional legal specialty, there is much work to be done to create a high functioning system throughout the country. A critical piece in that process is a comprehensive understanding of the competencies of child welfare. This book is intended to facilitate that understanding.

INTRODUCTION

Child Welfare Law and Practice: Purpose and Use of this Publication

This book is intended to serve as a resource for agency, parent, and children's attorneys who are preparing for the NACC child welfare law certification exam. But it is more than an exam study guide. The NACC believes that the material in this book represents the body of knowledge that defines child welfare law as a specialized field of legal practice. We believe this publication can serve as a general reference for the child welfare law practitioner and as a guide to develop and deliver much needed training for child welfare lawyers throughout the country.

This book and national certification standards would not have been possible, even a few years ago. Historically, child welfare law and practice have varied significantly from state to state. Recently, however, a national model of child welfare law has emerged through a culmination of federal law and policy and through national standards of lawyer practice. From the Child Abuse Prevention and Treatment Act through the Adoption and Safe Families Act, there is now considerable federal statutory direction in this field with which states must comply in order to secure significant amounts of federal funding for child protection and child welfare services. Additionally, national standards of practice now exist for both children's and agency attorneys, and parent attorney standards are in the drafting stage. The Child and Family Service Review process conducted by the federal government has resulted in Program Improvement Plans for states across the country that further define performance standards for attorneys and call for training and education consistent with the emerging national model. While child welfare law technically remains state law, it is heavily influenced by federal policy. What was once a provincial practice, varying considerably from state to state, has increasingly become a national model of practice.

The benefit of these developments is an increasing uniformity of the legal representation of children, parents, and state agencies. Now, for the first time, it is possible to produce a meaningful national practice book and to award specialty certification based on a mastery of the knowledge and skills presented here.

Since its inception in 1977, the National Association of Counsel for Children has worked to build an effective legal workforce for the legal representation of children, families, and agencies in child welfare cases. The child advocacy movement of the 1970's gave rise to previously unknown numbers of abuse, neglect, and dependency cases, and visionaries saw the need for an organization that could train attorneys to appear in these cases. The NACC was founded to fill that need. Yet this territory, particularly the representation of very young children, was uncharted, and the work required more than providing practice tips. It required the definition and creation of a new legal discipline. From the beginning, the NACC has worked not only to provide training and technical assistance to attorneys in the field, but also to establish the practice of child welfare law as a distinct legal specialty that would produce the highest quality legal service.

Certification of lawyers as specialists in child welfare law is an important step in the evolution of this area of practice. In the same way that pediatric medicine grew from obscurity to a recognized medical specialty, the NACC has sought to grow the practice of child welfare law. Whether called juvenile law, children's law, or even pediatric law, we are, as a profession, now poised to achieve the status of a legitimate and respected field of legal practice. In the same way that physicians are board certified in pediatrics, or other attorneys are board certified specialists in certain areas of law, this publication serves as the framework for certification in child welfare law. This has come about because of the dedication of numerous local, regional, and national organizations, and the dedication of thousands of lawyers who saw the value of this work in the service of children and families in our society. They worked tirelessly, without adequate compensation or recognition, and we stand on their shoulders now, as we take the next step—certification of attorneys as child welfare law specialists.

The NACC considered the concept of child welfare law certification for many years. For the longest time, we believed that the field was not ready for this step. Initially, we did not wish to discourage any lawyer who may have been interested in the field. We wanted the field to be accessible to as many committed people as possible. Even though we identified certain requisite competencies for practice, at the early stages we were careful not to make the conditions for entry into the field too burdensome. We thought it more important to nurture the field to maturity. At the same time, our clients, and the children these legal proceedings should ultimately serve, deserve the best we can offer. There comes a time when it is appropriate to advance and improve the competencies, even though raising expectations may make it more difficult to do child welfare work and may discourage some lawyers. It is a tricky balance.

In 2000, therefore, as the field reached a certain level of maturity, the NACC launched its Child Welfare Law Certification Program designed to improve the practice of law for children by offering lawyers who wish to distinguish themselves as elite practitioners the opportunity to become branded as child welfare law specialists. We are moved by the comment of a young lawyer working at the NACC, who said in response to the argument that we should not make it too difficult to do this work: "I don't want to be part of a practice that just anyone can do." And not just anyone can do this work well. Child welfare law is complex and demanding and requires a strong work ethic, high intelligence, extensive training, and empathy for our clients. Certification is a means to cultivate those qualities. By becoming a certified child welfare specialist, lawyers identify themselves as competent for the task.

In 2002, the NACC was awarded a three-year grant from the U.S. Department of Health and Human Services Children's Bureau to create the nation's first child welfare law certification program. The grant called on the NACC to create a program infrastructure, acquire designation from the

American Bar Association as an authorized certifying body, develop certification standards, draft a certification exam, prepare certification preparation material, pilot the program in selected states, evaluate the results, and present a plan for national dissemination. In February 2004, after careful review, the American Bar Association accredited the NACC to certify lawyers in the newly defined specialty of child welfare law.

This book is something more than a primer and less than a comprehensive treatise; it covers enough areas in adequate depth for the lawyer to develop a specialist's competence. While the editors do not pretend that everything one needs to know is in this book, we do believe that if an attorney comprehends and demonstrates mastery of the theory and practice of this manual, he or she will have presented, together with meeting the other standards of certification, indicia of expertise warranting certification as a child welfare law specialist. We also encourage readers to pursue the additional resources referenced throughout the text.

The NACC is indebted to many people and agencies, including those listed as contributing authors and organizations. We thank the dedicated professionals of the U.S. Children's Bureau who recognized the promise of certification and provided the essential funding to launch this ambitious endeavor. We thank the American Bar Association Standing Committee on Specialization who guided us through the rigorous and demanding accreditation process. Special thanks are also owed to NACC Staff Attorney Amanda George Donnelly for her considerable efforts on this publication.

Finally, we are indebted to the NACC Certification National Advisory Board members who guided the production of this manual and the entire certification development process. They are listed below.

Marvin Ventrell
Editor and Certification Program Co-Director
National Association of Counsel for Children

Donald N. Duquette
Editor and Certification Program Co-Director
Child Advocacy Law Clinic, University of Michigan Law School

NACC Child Welfare Certification National Advisory Board

John H. Stuemky, M.D.
Section Chief, General Pediatrics & Pediatric
Emergency Medicine
Children's Hospital of Oklahoma
Oklahoma City, OK

Katherine Walsh, M.A.
Courseware Author
Raytheon
San Diego, CA

Christopher N. Wu, J.D.
Supervising Attorney
California Administrative Office of the Courts
Center for Families, Children and the Courts
San Francisco, CA

I. THE CONTEXT OF CHILD WELFARE LAW

Chapter 1   AMERICA'S CHILDREN

by Amanda George Donnelly[1]

§ 1.1 Who Are America's Children and How Are They Doing?

The answers to this question give context to the thousands of children who enter the child welfare system each year, and in this way, these answers inform the work of the child welfare attorney.

The condition of children in America is difficult to access. It varies from state to state, and indicators of well-being can be subjective. That said, there is much that we do know. The following section, based largely on data developed by the U.S. Bureau of the Census, provides an overview of the United States general population and children in America. It is followed by a closer look at maltreated children and a discussion about America's children in foster care.

Children make up a significant proportion of the United States population. According to the U.S. Census Bureau, the total U.S. population in 2002 was approximately 288 million people.[2] There were roughly 73 million children under the age of eighteen in the United States, approximately 25 percent of the total population.[3] Youth have made up an increasingly growing percentage of the total population since 1984, when the number of youth in America hit a three decade low of 63 million.[4] The U.S. Census Bureau estimates that the youth population will increase 8 percent between 1995 and 2015.[5] The population of other segments of society is expected to increase at greater rates. The number of persons ages 18 to 24 is expected to increase 22 percent, the number of persons aged 25 to 64 will increase 18 percent, and the number of persons over 65 is expected

---

[1] Amanda George Donnelly, J.D., is a Staff Attorney at the National Association of Counsel for Children (NACC).

[2] POPULATIONS DIV., U.S. CENSUS BUREAU, ANNUAL ESTIMATE OF THE POPULATION FOR THE UNITED STATES AND STATES, AND FOR PUERTO RICO: APRIL 1, 2000 TO JULY 1, 2004, at tbl.NST-EST2004-01 (2004), *available at* http://www.census.gov/popest/states/tables/NST-EST2004-01.pdf.

[3] CHILDREN'S BUREAU, U.S. DEP'T OF HEALTH AND HUMAN SERVS., CHILD MALTREATMENT 2002, at 4 (Washington D.C.: U.S. Government Printing Office 2004), *available at* http://www.acf.hhs.gov/programs/cb/publications/cmreports.htm.

[4] HOWARD N. SNYDER & MELISSA SICKMUND, NAT'L CTR. FOR JUVENILE JUSTICE, JUVENILE OFFENDERS AND VICTIMS: 1999 NATIONAL REPORT 2 (1999).

[5] *Id.*

to increase 36 percent.[6] The experiences and well-being of these children, all living in the wealthiest nation in the world, vary dramatically.

§ 1.1.1 Indicators of Well-Being

There are many factors to consider when investigating the well-being of youth in America. Since 1990, the Annie E. Casey Foundation's annual Kids Count Data Book looks at a number of indicators they believe reflect the wide range of factors influencing children from birth through early adulthood.[7] In 2002, Kids Count employed ten measures to access the well-being of children in the United States, these indicators included: the percentage of low birth weight babies; infant mortality rates; child death rates; rate of teen deaths by accident, homicide, and suicide; teen birth rate; percent of teens who are high school dropouts; percent of teens not attending school and not working; percent of children living with parents who do not have full-time, year-round employment; percent of children in poverty; and the percent of families with children headed by a single parent.[8] According to Kids Count, all of these factors improved in the 1990s with the exception of the percentages of low-birth-weight babies and families with children headed by a single parent.[9]

Living Arrangements

A child's living arrangement directly impacts their well-being. Children in the United States grow up in a variety of different living arrangements. Although two-parent families have declined,[10] the majority of children, 69 percent, are raised in two-parent homes.[11] Two-parent homes can be comprised of biological, adoptive, or step parents. Single-parent homes are the second most common living arrangement for children. In 2002, 28 percent of children lived in a single parent home; 16.5 million children were being raised by a single mother and 3.3 million by a single father.[12] About 8 percent of children lived with grandparents or kinship caregivers.[13] Approximately 5.6 million children were living in a household with a grandparent in 2002.[14] The majority of these children lived in

---

[6] *Id.*

[7] *See generally* THE ANNIE E. CASEY FOUNDATION, 2004 KIDS COUNT DATA BOOK (2004) (summarizing child-related data through 2003), *available at* http://www.aecf.org/kidscount/.

[8] THE ANNIE E. CASEY FOUNDATION, 2002 KIDS COUNT DATA BOOK: STATE PROFILES OF CHILD WELL-BEING 27 (2002).

[9] *Id.*

[10] *Id.* at 8 (noting that 85 percent of children lived in two-parent homes in 1970 compared to 68 percent in 1997).

[11] JASON FIELDS, U.S. CENSUS BUREAU, CHILDREN'S LIVING ARRANGEMENTS AND CHARACTERISTICS: MARCH 2002, at 3 (Current Population Reports No. P20-547, 2003).

[12] *Id.* at 5.

[13] *Id.* at 6.

[14] *Id.* at 8.

their grandparent's home with a parent present.[15] Additionally, it is estimated that over one million homosexual people have children. There are approximately 594,000 same sex partners' households in the United States and 80,837 are raising children.[16] In addition to the make-up of a child's household, the educational attainment of a child's parent or guardian can significantly impact a child's environment.

Educational Attainment of Parents

Parental education is a predictor of child well-being and educational attainment. Americans who do not graduate from high school are more likely to be unemployed or in prison, to rely on public assistance, and to become single parents.[17] In 2003, approximately 87 percent of Americans between the ages of 25 and 29 had completed high school,[18] and 28 percent of this group had completed a bachelor's degree.[19] Parent's education levels are linked to educational expectations for their children, the likelihood that they read to their children, and their children's academic achievement.[20] Parents who have received a high school education or less are more likely to have low education expectations for their children.[21] Reading to children is considered a key factor of school readiness. Parents with a bachelor's degree are about 50 percent more likely to read to their children on a daily basis then parents who have a high school diploma or less.[22] Children whose parents are less educated are twice as likely to repeat a grade or be suspended from school.[23] Children whose parents have received a high school diploma or less are more likely to live in poverty.

---

[15] *Id.*

[16] Dan Black et al., *Demographics of the Gay and Lesbian Population in the United States: Evidence from Available Systematic Data Sources*, 37 DEMOGRAPHY 139, 150 (2000).

[17] JAY P. GREENE, THE MANHATTAN INST. FOR POLICY RESEARCH, HIGH SCHOOL GRADUATION RATES IN THE UNITED STATES: NOVEMBER 2001, at 1 (2002), *available at* http://www.manhattan-institute.org/cr_baeo.pdf; PHILLIP KAUFMAN ET AL., U.S. DEP'T OF EDUC., DROPOUT RATES IN THE UNITED STATES: 1999, at 1 (Nat'l Ctr. For Educ. Statistics, Statistical Analysis Report, NCES 2001-022, 2000).

[18] NICOLE STOOPS, U.S. CENSUS BUREAU, EDUCATIONAL ATTAINMENT IN THE UNITED STATES: 2003, at 3 (Current Population Reports No. P20-550, 2004), *available at* http://www.census.gov/prod/2004pubs/p20-550.pdf. *See generally* JAY P. GREENE, THE MANHATTAN INST. FOR POLICY RESEARCH, HIGH SCHOOL GRADUATION RATES IN THE UNITED STATES: NOVEMBER 2001, at 1 (2002).

[19] NICOLE STOOPS, U.S. CENSUS BUREAU, EDUCATIONAL ATTAINMENT IN THE UNITED STATES: 2003, at 3 (Current Population Reports No. P20-550, 2004).

[20] *See generally* TERRY A. LUGAILA, U.S. CENSUS BUREAU, A CHILD'S DAY: 2000 (SELECTED INDICATORS OF CHILD WELL BEING) (Current Population Reports P70-89, 2003) (presenting survey data regarding the characteristics and daily activities of children and their families), *available at* http://www.census.gov/prod/2003pubs/p70-89.pdf.

[21] *Id.* at 15 & tbl.9.

[22] *Id.* at 6 & tbl.3.

[23] *Id.* at 14-15 & tbl.8.

Poverty

Childhood poverty plagues many children in America. Although the national poverty rate has remained relatively steady since the turn of the twenty-first century, the number of children living in low-income families is increasing.[24] In 2002, 37 percent of children lived in low-income or poor families; 26 million children lived in low-income families and 11 million children in poor families.[25] The National Center for Children in Poverty defines "low-income" families as those with parents earning 200 percent of the federal poverty level, and "poor" families as those with parents earning the federal poverty level, which was $18,850 for a family of four in 2004.[26] Most children who live in low-income families have parents who work full-time and year-round.[27] These families often face material hardships, including difficulties maintaining stable housing, health insurance, and child care.

Health Insurance

Health insurance significantly contributes to a child's well-being. Most children receive health insurance from private health insurance providers, usually through a parent's employer. Children also receive health insurance from government sources, such as state Child Health Insurance Programs (CHIPS) and Medicaid.[28] In 2001, 9.2 million children, more than 12 percent, did not have health insurance.[29] Uninsured children are less likely to have a regular health care provider and more likely to fall behind on immunizations and well child care.[30] Children living in poverty, without proper health care or supervision, more frequently become victims of child maltreatment.

§ 1.2 Child Maltreatment

Child maltreatment, which encompasses physical abuse, sexual abuse, neglect, and emotional abuse, impacts a number of children in America. In 2002, there were 2.6 million reports of child maltreatment involving 4.6 million

---

[24] AYANA DOUGLAS-HALL & HEATHER KOBALL, NAT'L CTR. FOR CHILDREN IN POVERTY, LOW INCOME CHILDREN IN THE UNITED STATES (2004), *available at* http://www.nccp.org/media/cpf04-text.pdf.

[25] *Id.*

[26] *Id.*

[27] *Id.*

[28] SHAILESH BHANDARI & ELIZABETH GIFFORD, U.S. CENSUS BUREAU, CHILDREN WITH HEALTH INSURANCE: 2001, at 2 (2003).

[29] *Id.*

[30] Kevin H. Crenshaw, *The Laws of Health: Our Uninsured Population*, METRO NEWS, Vol. 1, No. 3 (Alabama Cooperative Extension System), March 2002.

children.[31] Of the 4.6 million children referred to states' child protective services, two-thirds of them were accepted for investigation, and approximately 896,000 children were confirmed victims of child maltreatment.[32] The most common type of child maltreatment is neglect (60.5 percent), followed by physical abuse (18.6 percent), sexual abuse (9.9 percent), and emotional or psychological abuse (6.5 percent).[33] In 2002, 1,400 children died as a result of child maltreatment.[34]

In 2002, youth of all ages, sex, socioeconomic class, and race were victims of child maltreatment. Children between the ages of zero to three accounted for the highest percentage of victims.[35] The rate that children are victimized decreases as children get older.[36] Although there were fewer females than males under the age of 18 in the United States,[37] girls were at a slightly higher risk of being maltreated then boys: 51.9 percent of child maltreatment victims were girls and 48.1 percent were boys.[38] Most child victims were maltreated by their mother; fathers were the second most common perpetrator, followed by both mother and father, and nonparental abusers.[39]

The number of child maltreatment investigations increased by 21 percent from 1990 to 2002. Nonetheless, the rate of victimizations decreased by 7.5 percent.[40] Every state has adopted some form of mandatory child abuse and neglect reporting law, which is required to obtain funding under the Child Abuse Prevention and Treatment Act.[41] This may account for a portion of the increase in reports and investigations. Most physical abuse victims were reported to child protective services by educators. Legal and justice personnel reported a significant portion of physical abuse victims, sexual abuse victims, and psychological

---

[31] CHILDREN'S BUREAU, U.S. DEP'T OF HEALTH AND HUMAN SERVS., CHILD MALTREATMENT 2002, at iii (2004). *See also* MADELYN FREUNDLICH ET AL., CHILDREN'S RIGHTS, TRENDS IN CHILD MALTREATMENT: 1996-2001 (tracking child maltreatment trends from 1996 through 2002), *available at* http://www.childrensrights.org/PDF/policy/maltreatment.pdf.

[32] CHILDREN'S BUREAU, U.S. DEP'T OF HEALTH AND HUMAN SERVS., CHILD MALTREATMENT 2002, at 21 (2004).

[33] *Id.* at 22.

[34] *Id.* at iii.

[35] *Id.* at 23.

[36] *Id.*

[37] In 2000, approximately 49 percent of children under the age of 18 were females and 51 percent were males. U.S. CENSUS BUREAU, CENSUS 2000, Summary File 1, Matrices P13 and PCT 12 (2004).

[38] CHILDREN'S BUREAU, U.S. DEP'T OF HEALTH AND HUMAN SERVS., CHILD MALTREATMENT 2002, at 23 (2004).

[39] *Id.* at 24.

[40] *Id.* at 21.

[41] Child Abuse Prevention and Treatment Act (CAPTA), 42 U.S.C. §§ 5101 through 5119 (1996) (current version amended and reenacted through the Keeping Children and Families Safe Act of 2003, Pub. L. No. 108-36).

maltreatment victims. Medical personnel reported 27 percent of medical neglect victims.[42]

§ 1.2.1 Poverty, Race, and Child Maltreatment

Poor and minority children are drastically overrepresented in the child welfare system. Although child maltreatment occurs in all cross-sections of society, poor children are at a higher risk for maltreatment than their wealthier counterparts. According to the Third National Incidence Study of Child Abuse and Neglect (NIS-3), poor children were over 20 times more likely to be maltreated, and over 40 times more likely to be neglected.[43] Minority children are more likely to live in poverty. In 2001, 11.7 percent of the total population lived in poverty, but 22.7 percent of blacks and 21.4 percent of Hispanics were poor.[44] Furthermore, 58 percent of African American children and 67 percent of Hispanic children lived in low-income families.[45]

In 2001, over one-half of child maltreatment victims were white (54.2 percent), 26.1 percent were African American, 11 percent Hispanic, and 1.8 percent American Indian or Alaskan Native.[46] This reflects a disproportionately large number of African American and American Indian children. African Americans and American Indians or Alaskan Natives comprised only 12.3 percent and .9 percent, respectively, of the total population.[47] According to the 2000 Adoption and Foster Care Analysis and Reporting System (AFCARS) report, 29 percent of children who entered care were African American, and 40 percent of children in foster care were African American.[48] Despite the disproportionate number of minority children found to be maltreated, the actual rate of maltreatment in all races appears to be about the same.[49]

Why are poor and minority children overrepresented? This is a source of great debate. There are a number of potential factors that may lend to the

---

[42] CHILDREN'S BUREAU, U.S. DEP'T OF HEALTH AND HUMAN SERVS., CHILD MALTREATMENT 2002, at 23 (2004).

[43] ANDREA J. SEDLAK & DIANE D. BROADHURST, U.S. DEP'T OF HEALTH & HUMAN SERVS., THE THIRD NATIONAL INCIDENCE STUDY OF CHILD ABUSE AND NEGLECT 5-4 (1996), *available at* http://nccanch.acf.hhs.gov/pubs/statsinfo/nis3.cfm#national.

[44] BERNADETTE D. PROCTOR & JOSEPH DALAKER, U.S. CENSUS BUREAU, CURRENT POPULATION REPORTS NO. P60-219, POVERTY IN THE UNITED STATES: 2001, at 3 tbl.1& n.4 (noting that Hispanics may be of any race for these calculations).

[45] *Id.*

[46] CHILDREN'S BUREAU, U.S. DEP'T OF HEALTH AND HUMAN SERVS., CHILD MALTREATMENT 2002, at 23 (2004).

[47] U.S. CENSUS BUREAU, 2000 CENSUS FACT FINDER, *available at* http://factfinder.census.gov/servlet/SAFFFacts?_sse=on.

[48] CHILDREN'S BUREAU, U.S. DEP'T OF HEALTH AND HUMAN SERVS., THE AFCARS REPORT: INTERIM FY 2000 ESTIMATES AS OF AUGUST 2002, NO. 7, at 2 (2002), *available at* http://www.acf.dhhs.gov/programs/cb/publications/afcars/report7.pdf.

[49] ANDREA J. SEDLAK & DIANE D. BROADHURST, U.S. DEP'T OF HEALTH & HUMAN SERVS., THE THIRD NATIONAL INCIDENCE STUDY OF CHILD ABUSE AND NEGLECT (1996).

disproportionate representation of poor and minority children. One argument is that poor families are more susceptible to state intervention because they are frequently involved with government agencies. For example, many poor families receive public assistance, use public transportation, and see public health care providers; this exposes them to more state agencies than middle class or wealthy families.[50] In fact, an estimated one-half of families referred to child protective services were receiving public assistance at the time of the referral.[51]

Some child advocates believe that today's child welfare system does not clearly distinguish child neglect from poverty. The original child protection movement was intended to save children from poverty. Child maltreatment was viewed as a social problem that could be treated with social welfare programs to help bring families out of poverty. The current system is based on a medical model, which some argue fails to sufficiently separate poverty from neglect. Advocates of this theory argue that state statutes should be designed to distinguish child neglect from child poverty and include an economic exception for neglect.[52]

Other scholars contend that the child welfare system is racially discriminate. Professor Dorothy Roberts argues that racial bias in the child welfare system dates back to the original child protection movement in the United States, which excluded African American children.[53] To support her argument, Professor Roberts points to the disproportionate number of African American children removed from their homes, the lack of services African American families receive, and the decreased likelihood that African American children will be returned home or adopted.

In light of the number of poor and minority families in the child welfare system, child welfare professionals must have a sense of cultural competency. Child welfare attorneys should use their lawyering skills to help ensure effective communication with people of differing cultures.[54]

§ 1.2.2 America's Children in Foster Care

Many maltreated children are removed from their homes. Adequately meeting the needs of children in foster care is one of the biggest challenges faced by child welfare professionals. The foster care system is frequently criticized for its inadequacies:

- Youth remain in foster care too long.

---

[50] Annette R. Appell, *Protecting Children or Punishing Mothers: Gender, Race, and Class in the Child Protection System*, 48. S.C. L. REV. 577, 584 (1997).

[51] DOROTHY ROBERTS, SHATTERED BONDS: THE COLOR OF CHILD WELFARE 29 (2002) (citing DUNCAN LINDSEY, THE WELFARE OF CHILDREN 89-126 (1994)).

[52] *Id.* at 38.

[53] *Id.* at 7.

[54] *See* Chapter 6, Cultural Context in Abuse and Neglect Practice: Tips for Attorneys.

- Children are often moved multiple times or placed in inappropriate settings, such as group homes instead of families.

- Oftentimes children do not receive the services they need.

The purpose of out-of-home placement is to protect dependent and neglected children. Placing children in family-like settings eventually emerged as the preferred placement option for children who were removed from their parents' care.

The Current System

The concept of foster care is not recent. It is connected to the child welfare movements of Elizabethan England and Colonial America. Historically, children who could not remain in their parent's care were bound out to caretakers who were to provide care, education, and training in the form of apprenticeships. Apprenticeships gave way in the nineteenth century to houses of refuge, reform, and orphanages. Child welfare professionals then came to believe that individualized family placements served children best, and by the twentieth century most dependent children lived in family homes.[55]

Today half a million children in America are living in out-of-home care.[56] In 2001, the median age of children in foster care was 10.6 years. The median age of children entering care was 8.7 years, and the median age for children exiting care was 10.2 years.[57] Forty-eight percent of children living in out-of-home placement were living in non-relative foster families. Twenty-four percent were living in relative placements, 18 percent in group homes or institutions, 4 percent in pre-adoptive homes, and 6 percent in other types of placement.[58] The majority of children (57 percent) who exited foster care in 2001 were reunited with their families. Eighteen percent were adopted, 13 percent went to live with a family member or guardian, and 7 percent were emancipated.[59]

Once children are removed from their homes, federal funds are available to provide services to them. In 2000, the federal government allocated $4.5 billion for foster care, $1 billion for adoption assistance, and $140 million for independ-

---

[55] JOHN E.B. MYERS, A HISTORY OF CHILD PROTECTION IN AMERICA 67 (Xlibris Corporation 2004). *See also* Chapter 7, The History of Child Welfare Law, for a discussion of the history of child welfare.

[56] NAT'L CLEARINGHOUSE ON CHILD ABUSE AND NEGLECT INFORMATION, FOSTER CARE NATIONAL STATISTICS 2 (2003), *available at* http://nccanch.acf.hhs.gov/pubs/factsheets/foster.pdf.

[57] *Id.* at 4.

[58] *Id.* at 2.

[59] *Id.* at 3.

ent living services.[60] The Urban Institute estimates that 9.1 billion dollars was spent that year on out-of-home care.[61] The majority of these funds go to state welfare agencies to administer services to foster children. This funding scheme has received criticism for its failure to provide services to families before children are placed in out-of-home care. Critics of the current foster care system argue that children are too quickly removed from their homes and that once a child is removed it is very difficult for the family to reunify.[62] The Adoption and Safe Families Act addressed some of the criticisms of foster care. Congress modified the national goal to not only promote family reunification, but also to reduce the time children spend in care. New federal policy encourages adoption once a child has been in placement for a certain amount of time.[63]

Challenges Faced by Foster Children

Emancipated foster children face a vast number of challenges. The foster care system is intended to be a temporary placement for children; however, many children spend lengthy amounts of time in care, and some are emancipated from care. This results in youth being cut off from social services between the ages of 18 and 21. Oftentimes these young adults do not have prior work experience or a support system to help them navigate adult life. In fact, one-third of foster children are teenagers.[64] A majority of these youth exit foster care without being reunified with their families or adopted. In 1999, Congress passed the Foster Care Independence Act to help assist youth exiting care.[65] The Act

---

[60] ADMIN. FOR CHILDREN AND FAMILIES, PROTECTING THE WELL-BEING OF CHILDREN (May 2000). The figures for 2002 are $5.05 billion for foster care, $1.4 billion for adoption assistance, and $140 million for independent living services, *available at* http://www.acf.dhhs.gov/news/facts/chilwelfpr.htm.

See generally THE FUTURE OF CHILDREN: CHILDREN, FAMILIES, AND FOSTER CARE (David and Lucille Packard Found., Los Altos, C.A.), Vol. 14, No. 1, Winter 2004 (providing a broad overview, analysis, and critique of the foster care system).

[61] NAT'L CLEARINGHOUSE ON CHILD ABUSE AND NEGLECT INFORMATION, FOSTER CARE NATIONAL STATISTICS 7 (2003).

[62] *See* Martin Guggenheim, *Commentary: The Foster Care Dilemma and What to do About it: Is the Problem that too Many Children Are Not Being Adopted Out of Foster Care or That Too Many Children Are Entering Foster Care,* 2 U. PA. J. CONST. L. 141 (1999).

[63] Adoption and Safe Families Act of 1997, Pub. L. No. 105-89, 111 Stat. 2115 (codified in scattered sections of 42 U.S.C.)

[64] Betsy Krebs & Paul Pitcoff, *Reversing the Failure of the Foster Care System,* 27 HARV. WOMEN'S L.J. 357, 358 n. 6 (2004) (citing Susan Vivian Mangold, *Extending Non-Exclusive Parenting and the Right to Protection for Older Foster Children: Creating Third Options in Permanency Planning,* 48 BUFF. L. REV. 835, 863 (2000); CHILDREN'S BUREAU, U.S. DEP'T OF HEALTH & HUMAN SERV., TITLE IV-E INDEPENDENT LIVING PROGRAMS: A DECADE IN REVIEW (1999), *available at* http://nccanch.acf.hhs.gov/pubs/otherpubs/il/execsum/cfm.

[65] Foster Care Independence Act of 1999, Pub. L. No. 106-169, 113 Stat. 1822 (codified as amended in scattered sections of 42 U.S.C.). *See also* Betsy Krebs & Paul Pitcoff, *Reversing the Failure of the Foster Care System,* 27 HARV. WOMEN'S L.J. 357, 358 n. 4 (2004).

provides money for low cost housing, health care, and job placement. The Act also requires the Secretary of the Department of Health and Human Services to develop outcome measures to access the well-being of youth who exit care.

Most child welfare professionals would agree that foster children are a complex and underserved population. Foster children are more likely then other children to have acute and chronic health conditions, developmental delays, and emotional adjustment problems.[66] Additionally, two-thirds of foster children have special needs or are classified as medically fragile.[67] Foster children are often exposed to genetic factors, prenatal substance exposure, and other physical health issues, making them more vulnerable to poor developmental outcomes.[68]

Educational attainment is one of many challenges foster youth face. Studies have shown that 30 to 96 percent of students in out-of-home care were below grade level in reading or math[69] and 26 to 40 percent are likely to repeat one or more grades.[70] Despite poor educational achievement, 70 percent of foster youth plan to attend college and 19 percent plan to continue their education beyond college.[71] According to The Casey National Alumni Study, former foster youth have a high school completion rate comparable to that of the general public.[72] Additionally, many of the former foster youth participating in the study were living in stable and positive environments, and the female Casey alumni had an employment rate higher than the national average.[73]

---

[66] Lisa Kraimer-Rickaby & Preston A. Britner, *Providing Child Care for Foster Children with Special Needs*, CHILD CARE CENTER CONNECTIONS, Vol. 9, Issue 3, 2000, at 1, *available at* http://www.canr.uconn.edu/ces/child/pdf/CCC93.pdf.

[67] *Id.*

[68] Brenda Jones Harden, *Safety and Stability for Foster Children: A Developmental Perspective*, THE FUTURE OF CHILDREN: CHILDREN, FAMILIES, AND FOSTER CARE (David and Lucille Packard Found., Los Altos, C.A.), Vol. 14, No. 1, Winter 2004, at 31, 37, *available at* http://www.futureofchildren.org/usr_doc/tfoc1401_c.pdf.

[69] Elisabeth Yu, *Improving Educational Outcomes for Youth in Care: A National Collaboration*, PERMANENCY PLANNING TODAY (Nat'l Res. Ctr. for Foster Care and Permanency Planning, New York, N.Y.), Winter 2003, at 9, *available at* http://www.hunter.cuny.edu/socwork/nrcfcpp/downloads/newsletter/ppt-winter-2003.pdf.

[70] *Id.*

[71] Curtis McMillen et al., *Educational Experiences and Aspirations of Older Youth in Foster Care*, 82 CHILD WELFARE 475, 483 (2003). *See generally* MARK E. COURTNEY ET AL., MIDWEST EVALUATION OF THE ADULT FUNCTIONING OF FORMER FOSTER YOUTH: CONDITIONS OF YOUTH PREPARING TO LEAVE STATE CARE (Chapin Hall Center for Children, University of Chicago, Feb. 2004) (examining the transition from foster care to adulthood for youth from selected states).

[72] PETER J. PECORA ET AL., ASSESSING THE EFFECTS OF FOSTER CARE: EARLY RESULTS FROM THE CASEY FOUNDATION NATIONAL ALUMNI STUDY 44 (2003). Complete results are available at: http://www.casey.org/NR/rdonlyres/CEFBB1B6-7ED1-440D-925A-E5BAF602294D/148/casey_alumni_studies_report1.pdf.

[73] *Id.* at 23, 36.

Improving the System

In 2004, the journal *The Future of Children*[74] devoted an entire issue to the foster care system. The purpose of the issue was to encourage informed debate about the most effective ways to improve the system. The journal made the following recommendations to help ensure the healthy development of foster children:

- All children in foster care should receive health screenings at entry and comprehensive pediatric assessments, and they should be assigned a "medical home" and receive ongoing assessments and treatment.

- States should quantitatively measure how well the education and health needs of children in foster care are being met.

- States should use existing programs to provide specialized services for children of different ages in foster care, ranging from early-childhood preschool programs to educational services and transitional support for older youth.

- Child welfare services need to enhance cultural competency by recruiting bilingual and culturally competent foster families and workers, and improve services to birth families by building partnerships with community-based organizations and integrating family focused models.

- Support systems and services should be developed to assist non-relative foster families and kin caregivers.

- Efforts should be made to support family relationships after a permanent placement to help promote the child's well-being after exiting the system.

- States should enhance accountability and public oversight by using external review boards and adequately investing in implementing performance improvement plans.

- The federal government should reauthorize and expand waivers available to states and revise outdated eligibility requirements to extend the flexibility and reach of federal foster care funds.

- State agencies should improve their efforts to coordinate services to children and families, including information sharing across programs and services.

---

[74] THE FUTURE OF CHILDREN: CHILDREN, FAMILIES, AND FOSTER CARE (David and Lucille Packard Found., Los Altos, C.A.), Vol. 14, No. 1, Winter 2004, *available at* http://www.future ofchildren.org/usr_doc/tfoc1401_full-1.pdf.

- Courts and child welfare agencies should support individualized planning and build continuity to promote effective collaboration between judges, caseworkers, children, and families in foster care.[75]

In 2003, the Pew Commission on Children in Foster Care[76] was formed to establish recommendations to improve outcomes for children in foster care. The Pew Commission is comprised of judges, child welfare experts, local child welfare agencies, social workers, foster and adoptive parents, former foster youth, and other child advocates. The Pew Commission focuses on preventing unnecessary foster care placements and expediting the placement of children in foster care into safe, permanent, and nurturing families. The work of the Pew Commission reflects a national interest in improving the foster care system and recognizing the needs of foster children.

Is today's foster care system providing a safer and healthier environment for dependent and neglected children? Yes. Family settings are clearly better for children than almshouses, apprenticeships, or orphanages. Despite the time and money spent on systemic improvement, many foster children live in group homes, experience multiple placements, and do not receive the services they need. Although as a nation we continue to improve the services offered to children in out-of-home care, we are a long way from truly meeting the needs of dependent and neglected children. Child welfare professionals will inevitably work with or represent children in foster care. It is crucial to keep in mind the needs and challenges of children in out of home placement.

§ 1.2.3 The Impact of Child Maltreatment on America

Child maltreatment indisputably impacts our society in a number of ways. It contributes to violent crime and has a significant impact on our economy. Child advocates play an important role, not only in improving the outcomes for children and their families, but in promoting systemic improvement.

Crime

Nationwide, studies indicate that child maltreatment contributes to future violence. Child victims of abuse or neglect are more likely to be arrested—as juveniles, as adults, and for violent crimes. When considering that the incidence of neglect is two and one-half times that of physical abuse, the importance of implementing procedures to identify and treat neglect are very significant.[77]

---

[75] Sandra Bass et al., *Children, Families, and Foster Care: Analysis and Recommendations*, THE FUTURE OF CHILDREN: CHILDREN, FAMILIES, AND FOSTER CARE (David and Lucille Packard Found., Los Altos, C.A.), Vol. 14, No. 1, Winter 2004, at 5-29.

[76] Additional information about The Pew Commission, including the Commission's research and reports, is *available at* http://pewfostercare.org/.

[77] CATHY S. WIDOM & MICHAEL G. MAXFIELD, U.S DEP'T OF JUSTICE, AN UPDATE ON THE "CYCLE OF VIOLENCE," 5 (Nat'l Inst. Of Justice: Research in Brief, NCJ 184894, 2001).

Child neglect may be more damaging to a child's development than physical abuse. The impacts of child malnutrition, a form of neglect, include attention deficit, poor emotional stability, and reduced social skills. Furthermore, victims of child neglect are arrested at nearly the same rates as victims of child abuse.[78]

Economic Impact

Additionally, child maltreatment has a significant economic impact on American society. In 2001, Prevent Child Abuse America estimated that the United States spent over $24 billion dollars annually on the direct costs of child abuse and neglect.[79] In calculating the direct costs of child maltreatment, Prevent Child Abuse America considered the costs of hospitalization, chronic health problems, mental health care, the child welfare system, law enforcement, and the judicial system. Additionally, an estimated $69 billion was spent annually on the indirect costs of child maltreatment, which included special education, mental health and health care, juvenile delinquency, lost productivity to society, and adult criminality.[80] Although these numbers are subjective, there is no question that child maltreatment costs our nation billions of dollars annually.

The Advocate's Role in Promoting Systemic Improvement

Working with maltreated children is a challenging and rewarding vocation. Most child welfare attorneys would agree that this work can often be disheartening and it may often seem like every child is maltreated or that one's advocacy efforts, in a less than perfect system, are for naught. It is important to remember that this is not true. Many families and children are healthy, and advocacy efforts improve outcomes for many children and families. Child welfare attorneys should appreciate the unique position they are in to advocate for children, families, and agencies and promote systemic improvement.

---

[78] *Id.*

[79] *See* SUZETTE FROMM, TOTAL ESTIMATED COST OF CHILD ABUSE AND NEGLECT IN THE UNITED STATES, PREVENT CHILD ABUSE AMERICA 2 (2001), *available at* http://www.preventchildabuse.org/learn_more/research_docs/cost_analysis.pdf.

[80] *Id.* at 3.

Chapter 2   PHYSICAL, SEXUAL, AND EMOTIONAL CHILD ABUSE AND NEGLECT

by Ann M. Haralambie[1]

§ 2.1 Physical Abuse

The modern child welfare system was largely a response to the concerns of pediatricians, such as C. Henry Kempe and his colleagues, who coined the term "battered child syndrome" to describe, in part, the existence of multiple fractures in different stages of healing.[2] Physicians now have half a century of study and training in forensic pediatrics to assist in diagnosing physical child abuse, and what began as a response to physical abuse has now come to also incorporate a legal response to sexual and emotional abuse as well as physical, medical, and educational neglect. However, not all physicians are well-versed in this information, and child welfare attorneys must ensure that the experts they use are well-trained and that their knowledge is up-to-date. For example, a family doctor may not be alert for signs of abuse and may accept a superficially plausible explanation from the parents.

One of the most common ways of diagnosing any non-accidental injury is recognizing a discrepancy between the physical findings and the parent's explanation of how the injury occurred. Parents are seldom knowledgeable enough or clever enough to invent a story that is totally consistent with the physical findings. Many parents change the story every time it is told, especially if they were questioned about the history before they had time to concoct a credible explanation. Stories created in haste are difficult to remember. If the parents were questioned separately, it is likely that they told versions different in at least some respects. Identifying those inconsistencies is helpful in showing that the stories did not reflect reality. The different stories also pose a challenge to the attorney to prove that none of the explanations is consistent with the physical findings.

Often parents of young children and infants explain that the child received the injury by doing something the child was developmentally incapable of doing. For example, parents of babies who cannot crawl or even creep may say that the baby fell after being left in the middle of a bed. The parents may say that the child injured himself or herself deliberately, but children rarely deliberately injure themselves. Other children are often accused of dropping, pushing, or hitting a

---

[1]   Ann M. Haralambie, J.D., is a certified family law specialist practicing in Tucson, Arizona. She is also an author and speaker in the fields of family and children's law. The NACC is grateful to Kathryn Wells, M.D., Medical Director, Denver Family Crisis Center, Assistant Professor in Pediatrics, University of Colorado Health Sciences Center, Attending Physician, Kempe Child Protection Team, for her services editing this chapter.

[2]   *See, e.g.*, C. Henry Kempe et al., *The Battered-Child Syndrome*, 181 JAMA 17 (1962).

younger sibling when the older child lacks the physical strength or agility to do so or to strike a blow with enough force to cause the injury sustained.

Most parents of children with accidental injuries seek medical help immediately. However, parents who have inflicted the injuries on the child themselves may fear detection of the abuse and, therefore, delay in seeking help. Any delay and the explanations offered for the delay are important parts of the medical history. The attorney attempting to prove physical abuse should obtain all chart notes and personal notes reflecting the history given, especially the parent's first explanation. In addition, the attorney should direct discovery to the parent, whether through interrogatories, depositions, or requests for admissions, seeking the parent's detailed explanation of how the injury occurred and a recitation of every explanation the parent has given. The physician to be used as an expert witness at trial should be provided with detailed information about each explanation, because he or she must be able to express an opinion as to whether that explanation is consistent with the findings.

§ 2.1.1 Fractures

Certain types of fractures are caused by different mechanisms. The biomechanics of the type of force used to result in a particular type of fracture can be explained, and the forces necessary to result in the fracture can be calculated,[3] although the amount of force varies depending on the age and skeletal development of the child. The most important factor to consider is whether or not the explanation given for the injury is consistent with the type of force required to cause the injury. The types of biomechanical forces involved in abusive fractures have been summarized as including:

- Transverse/greenstick fractures (bending or direct impact from a hand or other blunt object).

- Spiral/oblique fractures and periosteal striping with subperiosteal hemorrhage (twisting or torsion of the limb).

- Metaphyseal as well as epiphyseal complex fractures (shaking or pulling on the end of a limb).[4]

The expert who testifies at trial should be prepared to explain the mechanism of the fracture. Although the expert may not be able to calculate the actual amount of force needed to cause the injury, they should be able to testify that:

- The degree of force necessary to produce such a fracture would exceed that of normal child care.

---

[3] *See, e.g.*, Betty Spivak, *Biomechanics of Nonaccidental Trauma*, in CHILD ABUSE: A MEDICAL REFERENCE 61-78 (Stephen Ludwig & Allan Kornberg eds., 1992).

[4] *See* D. Merten et al., *Skeletal Manifestations of Child Abuse*, in CHILD ABUSE: MEDICAL DIAGNOSIS AND MANAGEMENT 26 (Robert M. Reece ed.,1994).

- The force is great enough that any reasonable person would recognize that it would hurt a child.

- Given the child's response, it did hurt the child.

Skeletal models or diagrams may be helpful in demonstrating how the fracture was inflicted. Some medical conditions and diseases may produce findings similar to those of abusive fractures and should be excluded by the medical expert. These include osteogenesis imperfecta, osteomyelitis, congenital syphilis, rickets, scurvy, leukemia, and Menkes' syndrome.[5]

The age of the fracture or fractures may be important to a determination of who had access to the child when the injury was inflicted and whether multiple fractures occurred on different occasions.[6] Very recent fractures may be accompanied by swelling or bruising, although there is frequently no external indication of fractures in abused children. Very recent fractures, particularly those in a very young infant, may be difficult to detect on initial radiographic evaluation and may be first identified at the time of a repeat x-ray taken at a two- or three-week follow-up. As fractures heal, they calcify, leaving a radiological record called a callous. New bone formation does not show up on x-rays initially, but in 5 to 14 days a thin layer of new bone is formed.[7] The younger the child, the more quickly healing will occur.[8] Additionally, a fracture may completely resolve in six months, so the absence of a fracture at the time of presentation doesn't absolutely exclude previous injury that has completely healed. It may be useful to consider the assistance of a pediatric radiologist to testify about the timing of a fracture.

§ 2.1.2 Bruises

Some of the most obvious physical injuries abused children display are bruises. Medical records may use several terms to describe a bruise. The terms used most often are:

- "Contusion" (any injury, usually caused by a blow, in which the skin is not broken).

- "Ecchymosis" (a purplish patch on the skin caused by an extravasation of blood into the surrounding tissue).

- "Petechiae" (tiny red or purple spots caused by an effusion of blood from ruptured capillaries).

---

[5] *See, e.g.*, Paul W. Brill & Patricia Winchester, *Differential Diagnosis of Child Abuse*, in DIAGNOSTIC IMAGING OF CHILD ABUSE 221 (Paul Kleinman ed., 1987).

[6] *See generally* John F. O'Connor & Jonathan Cohen, *Dating Fractures*, in DIAGNOSTIC IMAGING OF CHILD ABUSE 103-113 (Paul Kleinman ed., 1987).

[7] *See* Sandy C. Marks, *The Structural and Developmental Context of Skeletal Injury*, in DIAGNOSTIC IMAGING OF CHILD ABUSE 6-7 (Paul Kleinman ed., 1987).

[8] *See* John F. O'Connor & Jonathan Cohen, *Dating Fractures*, in DIAGNOSTIC IMAGING OF CHILD ABUSE 107 (P. Kleinman ed., 1987).

A violent blow to the skin may cause petechiae when the blood is forced "out of the capillaries under the area of contact into the surrounding unsupported vessels which rupture under the strain."[9] Strangulation injuries may produce something called Tardieu's ecchymoses, Tardieu's petechiae, or Tardieu's spots. The attorney may also see the word "purpura" in medical charts to describe a hemorrhage into the skin, which may be caused by disease, allergies, or fever rather than abuse. Redness of the skin produced by inflammation may be called "erythema."

As with other signs of physical abuse, the significant issue is not that the child has one or more bruises but whether the bruises were received accidentally or not. Children who play actively often have bruises on their bodies most of the time. They may not be able to remember how they received them. Typical accidental bruises occur on the skin overlying the bony prominences, such as elbows, knees, shins, chin, cheek bone, and forehead. Children who are not yet pulling to stand and walking along furniture, called cruising, should not have bruises, and the presence of bruises in these children should raise the suspicion of non-accidental trauma. Conversely, toddlers who are just learning to walk are particularly prone to falling and bumping into things. But bruises received from such falls and bumps are typically circular with irregular borders. Generally bruises received in a fall are on one plane of the body, unless it was a tumbling fall. In contrast, abusive bruises may be seen on unlikely parts of the body, such as the backs of the knees, genitals, lateral thighs, buttocks, back, fleshy part of the arm, neck, soft tissues of the cheek, or earlobes. Such bruises may result from blows to the child's body, grabbing, pinching, or squeezing. Two black eyes are almost always indicative of physical abuse[10] unless the child has a large bump on the forehead, in which case the blood can track down into the more dependant areas, such the area below the eyes. Bruises on the back, buttocks, and lateral thighs are generally the result of excessive discipline.[11]

Many times the implement that inflicted the injury leaves its outline in the bruise. Pinch mark bruises are round or oval bruises the size of fingertips. A larger thumb print bruise may be the appropriate distance away. Grab marks generally have the thumb bruise on one side of the limb and the fingertip bruises on the other side. Handprints may leave the outline of the hand, even including the spaces between the fingers and the lines of the finger joints. The shape of part of the implement may be quite visible in the bruise. For example, the loops of an electrical cord may be seen. Similarly, the width of a belt, sometimes even showing the holes, may be seen. The tapered end of a belt might leave a triangular bruise at the end of the linear bruise. This underscores the importance of the

---

[9]   *See* C. Cooper, *Child Abuse and Neglect: Medical Aspects*, in THE MALTREATMENT OF CHILDREN 9, 21 (Selwyn M. Smith ed., 1978).

[10] *Id.* at 22.

[11] *See, e.g.*, Baron D. Schmitt, *The Child with Nonaccidental Trauma*, in THE BATTERED CHILD 178, 180 (4th ed., Ray Helfer & Ruth Kempe eds., 1987).

investigator's effort to obtain potential weapons from the scene, which the medical expert can correlate with the injury. Sometimes there are ligature marks when the child has been bound or strangled. Ligature marks are typically seen as circumferential wounds around the extremities, particularly the wrists and ankles, or in the case of an attempted strangulation, around the neck. There may be abrasions and bruises around the ligature mark or grab marks elsewhere where the child was restrained while being bound. Bite marks also leave crescent-shaped linear bruises, often paired with individual tooth marks that are visible. A physician or dentist can measure the distances seen in the bruise and match them with the size of the abuser's bite. Parents often blame bite marks on other children; however, there is a significant variation between the size of a child's bite and that of an adult.

There are some medical conditions that cause bruise-like markings, such as leukemia and idiopathic thrombocytopenic purpura. In addition, some kinds of birth marks, such as Mongolian spots, nevi, or hemangiomas, may look like bruises but are not. Some disorders, such as hemophilia and Von Willebrand's disease, result in bruising with very little force. Bleeding disorder screens provide laboratory evidence concerning whether a bruise could have been spontaneous or the result of minor injury because of a coagulation disorder. Some cultures have medical practices, such as coining, which produce abrasions or bruises, and when accompanied by hot oil, may include some burning. Other potential causes of bruising should always be ruled out by a physician.

§ 2.1.3 Lacerations

Lacerations are cuts on the skin. Sometimes the pattern of the lacerations indicates abuse. If the child is hit with a switch, for example, there may be a number of parallel linear lacerations on the child's back or the back of the child's legs. The child may receive a torn frenulum of the upper lip or tongue from having a bottle forcibly shoved into his or her mouth. Such injuries are often seen in child abuse cases. Older children may tear the frenulum accidentally in a fall, but there is a history to fit the injury as these injuries typically bleed considerably. Lacerations in the mouth heal very quickly, and even within a few days there may be no evidence of the laceration. The impact of a fist, boot, or an object may leave a laceration as well as a bruise. Sometimes lacerations are intentionally inflicted by a knife or razor.

§ 2.1.4 Burns

Because children's skin is thinner than adults' skin, contact with a hot object for the same amount of time will leave a more severe burn on the child than on the adult. The burn pattern may well contain clues suggesting the agent, mode, direction, and time of injury. Dry burns often show the imprint of what caused them. Irons, electric range coils, hot plates, curling irons, radiator grates, fireplace pokers, branding irons, cigarettes, and cigars all may leave burns clearly indicative of what was used to burn the child. Inflicted burns tend to have sharp, clear borders from direct and sustained contact with the hot object. Accidental burns tend to be glancing burns, as the child pulls back from the accidental contact. Because the skin is in contact with the hot object for a shorter time, the resulting burns tend to be less severe than inflicted burns. The margins of the burn may be more diffuse and the depth of the burn both shallower and less symmetrical. For example, a child who accidentally walks into a lighted cigarette may have an oval or oblong burn deeper on one end than the other. In contrast, an inflicted cigarette burn may be perfectly round and deep. Especially in hot climates, accidental burns may result from contact with metal objects heated by the sun. For example, a seat belt buckle may leave a burn with distinct borders showing the shape of the buckle. Car seats may also burn the child. Sometimes children are "branded" with heated metal objects such as knife blades, fireplace pokers, and the metal tops of cigarette lighters. Cigarette lighters may also be used to inflict burns by holding a part of the child's body, often the palm, over the open flame.

Immersion burns leave imprints of the water level, with or without splash marks, which can allow a physician to recreate the child's exact posture when he or she was burned. "Stocking" and "glove" burns result from a child's foot or hand, respectively, being dunked in scalding water, leaving a burn pattern where the water touched the child. Frequently there is an absence of splash marks in these burns. A "doughnut" scalding burn occurs when a child is held down in a bathtub of scalding water. The pressure of the child's skin that is touching the relatively cool bottom of the tub is not burned, while the surrounding areas are burned from the scalding water. If the child was standing in the tub, the soles of the feet might not be burned for the same reason. Some children are held under running scalding water, causing particularly deep burns, because the water coming from the spigot is uniformly hot, with no time to cool down. Children who are still in diapers or who are being toilet trained are at particular risk of dunking burns. The parent may be frustrated at having to clean the child or may be angry that the child was not able to wait to use the toilet. The child is immersed in hot water either to clean the child's genital area or to punish the child for the lapse in toilet training.

Accidental scalds may be caused by a child tipping a pot or cup of boiling liquid. The hot liquid generally flows off the child and cools relatively quickly in the air, causing a less severe burn. The hot pot or tea kettle may also fall on the child, leaving a non-scald burn. If the child accidentally pulled the container of hot liquid onto himself or herself, the child will be burned mostly on the face, arms, and upper trunk, often including the underside of the chin and armpit on injured side, with the most severe burn at the point of initial impact and less severely burned areas flowing down from that area of burn. If those areas are not burned, it suggests that the hot liquid was actually thrown at or poured on the child. Correlation with history given is always critical.

Splash marks are often seen with scald burns, and their location indicates the direction from which the water or other hot liquid came. If the liquid was pulled down from above the child, the splash marks will be seen below the primary burn. If the liquid was thrown at the child, the splash marks may be at the same height, but beyond the primary burn, or may even be above the primary burn. If the child is restrained while being immersed in scalding water, there will be relatively few splash marks. There may be some from the water from the spigot splashing back when it hits the rest of the water in the tub. If the child is able to flail about, there may be many splash marks.

Scald burns around the mouth may result from hot liquid or a corrosive agent being forced into the child's mouth. Corrosive burns around and in the mouth and throat may also be caused accidentally if the child ingests corrosive agents found around the house. Poison control centers routinely deal with such mishaps. It is important to identify the corrosive agent causing the burn and to determine whether the child would have had access to it.

In all burns, scene investigations are extremely important to assist in the reconstruction of the circumstances around the injury. Additionally, as with all injuries, the element of delay in seeking medical treatment may help to differentiate between inflicted and accidental burns.

There are some things that produce injuries that look like inflicted burns but are not. For example, impetigo, a contagious infection, may look similar to an inflicted cigarette burn. Moxibustion is the burning of herbal agents on the skin as a counterirritant in the treatment of disease in traditional Chinese and Japanese medicine. It is important to be sure that the physician who testifies has considered and ruled out any such alternative explanation. The physician should also be asked to rule out conditions that may mimic burns, such as cutaneous infections, hypersensitivity reactions, and allergic reactions.

§ 2.1.5 Internal (Abdominal and Thoracic) Injuries

Serious internal injuries may occur as a result of abuse, frequently without any evidence of outward signs, such as bruises or lacerations. Such injuries may be the result of being punched, kicked, or thrown. Abdominal blows and severe crushing or squeezing of the trunk may cause internal injuries without leaving any bruises or other marks on the skin. When the child's abdominal wall is relaxed at the time of the blow, the internal organs absorb most of the energy from the blow, so there may be no abdominal bruising.[12] The most likely internal injuries will be to the abdominal organs, such as the liver, spleen, pancreas, gastrointestinal tract, or bladder, because the thoracic organs are protected by the rib cage.

Abusive abdominal and thoracic (chest) injuries have a poorer prognosis than those that occur as a result of an accidental cause. This is largely as a result of a delay in seeking care as well as poor or no history for the injury, making diagnosis and treatment difficult. Children who have sustained these injuries

---

[12] *Id.* at 190.

typically exhibit signs of the injury initially, but this may be followed by a period when the child seems to get better. This period ends when the child's injury progresses as a result of infection or other complications. Therefore, establishing the timing of the injury is challenging and dependant on careful history from the caregivers.

§ 2.1.6 Abusive Head Trauma

Head injury is a common presentation for child abuse. Children may sustain a head injury in an accidental manner, but there are certain features that are suggestive of and, in some cases, diagnostic of non-accidental injury. As with all child abuse, it is important to correlate the injury that the child sustains with the explanation given for that injury.

Very serious injuries or even death may result from shaking a child, especially an infant. Because infants have relatively large heads compared to their body size, and because they have relatively weak neck muscles, shaking an infant may cause serious injury or death. This injury may or may not be followed by rapid deceleration of the head against an object, constituting an impact that further increases the severity of the injury. The constellation of injuries commonly seen with shaking include intracranial head injuries, eye injuries, and skeletal injuries.

When a child is shaken, the rapid acceleration and deceleration of the child's head tears the cerebral veins, causing bleeding between the arachnoid and the dura mater (fibrous tissue layers that surround the brain), resulting in a subdural hematoma.[13] Subarachnoid hematomas may also occur when blood accumulates in subarachnoid space. Additionally, damage to the brain parenchyma (brain tissue) may occur as a result of the shaking itself as the axons (main nerve fibers that carry impulses) are injured. This may cause brain edema (swelling), which can be further exacerbated by apnea (intermittent cessation of breathing causing lack of oxygen to the tissues) and, frequently, delay in seeking medical care.

Eye injuries are frequently seen in children injured by a shaking mechanism. Retinal hemorrhages are the most common eye injury seen, but there may also be bleeding in the area behind the eye or around the optic nerve (seen only at autopsy). Retinal hemorrhages are described by their type, extent, and location. Severe retinal hemorrhaging may result in folding of the retina (called retinoschesis) or a detached retina.

Several skeletal injuries may also be seen in a child injured by shaking with or without impact. A skull fracture confirms some element of impact. Rib fractures may also be sustained when the perpetrator grabs the child around the chest during the shaking episode. Lateral rib fractures arise from anterior to posterior squeezing of the ribs, and posterior rib fractures are the result of the back of the rib bending against the spine, which acts as a fulcrum for the rib. These

---

[13] *Id.* at 188.

injuries are quite specific for a squeezing mechanism. As mentioned earlier, there may also be fractures to the end of the long bones called metaphyseal fractures. In addition to the acceleration and deceleration involved in shaking, shaking may involve sudden extension and flexion, which may result in spinal fractures or other neck injury.

Epidural hematomas occur when blood accumulates between the dura mater and the skull where arteries traverse. These injuries are the result of blunt force trauma to the head and are more commonly the result of an accidental injury. Subgaleal hematomas may form under the scalp from blunt trauma or as the result of a child's hair being pulled forcefully. Because subgaleal hematomas are between the scull and the scalp, they do not present the serious danger that subdural, subarachnoidal, and epidural hematomas do.

Other potential causes for the above injuries need to be ruled out, including accidental injury, infection, and metabolic illness. Serious head injury or death very rarely result from short falls or falls down stairs, although this is a common explanation given for these injuries, and when they do, the injury is either an epidural bleed or, rarely, a space-occupying subdural hematoma.

§ 2.1.7 Munchausen by Proxy Syndrome

Munchausen by proxy syndrome involves fabricating, simulating, or inducing symptoms in a child or tampering with laboratory samples or monitors, which in turn, results in unnecessary medical procedures being performed on the child for diagnosis or treatment.[14] Parents with Munchausen by proxy syndrome often have some medical knowledge; therefore, they may be quite clever in the fabrications. The parents, almost always mothers, are generally quite concerned and cooperative with the medical personnel, who become a team of medical detectives to explain and treat the child's problem. In retrospect, the mothers can be described as being overly involved and constantly with the child. The father is typically absent or very uninvolved. Preverbal children are the most likely victims of this type of maltreatment because they are not only under their parent's control, but they are also unable to give their own history to the medical personnel. The child's physicians may begin to suspect Munchausen by proxy only long after repeated testing fails to uncover the etiology of the child's problems. While occasionally the parent's action is captured on videotape (such as covert video surveillance in a hospital room recording a parent suffocating a child or contaminating an intravenous line), the diagnosis of Munchausen by proxy syndrome is most often made only after careful and exhaustive medical detective work.

---

[14] *See generally* HERBERT A. SCHREIER & JUDITH A. LIBOW, HURTING FOR LOVE: MUNCHAUSEN BY PROXY SYNDROME (1993); Roy Meadow, *What Is and What Is Not Munchausen Syndrome by Proxy?*, 72 ARCHIVES OF DISEASES IN CHILDHOOD 534 (1995); Donna A. Rosenberg, 27 CHILD ABUSE & NEGLECT 421-430 (2003).

§ 2.1.8 Medical Ramifications

In addition to diagnosing the child maltreatment, the medical expert should explain the ramifications of the maltreatment, both short-term and long-term. If the child will need special care, then the parent's ability and willingness to provide that care must be determined. The attorneys for the agency and child, in particular, will need to address any ancillary services the child will require, including follow-up medical care. The parent's attorney will need to determine whether specialized services are available to assist the parent in learning how to care for the child.

§ 2.2 Sexual Abuse

The Child Abuse Prevention and Treatment and Adoption Reform Act[15] defines sexual abuse for the purposes of that Act as including:

(A) the employment, use, persuasion, inducement, enticement, or coercion of any child to engage in, or assist any other person to engage in, any sexually explicit conduct or simulation of such conduct for the purpose of producing a visual depiction of such conduct; or

(B) the rape, and in cases of caretaker or inter-familial relationships, statutory rape, molestation, prostitution, or other form of sexual exploitation of children, or incest with children.

A more conceptual definition was provided by Drs. Ruth and C. Henry Kempe, who saw sexual abuse as "the involvement of dependent, developmentally immature children and adolescents in sexual activities that they do not fully comprehend, to which they are unable to give informed consent, or that violate the social taboos of family roles."[16]

§ 2.2.1 Intrafamilial Child Sexual Abuse

Intrafamilial child sexual abuse involves sexual contact or activity with a member of one's family or household, including sexual activity with one's natural or adopted children, stepchildren, or children of one's "significant other." It is often referred to as incest. Such sexual abuse does not require that there be intercourse, or even that there be actual contact. Having a child watch one masturbate or taking pornographic pictures of a child constitutes sexual abuse even when the adult never touches the child. Similarly, having children engage in sexual contact with one another while the adult watches constitutes sexual abuse. Fondling over clothing can also be sexual abuse. Fondling, oral-genital contact, romantic kissing, inserting objects in a child's vagina or anus, digital penetration,

---

[15] 42 U.S.C. § 5106g(4).

[16] *See* RUTH S. KEMPE & C. HENRY KEMPE, CHILD ABUSE 43 (1978).

and penile penetration are other forms of sexual abuse.[17] In some cases, both parents or parent-figures are actively engaged in molesting the child. More frequently, however, only one parent or parental figure molests the child. The other, whether out of ignorance, impotence, or complicity, simply fails to protect the child from the abuse.

§ 2.2.2 Pedophilia

The DIAGNOSTIC AND STATISTICAL MANUAL OF MENTAL DISORDERS[18] (DSM-IV), referring specifically to the disorder of pedophilia (302.2) states that:

> Individuals with Pedophilia who act on their urges with children may limit their activity to undressing the child and looking, exposing themselves, masturbating in the presence of the child, or gentle touching and fondling of the child. Others, however, perform fellatio or cunnilingus on the child or penetrate the child's vagina, mouth, or anus with their fingers, foreign objects, or penis and use varying degrees of force to do so. These activities are commonly explained with excuses or rationalizations that they have "educational value" for the child, that the child derives "sexual pleasure" from them, or that the child was "sexually provocative"—themes that are also common in pedophiliac pornography.[19]

In addition to the actual abuse, a person who molests a child may bribe or threaten the child to secure his or her acquiescence. This "complicity" by the child in the act of abuse may make the child feel responsible or guilty, especially if the child derived some pleasure from the molestation. This may contribute to the child's reluctance or unwillingness to disclose the abuse. The child may also be directly threatened not to disclose.

Prentky, Knight, and Lee report that while the DSM-IV diagnostic criteria "may succeed in isolating the 'pedophilic' child molester, it fails to capture those incest and extrafamilial offenders without known 6-month histories of sexualized interest in children . . . . [which will] inevitably screen out a large number of

---

[17] Psychiatrist David Jones divides "child sexual abuse" into direct sexual acts (contacting child's genital or anal area; anal, vaginal or oral penetration; and "other acts in which the child is the object of the adult's gratification," such as bondage, frotteurism, ejaculation onto the child, and fondling of a postpubertal child's breasts) and indirect sexual acts (genital exposure, production of pornographic material, encouraging children to have sex together, and exposing children to pornographic material). He defines "child sexual abuse" as "the actual or likely occurrence of a sexual act (or acts) perpetrated on a child by another person." *See* David P. H. Jones, *Assessment of Suspected Child Sexual Abuse*, in THE BATTERED CHILD 296, 296-297 & nn.1-2 (5th ed., Mary Edna Helfer et al. eds., 1997).

[18] AM. PSYCHIATRIC ASS'N, DIAGNOSTIC AND STATISTICAL MANUAL OF MENTAL DISORDERS (4th ed. 1994).

[19] DSM-IV at 527-528.

child molesters."[20] Therefore, Prentky believes that the DSM-IV will fail to provide adequate coverage in classifying most child molesters.[21]

The stereotypical picture of a child molester is the "dirty old man" in a trench coat hanging around playgrounds and elementary school fences. Such a person is typically a predatory pedophile, whose primary or only sexual attraction is to children. Most pedophiles do not fit this stereotype. Some people are sexually attracted to children in general and may seek out opportunities to be with children, often in socially accepted positions such as scout leader, coach, or Sunday school teacher. The DSM-IV points out that except where pedophilia is associated with sexual sadism, "the person may be attentive to the child's needs in order to gain the child's affection, interest, and loyalty and to prevent the child from reporting the sexual activity."[22] Other persons do not have primary sexual attraction to children but end up molesting children in their own household out of their improper responses to various stressful situations.[23] The DSM-IV classifies pedophilia, 302.2, as either Exclusive Type, where the sexual attraction is only towards children, or Nonexclusive Type, where the sexual attraction may also be to adults.[24]

The DSM-IV states that some pedophiles, particularly those who frequently victimize children, "develop complicated techniques for obtaining access to children" that can include winning the trust of the child's mother, marrying a woman who has an attractive child, trading children with other pedophiles, or "in rare instances, taking in foster children from nonindustrialized countries or abducting children from strangers."[25]

Further, the person may be attracted just to males, just to females, or to both.[26] While the disorder generally begins in adolescence, some pedophiles report "that they did not become aroused by children until middle age."[27] The frequency of the sexual activity "often fluctuates with psychosocial stress."[28] Marital discord, divorce, moving out of the family home, and the tension that often accompanies visitation and other communications during domestic relations litigation certainly constitute psychosocial stress, which may exacerbate the inappropriate sexual behavior.

---

[20] See ROBERT A. PRENTKY ET AL, U.S. DEP'T OF JUSTICE, CHILD SEXUAL MOLESTATION: RESEARCH ISSUES 4 (NIJ Research Report NCJ 163390, 1997).

[21] *See* Robert A. Prentky, *Child Sexual Molestation*, in HANDBOOK OF PSYCHOLOGICAL APPROACHES WITH VIOLENT OFFENDERS: CONTEMPORARY STRATEGIES AND ISSUES (Michel Hersen & Vincent B. Van Hasselt eds., 1999).

[22] DSM–IV at 528.

[23] The DSM-IV states that "[i]ndividuals may limit their activities to their own children, stepchildren, or relatives or may victimize children outside their families." *Id.*

[24] *Id.* at 527-528.

[25] *Id.* at 528.

[26] *Id.* at 527-528.

[27] *Id.* at 528.

[28] *Id.*

§ 2.2.3 Diagnosing Sexual Abuse

The perpetrator does not have to be an adult for the activity to constitute child sexual abuse. Any time there is a great disparity in power and authority, such as between a teenage child and a young sibling or step-sibling, sexual contact takes on the characterization of abuse.[29]

It is important to understand that while the presence of physical (medical) evidence is probative of sexual abuse, negative findings *are not* probative. History is probably the most important criterion in diagnosing child sexual abuse.[30] It is not uncommon for sexually abused children to have normal physical examinations, including normal genital examinations.[31] Most acts of child molestation would not be expected to leave evidence: fondling, oral-genital contact, digital penetration, exhibitionism, and nude photography. Many children are not injured in any way during the molestation. Young children might not have any sense that the contact is "wrong," and would not be expected, therefore, to exhibit signs of psychological trauma from the abuse. The attorney must keep in mind the entire context of the molestation and make sure that expert testimony is presented that will focus the judge on what is really relevant information.

There is sometimes medical evidence of vaginal or anal penetration in a child. Very recent traumatic penetration may be revealed by lacerations or bruising. Because the hymen is an elastic tissue, it is possible for there to have been penetration without tearing the hymen or leaving an enlarged opening.[32] Even pregnant adolescents, who have had intercourse, may have normal genital findings.[33] Sometimes medical findings have causes other than abuse.[34] For example, children may sustain straddle injuries from falling on playground equipment or bicycle bars. The abrasions and bruises resulting from such accidental injuries, however, tend to appear on the more exposed, superficial parts of the body, with

---

[29] For example, the DSM-IV diagnostic criteria for pedophilia require for that particular diagnosis that the perpetrator be at least 16 years old and at least 5 years older than the victim. *Id.*

[30] *See, e.g.,* Carolyn J. Levitt, *The Medical Examination in Child Sexual Abuse: A Balance Between History and Exam,* 1 J. Child Sexual Abuse 113 (1992).

[31] *Id.* at 114.

[32] *Id.* at 116.

[33] *See, e.g.,* Nancy D. Kellogg et al., *Genital Anatomy in Pregnant Adolescents: "Normal" Does Not Mean "Nothing Happened,"* 113 Pediatrics e67 (2004) (noting vaginal penetration generally does not result in observable evidence of healed injury to perihymenal tissues; only 2 of the 36 subjects had definitive findings of penetration).

[34] *See generally* Joyce Adams, *Significance of Medical Findings in Suspected Sexual Abuse: Moving Towards Consensus,* 1 J. Child Sexual Abuse 91, 93 (1992) (listing the following findings as non-specific: irregular vascularity, erythema of the vestibule, labial adhesions, urethral dilatation with labial traction, friability of the posterior fourchette, hymenal septa, transverse measurements of the hymenal orifice over 5 mm, using labial separation (supine), and vaginal discharge).

areas such as the hymen and vagina not receiving the blunt trauma.[35] Accidental penetrating injuries are much rarer.[36]

Infections may also create genital inflammations, rashes, and even bleeding.[37] Foreign objects in the vagina, such as pieces of toilet paper or feces, may cause vaginal discharge, which may be blood-tinged. Passage of large, hard stools may result in fairly superficial, straight, and narrow anal fissures.[38] However, if the fissures are deep, irregular, extending beyond the rugal folds, or are accompanied by swelling, bleeding, or hematomas, there is some suspicion of an abusive etiology.[39]

Medical findings that are suggestive of sexual abuse include abrasions, lacerations, swelling, bruising (only if the abuse was very recent), scarring or tearing of the hymen, absent or narrow hymenal tissue, scars, the presence of semen or sperm, bite marks, and the presence of sexually transmitted diseases.[40] A child who has been forcibly sexually abused may have grab mark bruises on the thighs. Because the vagina is very vascular, injuries heal quickly, often without leaving behind any medical evidence, even under magnification.[41] Therefore, negative medical findings may not be inconsistent with a history of trauma that is not very recent.

§ 2.3 Emotional Abuse

Emotional abuse is difficult to define, but it can damage a child in more far-reaching and pervasive ways than the more obvious physical abuse.[42] While emotional abuse may accompany physical or sexual abuse, it may also exist in the absence of other forms of maltreatment. The DSM-IV does not include a diagnosis for emotional abuse. The American Academy of Pediatrics Committee on Child Abuse and Neglect defines "psychological maltreatment"[43] as "a repeated pattern of damaging interactions between parent(s) and child that becomes typical of the relationship" and "occurs when a person conveys to a child that he or she is worthless, flawed, unloved, unwanted, endangered, or only

---

[35] *See, e.g.,* DAVID L. CHADWICK ET AL., COLOR ATLAS OF CHILD SEXUAL ABUSE 57 (1989).

[36] *Id.*

[37] *Id.* at 58-59 (1989) (listing vulvovaginitis, streptococcal perianal disease, diaper dermatitis, lichen sclerosis et atrophicus, and postinflammatory labial adhesions).

[38] *Id.* at 60.

[39] *Id.*

[40] *See, e.g.,* Am. Acad. of Pediatrics, Committee on Child Abuse and Neglect, *Guidelines for the Evaluation of Sexual Abuse of Children*, 87 PEDIATRICS 254 (1991).

[41] *See, e.g.,* Joyce Adams, *Significance of Medical Findings in Suspected Sexual Abuse: Moving Towards Consensus*, 1 J. CHILD SEXUAL ABUSE 91, 97 (1992).

[42] *See, e.g.,* JAMES GARBARINO ET AL., THE PSYCHOLOGICALLY BATTERED CHILD (1986).

[43] Although emotional and psychological abuse are used synonymously here, they may be distinguishable for professional diagnostic purposes.

of value in meeting another's needs. The perpetrator may spurn, terrorize, isolate, or ignore or impair the child's socialization."[44] The committee stated that:

> If severe and/or repetitious, the following behaviors may constitute psychological maltreatment:
>
> 1. Spurning (belittling, degrading, shaming, or ridiculing a child; singling out a child to criticize or punish; and humiliating a child in public).
>
> 2. Terrorizing (committing life-threatening acts; making a child feel unsafe; setting unrealistic expectations with threat of loss, harm, or danger if they are not met; and threatening or perpetrating violence against a child or child's loved ones or objects).
>
> 3. Exploiting or corrupting that encourages a child to develop inappropriate behaviors (modeling, permitting, or encouraging antisocial or developmentally inappropriate behavior; encouraging or coercing abandonment of developmentally appropriate autonomy; restricting or interfering with cognitive development).
>
> 4. Denying emotional responsiveness (ignoring a child or failing to express affection, caring, and love for a child).
>
> 5. Rejecting (avoiding or pushing away).
>
> 6. Isolating (confining, placing unreasonable limitations on freedom of movement or social interactions).
>
> 7. Unreliable or inconsistent parenting (contradictory and ambivalent demands).
>
> 8. Neglecting mental health, medical, and educational needs (ignoring, preventing, or failing to provide treatments or services for emotional, behavioral, physical, or educational needs or problems).
>
> 9. Witnessing intimate partner violence (domestic violence).[45]

Some state statutes tie the definition of emotional abuse to a psychological or psychiatric diagnosis in the child and a causal connection between the disorder

---

[44] *See* Steven W. Kairys et al., *The Psychological Maltreatment of Children—Technical Report*, 109 PEDIATRICS e68 (2002).

[45] *Id. See also* Stephanie Hamarman & William Bernet, *Evaluating and Reporting Emotional Abuse in Children: Parent-Based, Action-Based Focus Aids in Clinical Decision-Making*, 39 J. AM. ACAD. CHILD & ADOLESCENT PSYCH. 928 (2000).

and improper conduct by the parent.[46] The statutes may require that emotional abuse be proven based on the testimony of a licensed physician or psychologist.[47]

§ 2.4 Neglect

In this section, the following types of neglect are discussed: emotional neglect, physical neglect, medical neglect, failure to thrive, and educational neglect.

§ 2.4.1 Emotional Neglect

Even if the parent provides for the child's physical needs, the child's emotional needs may be neglected. Children who experience chronic emotional neglect may grow up without the ability to form emotional bonds, resulting in antisocial behavior and crime. It is difficult to define what constitutes psychological or emotional neglect. Garbarino, Guttmann, and Seeley identify five forms of "psychically destructive behavior": rejecting, isolating, terrorizing, ignoring, and corrupting.[48] It might be said that the rejecting, isolating, and ignoring forms constitute emotional neglect, while the terrorizing and corrupting forms constitute emotional abuse. Emotional or psychological neglect may also arise from the emotional unavailability of the parent to the child. The DSM-IV describes the psychiatric diagnosis of Reactive Attachment Disorder of Infancy or Early Childhood (313.89) as "markedly disturbed and developmentally inappropriate social relatedness in most contexts that begins before age five and is associated with grossly pathological care."[49] Among the listed causes for the diagnosis are that the care giver neglects the "child's basic emotional needs for comfort, stimulation and affection" or neglects the "child's basic physical needs."[50]

Despite the adverse consequences to the emotionally neglected child, courts are not as likely to sustain an adjudication based on emotional or psychological neglect as for physical or medical neglect.

§ 2.4.2 Physical Neglect

There are a number of types of neglect, including physical neglect, medical neglect, failure to thrive, educational neglect, and emotional neglect. Neglect

---

[46] *See, e.g.,* COLO. REV. STAT. § 19-1-103(1)(a)(IV), which defines emotional abuse as "an identifiable and substantial impairment of the child's intellectual or psychological functioning or development or a substantial risk of impairment of the child's intellectual or psychological functioning or development."

[47] For a useful set of guidelines on evaluating emotional abuse, *see* the AM. PROF. SOC. ON THE ABUSE OF CHILD., GUIDELINES FOR PSYCHOSOCIAL EVALUATION OF SUSPECTED PSYCHOLOGICAL MALTREATMENT IN CHILDREN AND ADOLESCENTS.

[48] JAMES GARBARINO ET AL., THE PSYCHOLOGICALLY BATTERED CHILD (1986).

[49] AM. PSYCHIATRIC ASS'N, DIAGNOSTIC AND STATISTICAL MANUAL OF MENTAL DISORDERS 116 (4th ed. 1994).

[50] *Id.*

can be based on the parent's own actions or inactions or by the parent's failure to protect the child from abuse or neglect by others. Neglect does not require a finding of parental fault, only the inability or unwillingness to provide proper care for the child. The failure to perform an affirmative parental duty constitutes neglect. Neglect can encompass neglect of physical needs (such as food, shelter, and clothing), medical needs (either regular care or a special medical procedure), supervision, or emotional needs (such as attention, affection, and intellectual stimulation). In its most extreme form, neglect may result in abandonment, the *de facto* forfeiture of parental care for a child. While society often views neglect as being more benign than abuse, research has shown that neglect, particularly emotional neglect, can leave far deeper and more debilitating scars in a child.

It is important to distinguish neglect from poverty. There are often various programs available to assist parents who find it difficult to meet their children's needs because of their poverty. A parent who is unable to provide personally for the child's physical needs, but who leaves the child in a good environment that does provide for those needs, has not neglected the child. However, the fact that a parent is poor is not a defense to the failure to meet the child's basic needs. In proving neglect, it is important to address the role that poverty plays in the failure to provide what the child needs, with particular emphasis placed on the parent's refusal or misuse of available services and assistance.

It is also important for the attorney to be aware of the broad range of cultural standards sometimes labeled as neglect. By keeping in mind the need to *prove* some actual detriment or unacceptable risk of harm to the child, the attorney should be able to differentiate between neglect warranting court intervention and simply different, but acceptable, cultural norms.

§ 2.4.3 Medical Neglect

In *Parham v J.R.*,[51] the United States Supreme Court stated that parents have "a 'high duty' to recognize symptoms of illness and to seek and follow medical advice."[52] Failure to obtain appropriate medical care for a child may constitute medical neglect. If the parent never takes the child for medical care, and the child's health is adversely affected because of that failure, the court may find medical neglect. The important issue of proof is the adverse affect of the failure on the child's medical health. Most medical neglect cases come to the attention of the court when a child has a particular medical crisis or condition and the parent refuses to follow a physician's advice concerning treatment. Where the parent acts contrary to medical advice without competent medical advice supporting the parent's decision, the court may find medical neglect. However,

---

[51] 442 U.S. 584 (1979) (ruling on requirements for parents voluntarily admitting their minor children to mental health institutions).

[52] *Id.* at 602.

where there is considerable risk in the proposed procedure or the parents are acting on medical advice, courts have accorded great deference to the parents' judgment in choosing medical treatment. Where the medical condition is life-threatening, and the risks of withholding the proposed treatment are much greater than the risks associated with the treatment, courts are more likely to find medical neglect and order the recommended treatment.

Medical neglect cases often involve religious issues, and a number of states have specific statutory provisions providing some special protections in such circumstances. However, in *Prince v. Massachusetts*[53] the U.S. Supreme Court stated that the "right to practice religion freely does not include liberty to expose the community or the child to communicable disease or the latter to ill health or death."[54] The Supreme Court has held that the constitution does not forbid a finding of medical neglect when the parent's religiously motivated failure to provide medical care seriously endangers the child.[55]

§ 2.4.4 Failure to Thrive

Babies who are denied attention and affection may suffer from nonorganic failure to thrive syndrome (FTT). These babies are born with a normal weight but do not gain weight and develop normally. Their failure to grow as expected is not because of a physical problem. Sometimes the baby does not gain weight normally at home because the family is too poor to obtain proper food or formula or because the inexperienced parents do not know how or how often to feed the child. This possible cause for the baby's condition is usually determined by an initial interview by a doctor, nurse, or social worker. Such a cause is not FTT, but may constitute neglect by virtue of the failure to provide adequate nutrition. Sometimes the child has an organic defect or disease that prevents proper absorption of nutrients. Sometimes the child is genetically small for gestational age (SGA), just as some adults are short. The parents are not to blame for these conditions, and no neglect is involved, except to the extent that the parents of a child with an organic problem did not seek proper medical attention or follow through with the medical advice prescribed. Such children are not FTT babies. The final diagnosis of FTT is often made by placing the baby in a controlled environment, sometimes a foster home, but more typically a hospital, where the baby gains weight rapidly.

---

[53] 321 U.S. 158 (1944) (ruling on whether a parent may be convictied for providing children with religious literature to sell on the street in violation of child labor laws).

[54] *Id.* at 166-167

[55] *See Jehovah's Witnesses in State of Washington v. King County Hospital Unit No. 1*, 390 U.S. 598 (1968) (per curiam), aff'g, 278 F. Supp. 488 (W.D. Wash. 1967) (upholding state statute authorizing dependency when parents refuse to allow their children to have blood transfusions).

§ 2.4.5 Educational Neglect

States generally require children to attend school through a certain grade or until a certain age. If the parent does not send the child to school or is unable to enforce school attendance, the parent may be said to have educationally neglected the child. States that permit home-schooling generally have some pre-requisites or require certain performance on standardized tests. Where home schooling is inadequate, the child may found to be neglected. Where the state requires certain qualifications of the home teacher, proof that the parent lacks the minimum qualifications may be sufficient to show educational neglect.

Chapter 3   MENTAL HEALTH AND RELATED PROFESSIONAL EVALUATIONS IN CHILD WELFARE PROCEEDINGS*

by Ann M. Haralambie[1] and Christina Little[2]

§ 3.1 Introduction

Mental health and related professional evaluations of child and adult parties involved in child welfare proceedings are essential in terms of treatment planning and case disposition. For example, parents involved in child welfare proceedings often have diagnosed or diagnosable mental health or substance abuse conditions and require proper identification and treatment.[3]

Children also often have developmental, medical, or mental health conditions that can challenge parenting and require specialized services.[4] Many states' laws provide that the mental illness of a parent may constitute grounds for dependency or termination of parental rights. The mere fact of a diagnosis, however, is only the beginning of the inquiry. The crucial determination is the effect of the mental illness on the parent's ability to care for the child. If the parent neglects or abuses the child or places the child in physical or emotional jeopardy, then the mental illness is relevant. A parent's mental illness may also impair his or her ability to benefit from services, or it may impact which types of services are effective. On the other hand, if the mental illness manifests itself as nothing more serious than eccentricity or problems similar to those of parents who are not labeled mentally ill, or if the mental illness is being controlled by medication or other therapy and the parent is treatment adherent, then it is not relevant.

---

* Portions of this chapter were adapted from *Handling Child Custody, Abuse and Adoption Cases*, by Ann Haralambie, and used with permission of West, a Thomson business. For more information about this publication please call 800-328-9352 or visit http://www.west.thomson.com. Additionally, portions were adapted with permission from other works by Ann Haralambie. The excerpts were previously published in The Child's Attorney: A Guide to Representing Children in Custody, Adoption, and Protection Cases and Child Sexual Abuse in Civil Cases: A Guide to Custody and Tort Actions, published by the American Bar Association, copyright 1993 and 1999, respectively. All rights reserved. Reprinted by Permission.

[1] Ann M. Haralambie is a certified family law specialist practicing in Tucson, Arizona. She is also an author and speaker in the fields of family and children's law.

[2] Christina Little, Ph.D., is a licensed psychologist and the Director of Research and Evaluation for the Infants in Foster & Kinship Care Program at the Kempe Children's Center, Department of Pediatrics, University of Colorado School of Medicine.

[3] U.S. DEP'T OF HEALTH AND HUMAN SERVS., BLENDING PERSPECTIVES AND BUILDING COMMON GROUND: A REPORT TO CONGRESS ON SUBSTANCE ABUSE AND CHILD PROTECTION (1999).

[4] R.B. Clyman, B. Jones Harden & C. Little, *Assessment, Intervention, and Research with Infants in Out-of-Home Placement*, INFANT MENT. HEALTH J., 23(5), 435-453 (2002).

If the state removes a child from a parent's custody, the state is obligated under the Adoption and Safe Families Act (ASFA)[5] to provide rehabilitative services to reunify the family if possible. Before a parent's rights may be terminated, however, courts generally require a finding that the parent is unfit and unlikely to become fit within a reasonable period of time. Mere progress by a parent, however, will not be sufficient if the child is still at risk. Under ASFA, the relevant time periods have been shortened. Therefore, the parent's attorney should move quickly to get the parent involved in effective treatment.

§ 3.2 Mental Health Professionals

While different types of mental health professionals may be involved in the child welfare case, the following professionals have the general capacity to evaluate and treat mental illness and should be certified or licensed by a governing body. The disciplines of psychiatry, psychology, and social work each have diverse aspects of training and, by nature of the discipline, these professionals often possess specialized expertise in one or more areas. Further specialization is possible within each discipline. Infants and toddlers are a critical population within the child welfare system that requires specialized expertise in evaluation and treatment. Children three years and under were the largest single group of victims, and were more likely than older children to re-experience maltreatment within six months of the first substantial report.[6] The large majority of children entering foster care is under three years old, and infants and toddlers tend to remain in foster care longer than older children.[7] While resources may be scarce in many communities, there are mental health professionals who sub-specialize in the field of infant mental health.[8]

Some other types of mental health practitioners (*e.g.*, marriage and family therapists) may or may not be licensed or certified. Licensure or certification allows the lawyer and the court to have an "objective evaluation" of a professional's *entry-level* competence for practice.[9] For all professionals, the theoretical underpinnings of various types of training may be quite different.

---

[5] Pub. L. No. 105-89, codified at various sections of Title 42 of the United States Code.

[6] ADMIN. FOR CHILDREN & FAMILIES, U.S. DEP'T OF HEALTH AND HUMAN SERVS., CHILD MALTREATMENT 2002: REPORTS FROM THE STATES TO THE NATIONAL CHILD ABUSE AND NEGLECT DATA SYSTEMS – NATIONAL STATISTICS ON CHILD ABUSE AND NEGLECT (2004).

[7] R.M. Goerge & F. Wulczyn, Placement Experiences of the Youngest Foster Care Population: Findings from the Multistate Foster Care Data Archive, ZERO TO THREE, 19(3), 8-13 (1998).

[8] The Zero to Three organization published a diagnostic manual specific to the birth to three population. "The diagnostic framework presented in Diagnostic Classification of Mental Health and Developmental Disorders of Infancy and Early Childhood (DC: 0-3) seeks to address the need for a systematic, developmentally based approach to the classification of mental health in the first four years of life." (p.3). For information and resources on infant mental health resources, *see* http://zerotothree.org/ztt_professionals.html.

[9] Celia B. Fisher, *American Psychological Association's (1992) Ethics and the Validation of Sexual Abuse in Day-Care Settings*, PSYCHOL. PUB. POL'Y & L., 1(2), 461-478 (1995).

§ 3.2.1 Psychiatrists

A psychiatrist is a licensed medical doctor who specializes in the diagnosis, treatment, and prevention of mental illnesses. Psychiatrists have had an internship and residency in psychiatry following graduation from medical school. If a psychiatrist is "board certified," it means that he or she has met national criteria and passed a rigorous examination in the field by a national specialty board, such as the American Board of Psychiatry and Neurology or the American Board of Forensic Psychiatry. Psychiatrists follow the code of ethics of the American Psychiatric Association. Psychiatrists may be the experts of choice where a party has complex psychiatric diagnoses or is on psychotropic medication. Many psychiatrists pursue training and board certification in subspecialty areas with relevance to child welfare proceedings, including: (1) child and adolescent psychiatry; and (2) substance abuse. In cases where children need to be evaluated and possibly treated with medication, it is important for a psychiatrist specifically trained in child and adolescent psychiatry to be involved.

§ 3.2.2 Psychologists[10]

A psychologist involved in child welfare proceedings is typically a licensed or certified mental health professional who has a Ph.D. (doctor of philosophy) in a field of psychology (generally Clinical Psychology) or a Psy.D (doctor of psychology). In some states, professionals with a Master's degree in Clinical Psychology can also practice as psychologists. In order to be licensed as a psychologist, supervised pre- and post-doctoral mental health internships must be completed and a state licensing examination must be passed. Each state has its own certification or licensing requirements. In addition to the diagnosis and treatment of mental illness and other psychosocial problems, psychologists are extensively trained in psychometric testing and research methodology. Psychologists follow the code of ethics of the American Psychological Association (APA). The APA provides a national procedure for becoming recognized as a diplomate in various psychological specialties, which reflects a certain level of expertise; however, use of the diplomate procedure is not as frequent among psychologists as board certification is for psychiatrists. There is an annual national register of psychologists that lists all psychologists who are certified as health service providers, showing particular qualifications to provide treatment.[11]

---

[10] *See* AMERICAN PSYCHOLOGICAL ASSOCIATION COMMITTEE ON PROFESSIONAL PRACTICE AND STANDARDS, GUIDELINES FOR PSYCHOLOGICAL EVALUATIONS IN CHILD PROTECTION MATTERS (Washington, D.C.: American Psychological Association 1998), *available at* http://www.apa.org/practice/childprotection.html.

[11] COUNCIL FOR THE NAT'L REGISTER OF HEALTH SERV. PROVIDERS IN PSYCHOLOGY, NATIONAL REGISTER OF HEALTH SERVICE PROVIDERS IN PSYCHOLOGY, *available at* http://www.national-register.com.

§ 3.2.3 Social Workers

Social workers who practice mental health evaluation and treatment are specifically titled "Clinical Social Workers." They must complete a Master's Degree in Social Work and are trained in the diagnosis and treatment of mental illness. As part of this degree, they complete extensive internships in clinical settings. Licensing is certified by each state and licenses are not necessarily transferable across states. States require examination as well as completion of an MSW degree. Social workers follow a code of ethics adopted by the National Association of Social Workers (NASW). Experienced licensed clinical social workers may apply to the NASW for Board Certified Diplomate status, which confirms a high level of experience and expertise. Social workers may also pursue doctoral degrees in social work.

§ 3.2.4 Evidentiary Privilege and Confidentiality

In general, patients have an evidentiary privilege protecting their communications with mental health professionals. The privilege is based on state law. States frequently provide such a privilege for psychiatrists, physicians, and psychologists. Some states also extend the privilege to other certified mental health professionals, such as social workers, marriage counselors, and rape crisis counselors. However, the privilege does not arise for communications made during a court-ordered evaluation.[12]

§ 3.3 Evaluations

Child welfare attorneys and evaluation professionals should be mutually clear on the purpose of an evaluation and how it is to be subsequently used. In any written evaluation report, the evaluator should describe the methods used and the reasoning for conclusions and recommendations. The specific reason for an evaluation referral should dictate what type of assessment methods are used and, at times, by what type of professional. A mental health, psychiatric, or psychological evaluation addresses an individual's mental and emotional status, provides diagnostic information, and offers recommendations if appropriate. However, the comprehensive child welfare evaluation should include more than merely a psychiatric or psychological evaluation of each party. In terms of treatment planning for the family and information regarding case disposition, evaluations geared specifically to parenting competencies and the quality of the parent-child relationship are often the most useful for child welfare proceedings.

Three United States Supreme Court cases have changed the foundational requirements for expert testimony: *Daubert v. Merrell Dow Pharmaceuticals*,

---

[12] For a discussion of confidentiality in reporting and investigating child maltreatment, *see* Chapter 10, A Child's Journey Through the Child Welfare System.

Inc.,[13] *G.E. Co. v. Joiner*,[14] and *Kumho Tire Co. v. Carmichael*.[15] Taken together, these cases place great responsibility on the trial court as gatekeepers for determining the reliability of expert testimony and the methods by which the experts arrived at their opinions and conclusions. Therefore, it is important for attorneys to understand the different types of psychological testing and other methods used in an evaluation.

§ 3.3.1 Evaluating the Evaluation

The first thing the attorney needs to do is to evaluate the evaluation on several levels. In child welfare evaluations, the mental health professional should adhere to the same ethical and practice principles that would be used in any other type of evaluation specific to his or her field. Evaluation methods that are culturally insensitive or inappropriately used or interpreted, overstating the reliability or validity of instruments, and otherwise inadequate evaluations can result in unwise decisions by the court in the child welfare proceeding. The credibility and persuasiveness of the report can never exceed those of the expert who made the evaluation. Therefore, the attorney must review the qualifications of the evaluator. The attorney should determine what type of expert conducted the evaluation and how much expertise he or she has in the particular areas involved in the case. For example, if psychometric tests are administered or interpreted as part of the evaluation, the expert should have training in psychometric testing. In child evaluations, the expert must have specialized training in child development and assessment. It is also essential for the evaluator to consider the emotional status of the persons being evaluated. Involvement in child welfare proceedings occur in the context of stress and possible crisis for the family, and the timing of any evaluation in the course of the proceedings should be kept in mind. Examples may include whether or not a traumatizing physical or psychological event has just occurred or the presence of possible separation effects on both parents and children if the child has been removed from the home. Behavior and performance in evaluations may change over time. For example, performance may change in response to intervention, or for children, placement changes. It is recommended that all types of evaluations be based on multiple methods, multiple sources, and multiple sessions.[16] It is important to know exactly how much time the evaluator spent with the persons being evaluated and how that time was used. For example, the attorney should know who participated in the evaluation (some of the parties, all of the parties, friends and relatives, teachers, physicians,

---

[13] 509 U.S. 579 (1993).

[14] 522 U.S. 136 (1997).

[15] 526 U.S. 137 (1999).

[16] Karen S. Budd, Erika D. Felix, LaShaunda M. Poindexter, Anjali T. Naik-Polan, & Christine F. Sloss, *Clinical Assessment of Children in Child Protection Cases: An Empirical Analysis*, PROFESSIONAL PSYCHOLOGY: RESEARCH AND PRACTICE, 33(1), 3-12 (2002).

and other professionals involved with the child or parents), the length of the evaluation, and the procedures used. Further, the attorney should ascertain whether various people were seen individually or together. An evaluation made over a period of time is more likely to be reliable than one made after a one-time visit; however, most agency evaluations of parents or children are made after only one visit. Therefore, there may be a question about whether the findings, particularly those based on one method or source of information, can be generalized. The mental health professional should address the limitations of the evaluation and the generalizability of the findings in the report.

§ 3.3.2 Mental Health Evaluations

Psychological and psychiatric evaluations are performed for many different reasons, and they address problems and competencies that may or may not be relevant to the legal and social issues presented by child welfare proceedings. Therefore, child welfare attorneys need to understand the context and purpose of any procedures and records that are being used. From a mental health professional's standpoint, evaluations can be thought of as forensic or clinical. Forensic evaluations are intended to address a legal issue or question, while clinical assessments are most relevant for treatment needs and planning.[17] Mental health professionals must be cautious not to engage in "multiple relationships," which generally contraindicates the same professional acting as both an evaluator and mental health treatment provider.[18] To understand the treatment needs of a parent or child, a mental health evaluation could focus on one or more different domains, including but not limited to the need for services targeted toward a specific diagnosis of mental illness, substance abuse treatment, or the potential need for psychiatric medication. Specific referral questions regarding a child could also address the psychological and developmental impacts of maltreatment or separation from family, types of services needed in multiple domains, or the impact of visitation or reunification with the birth family.

The attorney should be familiar with the current edition of the American Psychiatric Association's DIAGNOSTIC AND STATISTICAL MANUAL OF MENTAL DISORDERS (DSM),[19] which represents the most recent classification of mental

---

[17] American Academy of Child and Adolescent Psychiatry, *Practice Parameters for the Forensic Evaluation of Children and Adolescents Who May Have Been Physically or Sexually Abused*, J. AM. ACAD. CHILD AND ADOLESCENT PSYCHIATRY, 36 (suppl.), 37S-56S (1997).

[18] American Psychological Association, *Ethical Principles of Psychologists and Code of Conduct*, 57 AM. PSYCHOLOGIST 1060-1073 (2002); Karen S. Budd, Erika D. Felix, LaShaunda M. Poindexter, Anjali T. Naik-Polan, & Christine F. Sloss, *Clinical Assessment of Children in Child Protection Cases: An Empirical Analysis*, PROFESSIONAL PSYCHOLOGY: RESEARCH AND PRACTICE, 33(1), 3-12 (2002); David E. Arredondo & Hon. Leonard P. Edwards, *Attachment, Bonding, and Reciprocal Connectedness: Limitations of Attachment Theory in the Juvenile and Family Court*, 2 JOURNAL OF THE CENTER FOR FAMILIES, CHILDREN & THE COURTS 109 (2000), *available at* http://www.courtinfo.ca.gov/programs/cfcc/pdffiles/109arredando.pdf.

[19] AM. PSYCHIATRIC ASS'N, DIAGNOSTIC AND STATISTICAL MANUAL FOR MENTAL DISORDERS, TEXT REVISION (DSM-IV-TR) (4th ed. 2000) is the current edition.

disorders for both adults and children. Disorders are arranged by categories, and within the categories, more specific disorders are described and assigned a diagnostic number. Each category is explained in general terms, and each specific disorder is described according to essential features, associated features, predisposing factors, and other parameters. Some disorders are further broken down into subtypes, and differential diagnoses for those are listed. The most useful features for attorneys are the diagnostic criteria and differential diagnosis sections. Psychiatric and psychological evaluations frequently contain the DSM diagnosis number. The DSM sets forth five axes on which the individual is to be evaluated. They are:

- Clinical syndromes (Axis I).

- Personality disorders and specific developmental disorders (Axis II).

- Physical disorders and conditions (Axis III).

- Severity of psycho-social stressors (Axis IV).

- Highest level of functioning past year (Axis V).

The Axis I clinical syndromes include disorders such as those involving depression, anxiety (including Post-Traumatic Stress Disorder), psychosis, and substance abuse. Axis I clinical syndromes may be acute or chronic. Axis II disorders, such as Borderline Personality Disorder, tend to be fairly persistent parts of the person's make-up, but currently there are treatment strategies targeted toward some personality disorders.[20] Both Axis I and Axis II conditions require treatment by mental health professionals with expertise in that specific disorder.

§ 3.3.3 Parent-Child Relationship Evaluations

Evaluations of the parent-child relationship are complex and require a great deal of specialized expertise. Evaluations should incorporate multiple methods of gaining information including direct observation of parent and child interactions, preferably in multiple sessions and in natural surroundings, and a consideration of strengths as well as problems. Although there are some general professional guidelines for parent-child evaluations,[21] there are currently no standardized protocols that are widely used. However, promising measures include clinical

---

[20] Marsha M.Linehan, Bryan N. Cochran & Constance A. Kehrer, *Dialectical Behavior Therapy for Borderline Personality Disorder*, in CLINICAL HANDBOOK OF PSYCHOLOGICAL DISORDERS: A STEP-BY-STEP TREATMENT MANUAL, 3rd ed. (David H. Barlow ed., 2001) (New York, NY: The Guilford Press), pp. 470-522.

[21] AMERICAN PSYCHOLOGICAL ASSOCIATION COMMITTEE ON PROFESSIONAL PRACTICE AND STANDARDS, GUIDELINES FOR PSYCHOLOGICAL EVALUATIONS IN CHILD PROTECTION MATTERS (Washington, D.C.: American Psychological Association 1998), *available at* http://www.apa.org/practice/childprotection.html.

adaptations of the Crowell Assessment[22] and the Emotional Availability Scales.[23] Relationship evaluations may be useful in many aspects of a child welfare case, such as providing specific parent and child mental health treatment recommendations, and providing information for making placement and visitation decisions and case dispositions. In very general terms, this type of evaluation should assess the relationships among the relevant adult parties and the child, the needs of the child, and the abilities of the parents or other caregivers to meet those needs.[24]

Specific referrals for evaluation regarding parental capacities, parent-child treatment planning, and case disposition are often variably termed "parent-child interactionals," "attachment studies/evaluations," or "bonding studies/evaluations." There are important distinctions between the meaning of the terms "attachment" and "bonding" from a theoretical child development perspective, and there has been some criticism that the terms are used with a lack of precision in forensic/clinical practice.[25] The concepts of secure and insecure attachment derived from theory and research[26] can be useful in describing child behavior with the caregiver. But from a research perspective, attachment is one aspect of the caregiver-child relationship, and it refers specifically to behavior exhibited by the child in the context of separations and reunions. Empirical research has shown that the majority of maltreated children exhibit disorganized attachment patterns;[27] therefore, observing the specific behaviors of each adult and child with one another is crucial. In making treatment or dispositional recommendations, it is not sufficient to rely solely on broadly termed attachment behavior in a forensic or clinical evaluation. The evaluation should focus on *reciprocal* relationship behaviors between adult and child on a number of dimensions (*e.g.*, parental warmth and control, the ability to read child cues appropriately, and child responsivity to the parent). Additionally, an evaluation of par-

---

[22] Cindy S. Lederman & Joy D. Osofsky, *Infant Mental Health Interventions in Juvenile Court: Ameliorating the Effects of Maltreatment and Deprivation*, PSYCH. PUB. POL'Y & L., 10(1), 162-177 (2004); Judith A. Crowell & Melissa A. Fleischmann, *Use of Structured Research Procedures in Clinical Assessments of Infants*, in CHARLES H. ZEANAH, JR. (Ed.), HANDBOOK OF INFANT MENTAL HEALTH 210-221 (New York, NY: The Guilford Press 1993).

[23] Z. Biringen, J.L. Robinson & R.N. Emde, *The Emotional Availability Scales*, Unpublished Manuscript, University of Colorado, Health Science Center, Denver (1998, 1993).

[24] AMERICAN PSYCHOLOGICAL ASSOCIATION COMMITTEE ON PROFESSIONAL PRACTICE AND STANDARDS, GUIDELINES FOR PSYCHOLOGICAL EVALUATIONS IN CHILD PROTECTION MATTERS (Washington, D.C.: American Psychological Association 1998), *available at* http://www.apa.org/practice/childprotection.html.

[25] David E. Arredondo & Hon. Leonard P. Edwards, *Attachment, Bonding, and Reciprocal Connectedness: Limitations of Attachment Theory in the Juvenile and Family Court*, 2 JOURNAL OF THE CENTER FOR FAMILIES, CHILDREN & THE COURTS 109 (2000), *available at* http://www.courtinfo.ca.gov/programs/cfcc/pdffiles/109arredando.pdf.

[26] *See* Chapter 4, The Impact of Maltreatment on Child Development.

[27] *See* D. Cicchetti & S.L. Toth, *A Developmental Psychopathology Perspective on Child Abuse and Neglect*, J. AM. ACAD. CHILD ADOLESC. PSYCHIATRY, 34(5), 541-563 (1995).

enting capacity should consider the ability to provide adequately for a child's basic needs and safety.

It is possible that the particular needs (*i.e.*, developmental, medical, or mental health) of a specific child may exceed the ability of a specific parent to address them.[28] Prior experience with problematic caregiving can promote child behaviors that, while adaptive in the previous context with an abusive or neglectful parent,[29] can challenge even a typically sensitive caregiver. The child's developmental stage should also be considered in conjunction with specific parenting capacities. If the evaluation identifies parenting deficiencies, the evaluation should include: (1) a description of the specific nature of the deficiencies; (2) a prognosis and recommendations for what would be needed to remediate the problems; and (3) a reasonable estimate of the time the remediation might take. A time estimate is important to assist the parties and the court to determine whether the remediation is likely to occur within the state- and federally-mandated time frames. Subsequent treatment that targets parenting problems should be provided by a mental health professional experienced in parent-child therapy. For infants and toddlers, treatment needs to take place jointly with the primary caregivers and the child. If the child is in non-parental care and reunification is indicated, treatment should occur with the parent and child, for example through therapeutic visitation.[30]

§ 3.4 Psychological Tests

For both adults and children, referral for testing by a psychologist can target functioning in different domains of cognition or other development, provide further information regarding emotional issues, and provide further recommendations for treatment. Child welfare attorneys should be familiar with the most commonly used psychological tests. Consultation with a qualified psychologist can be very useful in helping to understand the tests used in an evaluation, the appropriateness of using the tests, and how they were used and interpreted.

---

[28] AMERICAN PSYCHOLOGICAL ASSOCIATION COMMITTEE ON PROFESSIONAL PRACTICE AND STANDARDS, GUIDELINES FOR PSYCHOLOGICAL EVALUATIONS IN CHILD PROTECTION MATTERS (Washington, D.C.: American Psychological Association 1998), *available at* http://www.apa.org/practice/childprotection.html; Corina Benjet, Sandra T. Azar & Regina Kuersten-Hogan, *Evaluating the Parental Fitness of Psychiatrically Diagnosed Individuals: Advocating a Functional-Contextual Analysis of Parenting*, J. FAM. PSYCHOL., 17(2), 238-251 (2003).

[29] P.M. Crittenden, *Attachment and Risk for Psychopathology: The Early Years*, J. DEV. BEHAV. PEDIATR., 16(3), S12-S15 (1995).

[30] A.F. Lieberman, R. Silverman, & J. Pawl, *Infant-Parent Psychotherapy: Core Concepts and Current Approaches*, in CHARLES H. ZEANAH, JR. (Ed.), HANDBOOK OF INFANT MENTAL HEALTH 472-484 (New York: The Guilford Press 2000); M. Dozier et al., *Intervening with Foster Infants' Caregivers: Targeting Three Critical Needs*, INFANT MENT. HEALTH J., 23(5), 541-554 (2002); C.H. Zeanah, J.A. Larrieu, S.S. Heller, J. Valliere, S. Hinshaw-Fuselier, Y. Aoki et al., *Evaluation of a Preventative Intervention for Maltreated Infants and Toddlers in Foster Care*, J. AM. ACAD. CHILD AND ADOLESCENT PSYCHIATRY, 40(2), 214-221 (2001).

There are hundreds of psychological (psychometric) tests. Some are widely used, and others are not. Some have a solid empirical basis, and others do not. Methods of finding information on test characteristics, test usage, and tester qualifications can be accessed through the American Psychological Association.[31]

If the evaluator used psychological tests, the attorney should know what the tests were, whether they were used properly, and whether the evaluator personally administered the tests and interpreted the results. Tests used as the basis for expert testimony should be used widely in the profession, the norms should be standardized for the population to whom they are being applied, and the tests should be validated for the purposes for which they are used.[32] "Reliability" in a psychological instrument refers to a test being administered and interpreted in the same way by different clinicians. "Validity" refers to whether the instrument really measures what it claims to measure. Attorneys should find out whether the psychological tests used have been established as both reliable and valid. The education, reading ability, and language fluency of the test-taker all affect whether the person being evaluated understands the task he or she is being asked to complete. A perfectly acceptable test can be useless if the test-taker is not able to understand and comply with the requirements of the test. In many evaluation contexts, test takers can be prone to give socially desirable answers and have varying motivation to fully participate. In child welfare proceedings, these issues can be heightened and many factors may influence the willingness of the test taker's compliance, honesty, and willingness to be complete in giving answers. The evaluator should explicitly take the assessment context and the test taker's behavior into consideration when interpreting the results and offering recommendations.

§ 3.4.1 Psychometric Tests

Psychometric tests sample certain information, and the interpretation generalizes from the responses, making assumptions and predictions about a person based on that sampling in comparison to the scores obtained by other people. Psychometric tests are either objective or projective. Objective tests involve standardized administration, scoring, and interpretation that does not require clinical judgment, although clinical judgment should be used to interpret test results for the particular person and context. Projective tests generally examine how a person responds to ambiguous stimuli and rely on clinical interpretation to score as well as to interpret the results. They permit great flexibility in how the person tested responds to the stimulus given. Some tests are based on self-reports, others involve completion of checklists by lay persons such as parents,

---

[31] *See* http://www.apa.org.

[32] A test can be valid and reliable for some uses but not for others. For example, the MMPI (discussed in the section below in *Personality Tests*), is useful for many purposes, but it cannot diagnose someone as a pedophile. Therefore, it is important to know whether there is empirical support for using the test to answer the specific questions being addressed.

foster parents and teachers, and still others rely on direct measurement of performance.

§ 3.4.2 Personality Tests

Personality tests are used in most evaluations in child welfare cases. They measure personality traits, temperament, psychological functioning, and adjustment. They can be either objective or projective tests. The best known objective personality test is the Minnesota Multiphasic Personality Inventory (MMPI), now in a revised edition (MMPI-2),[33] for adults and the MMPI-Adolescent Version (MMPI-A)[34] for adolescents. The test publisher, the University of Minnesota, does not continue to sell the original MMPI, supporting only the MMPI-2. The MMPI-2 is a 567-item true/false test that the test-taker answers by filling in a scoring sheet. Interpretation includes validity scales, clinical scales, and a number of supplemental scales. Another personality test is the Millon Clinical Multiaxial Inventory, now in a revised edition (MCMI-III)[35] and Millon Adolescent Clinical Inventory (MACI).[36] The MCMI-III is a 175-item true/false test that the test-taker answers by filling in a scoring sheet. Interpretation includes validity and clinical scales. The MACI is a similar, 160-item true/false test administered to adolescents between 13 and 19 years of age.

§ 3.4.3 Projective Tests

Projective tests, such as the Rorschach Ink Blot Technique,[37] are very subjectively interpreted. In a projective test, the test taker explains what various ambiguous pictures or situations look like or mean to him or her. The theory behind projective testing is that people will project their personality, experiences, and thought structure into their stories, explanations, or drawings. While the explanations may suggest certain personality characteristics or psychological traits or dynamics, they are not conclusive. There may or may not be well accepted methods for interpreting the results of particular projective tests. For example, the Rorschach may be interpreted based on the Comprehensive System.[38] In the Rorschach, the test-taker observes ten abstract inkblot cards and describes what he or she sees. Responses on the Rorschach or other projective tests, such

---

[33] STARKE R. HATHAWAY & J. CHARLNEY MCKINLEY, MINNESOTA MULTIPHASIC PERSONALITY INVENTORY-2 (1989).

[34] JAMES N. BUTCHER ET AL., MMPI-A: MINNESOTA MULTIPHASIC PERSONALITY INVENTORY-ADOLESCENT: MANUAL FOR ADMINISTRATION, SCORING, AND INTERPRETATION (The University of Minnesota Press MMPI Adolescent Project Committee 1992).

[35] THEODORE MILLON, THE MILLON CLINICAL MULTIAXIAL INVENTORY-III MANUAL (3d ed.) (Minneapolis: National Computer Systems 1987).

[36] THEODORE MILLON ET AL., MANUAL: THE MILLON ADOLESCENT CLINICAL INVENTORY (1994).

[37] HERMANN RORSCHACH, PSYCHODIAGNOSTIK (1932).

[38] JOHN E. EXNER, 1 THE RORSCHACH: A COMPREHENSIVE SYSTEM: BASIC FOUNDATIONS (Wiley 1993).

as the various Draw-a-Person Tests (DAP),[39] and Sentence Completion Tests,[40] Thematic Apperception Test (TAT)[41] and Children's Apperception Test (CAT),[42] may be less reliable when administered to highly creative people, whose unusual responses may be a function of their creativity rather than personality traits or emotional disturbances. With the TAT and CAT, the test-taker is shown a number of cards depicting an ambiguous activity and asked to tell a story about what is depicted.

If interpretation of a child's drawings or paintings is part of the evaluation, the attorney should become familiar with the methodology used in interpreting artwork. The attorney should also determine whether the artwork was created as part of a therapeutic exercise or done outside of the direct evaluative process. If the art was produced outside of the evaluation, it is important to know the circumstances of the creation. For example, the interpretation of a drawing made during free play may differ from that of a drawing responsive to a particular school assignment. While projective tests are often used in clinical practice, because of lack of validity and reliability, they are less useful in a forensic child welfare evaluation.

§ 3.4.4 Developmental and Intelligence Tests

Because children involved with the child welfare system often show developmental delays and because developmental levels are relevant to child welfare proceedings, tests are often given to locate the child's progress and functioning relative to other children of the same age. Even very young babies can be evaluated in terms of their achievement of developmental milestones as well as the quality of their developmental progress (*e.g.*, motor movement quality). Specialized training in infant assessment is necessary for identifying problems and competencies in this age group. Common developmental tests for infants and toddlers are the Denver Development Screening Test[43] and the Bayley Scales of Infant Development-II.[44] Developmental evaluations for all children should take into account the child's prenatal experience (*e.g.*, exposure to alcohol and illegal substances), risk factors at birth (*e.g.*, low birth weight, prematu-

---

[39] *See* EDWARD STEINBERG, CLINICAL JUDGMENT AND THE VALIDATION OF THE DAP (Ann Arbor, Mich.: University Microfilms 1973).

[40] *See generally* JAMES QUINTER HOLSOPPLE & FLORENCE R. MIALE, SENTENCE COMPLETION: A PROJECTIVE METHOD FOR THE STUDY OF PERSONALITY (Springfield, Illinois: Charles C. Thomas 1954).

[41] HENRY MURRAY AND LEOPOLD BELLAK, THEMATIC APPERCEPTION TEST (1973). *See also* LEOPOLD BELLAK, THEMATIC APPERCEPTION TEST, THE CHILDREN'S APPERCEPTION TEST, and THE SENIOR APPERCEPTION TECHNIQUE IN CLINICAL USE (Boston: Allyn and Bacon 1997).

[42] HENRY MURRAY AND LEOPOLD BELLAK, CHILDREN'S APPERCEPTION TEST (1974).

[43] WILLIAM FRANKENBURG, DENVER DEVELOPMENTAL SCREENING TEST (Denver: Ladoca Project & Publishing Foundation 1970).

[44] N. BAYLEY, MANUAL FOR THE BAYLEY SCALES OF INFANT DEVELOPMENT (2nd ed., 1993) (San Antonio, TX: The Psychological Corporation).

rity), and other pediatric issues. It is important for the attorney to facilitate the evaluator's ability to review this collateral information because it can be very difficult to obtain for children involved in the child welfare system.

For older children and adults, several intelligence tests are available, the most widely used being the Wechsler Adult Intelligence Scale-III (WAIS-III),[45] the Wechsler Intelligence Scale for Children-IV (WISC-IV),[46] and the Wechsler Preschool and Primary Scale of Intelligence-III (WPPSI-III).[47] These tests are comprised of separately scored subtests, which measure various aspects of general intelligence. The subtests fall within two categories: verbal and performance. The combined subtest scores yield verbal IQ and performance IQ scores, which are then combined again to yield a full-scale IQ score. Although the performance subscales are designed to assess non-language-based capacities, success on many of these tasks does require some receptive language abilities in order to understand the directions. Significant differences (as specified in each test manual) within and between verbal and performance IQ scores can indicate the possibility of a learning disability or other problematic cognitive process. This pattern then indicates further specialized testing to understand the full impact of intellectual functioning on the person's behavior and to refine recommendations for treatment.

§ 3.4.5 Neuropsychological Tests

Neuropsychological testing can help to identify behavioral indicators of organic brain disorders and provide more specific information about cognitive functioning and thought processes. Neuropsychological testing can illuminate possible connections between brain functioning and specific types of problematic behaviors and help to differentiate them from more psychologically-based disorders. A common test used to measure vulnerabilities in brain functioning is the Bender Visual-Motor Gestalt Test. (Bender-Gestalt II).[48] It measures psychomotor development, orientation, memory, calculation, learning, knowledge, and judgment abilities and changes. A leading group of neuropsychological tests is the Halstead-Reitan Neuropsychological Battery.[49]

§ 3.4.6 Achievement Tests

Achievement tests measure mastery over specific fields of information. Schools are required to administer some achievement tests to their students.

---

[45] DAVID WECHSLER, WECHSLER ADULT INTELLIGENCE SCALE - III (Harcourt Assessment, 1997).

[46] DAVID WECHSLER, WECHSLER INTELLIGENCE SCALE FOR CHILDREN - IV (Harcourt Assessment, 2003).

[47] DAVID WECHSLER, WECHSLER PRESCHOOL AND PRIMARY SCALE OF INTELLIGENCE - III (Harcourt Assessment, 2002).

[48] LAURETTA BENDER & THE AMERICAN. ORTHOPSYCHIATRIC ASSOCIATION, INC., BENDER VISUAL-MOTOR GESTALT TEST (Bender-Gestalt II).

[49] WARD HALSTEAD & RALPH REITAN, HALSTEAD-REITAN NEUROLOGICAL BATTERY (1959, 1979).

Commonly used achievement tests are the Stanford Achievement Test, 10th edition (SAT-10),[50] the Peabody Individual Achievement Test-R,[51] Wide Range Achievement Test-3 (WRAT-3),[52] and the Woodcock-Johnson III Complete Battery.[53] The use of achievement tests in conjunction with intelligence tests and other cognitive tests can provide information regarding psycho-social or other issues that may interfere with school or vocational achievement. For example, a pattern of average or high cognitive abilities in combination with low achievement suggests that further assessment is warranted.

§ 3.4.7 Checklists and Inventories

There are also a variety of checklists and inventories for use with children and adults, such as the Achenbach Child Behavior Checklist,[54] Beck Depression Inventory (2nd edition),[55] Parenting Stress Index,[56] Parent-Child Relationship Inventory,[57] the Child Abuse Potential Inventory,[58] and the Child Sexual Behavior Inventory.[59] The information provided in these checklists and inventories varies in usefulness based on who is filling out the form.

§ 3.4.8 Scoring and Interpreting Test Results

Some experts have the tests interpreted by a computer program or another person. For example, the MMPI-2 and the MCMI-III are often scored by computer. A computer report, in addition to listing the various scores, may also contain text interpretations. However, these interpretations do not take into account various relevant clinical factors and case-specific facts that are important to understanding the family functioning and creating a usable case plan. For many tests, clinical interpretation, based on the evaluator's knowledge of the client, is essential in interpreting the test results. In addition, some test results

---

[50] HARCOURT ASSESSMENT, STANFORD ACHIEVEMENT TEST (10th ed.) (Harcourt Assessment, Gallaudet Research Institute 2003).

[51] LLOYD DUNN, PEABODY INDIVIDUAL ACHIEVEMENT TEST (Circle Pines, Minnesota: American Guidance Service, Inc. 1970).

[52] GARY WILKINSON, WIDE RANGE ACHIEVEMENT TEST (WRAT-3) (Wilmington, DE: Wide Range, Inc. 1993).

[53] RICHARD W. WOODCOCK ET AL., WOODCOCK-JOHNSON III COMPLETE BATTERY (The Riverside Publishing Company 2001).

[54] THOMAS M. ACHENBACH, CHILD BEHAVIOR CHECKLIST (University of Vermont Psychiatry Department 1991).

[55] AARON BECK, ROBERT A. STEER & GREGORY K. BROWN., BECK DEPRESSION INVENTORY MANUAL (2d ed.) (San Antonio, Texas: Psychological Corp. 1996).

[56] RICHARD ABIDIN, PARENTING STRESS INDEX (Pediatric Psychology Press 1990).

[57] ANTHONY B. GERARD, PARENT-CHILD RELATIONSHIP INVENTORY (Western Psychological Services 1994).

[58] JOEL S. MILNER, CHILD ABUSE POTENTIAL INVENTORY MANUAL (2d ed. 1986) (Lutz, FL: Psychological Assessment Resources, Inc.).

[59] *See* William N. Friedrich et al., *Child Sexual Behavior Inventory: Normative and Clinical Comparisons*, PSYCHOLOGICAL ASSESSMENT 4, 303-311 (1992).

are affected by race, sex, socioeconomic group, or education. Standardized tests compare the test-taker's answers with those of other persons. Therefore, it is important that the standard group be fairly representative. Some tests have never been standardized. Some tests are standardized to a very small or a racially skewed sample. Some tests are standardized on a clinical or incarcerated population, which may, therefore, suggest a higher level of pathology.

Computer scoring can be extremely helpful to reduce scoring errors and to compile various subsets of information, such as scoring the supplemental scales in the MMPI-2. Computer-generated interpretations of tests, particularly personality tests raise difficult problems because they are based on assumptions that may not apply to the person being tested and can be oversimplified. It is important for clinical information to be included in any interpretation of results. For example, the test-taker's education, socioeconomic background, occupation, and context of taking the test must be taken into consideration. Results for people in a forensic setting may need to be interpreted differently than for people in a clinic or research setting.

§ 3.5 Child Sexual Abuse Evaluations

Most child sexual abuse cases do not have any positive medical findings,[60] making the mental health evaluation particularly important. However, evaluations in the area of child sexual abuse raise many issues, and the empirical data continues to be compiled concerning best practices.[61] Several professional organizations have provided practice guidelines regarding the evaluation of child sexual abuse.[62] In addition, structured interview protocols have also been developed, but they are not widely used in clinical practice.[63] Child welfare attorneys should keep up-to-date with the professional literature to assist them in critically reviewing evaluations of alleged victims and alleged perpetrators, and evaluating "risk assessments," which attempt to address whether a person is likely to have molested a child or whether someone who has molested a child is likely to re-molest.

While practice guidelines vary, there are some general consistencies regarding interviewing children in sexual abuse evaluations largely due to continuing

---

[60] For further discussion of sexual abuse, *see* § 2.2, Sexual Abuse.

[61] *See generally* ANN M. HARALAMBIE, CHILD SEXUAL ABUSE IN CIVIL CASES: A GUIDE TO CUSTODY AND TORT ACTIONS, Ch. 6 (American Bar Association 1999).

[62] W. Bernet, *Practice Parameters for the Forensic Evaluation of Children and Adolescents Who May Have Been Physically or Sexually Abused*, J. AM. ACAD. CHILD & ADOLESC. PSYCHIATRY, 36 (10 Suppl), 37S-56S (1997).

[63] Yael Orbach et al., *Assessing the Value of Structured Protocols for Forensic Interviews of Alleged Child Abuse Victims*, CHILD ABUSE & NEGLECT, 24(6), 733-752 (2000); Web site for the National Institute of Child Health and Human Development (NICHD), *available at* http://www.nichd.nih.gov; Web site for the National Institutes of Health, *available at* http://www.nih.gov.

research in child development and related fields. For example, most guidelines recommend the reliance on free-recall prompts (*i.e.*, invitations "to report remembered information without input from the interviewer)[64] at least as an initial strategy when interviewing children because this method provides greater accuracy.[65] The diagnostic use of anatomically detailed dolls is specifically disapproved by all of the protocols and guidelines that mention the issue. There is no MMPI scale or profile that can identify an incestuous offender or a molested child. Similarly, there is no item or cluster of items on the Child Sexual Behavior Inventory (CSBI) that can determine whether a child has or has not been sexually abused. A National Institute of Justice Research Report says:

> The sexual abusers of children are highly dissimilar in terms of personal characteristics, life experiences, and criminal histories. No single "molester profile" exists. Child molesters arrive at deviancy via multiple pathways and engage in many different sexual and nonsexual "acting out" behaviors.[66]

While there may not be a profile or syndrome that is diagnostic of child sexual abuse, experts may testify that various behaviors, symptoms, and disorders are consistent with sexual abuse. Testimony about any such patterns or profiles, however, must be based on the foundational showing of reliability and acceptance in the field of the pattern or profile. Explicit sexualized play in the absence of a history explaining the child's knowledge (such as exposure to watching people engaged in sexual activity or exposure to sexually explicit pornographic material) is a frequently discussed behavior that may be indicative of sexual abuse.[67] However, not all molested children engage in sexualized play, and not all children who engage in sexualized play have been molested.

The term "syndrome" has been used very loosely, with a great deal of confusion in the legal arena. The syndromes used in sexual abuse cases are generally not really syndromes in the diagnostic sense. The most prominent syndrome that had been used to understand children's behavior is the Child Sexual Abuse Accommodation Syndrome (CSAAS),[68] which suggested that many children share a pattern of response to sexual abuse that includes feelings and behaviors of secrecy, helplessness, entrapment and accommodation, and delayed, conflict-

---

[64] Jan Aldridge et al., *Using a Human Figure Drawing to Elicit Information from Alleged Victims of Child Sexual Abuse*, J. Consult. Clin. Psychol., 72(2), 304-316 (2004).

[65] American Professional Society on the Abuse of Children, Guidelines for Psychosocial Evaluation of Suspected Sexual Abuse in Young Children (Rev. ed., 2002) (Chicago: APSAC).

[66] Robert A. Prentky et al., U.S. Dep't of Justice, Child Sexual Molestation: Research Issues 2 (NIJ Research Report NCJ 163390, 1997).

[67] *See generally* William N. Friedrich, *Sexual Victimization and Sexual Behavior in Children: A Review of Recent Literature*, 17 Child Abuse & Neglect 59 (1993).

[68] *See, e.g.*, Roland Summit, *The Child Sexual Abuse Accommodation Syndrome*, 7 Child Abuse & Neglect 177 (1983).

ed, and unconvincing disclosures and retraction. While sexually abused children may individually experience these feelings and show these behaviors, the validity of the CSAAS is not widely accepted,[69] and there has been little empirical evidence supporting this theory. One exception is that research has consistently indicated that the majority of children who have been sexually abused do considerably delay disclosure of the abuse.[70]

Not every physician or mental health professional is an expert in intrafamilial child sexual abuse, which is an extremely specialized field. Especially where the sexual abuse allegations arise where there is also family law litigation, a circumstance that often raises a high level of skepticism, it is essential that a properly qualified expert evaluate the allegations. As with other areas of forensic evaluation, sexual abuse evaluators must keep current with the latest research on relevant scientific topics, such as children's memory and response to interviewing techniques, in addition to professional practice guidelines.

§ 3.6 Conclusion

Several types of evaluations performed by mental health professionals can be helpful in appropriate treatment planning and to assist the court in case disposition at all stages. As child welfare cases overwhelmingly involve families with multiple problems and service needs, evaluations tapping into different domains of functioning will likely be required to identify the individual needs of parents and children, as well as the quality and treatment of the parent-child relationship itself. When involved in making referrals it is important for the child welfare lawyer to communicate to the evaluator what specific information is necessary for the case and how the evaluation results and recommendations are intended to be utilized. Familiarity with the professional codes of ethics and most recent practice guidelines for varied mental health professionals will assist the child welfare attorney in ensuring that evaluations provided on the behalf of parent and child clients will be of high quality and useful in directing treatment planning and case disposition.

---

[69] Kamala London, Maggie Bruck, Stephen J. Ceci, & Daniel W. Shuman, *Disclosure of Child Sexual Abuse: What Does the Research Tell Us About the Ways that Children Tell?*, PSYCHOL. PUB. POL'Y & L., 11(1), 194-226 (2005); Celia B. Fisher, *American Psychological Association's (1992) Ethics and the Validation of Sexual Abuse in Day-Care Settings*, PSYCHOL. PUB. POL'Y & L., 1(2), 461-478 (1995).

[70] Kamala London, Maggie Bruck, Stephen J. Ceci, & Daniel W. Shuman, *Disclosure of Child Sexual Abuse: What Does the Research Tell Us About the Ways that Children Tell?*, PSYCHOL. PUB. POL'Y & L., 11(1), 194-226 (2005).

Chapter 4 THE IMPACT OF MALTREATMENT ON CHILD DEVELOPMENT*

by Ann M. Haralambie[1] and Stacy A. Klapper[2]

§ 4.1 Child Development

Child welfare attorneys need to have a general understanding of child development and a realization that children's needs will vary significantly, depending on the age and developmental stage of the child. All attorneys in the case need to review the child's statements and behaviors in light of the individual child's developmental level. Additionally, as the ABA and NACC/ABA Standards[3] provide, the child's attorney should always consider the child's developmental level—both when communicating with the child and when making legal decisions for the child. This should include an assessment of the child's "emerging behavioral repertoire, cognitive and language functions, social and emotional processes, and changes occurring in anatomical structures and physiological process of the brain."[4]

From birth through adolescence, the needs of children are ever changing. Development involves progressive changes throughout the life span, with changes being more rapid and definitive in the early years than in later years. "Developmental psychopathologists perceive development as consisting of a number of important age and stage-appropriate tasks which, upon emergence, remain critical to the child's continual adaptation, although decreasing in salience relative to newly emerging tasks."[5] Chronological age provides only an

---

*   Portions of this chapter were adapted from *Handling Child Custody, Abuse and Adoption Cases*, by Ann Haralambie, and used with permission of West, a Thomson business. For more information about this publication please call 800-328-9352 or visit http://www.west.thomson.com. Additionally, portions of this chapter were adapted from Jean M. Baker & Rachel B. Burkholder, *Child Development and Child Custody*, previously published in <ins>The Child's Attorney: A Guide to Representing Children in Custody, Adoption, and Protection Cases</ins>, published by the American Bar Association, copyright 1993. All rights reserved. Reprinted by Permission.

[1] Ann M. Haralambie, J.D., is a certified family law specialist practicing in Tucson, Arizona. She is also an author and speaker in the fields of family and children's law.

[2] Stacy A. Klapper, Psy.D., is a licensed clinical psychologist, specializing in infant mental health. Dr. Klapper is on the faculty of the Irving Harris Program in Child Development and Infant Mental Heath at the University of Colorado Health Sciences Center. She is the team psychologist for the Infant Program at the Kempe Children's Center/Children's Hospital in Denver, Colorado, and she maintains a small private practice.

[3] *See* Appendix A-2, American Bar Association Standards of Practice for Lawyers Who Represent Children in Abuse and Neglect Cases.

[4] D. Cicchetti & S.L. Toth, *A Developmental Psychopathology Perspective on Child Abuse and Neglect*, J. AM. ACAD. CHILD ADOLESC. PSYCHIATRY, 34(5), 541-563 (1995).

[5] J.W. Pearce & T.D. Pezzot-Pearce, *Attachment Theory and its Implications for Psychotherapy with Maltreated Children*, CHILD ABUSE & NEGLECT, 18(5), 425-438 (1994).

estimate of a child's developmental level, as typical development often follows an uneven course.[6] For example, a child may be verbally precocious, but lack age-appropriate competency in peer skills or emotional regulation. Developmental competencies in many areas, such as emotional regulation and attachment, continue to unfold across the lifespan, with new experiences shaping new opportunities for growth.[7] "As such, individuals will experience the same events differently depending on their level of functioning across all domains of psychological and biological development."[8] This has important implications for understanding the developmental consequences resulting from childhood maltreatment.

The experience of being maltreated will have different meaning for individual children according to their level of functioning at the time of the maltreatment.[9] For example, a child with well-developed language skills will have a different skill set for understanding and containing the maltreatment experience than a pre-verbal child.[10] While not all children who have been maltreated will display symptoms at the time of court involvement, there is clear evidence that abuse and neglect impact interconnected areas of development across the lifespan.[11] Therefore, even the asymptomatic child warrants assessment following the experience of maltreatment, and children who have completed a successful course of treatment may experience a resurgence of symptomatology as new developmental challenges emerge.

Although there is no one unified approach, child development is historically described as an unvarying series of stages, each one being qualitatively distinct from the preceding one, and being reflected by dramatic changes in physical, cognitive, language, and social/emotional characteristics. There are numerous

---

[6] T.B. Brazelton, Touchpoints: Your Child's Emotional and Behavioral Development (Reading, MA: Perseus Books 1992).

[7] D. Cicchetti & S.L. Toth, *A Developmental Psychopathology Perspective on Child Abuse and Neglect*, J. Am. Acad. Child Adolesc. Psychiatry, 34(5), 541-563 (1995).

[8] *Id.*

[9] *Id.*

[10] T. Gaensbauer, *Trauma in the Preverbal Period: Symptoms, Memories, and Developmental Impact*, 50 The Psychoanalytic Study of the Child 122-149 (Albert J. Solnit, Peter B. Neubauer, Samuel Abrams & A. Scott Dowling, eds.) (Yale University Press 1995); M. Sugar, *Toddlers' Traumatic Memories*, 13 Infant Ment. Health J. 245-251 (1992); R.A. Thompson & J.M. Wyatt, *Current Research on Child Maltreatment: Implications for Educators*, Educational Psychology Review, 11(3), 173-201 (1999).

[11] D.J. Kolko, *Child Physical Abuse*, in The APSAC Handbook on Child Maltreatment 21-50 (J. Briere & L. Berliner, eds.) (Thousand Oaks, CA: Sage Publications 1996); R. Malinosky-Rummell & D.J. Hansen, *Long-term Consequences of Child Physical Abuse*, Psychological Bulletin, 114(1), 68-79 (1993); R.C. Pianta, B. Egeland & M.F. Erickson, *The Antecedents of Maltreatment: Results of the Mother-Child Interaction Research Project*, in Child Maltreatment: Theory and Research on the Causes and Consequences of Child Abuse and Neglect 203-253 (D. Cicchetti & V. Carlson, eds.) (New York: Cambridge University Press 1989); R.A. Thompson & J.M. Wyatt, *Current Research on Child Maltreatment: Implications for Educators*, Educational Psychology Review, 11(3), 173-201 (1999).

theories of child development, each of which traces the child's growth through a number of distinct stages. Each of these theories describes the particular activities or behaviors that are most significant for the child at the given stages of development. Certain developmental theorists have focused on specific aspects of development. For example, Piaget[12] focused on cognitive development, and Erik Erikson[13] focused on psychosocial development. Others have taken a more comprehensive approach and have written detailed descriptions of children's overall growth and development at various ages.[14]

While stage models of development provide a framework for placing skills and abilities within a predictable context, it is important to remember that the range of normal behavior is vast and varied. Brazelton notes that, "no developmental line in a child proceeds in a continuous upward course."[15] Typically developing children display widely divergent behaviors, and tasks of infancy have implications across the lifespan.[16] With maturation, a child will re-work earlier developmental stages, consolidating skills and acquiring more sophisticated understanding and solutions to problems. In this way, developmental tasks of childhood remain salient throughout the lifespan, as greater maturational strength is applied to previously acquired competencies. Similarly, stressors such as losses, illness, moves, and changes in caregiving relationships can impact developmental functioning, such that children appear to lose competencies for a time. For example, a child who has successfully completed toilet training may lose this skill under stress. In addition, as new developmental challenges emerge, such as the onset of walking, children may experience a brief regression in skills in other areas, such as verbal communication.[17]

> We have at all times to think in terms of the interactions and transactions that are constantly occurring between an ever-developing personality and the environment, especially the people in it. This means that it is necessary to think of each personality as moving through life along some developmental pathway, with the particular pathway followed always being determined by the interaction of the personality as it has so far developed and the environment in which it then finds itself.[18]

---

[12] *See, e.g.,* JEAN PIAGET, THE LANGUAGE AND THOUGHT OF THE CHILD (1955).

[13] *See, e.g.,* ERIC ERICKSON, CHILDHOOD AND SOCIETY (1950).

[14] *See, e.g.,* ARNOLD GESELL & FRANCES L. ILG, THE CHILD FROM FIVE TO TEN (1946); BURTON WHITE, THE FIRST THREE YEARS OF LIFE (2d ed. 1985).

[15] T.B. BRAZELTON, TOUCHPOINTS: YOUR CHILD'S EMOTIONAL AND BEHAVIORAL DEVELOPMENT (Reading, MA: Perseus Books 1992).

[16] JOHN BOWLBY, 1 ATTACHMENT AND LOSS: ATTACHMENT (1969); DANIEL STERN, THE INTERPERSONAL WORLD OF THE INFANT: A VIEW FROM PSYCHOANALYSIS AND DEVELOPMENTAL PSYCHOLOGY (New York: Basic Books 1985).

[17] T.B. BRAZELTON, TOUCHPOINTS: YOUR CHILD'S EMOTIONAL AND BEHAVIORAL DEVELOPMENT (Reading, MA: Perseus Books 1992).

[18] J. Bowlby, *Developmental Psychiatry Comes of Age*, 145 AM. J. PSYCHIATRY 1-10 (1988).

Most importantly, successful development depends on the health of the relationship between the child and the caregiving environment. The child and the caregiver bring particular strengths and challenges to the relationship, and the "goodness of fit" between what the child needs and what the parent has to offer sets the stage for developmental risk or healthy outcomes. "Virtually all contemporary researchers agree that the development of children is a highly complex process that is influenced by the interplay of nature and nurture . . . In simple terms, children affect their environments at the same time that their environments are affecting them."[19]

§ 4.1.1 Physical Development

Children require a caregiving environment that supports their physical growth. "Despite a tendency to see infants as objects existing in a material world where their talents unfold in some maturational sequence, the reality is that, from conception, the infant is embedded in relationships with others who provide the nutrition for both physical and psychological growth."[20] Studies of children who have experienced severe environmental deprivation reveal that when a child lacks appropriate environmental stimulation and support for exploration, the child's physical development, in addition to his or her cognitive and social-emotional development, may move off track.[21] The physical development of children follows a sequential course that is quite consistent in all normal children who are raised without any extreme environmental deprivations. A child's muscle control will develop without any attempt on the parent's part to teach the child, however parents can optimize their child's motor development by providing opportunities for supervised play and exploration, encouraging the child to use his or her body to actively learn about the child's surroundings.[22] The elemental human desire to explore one's environment and gain mastery through experience drives much of early motor development.[23] The age range during

---

[19] National Research Council and Institute of Medicine, FROM NEURONS TO NEIGHBORHOODS: THE SCIENCE OF EARLY CHILDHOOD DEVELOPMENT, Committee on Integrating the Science of Early Childhood Development, Board on Children, Youth, and Families (Jack P. Shonkoff & Deborah A. Phillips, eds.) (Washington, D.C.: National Academy Press 2000), *available at* http://books.nap.edu/catalog/9824.html?onpi_newsdoc100300.

[20] A.J. Sameroff & B.H. Fiese, *Models of Development and Developmental Risk in* C.H. Zeanah, Jr. (Ed). HANDBOOK OF INFANT MENTAL HEALTH (2nd Ed., 2000) (New York: The Guilford Press).

[21] National Research Council and Institute of Medicine, FROM NEURONS TO NEIGHBORHOODS: THE SCIENCE OF EARLY CHILDHOOD DEVELOPMENT 24, Committee on Integrating the Science of Early Childhood Development, Board on Children, Youth, and Families (Jack P. Shonkoff & Deborah A. Phillips, eds.) (Washington, D.C.: National Academy Press 2000), *available at* http://books.nap.edu/catalog/9824.html?onpi_newsdoc100300.

[22] T.B. BRAZELTON, TOUCHPOINTS: YOUR CHILD'S EMOTIONAL AND BEHAVIORAL DEVELOPMENT (Reading, MA: Perseus Books 1992).

[23] R. MacTurk & G. Morgan (Eds.), *Mastery Motivation: Origins, Conceptualizations, and Applications: Advances in Applied Developmental Psychology*, Vol. 12. (Norwood, NJ: Ablex Publishing Corporation 1995).

which the various motor skills typically emerge is relatively narrow. Here are some of the physical milestones of young children:

turning	4-6 months
reaching for objects	4-6 months
unaided sitting	5-8 months
crawling, scooting	6-12 months
climbing (up to 6 inches)	8-10 months
walking while holding onto support	9-15 months
climbing (up to 12 inches)	11-12 months
unaided walking	9-15 months
unaided stair climbing	25-30 months
ability to turn door knob	25-30 months
ability to remove jar lids	25-30 months
anal sphincter muscles in control	31-36 months

Between the ages of three to six, children's gross and fine motor skills expand significantly. Their movements smooth out and become more automatic. Their sense of balance improves, and the ability to draw, copy, cut, and pick up tiny objects becomes increasingly proficient. By age six many children can ride a small bicycle and will attempt to accomplish many physical feats that involve increasingly refined coordination and skill. Physical growth for the school-aged child tends to slow down. Body proportions become more similar to those of adults. Both gross and fine motor skills improve until they gradually almost resemble those of adults.

§ 4.1.2 Cognitive Development

Cognitive development refers to the process of intellectual growth. "Abundant evidence indicates that brain development begins well before birth, extends into the adult years, and is specifically designed to recruit and incorporate experience into its emerging architecture and functioning."[24] The process of cognitive development enables a human being to progress from the initial state of infancy to a well-organized, well-ordered understanding of the world typical of the average adult. For this to occur, all children must pass through certain

---

[24] National Research Council and Institute of Medicine, FROM NEURONS TO NEIGHBORHOODS: THE SCIENCE OF EARLY CHILDHOOD DEVELOPMENT 216, Committee on Integrating the Science of Early Childhood Development, Board on Children, Youth, and Families (Jack P. Shonkoff & Deborah A. Phillips, eds.) (Washington, D.C.: National Academy Press 2000), *available at* http://books.nap.edu/catalog/9824.html?onpi_newsdoc100300.

developmental sequences in each important area of intellectual understanding. This means that a child must have reached a given stage of maturation and experience before certain concepts can be taught or understood. The exact age at which individual children will reach given stages of cognitive development can vary considerably, and children's capacities to make sense of the world is embedded in relational, familial, and cultural contexts.[25]

Overall, cognitive development seems to be robust in young children. "Both language development and the emergence of early learning capabilities appear to be relatively resilient processes. This means that they are relatively protected from adverse circumstances, that it may take more to undermine these processes than is the case for other aspects of development, and that they can show surprising recovery if children exhibiting delays are placed in more advantageous environments."[26] Fortunately, even children who have experienced extreme cognitive deprivation and trauma show a remarkable capacity for learning and growth once provided with a reparative circumstance.[27] Nonetheless, deficits in attention, emotional regulation, and behavioral control often remain.[28] "The neuroscientific research on early brain development says that the young children warranting the greatest concern are those growing up in environments, starting before birth, that fail to provide them with adequate nutrition and other growth-fostering inputs, expose them to biological insults, and subject them to abusive and neglectful care."[29]

In typically developing children, the progression of cognitive development in early years has been described by Piaget as following a fairly predictable course, with the evolution of competencies being acquired in a universal manner. "Children from birth to age five engage in making sense of the world on many levels: language, human interactions, counting and quantification, spatial reasoning, physical causality, problem solving, categorization. Indeed, even pre-

---

[25] *Id.*

[26] *Id.* at 125.

[27] E.W. Ames, *The Development of Romanian Orphanage Children Adopted to Canada: Final Report to the National Welfare Grants Program: Human Resources Development Canada* (Burnaby, British Columbia: Simon Fraser University 1997); M. Rutter & the English and Romanian Adoptees (ERA) Study Team, *Developmental Catch-up, and Deficit, Following Adoption After Severe Global Early Privation*, J. CHILD PSYCHOL. PSYCHIATRY, 39(4), 465-476 (1998).

[28] National Research Council and Institute of Medicine, FROM NEURONS TO NEIGHBORHOODS: THE SCIENCE OF EARLY CHILDHOOD DEVELOPMENT, Committee on Integrating the Science of Early Childhood Development, Board on Children, Youth, and Families (Jack P. Shonkoff & Deborah A. Phillips, eds.) (Washington, D.C.: National Academy Press 2000), *available at* http://books.nap.edu/catalog/9824.html?onpi_newsdoc100300.

[29] National Research Council and Institute of Medicine, FROM NEURONS TO NEIGHBORHOODS: THE SCIENCE OF EARLY CHILDHOOD DEVELOPMENT 271, Committee on Integrating the Science of Early Childhood Development, Board on Children, Youth, and Families (Jack P. Shonkoff & Deborah A. Phillips, eds.) (Washington, D.C.: National Academy Press 2000), *available at* http://books.nap.edu/catalog/9824.html?onpi_newsdoc100300.

verbal infants show surprisingly sophisticated understandings in each of these areas."[30] Piaget organized his theory of cognitive development into four stages. The first stage is called the sensorimotor period and lasts from birth to around eighteen months or two years. The sensorimotor stage describes the development of object permanence and causality. "A baby's expectations for certain kinds of reactions from important individuals around the baby are signs of learning about predictability. As early as one month, a baby will have different expectations for a father and a mother,"[31] demonstrating a capacity for memory based on patterns of interaction over time. In the first two years of life, babies "prefer consequences that they control directly over those that are uncontrollable. Infants 12 and 18 months old respond more positively to strangers who act in predictable ways that allow them more control to strangers who are less predictable."[32] During this period, the child's thinking is displayed in concrete actions rather than language. The child is focused on building motor and sensory skills, on his body movements, and on manipulation of concrete objects.

The next broad phase of cognitive development is called preoperational, during which language begins to govern the child's mental life. The emergence of language marks the development of a symbolic function, allowing play to serve an important role in communicating thoughts and feelings. The first part of this stage, which lasts roughly from two to four years, is called preconceptual. During this time thought is extremely egocentric and still quite concrete. Children's reasoning at this stage is often distorted because they are able to focus on only one salient aspect of a situation at a time. The second half of the preoperational stage lasts from age four to about age seven and is referred to as the intuitive phase. The child during this period is gradually becoming able to construct more complex thoughts and images. "By age five [the ability to take on another's perspective] has developed into a full-blown theory of mind, in which children can predict others' intentions, deceive others successfully, and recognize that beliefs don't always correspond to reality."[33]

Piaget's third broad stage is called concrete-operational and lasts from about age seven to approximately age eleven. Caplan and Caplan describe this stage as follows: "During this time the child develops the ability to do in his head what he previously would have had to do through physical action. He can make

---

[30] *Id.* at 147.

[31] T.B. BRAZELTON, TOUCHPOINTS: YOUR CHILD'S EMOTIONAL AND BEHAVIORAL DEVELOPMENT (Reading, MA: Perseus Books 1992).

[32] National Research Council and Institute of Medicine, FROM NEURONS TO NEIGHBORHOODS: THE SCIENCE OF EARLY CHILDHOOD DEVELOPMENT 147, Committee on Integrating the Science of Early Childhood Development, Board on Children, Youth, and Families (Jack P. Shonkoff & Deborah A. Phillips, eds.) (Washington, D.C.: National Academy Press 2000), *available at* http://books.nap.edu/catalog/9824.html?onpi_newsdoc100300.

[33] *Id.* at 148.

estimates and is able to understand the concepts of relative length, amount, etc. His ways of thinking are becoming increasingly like those of an adult."[34]

Piaget's fourth stage is called the stage of formal operations. It begins at about age twelve. The child is now able to think abstractly and use abstract rules and is also capable of considering a number of different hypothetical possibilities in a given situation or in solving a given problem.

Research on early learning and brain development reveals that infants come into the world "wired to learn" with "inborn motivation to develop competencies."[35] "The exciting discoveries that have characterized research on cognitive development have led some to argue that young minds—so active and capable—require special, heightened cognitive stimulation. Certainly, as more is learned about the remarkable capabilities of young children and their eagerness to learn, one naturally wants to provide them with environments that will support them in their task of becoming the most competent children, and ultimately adults, that they can be."[36] However, research has not shown that special toys or exposure to certain music, such as Mozart, optimizes cognitive growth. Instead, "as with every other task of early development . . . this literature emphasizes parents' interactions with their young children, their beliefs about learning and their children's capabilities, the home learning environment, and family organization."[37]

§ 4.1.3 Language Development

Language development, like other aspects of development, follows a regular sequential course in all children who are not physically, mentally, or emotionally impaired. However, there is a great deal of variation in the ages at which language acquisition and usage takes place. Also, language development is highly influenced by the environment, particularly by the amount of language stimulation provided by the parents or other adults. "Language learning turns out to be remarkably similar across cultures. Children exposed to markedly different languages follow similar developmental trajectories as they learn their native

---

[34] *See* Teresa Caplan & Frank Caplan, The Early Childhood Years: The 2 to 6 Year Old 1 (1983).

[35] National Research Council and Institute of Medicine, From Neurons to Neighborhoods: The Science of Early Childhood Development 148, Committee on Integrating the Science of Early Childhood Development, Board on Children, Youth, and Families (Jack P. Shonkoff & Deborah A. Phillips, eds.) (Washington, D.C.: National Academy Press 2000), *available at* http://books.nap.edu/catalog/9824.html?onpi_newsdoc100300.

[36] National Research Council and Institute of Medicine, From Neurons to Neighborhoods: The Science of Early Childhood Development 155, Committee on Integrating the Science of Early Childhood Development, Board on Children, Youth, and Families (Jack P. Shonkoff & Deborah A. Phillips, eds.) (Washington, D.C.: National Academy Press 2000), *available at* http://books.nap.edu/catalog/9824.html?onpi_newsdoc100300.

[37] *Id.* at 156-158.

language."[38] At all given stages of language acquisition, the child usually comprehends approximately twice as many words as he or she is able to speak.

The period from age two to age five is the most notable in terms of the acquisition and mastery of language. However, the precursors of language are evident almost from birth. For example, during the second and third month, infants usually begin to make non-crying, squalling, gurgling sounds called cooing. By the end of the fourth or fifth month the infant has started to babble, *i.e.*, make sounds that resemble one syllable utterances such as ma, mu, da, etc. Babbling becomes more frequent with identifiable, single words emerging around the end of the first year. Signs of understanding some words and commands is also evident at this time. Children usually start to combine words into simple two word sentences at 18 to 24 months. By 36 months the child's utterances consist of at least two words, and the child may even use three to five word sentences. By the age of four language is usually well established, and the child is starting to master the complex rules of grammar. By this age the average number of words in the child's spoken vocabulary is about 1,500.

By the age of five, speech is becoming more fluent and grammatically correct. The child can usually give his or her name, age, and address. The number of words of the vocabulary of the average five-year-old is approximately 2,200.[39] Even though five- and six-year-old children are becoming more and more competent in language skills, there are limits to what children under seven can convey with words alone. The adult needs to observe the child's nonverbal behavior in order to fully comprehend the meaning of the child's language. The young child's language is closely tied to action and is embedded in the ongoing situation. The child of this age is very easy to misunderstand, and it is not until about the age of six, at the earliest, that the child can pay attention to language per se without external support, actions, or physical cues.

After age six or seven, the child's expressive language gradually becomes more and more adult-like, and communication with others is significantly easier to understand. Written language expands, and as children move into elementary school age, they can express much more clearly their ideas and intentions. The language and communication skills of adolescents differ little from those of adults.

§ 4.1.4 Social and Emotional Child Development

The child's experiences with adult caretakers during the first few years of life lay the foundation for his or her social, emotional functioning throughout life. Thus, rejection, neglect, and abuse during childhood may result in serious interference with the child's social and emotional development. Erik Erikson has described a series of psychosocial stages that children move through as they

---

[38] *Id.* at 127.

[39] *See, e.g.,* FRANK CAPLAN, THE PARENTING ADVISOR 301 (1978).

mature.[40] During each of the stages there is a major task for the individual to accomplish if development is to proceed normally and positively. These stages will be described in some detail because Erikson's theories are highly applicable to child welfare cases. An understanding of these stages and the tasks associated with each will help the attorney to understand children's social and emotional growth at different times of their lives, and thus, what children may need in terms of parenting at each of these developmental stages.

Stage 1 — Basic Trust vs. Mistrust

This stage lasts from birth until approximately 18 months of age. The major developmental task to be accomplished by the developing infant is to establish "basic trust." This sense of trust is established during the first year or so of life. "By the end of the first year of life, infants are acutely sensitive to the emotional cues of other people, especially in uncertain or potentially threatening circumstances. In a process researchers call social referencing, infants take their cues from the reassuring or anxious expression of a caregiver, which, in turn, can affect whether they continue to play comfortably or freeze in their tracks."[41] Infants require consistent, responsive interactions to develop a secure belief that their needs will be met. The child's ability to love other people and to relate positively to others is also best established during this very important period of development.

The infant learns to trust by having his or her physical and emotional needs met by a nurturing, responsive, non-abusive caretaker. If these needs are not met during the first year or so of life, the child's capacity to relate to and trust other people is likely to be permanently impaired. "The findings on the prevalence and stability of insecure and atypical attachments in maltreated children point to the extreme risks these children face in achieving adaptive outcomes in other domains of interpersonal relationships."[42] It is during this stage that the child is, thus, particularly vulnerable to physical or emotional neglect. Neglect at this stage includes not meeting the child's needs for food, comfort, soothing, physical contact, and appropriate stimulation. The promptness with which the child's needs are met is especially important at this stage. The young infant does not have the capacity to wait for long periods of time while the parent takes care of other things.

Infants are at much greater risk of physical abuse and neglect than older children due to their physical fragility and extreme helplessness. Also, the con-

---

[40] *See* ERIC ERICKSON, CHILDHOOD AND SOCIETY (1950).

[41] National Research Council and Institute of Medicine, FROM NEURONS TO NEIGHBORHOODS: THE SCIENCE OF EARLY CHILDHOOD DEVELOPMENT 107, Committee on Integrating the Science of Early Childhood Development, Board on Children, Youth, and Families (Jack P. Shonkoff & Deborah A. Phillips, eds.) (Washington, D.C.: National Academy Press 2000), *available at* http://books.nap.edu/catalog/9824.html?onpi_newsdoc100300.

[42] D. Cicchetti & S.L. Toth, *A Developmental Psychopathology Perspective on Child Abuse and Neglect*, J. AM. ACAD. CHILD ADOLESC. PSYCHIATRY, 34(5), 541-563 (1995).

sequences of certain types of physical maltreatment (*e.g.*, shaking, tossing in the air, jerking an arm or leg, hitting, or spanking) can be extremely damaging to the young child and can result in serious physical injury, neurological damage, and even death. The same acts perpetrated upon an older child might result in only minor injury. Therefore, physical abuse of the child at this particular development level must be considered a much more serious event than at older age levels.

Even though children at this very early developmental stage are more at risk of abuse or neglect, they are also more at risk of being emotionally damaged by being removed from a parent to whom they are attached even though that parent may be abusive or neglectful. It is generally accepted among health professionals and child development specialists that it can be extremely damaging to separate a young child from a primary caretaker. Bowlby, among others, has expressed the opinion that states of anxiety, depression, and other forms of adult pathology may have their origins in earlier experiences of separation and loss.[43]

Despite the risks associated with removal, however, there are certain types of abuse, particularly at this early stage of development, where the risk of severe injury or death is so great that nothing but removal should be considered. A parent who is capable of intentionally and severely abusing a tiny infant is not likely to be rehabilitated, and termination of parental rights should be considered. There are also parents who, even though they may not severely abuse their child, are so inadequate and so unable to recognize the helplessness of a baby that their ability to provide protection must be questioned. Bolton,[44] in his discussion of parents who are unable to form attachments, warns that a failure to view the infant's helplessness realistically suggests that such a parent, because of his or her own selfishness and inability to care for a helpless infant, may never be able to adequately fulfill a parental role, nor is such a parent likely to benefit from treatment or education. In these instances, it is necessary to consider the termination of parental rights as early as possible.

Stage 2 — Autonomy vs. Shame and Guilt

Sometime beginning in the second year of life and extending until around the age of three years, the child goes through the second stage of development. Erikson has called this the stage of autonomy. He describes the child's primary developmental task during this period as that of developing a sense of independence and self-control. The child's striving for independence during this stage repeatedly brings the child into conflict with what society and parents expect. The child begins to encounter the word "no" and to resist the prohibitions that accompany this word. The child at this stage needs opportunities to assert his or her will to some extent, to make choices, and to feel he or she is having an impact on the world in which the child lives. At the same time, the child needs to learn

---

[43] *See, e.g.,* JOHN BOWLBY, 2 ATTACHMENT AND LOSS: SEPARATION, ANXIETY, AND ANGER (1973).

[44] *See, e.g.,* FRANK BOLTON, WHEN BONDING FAILS: CLINICAL ASSESSMENT OF HIGH RISK FAMILIES 184 (1983).

that there are limits and some external controls over his or her behavior. The capacity for later self-control may be very much related to the opportunity to practice making mistakes and experiencing natural consequences. As the child gets closer to the age of two, the child often becomes more and more negative and rebellious. This negativism is actually a positive sign of good emotional adjustment. The child is learning to assert himself or herself and to develop confidence in his or her own abilities. Failure to receive proper support and guidance during this period of life may result in deep-seated feelings of shame and guilt.

The risk for physical abuse at this stage often revolves around the child's struggle for independence and need to explore. At this stage of development, the child requires a parent who can allow the child to make choices and decisions while not becoming punitive or overly invasive in an attempt to control the child's behavior. The parent of a child at this stage needs to be patient and not overly rigid. The capacity for later self-control requires that the child be allowed some freedom at this stage and not be shamed for making mistakes. Because language and cognitive development are still limited, children at this stage often do not comprehend verbal instructions, and may require reminders of what is expected. When the parents do not understand these limitations and they lack understanding of positive ways to manage the child's negativistic and rebellious behavior, they may falsely assign malevolent intentions to their child's attempts at autonomous exploration.

Simple punishments such as light spanking may escalate to increasingly punitive and abusive treatment of the child. Again, parents often have unrealistic expectations of children's capabilities. When the child does not obey verbal instructions or is uncooperative with toilet training or does not pick up the toys, the parent may interpret the child's behavior as disrespectful or disobedient rather than as a function of his or her developmental level. This may lead to excessive punishment and abuse. Children at this age are physically fragile and unable to defend themselves. Therefore, although they are not quite as vulnerable as during the first year or so of life, children in this stage are still at high risk for very serious physical abuse.

It is also at this stage that emotional abuse and emotional neglect may become more evident. Although emotional abuse is a complex phenomenon and there are no clear-cut guidelines as to when it exists, it is important to realize that emotional abuse may be as damaging—or even more damaging—than physical abuse. Diagnosis of emotional abuse usually requires an evaluation by a child psychologist or child psychiatrist who can differentiate between emotional abuse and psychiatric disturbance arising from other causes. For example, Attention Deficit Disorder with or without Hyperactivity, Pervasive Developmental Disorders, and organic problems may need to be ruled out. Emotional abuse and neglect are often manifested at this stage by a lack of parental responsiveness to the child's normal needs for attention, approval, and affection. At this stage, the child is also particularly vulnerable to being shamed or belittled, especially around the issues of toilet training and obedience. During toilet training, a parent who is critical and negative can seriously damage the child's sense of autonomy and self respect.

Children in this age range are also extremely vulnerable to physical neglect as they are still dependent upon an adult to provide a safe and healthy environment. Lack of supervision is often a serious neglect issue because the child cannot provide for his or her own physical needs, does not have a cognitive understanding of danger, and requires protection in almost all settings.

Separation of children from their parents is still extremely traumatic at this age, and alternatives to removal should be considered, except in very high risk situations. If a child of this age has been removed from parental custody because of abuse or neglect, a careful assessment should be made by a qualified professional in creating a visitation plan.

Stage 3 — Initiative vs. Self-Doubt

The third stage is the stage of initiative. It develops during the third year and lasts up until around six years. The child's growth in physical coordination, in language, and in imagination is most important in terms of development. These developmental skills enable the child to accomplish the main developmental task of this period, which is to find out what kind of person he or she is going to be. The child's great store of energy and growing skills allow the child to plan and carry out many new activities. A child at this stage may be more aware of sexual impulses. One of the problems at this stage may be that of excessive feelings of guilt.

Excessive guilt can result in an overly strict conscience. The child does need to learn to experience some guilt about his or her inappropriate behavior because this is the stage when the conscience (feelings of right and wrong) is being established. However, it is also possible for the child to feel very little remorse about destructive or negative behaviors and thus fail to develop appropriate feelings about right and wrong.

At this stage, the child is particularly interested in the activities of adults and may imitate and identify with the parents even more than he or she did at younger ages. Because of the increase in imaginative powers and the desire to imitate adults, the child engages in a great deal of fantasy and playing out the roles of adults. A child who successfully negotiates this phase of development will establish a sense of playfulness and creativity.

At this stage the child is more active and physically coordinated and also can move about much more freely. Children at this stage are at a high risk of neglect, especially lack of appropriate parental supervision and exposure to household and neighborhood dangers. Unrealistic expectations for the child may lead the parent to believe the child is capable of avoiding these dangers and may also lead the parent to treat the child as older than he or she is developmentally. For example, parents may leave three- to six-year-olds alone in the house or may even leave them alone to supervise younger children. Parents may also expect children at this age to be able to assume household responsibilities that they are not capable of—such as cleaning the house, keeping their rooms picked up and neat, and preparing their own meals—all without adult supervision. When the child does not perform these tasks or performs them poorly, the parent may believe that the child is being deliberately disobedient and, thus, deserving of punishment that can be excessive, physical, and even abusive.

At this stage, the risk from physical abuse is still quite high, but the likelihood of serious physical injury is not quite as great as at earlier ages because the child is less fragile physically and more mobile (*e.g.*, the child can run away from a momentarily angry parent). Also, because children at this age have significantly better language and cognitive skills, they can understand simple verbal instructions and explanations, making it somewhat easier to discipline them without resorting to physical punishment.

Children at the stage of initiative need opportunities to plan and initiate their own activities and develop competencies and confidence. They need help in language development and encouragement in pre-school and school attendance and activities. Rewarding a child's accomplishments and achievements with attention and praise helps the child to experience success and not develop feelings of hopelessness and failure. Encouraging a child to establish good relationships with peers and providing opportunities for this to occur are important goals at this stage. The parent must have the willingness and the time to carry out these many parenting responsibilities. If parents berate or make fun of their children or prevent them from participating in activities and experiences in which they can achieve mastery and competence, children begin to doubt themselves and suffer impairment of self-esteem. Such treatment can reach the level of emotional abuse, wherein the child may feel totally rejected or terrorized by the parent's threats or by their extremely harsh punishments.

Sexual abuse in the family is an increasing danger at this age, even more so when the adult male in the home is not biologically related to the child.[45] It is also possible that a child may have repeatedly observed adult intercourse in the home or may have viewed explicit sexual activities on cable or satellite television channels or on video or DVD movies. These kinds of experiences, by prematurely exposing a child to sexual stimuli, can lead to early sexualization of the child. Thus, some children who are observed to behave in very sexualized ways and are thought to have been sexually molested, may have, instead, witnessed adult sexual activity. Some authorities consider such experiences to be a form of sexual abuse. Elevated sexual behavior, particularly certain types of sexual behavior, has been found to occur more frequently in sexually abused children.[46]

---

[45] *See, e.g.*, DIANA RUSSELL, THE SEXUAL TRAUMA: INCEST IN THE LIVES OF GIRLS AND WOMEN (1986).

[46] *See, e.g.*, WILLIAM N. FRIEDRICH, PSYCHOTHERAPY OF SEXUALLY ABUSED CHILDREN AND THEIR FAMILIES (1990). Friedrich has published a CHILD SEXUAL BEHAVIOR INVENTORY FOR CHILDREN, AGES 2 TO 12 (1990) which has been helpful in distinguishing those specific sexual behaviors which are more diagnostic of sexual abuse from those which are exhibited generally in non-abused children.

Although temporary separation from a primary parenting figure can be better tolerated than at younger ages, regular contact with the parents is still very important and should be maintained except in extreme situations.

Stage 4 — Industry vs. Inferiority

Stage 4 begins at about the time the child enters elementary school and lasts until puberty begins. This stage is sometimes referred to as the latency period, during which a child earns recognition from others by learning to apply himself or herself to skills and tasks that go beyond play and pleasure. The child's major task is to develop a sense of industry, both at home and at school, learning the basic skills of survival and thereby avoiding feelings of inferiority and inadequacy. This is also a very decisive stage socially because it involves doing things cooperatively with others, resulting in a sense of self-worth.

Of prime importance during this stage of development is the parents' support of and interaction with their child's educational program and activities. This is also the time in a child's life when the development of social skills and strong peer relationships become highly significant. The child needs to have numerous successes to avoid a sense of inferiority. Providing consistent and fair rules and guidelines during these developmental years helps the child to learn to live within societal limits and develop a sense of right and wrong. The child's participation in school and social activities is very important and should not be disrupted if possible. Peers are also extremely important at this stage of development, and disruption of peer relationships can be damaging to the child's social and emotional development.

The child at this developmental stage is gradually becoming more and more independent and is not so helpless or physically fragile. He or she is less vulnerable to serious injury from abuse and less in danger from neglect or lack of supervision. Because the child is cognitively and linguistically more advanced, he or she is able to listen to reasoning and to respond to verbal discipline. However, because children at this stage can reason, they may talk back to parents when the parents are illogical or ill informed. This talking back is often perceived as a lack of respect and may lead to abuse.

The child's emotional and social needs during this stage include the establishment and maintenance of peer relationships. Achieving some independence from parental figures is another important need, particularly toward the end of this age period. The parent who is unable to recognize the child's emotional and social needs is likely to become involved in conflict with the child. School is particularly important during this stage of development, and success in school helps the child to avoid feelings of inferiority. However, if the child is not doing well in school and the parental expectations are for school success, serious conflict may occur in the parent-child relationship. Slow-learning children or children with unidentified learning disabilities are especially vulnerable to parental abuse when they bring home poor grades. Punishment related to poor grades is common and often so severe that it can be considered abusive.

Children who have attention deficit or hyperactivity disorders are particularly susceptible to abuse because they are so impulsive and do not learn as readily from consequences as do other children. Children who are suspected of being hyperactive are usually not identified as hyperactive until they enter school. These children, whether in abuse/neglect cases or divorce cases, need thorough evaluations by a child psychiatrist and a child psychologist because they may need medical management and other forms of psychological treatment.

Another significant issue at this developmental stage is sexual abuse. Research studies have found that children are most vulnerable to sexual abuse between the ages of eight to twelve years old.[47] In addition, there are risks of inappropriate exposure to adult sexuality through observation of adults in the home or from watching overtly sexual videotapes or movies in the home.

At this developmental stage, separation from abusive parents through removal from parental custody does not usually result in the severe trauma that separation at younger ages does. Separation may be dangerous to the child's mental health, however, due to disruption of schooling and peer relationships, particularly if the child is moved to a different neighborhood because of being placed in foster care or with relatives. Also, children at this age may be extremely resistant to removal from their home, despite the abuse. The child's own desires are particularly important to the child's attorney, even when the child's desires may not represent what the attorney considers to be the child's best interest. All of these issues must be taken into consideration by the child's attorney in making legal recommendations.

If it is necessary to remove the child from the home, an attempt should be made to locate an appropriate placement for the child that will be in or close to the child's own neighborhood and in the same school district. The child may be able to suggest relatives or friends who may be willing to take the child in or even to become specially licensed foster parents for the child. If not, placement should be sought in a foster home as close as possible to the child's parents' home, with the child to be transported to the same school and, if at all possible, be allowed to continue established activities and maintain contact with his or her family.

Stage 5 — *Identity vs. Role Confusion*

This final developmental stage before reaching adulthood is one of rapid physical growth and evolving sexual maturity. Each youth is now faced with the formidable task of integrating his or her physiological upheaval with his or her natural aptitudes, acquired skills, and newly developing social roles into a sense of personal identity. The danger at this stage is one of "role confusion" sexually, vocationally, and socially, which may result in a tendency to over identify with accessible heroes who are revered by those in his or her age group. In particular,

---

[47] *See, e.g.*, David Finkelhor & Larry Baron, *High-Risk Children,* in A SOURCEBOOK ON CHILD SEXUAL ABUSE 60 (David Finkelhor ed., 1986).

the young individual is eager to be affirmed by his or her peers while grappling with the morality he or she learned as a child and the ethics to be developed for the adult years ahead.

When children enter the changing turbulent years of adolescence, the role of the parent also changes. As the young person attempts to clarify and solidify his or her identity, parents often become the foil against whom the child tries out new and sometimes controversial ideas. Walking the fine line between maintaining necessary and consistent boundaries and rules, while allowing the child to gradually become more self-sufficient and independent is a parental requirement at this stage. As a result of the drastic changes involved in the rapid physical growth and maturation, adolescents generally experience a great deal of emotional turmoil. A child who has previously been compliant and easy to get along with may suddenly become rebellious and demanding. This places pressure on parents, who may have gotten along relatively well with the child so long as the child was following family rules and adhering to family values. As the child's cognitive and language abilities mature and he or she is trying to establish a healthy sense of his or her own identity, the parents may become increasingly frustrated in their attempts to control the child. Conflict can erupt, leading to escalation of discipline on the part of the parents, which in turn may result in actual physical or emotional abuse.

Although the risk of serious harm or injury is much less at this age than when the child was younger, there still may be some situations in which the child is so at risk that removal from parental custody may need to be considered. However, the attorney should recognize that alternative placements in state custody are quite limited for adolescents and that few foster homes are equipped to deal with a rebellious adolescent. In addition, many adolescents, despite their conflict with their parents and even abuse by one or both parents, may still not wish to be removed from their present home or placed in foster care. Also, because adolescents are able to reason and think abstractly, much like an adult, they are able to consider various alternatives to their family situations and the consequences of these alternatives. Therefore, the adolescent's choice must be respected, unless remaining in parental custody would involve extreme risk. Attorneys should be reluctant to recommend asking the state to take custody of adolescent clients. An alternative may be to consider placing the adolescent in a temporary shelter facility to reduce immediate stress, to allow mediation between parent and child, and to locate therapy services that might resolve the family conflicts.

Emotional abuse may be more likely to occur with adolescents than physical abuse. However, again, attempting to define and prove emotional abuse is a very difficult task, and the diagnosis usually requires the services of a psychiatrist or psychologist who can differentiate between emotional symptoms that are caused by emotional abuse and those where the cause lies elsewhere. The most serious neglect, as well as abuse, may arise in situations where parents are severe alcoholics or drug abusers. Such situations present very complex legal decisions, requiring a delicate balance between risk of leaving the adolescent in such a family situation versus the risk of removing the child and all the attendant problems that go along with that removal, such as: changing schools, separation from friends, and the difficulties of adjusting to foster families.

Another area of family conflict that often emerges during adolescence is related to the adolescent's interest and involvement in sexual experimentation. This is likely to create significant anxiety on the part of the parents, often leading to attempts to control the child's sexual activity and consequently to situations that may become abusive. Another significant issue that may first emerge at this developmental level is that of a child's emerging homosexual orientation. Gay and lesbian youth are more likely to be abused and rejected by their families than are heterosexual youth, and research indicates that many run away from home, attempt suicide, and abuse substances.[48] The unusually high rate of suicide among gay adolescents has been repeatedly demonstrated, and is a phenomenon with which child welfare attorneys should be familiar.

§ 4.1.5 Attachment, Separation, and Loss

The concepts of attachment, separation, and loss are significant in understanding children's social and emotional needs at different developmental stages. John Bowlby[49] and Mary Ainsworth[50] were among the earliest professionals to describe the importance of a child's attachment to his or her primary caretaker as well as the child's reactions to separation from that caretaker. It is extremely important for a child's attorney to be knowledgeable about these issues because of their significance at different stages of a child's development. For example, in Bowlby's description of attachment, he states that most infants have begun to respond differently to the mother (or other primary caretaker) as compared to other people in the infant's life.[51] It is now commonly believed that the attachment process continues to develop over the course of the first year of life and beyond. If the child's basic physical needs and the needs for comfort, touch, nurturing, and stimulation have been met, the child will develop an increasing attachment to the caretaker who meets these needs most consistently.

Ainsworth described three patterns of attachment: secure, anxious/avoidant, and anxious/resistant. These types of attachment are observed in the "Strange Situation," in which a child between one and two years old is separated from and

---

[48] *See, e.g.*, Gary Remafedi, *Adolescent Homosexuality: Medical and Psychological Implications*, 79 PEDIATRICS 331-337 (1987); Gary Remafedi, *Homosexual Youth: A Challenge to Contemporary Society*, 258 J. AM. MED. SOC. 222-225 (1987).

[49] *See, e.g.*, JOHN BOWLBY, 1 ATTACHMENT AND LOSS: ATTACHMENT (1969); JOHN BOWLBY, 2 ATTACHMENT AND LOSS: SEPARATION, ANXIETY AND ANGER (1973).

[50] *See, e.g.*, M. D. S. Ainsworth, *Infant-Mother Attachment*, 34 AMERICAN PSYCHOL. 34 (1979); M. D. S. Ainsworth, *Attachments Beyond Infancy*, 44 AM. PSYCHOL. 709 (1989).

[51] *See* JOHN BOWLBY, 1 ATTACHMENT AND LOSS: ATTACHMENT (1969).

reunited with a parent or primary caretaker, and the evaluator observes the child's reactions.[52] The securely attached child protests the separation and is happy and easy to console upon reunification. Securely attached children have a secure base from which to explore their environment. They are expected to show separation anxiety and to be more easily consoled by their parents than by other adults. The insecurely attached, anxious/avoidant child is not distressed during separation and avoids the parent at the time of reunification. Children with anxious/avoidant attachment are presumed to have had experiences where their emotional arousal was not reestablished by the parent or where they were overly aroused through intrusive parenting; so they over-regulate their affect and avoid situations that are likely to be distressing. The insecurely attached, anxious/resistant child is clingy from the beginning, anxious during separation, and angry upon reunification. Children with anxious/resistant attachment under-regulate their affect, heightening their expression of distress and becoming pre-occupied with having contact with the parent, but becoming frustrated even when the parent is available.

Main and Solomon have identified a fourth pattern of attachment, with the child demonstrating seemingly undirected behavior, freezing, hand clapping, head banging, and the wish to escape the situation even in the presence of the parent. They call this pattern of attachment "disorganized/disoriented."[53] Children with disorganized/disoriented attachment are presumed to have had experiences where the parent was a source of both fear and reassurance, so arousal of the attachment behavioral system produces strong conflicting motivations. A history of serious neglect or physical or sexual abuse is often associated with this pattern.[54]

Attachment patterns in infancy affect a child's ability to form future attachments, including attachments to subsequent caretakers. Children whose attachments are repeatedly broken—by being placed in multiple placements, for example—may have difficulty forming secure attachments anywhere. Children with insecure attachments from their homes of origin or multiple out-of-home placements need stability and specialized therapy to increase the likelihood of

---

[52] *See, e.g.*, M. D. S. Ainsworth et al., Patterns of Attachment: A Psychological Study of the Strange Situation (1978).

[53] *See, e.g.*, Mary Main & Judith Solomon, *Procedures for Identifying Infants as Disorganized/Disoriented during the Ainsworth Strange Situation*, in Attachment during the Preschool Years: Theory, Research and Intervention 121-160 (Mark T. Greenberg et al. eds.) (University of Chicago Press 1990).

[54] *See, e.g.*, Dante Cicchetti & Marjorie Beeghly, *Symbolic Development in Maltreated Youngsters: An Organizational Perspective*, 36 Atypical Symbolic Development: New Directions for Child Development 5-29 (Dante Cicchetti & Marjorie Beeghly eds.) (Jossey-Bass 1987); Mary Main & Erik Hesse, *Parents' Unresolved Traumatic Experiences Are Related to Infant Disorganized Attachment Status: Is Frightened and/or Frightening Parental Behavior the Linking Mechanism?* in Attachment in the Preschool Years: Theory, Research and Intervention 161-182 (Mark T. Greenberg et al. eds.) (University of Chicago Press 1990).

their being able to form secure attachments, even in their subsequent adult relationships.

A great deal has been written about children's reactions to separation from their primary caretakers.[55] It is generally accepted among mental health professionals and child development specialists that it can be extremely damaging to separate a child from a primary caretaker. Among the first writers to point out the extremity of children's reactions to such separations were Dorothy Burlingham and Anna Freud.[56] They describe their experiences with young children who were separated from their parents in England during World War II to protect them from bombing raids. Concerning children who they observed in the Hampstead Nursery where they were cared for during this separation, Burlingham and Freud commented that the child who was between the ages of one and three was particularly affected. "Reactions to parting at this time of life are particularly violent. . . . This new ability to love finds itself deprived of the accustomed objects (parents) and his greed for affection remains unsatisfied. His longing for his mother becomes intolerable and throws him into states of despair."[57] Bowlby, among others, has referred to these findings and expressed the opinion that states of anxiety, depression, and other forms of adult pathology may have their origins in earlier experiences of separation and loss.[58]

Because the attachment process is important to the child's sense of security and trust, it is necessary to carefully consider the child's possible reactions to separation from, or loss of, his or her primary attachment figures, whether these result from parental divorce or from involvement by the child welfare system. The risks associated with separation vary at different stages of the child's development and with the length of the separation. In general, the younger the child, the more difficult a separation will be. After the age of three, some children can tolerate temporary separation from parent figures more readily than at earlier ages. Because of their increased language and cognitive abilities, the parent's absence can be explained to the older child, and the child has the ability to understand that the absence will be temporary.

It is extremely important for the child's attorney to recognize the risks of separation and to realize that even in cases of abuse and neglect, it is necessary to weigh the risks of removal of the child from the home just as carefully as the risks of leaving the child in the home with an abusive or neglecting parent. In abuse or neglect situations, one possible solution may be for the attorney to

---

[55] *See, e.g.*, M. D. S. Ainsworth & M. Boston, *Psychodiagnostic Assessments of a Child After Prolonged Separation in Early Childhood*, 25 BRITISH J. OF MED. PSYCHOLOGY (1952); JOHN BOWLBY, 1 ATTACHMENT AND LOSS: ATTACHMENT (1969); JOHN BOWLBY, 2 ATTACHMENT AND LOSS: SEPARATION, ANXIETY AND ANGER (1973).

[56] *See, e.g.*, DOROTHY BURLINGHAM & ANNA FREUD, INFANTS WITHOUT FAMILIES (1944); DOROTHY BURLINGHAM & ANNA FREUD, YOUNG CHILDREN IN WAR-TIME (1942).

[57] *See* DOROTHY BURLINGHAM & ANNA FREUD, YOUNG CHILDREN IN WAR-TIME 388 (1942).

[58] *See, e.g.*, JOHN BOWLBY, 2 ATTACHMENT AND LOSS: SEPARATION, ANXIETY AND ANGER (1973).

recommend that the state take legal custody but leave the child in the physical custody of the parent. Danger can be minimized by asking the court to order monitoring and intensive services to be provided to the family in the home in order to ensure that the child's developmental needs are being met and that the child is not in danger of serious abuse or neglect.

§ 4.2 Long-term Effects of Maltreatment

Abuse and neglect may have long-term physical consequences. Children of alcoholic and substance-abusing mothers may be born with physical limitations. For example, children whose mothers consume alcohol during their pregnancy may be born with fetal alcohol syndrome, which can include physical, behavioral, and learning disabilities that may persist into adulthood. Infants and toddlers who are violently shaken may suffer from shaken baby syndrome, which can cause death, paralysis, blindness, brain damage, learning disabilities, and mental retardation. Being exposed to a violent or chaotic home in the earliest years of life can change the way neurons form in the brain, affecting the child cognitively, emotionally, and behaviorally. Inadequate nutrition in infancy and early childhood can alter all types of physical development, including development of the brain. Serious physical injuries can result in life-long disabilities and deficits. Beyond these direct, physical consequences, maltreatment can change who the child is: how the child views himself or herself, the child's worth, and the child's ability to relate to his or her world and the people in it.[59] Maltreated children may suffer from post-traumatic stress disorder, depression, anxiety disorders, dissociative disorders, eating disorders, and attachment disorders as a result of their maltreatment. These disorders may affect the child for his or her lifetime.

Children who are abused and neglected may be more likely to have various social problems, including substance abuse, school disciplinary problems, and delinquency. These problems may persist into adulthood, particularly when children age out of the child welfare system with multiple foster care and group home placements. These children are at a greater risk of experiencing homelessness and incarceration as young adults. Adults who have juvenile histories of poor academic performance, behavioral problems, substance abuse, and delinquency are less likely to be welcomed into good schools or to be offered good jobs.

Responses to child abuse and neglect are very individual. Some resilient children are able to overcome even serious abuse and flourish, while other children are seriously impaired in their life-long ability to function as adults. A number of factors have been identified that affect outcomes, including:

- The child's age and stage of development at the time the abuse occurred.

- The severity, frequency, and duration of the abuse, the type of abuse.

---

[59] *See generally* YOUNG CHILDREN AND TRAUMA (Joy D. Ofofsky ed., 2004).

- The relationship between the child and the abuser.

- The child's temperament.

- The child's physical and emotional health.

- The degree of family or community support systems.

- The presence of a healthy, nurturing relationship between the child and an adult, who need not be a relative.

§ 4.3 Importance of Developmental Level for Child Abuse/Neglect Issues

Many researchers and child abuse specialists have observed that the likelihood of being abused is greatest for children who are from three months to three years of age. Possible reasons for this phenomenon are that the younger children tend to place much higher emotional and physical demands on their parents. Also, they are more disruptive to the parents' activities than are older children. Thus, it should be recognized that the period of greatest risk for children coincides with the period of greatest vulnerability, helplessness, and need. Certain children are even more at risk during this age period, such as children who have any type of physical or developmental handicap, children who are born prematurely, children with difficult temperaments who may cry excessively, or children who, for any reason, require more than the usual amount of attention and care giving. These children tend to remain at high risk of abuse throughout their childhood.

Since children have differing cognitive, physical, emotional, and language capabilities at different stages of their development, the parents need to take these capabilities into account when forming expectations for their children. Abusive parents have often been found to have unrealistic expectations for their children, based on their lack of understanding of the child's developmental needs. When the child does not respond according to the parents' expectations, this may lead to anger in the parents, and abuse may occur.

It is important to understand that abuse and maltreatment exist on a continuum of severity. Bolton describes that "the maltreating family may be drawn from a wide distribution of social/emotional/parenting pathology. These families range from those who repeatedly inflict grievous injury on their children and seem impervious to treatment to those who make minor child care errors out of ignorance."[60] Depending on the nature and severity of abuse and the parent's potential for benefiting from treatment, intervention approaches other than removing a child from an abusive home should be considered. Since separation from a primary caretaker is known to be extremely damaging, particularly to

---

[60] *See, e.g.,* FRANK BOLTON, WHEN BONDING FAILS: CLINICAL ASSESSMENT OF HIGH RISK FAMILIES 184 (1983).

very young children, other alternatives should usually be considered. The following are among the possible alternative interventions:

- Parent education.

- Parent counseling.

- Supervision and close monitoring by Child Protective Services.

- In-home family therapy.

- Parent aides in the home.

Use of multidisciplinary teams can be extremely valuable in long term planning for difficult cases.

It is important to recognize that children who have been victims of abuse and/or neglect often need mental health treatment themselves. For example, if the child appears to be displaying signs of anxiety, depression, aggression, or extreme noncompliance, evaluation and treatment by a mental health professional may be necessary. Abused children who need treatment and do not receive it at the appropriate time may experience life-long adjustment and emotional problems.

§ 4.3.1 Communicating with the Child

The child's way of communicating is considerably different from that of an adult and varies according to the child's developmental level. Vocabulary, syntax, concepts, and length of interview must all be tailored to the child's developmental abilities and needs. Also, the child's ability to accurately express his or her opinions and wishes differs significantly from that of an adult. For example, children under the age of about three and one-half to four have fairly limited vocabularies and are often intimidated by unfamiliar adults. Therefore, an attorney will gain little from an interview with a child of this age. Observing the child with the parent or parents and interviewing the significant others in the child's life are likely to be more helpful than are interviews with the child. For children above the age of three and one-half there are several issues to consider in terms of how to talk to the child and how to interpret his or her communications. For example, it is important to approach the child in a very positive, soft-spoken, informal manner. The neutral, objective manner that an attorney might typically use with an adult is usually quite inappropriate with the young child and even with most somewhat older children. It is also important for the attorney to put himself of herself at the child's level physically, for example, by sitting on the floor or by sitting in a low chair beside the child.

It should also be noted that young children seek to please adults and are easily influenced and intimidated by adults. Therefore, leading questions should be avoided, and the child's response to direct questions cannot always be taken as factual since the child may merely be saying what he thinks the adult wants or expects to hear. The child may misinterpret questions and will seldom say that he does not understand. If the attorney is asking a complex question, or if a difficult concept is being used, it may be helpful to ask the child to say what he thinks the concept or question means and to explain in his own words. If it appears that the child is confused, the question should be rephrased in a simpler manner.

Young children have fairly limited vocabularies (*e.g.*, two-year-old children have a vocabulary of approximately 250 words; by the age of four and one-half the average vocabulary is approximately 1900 words; by the age of six the average is around 2200 words) and they usually have limited understanding of abstract concepts. Therefore, the attorney should communicate briefly and simply, preferably using only one main thought in each sentence or question.

Attention span must also be considered. Although this varies considerably among children, the majority of young children are unlikely to comfortably participate in an interview for much longer than a half hour if they are between the ages of four and five, and possibly slightly longer for a six- or seven-year-old child. It may be necessary to see the child on several different occasions if more information is needed. Subsequent interviews are often necessary because rapport with the child may not be established in one interview.

If the attorney wishes to elicit the child's preference about placement, it must be noted that children younger than six or seven years old are unlikely to be mature enough to understand the ramifications of such a choice or even to be consistent in their responses from one occasion to another. Observing the child's interactions with each parent may be a better way of assessing the child's preference or attachment strength. For the older child, the attorney may directly ask the child's preference, but should also attempt through close questioning to determine the motivation for the child's preference. While children's preferences should be considered at all developmental levels, it is important to note that children should never be made to feel responsible for adult decisions.

An essential resource for any attorney who speaks to children or must face children's statements or testimony is Anne Graffam Walker's book, HANDBOOK ON QUESTIONING CHILDREN: A LINGUISTIC PERSPECTIVE (2nd ed. American Bar Association, 1999).

§ 4.4 Conclusion

While not every child who experiences abuse or neglect will develop a diagnosable disorder, many children do display symptoms that warrant treatment. Children who experience abuse and neglect are at risk for developing complex, interconnected developmental problems. In order to better meet the needs of maltreated children, we must understand the developmental challenges occurring at the time of the trauma. Because there exists a variety of responses to maltreatment, careful assessment and diagnosis by a qualified professional is imperative.

Diagnosing problems in young children is difficult for many reasons. Adults often assume that problems of childhood will work themselves out over time— that children go through stages and that problems don't require intervention.

Adults worry about labeling young children and fear that labels will become self-fulfilling prophecies. Recognizing problems in children forces adults to examine painful feelings of guilt and inadequacy, especially when the child is experiencing problems as a result of adult behavior. These difficulties are particularly present in cases of child maltreatment.

Children look different from adults in terms of their physical, social, cognitive, emotional, neurological, and developmental capacities. Despite the difficulty of recognizing problems, young children continue to experience symptoms that benefit from intervention. Children who have experienced maltreatment should receive a thorough professional evaluation. Even subtle delays in motor planning, speech-language, and social-emotional arenas can negatively impact a child's functioning and interfere with effective learning. While typically developing children can focus on gaining new skills and taking good advantage of a stimulating environment, children who suffer from abuse and neglect are often more focused on basic survival. Their systems are revved up and they are exquisitely aware of events in their environment. This hypervigilance served a protective function at one point for the child who needed to be aware of his or her surroundings in order to find protection from a perpetrator of abuse. Unfortunately, children often hang onto old patterns of behavior long beyond their usefulness has been served. Children must feel safe and secure in order to begin to let go of protective defenses. This is particularly relevant in terms of children's relational functioning. The experience of being abused or neglected at the hands of adults who are supposed to love and protect their children has repercussions across the lifespan. Maltreated children are faced with the challenge of re-working maladaptive relationship patterns—a task requiring new, reparative models of interaction and a safe environment that promotes growth and healing.

Chapter 5   FAMILY DYNAMICS IN CHILD MALTREATMENT

by Donald C. Bross[1] *and Terri James-Banks*[2]

"Every happy family is the same, but every unhappy family is different."

—*The opening lines of Anna Karenina by Leo Tolstoy*

§ 5.1 Introduction

Clinical observations, rather than controlled research, form the primary basis for current beliefs and understanding about family dynamics in child abuse. No single explanation for child maltreatment is established, but there are many risk factors and indicators of the psychological, social-psychological, and situational, contextual, or ecological realities most likely to be present when children are abused. Thus, even though there is uniqueness to each specific situation of child maltreatment, certain factors are present singly or in combination in almost every confirmed child abuse or neglect case:

- How parents were cared for in their own childhood.

- The existence of one or more types of "crisis" in the home.

- Some feature or behavior of the child that "triggers" parental anger or falls short of parental expectations.

- Isolation from needed support or intervention from other adults.

Adequate legal representation requires the child's lawyer to know enough about contemporary views of child abuse dynamics to ask informed questions before hearings, of witnesses at trial, and of treatment plans that purport to address the question of whether a given parent can safely and at least minimally adequately respond to the needs of the child client. Addressed below are various behavioral theories of child maltreatment; important features of children's development that challenge parents; the limited research on treatment interventions; and an assessment of treatment progress, treatment failure, and cases in which treatment is most unlikely to be successful.

§ 5.2 Circumstances in Which Child Maltreatment Occurs

"The term *child maltreatment* covers a large, complex group of human behaviors characterized by traumatic interactions between parents or other

---

[1]   Donald C. Bross, J.D., Ph.D., is Legal Counsel and Education Director of the Kempe Children's Center in Denver, Colorado.

[2]   Terri James-Banks, M.S.W., L.C.S.W., is Director of the Community Caring Program at the Kempe Children's Center in Denver, Colorado.

caretakers and the infants and children of all ages under their care."[3] There are many differences in how parents view children, and how parents were themselves cared for in their own childhood. The inherent vulnerability of human infants and toddlers makes manifest that children need parents. On the other hand, to what extent does a parent "need" the child? Normal child development requires parents who can meet the needs of their child, subordinating the parents' own needs (*e.g.*, the parents' needs for emotional reassurance that the parents are not inadequate, for emotional closeness, or for love) to the needs of the child. Maltreatment can occur whenever a parent's needs overwhelm his or her ability to give a dependent child what the child must have to be safe and develop normally.

§ 5.2.1 Lack of Empathy

Knowledge about children's changing needs as each need develops over time is essential for every adequate caregiver. How does someone learn to be a parent? Books can help, but clinical observation suggests that much of what parents carry with them into the parenting role is the experience of being cared for by others. Just as we best learn dancing by the act of having someone dance with us, we best learn care giving by being cared for. Parents who did not receive adequate care themselves as children must acquire not only cognitive but social and emotional facility if they are to provide adequate care. The difficulty of understanding the challenge can be illustrated by the difference between the words empathy and sympathy. If a person is sympathetic it is because he or she is similar to another person or has similar experiences on which to draw. If a person is empathic, it is because he or she can to some degree accurately assess how the other person might be feeling without necessarily being like the other person. With empathy, the differences between the two persons do not block meaningful and appropriate interaction. Developmentally, children are always different from their adult caregivers. Parents who expect developmentally unrealistic ideas, attitudes, or behaviors from their children—for example, about crying or toilet training—are not demonstrating a capacity for empathy. Instead the parent's behavior might be based entirely on the parent's needs or the parent's belief that the child must think or understand in the same way the parent does.

Parents who have not been empathically cared for can be less resilient and less prepared to deal with the many types of "crisis" that can occur in a home. Crises can include substance abuse, marital discord, domestic violence, job loss and job demands, mental illness, mental retardation, or physical illness. While the parent might contribute to these problems, parents cannot control all aspects of their lives; it is a mistake to assume that "fault" is at the core of resolving these crises, even though improved self-efficacy is usually part of treatable situations.

---

[3] Brandt F. Steele, *Psychodynamics and Biological Factors in Child Maltreatment, in* THE BATTERED CHILD 73-103 (5th ed., Mary Edna Helfer et al. eds., 1997).

Few would consider mental illness or mental retardation as the "fault" of the parent. Many would, however, feel that parents can control how they respond to each of these problems. From the perspective of child protection, the essential question is not whether a parent is at "fault" but whether the parent has the "capacity" to provide minimally adequate (or preferably reasonably adequate) care for a given child.

§ 5.2.2 "Trigger" Behaviors

While parents vary greatly in their ability to adapt to the needs of different types of children, everyone would have difficulty caring for some children. Even for children fairly easy to care for, for each person, there might be some feature or behavior of a child that can "trigger" an angry or nonempathic response to the child's behavior. For example, when a child falls short of parental expectations—even expectations that can be unrealistic, such as expecting an infant not to cry—this small bit of "misbehavior" might be intolerable. The parent's capacity to care must be measured in terms of the child's needs, and the standard is higher for some children for whom it will be very much more demanding to provide care. In addition to crying, other "triggers" identified in child abuse fatalities are feeding difficulties and toilet training accidents. Again, in each of these areas, experienced caregivers and child care professionals may understand, tolerate, and respond empathically to the child's behavior, but the abusive individual will often view that same behavior as a personal affront, deliberate disobedience, or intolerable.

§ 5.2.3 Domestic Violence

Domestic violence[4] and substance abuse are among a number of co-existing problems that are frequently encountered in families where children are abused or neglected. Children who witness domestic violence are at risk for injury as bystanders, and some research indicates that they are at risk for developing emotional or behavioral problems as a result of pervasive exposure to violence occurring to a parent, usually the mother. Some courts have accepted testimony supporting actual injury or substantial risk of injury to children living in homes where domestic violence occurs, as a separate basis for adjudication. Efforts to support women who are battered often emphasize empowering women to begin managing their lives better. Efforts to protect children through involuntary child protection interventions can, but do not necessarily, create conflicts between individuals and agencies trying to work with the mother and her children. The child's attorney or guardian ad litem must try to support any appropriate treatment for a mother or a father that will help assure that a child's needs are met, so long as the safety and treatment issues of the child client are addressed

---

[4] *See* Jeffrey L. Edleson, *Introduction to Special Issue, Interventions and Issues in the Co-Occurrence of Child Abuse and Domestic Violence*, 4 CHILD MALTREATMENT 91-92 (1999).

completely and not subordinated to the treatment of the parent. Each proposal for treatment of a parent and a child must be evaluated thoroughly, requiring an examination of whether or not there are alternatives that have different relative success rates or reputations, and whether any of the potential alternatives will guarantee not only treatment and safety for a parent but also safety and treatment for the child.

§ 5.2.4 Substance Abuse

Along with domestic violence, substance abuse is one of the most common co-occurring problems for families in which maltreatment occurs. Screening for substance abuse can be used by generalist caseworkers for the purpose of establishing that a formal substance use disorder evaluation should be offered or court ordered. If substance abuse is not detected and addressed—and for some families even if it is—the prognosis for maltreated children being safe and developing well in the future is guarded.[5] Recent research and experience by respected substance abuse professionals working with substance abusing mothers has provided reason for optimism that a number of substance abusing families can be treated successfully with the right interventions and enough time.[6]

§ 5.2.5 Mental Conditions; Postnatal Depression

Severe, co-existing mental illness, such as psychotic conditions, is not found in most situations of child maltreatment. While there are numerous mental conditions that can contribute to the risk of child maltreatment, postnatal depression is receiving special attention because it is not uncommon and can have fatal consequences. Research and programs to address postnatal depression are becoming more available.[7]

§ 5.2.6 Isolation

Clinicians responding to abuse soon recognized that many maltreating parents are isolated from supportive family and friends, and thus lack a "life line" that could change the parental and family dynamic. Parents who have extended

---

[5] R. Famularo et al., *Parental Substance Abuse and the Nature of Child Maltreatment*, 16 CHILD ABUSE & NEGLECT 475-483 (1992); J. M. Murphy et al., *Substance Abuse and Serious Child Mistreatment: Prevalence, Risk, and Outcome of a Court Sample*, 15 CHILD MALTREATMENT 279-291 (1991).

[6] RICHARD MCGOURTY & IRA CHASNOFF, POWER BEYOND MEASURE (Chicago: NTI Publishing 2003).

[7] Karen A. Frankel & Robert J. Harmon, *Depressed mothers: They Don't Always Look As Bad As They Feel*. 35 J. OF THE AM. ACAD. OF CHILD AND ADOLESCENT PSYCHIATRY 289-298 (1996); Ruta M. Nonacs & Lee S. Cohen, *Postpartum Mood Disorders: Diagnosis and Treatment Guidelines*, 59 J. OF CLINICAL PSYCHIATRY 34-40 (Supp. 2 1998); M. W. O'Hara & Lee S. Cohen, *Rates and Risk of Postpartum Depression: A Meta-Analysis*. 8 INT'L REV. OF PSYCHIATRY 37-54 (1996).

family available who unfortunately reinforce parental abuse or neglect are still considered "isolated" from healthy support systems. If nothing else, once a child is abused or neglected, appropriate intervention at least decreases the damaging isolation of families in which maltreatment is occurring.

§ 5.3 Perspectives for Understanding Abusive or Neglectful Parenting

§ 5.3.1 Psychodynamic Theory and Practice

Following identification of the battered child syndrome in 1962,[8] psychodynamic theory and practice provided an early foundation for understanding maltreating families. From the beginning, early life experience was identified an important feature of why some parents abused their children and others did not. Attachment and bonding research extended this approach to detailed examination of early mother-child interaction patterns, including a range of secure to insecure attachments between mothers and infants. Almost from the beginning of modern attention to child maltreatment, it has been understood that some children are resilient—they do not seem as devastated by their abuse as one might expect, but rather survive the harm done to them extremely well and for various reasons are resilient despite their mistreatment. It has also repeatedly been noted that many children who were abused will not later abuse their own children. As also noted below, however, some maltreated children do very poorly.

§ 5.3.2 Social and Economic Ecology

Social and economic ecology, including different cultural traditions and degrees of economic poverty, have also been shown to create risk for abuse and neglect. While no culture has been shown to be immune to child abuse, some seem to experience less abuse and others more.[9] In the United States, poverty is more strongly associated with physical abuse and neglect than with sexual abuse, which is more likely to be reported from all of the socio-economic classes.[10] "Brofenbrenner's 1979 ecological model often has been used to integrate research on multiple risks for family violence at four levels of analysis: (a) individual characteristics, (b) the immediate social context, (c) the broader ecological context, and (d) the societal and cultural context."[11]

---

[8]   *See, e.g.*, C. Henry Kempe et al., *The Battered-Child Syndrome*, 181 JAMA 17 (1962).

[9]   Jill E. Korbin, *Culture and Child Maltreatment, in* THE BATTERED CHILD 29-48 (5th ed., Mary Edna Helfer et al. eds., 1997).

[10]   David Finkelhor, A SOURCEBOOK OF CHILD SEXUAL ABUSE (Thousand Oaks, CA: Sage Publications 1986).

[11]   Robert E. Emery & Lisa Laumann-Billings, *An Overview of the Nature, Causes, and Consequences of Abusive Family Relationships: Toward Differentiating Maltreatment and Violence*, 53 AM. PSYCHOL. 121, 126 (1998).

§ 5.3.3 Biology

More recently, developing knowledge of human biology has been evaluated for the possible influences of intrinsic biological differences in parents and children on the risk for child abuse and risk from the consequences of child maltreatment. Genetics, which might underpin some of the risk for postnatal depression and which, in one prospective study, has been shown to create higher odds for physically abused males to exhibit negative behavioral effects from abuse than females, is currently a major focus.[12] Other factors with genetic underpinnings, such as substance abuse especially and mental illness to a lesser extent, are known to be significant cofactors in many maltreating families, and different studies are being undertaken to develop tailored approaches when these factors are present.

§ 5.3.4 Developmental Psychopathology

Developmental psychopathology is a newly evolving approach that combines many different disciplines and theories to understand individual pathology as it relates to a multitude of risk factors and developmental pathways.

> Theorists and researchers in the field of developmental psychopathology seek to unify, within a life-span framework, the many contributions to the study of individuals at high risk for developing mental disorders and those who have already manifested such disorders. Developmental psychopathologists strive to engage in a comprehensive evaluation of biological, psychological, social and cultural processes and to ascertain how these multiple levels of analysis may influence individual differences, the continuity of discontinuity of adaptive or maladaptive behavioral patterns, and the pathways by which the same developmental outcomes may be achieved. In a discussion of the importance of basic and applied research, and of a multidomain and interdisciplinary perspective for the field of neuroscience Miller (1995) enunciated the view that all of the different specialities—ranging from the basic to the applied and from the biological to the social and cultural—are needed to advance our common goal of better understanding human behavior.[13]

§ 5.3.5 Conclusions

In reviewing the literature, both trauma and resilience interplay in complex ways that are only barely appreciated. Yet early intervention is relevant to all theoretical frameworks, given studies that suggest that reduction of maltreat-

---

[12] Avshalom Caspi et al., *Role of Genotype in the Cycle of Violence in Maltreated Children*, 297 SCIENCE 851-854 (2002).

[13] Dante Cicchetti & L. Alan Sroufe, *Editorial, The Past As Prologue to the Future: The Times, They Have Been A-Changin'*, 12 DEV. AND PSYCHOPATHOLOGY 255-264 (2000).

ment can yield both short-term and long-term beneficial effects.[14] Anyone hoping to represent a maltreated child well must continue learning of the developments that are leading to the most appropriate, effective interventions.

§ 5.4 Consequences of Maltreatment

The consequences of child abuse and neglect have been better documented during the last 40 years.[15] The consequences vary depending on many factors, for example on the gender of the victim, with males more likely to "externalize" the effects of maltreatment and females more likely to "internalize" various forms of maltreatment. Cathy Spaatz Widom followed more than 1,000 young males from a midwestern American state, some of whom had official records of having been abused or neglected and others without such a record, but from the same neighborhood, and found that a history of physical abuse or neglect increased the odds of arrest as a minor or as an adult by 60 percent.[16] Dorothy Otnow Lewis[17] and her colleague Jonathan Pincus, a neurologist, have interviewed hundreds of violent offenders in the United States over a period of more than two decades. They found that a combination of severe child maltreatment and organic brain injury, from accident or abuse, is associated with the most violent offenders, including serial killers.

Moeller, Bachmann, and Moeller[18] reported on the results of interviews with 668 middle-class women, 47 percent of whom reported experiencing one or more forms of child maltreatment. The physical and psychological health problems reported by the women were significantly different for the two groups. For example, none of the non-abused group reported being alcoholic or experiencing a drug overdose, but 2.5 percent of the abused group were alcoholic and 1.4 percent had experienced a drug overdose, and 5.4 percent reported excessive drug use (as compared to 0.3 percent of the non-abused comparisons. Being a victim of a crime was 6 times more likely for the abused group (6.2 percent vs. 1

---

[14] David L. Olds et al. *Long-Term Effects of Home Visitation on Maternal Life Course and Child Abuse and Neglect: 15-Year Follow-up of a Randomized Trial*, 278 JAMA 637-643 (1997). Note: This article won the 1997 NIHCM Foundation Health Care Research Award.

[15] An excellent and detailed listing of references on developmental consequences of child abuse and treatment of child abuse and neglect can be found at http://nccanch.acf.hhs.gov/pubs/user-manuals/treatmen/index.cfm.

[16] Cathy Spatz Widom & Michael G. Maxfield, *A Prospective Examination of Risk for Violence Among Abused and Neglected Children*, 794 ANNALS OF THE N.Y. ACAD. OF SCI. 224-237 (New York: New York Academy of Sciences Press 1996).

[17] DOROTHY OTNOW LEWIS, GUILTY BY REASON OF INSANITY: A PSYCHIATRIST EXPLORES THE MINDS OF KILLERS (New York, New York: Ballantine Publishing Group 1998). This book is written for a general audience but summarizes results published in peer-reviewed journals and will make readers familiar with our entire line of research.

[18] Tamerra P. Moeller et al., *The Combined Effects of Physical, Sexual, and Emotional Abuse During Childhood: Long-term Health Consequences for Women*, 17 CHILD ABUSE & NEGLECT 623-640 (1993).

percent), suicide attempts were 6 times more likely (4.5 percent vs. 0.7 percent), and thoughts of hurting oneself were 9 times more likely (9.6 percent vs. 1.0 percent). Other areas in which the maltreated group experienced more problems were with physical health, missing work due to illness, depressed feelings, frequent emotional outbursts, frequent conflicts, and problems in many other areas. The authors provided data that physical abuse, neglect, or sexual abuse, alone or in combination, can each create a risk of many different problems for adults who were maltreated as children.

Working with a small but scientifically defined population, researchers in Minnesota reported statistically significant differences between a group of children under age five with a history of abuse or neglect and a control group of children with no such history. The maltreated children generally were more negative, nonaffectionate, avoidant of their mothers, and lacked enthusiasm and persistence in age appropriate tasks. They were more likely to be angry, showed a lack of ego control, and were judged to be avoidant and low in self-esteem. At age 54 months through kindergarten, physically abused children were identified by teachers as "extremely inattentive, unpopular, aggressive, and overactive. They were more likely than children in the control group to engage in self-destructive and obsessive-compulsive behavior."[19]

With time, there has been increasingly careful documentation of the short- and long-term harms to children who are abused and neglected. The resiliency and specific vulnerabilities of each child (*e.g.*, a child with disabilities)[20] are known to be part of the picture of both who is targeted and how experiencing trauma plays out for individuals.

§ 5.5 Treatment for Abused and Neglected Children

Family dynamics depend not only on the nature of individual parents but also on the nature of individual children. Some children are much more difficult to parent than others. Children who have been maltreated can need care and treatment that is well above average in quality for the child to recover and develop normally. Thus, treatment is needed for abused and neglected children, their parents, and the child and parents together. However, both controlled studies of treatment of parents who abuse or neglect children and studies of the effects

---

[19] Martha Ferrell Erickson et al., *The Effects of Maltreatment on the Development of Young Children*, *in* CHILD MALTREATMENT THEORY AND RESEARCH ON THE CAUSES AND CONSEQUENCES OF CHILD ABUSE AND NEGLECT 647-684 (Dante Cicchetti & Vicki Carlson eds., 1989).

[20] DICK SOBSEY, VIOLENCE AND ABUSE IN THE LIVES OF INDIVIDUALS WITH DISABILITIES: THE END OF SILENT ACCEPTANCE? (Baltimore: Paul H. Brookes Publishing 1994).

of therapy for maltreated children[21] are too few in number and quality.[22] Notwithstanding limits on available research, it appears that children who actually receive competent psychotherapy appear to do better than children who receive no competent therapy; and yet children do not receive treatment to the extent needed. In the United States, approximately 20 percent of all children have a diagnosable emotional or behavioral disorder,[23] but nearly 50 percent of children reported for abuse or neglect, ages 2-14 years of age, have "clinically significant emotional or behavioral problems."[24] As discussed previously, maltreated children are at a highly increased risk of experiencing a wide variety of emotional and behavioral disorders. Unfortunately, this fact has not generally led to specific treatment for abused children other than any benefit that might accrue from being in foster care and any improvements that might occur indirectly in the children's lives through treatment of the parents.

There are some treatment modalities that have promising indicators of success, including:

- Therapeutic preschools.

- Individual therapy.

- Group therapy.

- Home-based services with a multi-systemic approach.

- Treatment that helps foster parents address children's needs.

- Case work.

Psychotropic medications can be helpful but cannot alone address the needs of maltreated children.[25] Only rarely do maltreated children receive the direct benefits from any of these therapies. Assuring that abused and neglected children have a "right to treatment" that is enforced represents one of the major challenges to the child's attorney or guardian ad litem. When asking questions and challenging treatment professionals to address the treatment needs of abused

---

[21] David Finkelhor & Lucy Berliner, Research on the treatment of sexually abused children: A review and recommendations. 34 J. OF THE AM. ACAD. OF CHILD & ADOLESCENT PSYCHIATRY 1408-1425 (1995); R. Kim Oates & Donald C. Bross, *What Have We Learned About Treating Child Physical Abuse? A Literature Review of the Last Decade*, 19 CHILD ABUSE & NEGLECT 463-473 (1995).

[22] A good quick source of information on treatment of abused and neglected children is found at http://nccanch.acf.hhs.gov/pubs/usermanuals/treatmen/index.cfm.

[23] Adrian Angold & E. Jane Costello, *Assessment to Intervention, in* ASSESSMENT AND TREATMENT OF CHILDHOOD PROBLEMS (Carolyn S. Schroeder & Betty N. Gordon eds., 1995).

[24] Barbara J. Burns et al., *Mental Health Need and Access to Mental Health Services by Youth Involved with Child Welfare: A National Survey*, 43 J. OF THE AM. ACAD. OF CHILD & ADOLESCENT PSYCHIATRY 960-970 (2004).

[25] TIMOTHY E. WILENDS, STRAIGHT TALK ABOUT PSYCHIATRIC MEDICATIONS FOR KIDS (New York: Guilford Press 1998).

and neglected children, the guardian ad litem should avoid any formulaic approach to the client's needs and be the best possible "consumer" on behalf of the child to increase the chances of an appropriate, scientifically-based (where possible), and individually tailored plan.

In many respects, foster care has become the default mental health intervention in the lives of maltreated children. Children can fare both worse and better in foster care. To the extent that they fare much better in foster care, it is a diagnostic indication that their previous home environment was sorely lacking in physical, emotional, and psychological support. Gradually, a picture is being established of improvements in the life prospects for many children who, for good and sufficient reasons, must be placed in foster care, notwithstanding the losses in relationships with their families of origin.[26]

§ 5.6 Treatment for Parents

§ 5.6.1 Treatment Goals

The goals of treatment for parents include:

- Stopping abuse or reversing neglect.

- Ensuring adequate care giving.

- Improving the parental capacity for positive interpersonal relationships with any child in the family who has been the subject of maltreatment and other family members.

- Addressing any symptoms of psychological disorder.

- Managing any sexually aggressive violent or exploitative behavior that is directed toward the child.

The phases of treatment for parents include the acknowledgment of the abuse and its effects and the development of increased parental competence and sensitivity to the child. Resolution is the beginning of more adaptive family functioning so far as the child is concerned.[27]

§ 5.6.2 Effectiveness of Voluntary and Court-Ordered Treatment

A review[28] of 10 years of studies in peer-reviewed journals of the effectiveness of various types of behavioral treatment for parents who were physically

---

[26] *See, e.g.,* Heather Taussig et al., *Children Who Return Home from Foster Care: A Six-Year Prospective Study of Behavioral Health Outcomes in Adolescence,* 108 PEDIATRICS e10 (2001), *available at* http://pediatrics.aappublications.org/.

[27] David P. H. Jones, *Treatment of the Child and Family, in* THE BATTERED CHILD 521-542, 524, 525 (5th ed. Mary Edna Helfer et al. eds., 1997).

[28] R. Kim Oates & Donald C. Bross, *What Have We Learned About Treating Child Physical Abuse? Literature Review of the Last Decade,* 19 CHILD ABUSE & NEGLECT 463-473 (1995).

abusing their children found just 13 studies with a "rigorous research design," such as comparison groups or before-treatment and after-treatment testing. Taking into account these limitations, positive results were reported as having been obtained with parents. These results included:

- Better anger control.

- Increased goal attainment, including attaining social goals.

- Reduced or fewer psychiatric symptoms.

- Increased knowledge of alternatives to physical punishment.

- Increased use of praise.

- Increased chances of good parent-child relationships when parents acknowledged their abuse.

The studies usually addressed only one or two of these outcomes, and none of the studies attempted to measure success in all of these areas. Positive results were also found for treatment of children. Most notably, only 1 of 25 studies looked at the effects of treating both parents and children in the same intervention, with positive results reported.

One of the important assumptions of the American child protection system, and of court involvement in the lives of maltreating families, is that mandatory rather than voluntary intervention can protect children and help parents, more than it will harm them. The earliest attempt to determine if court-ordered intervention might have a positive effect was published in 1980.[29] With 71 physically abusing parents referred for treatment, 46 of whom voluntarily agreed to treatment and 25 of whom were court-ordered to treatment, the court-ordered families were found to have been 5 times more likely to have completed treatment. The percentage of court-ordered families viewed as "successful" from treatment (17 of 25 or 68 percent) was also much higher than the percentage of voluntary families who were successfully treated (6 of 46 or 13 percent). A later study also concluded that families in both voluntary and involuntary treatment significantly increased their use of praise in interaction with their children and drastically reduced their use of criticism.[30]

A five-year follow-up study of 53 infants who were born positive for substance abuse exposure, all of whose mothers were court-ordered into treatment, found that 66 percent of the infants were reunited with at least one parent and that only one child (whose mother did not attend therapy or comply with toxicol-

---

[29] David A. Wolfe et al., *The Importance of Adjudication in the Treatment of Child Abusers: Some Preliminary Findings*, 4 CHILD ABUSE & NEGLECT 127-135 (1980).

[30] Ana Maria Irueste-Montes & Francisco Montes, *Court-Ordered vs. Voluntary Treatment of Abusive and Neglectful Parents*, 12 CHILD ABUSE & NEGLECT 33-39 (1988).

ogy screening) was subsequently abused.[31] A study published in 1990 asked parents whether their families were either better off or worse off after involuntary reports and services.[32] Of the 176 parents responding, 20 percent of the parents did not answer the question, 20 percent said their families were "worse off," and 60 percent of the parents responding said their families were "better off." All of the studies cited are limited by relatively small numbers of subjects and a lack of randomized control groups, or even matched individuals, for comparison purposes. The results are enough to suggest, however, that the effects of legally mandated intervention are not necessarily bad and indeed seem to be beneficial beyond mere protection, when warranted by underlying documented abuse or neglect.

§ 5.6.3 Measuring Change in Parenting Capacity

In 1993, the National Research Council published a review of available research on the etiology of child maltreatment.[33] They identified more than 55 variables that had been associated with occurrence of child maltreatment. Twelve of the variables specifically related to aspects of the interaction between child and caregiver. Among the reported findings regarding a caregiver's relationship with the child were:

- Unrealistic expectations of the child.
- Views child's behavior as extremely stressful.
- Negative attitudes about the child's behavior.
- Perceives the child as more aggressive, intentionally disobedient, annoying, and less intelligent.
- Abusive mothers are more likely to perceive their child's negative behavior as the result of stable internal factors such as a personality trait, but her behaviors as a result of unstable external factors.
- Low involvement, nurturance, control, and monitoring.
- Authoritarian, involving punitiveness, coercion, restrictiveness, and low warmth and respect.
- Less supportive, affectionate, playful, and responsive with their children.
- With infants, abusing parents are more controlling, interfering, and covertly if not overtly hostile.
- Neglectful parents tend to be unresponsive to infants and children.

---

[31] James R. MacMahon, *Perinatal Substance Abuse: The impact of Reporting Infants to Child Protective Services*, [Electronic version] 100 PEDIATRICS e1 (1997), *available at* http://pediatrics.aappublications.org/.

[32] George E. Fryer, Jr. et al., *Good News for CPS Workers: An Iowa Survey Shows Parents Value Services*, 48 PUBLIC WELFARE 38-41,46 (1990).

[33] NAT'L RES. COUNCIL, UNDERSTANDING CHILD ABUSE AND NEGLECT (Washington, D.C.: National Academy Press 1993).

- Neglectful parents do not initiate interaction with their children and do not respond to initiations by their children.

- Abusive parents are more likely to use punishment, threats, coercion, and power, and they are less likely to use reasoning and affection in controlling their children.

In considering the development of case or treatment plans, this information suggests that evaluators responsible for determining whether change has occurred in important problems of care giving that might have lead the case to court should be able to understand and measure parental attitudes and behaviors in the areas noted by the National Science Foundation and in similar areas of interaction and care giving. While psychological testing might be sensitive enough to measure change in some situations, the ability to interview and observe parents and children will almost always form the basis for the most compelling insights. Sometimes, observation of parent-child interactions, if not too distressing to the child, may be essential for clarity. Sometimes the individual behaviors of either the parent or the child in isolation from each other can be so dramatic that the information is compelling. Thus, a child's significant improvement in foster care can provide evidence that whatever the nature of some of the parent's interactions with the child, there are also prevailing parental acts or omissions that are destroying the child's chances for reasonable development. It is important that attention be given to the more subtle and unique aspects of caregiver and child interactions rather than solely relying on identifying issues—such as substance abuse, mental health issues, domestic violence or other problems—as the primary guide for intervention strategies. A major challenge for the child's advocate is to become a "good consumer" of evaluation and therapeutic providers to determine if they are able to perform reliably and validly at the level of understanding and insight required.

Maltreatment may be exacerbated by conditions such as substance abuse or mental illness, but clinical experience and reports also suggest that harm to children also separately derives from certain aspects of the interactions of caretaker and child. Therefore, expertise in analyzing parent-child interactions in formulating a case plan is essential if many of the more difficult issues that have resulted in child maltreatment are truly to be addressed and changed in a meaningful and sustained manner.

§ 5.6.4 Parents Who Are the Most Difficult to Treat

David P. H. Jones, a child psychiatrist in Oxford, England, published a typology of "treatability" or "untreatability" in the mid-1980's that has not been replaced by any better approach.[34]

---

[34] David P. H. Jones, *The Untreatable Family*, 11 CHILD ABUSE & NEGLECT 409-420 (1987).

- There are some families who simply will not change. They do not want or intend to change.

- Some parents persistently deny abusive behavior in the face of clear evidence to the contrary.

- Some families cannot change in spite of a will to do so. There may be a subgroup here of families who are willing to change but resources to help them are not available.

- Some parents can change, but not "in time" for their child's developmental needs. For example, a six-month old baby's abusive parents, who after two years become less impulsive and dangerous, but in the meantime whose baby has developed a strong attachment to a surrogate parent.

- Similarly, other parents may change in time for their next child but not for the index one.

- Finally, there is the category of untreatable parents who fail to respond to one treatment approach but who may be amenable to another agency or approach.

Parents with personality disorders (Axis II in DSMIV-R) are an example of persons that can be particularly difficult to treat, and parents with personality disorders are not uncommon to abusive situations. Included within this general diagnostic category are narcissistic, borderline, obsessive-compulsive, and anti-social personalities. With these diagnoses, it is common for the parent to lack the ability to recognize and respond to the needs of anyone except themselves. In treatment, they often are unable to see any problem with their behavior; they tend to define the problem in terms of the failures of others. The same features that make addressing the needs of children difficult for a parent with a personality disorder tend to make treatment of the same individual both intensive and long term.

As another example of treatment difficulty, persons with multiple problems (*e.g.*, dual diagnoses of mental illness and substance abuse) require carefully tailored and often prolonged courses of treatment. It is not always possible for parents confronting a difficult course of treatment to improve sufficiently and in time to meet the minimal needs of developing children, who cannot wait for adequate care.

§ 5.7 Decisions Regarding Placement, Reunification, and Termination

Thanks to the work of Goldstein, Freud, and Solnit in their seminal series on the "best interests of children,"[35] any attorney who has represented infants and very young children is aware that time can be of the essence in the secure attachment of children. In other words, it is not good for children to be moved from one caregiver, parent, or foster parent to another for more than a very limited time, generally measured in hours for infants and days for toddlers, without very important reasons of safety or, in some situations, a clear diagnostic purpose. Every move must have an impact on the child and, unless carefully considered, may cause the child to experience a sense of loss and even depression. Thoughtful and planned changes with transition objects, preparation, and support for the child and caregivers throughout the process are not only the ideal but essential to the child's well being. Using attachment or bonding is not the only consideration of course, and the meaning of the terms and the proper application of the concepts is only part of the reciprocal connectedness that must be considered by courts in making decisions about child placements.[36]

Safety is always the first consideration in decisions for reunification. If issues of safety have been addressed, then reunification must encompass the needs of the child and caregivers for continued support, since reunification also means a different set of hourly and daily interactions between child and parent and every other person in the environment of each. This means lots of work and stress for the child and the parent, as understanding and reciprocity is renegotiated.

Termination may be the only option for not only the child but the parent to transcend their dysfunction, given court-adjudicated abuse or neglect, a treatment plan that has been refused or failed, continued parental incapacity that relates directly to meeting the child's minimally adequate needs, and if and when involuntary dissolution of the child-parent legal relationship is otherwise in the child's best interests. Thus a child who is much older or appears very difficult to adopt might not be benefited by termination.

§ 5.8 Summary

An understanding of the family dynamics that create risk and anticipate child abuse, child sexual abuse, and various forms of neglect is important for

---

[35] See JOSEPH GOLDSTEIN ET AL., BEYOND THE BEST INTERESTS OF THE CHILD (New York: Free Press 1973); JOSEPH GOLDSTEIN ET AL., BEFORE THE BEST INTERESTS OF THE CHILD (New York: Free Press 1979); JOSEPH GOLDSTEIN ET AL., IN THE BEST INTERESTS OF THE CHILD: PROFESSIONAL BOUNDARIES (New York: Free Press 1986).

[36] David E. Arredondo & Leonard P. Edwards, *Attachment, Bonding, and Reciprocal Connectedness: Limitations of Attachment Theory in the Juvenile and Family Court*, 2 J. OF THE CENTER FOR FAMILIES, CHILD. & THE CTS. 109-127 (2000).

adequate evaluation of the existence of maltreatment, and essential for crafting interventions to address the child's and family's problems of abuse and neglect. Such an understanding is also the foundation for determining where children can be placed appropriately at any stage of child protection proceedings. The intrinsic biological factors of parent and child, factors in the childhood of the parents, and the nature of the relationships that have developed between the child, the parent, and significant others in the child's life are all informed by experience and research on family dynamics in child abuse and neglect settings. Both the importance of general factors of maltreatment and resiliency and the uniqueness of each child's situation is a responsibility for each child's attorney to address.

Chapter 6 CULTURAL CONTEXT IN ABUSE AND NEGLECT PRACTICE: TIPS FOR ATTORNEYS*

by Karen Aileen Howze[1]

§ 6.1 Introduction

The men and women who serve as attorneys, judges, and social workers in abuse and neglect cases bring their total life experiences—and the assumptions that those experiences create—to each case. It is a lofty goal to expect that attorneys, judges, and social workers can set aside assumptions that are based on our perceptions of race, ethnic background, religion, poverty, substance abuse, literacy, language differences, gender, age, and sexual orientation.

Yet, central to the role of attorneys for children, parents, and the child welfare agencies is the examination of the specific needs of each family and each child so that permanency can be achieved in a timely manner. Central to the determination of the specific needs of the family and the effectiveness of services provided to promote permanency is the exploration of the cultural and subcultural context that creates the mosaic of each family.

§ 6.2 Defining Cultural and Subcultural Context

Cultural and subcultural context is the application of culture (race, ethnicity, and religion) and subculture (poverty, language, mental and physical disability, literacy, gender, sexual orientation, age, religion, or faith) to improve the decision making and services that are designed to meet the needs of children and families as they move toward a permanent resolution of conditions that necessitated court intervention.

As attorneys, judges, and social workers work to rebuild families in abuse and neglect cases, the reality is clear: The law is color blind. The law is blind to economic differences. The law balances the interests of the parties based solely on the facts presented. These are the cornerstones of the culture of American jurisprudence. At the same time, our society is filled with differences that affect a person's interpretation of the facts that are central to the application of the rules of law. In no other area of law are the differences more pronounced and more likely to affect the outcome of a case than in the area of child abuse and neglect.

---

* This chapter is adapted from KAREN AILEEN HOWZE, MAKING DIFFERENCES WORK: CULTURAL CONTEXT IN ABUSE AND NEGLECT CASES (American Bar Association 1996).

[1] Karen Aileen Howze, J.D., is a Magistrate Judge, Superior Court of the District of Columbia.

The facts:

- The majority of child welfare cases across the United States involve people who live at or below the poverty line.

- Frequently, the mothers in abuse and neglect cases are single and rearing more than one child.

- Drug addiction, mental illness, and developmental and cognitive issues create permanent disabilities that impact services and planning for permanency.

- The number of African American and Hispanic children in foster care is disproportionate to their representation in the general population across the United States.[2]

- Youth in foster care have a greater incidence of emotional, behavioral, and developmental problems than other adolescents.

- There are no societal norms that apply to all people.

The Adoption and Safe Families Act—with its tight timeframes for the achievement of permanency in abuse and neglect cases and its focus on the well being and safety of children under court supervision—requires that attorneys understand and employ different approaches to management of their cases, regardless of whether they represent parents, children, or agencies. ASFA requires that, to achieve permanency, the focus *must* be on the specific needs of each child and parent or custodian. Compliance with the rule of law in abuse and neglect cases mandates an examination and responsiveness to the specific needs of each family.

Attention to the important cultural context of a child must also be within the mandates and limits of the Multi-Ethnic Placement Act (MEPA).[3] MEPA prohibits denying any person the opportunity to become an adoptive or foster parent on the basis of the race, color, or national origin of the person or the child involved. MEPA also prohibits denial or delay of placement of a child based on race, color, or national origin. The Act also requires diligent recruitment of potential adoptive and foster parents that reflect the ethnic and racial diversity of children in the state for whom foster and adoptive homes are needed.[4]

---

[2] Michelle Y. Green, *Minorities as a Majority; Disproportionality in Child Welfare and Juvenile Justice*, CHILDREN'S VOICE (November/December 2002), *available at* http://www.cwla.org/articles/cv0211minorities.htm).

[3] 42 U.S.C. § 1996b.

[4] For a full discussion of MEPA, *see* Chapter 8, Federal Child Welfare Law and Policy: Understanding the Federal Law and Funding Process.

§ 6.3 The Players

The greatest challenge facing attorneys, regardless of whether they are guardians ad litem, parents' counsel, or agency counsel, is the development of a professional framework to recognize when the attorney's individual perceptions and assumptions of the cultural and subcultural context are getting in the way of effective advocacy and decision making. In most areas of the law, the assumptions and perceptions of attorneys and judges are of little if any consequence because resolution of the issues before the court depends on the application of the law to the facts of the case. In abuse and neglect cases, the law also rules, but the facts are always colored by the cultural and subcultural context. Once the law is applied, case resolution depends on the appropriate application of the cultural and subcultural context that is wrapped around each child, each parent, and each permanent placement family. Although an adversarial stance is required at various stages in child abuse and neglect proceedings, attorneys who are successful are also able to create a cooperative, problem-solving atmosphere while keeping in mind the context of the children and families. The critical issue for attorneys—whether they represent the agency, children, or adults—is understanding their own cultural and subcultural assumptions and perceptions. Attorneys should let those assumptions and perceptions give way to a methodical approach to questioning the reality of the lives of the children and families the attorneys serve.

§ 6.3.1 Parents' Attorney

Parents' attorneys serve as advocates and counselors. As counselor, the attorney guides the parent in making choices early in the case in the hopes that those choices will facilitate rebuilding family and the return of the child to the home. As counselor, the attorney encourages parents to put aside their reactions and feelings that "they took my child" so the rebuilding process can begin immediately.

§ 6.3.2 Guardians Ad Litem

Assisting the court as representative of the child is a powerful position with an awesome responsibility. If a guardian ad litem does not understand how to evaluate and use cultural and subcultural context in performing these responsibilities, the child is disserved. Consider this: How can the attorney purport to speak for the child when the attorney does not understand who the child is? If the attorney is to advocate for the best interests of the child, under whose norms or standards will "best interests" be defined?

There are no clear-cut answers to these questions. Good practice requires that each attorney acting as a child's representative understand who the child is and the child's context. In short, the child's attorney has a special duty that requires constant self-awareness and the ability to set aside one's background and discern what is important to a child who may not be able to define what is important for himself or herself.

The exploration of cultural and subcultural context is not as complex as it may seem. The information that follows is designed to help attorneys develop a framework for understanding cultural context in abuse and neglect cases.

§ 6.4 Beginning the Process

Creating a balance between cultural context and compliance with the law at every stage of abuse and neglect proceedings is a challenge. The populations that are frequently before the court in these matters are overwhelmingly poor. They have less education. They are often mentally ill or developmentally delayed. Many cannot read or write. Many do not speak English. Many are immigrants. Yet each has a unique family system and structure that may not mirror the personal histories of the lawyers who represent them. The following principles apply to all:

- Each family is unique.

- Each family is different in key aspects of each family member's life.

- The solutions needed to repair the family or to successfully move toward adoption, guardianship or an alternate plan must be based on a clear and careful examination of family differences and family uniqueness.

- To accomplish permanency for children, attorneys must develop a disciplined method of questioning the facts in each case to determine what role culture plays throughout each phase of the abuse and neglect proceedings.

The first step in the examination process requires that the scope of relevant facts be expanded to include the total life experiences of adults and children before the court.

The principles guiding the examination are:

- *Culture does not shape the law within the abuse and neglect framework.* Rather, cultural and subcultural context provide a backdrop on which judges, attorneys, and social service agencies can determine the levels of service, the types of services, and the anticipated impact of those services on the outcome of each case.

- *Cultural context encompasses more than race and ethnicity.* Other areas that must be explored in each case are: economic status, literacy, language, immigration status, mental and physical disabilities, education, gender, age, and sexual orientation.

- *Learning a few generalizations about the characteristics of African-Americans, Hispanics, Asians, Native Americans, or the poor does not meet the requirements for working within cultural context.* Rather, learning to question why parents or children respond the way they do will lead to an effective use of cultural and subcultural context.

- *Cultural and subcultural context must be explored through methodical questioning.* The facts of abuse and neglect must be balanced against the law with a constant eye on the impact of culture and subculture in shaping the permanency outcome.

- *Cultural and subcultural context requires an understanding of when and how cultural factors affect the way families function.* Examine each family with the assumption that each is a unique entity working within its own environment, which is affected by race, economics, language, disabilities and more.

§ 6.4.1 Begin at the Commencement of the Case

Attorneys are in a unique position to lead the assessment of the cultural and subcultural context as each case moves from petitioning through permanency. Attorneys cannot assume that cultural and subcultural context is the purview of the social workers just because they are specially trained in working with people. Attorneys must look at cultural and subcultural context as a critical element in their management of each case. Whether advocating for the child or representing the parent, the context of the client must be in the forefront of the services provided to determine whether reunification is in the best interest of the child or whether adoption, guardianship, or an alternate plan are appropriate. It is through the examination of cultural and subcultural context that attorneys, judges and social workers can evaluate the individual service needs of each family member and determine whether the services are effective based on the individual needs of each family member.

Central to the ability of attorneys to address the issues raised through the examination of cultural and subcultural context is the need to look beyond what we know through our personal life experiences. Attorneys must develop a method of interacting, assessing, and communicating with children and families through a methodical questioning process that assumes there is validity in examining the total family environment in each case to determine how we can assist families toward permanency without negating their histories. Judges, commissioners, and referees must ask the questions that may not be asked by the attorneys, social workers, or other professionals so that cultural and subcultural context are applied appropriately during all phases of the case.

§ 6.4.2 Beginning the Questioning Process

Applying cultural context to child abuse and neglect cases is a complex process. It requires:

- Knowledge of the overall community and the resources available to children and families in their communities of origin.

- Understanding of the meaning of community diversity and what community diversity means to that children and families.

- Understanding how culture and subculture affect the ability of children and families to participate in the rehabilitation process and achieve permanency while ensuring the well-being and safety of each child.

§ 6.5 At the Initial Hearing

From the instant a case is petitioned, the court's goal must be to remove the child from neglectful or abusive relationships without removing the cultural context that may be at the heart of the child's sense of self.[5]

At the initial hearing, decisions are made regarding where the child should be placed. The court enters orders to initiate services for the family and the child. Often these processes occur with little chance for a full investigation of the social and emotional status of the parents and the children. The quality of the questioning inquiries by the court, attorneys for the parties, and social workers between initial hearing and disposition often have a greater impact on case resolution than at any other time in the proceedings.

CASE SCENARIO:

James is one of three children. He is five years old and has lived in his inner-city neighborhood his entire life. His mother allegedly beat him with a belt; marks were left on his back and legs. At the initial hearing, the mother is present. It is alleged that she beat her 5-year-old son, James, with a belt. Her attorney talks with her about the case and the case is called. The child is removed and placed in the home of an unrelated foster parent in a rural community about 50 miles from home. The guardian ad litem has not met with the child; however, the maternal grandmother tells her that the 5-year-old has physical and emotional issues. The grandmother is unable to care for the child. The plan: once the mother is drug free, the child will be allowed to return home. The mother also must secure her GED.

The case plan does not address the cultural context issues. What information is missing that could be gleaned before, during and after the hearing to develop a sense of the cultural and subcultural context of the mother and child and to shape the case plan?

CULTURAL CONTEXT: There are no apparent issues of race, ethnicity, or religion.

---

[5] KAREN AILEEN HOWZE, MAKING DIFFERENCES WORK: CULTURAL CONTEXT IN ABUSE AND NEGLECT CASES 9 (ABA Center on Children and the Law 1996).

SUBCULTURAL CONTEXT: Consider possible mental illness, emotional and developmental issues for parent and child, religion/faith community, and neighborhood.

Why is information regarding cultural and subcultural context needed at the initial hearing? The mother may be mentally ill or cognitively impaired, requiring more specialized treatment than is provided in a standard drug treatment program. If the mother begins and fails in an inappropriate program, the clock continues to tick, and reunification may become less and less likely as the mother moves from program to program or gives up because the services provided did not meet her specific needs. Without at least an inquiry about the child's functioning, the child may be placed inappropriately based on his functioning and also based on the impact of moving the child a distance from whatever level of security that the child may have had in his environment.

Examine the questions that should be asked to provide context.

THE QUESTIONS:

- *The child:* What is the child's relationship with the maternal grandmother and, though she cannot care for him, does she wish to be involved in his life? How? Does the child participate in a church? Do the foster parents participate in church? How important is church participation to the respondent? To his family? Can the family participate in ensuring that his connections to his church are maintained? Are the religious affiliations of the foster parent compatible with the church affiliation that the child is accustomed to? What issues should be addressed to ensure that the respondent, a city kid, is comfortable and feels safe in a rural environment 50 miles from home?

- *The mother:* Though drug addiction is not a subcultural context, other issues related to mental health and cognitive functioning are. Is the birth mother diagnosed with a mental illness? Is she literate? Is English her primary language? If she is not literate or is developmentally disabled, is the plan to secure a GED realistic in the context of her life and the timelines required under ASFA?

Even though the answers to these questions may not be available at the initial hearing, the mere questioning begins to shape services and case planning at the earliest possible point in the case. The goal in the questioning process is to address issues that may affect the well being of the child when in foster care, and ensure that a realistic plan is developed to move toward return home because the birth mother is able to comply with the orders entered as early as the initial hearing.

§ 6.6 Between Disposition and the First Permanency Hearing

Disposition—and the reviews that follow—is one of the most critical stages in abuse and neglect cases. The timelines for reunification are short; termination of parental rights may loom on the horizon; the child experiences many changes, including the loss of a parent figure in many cases and adjustment to new ways of living when the child is placed in a non-relative foster placement. Between removal and disposition, some children change placements multiple times. Each move affects the child in unique ways, and each move affects the ability of the attorneys, social workers, and judges to assure timely permanency as required by law. On the other hand, once disposition occurs, the court will regularly examine progress made by the parents to achieve the dispositional goal. Without an early examination of the cultural and subcultural context of the child's life and the parent's life, achieving permanency will become an elusive and somewhat painful process for all.

DISPOSITION CASE SCENARIO:

Joseph is a 15-year-old Vietnamese youth who resided with his mother, father and two siblings (ages 5 and 9) in a community that is primarily African American. Joseph called the authorities to ask that he and his siblings be removed. He says he cannot live with his dumb parents any longer. Joseph says his parents use drugs and, because of that, the family is facing eviction. He and his younger siblings were placed in a foster home in a predominantly white community in a different city than his home of origin. The goal at disposition is reunification for all three children. The birth mother speaks some English. The birth father does not speak English. The children speak both English and Vietnamese. The birth parents have substance abuse issues. For reunification to occur, the birth mother must secure housing, undergo drug treatment, and participate in individual and family therapy to address the domestic violence between the parents. The disposition hearing sets a six-month deadline for reunification. The birth mother says she will kick her drug habit on her own. The birth father claims he does not have a drug habit.

CULTURAL CONTEXT: Ethnicity and race (Vietnamese family).

SUBCULTURAL CONTEXT: Language barriers (internal and external to the family), possible mental health issues, literacy issues.

THE QUESTIONS:

- How do we determine whether traditional cultural practices should be a factor in the services that are provided to the family? Are there differences in the level of receptiveness to those services by the parents and each child?

- How do we determine what is an appropriate placement for an adolescent (family foster placement vs. group home setting) who is slowly losing the connection between the family's culture of origin and the adolescent's acculturation into American culture? Does the ethnic or racial composition of the foster home matter if a family setting is appropriate?

- How do we communicate with an adolescent when English is not the first language and nuances of communication are lost because of the lack of proficiency in English?

- What are Joseph's views of his culture of origin? Can his positive views be used to help him understand that he may be able to function in the world of his family's culture and in his new American world? How do we address the apparent lack of interest and disrespect that Joseph exhibits toward his culture of origin in a manner that will make it easier for him to "live in two worlds?"

- Can we identify service providers to assist in developing the service plan, explore the issues presented by Joseph and his family, and possibly provide direct services to this family beginning soon after the removal?

- Does the reunification plan include helping the birth parents understand and cope with Joseph's Americanized behaviors?

- What services will be needed to ensure a successful reunification for Joseph? Does the language spoken by the service provider matter? Who will provide the services, and will they be able to work effectively with Joseph and other family members?

- What will the parents need to help them understand the cultural and subcultural context of their son's life to ensure the success of the reunification effort?

- Are service providers who are experienced in working with these cultural issues available to work with the family consistently until permanency is resolved?

Clearly, there are no pat answers or cookie-cutter solutions to this scenario or those that follow. However, by simply raising the questions that arise from the facts of the case, the attorney will provide invaluable assistance to the court in setting realistic timeframes for reunification and defining the quality and type of service needed by the birth family. Raising the questions may assist in predicting issues that the children may face as the reunification effort progresses, and raising the questions early in the case reduces the likelihood that the issues will divert attention from rebuilding the family of origin on stronger footing to achieve the permanency goal. By raising the questions, the attorney has a basis to question whether the disposition plan should be the same for all three children or whether the time frame for reunification may differ based on the needs of each child.

Frequently, the failure to identify cultural and subcultural context derails or delays the achievement of permanency. Ultimately, the judicial officers who are responsible for the lives of the children and families must hold the child's attorney, the social worker, counsel for the birth parents where appropriate, agency counsel, and service providers accountable for ensuring that the questioning process is in full force at the disposition hearing—and at all subsequent permanency hearings.

THE GUIDELINES:

- Recognize that the cultural framework of each family of origin remains with each child no matter how long the youth is in foster care. While the child is in care, that framework must continue to be nurtured or the child will lose an important part of who that child is, which will affect permanency planning and the child's well being as permanency moves forward.

- Question the cultural and subcultural context in the permanency planning process, and allow that context to inform case planning and progress toward case resolution.

§ 6.7 From the First Permanency Hearing through Case Resolution

Regardless of how long a child has been away from his or her birth family, the reintegration into the family after foster care is often fraught with cultural and subcultural issues that were not explored while the family received reunification services. Joseph's case provides an example of the need to address cultural and subcultural issues immediately upon removal or state intervention. Take a look at Joseph's situation as permanency planning proceeds:

DISPOSITION CASE SCENARIO (CONT.):

Joseph decides that he does not wish to return home even though his sister and brother will be going home in a few months. Joseph says he no longer considers himself Vietnamese. He is American. He also does not want to live in a white community because he is more comfortable around African Americans. A permanency plan must be developed for Joseph. The case has been open for 16 months.

Joseph's circumstances present a clear picture of the impact that failing to explore cultural and subcultural context can have on the resolution of the case.

THE QUESTIONS:

- The primary question: Is adoption an option for Joseph? Is there anyone who is a possible adoptive resource for him?

- What impact does Joseph's rejection of his culture of origin have on his continued relationship with his siblings? His parents?

- What is the view of adoption in the Vietnamese community?

- Would the change in the goal and identification of an appropriate pre-adoptive family have been easier if Joseph's familiarity and comfort with one culture (African Americans) had been taken into account at his— and his siblings'—placement in shelter care?

Questions like these are central to the effective exploration and preparation of children for any permanency plan. Failing to ask cultural and subcultural context questions can and does result in frustration during permanency planning, and it may mean the difference between successful resolution and continued foster care for some children.[6]

If reunification cannot be achieved and Joseph is to find permanency, attention must be focused on the best solution. It is never too late to begin the questioning process.

PERMANENCY PLANNING SCENARIO:

Jeremiah is a 12-year-old African American who visits with his birth family occasionally. Substance abuse was the primary issue that led to the finding of neglect in his case. For two years, his goal has been adoption. He has been placed with one foster family since his removal. The foster parents are African American and they are Muslim. Jeremiah grew up participating in services with his grandmother, who is a Jehovah's Witness. The family has indicated their intent to adopt Jeremiah, but he is not willing to explore adoption. In addition, he is not enthusiastic about meeting prospective adoptive parents. The social worker recommends that Jeremiah's goal be changed to an Alternate Planned Permanent Living Arrangement so that he can remain with the current foster parents until he is emancipated.

---

6   Forty-seven states, the District of Columbia, American Somoa, Guam, and the Northern Mariana Islands, Puerto Rico, and the Virgin Islands require that adolescents consent to their adoption. Twenty-three states and the Virgin Islands require 14-year-olds to consent; eighteen states, American Somoa, and Guam require consent from 12-year-olds; and seven states, the Northern Mariana Islands, and Puerto Rico require the consent of youth age 10 and above. Similar laws apply in custody and guardianship proceedings. For Native American children, when ICWA applies and the tribal court holds jurisdiction, the issue of whether an adolescent must consent to adoption, guardianship, or custody is based on the tribe's laws. In cases where the state has jurisdiction over the adolescent, state consent laws apply.

CULTURAL CONTEXT: Religion (Muslim faith of the foster parents).

SUBCULTURAL CONTEXT: Religion (Faith community of the family of origin).

THE QUESTIONS:

- Did anyone involved in the case know that Jeremiah was a Jehovah's Witness?

- Was the Agency aware of the foster family's practices and beliefs before the placement?

- Were the foster parents provided with guidance regarding how to introduce their religious and cultural practices to Jeremiah before his placement? Has there been any discussion regarding his feelings about abandoning the religious experiences he had with his grandmother prior to his placement in foster care?

- Was there an opportunity for Jeremiah to learn about their practices and beliefs before he was placed in the home?

- Once he was in the family home did anyone discuss how Jeremiah felt about the Muslim faith? After he was placed in foster care, was he given an opportunity to participate in services and activities through his grandmother's church?

- Is Jeremiah's reluctance to be adopted by the foster parents based on their beliefs, practices, and traditions, or is it based on his conflicts regarding his birth family?

- Has anyone discussed the conflicts facing Jeremiah with his birth parents?

Because these cultural and subcultural context questions were not explored at the time of placement, the opportunity has more than likely been lost for this foster home to serve as the permanent placement should an Alternate Planned Permanent Living Arrangement be set as Jeremiah's permanency plan. Again, there are no pat answers or cookie-cutter solutions, and it is never too late to begin the questioning process.

PERMANENCY PLANNING SCENARIO:

Maria is a 10-year-old who was born in Mexico. She and her five siblings have been placed in a foster home where no one speaks Spanish. English is the second language for the children. They visit their birth mother weekly and attempt to keep up their native language skills during those visits. The adoption goal was set six months ago during the first permanency hearing and within weeks of their placement in the current foster home. The foster family has indicated an interest in adopting the children, but Maria is not interested. Recently, Maria informed the court that she does not want to remain in the home because the family does not allow the children to speak Spanish. Her siblings are three and four years old, and Maria does not want to leave her siblings.

CULTURAL CONTEXT: Ethnicity and race.

SUBCULTURAL CONTEXT: Language.

THE QUESTIONS:

- What can be done to resolve the issues presented for Maria and her siblings? Should there be a search for a placement that will respect the language and culture of all three children?

- What should be done to determine whether the pre-adoptive family has the capacity to view the children's culture and language with respect and allow them to continue to participate actively in that culture? Who will assess their capacity?

- Even with appropriate assessment and intervention, is it too late to rectify the situation for Maria? What will become the best permanency option for Maria and her siblings, and what interventions will be necessary to ensure that they can remain together and have a permanent home?

- Has the situation with the current foster parents affected Maria's interest in pursuing adoption as a goal, or is her refusal to participate in the adoption process based on her relationship with her birth mother?

- What harm will be caused to Maria if she is placed elsewhere and the younger children remain in the current foster home? What harm will be caused to the younger children if they remain in a home that does not value their heritage? What impact will this dynamic have on their overall development? What impact will the lack of respect for culture have on their relationships with each other and with Maria if she begins to resist remaining in the home as adoption plans progress?

- What is the family of origin's cultural view of adoption? Termination of Parental Rights?

Consider the following permanency scenarios:

- How do the cultural norms of the 7-year-old Native-American boy affect his ability to integrate into a new family structure and a new community that is primarily white and in a new state? What supports will be required if he is placed in a Caucasian family for adoption?[7]

- A 16-year-old girl from a farming community in the South is placed with a family in a metropolitan area in New York State. What assistance will this adolescent need to help her become acclimated to her new environment? What assistance will she and her new family need to help her adjustment in the home, at school, and in the community?

If attention is not paid to the cultural and subcultural context, opportunities are missed to ensure appropriate placement to meet the contextual needs of each child. Each of the reunification and adoption scenarios presented above rest on the edge of an alternate planned permanent living arrangement because cultural and subcultural context were not addressed early in the permanency planning process. What will be the goal for Maria, Jeremiah and Joseph if the questions are not explored and issues resolved with an eye to cultural and subcultural context?

§ 6.8 APPLA is the Final Option

APPLA SCENARIO:

Catherine is 15 years old, and she has been in foster care since she was 10. She has been involved in two failed attempts to reunify with her birth mother and has decided she does not wish to live with her mother. Catherine's family—maternal and paternal—are very religious. Over the past 18 months, she was placed successively with her maternal grandmother and a paternal aunt. Each relative asked for her removal because of the friends she associates with and her mode of dress. She says she is a lesbian, though she states she has never had a relationship with anyone. She is seriously depressed and has tested as mildly mentally retarded. The Agency has identified a foster home, but Catherine is not interested in placement in a family setting.

CULTURAL CONTEXT: Religion.

---

[7] The Indian Child Welfare Act (ICWA), Pub. L. No. 95-608, 25 U.S.C. §§ 1901 through 1963, sets jurisdiction for Native American children. ICWA is based on recognition that child welfare officials and workers do not share the same values as Indian families and authorities. The Act requires the involvement of the tribe in decisions related to children and families and promotes the placement of Native American children with Native families. Two excellent resources for permanency planning for this population are the INDIAN CHILD WELFARE ACT CHECKLIST, PERMANENCY PLANNING FOR CHILDREN DEPARTMENT, NAT'L COUNCIL OF JUV. AND FAM. CT. JUDGES (2003) and THE NATIVE AMERICAN RESOURCE DIRECTORY FOR JUVENILE AND FAMILY COURT JUDGES, PERMANENCY PLANNING FOR CHILDREN DEP'T, NAT'L COUNCIL OF JUV. AND FAM. CT. JUDGES (2003).

SUBCULTURAL CONTEXT: Sexual orientation, mental health issues, emotional/developmental issues, and faith/religion.

THE QUESTIONS:

- Can the social worker and the Court ensure that Catherine is placed in a safe environment where she is able to grow into herself without feeling she is not a healthy person? If safety cannot be certain in a group setting, what discussions will the worker have with Catherine to determine whether she will agree to a foster home placement and under what circumstances?

- What role does faith play in Catherine's life? Is there a faith organization that will be accepting of Catherine where she can continue to maintain a faith connection despite her past rejection?

- Has anyone explored identifying a specialized placement for Catherine with a foster parent who has been trained in working with adolescents who have sexual identity issues?

- Has anyone explored whether a safe group setting can be identified that does not leave Catherine vulnerable to attack because of her dress, her friends and associates, and her intellectual functioning?

- What impact does Catherine's diagnosis as mildly mentally retarded have on her ability to process and advocate for herself regarding her sexual identity issues?

- Has Catherine been referred to community-based organizations that assist youth who are questioning their sexual identity? Has anyone helped Catherine identify a professional who can assist her in resolving the rejection that she has experienced from her family members because of her dress and her friends?

APPLA CASE SCENARIO:

Michael is a 17-year-old Native American who is under state court jurisdiction. The tribal court agreed to state jurisdiction because services were available through the state that would not have been available through the tribe. Michael was discharged from residential treatment six months ago. He has done well in his placement and in the community, and he is excelling in school. Michael, whose parents are deceased, remains connected to the tribe. The social worker who was assigned to the case two months ago reports to the court that she is frustrated because Michael seems to not be fully invested in his emancipation planning. He arrives late for critical meetings and can never look her in the eye. That behavior, she says, makes her believe she cannot trust him or the information he provides to her about his compliance with his Independence

Transition Plan. She recommends that the court end supervision because Michael is not participating in the process and says that he has members of his tribe who will provide support for him once court supervision ends. The social worker has not met with any of Michael's support network from the tribe.

CULTURAL CONTEXT: Ethnicity and race.

SUBCULTURAL CONTEXT: Age and neighborhood.

THE QUESTIONS:

- Are the conclusions of the social worker based in reality or are they perceptions of Michael's presentation that do not reflect his involvement in his emancipation planning? Are some of her complaints, such as eye contact and punctuality, based on cultural norms?

- What can the court do to bring together Michael's supportive adults from the tribe to participate in the last year of planning for Michael and place his response in the process in the proper perspective so that Michael can be successful?

- How can Michael be encouraged to involve the tribe in the planning process? Who can help him in this process? Can the judge contact the tribal court to discuss Michael's situation and forge a partnership with the tribe, regardless of who has jurisdiction?

§ 6.9 Conclusion

Clearly, there are no answers to the questions presented with each of the permanency scenarios. However, the questions in each scenario clearly exhibit that by asking questions, attorneys, judges, and social workers begin to peel the onion to reach the core issues that may ensure that each child in foster care reaches permanency in a timely and appropriate manner.

In some cases, the examination of cultural and subcultural context can mean the difference between a permanent home through reunification, adoption, or guardianship versus an Alternate Permanent Planned Living Arrangement.

These are the critical factors that ring true in all cases:

- There are numerous cultural and subcultural issues involved in each case. No one can decide which issue is paramount.

- The family defines which issues are paramount—even if the professionals believe the priorities set by the family do not comport with the professional's view of what will be required to achieve permanency. Attorneys, social workers, and judges will not be able to craft a plan that will be successful without the understanding of the cultural and subcultural context of the family and each member involved in the case.

In the end, by working with the cultural context of each child and adult in abuse and neglect cases, we will make the differences within our communities work to maximize the potential of each child and adult to rebuild families or successfully move children to new families if reunification is not possible.

II. THE LEGAL FRAMEWORK OF CHILD WELFARE LAW

Chapter 7 THE HISTORY OF CHILD WELFARE LAW*

by Marvin Ventrell[1]

§ 7.1 Introduction

Juvenile law and the juvenile court are comprised of two distinct but historically related components: delinquency (juvenile justice) and dependency (child welfare).[2] Much has been written about the history of delinquency but very little about dependency. The history of child welfare law and the dependency side of the juvenile court are commonly seen as beginning with the anomaly of the child abuse case of "Little Mary Ellen" toward the end of the nineteenth century, followed many years later by society's recognition of child maltreatment in the 1960s, culminating in the federal Child Abuse Prevention and Treatment Act in 1974. Although these are significant events leading to the current child welfare system, they do not explain the whole story. The early juvenile court actually had a dependency component that evolved into the modern dependency system. That dependency component, like its delinquency counterpart, has a lengthy and important history. To more fully understand current child welfare law and policy and to inform system improvement, it is useful to know something about its development. What follows is primarily an attempt to summarize and give context to existing research[3] on the development of child welfare law and the dependency court.

§ 7.2 Dependency Court Jurisdiction

The dependency court is that part of the juvenile court that handles child maltreatment cases. A child who has been adjudicated maltreated or is under

---

* This chapter is adapted with permission from Marvin Ventrell, *Evolution of the Dependency Component of the Juvenile Court,* Juv. AND FAM. CT. J., Fall 1998, Vol. 49, No. 4, at 17.

[1] Marvin Ventrell, J.D., is the President/CEO of the National Association of Counsel for Children (NACC).

[2] *See* Leonard P. Edwards, *The Juvenile Court and the Role of the Juvenile Court Judge,* Juv. FAM. CT. J., Spring 1992, Vol. 43, No. 2, at 5 (1992).

[3] This analysis draws heavily on the scholarship of Sanford J. Fox (former Professor of Law, Boston College School of Law); Jean Koh Peters (Clinical Professor of Law, Yale University School of Law); John C. Watkins, Jr. (University of Alabama); Mason P. Thomas, Jr. (Professor of Public Law and Government, Institute of Government, University of North Carolina); and Douglas R. Rendleman (Professor of Law, University of Alabama School of Law).

state custody is often referred to as a dependent child.[4] Child maltreatment is the general term used to describe all forms of child abuse and neglect that give rise to dependency court jurisdiction.[5] There is no one commonly accepted definition of child abuse and neglect. The federal government defines child abuse and neglect in the Child Abuse Prevention and Treatment Act as "at a minimum, any recent act or failure to act on the part of a parent or caretaker, which results in death, serious physical or emotional harm, sexual abuse or exploitation, or an act or failure to act which presents an imminent risk of serious harm"[6] Each state provides its own definition of child abuse and neglect.[7] Child maltreatment encompasses physical abuse, sexual abuse, neglect, and emotional abuse, which can be defined as follows:

- *Physical Abuse: Nonaccidental physical injury as a result of caretaker acts.* Physical abuse frequently includes shaking, slapping, punching, beating, kicking, biting, and burning.[8]

- *Sexual Abuse: Involvement of dependent, developmentally immature children and adolescents in sexual activities that they do not fully comprehend and to which they are unable to give informed consent.* Sexual abuse includes touching, fondling, and penetration.[9]

- *Neglect: Failure of caretakers to provide for a child's fundamental needs.* Although neglect can include children's necessary emotional needs, neglect typically concerns adequate food, housing, clothing, medical care, and education.[10]

- *Emotional or Psychological Abuse: The habitual verbal harassment of a child by disparagement, criticism, threat, and ridicule.* Emotional or psychological abuse includes behavior that threatens or intimidates a child. It includes threats, name calling, belittling, and shaming.[11]

These categories make up the jurisdiction of the modern juvenile dependency court. The first juvenile court was founded in Chicago in 1899, and the dependency categories were quite different.[12] The word "abuse" does not

---

[4] *See* INGER SAGATUN & LEONARD EDWARDS, CHILD ABUSE AND THE LEGAL SYSTEM 17 (1995).

[5] *Id.*

[6] 42 U.S.C. § 5106(g)(2) (2004).

[7] *See,* 1 NAT'L CENTER ON CHILD ABUSE AND NEGLECT, CHILD ABUSE AND NEGLECT STATE STATUTES SERIES (1997), for a compilation of state maltreatment statutes.

[8] KIM OATES, THE SPECTRUM OF CHILD ABUSE (1996). *See also* INGER SAGATUN & LEONARD EDWARDS, CHILD ABUSE AND THE LEGAL SYSTEM 17 (1995).

[9] KIM OATES, THE SPECTRUM OF CHILD ABUSE (1996).

[10] *Id.*

[11] *Id.*

[12] *See* § 7.3.6 for a detailed discussion of the dependency categories of the 1899 court.

appear in the act, although parental neglect and cruelty are mentioned. While with a little ingenuity, modern categories of child abuse and neglect can be made to fit the 1899 categories, the jurisdictional dependency language of the early court suggests a different emphasis. Tracking the evolution of current dependency court jurisdiction begins with a review of the historical treatment of children.

§ 7.3 Origins of Child Maltreatment and Protection

§ 7.3.1 Maltreatment

There are approximately one million substantiated cases of child abuse and neglect in the United States each year, and millions of additional cases are reported.[13] Child maltreatment is appropriately described by the U.S. Advisory Board on Child Abuse and Neglect as a national emergency to which inadequate attention and resources are paid.

Child maltreatment is not a recent phenomenon, nor is it unique to certain nations and cultures.[14] It appears children have always been abused and neglected.[15] A number of essays on child maltreatment have included the familiar quote by Lloyd deMause:

> The history of childhood is a nightmare from which we have only recently begun to awaken. The further back in history one goes, the lower the level of child care, and the more likely children are to be killed, abandoned, beaten, terrorized, and sexually abused.[16]

One the one hand, history seems to bear out deMause. History is replete with incidents of infanticide, sexual abuse, beatings, and inadequate responses to these tragedies.[17] At the same time, it is a mistake to assume that the history of childhood has been a nightmare for most children or that significant efforts have not been made to protect children. To the contrary, one can make the case, as does John E.B. Myers, that history shows continual humanitarian progress to value and protect children. Professor Myers begins his recent book on the history of child protection as follows:

---

[13] CHILDREN'S BUREAU, U.S. DEP'T OF HEALTH AND HUMAN SERVS., CHILD MALTREATMENT 2002, at 4 (Washington, DC: U.S. Government Printing Office, 2004).

[14] Robert W. ten Bensel et al., *Children in a World of Violence: The Roots of Child Maltreatment,* in THE BATTERED CHILD 3, 3-5 (Mary Edna Helfer et al. eds., 5th ed. 1997).

[15] *Id.*

[16] Lloyd deMause, *The Evolution of Childhood,* in THE HISTORY OF CHILDHOOD 1 (Lloyd deMause, ed., Jason Aronson, Inc. 1995).

[17] Lloyd deMause, *The Evolution of Childhood,* in THE HISTORY OF CHILDHOOD 1 (Lloyd deMause, ed., Jason Aronson, Inc. 1995); William L. Langer, *Foreword,* in THE HISTORY OF CHILDHOOD i, i-ii (Lloyd deMause, ed., 1974); Robert W. ten Bensel et al., *Children in a World of Violence: The Roots of Child Maltreatment,* in THE BATTERED CHILD 3, 4-5 (Mary Edna Helfer et al. eds., 5th ed. 1997).

Throughout history, parents adored their children. Something deep within us created a bond between parent and child; a bond that is without parallel in human experience. Because of this bond, and for other reasons as well, the vast majority of parents do not abuse or neglect their children. Competent parenting is the rule, abuse and neglect the exception.... Efforts to protect children from abuse and neglect are as old as maltreatment itself.[18]

These two views are entirely reconcilable. From the perspective of education and awareness, it is necessary to point out the horrors of child maltreatment and society's inadequate response. At the same time, we should be mindful that most children are not abused or neglected and that while we are not there yet, great strides have been made in child protection.

§ 7.3.2 Child Protection

Pre-sixteenth-century legal and humanitarian efforts to protect maltreated children were minimal. To the extent services or prohibitions against maltreatment were afforded children, the work was private or church driven. A review of some historic pro-child developments does reveal a gradual increase in child protection and children's rights. Robert W. ten Bensel[19] reports that esteem for the child slowly began to appear in the following historic events:

- The Bible commands, "Do not sin against the child" (Gen. 42:22).

- The laws of Solon, in 600 B.C., required the commander of an army to protect and raise, at government expense, children of citizens killed in battle.

- Athens and Rome had orphan homes.

- The Christian church fathers in the fourth century, in line with the Judaic injunction "Thou shalt not kill," equated infanticide with murder. A succession of imperial edicts after that guaranteed a child's right to life.

- Orphanages were mentioned in 529 in the laws of Justinian.

- By the sixth century, the "orphanage" at Trier included a marble receptacle in which a child could be safely deposited.

- The first foundling hospital was established in Milan in 787.

- Pope Innocent III started the Hospital of the Holy Spirit in 1066.

---

[18] JOHN E.B. MYERS, A HISTORY OF CHILD PROTECTION IN AMERICA, 17 (Xlibris Corporation 2004).

[19] Robert W. ten Bensel et al., *Children in a World of Violence: The Roots of Child Maltreatment, in* THE BATTERED CHILD 3, 16-21 (Mary Edna Helfer et al. eds., 5th ed. 1997).

- A foundling hospital was established in Florence in 1444, and was known as the Hospital of the Innocents.

- Vincent de Paul established a foundling hospital in Paris in 1650 when he became concerned about the children abandoned on the steps of Notre Dame.

While these events may in some way represent the origins of modern child protection, it is difficult to argue that children's status, even as late as the sixteenth and seventeenth centuries, was such that children were meaningfully protected from maltreatment. The family's autonomy to do essentially as it saw fit with its children was untouched. The first direct link with juvenile dependency court protections appears in sixteenth-century England.

§ 7.3.3 Sixteenth- and Seventeenth-Century England: Creation of a System of Family Law

The development of American family law most likely has its origins in the sixteenth and seventeenth centuries when society moved from communal living arrangements to family groups.[20] From there, it is argued that the relationship of those family groups to the church and state, and the institutions that resulted from them, form the basis of the law that led to the creation of the juvenile court.[21] This period is characterized by nonintervention into the family except to the extent a driving social policy warranting intervention arose.[22] The two driving policies that justified intervention were the regulation of poverty and the regulation of wealth.

Jacobus tenBroek describes family law of sixteenth- and seventeenth-century England as a "dual system."[23] More recently, Jean Koh Peters has supplemented this analysis by reviewing the theory of the dual system of family law in the context of the development of child protection law.[24] The theory of the dual system of family law is that, to the extent that families of sixteenth- and seventeenth-century England experienced legal intervention, they experienced one of two distinct types of intervention according to their social class. On one side of the spectrum was a legal system designed to ensure the orderly passage of property of the rich. On the other side of the spectrum was a legal system of

---

[20] *See* Douglas R. Rendleman, Parens Patriae: *From Chancery to the Juvenile Court,* 23 S.C. L. REV. 205 (1971) (tracing the evolution of the juvenile court system from feudal England to modern times).

[21] *See, e.g., id.*

[22] JEAN KOH PETERS, REPRESENTING CHILDREN IN CHILD PROTECTIVE PROCEEDINGS: ETHICAL AND PRACTICAL DIMENSIONS app. (2nd ed. 2001).

[23] Jacobus tenBroek, *California's Dual System of Family Law: Its Origin, Development and Present Status* (pt. 1), 16 STAN. L. REV. 257, 257-258 (1964).

[24] JEAN KOH PETERS, REPRESENTING CHILDREN IN CHILD PROTECTIVE PROCEEDINGS: ETHICAL AND PRACTICAL DIMENSIONS app. (2nd ed. 2001).

intervention designed to control the family relationships of the poor. In the middle were the majority of people who experienced no legal intervention into the accepted patriarchal system.[25]

Family Law for the Wealthy

The wealthy experienced no family intervention except to the extent it was necessary to insure the passage of wealth. The state had an interest in taxing the transfer of property from one generation to the next. Under primogeniture, court or crown involvement was generally unnecessary. However, where a patriarch died prior to his heir's majority, or where there was a dispute as to the identity of the heir or the character of land tenure, the crown became interested in the child to ensure proper passage of wealth and to collect tax on the property. It is in these proceedings that we first see the appointment of a representative for the child in the form of the guardian ad litem.[26]

Family Law for the Poor

As the chancery court was deciding the property and custody issues of the aristocracy, a statutory scheme dealing with the custody of poor children was developing.[27] Two concepts began to emerge in sixteenth-century England out of what became the Elizabethan Poor Laws, which serve to connect this period in history to the juvenile court. The first is the government's assumption of the authority and obligation to care for poor children as a kind of ultimate parent. The second is the mechanism of apprenticeships as a means of that parentage.

At the decline of the feudal age, motivated by the emergence of an underclass of poor children, and the vagrancy and crime attributed to the poor, combined with the post reformation decline of the church as an instrument of social welfare, Parliament passed the Statute of Artificers[28] in 1562 and later the Poor Law Act of 1601.[29] The Statute of Artificers provided that poor children could be involuntarily taken from their parents and apprenticed. The Poor Laws were a series of statutes authorizing the removal of poor children from their parents at the discretion of overseer officials and the "bounding out" of children to a local resident as an apprentice until the age of majority.[30] In addition to this forced labor, the Poor Laws also provided for cash for those unable to work.[31]

---

[25] *Id.*

[26] *Id.*

[27] *See, e.g.,* Douglas R. Rendleman, Parens Patriae: *From Chancery to the Juvenile Court,* 23 S.C. L. REV. 205, 210 (1971).

[28] 5 Eliz. c. 4 (1562).

[29] 43 Eliz. c. 2 (1601).

[30] Jacobus tenBroek, *California's Dual System of Family Law: Its Origin, Development and Present Status* (pt. 1), 16 STAN. L. REV. 257, 279-282 (1964).

[31] Douglas R. Rendleman, Parens Patriae: *From Chancery to the Juvenile Court,* 23 S.C. L. REV. 205, 211 (1971).

These laws resulted in considerable family intervention and are seen as the beginning of "state-run welfare."[32]

The Elizabethan state-run welfare program was cleverly structured without state funding. The law provided that each community, through its parish, would administer the law by providing relief, removing children, apprenticing children, and using punishment.[33] Peters points out that the Poor Laws effected the poor in three basic ways:[34]

1. *Labor.* The Poor Laws controlled labor of the poor in the following ways:

    - By mandating that an unmarried laborer could not refuse work in his apprenticed trade.

    - Laborers' wages were capped.

    - Women who labored had to be over 12, under 40, and unmarried.

    - There were to be restrictions on both apprenticeship and laboring.

    - Rules were to be adopted regarding the dismissal of an apprentice.

    - The apprenticing of nonpoor children was to be regulated by provided rules.

2. *Travel.* Poor persons' travel and residency were restricted in these ways:

    - Poor persons were often restricted from moving to healthier economies.

    - The parish had the authority to remove the poor.

    - Regulations determined who were local and foreign and not the responsibility of the parish.

3. *Family Support.* The Poor Laws shaped family life for poor persons by:

    - The doctrine of intra-familial support that demanded three generations of ascending and descending support, mandating parental support of children.

    - Restricting the freedom of the poor to marry through tactics to prevent the poor from marrying and producing children.

    - Restricting a poor woman's right to bear children through bastardy laws that could result in punishments for mothers of illegitimate children of up to one year labor in a house of corrections.[35]

---

[32] JEAN KOH PETERS, REPRESENTING CHILDREN IN CHILD PROTECTIVE PROCEEDINGS: ETHICAL AND PRACTICAL DIMENSIONS 238 (2nd ed. 2001).

[33] 43 Eliz. c. 2 s.1. (1601).

[34] JEAN KOH PETERS, REPRESENTING CHILDREN IN CHILD PROTECTIVE PROCEEDINGS: ETHICAL AND PRACTICAL DIMENSIONS 239-240 (2nd ed. 2001).

[35] Mothers could also be forced to pay relief to the state for having an illegitimate child and then receive no state assistance with which to feed the child. This practice led to an increase in infanticide, which was itself punished. *Id.* at 249 n.76 (quoting PETER C. HOFFER & N. E. HULL, MURDERING MOTHERS: INFANTICIDE IN ENGLAND AND NEW ENGLAND, 1558-1803 (1981)).

It is generally accepted that the Poor Laws authorized significant intervention into the lives of the poor in exchange for poverty relief. In truth, the Poor Laws served less as a system of welfare and more as a mechanism of social control of the poor.[36]

In a frequently used quote, William Blackstone summarized the dual system of family law and the rise of the state as the ultimate parent:

> Our laws, though their defects in this particular cannot be denied, have in one instance made a wise provision for breeding up the rising generation; since the poor and laborious part of the community, when past the age of nurture, are taken out of the hands of their parents, by the statutes for apprenticing poor children; and are placed out by the public in such manner, as may render their abilities . . . of the greatest advantage to the commonwealth. The rich indeed are left at their own option, whether they will breed up their children to be ornaments or disgraces to their family.[37]

§ 7.3.4 Colonial America: Transplanting and Developing the English System

The English dual system of family law was transplanted with the colonists into seventeenth- and eighteenth-century America[38] and then modified in a number of ways.[39] For the majority of colonists, there continued to be little or no intervention into patriarchal, autonomous family life. Only the rich and poor were affected, and the rich only minimally. In fact, it is argued that system number one in colonial America is characterized by even less intervention than occurred in England. Peters argues that the American colonists actually expanded the autonomous, nuclear patriarchal family for the nonpoor through two major changes:

1. *Abolition of Feudal Land Tenures.* The most significant example of this was the creation of private bequeathal such that property passed not by primogeniture, but by the choice of the testator. In this way, the transfer of property bypassed any feudal structure that ensured payment of taxes to the government.

---

[36] *Id.* at 241.

[37] *Id.* at 235 (quoting WILLIAM BLACKSTONE, COMMENTARIES ON THE LAWS OF ENGLAND 452 (1826)). *See also* Douglas R. Rendleman, Parens Patriae: *From Chancery to the Juvenile Court,* 23 S.C. L. REV. 205, 211 (1971).

[38] Stefan A. Riesenfeld, *The Formative Era of American Public Assistance Law,* 43 CAL. L. REV. 175, 177-178 (1955).

[39] Douglas R. Rendleman, Parens Patriae: *From Chancery to the Juvenile Court,* 23 S.C. L. REV. 205, 211 (1971); JEAN KOH PETERS, REPRESENTING CHILDREN IN CHILD PROTECTIVE PROCEEDINGS: ETHICAL AND PRACTICAL DIMENSIONS 242 (2nd ed. 2001).

2. *Private Property Matters in Secular Chancery Courts.* Correspondingly, private property matters were taken away from church or crown control and placed in local secular chancery courts.

These actions seem consistent with the view that colonists settled America in rejection of excessive governmental and religious intervention into their lives.[40]

The English Poor Law, however, was transplanted firmly into the colonies and even enhanced. Mobility restrictions were transplanted as part of the colonial poor laws. The New Plymouth code required settlements to take responsibility for their poor and restrict settlement; the Massachusetts Bay code prohibited new settlers coming in without town council approval; Connecticut codes required proof of property ownership for settlement; and New York provided relief to poor nonresidents only if they brought proof that their community had no funds to support them.[41]

Involuntary apprenticeship of poor children became an integral part of colonial North American Poor Law.[42] Such apprenticeships were frequently used throughout the colonies.[43] Douglas Rendleman makes the case that it is at this point we see an enhancement of English Poor Law into a "poor plus" system.[44] In eighteenth-century Virginia for example, children could be removed and apprenticed not only because of their poverty but because their parents were not providing "good breeding, neglecting their formal education, not teaching a trade, or were idle, dissolute, unchristian or uncapable."[45] Rendleman suggests this is an example of the state's belief that poor children needed to be protected, not just from poverty, but from certain environmental influences commonly associated with the poor.[46] Apprenticeships were in many ways the ideal anchor in the poor law system because the child paid his or her own way, the

---

[40] JEAN KOH PETERS, REPRESENTING CHILDREN IN CHILD PROTECTIVE PROCEEDINGS: ETHICAL AND PRACTICAL DIMENSIONS 242 (2001). *See* John Seymour, Parens Patriae *and Wardship Powers: Their Nature and Origins,* 14 OXFORD J. LEGAL STUD. 159, 164-165 (1994); HASSELTINE BYRD TAYLOR, LAW OF GUARDIAN AND WARD 23-24 (1935).

[41] JEAN KOH PETERS, REPRESENTING CHILDREN IN CHILD PROTECTIVE PROCEEDINGS: ETHICAL AND PRACTICAL DIMENSIONS 243 (2nd ed. 2001). For an examination of poor law statutes in the American colonies, *see* Judith Areen, *Intervention Between Parent and Child: A Reprisal of the State's Role in Child Neglect and Abuse Cases,* 63 GEO. L.J. 887, 899-900 (1975); Gerald L. Neuman, *The Lost Century of American Immigration Law 1776-1875),* 93 COLUM. L. REV. 1833, 1846 (1993); Stefan A. Riesenfeld, *The Formative Era of American Public Assistance Law,* 43 CAL. L. REV. 175, 206 & n.179, 212, 219 (1955).

[42] Stefan A. Riesenfeld, *The Formative Era of American Public Assistance Law,* 43 CAL. L. REV. 175, 214 (1955).

[43] MARCUS WILSON JERNEGAN, THE LABORING AND DEPENDENT CLASSES IN COLONIAL AMERICA, 1607-1783, at 157 (1960).

[44] Douglas R. Rendleman, Parens Patriae: *From Chancery to the Juvenile Court,* 23 S.C. L. REV. 205, 212 (1971).

[45] *Id.* at 212 (citing MARCUS WILSON JERNEGAN, THE LABORING AND DEPENDENT CLASSES IN COLONIAL AMERICA, 1607-1783, at 104, 151, 149, 161 (1960)).

[46] *Id.*

child was trained in skilled labor, relief costs were kept down, and society experienced reduced idleness and unemployment.[47] As a reflection of the state in the role of beneficent ultimate parent, however, the system left much to be desired, since the quality of the child's care was suspect and the child operated frequently as nothing more than a slave subject to a business proposition.[48]

In addition to Rendleman's "poor plus" modification of the dual system of family law, Peters has recently suggested that an additional condition unique to the colonies created a third system of family law for the black slave family.[49] Prior to the civil war, there was no legal recognition of the black slave family. Legally, blacks were not persons, but were instead property of their masters, and secondarily subject to all white people.[50] Black men and woman living in a long-term committed relationship were not recognized as lawfully married, and therefore their children were considered illegitimate.[51]

Peters points out that it was even difficult for blacks to maintain a *de facto* family life because the white master exercised total control over the slave's education, labor, diet, living arrangements, mates, and children. The result was the creation of a unique "family relationship" in which slave families lived apart and children were regularly sold away from their biological parents. A third system of family law clearly did exist in the colonies as to black slave families, a system that prohibited traditional family relationships for an entire segment of society.[52]

While governmental intervention due to child abuse per se was exceptionally rare in colonial America, Robert Bremner has recorded three seventeenth-century American cases. The 1655 Massachusetts case of twelve-year-old apprentice John Walker who was killed by his master may be the first recorded American case of child abuse. John was brutally beaten and neglected until his death. His master was convicted of manslaughter. In addition, in Massachusetts, Samuel Morison in 1675 and Robert Styles in 1678 had their children removed by the court for failure to provide suitable homes.[53]

In summary, the developing American system of intervention into the life of the child was characterized by the absence of intervention except on very rare

---

[47] *Id.*

[48] *Id.*

[49] JEAN KOH PETERS, REPRESENTING CHILDREN IN CHILD PROTECTIVE PROCEEDINGS: ETHICAL AND PRACTICAL DIMENSIONS 243 (2nd ed. 2001).

[50] *Id. See also* GEORGE M. STROUD, A SKETCH OF THE LAWS RELATING TO SLAVERY 154 (2d ed. 1856).

[51] JEAN KOH PETERS, REPRESENTING CHILDREN IN CHILD PROTECTIVE PROCEEDINGS: ETHICAL AND PRACTICAL DIMENSIONS 243 (2nd ed. 2001). *See also* HERBERT G. GUTMAN, THE BLACK FAMILY IN SLAVERY AND FREEDOM 1750-1925, 9 (1976).

[52] JEAN KOH PETERS, REPRESENTING CHILDREN IN CHILD PROTECTIVE PROCEEDINGS: ETHICAL AND PRACTICAL DIMENSIONS 245 (2nd ed. 2001). Peters also points out the importance of studying this neglected area of the development of child intervention law as black families struggle for normalcy and develop family models following the civil war.

[53] 1 CHILDREN AND YOUTH IN AMERICA 123-124; 41-42 (Robert H. Bremner, ed., 1970).

occasion or where the very poor were concerned. Family autonomy for the self-sufficient was paramount. The majority of children in Colonial America received no protection from abuse and neglect. The Massachusetts Stubborn Child Law of 1646, for example, even allowed parents to classify their child as stubborn and seek state punishment, including capital punishment.[54] In the case of the poor, the state felt authorized to remove poor children and apprentice them for the common good. It was in no way, however, a system designed to protect maltreated children, and little welfare was actually provided to children and their families in exchange for lost autonomy. This doctrine remained intact and was emulated in the states and territories of the west through the eighteenth century.[55]

§ 7.3.5 Nineteenth-Century America: The Rise of the *Parens Patriae* System

Although children in the twentieth century exist as a recognized social class,[56] children first developed class identification in the nineteenth century. The child's identity as it developed was as both a resource and a danger to society.[57]

Major social change is a theme of the nineteenth century. Early nineteenth-century America was dominated by the "rural-communitarian-protestant triad."[58] That triad began to come apart in the nineteenth century with the industrialization and urbanization of America. Additionally, the industrialized urban areas became populated with European and Asian immigrants. An 1824 report concluded, for example, that there were approximately 9,000 children under age 14 living in poverty in New York State, and that three-fourths of the children receiving public relief were immigrant children.[59] The response to this condition gives rise to a special system for treatment of children.

---

[54] NATHANIAL B. SHURTLEFF, RECORDS OF THE GOVERNOR AND COMPANY OF THE MASSACHUSETTS BAY IN NEW ENGLAND 1628-1686, at 101 (1854).

[55] Douglas R. Rendleman, Parens Patriae: *From Chancery to the Juvenile Court,* 23 S.C. L. REV. 205, 212 (1971). For a discussion of specific jurisdictions, *see, e.g.,* JOHN LEWIS GILLIN, HISTORY OF POOR RELIEF LEGISLATION IN IOWA (1914); ROBERT W. KELSO, HISTORY OF PUBLIC POOR RELIEF IN MASSACHUSETTS 1620-1920 (1922); ISABEL BRUCE & EDITH EICKHOFF, THE MICHIGAN POOR LAW (1936); Jacobus tenBroek, *California's Dual System of Family Law: Its Origin, Development and Present Status* (pt. 2), 16 STAN. L. REV. 900, 965 (1964). *See also generally* Stefan A. Riesenfeld, *Lawmaking and Legislation Precedent in American Legal History,* 33 MINN. L. REV. 103 (1949).

[56] Whether we treat the class of children empathicly, or merely as a "reflection of adult concerns and agendas" is debatable, but children are seen in the twentieth century as an identifiable interest group. *See* JEAN KOH PETERS, REPRESENTING CHILDREN IN CHILD PROTECTIVE PROCEEDINGS: ETHICAL AND PRACTICAL DIMENSIONS 249 (2nd ed. 2001).

[57] JOHN C. WATKINS, JR., THE JUVENILE JUSTICE CENTURY 3 (1998).

[58] *Id.* at 4.

[59] Sanford J. Fox, *Juvenile Justice Reform: An Historical Perspective,* 22 STAN. L. REV. 1187, 1200 & n.72 (1970) (citing J. YATES, REPORT OF THE SECRETARY OF STATE IN 1824 ON THE RELIEF AND SETTLEMENT OF THE POOR, *reprinted in* I NEW YORK STATE BOARD OF CHARITIES, ANNUAL REPORT NO. 34, at 937, 942).

The House of Refuge Movement

In response to the creation of the underclass of urban poor children, the House of Refuge Movement, a movement that has been called the first great event in child welfare, was launched.[60] The movement began with the Society for Prevention of Pauperism, which believed that poverty was a cause, if not the primary cause, of crime committed by children. The Society issued a report in 1819 raising concern for the number of children confined with adults in Bellevue Prison, and in 1823 the Society issued a now famous statement describing the streets as overrun with pauper children in need of saving. On January 1, 1825, New York City opened the first "House of Refuge."[61]

The New York House of Refuge was authorized by New York Law[62] that provided a charter to the Society for the Reformation of Juvenile Delinquents, the successor to the Society for Prevention of Pauperism.[63] The authorizing legislation allowed managers of the Society to take into the house children committed as vagrants or convicted of crimes by authorities. Criminal conviction was not a condition to incarceration in the House of Refuge. Children could even be committed by administrative order or application of their parents.[64] Neither was there any right to indictment or jury trial,[65] as summary conviction of disorderly persons had previously been upheld in New York in the case *In re Goodhue.*[66]

It is a mistake to assume that the House of Refuge served as a haven for youth otherwise guilty of serious crime. Those youth were still maintained in the adult system. In the first two years of operation of the New York House of Refuge, approximately 90% of the children were housed as a result of vagrancy or minor offenses.[67] Since such minor offenses tended to go unpunished by the law, it is unlikely that these children would have fallen under the authority of the state without a House of Refuge.[68]

Neither, however, was the Refuge movement one to protect abused children from their caretaker's authority. There is no evidence that children were placed as a result of caretaker cruelty. To the contrary, severe corporal punishment was clearly part of the House of Refuge system. In fact, conditions in many Houses

---

[60] *Id.* at 1187. *See also* DAVID M. SCHNEIDER, THE HISTORY OF PUBLIC WELFARE IN NEW YORK STATE 1609-1866, at 317 (1938).

[61] JOHN C. WATKINS, JR., THE JUVENILE JUSTICE CENTURY 4 (1998).

[62] *See* Sanford J. Fox, *Juvenile Justice Reform: An Historical Perspective,* 22 STAN. L. REV. 1187, 1190 & n.20 (1970) (referring to Laws of New York, 47th Session, Ch. CXXVI at 110 (1824)).

[63] *Id.*

[64] THOMAS J. BERNARD, THE CYCLE OF JUVENILE JUSTICE (1992).

[65] Sanford J. Fox, *Juvenile Justice Reform: An Historical Perspective,* 22 STAN. L. REV. 1187, 1191 (1970).

[66] *Id.* at n.28 (citing *In re Goodhue,* 1 N.Y. City Hall Recorder 153 (1816)).

[67] *Id.* at 1192.

[68] *Id.* at 1194.

were quite abusive by modern standards, including solitary confinement and beatings.[69]

Poor "vagrant" children were the focus of the Refuge movement. In short, seriously criminal children tended to remain in the adult system, the majority of children in families saw no intervention, and children who might today be considered status cases, were rounded up off the streets. The Refuge movement was a pre-delinquency movement, which focused on saving "salvageable," probably neglected, poor children. In that sense, as Sanford Fox has pointed out, the Refuge movement was, although motivated in part by humanitarianism, very much a "retrenchment in correctional practices" and "a regression in poor-law policy."[70] The movement also involved a coercive religious intolerance, as all children were required to adopt the Protestant teachings of their reformers.[71] When viewed in the context of protection for abused and neglected children, it did not represent progress. It did represent continued intervention, but little welfare, for neglected poor children.

The Refuge movement spread from New York to Boston (1826) to Philadelphia (1828) to New Orleans (1847) to Baltimore (1849) to Cincinnati (1850) to Pittsburgh and St. Louis (1854). By 1860, 16 Houses of Refuge were opened in the United States.[72] Legislation authorizing the intervention and placement of delinquent and dependent children similarly spread throughout the jurisdictions.[73]

In addition to Houses of Refuge, Reformatories, which were entirely state-financed, began to emerge toward the middle of the century. John Watkins points out that the reformatory movement was initiated by a number of influential individuals who believed the House of Refuge system had not slowed the rate of delinquency.[74] Reformatories were to be progressive institutions where, through civic and moral training, the youth would be reformed by his or her surrogate parent. In reality, Reformatories tended to be coercive, labor-intensive incarceration.[75]

Houses of Refuge dominated the first half, and Reformatories the last half of the century. They were characterized by an ultimate parent philosophy

---

[69] *Id.* at 1195 (citing SOCIETY FOR THE REFORMATION OF JUVENILE DELINQUENTS, ANNUAL REPORT NO. 3 (1828), *reprinted in* SOCIETY FOR THE REFORMATION OF JUVENILE DELINQUENTS, DOCUMENTS RELATIVE TO THE HOUSE OF REFUGE 138 (N. Hart ed. 1832) and R. PICKETT, HOUSE OF REFUGE 24 (1969)).

[70] Sanford J. Fox, *Juvenile Justice Reform: An Historical Perspective*, 22 STAN. L. REV. 1187, 1195 (1970).

[71] *Id.*

[72] JOHN C. WATKINS, JR., THE JUVENILE JUSTICE CENTURY: A SOCIOLEGAL COMMENTARY ON AMERICAN JUVENILE COURTS 5 (1998).

[73] *Id.* at 7.

[74] *Id.* at 8.

[75] *Id.* at 9.

toward the poor, which ties the movement to the poor laws. Another link to the past was the use of apprenticeship in the Refuge movement. As Houses of Refuge became overcrowded, many children were "placed out" by being transported to rural areas of the state or placed on trains headed to the developing west where they were apprenticed until they reached age 21. It was thought, or at least stated, that rural agrarian lifestyle would reform children from the effects of urban poverty.[76]

Ex parte Crouse *and* Parens Patriae

The House of Refuge movement may not have had significant impact on the ultimate development of the juvenile court if the judicial system had not validated it. In a number of cases during this period, courts affirmed and authorized the practice of intervention into the lives of children through the English doctrine of *parens patriae,* which means ultimate parent or parent of the country. The courts accepted the Reformers' logic that they were entitled to take custody of a child, regardless of the child's status as victim or offender, without due process of law, because of the state's authority and obligation to save children from becoming criminal.

The 1839 Pennsylvania decision of *Ex parte Crouse*[77] is thought to be the first case upholding the Refuge System. The child, Mary Ann Crouse, was committed to the Philadelphia House of Refuge by a Justice of the Peace Warrant. The warrant, executed by Mary Ann's mother, essentially provided that it would be in Mary Ann's interests to be incarcerated in the House because she was "beyond her parent's control." The reported case is an appeal from a denial of the father's subsequent *habeas corpus* petition for his daughter's return. The father argued that the law allowing commitment of children without a trial was unconstitutional. The court summarily rejected the father's argument on the basis that the House was not a prison (even though Mary Ann was not free to leave), and the child was there for her own reformation, not punishment (even though Mary Ann was probably treated very harshly, a fact the court did not review). The court essentially accepted the rhetoric of the representatives of the House of Refuge. In doing so, the court acknowledged and sanctioned the state's authority to intervene into the family as ultimate parent via the doctrine of *parens patriae.* The case and the doctrine became the cornerstones of juvenile proceedings throughout the century and through the pre-*Gault* years of the juvenile court. The case was generally relied on to support "the right of the state to make coercive predictions about deviant children."[78] Although the distinction may have been irrelevant at the time, the case involved a dependent—not delinquent—child, and in

---

[76] *Id.* at 7.

[77] 4 Whart. 9 (Pa. 1839).

[78] Sanford J. Fox, *Juvenile Justice Reform: An Historical Perspective,* 22 STAN. L. REV. 1187, 1207 (1970).

dicta, as Rendleman points out, the court argued that the state has authority to intervene into the parent-child relationship for the good of the child:

> To this end may not the natural parents, when unequal to the task of education, or unworthy of it, be superseded by the parens patriae, or common guardian of the community? . . . . That parents are ordinarily intrusted with it is because it can seldom be put into better hands; but where they are incompetent or corrupt, what is there to prevent the public from withdrawing their faculties, held, as they obviously are, at its sufferance? The right of parental control is a natural, but not an unalienable one.[79]

The *Crouse* court was making the case for state intervention into the family where the parents fail, in the state's view, to perform adequately, and the state is needed to care for the child. The reality that the state was probably caring for the child very poorly does not diminish the precedent for intervention in dependency cases.

The lead of the *Crouse* court was followed in a series of cases involving delinquent and dependent children. In Maryland, *Roth v. House of Refuge*,[80] in Ohio, *Prescott v. State*,[81] in Wisconsin, *Milwaukee Indus. School v. Supervisors of Milwaukee County*,[82] and in Illinois, *In re Ferrier*,[83] courts adopted the *Crouse* policy that the state's *parens patriae* duty and authority permitted seemingly unlimited intervention into family autonomy, including the child's deprivation of liberty.

The 1882 Illinois *Ferrier* case is particularly illustrative of the development of child protection law for two reasons. First, it involved a very young dependent, rather than delinquent, child. Nine-year-old Winifred Bean came to the court's attention, in significant part because her parents were viewed as incompetent to provide necessary parental care. Testimony was even taken that the parents were neglectful. Winifred was adjudicated dependent by a jury and committed to an industrial school for girls. In language typical of *Crouse* and its progeny, the court approved of both the state's authority to interrupt the rights of parents and children to the parent-child legal relationship, as well as the right to deprive the child of a degree of personal liberty through a state placement. While acknowledging that the Refuge movement did not distinguish between dependent and delinquent children (as the focus was delinquency prevention, not humanitarian protection), *Ferrier* was not just another case of picking up a vagrant child. It was a case of forced removal due to parental neglect.

---

[79] *Ex parte Crouse*, 4 Whart. 9, 11 (Pa. 1839).

[80] 31 Md. 329 (1869).

[81] 19 Ohio St. 184 (1869).

[82] 40 Wis. 328 (1876).

[83] 103 Ill. 367 (1882).

Second, *Ferrier* repudiated a serious effort to create precedent limiting the state's *parens patriae* authority. Twelve years earlier, the Illinois court had issued a decision that, if followed, would have repudiated the *parens patriae* Refuge system in *People ex rel. O'Connell v. Turner.*[84] The Illinois court released Daniel O'Connell from the custody of the Chicago Reform School because his confinement as a dependent child was unconstitutional. The court wrote: "in our solicitude to form youth for the duties of civil life, we should not forget the rights which inhere both in parents and children. The principle of the absorption of the child in, and its complete subjection to the despotism of, the State, is wholly inadmissible in the modern civilized world."[85] The case was not followed, however, and was then overruled by *Ferrier*. "The decision was ultimately looked upon as an aberrant pronouncement that could not and would not stand in the way of Progressive social engineering."[86]

As the final third of the nineteenth century approached, state legislatures had created, and the courts had approved, a system of family law and intervention that focused on "saving," by removal and placement, children of the expanding poor urban population. In doing so, authorization was given to disrupt the parent-child legal relationship and infringe on children's liberty solely because the child was not, in the state's view, cared for properly. The focus of the intervention was status-offending poor street children, with an occasional neglect scenario and, although an occasional reference to parental cruelty was made, little if any intervention for the abused child.

Special Cases of Child Abuse

Absent from many histories of the dependency court, but present in histories of child abuse and neglect, are the several documented nineteenth-century cases of legal intervention on behalf of children who were physically abused by their caretakers. Clearly, these are not the types of cases the Reformers of the nineteenth century envisioned as part of the movement to save children. Society did not view even severe corporal punishment or discipline as beyond the autonomy of the family, except in particularly heinous cases. In addition, even in such cases, criminal punishment of the parent, rather than removal and care of the child, was the focus.[87] Mason Thomas points out that the lack of civil cases can be explained in part by the then existing common law doctrine that a minor could not sue his parents in tort. The view that, at best, a child may get protection by way of criminal prosecution of parents was stated in the 1891 Mississippi case, *Hewellette v. George,*[88] where the court wrote: "The state, through its crim-

---

[84] 55 Ill. 280 (1870).

[85] *Id.* at 284.

[86] JOHN C. WATKINS, JR., THE JUVENILE JUSTICE CENTURY 25 (1998).

[87] 2 CHILDREN AND YOUTH IN AMERICA 119-124 (Robert H. Bremner, ed., 1971).

[88] 68 Miss. 703 (1891).

inal laws, will give the minor child protection from parental violence and wrong-doing, and this is all the child can be heard to demand."[89]

Why these cases did not come to the developing *parens patriae* court's attention is not entirely clear, but the explanation is probably basic—those officials in charge of executing the Reformers' child-saving plans did not include caretaker-abused children within their net, and society did not view even brutal treatment of children by their nonpoor caretakers as outside the bounds of family autonomy. Such an illustration is found in the 1840 Tennessee case, *Johnson v. State*,[90] where the court reversed the parents' criminal conviction for the brutal treatment of their daughter. The court's analysis of whether the parents' exceeded their authority to control and discipline included the following language:

> The right of parents to chastise their refractory and disobedient children is so necessary to the government of families, to the good order of society, that no moralist or lawgiver has ever thought of interfering with its existence, or of calling upon them to account for the manner of its exercise, upon light or frivolous pretenses. But, at the same time that the law has created and preserved this right, in its regard for the safety of the child it has prescribed bounds beyond which it shall not be carried.[91]

Nonetheless, some jurisdictions specifically mentioned cruelty as a justification for removal in their reform laws, and those that did not could have accommodated abused children in their dependency statutory scheme, but they did not.

Which brings us to the myth that the Mary Ellen case is the first documented child abuse case. That is not accurate for the reasons just discussed. Additionally, it now appears there was a similar case, also involving Henry Bergh (who intervened for Mary Ellen), before Mary Ellen. Steven Lazoritz and Eric Shelman published an article entitled *Before Mary Ellen*[92] that, based on the unpublished notes of the biographer of Henry Bergh, recounts the story of the intervention to protect the child Emily Thompson several years before the case of Mary Ellen. As the biographer's notes state, according to Lazoritz and Shelman, in June of 1871, a woman approached Henry Bergh, founder of the Society for Prevention of Cruelty to Animals, and sought his assistance to save 8-year-old Emily Thompson, who she said she frequently observed from her window being brutally beaten and whipped for up to an hour at a time. Bergh sent investigators who found the child to be battered. Additional neighbors

---

[89] Mason P. Thomas, Jr., *Child Abuse and Neglect*, 50 N. C. L. Rev. 293, 304 & n.43 (1972) (quoting *Hewellette v. George*, 68 Miss. 703, 711 (1891)).

[90] 21 Tenn. (2 Hum.) 282 (1840).

[91] Mason P. Thomas, Jr., *Child Abuse and Neglect*, 50 N. C. L. Rev. 293, 305 (1972) (citing *Johnson v. State*, 21 Tenn. (2 Hum.) 282, 283 (1840)).

[92] Stephen Lazoritz & Eric A. Shelman, *Before Mary Ellen*, 20 Child Abuse & Neglect: The Int'l J. 235, 235-237 (1996).

came forward to confirm the almost daily beatings. Bergh acquired a writ—probably the same writ later used in Mary Ellen's case—and the child was removed. Emily was presented to New York Court of Special Sessions where Judge Barnard took jurisdiction, apparently as a criminal matter. Although the child was visibly battered, Mary Ann Larkin, who was Emily's nonbiological caretaker, denied the abuse, as did Emily. The judge found Ms. Larkin "guilty," suspended her sentence, and returned the child to her care. Later, however, Emily's grandmother, who thought the child dead, read a newspaper account of the matter and contacted Bergh. Bergh brought Emily again to Judge Bernard on a writ. Judge Bernard then removed Emily from Ms. Larkin and placed her with her grandmother. It is not indicated whether the court viewed the removal and placement as a continuation of the criminal action against the caretaker or under some theory of protection jurisdiction. The trial-level action was apparently never reviewed.

As for Mary Ellen, the case has traditionally been used to support the proposition that at the time of the case, society had no child protection law, and after the case, due to the clever use of an animal rights theory and sympathy created by the case, child abuse protection began. As we have seen, that proposition is not supported by fact. New York, Mary Ellen's residence, as we have seen, had a massive child welfare scheme, albeit not focused on removing middle class children, but prevalent enough to have had a hand in placing the child in the abusive setting in the first place. Using Bremner's documentary history, Thomas sorted out the facts as follows:

> The case arose in 1874, when Mary Ellen probably was ten years old. Laws to protect children (criminal laws forbidding assault and statutes dealing with the neglect of children) were not lacking but were not enforced systematically. The case was not brought into court by the Society for the Prevention of Cruelty to Animals on the theory that this child was entitled to the legal protection afforded animals; rather, it was initiated by the founder of this society acting as an individual, using the Society's attorney, by a petition for a writ *de homine replegiando*, on the basis of which the court issued a special warrant to bring the child before the court. Mary Ellen was not placed with the church worker but instead was placed temporarily (exactly where is unknown) for seven months pending efforts to locate relatives; when none could be found, she was committed to the "Sheltering Arms," an orphan asylum.

> Various issues of the *New York Times* during April 1874 summarize the evidence presented in the several court hearings that involved this case: Mary Ellen Wilson, an infant girl whose birth date apparently was unknown, was left at the office of the Superintendent of Outdoor Poor, Department of Charities, New York City, on May 21, 1864, by a woman who had cared for the child while she received eight dollars per month for her support. When the support stopped, she turned the child over to

the Department. When Mary Ellen was eighteen months old, she was apprenticed to Mary and Thomas McCormack under an indenture that required the foster parents to teach her that there was a God, and what it meant to lie, and to instruct her "in the art and mystery of housekeeping." The indenture also required the foster parents to report to the Department annually on the child's condition. The placement was made on January 2, 1866, and the indenture was signed on February 15. When the placement was made, the Department checked with one reference – Mrs. McCormack's physician. Unbeknown to the Department of Public Charities, Mary Ellen Wilson was actually the illegitimate child of Thomas McCormack by a "good-for-nothing" woman whose name was unknown.

The case arose in 1874, when Mary Ellen was about ten years old. By that time, Thomas McCormack had died and Mary McCormack had married Francis Connolly. Mary Ellen could not remember having lived with anyone other than the Connollys. She believed that her parents were dead; she did not know her exact age; and she called Mrs. Connolly "Mamma." She could not recall ever having been kissed by anyone.

The Superintendent of Outdoor Poor, who had made the placement, testified that he could remember nothing about the case except what was contained in his written record, since he had placed five hundred children through his department during 1874. Clearly, the Department of Charities had lost contact with Mary Ellen and the Connollys, as only two of the required annual reports on the child's condition had been made between 1866 and 1874.

The evidence indicated both abuse and neglect: Mrs. Connolly had whipped Mary Ellen almost every day with a cane and a twisted whip – a rawhide that left black and blue marks – and had struck her with a pair of scissors (which were produced in court) that had cut her on the forehead; the child was locked in the bedroom whenever "Mama" left home; she was not allowed to leave the room where the Connollys were; she was not allowed to play outside or with other children; and she was inadequately clothed and slept on a piece of rug on the floor.

Mrs. Connolly was prosecuted under indictments for felonious assault with a pair of scissors on April 7, 1874, and for a series of assaults during 1873 and 1874. The jury found her guilty of assault and battery and sentenced her to one year in the penitentiary at hard labor.[93]

---

[93] Mason P. Thomas, Jr., *Child Abuse and Neglect*, 50 N. C. L. Rev. 293, 308-310 (1972) (citations omitted); for a description of events in Mary Ellen's later life, see Stephen Lazoritz, *Whatever Happened to Mary Ellen?*, 14 Child Abuse and Neglect: The Int'l J. 143-149 (1990).

The Mary Ellen case, together with the founding of the New York Society for Prevention of Cruelty to Children (NYSPCC), did have significant impact on child welfare. Its founder, Elbridge Gerry, recognized the void in the Refuge system for abused and neglected children outside the pre-delinquency net. He also recognized that law enforcement did not typically become involved in "family matters." Eventually, the NYSPCC acquired police power and controlled the welfare of many of New York's abused and neglected children. By 1900, 161 similar "cruelty" societies existed in the United States.

By the end of the nineteenth century, there was a developing *parens patriae* jurisprudence that enabled saving children from the effects of poverty and a related movement began to concern itself with child abuse and neglect within the family.

A Scientific Development

An important scientific development in the recognition of child abuse and neglect occurred in France in 1860. A French physician, Ambrose Tardieu, conducted a study of 32 children whom he believed died of child abuse. Tardieu's findings describe medical, psychiatric, social, and demographic features of the condition of child abuse as a syndrome.[94] This groundbreaking work went largely unrecognized until the mid-twentieth century.

§ 7.3.6 The Juvenile Court: Institutionalizing and Developing the *Parens Patriae* System

Founding and Dependency Philosophy

The events of the last decades of the nineteenth century that lead to the founding of the first juvenile court were very much an extension of the nineteenth-century refuge/reform movement, which in turn were an outgrowth of poor law policy. While the founding of the court has traditionally been treated as a revolutionary humanitarian advancement for children, more recent scholarship has shown the inaccuracy of that belief.[95] This is not to say the founding of the court was not an historic event; it was just not a revolutionary one. It was a culmination of, not a departure from, nineteenth-century reform.

The legislation, which led to the creation of a special tribunal that came to be called the juvenile court, was "An Act to Regulate the Treatment and Control of Dependent, Neglected and Delinquent Children."[96] The Juvenile Court of Cook County, Illinois opened on July 1, 1899.[97] Although it is accurate that the Cook

---

[94] Selwyn M. Smith, Tardieu, Etude Medico-Legale Sur Les Services Et Mauvais Traitements Exerces Sur Des Enfants (1860), The Battered Child Syndrome (1975).

[95] Fox, *Juvenile Justice Reform: An Historical Perspective*, 22 Stan. L. Rev. 1187 (1970).

[96] Act of Apr. 21, 1899, [1899] Ill. Laws 131.

[97] J. Watkins, Jr., The Juvenile Justice Century: A Sociolegal Commentary On American Juvenile Courts (1998) at 43.

County Court was the first fully formalized tribunal of its kind, Massachusetts (in 1874) and New York (in 1892) had actually passed laws separating minors' trials from adults. While it is a mistake to assume all subsequent juvenile courts simply copied the Illinois legislation, it did serve as a model, and in less than 20 years similar legislation had been passed in all but three states.[98]

The Illinois legislation was largely the product of a Progressive Era movement called Child Saving. The Child Savers were individuals who viewed their cause of saving "those less fortunately placed in the social order"[99] as a matter of morality. The Child Savers were dominated by bourgeois women, although many were considered liberals. The movement, which was supported by the propertied and powerful, "tried to do for the criminal justice system what industrialists and corporate leaders were trying to do for the economy—that is, achieve order, stability, and control, while preserving the existing class system and distribution of wealth."[100] The Child Savers' rhetoric envisioned a juvenile court that would serve children and society by removing children from the criminal law process and placing them in special programs.[101] The movement in Chicago was supported by the Illinois Conference of Charities, The Chicago Bar Association, and the Chicago Woman's Club.

The Illinois act provided for jurisdiction in a special court for delinquent and dependent and neglected children. A delinquent child was any child under age 16 who violated a law or ordinance, except capital offenses.[102] Dependency and neglect was defined as follows:

1. Any child who for any reason is destitute or homeless or abandoned;

2. Has not proper parental care or guardianship;

3. Who habitually begs or receives alms;

4. Who is found living in any house of ill fame or with any vicious or disreputable person;

5. Whose home, by reason of neglect, cruelty, or depravity on the part of its parents, guardian or other person in whose care it may be, is an unfit place for such a child;

6. Any child under the age of 8 years who is found peddling or selling any article or singing or playing any musical instrument upon the street or giving any public entertainment.[103]

---

[98] ANTHONY M. PLATT, THE CHILD SAVERS 10 (2nd ed. 1977).

[99] *Id.* at 3.

[100] *Id.* at xxii.

[101] *Id.* at 10.

[102] Act of Apr. 21, 1899, [1899] Ill. Laws 131.

[103] Act of Apr. 21, 1899, [1899] Ill. Laws 131.

The categories are remarkably familiar to the Refuge movement conditions of eliminating vagrancy through confinement. As Fox has noted, the juvenile court was very much a continuation of a system of coercive predictions begun at the beginning of the century.[104]

There also appears to be little, if any, support for the proposition that the juvenile court began a system of benevolent caretaking of youth by substituting a kind of therapeutic jurisprudence for harsher and limiting criminal procedure. First, serious older offenders stayed in the adult criminal system. Second, the nineteenth-century case law reveals that juveniles brought to court under delinquency and dependency concepts received no due process. *Ex parte Crouse*[105] served to inform us they were entitled to none.

This is not to suggest that the juvenile court was a step backward. It was progress in the form of codification and institutionalization of the nineteenth-century *parens patriae* system. As an institution, the juvenile court stressed centrality for dependent children. Rather than being subject to random placements without follow up, it was believed that a court could function as a centralized agency responsible for all such children from start to finish. The new court implemented the concept of probation, and the founders made minimal progress toward improving placement conditions for children. Dependent children could be placed with an agency or put on probation. To at least some extent, the Child Savers' mission of creating a juvenile "statutory, non-criminal, stigma-neutral, treatment-oriented" system was achieved.[106]

As for abused and neglected children, although cruelty societies helped, state intervention under the juvenile court acts was modest. The condition of poverty, which brought children into the Refuge system, continued as a *de facto* prerequisite for juvenile court intervention. Saving nonpoor abused and neglected children from their lawful caretakers was not a goal of the Child Savers either. Nonetheless, the *parens patriae* authority to do so became the central component of the juvenile court.

The early years of the court were characterized by continued commingling of dependency and delinquency under the courts' *parens patriae* authority. Minimal numbers of appeals validated that authority. Families remained autonomous.

The delinquency and dependency components of the juvenile court, historically connected by a "child saving" philosophy, began to separate into distinct functions in the 1960s. Driven by judicial process in delinquency, and social progress in dependency, both components were transformed.

---

[104] Fox, *Juvenile Justice Reform: An Historical Perspective*, 22 STAN. L. REV. 1187 (1970).

[105] 4 Whart. 9 (Pa. 1839). *See* § 7.3.5, Nineteenth-Century America: The Rise of the Parens Patriae System.

[106] JOHN C. WATKINS, JR., THE JUVENILE JUSTICE CENTURY: A SOCIOLEGAL COMMENTARY ON AMERICAN JUVENILE COURTS 50 (1998).

Gault *and the Transformation of Delinquency out from* Parens Patriae

The delinquency component of juvenile court was transformed in the late 1960s by two U. S. Supreme Court cases. In 1966, in *Kent v. United Sates*,[107] the court set the stage for dismantling the *parens patriae* authority of the juvenile delinquency court by holding that the action of transferring a juvenile to criminal court required procedural due process. Then, in 1967, the Court struck down the *parens patriae* authority of the juvenile court in the context of delinquency adjudication in *In re Gault*.[108] The Court declared that "neither the Fourteenth Amendment nor the Bill of Rights is for adults alone."[109] In his famous opinion, Justice Fortas reviewed the shortcomings of the juvenile process, which had been in operation since the founding of the court. Justice Fortas stated that the belief that the juvenile court could best care for children without the distractions of due process was a myth, and that due process, not benevolent intentions, produced justice. Among the rights *Gault* created for juveniles were notice of charges, confrontation and cross-examination, prohibition against self-incrimination, and the right to counsel. The decision continues to be hailed by some as a great advancement in children's rights and by others as the criminalization of the juvenile court and the beginning of the end of the court's authority to treat children like children rather than adults. The difference of opinion goes to the heart of the debate over the purpose and future of the delinquency court.

While *Gault* did not instruct juvenile courts across the country to wholly substitute adult criminal procedure for juvenile practice, that is very much what happened. The delinquency court separated from the dependency court and the traditional commingling of all children in a predelinquency/criminal prevention program began to come to an end.

For the future of dependency proceedings it is critical to focus on what *Gault* did *not* do: *Gault* did not dismantle, or even limit, the *parens patriae* authority of the dependency court. The *Gault* Court focused on juvenile misconduct, as opposed to victimization, and stated, "[w]e do not in this opinion consider the impact of these constitutional provisions upon the totality of the relationship of the juvenile and the state."[110] The state, therefore, was free to continue separately "saving" dependent children, whoever they may be, under the *parens patriae* duty and authority of the state.

"The Battered Child," *CAPTA, and the Evolution of Dependency Within* Parens Patriae

The dependency court underwent a transformation in the last half of the twentieth century, not away from, but within the state's *parens patriae* authority.

---

[107] 383 U.S. 541 (1966).

[108] 387 U.S. 1 (1967).

[109] *Id.* at 13.

[110] *Id.*

Grounded in a new public awareness of the need to protect children from mal-treatment, the dependency court moved from a system of coercive predictions for poor dependent children to a system of intervention into the family to pro-tect abused and neglected children. This "evolution" can be seen in the follow-ing events:[111]

- In 1912, as a result of President Roosevelt's 1909 White House Conference on Children, Congress created the United States Children's Bureau.

- In 1921, Congress passed the Shappard-Towner Act, which established Children's Bureaus at the state level and promoted maternal-infant health.

- In 1944, the Supreme Court of the United States confirmed the state's authority to intervene in family relationships to protect children in *Prince v. Massachusetts*.[112]

- In 1946, Aid to Dependent Children was added to the Social Security Act.

- In 1946, Dr. Caffey, a pediatric radiologist in Pittsburgh, published the results of his research showing that subdural hematomas and fractures of the long bones in infants were inconsistent with accidental trauma.[113]

- In 1962, following a medical symposium the previous year, several physi-cians headed by Denver physician C. Henry Kempe, published the land-mark article *The Battered Child Syndrome* in the Journal of the American Medical Association. Through the article, Kempe and his colleagues exposed the reality that significant numbers of parents and caretakers bat-ter their children, even to death. *The Battered Child Syndrome* describes a pattern of child abuse resulting in certain clinical conditions and estab-lishes a medical and psychiatric model of the cause of child abuse. The article marked the development of child abuse as a distinct academic subject. The work is generally regarded as one of the most significant events leading to professional and public awareness of the existence and magnitude of child abuse and neglect in the United States and through-out the world.[114]

---

[111] *See generally* INGER SAGATUN & LEONARD EDWARDS, CHILD ABUSE AND THE LEGAL SYSTEM (1995) (describing and identifying many of these events).

[112] 321 U.S. 158 (1944).

[113] John Caffey, *Multiple Fractures in the Long Bones of Infants Suffering from Chronic Subdural Hematoma*, 56 AM. J. ROENTGENOLOGY 163 (1946).

[114] C. Henry Kempe et al., *The Battered Child Syndrome,* 181 JAMA 17 (1962).

- In 1962, in response to *The Battered Child Syndrome*, the Children's Bureau held a symposium on child abuse, which produced a recommendation for a model child abuse reporting law.

- By 1967, 44 states had adopted mandatory reporting laws. The remaining six states adopted voluntary reporting laws. All states now have mandatory reporting laws. Generally, the laws require physicians to report reasonable suspicion of child abuse. Reporting laws, now expanded to include other professionals and voluntary reporting by the public, together with immunity for good faith reporting, are recognized as one of the most significant measures ever taken to protect abused and neglected children. Reporting is recognized as the primary reason for the dramatic increases in cases of child abuse and neglect.

- In 1971, the California Court of Appeals recognized the Battered Child Syndrome as a medical diagnosis and a legal syndrome in *People v. Jackson.*[115]

- In 1974, Congress passed landmark legislation in the federal Child Abuse Prevention and Treatment Act (CAPTA).[116] The Act provides states with funding for the investigation and prevention of child maltreatment, conditioned on states' adoption of mandatory reporting law. The Act also conditions funding on reporter immunity, confidentiality, and appointment of guardians ad litem for children. The Act also created the National Center on Child Abuse and Neglect (NCCAN) to serve as an information clearinghouse. In 1978, The Adoption Reform Act was added to CAPTA. In 1984, CAPTA was amended to include medically disabled infants, the reporting of medical neglect and maltreatment in out-of-home care, and the expansion of sexual abuse to include sexual exploitation.

- In 1980, Congress passed the Adoption Assistance and Child Welfare Act,[117] designed to remedy problems in the foster care system. The Act made federal funding for foster care dependent on certain reforms. In 1983 the Act was amended to include "reasonable efforts." The reasonable efforts amendment provided for special procedures before removing a child and reunification strategies after removal. Important provisions for case review were also included. The Act and its amendment essentially provided fiscal incentives to encourage states to prevent

---

[115] 18 Cal. App. 3d 504, 506-508 (1971). *See also Estelle v. McGuire*, 502 U.S. 62 (1991) and *State v. Henson*, 33 N.Y.2d 63 (1973) (describing Battered Child Syndrome).

[116] Pub. L. No. 93-273; 42 U.S.C. §§ 5101 through 5119 (1996) (current version amended and reenacted through the Keeping Children and Families Safe Act of 2003, Pub. L. No. 108-36).

[117] Pub. L. No. 96-272; 42 U.S.C. §§ 670 through 676 (2004).

unnecessary foster care placements and to provide permanent homes for children in placement as quickly as possible. The law also gave courts a new oversight role.

- In 1981, Title XX of the Social Security Act was amended to include the Social Services Block Grant to provide child protective services funding to states. This became the major source of state social service funding.

- In 1986, Congress passed the Child Abuse Victims' Rights Act, which gave a civil damage claim to child victims of violations of federal sexual exploitation law.

- In 1991, Congress passed the Victims of Child Abuse Act of 1990, aimed at improving the investigation and prosecution of child abuse cases.

- In 1993, as part of the Omnibus Budget and Reconciliation Act, Congress provided funding for state courts to assess the impact of Public Law 96-272 (the Adoption Assistance and Child Welfare Act) on foster care proceedings, to study the handling of child protection cases, and to develop a plan for improvement. Funds were made available to states through a grant program called the State Court Improvement Program. The program was the impetus behind a nationwide movement to improve court practice in dependency cases.

- In 1997, Congress Passed the Adoption and Safe Families Act of 1997 (ASFA).[118] ASFA represents the most significant change in federal child welfare law since the Adoption Assistance and Child Welfare Act of 1980. ASFA includes provisions for legal representation, state funding of child welfare and adoption, and state performance requirements. In general, ASFA is intended to promote primacy of child safety and timely decisions while clarifying "reasonable efforts" and continuing family preservation. ASFA also includes continuation funding for court improvement.[119]

These events, particularly recognition of the "battered child," mandatory reporting and the passage of CAPTA, exemplified a new recognition of both the presence of child maltreatment and the need to protect its victims. As a result, the dependency court, once reserved primarily for pre-delinquent vagrant children of the poor, was transformed into an active tribunal to determine whether a child is abused and neglected, and if so, what disposition is appropriate. Criminal prosecutions of adults for child maltreatment were no longer viewed as the child's exclusive "remedy."

---

[118] Pub. L. No. 105-89.

[119] Rollin, *Legislative Update*, 16 A.B.A. CHILD LAW PRAC. 11, 166-171 (1998).

As juvenile court legislation was transformed in the delinquency context to provide procedures to satisfy the *Gault* requirements, the dependency court was left to continue its *parens patriae* jurisdiction over children and families. Within that context, states' dependency codes were modified to provide special processes for the intake, adjudication, and disposition of the newly recognized class of maltreated children. The result is child protection codes that contain language describing child abuse and neglect, rather than the early dependency language that described social conditions warranting intervention. Although vestiges of the commingling of delinquency and dependency can still be seen in some juvenile codes, the combination of the *Gault* influence on delinquency and the recognition of child maltreatment on dependency cause a clear separation of the two components of the juvenile court.[120]

The Dependency Court at the Beginning of the Twenty-First Century

The early twenty-first-century dependency court is very different from the "vagrancy" dependency court that began the twentieth century. Child abuse and neglect cases, once unrecognized, dominate the court calendar.

Incidence of Maltreatment

Although it is difficult to accumulate precise statistics for child maltreatment nationally, methodology has been developed for accumulating the incidence of child maltreatment from the states.[121] Once thought to be a problem involving only a few thousand children a year, child maltreatment has since been identified as nothing less than a national emergency.[122] See Chapter One, America's Children, for a full description of the condition of children in America and the incidence of child maltreatment.

In response to growing evidence of child maltreatment state legislatures enacted child protection legal procedures within their juvenile dependency codes. The juvenile dependency court became the primary forum for the oversight and the resolution of these child maltreatment and foster care cases. Where once child maltreatment cases occupied little, if any, of the juvenile court's time, they have recently become the central business of the dependency court.

Today's abused children were simply not part of the early dependency court. Likewise, the current dependency system reaches far beyond the neglected "pauper" children before the emergence of the juvenile court and during the

---

[120] It is even uncommon for attorneys representing children to "cross over" from one forum to the other. Katner, *Addressing the "Unmet Need" for Counsel to Handle Delinquency As Well As Dependency Cases*, GUARDIAN, Vol. 20, No. 2, 3 (1998).

[121] ANDREA J. SEDLAK & DIANE D. BROADHURST, U.S. DEP'T OF HEALTH & HUMAN SERVS., THE THIRD NATIONAL INCIDENCE STUDY OF CHILD ABUSE AND NEGLECT (1996). *See also* CHILDREN'S BUREAU, U.S. DEP'T OF HEALTH AND HUMAN SERVS., CHILD MALTREATMENT 2002.

[122] U.S. Advisory Committee on Child Abuse and Neglect.

early juvenile court. A significant number of abused and neglected children come to the system from the middle class.[123] These statistics reflect a legal and social willingness to intervene into the family and protect children. The dependency court can no longer be classified as a system of coercive predictions for pre-delinquent children. The poor law philosophy, which clearly found its way into the early court, no longer dominates the dependency court. There is consider-able evidence of continuing class bias in the contemporary dependency court, however. The Third National Incidence Study of Child Abuse and Neglect (NIS-3) reports the highest correlation of family income to maltreatment exists in families with an annual income of $15,000 or less, and the lowest correlation in families with annual income of $30,000 or more.[124] This and the disproportion-ate representation of minority children in dependency cases should be taken seriously, particularly in light of the medical view that child abuse knows no class or race boundaries.[125] Whether reporting accurately captures maltreatment in higher income households, and whether intervention is racially and culturally competent, are issues that warrant investigation.[126]

Dependency Court Operation: Best Interests and Family Preservation

While *parens patriae* continues as the underlying authority for intervention, the modern dependency court is not without legal process. The process is intend-ed, within limitations protecting parental autonomy, to serve "the best interests of the child." The best interests standard is the governing principle of the mod-ern dependency court. "Best interests" represents an advancement in child pro-tection compared with the early court, which tended to view child welfare through society's eyes. "Best interests" is a child-centered principle that repre-sents real progress in the dependency system.

"Best interests" is not, however, an entirely objective standard, and as we are quick to congratulate the current court for the principle, we must recognize that the litigants' perspectives influence the position taken on the child's interests. The caretakers' interest in parental rights and the state's fiscal concerns may pro-hibit empathic consideration from the child's perspective. One of the most sig-nificant innovations of the modern juvenile court is the use of a representative for the child whose function is to view the best interests standard through the eyes of the child. CAPTA requires the appointment of a guardian ad litem, a vestige

---

[123] ANDREA J. SEDLAK & DIANE D. BROADHURST, U.S. DEP'T OF HEALTH & HUMAN SERVS., THE THIRD NATIONAL INCIDENCE STUDY OF CHILD ABUSE AND NEGLECT 5-3 (1996).

[124] *Id. See also* Michael R. Petit & Patrick A. CURTIS, CHILD ABUSE AND NEGLECT: A LOOK AT THE STATES (Child Welfare League of America 1997).

[125] Jill E. Korbin, *Culture and Child Maltreatment, in* THE BATTERED CHILD 29, 29-48 (Mary Edna Helfer et al. eds., 5th ed. 1997).

[126] Apart from *parens patriae* jurisdiction, this may be the thread that ties the late twentieth cen-tury dependency court to its poor laws heritage.

of the dual system of English family law, to protect the child's interest.[127] While attorney representatives for children were absent from the early court, there is now a consensus among dependency court professionals that quality legal representation for children is necessary to a high functioning court process.[128]

Coexisting with the "best interests" is the dependency court policy of "family preservation and reunification." Begun as an amendment to the federal Adoption Assistance and Child Welfare Act, the policy continues, as modified, in the federal Adoption and Safe Families Act. While keeping child safety paramount, the policy calls for recognition that families should be kept together. While more and different types of families experience intervention in the modern dependency court, the intervention occurs within the context of a policy of family integrity. Today's courts operate with "best interests of the child" and "family preservation" as the guideposts.

Criticism and Improvement

Criticism of the juvenile dependency court tends to take two forms. The first is a "parental rights" criticism, which seems to come from a vocal minority and suggests that the child protective system overreaches into the autonomy of the family and that families should be allowed, without governmental interference, to raise, educate, and discipline children as they see fit. The criticism is flawed in two basic ways. First, the position requires one to accept either that children are not seriously maltreated by their caretakers, or that society should allow over one million children a year to be maltreated by their caretakers as a price of parental autonomy. In reality, child maltreatment data, if flawed, is probably understated.[129] Further, an argument that societal tolerance of large-scale child abuse and neglect is the legitimate price of parental autonomy is morally unacceptable.

The second flaw of the "parental rights" criticism is found in the absence of data showing overreaching. While system accountability and awareness of abuse of authority must be part of the process, there is a lack of evidence that the child protective system unfairly intrudes into the American family. The vast majority of families will simply never experience any form of intervention from the state. It is a myth that the state possesses unfettered authority to substitute its parenting

---

[127] 42 U.S.C. § 5106(a) (1988).

[128] MARK HARDIN et al., A.B.A. CENTER ON CHILD. AND THE LAW, COURT IMPROVEMENT PROGRESS REPORT, 1998 (1998). Additionally, the representation of children in the dependency court has also evolved from the 1970s paternal model to the current tendency toward an independent child's attorney. *See, e.g.*, Brian G. Fraser, *Independent Representation for the Abused and Neglected Child: The Guardian Ad Litem*, 13 CAL. W. L. REV. 16 (1976); Ann M. Haralambie, *Current Trends in Children's Legal Representation*, 2 CHILD MALTREATMENT 193 (1997); Marvin Ventrell, *Rights and Duties: An Overview of the Attorney-Child Client Relationship*, 26 LOY. U. CHI. L. J. 259 (1995).

[129] CHILDREN'S BUREAU, U.S. DEP'T OF HEALTH AND HUMAN SERVS., CHILD MALTREATMENT 2002.

judgment for that of parents. States may not substitute judgment of a child's interests except in rare circumstances. The "best interests of the child" standard is invoked only where a threshold finding of abuse or neglect is supported through a judicial determination after a hearing in which parental fitness is presumed. Further, even where dependency adjudications are made, many children are never, even temporarily, removed from the home. The state's authority to terminate the parent-child legal relationship is even further restricted. Family preservation remains the underlying policy of the juvenile court under federal law.[130] Additionally, parents have a constitutionally protected right to raise their biological children, and the minimum burden of proof required to terminate parental rights is clear and convincing evidence. Under the due process clause of the Fourteenth Amendment, "the fundamental liberty interest of natural parents . . . does not evaporate simply because they have not been model parents or have lost temporary custody of their child to the State."[131]

The second primary criticism of the dependency court process is that it does not produce adequate outcomes for many children. While many children are well served by the system, this criticism is valid. Problems including failure to remove children in danger, inappropriate removal, inadequate services to children at home and in placement, lack of high quality social work and legal representation for children, untimeliness of proceedings, and failures to develop permanent solutions exist and must be acknowledged and corrected. Efforts such as the federal Child and Family Service Reviews and the corresponding Program Improvement Plans, together with the Court Improvement Program, are addressing many of these issues.

§ 7.4 Conclusion

The modern juvenile dependency process is an outgrowth of early juvenile court dependency jurisdiction, which itself has origins in the nineteenth-century reform and child-saving movements. The current dependency court, grounded in the *parens patriae* jurisdiction of the early court, evolved from a system of criminal predictions, to a comprehensive child welfare system. As such, it represents an evolving dependency philosophy where children are protected legally from child maltreatment to a greater extent than ever before.

---

[130] Rollin, *Legislative Update*, 16 A.B.A. CHILD LAW PRAC. 11, 166-171 (1998).

[131] *Santosky v. Kramer*, 455 U.S. 745, 753 (1982).

Chapter 8   FEDERAL CHILD WELFARE LAW AND POLICY: UNDERSTANDING THE FEDERAL LAW AND FUNDING PROCESS

by Miriam Rollin,[1] Frank Vandervort,[2] and Ann M. Haralambie[3]

This chapter provides an overview of federal and uniform statutes that impact the practice of child welfare law.[4]

§ 8.1 Introduction to Federal Child Welfare Funding Legislation

Federal statutory child welfare policy is a patchwork of overlapping and confusing provisions. But viewed in a historical context, the federal statutory framework tells a story of a field of child protection that has evolved to address a successive series of challenges, as the perception of each of those challenges reached a "critical mass" over the last 30 years. In truth, some federal statutory changes in the child welfare area over the last 30 years have represented less of a linear progression and more of a pendulum swing back and forth from one extreme to another. The pendulum has swung from a tendency toward protecting children and removing them from their homes (and even terminating parental rights and moving children to adoption), to a tendency toward providing services to parents to prevent placements and return children home as soon as possible, and back again.

Concerned about the problems presented by child protection and foster care systems, in the mid-1970s the United States Congress began an effort to reform child welfare by enacting a series of incentive-based funding statutes. The general aim of these statutes is to encourage the states to take steps to reform their child welfare systems by funding the reforms Congress believes are

---

[1] Miriam Rollin, J.D., is the Policy Representative for the National Association of Counsel for Children in Washington, D.C.

[2] Frank Vandervort, J.D., is Clinical Assistant Professor of Law at the Child Advocacy Law Clinic of the University of Michigan Law School.

[3] Ann M. Haralambie, J.D., is a certified family law specialist practicing in Tucson, Arizona. She is also an author and speaker in the fields of family and children's law.

[4] The Federal Regulations issued by the Department of Health and Human Services or other federal agency responsible for the implementation of the various statutes discussed in this chapter are critically important to a thorough understanding of how these statutes are applied. *See generally*, THEODORE J. STEIN, CHILD WELFARE AND THE LAW (Revised Edition, 1998). The Children's Bureau's Web site contains a wealth of information: http://www.acf.hhs.gov/programs/cb.

important. The federal government's influence over child welfare practice has steadily grown over the past 30 years. While most of the federal statutes are concerned with financing systemic reform, in a few instances Congress explicitly indicated that federal law provides substantive law that supplants state law. In other circumstances, Congress has provided specific enforcement authority to individuals—*e.g.*, a child or a prospective foster parent—involved in the child welfare system.

In most instances, a state's compliance with the federal statutes is voluntary. That is, a state may choose to forego the federal financial assistance and be fully responsible for the costs of its own child welfare system. The funding incentives—in the hundreds of millions of dollars annually for larger states—are sufficient so that each state has determined it is in its interest to take the money. When a state avails itself of the federal financial support, it must comply with the requirements of the federal law.

One crucial element of the history of federal child welfare policy making is that the protection of children who are at risk of abuse or neglect, and of children who have been abused or neglected, has been overwhelmingly bipartisan. For example:

- The fully bipartisan co-sponsorship of the Child Abuse Prevention and Treatment Act in 1974.

- The 401-2 vote in the House of Representatives (and voice vote in the Senate) on the Adoption Assistance and Child Welfare Act of 1980.

- The bipartisan co-sponsorship of the Adoption and Safe Families Act of 1997 and its 416-5 vote in the House (and unanimous consent approval in the Senate).

- In the most recent vote on a child welfare policy bill, the 2003 vote on CAPTA reauthorization legislation (S. 342), the House of Representatives passed the Conference Report by a vote of 421-3, while the Senate adopted it by unanimous consent.

It will be to the benefit of these vulnerable children if Congress is able to continue to work together on both sides of the aisle as further child welfare policy improvements are made in the future.

In some ways, federal child welfare policy history is still very much a part of current child welfare policy—especially when one observes the link that is still maintained between Title IV-E foster care eligibility and the old AFDC income eligibility standards as applied to the child's family of origin, even though AFDC no longer exists.

Therefore, a timeline of major child welfare legislation—from the 1960s to the present—is listed in Section 8.2 below, to provide the historical context that is so essential to full comprehension of the labyrinth of current federal child welfare statutory law. Then, Section 8.3 of this chapter provides a snapshot of the current federal support designed to address child abuse and neglect, while

Section 8.4 provides information on key federal statutory requirements that may apply to various child welfare cases. Section 8.5 reviews other relevant federal and uniform statutes, and Section 8.6 reviews other current federal support that can assist abused and neglected children and their families. Finally, Section 8.7 demonstrates how a number of these federal statutory provisions apply to a particular child welfare case.

§ 8.2 Timeline of Major Federal Child Welfare Legislation[5]

1960s — Title IV-A, the Aid to Families with Dependent Children (AFDC) entitlement, is amended to allow use of funds for foster care expenses if the child comes from an AFDC-eligible family and a court determines it is in the child's best interest to be removed.

1974 — Child Abuse Prevention and Treatment Act is enacted.[6] It is the only federal legislation exclusively dedicated to the prevention, identification, and treatment of child abuse and neglect. Funding for states is conditioned on their adoption of mandatory reporting laws, reporter immunity, confidentiality, and appointment of guardians ad litem for children.

1978 — Indian Child Welfare Act (ICWA) is adopted,[7] establishing requirements for child welfare agencies when serving Native American children and families, including the requirement that tribes play a greater role in placement decisions regarding the children.

1980 — Enactment of the Adoption Assistance and Child Welfare Act of 1980[8] establishes a new Title IV-E Foster Care and Adoption Assistance entitlement program, and requires that state agencies make "reasonable efforts" to prevent the removal of a child from his or her home and to reunify a child with parent(s), and specifies case review requirements for courts.

1981 — Title XX Social Services Block Grant to states is established[9] to address a number of social services needs, including preventing child abuse.

1986 — Title IV-E Independent Living Program is established[10] for foster care children ages 16 and over, to prepare them to live independently upon leaving foster care.

---

[5] This Section 8.2 is adapted from a document entitled TIMELINE OF MAJOR CHILD WELFARE LEGISLATION, created by the Child Welfare League of America and posted on their Web site. Copyright Child Welfare League of America. All rights reserved. Available at: http://www.cwla.org/advocacy/financingtimeline.htm (last visited December 22, 2004).

[6] Pub. L. No. 93-247.

[7] Pub. L. No. 95-608.

[8] Pub. L. No. 96-272.

[9] Pub. L. No. 97-35.

[10] Pub. L. No. 99-272.

1993 — Title IV-B is amended to create a new Family Preservation and Support Services program, as well as a new State Court Improvement program for courts handling foster care and adoption cases.[11]

1994 — Multi-Ethnic Placement Act (MEPA) is enacted[12] to prohibit delay or denial of foster care or adoptive placements on the basis of race, color, or national origin of the child or prospective family.

1996 — Temporary Assistance for Needy Families (TANF) block grant is created,[13] thus eliminating AFDC as an individual entitlement. While TANF replaces AFDC, the law requires states to continue to base Title IV-E Foster Care and Adoption Assistance eligibility on AFDC standards that were in place before the creation of TANF.

1997 — Adoption and Safe Families Act is enacted.[14] It makes explicit the primacy of child safety in placement decisions, creates timelines for moving children to permanency, and provides adoption bonuses for states. The law also renames the Family Preservation and Support Services program to Promoting Safe and Stable Families and expands the use of funds to two additional categories of service: time-limited family reunification services and adoption promotion and support services.

1999 — Through the Foster Care Independence Act,[15] the Independent Living program is expanded, strengthened, and renamed in honor of Senator John H. Chafee (R-RI).

2002 — Promoting Safe and Stable Families is reauthorized, together with Court Improvement. The law also amends the Chafee Independent Living program to provide funding for education and training vouchers for foster youth and creates new funding for mentoring of children of incarcerated parents.[16]

Note: For further information on the public laws listed above, visit the Library of Congress's legislative information Web site at http://thomas.loc.gov.

§ 8.3 Summary of Federal Funding Sources for Child Abuse and Neglect

§ 8.3.1 Foster Care Reimbursements to States

Title IV-E foster care reimbursements to states[17] constitute by far the largest federal expenditure to address child abuse and neglect. These payments are matched with state dollars to pay the costs of each of the following:

---

[11] Pub. L. No. 103-66.

[12] Pub. L. No. 103-382; *see* 42 U.S.C. § 1996b.

[13] Pub. L. No. 104-193.

[14] Pub. L. No. 105-89.

[15] Pub. L. No. 106-169.

[16] Pub. L. No. 107-133.

[17] Social Security Act, Title IV-E.

- "Foster care maintenance" (*i.e.*, housing, food, clothing, and supervision for a foster child).

- "Foster care administration" (*i.e.*, eligibility determinations, referrals to services, placing children, case plans, case reviews, case management and supervision, recruitment and licensing of foster homes, data collection and reporting, and other administrative functions).

- "Foster care training" (*i.e.*, training for foster care workers, as well as for foster parents).

Title IV-E foster care does not pay for services to prevent initial child abuse or neglect, to heal children who have been abused or neglected, or to help families care for abused or neglected children.

§ 8.3.2 Adoption Assistance Reimbursements to States

The second largest federal expenditure related to child abuse and neglect is Title IV-E Adoption Assistance.[18] Adoption Assistance payments are also matched with state funds to support "maintenance" (subsidy payments to adoptive families of special needs children), "administration," and "training," as well as nonrecurring adoption expenses, but do not support prevention or treatment services for children, or services to help parents.

§ 8.3.3 Promoting Safe and Stable Families Program (PSSF)

The Promoting Safe and Stable Families Program (PSSF)[19] is the largest dedicated source of federal child abuse/neglect prevention and intervention services (as opposed to placement) funding, and it includes funding that is specifically targeted toward prevention services and court improvement.

§ 8.3.4 Child Welfare Services Program

The Child Welfare Services Program[20] is the second largest dedicated source of federal child abuse/neglect services funds. It is very flexible; it has no funding targeted toward specific uses.

§ 8.3.5 Chafee Foster Care Independence Program

The Chafee Foster Care Independence Program[21] is the only dedicated source of federal funding for the care of and services to youth aging out of foster care, to enhance their opportunities to become productive adults.

---

[18] Social Security Act, Title IV-E.
[19] Social Security Act, Title IV-B, Subpart 2.
[20] Social Security Act, Title IV-B, Subpart 1.
[21] Social Security Act, Title IV-E.

§ 8.3.6 Child Abuse Prevention and Treatment Act Programs (CAPTA)

Child Abuse Prevention and Treatment Act Programs (CAPTA)[22] includes three funding streams:

- Community-based funding for child abuse/neglect prevention ($33 million in 2004).

- Child Abuse State Grants ($22 million in 2004).

- Child Abuse Discretionary (research/demonstration) Grants ($34 million in 2004).

§ 8.3.7 Other Smaller Federal Funding Sources

Other smaller federal funding sources to address child abuse and neglect include:

- The Children's Justice Act (CJA) provides grants to states to improve the investigation, prosecution, and judicial handling of cases of child abuse and neglect, particularly child sexual abuse and exploitation, in a manner that limits additional trauma to the child victim. In fiscal year 2003, $17 million in CJA funds were available. Funding comes from the Crime Victims' Fund, which collects fines and fees charged to persons convicted of federal crimes.

- Victims of Child Abuse Act (VOCA) and related programs: for "children's advocacy centers" (multi-disciplinary interviewing centers) efforts ($13 million in 2004); for Court Appointed Special Advocates (citizen volunteers trained to assist in individual cases) programs ($12 million in 2004); for Judicial Training ($2 million in 2004); and for televised testimony ($1 million).

- Adoption Opportunities ($27 million in 2004), Adoption Incentives ($7 million in 2004), and Adoption Awareness ($13 million in 2004).

- "Safe Haven" supervised visitation ($15 million in 2004).

- Abandoned Infants Assistance ($12 million in 2004).

- Child Welfare Training grants to higher education institutions ($7 million in 2004).

---

[22] 42 U.S.C. §§ 5101 through 5107.

§ 8.4 Key Federal Statutory Requirements

§ 8.4.1 The Child Abuse Prevention and Treatment Act

The Child Abuse Prevention and Treatment Act (CAPTA) was initially enacted in 1974, and it must be periodically reauthorized.[23] CAPTA was most recently reauthorized in 2003 as part of the Keeping Children and Families Safe Act, which was signed into law by President Bush in June of that year.[24] In general, CAPTA provides federal funding to support states' efforts aimed at preventing child maltreatment and responding to reports of child abuse and neglect.

CAPTA permits the Secretary of the Department of Health and Human Services (DHHS) to appoint an advisory board on child abuse and neglect, the purpose of which is to make recommendations to the Secretary of DHHS and to the relevant congressional committees regarding issues involving child maltreatment.[25] CAPTA also establishes the National Clearinghouse for Information Relating to Child Abuse (Clearinghouse).[26] The Clearinghouse gathers, analyzes, and disseminates data regarding child abuse and neglect. The Secretary of DHHS is charged with carrying out a program of research regarding child abuse and neglect, which may include—among other areas of consideration—"appropriate, effective and culturally sensitive investigative, administrative, and judicial systems, including multidisciplinary, coordinated decision-making procedures with respect to cases of child abuse"[27] as well as information on the national incidences of child abuse and neglect.[28]

If a state wishes to avail itself of the money available through CAPTA, the state must apply to the DHHS and its application must address each of the areas of concern as established in the statute.[29] In essence, the state's application must establish a comprehensive program for: (1) mandated reporting of suspected child maltreatment; (2) responding to those reports with assessment methods that will separate valid reports from those that do not present sufficient evidence to be deemed valid; and (3) taking action appropriate to the level of risk of harm to the children involved.[30]

Several provisions of CAPTA are of particular interest to lawyers who practice child welfare law. First, if judicial proceedings are needed to ensure the protection of the child, CAPTA requires the appointment of a guardian ad litem

---

[23] Pub.L. No. 93-247; 42 U.S.C. § 5101. For a detailed consideration of the most recent version of CAPTA, *see:* http://www.acf.hhs.gov/programs/cb/laws/capta03/capta_manual.pdf.

[24] Pub. L. No. 108-36.

[25] 42 U.S.C. § 5102.

[26] 42 U.S.C. § 5104.

[27] 42 U.S.C. § 5105(a)(1)(C).

[28] 42 U.S.C. § 5105(a)(2).

[29] 42 U.S.C. § 5106a.

[30] *Id.*

"who may be an attorney" for the child.[31] CAPTA provides money to states to train professionals involved in preventing and responding to child abuse and neglect.[32] These training programs must include guardians ad litem who represent children and for "the training of personnel regarding the legal duties of such personnel and their responsibilities to protect the legal rights of children and families."[33] It also provides funding for:

> improving legal preparation and representation, including—
> (i) procedures for appealing and responding to appeals of substantiated reports of abuse or neglect; and
> (ii) provisions for the appointment of an individual to represent a child in judicial proceedings[34]

CAPTA requires each state that wants to avail itself of the federal funds provided under the statute to reapply every five years and to submit a plan that complies with CAPTA's various provisions. Part of that plan must be an assurance:

> that in every case involving an abused or neglected child which results in a judicial proceeding, a guardian ad litem, who has received training appropriate to the role, and who may be an attorney or a court appointed special advocate who has received training appropriate to that role (or both), shall be appointed to represent the child in such proceedings—
> (I) to obtain first-hand, a clear understanding of the situation and the needs of the child; and
> (II) to make recommendations to the court concerning the best interests of the child.[35]

The 2003 CAPTA amendments let the individual states determine whether court proceedings regarding the adjudication of abuse and neglect may be open to the public.[36]

The CAPTA requires that the state's plan "shall, to the maximum extent practicable, be coordinated with the State plan under part B of title IV of the Social Security Act [42 U.S.C. §§ 620 et seq.] relating to child welfare services and family preservation and family support services . . . ."[37] Thus, CAPTA, when applied in conjunction with Titles IV-B and IV-E, provides for a comprehensive federal funding scheme to respond to alleged child maltreatment.

---

[31] 42 U.S.C. § 5106a(b)(2)(A)(xiii).

[32] 42 U.S.C. § 5106(a)(1).

[33] 42 U.S.C. § 5106(a)(1)(F).

[34] 42 U.S.C. § 5106a(a)(2)(B).

[35] 42 U.S.C. § 5106a(b)(2)(A)(xiii).

[36] 42 U.S.C. § 5106a(b).

[37] 42 U.S.C. § 5106a(b)(2).

§ 8.4.2 Titles IV-B and IV-E of the Social Security Act

The purpose of Titles IV-B and IV-E is to establish a funding scheme whereby a state's child welfare agency may receive federal funds to support its child protection efforts if it develops a comprehensive plan, in conjunction with DHHS and which the Secretary of the DHHS approves, that addresses all aspects of child welfare practice from prevention to provision of alternative permanent plans for children who cannot be safely maintained or returned to their natural families.[38] It should be noted that most provisions of these statutory schemes are not intended to and do not establish substantive law that applies to individual cases.[39] Rather, failure to adequately implement the state's plan or failure to abide by a corrective action plan established to address failures to adequately comply with the plan may result in financial penalties being assessed against the state.[40] These financial penalties can be substantial. The loss of the federal dollars may result in a diminution in critically important programming for children and families at the state and local level, so it is important that the various provisions of Titles IV-B and IV-E be complied with.

The federal government's concern about foster care was prompted by a growing consensus that too many children were entering the nation's foster care system, that they remained in that system too long and that too little effort was being made either to reunite foster children with their families of origin or to free them for adoption.[41] It was against this background that Congress acted.

---

[38] *See* 42 U.S.C. § 622 ("In order to be eligible for payment under this subpart, a State must have a plan for child welfare services which has been developed jointly by the Secretary and the State agency. . . ."); 42 U.S.C. § 670 ("The sums made available under this section shall be used for making payments to States which have submitted, and had approved by the Secretary, State plans under this part.").

[39] The 1997 ASFA amendments to Title IV-E make it explicitly clear that state agencies and state courts retain the right to take whatever action in an individual case that is necessary to protect the well-being of the child(ren) involved in that particular case. *See* 42 U.S.C. § 678 and Rule of Construction following 42 U.S.C. § 675. *See also, Suter v. Artist M.*, 503 U.S. 347 (1992) (federal statutory requirement that agency make reasonable efforts does not confer right to reasonable efforts on individual children in the foster care system); *Gonzaga Univ. v. Doe*, 536 U.S. 273 (2002) (citing federal child welfare legislation and *Artist M.* as an example of exercise of federal spending power that is not intended to confer individual rights); *but see, Jeanie B. v. Thompson*, 877 F. Supp. 1268 (E.D. Wis. 1995) (in a class action suit, the court denied a motion for summary judgment because the class of children stated a claim); *Brian A. v. Sunquist*, 149 F. Supp. 2d 941 (M.D. Tenn. 2000) (in class action suit brought by children in foster care, those children were the intended beneficiaries of various provisions of the act).

[40] *See generally* 42 U.S.C. § 674.

[41] Two U.S. Supreme Court cases from that era illustrate a number of the problems presented by the foster care system. In *Smith v. Organization of Foster Families for Equality & Reform*, 431 U.S. 816 (1977), the court considered the due process claims of foster parents and foster children to remain together as a family where children in the New York foster care system had been placed with their foster parents for a median length of four years. Similarly, in the seminal case of *Santosky v. Kramer*, 455 U.S. 745 (1982), which establishes the constitutionally minimum burden of proof for termination of parental rights, the children at issue in the case had been in the foster care system for some five years before the state sought to terminate the parental rights of Mr. and Mrs. Santosky.

Adoption Assistance and Child Welfare Act of 1980

Congress passed and President Jimmy Carter signed into law the Adoption Assistance and Child Welfare Act of 1980 (AACWA).[42] The AACWA sought for the first time to establish a comprehensive federal scheme to reform the nation's foster care system. It did so by establishing a program of contingent funding for the states. If a state developed child welfare and foster care programming consistent with the federal government's view of how such programs should be structured, then the state would be eligible to receive federal assistance in funding those services. Typically, the funds provided by the federal government require a state match, which is sometimes 25 percent and sometimes 50 percent.[43]

The federal government's reform efforts fell into three broad categories. First, Congress sought to stem the flow of children into the foster care system by requiring that states make "reasonable efforts" to maintain children in their families by providing services aimed at preventing the unnecessary removal of children from their parents.[44] Next, beginning in 1983, the AACWA required states to make "reasonable efforts" to reunify children with their parents for a time-limited period, originally requiring a move toward permanency after 18 months.[45] Finally, the federal government sought to encourage the adoption of children from the foster care system by providing adoption subsidies to meet the needs of those children for whom financial considerations (such as special medical conditions) created a barrier to adoption. Similarly, the law sought to provide financial incentives to encourage the adoption of children with other special needs, such as emotional disturbance or behavioral problems.

Congress acted again in 1997.[46] Concerned that its intent with regard to the handling of child welfare cases—and especially that its intentions regarding the application of the "reasonable efforts" and family preservation provisions of the

---

[42] Pub. L. No. 96-272.

[43] *See, e.g.*, 42 U.S.C. § 674 (detailing percentages of reimbursements from the federal government).

[44] Title IV-B, 42 U.S.C. §§ 620 through 629i, seeks to provide, among other things, funding for an array of preventive services and to require as a prerequisite to receiving that funding that states coordinate their various child well-being related efforts.

[45] The federal law does not define "reasonable efforts." For helpful guidance in understanding the reasonable efforts concept and its application in practice, see ABA CENTER ON CHILDREN AND THE LAW, MAKING SENSE OF THE ASFA REGULATIONS (2001); CECILIA FIERMONTE & JENNIFER RENNE, ABA CENTER ON CHILDREN AND THE LAW, MAKING IT PERMANENT: REASONABLE EFFORTS TO FINALIZE PERMANENCY PLANS FOR FOSTER CHILDREN (2002).

[46] Between 1980 and 1997, there were several additions and modifications to the federal law governing child welfare, but they were relatively modest in comparison to the sweeping changes wrought by the AACWA and the ASFA. *See, e.g.*, the Safe and Stable Families Act of 1993 (reauthorized by the Promoting Safe and Stable Families Act of 2001), 42 U.S.C. §§ 629 through 629i. The Web site of the National Resource Center for Family-Centered Practice and Permanency Planning contains helpful information regarding family preservation and permanency planning efforts: http://www.hunter.cuny.edu/socwork/nrcfcpp.

AACWA—had been misunderstood and misapplied,[47] Congress passed the Adoption and Safe Families Act (ASFA), which was signed into law by President Clinton in November 1997.[48]

ASFA maintained the basic formula established in the AACWA. First, it reaffirmed the federal government's commitment to family preservation as a means of reducing the number of children who are removed from their home and in need of foster care placement. Similarly, ASFA maintained the requirement that in most cases state child welfare agencies were required to make "reasonable efforts" to maintain familial integrity and substantially increased the funding available to states for family preservation services. However, in doing so, it specifically sought to make clear its intention that "in determining reasonable efforts to be made with respect to a child . . . the child's health and safety shall be the paramount concern."[49]

Next, when a child's safety within his or her family cannot be ensured and court action is necessary, ASFA requires states to implement a differential response.[50] In cases of serious child abuse that result in criminal conviction or where a parent has previously experienced involuntary termination of parental rights, ASFA excuses the reasonable efforts requirement and requires, as a prerequisite to receiving federal funds, that the state child welfare agency immediately initiate or join an effort to terminate parental rights or otherwise place the child permanently.[51]

ASFA also invites, but does not require, each state to establish for itself a set of "aggravated circumstances" cases, which the state determines (by statute or policy) will render the parent ineligible for either family preservation or family reunification services.[52] While the federal legislation lets each state determine

---

[47] *See generally* RICHARD J. GELLES, THE BOOK OF DAVID: HOW PRESERVING FAMILIES CAN COST CHILDREN'S LIVES (1996) (arguing that family preservation had become the "central mission" of the child welfare system and that it placed children at an unacceptable and unnecessary risk of harm).

[48] Pub. L. No. 105-89.

[49] 42 U.S.C. § 671(a)(15).

[50] This term is borrowed from Professor Jane Waldfogel, who defines a "differential response" as one:

> [I]n which CPS and its partners tailor their approach and services to fit each family's problems, needs, and resources. At the most general level, a differential response implies there are at least two pathways for families referred for abuse or neglect: a mandatory investigation for high-risk families, and an assessment- and service-oriented response for low-risk families. Within each pathway, the approach of the caseworkers and the services they recommend will be customized to fit the family's situation.

See Jane Waldfogel, *Rethinking the Paradigm for Child Protection*, 8 THE FUTURE OF CHILDREN (1998), *available at* http://www.futureofchildren.org/information2826/information_show.htm?doc_id=75380.

[51] 42 U.S.C. § 671(a)(15)(D)(ii); *see* 45 C.F.R. § 1356.21(b)(3) (requiring that the parent be convicted on the relevant crime before the mandatory termination provision of ASFA is triggered).

[52] 42 U.S.C. § 671(a)(15)(D)(i).

the specific types of cases that will fall within the "aggravated circumstances" designation, it suggests that appropriate cases may include situations where the parent has subjected the child to "abandonment, torture, chronic abuse and sexual abuse."[53] Finally, ASFA permits the state child welfare agency to seek, and the court to grant, a request for immediate or early termination of parental rights in any case where the facts and circumstances of that particular child's situation warrant such action.[54]

Some states allow the child's advocate to petition the court to terminate parental rights or to otherwise move to permanency at any time after the case is filed.[55] If your state permits such action, it is a good practice for the child's advocate to consider in every case whether the facts of the case merit an effort to seek immediate or early termination or if continued efforts to reunify the family will best serve the child.

Unless the court has determined that no "reasonable efforts" are required and permits a party to immediately implement an alternative permanent plan, the state must make "reasonable efforts" to reunify the child with his or her parent. While the federal law requires reasonable efforts in most cases, it does not define the term. Defining what constitutes "reasonable efforts" in a way that is truly helpful and provides practitioners with the guidance they need has proven elusive. Missouri, for example, uses this definition:

> "reasonable efforts" means the exercise of reasonable diligence and care
> . . . to utilize all available services related to meeting the needs of the
> juvenile and the family. In determining reasonable efforts to be made
> and in making such reasonable efforts, the child's present and ongoing
> health and safety shall be the paramount consideration.[56]

---

[53] *Id.* Note, again, that this list is merely suggestive and each state is free to determine for itself whether or not to include these or other groups of cases. For example, Michigan has adopted a definition of "aggravated circumstances" cases that includes child sexual abuse involving penetration or attempt to penetrate, but has not included sexual abuse that involves only fondling. *See* MICH. COMP. LAWS. ANN. § 722.638 (requiring state child welfare agency to petition the court and to seek termination of parental rights at the initial dispositional hearing); MICH. COMP. LAWS. ANN. § 712A.19b(3)(k) (establishing basis for termination of parental rights). For more information regarding aggravated circumstances provisions of state laws, visit the Web site of the National Clearinghouse on Child Abuse and Neglect Information: http://nccanch.acf.hhs.gov.

[54] *See* Rule of Construction following 42 U.S.C. § 675 (Pub. L. No. 105-89, § 103(d)). *See generally U.S. v. Welden*, 377 U.S. 95, fn 4 (1964); 42 U.S.C. § 678 (permitting state court to take any action necessary to protect the health and safety of a child in a particular case unless immediate permanency is required because the parent has murdered his or her child, committed manslaughter, aided or abetted murder or manslaughter, or has committed a felony assault that has resulted in serious bodily injury). *See, e.g.*, 705 ILL. COMP. STAT. ANN. § 405/1-2(1)(c) (permitting immediate termination "in those extreme cases in which the parent's incapacity to care for the child, combined with an extremely poor prognosis for treatment or rehabilitation, justifies expedited termination of parental rights.").

[55] *See, e.g.*, MICH. COMP. LAWS ANN. § 712A.19b(1).

[56] MO. ANN. STAT. § 211.183.

In order to operationalize the definition, some states have combined a definition of "reasonable efforts" with criteria to assist courts in determining whether the state agency has made reasonable efforts. Iowa provides an example of this approach:

> "reasonable efforts" means the efforts made to preserve and unify a family prior to the out-of-home placement of a child in foster care or to eliminate the need for removal of the child or make it possible for the child to safely return to the family's home. . . . Reasonable efforts may include intensive family preservation services or family-centered services, if the child's safety in the home can be maintained during the time the services are provided. In determining whether reasonable efforts have been made, the court shall consider both of the following:
>
> (1) The type, duration, and intensity of services or support offered or provided to the child and the child's family. If intensive family preservation services were not provided, the court record shall enumerate the reasons the services were not provided, including but not limited to whether the services were not available, not accepted by the child's family, judged to be unable to protect the child and the child's family during the time the services would have been provided, judged to be unlikely to be successful in resolving the problems which would lead to removal of the child, or other services were found more appropriate.
>
> (2) The relative risk to the child of remaining in the child's home versus removal of the child.[57]

Despite the definitional difficulties, when "reasonable efforts" must be made, the state's child welfare agency must establish a "case plan." The plan must include a description of the child's placement; a schedule of services to be provided to the child, the child's parents, and the foster parents to facilitate reunification; and other similar matters.[58] If the child is 16 years of age or older, the plan must include services aimed at helping the youth to prepare for independence.[59] If the permanency plan for the child is adoption or some other alternative permanent plan (*e.g.*, permanent guardianship), then the case plan must include a description of the "reasonable efforts" made to achieve that alternative goal.[60]

---

[57] IOWA CODE § 232.102.

[58] *See* 42 U.S.C. § 675(1) (defining "case plan").

[59] *See* the discussion of the Foster Care Independence/Chafee Act below. It should also be noted that some states have made these services available to youth younger than 16. You should consult your state law and policy to determine your state's approach to this question.

[60] 42 U.S.C. § 675(1)(E).

In addition to the provisions that obviate the need to make "reasonable efforts," ASFA made numerous procedural changes aimed at expediting children's moves through the child welfare system. For example, the state's plan for providing foster care must include a "case review system" that provides for periodic review of the case by a court or an administrative agency at least every six months, as well as a permanency planning hearing to be held at least once every 12 months for as long as the child remains in foster care.[61] Subject to several specific exceptions, when a child has been in foster care for 15 of the most recent 22 months, the state agency must seek termination of parental rights.[62] At least one state supreme court, however, has required more than merely the passage of time when considering termination based on this provision of ASFA.[63]

ASFA continues the AACWA's effort to get children out of the child welfare system and into permanent placements by permitting the use of concurrent planning, expanding the use of adoption assistance, and expanding the permanency options available to the states. First, ASFA gives states the option to begin using concurrent planning without suffering financial penalties.[64] Concurrent planning allows the state to simultaneously pursue efforts aimed at reunification as well as efforts to place the child in an alternative permanent setting if a family reunification cannot be achieved. Such a concurrent approach to permanency planning can shorten the child's stay in temporary foster care.

Next, in addition to continuing the subsidies available to individual families to assist with the expenses of adoption, the ASFA provides each state a financial incentive to focus on efforts to move children who cannot be returned to their family of origin into adoptive homes. It does this by establishing a baseline of the number of adoptions and then paying the state a bonus for each adoption from foster care finalized in excess of that baseline.[65]

Finally, ASFA expands the available permanency options.[66] For example, permanent guardianship was specifically recognized in ASFA as a form of permanency.[67] Illinois, for example, has established statutory scheme for subsidized

---

[61]   42 U.S.C. § 675(5).

[62]   42 U.S.C. § 675(5)(E).

[63]   *In re H.G.*, 757 N.E.2d 864 (Ill. 2001) (termination based merely on child's placement in foster care for 15 of most recent 22 months violated parent's substantive due process right to custody of her or his child).

[64]   42 U.S.C. § 671(a)(15)(F); for a detailed discussion of concurrent planning, *see* LINDA KATZ ET AL., CONCURRENT PLANNING: FROM PERMANENCY PLANNING TO PERMANENCY ACTION (Lutheran Social Services of Washington and Idaho, 1994).

[65]   42 U.S.C. § 673b.

[66]   *See generally* DONALD N. DUQUETTE & MARK HARDIN, GUIDELINES FOR PUBLIC POLICY AND STATE LEGISLATION GOVERNING PERMANENCE FOR CHILDREN (Children's Bureau, 1999) *available at* http://www.acf.hhs.gov/programs/cb/publications/adopt02/02final.htm.

[67]   42 U.S.C. § 675(7) (defining "legal guardianship" as a judicially created relationship that is intended to be permanent).

guardianship to be used when adoption is not a realistic option for a case, but it has been determined that the child cannot be returned home.[68] Some states have been granted Title IV-E waivers to provide financial subsidies to support permanent guardianships.

§ 8.4.3 The Indian Child Welfare Act

In 1978, the federal government responded to long-term advocacy by Native American groups and enacted the Indian Child Welfare Act (ICWA).[69] Unlike most of the federal legislation discussed in this chapter, the ICWA is substantive law. That is, if a state court determines that the ICWA applies to a case before it, the state court must apply the specific provisions of the ICWA to that case rather than applying the state's law.

The ICWA is an attempt to respond to the historical discrimination experienced by Native American families and tribes when their children were unnecessarily removed from their care in an effort to assimilate Native Americans into the dominant culture. The ICWA seeks to preserve the rights of both Indian families and Indian tribes to make decisions regarding their children.[70] Thus, tribal court orders regarding child custody are entitled to full faith and credit.[71]

Jurisdiction and Standing

An Indian tribe has exclusive jurisdiction over child protection proceedings that involve children who are domiciled on its reservation.[72] Despite a tribe's exclusive jurisdiction over a child residing or domiciled on the reservation, a state court may enter emergency orders to protect an Indian child who is domiciled on a reservation but who is found off the reservation "in order to prevent imminent physical damage or harm to the child."[73] If a case involves an Indian child, the child's tribe has the right to request transfer of the case from the state court to the tribal court.[74] Such a request "shall be made promptly after receiving notice of the proceedings."[75] A state court must grant the tribe's request to

---

[68]   705 ILL. COMP. STAT. ANN. § 405/2-27.

[69]   25 U.S.C. §§ 1901 through 1963; *see* Bureau of Indian Affairs, Guidelines For State Courts; Indian Child Custody Proceedings, 44 Fed. Reg. 67584 (November 26, 1979), *available at* http://www.nicwa.org/policy/regulations/icwa/ICWA_guidelines.pdf. For an excellent detailed discussion of the ICWA's provisions and impact, *see* B.J. JONES, THE INDIAN CHILD WELFARE ACT HANDBOOK. The National Indian Child Welfare Association's Web site also contains a wealth of helpful information: http://www.nicwa.org.

[70]   *See* 25 U.S.C. §§ 1901-1902.

[71]   42 U.S.C. § 1911(d).

[72]   25 U.S.C. § 1911(a).

[73]   25 U.S.C. § 1922.

[74]   25 U.S.C. § 1911(b).

[75]   Bureau of Indian Affairs, Guidelines For State Courts; Indian Child Custody Proceedings, 44 FED. REG. 67584, Sec. C.1 (November 26, 1979), *available at* http://www.nicwa.org/policy/regulations/icwa/ICWA_guidelines.pdf.

transfer the case unless there is "good cause" to deny it or a parent objects to the transfer.[76]

Even if the tribe declines to remove a case from the state child protective proceeding process, the tribe has standing to intervene in the state court proceeding at any point.[77]

Application

The ICWA applies to any child protective proceeding in which the right to custody of an "Indian child" is at issue.[78] Additionally, ICWA applies to cases in which an Indian child's parent wishes to voluntarily place a child in foster care or for adoption.[79] An "Indian child" is a child whose parent is a member of a federally recognized Indian tribe or band and who is also eligible for such membership.[80] Each Indian tribe has the exclusive right to determine its eligibility requirements. While some tribes have a blood quantum requirement for eligibility, this is not a universal measure of eligibility.

Notice

When a child welfare proceeding may involve an Indian child, the ICWA requires that notice be provided to the child's parents or "Indian custodian" and to the child's tribe.[81] The ICWA provides for notice to be provided "where the court knows or has reason to know that an Indian child is involved."[82] Clearly, ICWA's notice requirement is very broad, requiring that notice be provided when there is any hint of Native American heritage.[83] Providing notice to the child's parents is routine for state courts. However, notice may be complicated in

---

[76] 42 U.S.C. § 1911(b). The federal statute does not define "good cause" to decline transfer. The Bureau of Indian Affairs Guidelines, however, establishes four bases on which a state court may decline to transfer a case to a tribal court. Bureau of Indian Affairs, Guidelines For State Courts; Indian Child Custody Proceedings, 44 FED. REG. 67584, Sec. C.3 (November 26, 1979), *available at* http://www.nicwa.org/policy/regulations/icwa/ICWA_guidelines.pdf.

[77] 25 U.S.C. § 1911(c).

[78] The ICWA defines "custody" to include only cases in involving child protection, guardianship and status offense cases. The ICWA does not apply in the divorce context or to delinquency cases.

[79] *See* 25 U.S.C. § 1913; *Mississippi Band of Choctaw Indians v. Holyfield*, 490 U.S. 30; 109 S. Ct. 1597; 104 L. Ed. 2d 29 (1989).

[80] 25 U.S.C. § 1903(4).

[81] *Id.*

[82] *Id.*

[83] *Id. See In re I.E.M.*, 599 N.W. 2d 772 (Mich. 1999) (where mother mentioned at a preliminary hearing that there was some Native American heritage in her family, failure to provide notice pursuant to ICWA was error); *In re Colnar*, 757 P.2d 534 (Wash. App. 1988) (mother's claim that child was Indian child sufficient to trigger notice requirement); *In re M.C.P.*, 571 A.2d 627 (1989) (notice requirement triggered when court had reason to believe child was Indian child); *but see, In re O.K.*, 106 Cal. App. 4th 152; 130 Cal. Rptr. 2nd 276 (2003) (grandmother's statement that child may qualify as Indian child not sufficient to trigger notice requirement).

an ICWA case because if the whereabouts of the child's parents are unknown, notice must be provided to the Secretary of the Interior.[84] Moreover, some courts struggle with the concept of a child's "Indian custodian" because such a relationship may be established by either tribal law or tribal custom.[85] Similarly, providing notice to the tribe can be complicated if membership is uncertain. If the child's tribe is known, then notice must be provided directly to the tribe.[86] If tribal affiliation is uncertain, then notice must be provided to the Secretary of the Interior.[87] In some instances, a parent may communicate an affiliation with an Indian Nation that has more than one federally recognized tribe or band; for example, a parent may say, "My grandfather was Cherokee." In such a case, it is best practice that notice be provided to each federally recognized Cherokee tribe or band as well as the Secretary of the Interior.[88] Pursuant to the ICWA, notice must be provided by registered mail, return receipt requested.[89]

The notice provisions of the ICWA are critically important. Counsel should make every effort to carefully document efforts made to notify the parents, the Indian custodian, and the Secretary of the Interior. As a practical matter, counsel should file with the court copies of any notice sent. Similarly, copies of any responses received from tribes or the Secretary of the Interior should be filed with the court.

Higher Standards of Evidence

ICWA requires that state courts apply higher standards of evidence before removing an Indian child from his or her parent or Indian custodian and when seeking termination of parental rights. At any stage in a proceeding where the state standard and the federal standard differ, the court must apply the higher of the two standards.[90] When removal from parental custody is sought, the petitioner must demonstrate by clear and convincing evidence—supported by expert testimony—that "continued custody by the parent or Indian custodian is likely to result in serious emotional or physical damage to the child."[91] A court may terminate the parental rights of an Indian child only upon a showing beyond a reasonable doubt (again supported by expert testimony) that custody of the child by the parent or Indian custodian "is likely to result in serious emotional or physical damage to the child."[92]

---

[84]   25 U.S.C. § 1912(a).

[85]   25 U.S.C. § 1903(6).

[86]   25 U.S.C. § 1912(a).

[87]   *Id.*

[88]   *See, e.g., In re N.E.G.P.,* 626 N.W. 2d 921 (Mich. Ct. App. 2001).

[89]   25 U.S.C. § 1912(a).

[90]   25 U.S.C. § 1921.

[91]   25 U.S.C. § 1912(e).

[92]   25 U.S.C. § 1912(f).

Placement

When the facts of a case warrant the removal of an Indian child from his or her home, the ICWA establishes placement criteria that must be followed.[93] When placing an Indian child into foster care or for adoption, the child must be placed as follows:

(1) with a member of the child's extended family;

(2) if no placement with a family member is available then the child must be placed in a foster home licensed or approved by the Indian child's tribe (this may include placement in a non-Indian foster home);

(3) if neither 1 or 2 are available, then the child is to be placed with an Indian foster family that is approved by a non-Indian licensing authority; or

(4) finally, if none of these are available, the child may be placed in an institution approved by a tribe or operated by an Indian organization.

It should be noted that this placement criteria, which specifically considers a child's Native American heritage, is in direct contrast to the typical scheme for placement of children into foster care established by the MEPA-IEP.

Failure to Comply

While the ICWA applies to a relatively small number of child welfare proceedings, when it does apply it is critically important to strictly adhere to its provisions. The ICWA provides that any improper removal of a child from parental custody or termination of parental rights may be invalidated by a court of competent jurisdiction.[94] This point is illustrated by what happened in *Mississippi Band of Choctaw Indians v. Holyfield*,[95] where the U.S. Supreme Court invalidated a voluntary adoption of two Indian children three years after the adoption because the ICWA's requirement for tribal notification was not complied with. Such actions, obviously, can disrupt even long-term placements and can be damaging to children.

Inapplicable to Some Native American Children

It is possible that a child could have substantial Native American heritage (and, therefore, cultural needs that should be considered) even though he or she is not eligible for membership in a particular tribe. Indeed, it is possible for a child to be fully Native American but still not meet the eligibility requirements for membership in any single federally recognized tribe. For example, this author was recently involved in a case where the child was descended from Native

---

[93] 25 U.S.C. § 1915.

[94] 25 U.S.C. § 1914.

[95] *See Mississippi Band of Choctaw Indians v. Holyfield*, 490 U.S. 30 (1989).

American heritage on both his maternal and paternal sides, but because of tribal blood quantum membership requirements the child was not eligible for membership in any single tribe. Such a child still has important cultural concerns that should be considered.[96] Similarly, the ICWA applies only to children who are members or eligible for membership in tribes or bands recognized by the United States government. It does not apply to a Native American child whose tribe has not been recognized nor does it apply to a child descended from a Canadian tribe.

§ 8.4.4 The Multi-Ethnic Placement Act

In 1994, Congress enacted the Multi-Ethnic Placement Act (MEPA), which it amended by passage of the Interethnic Adoption Provisions of the Small Business Job Protection Act in 1996 (IEP).[97] In general, the MEPA-IEP contains two broad goals. First, it seeks to eliminate the consideration of a person's race, color, or national origin with regard to licensing foster parents and making placement decisions regarding either the foster or adoptive placement of children.[98] Specifically, MEPA-IEP provides:

> neither the State nor any other entity in the State that receives funds from the Federal Government and is involved in adoption or foster care placements may—
> (A) deny to any person the opportunity to become an adoptive or a foster parent, on the basis of race, color, or national origin of the person, or of the child involved; or
> (B) delay or deny the placement of a child for adoption or into foster care, on the basis of race, color, or national origin of the adoptive or foster parent, or the child, involved.

The second overarching goal of MEPA-IEP is to "provide for the diligent recruitment of potential foster and adoptive families that reflect the ethnic and racial diversity of children in the State for whom foster and adoptive homes are needed."[99]

Application

Despite the categorical language of the MEPA-IEP, the state may in narrow circumstances consider race, color, or national origin when making placement

---

[96] *See* Chapter 6, Cultural Context in Abuse and Neglect Practice: Tips for Attorneys .

[97] MEPA-IEP's various provisions are codified in large part within Titles IV-B and IV-E. *See* 42 U.S.C. § 622(b)(9); 42 U.S.C. § 671(a)(18); 42 U.S.C. § 674(d). For an excellent detailed discussion of the MEPA-IEP, *see* JOAN HEIFETZ HOLLINGER & THE ABA CENTER ON CHILDREN AND THE LAW, A GUIDE TO THE MULTIETHNIC PLACEMENT ACT OF 1994 AS AMENDED BY THE INTERETHNIC ADOPTION PROVISIONS OF 1996 (American Bar Association 1998), available from the Children's Bureau's Web site at http://www.acf.hhs.gov/programs/cb/publications/mepa94/index.htm.

[98] 42 U.S.C. § 671(a)(18).

[99] 42 U.S.C. § 622(b)(8).

decisions.[100] When a child has a specific need relating to race, color, or national origin, this need should be carefully documented and may be considered.[101] Professor Hollinger has observed that "agencies may not routinely assume that children have needs related to their race, color, or national origin. Nor may agencies routinely evaluate the ability of prospective foster and adoptive parents to meet such needs."[102] However, she goes on to point out that, "As amended by IEP, MEPA does not prohibit agencies from the nondiscriminatory consideration of a child's cultural background and experience in making an individualized placement decision," although consideration of race, color, or national origin "should not predominate" the placement decision.[103] So for example, if an older child expresses particular concern regarding a cross-racial placement or if a child speaks only Spanish, this fact may be taken into consideration when selecting a foster or adoptive home.

Strict scrutiny applies to any placement decision in which race, color, or national origin is considered.[104] Thus, agency personnel must seek the least restrictive and most narrowly tailored means of addressing the concern. In the earlier example, the use of counseling to allay the child's concern about cross-cultural placement or providing English lessons to the child and/or Spanish lessons to the foster care provider should be considered before the placement is denied. Such consideration should never affect placement decisions regarding infants.[105] Moreover, it is the intent of the "diligent recruitment" provision of the statute to reduce the necessity of such considerations by diversifying the pool of foster and adoptive homes. To meet the goal of more diverse placement resources, MEPA-IEP has been interpreted as eliminating even race-neutral licensing criteria that have a disparate impact on licensing particular groups of applicants.[106] For example, a state cannot mandate home ownership as a prerequisite to licensing foster homes if doing so would disproportionately impact applicants of a particular racial group for a foster care license.

Enforcement

The MEPA-IEP contains two basic enforcement mechanisms. First, as with the other federal child welfare legislation, violation of MEPA-IEP may result in financial penalties. If the state agency violates this statute, then it will suffer a

---

[100] JOAN HEIFETZ HOLLINGER & THE ABA CENTER ON CHILDREN AND THE LAW, A GUIDE TO THE MULTIETHNIC PLACEMENT ACT OF 1994 AS AMENDED BY THE INTERETHNIC ADOPTION PROVISIONS OF 1996, 22 (American Bar Association 1998), available from the Children's Bureau's Web site at http://www.acf.hhs.gov/programs/cb/publications/mepa94/index.htm.

[101] *Id.* at 22-23.

[102] *Id.* at 22.

[103] *Id.* at 22-23.

[104] *Id.* at 23.

[105] *Id.* at 25.

[106] *Id.* at 12, *citing* Policy Guidance, 60 FED. REG. 20272, 20275.

two percent reduction in the amount of federal funds it is eligible to receive in the period during which the first offense occurs. If a second violation is identified, the state agency will lose three percent of its federal funding for that period. For a third or subsequent violation, the state will lose five percent of its funding for that fiscal year.[107] Similarly, but more severe still, if a private agency (*e.g.*, a private foster care agency that contracts with the state to provide services) violates MEPA-IEP's provisions, it will be required to remit to the DHHS all the funds it received for the fiscal quarter.[108]

In addition to the public enforcement mechanism just described, MEPA-IEP provides for private enforcement by any individual—child or prospective foster or adoptive parent—who has been aggrieved by a violation of the statute.[109] Such enforcement may be brought in the form of a lawsuit "seeking relief" in a federal district court. Such a suit must be filed within two years of the violation.[110]

MEPA-IEP specifically states that its enactment does not in any way affect the application of the Indian Child Welfare Act.[111]

§ 8.4.5 Special Immigrant Juvenile Status

Many federal laws have specific provisions governing the law's application to noncitizens. For example, the law creating Temporary Assistance for Needy Families (TANF)[112] in 1996 made substantial eligibility changes for immigrants that affected not only TANF but also other federal benefits. Attorneys handling cases involving immigrants should research applicable statutes for provisions specific to immigrant populations. One immigration law provision, however, specifically relates to juvenile court proceedings (and young immigrants' ability to remain in the United States after leaving foster care) and is included below—a provision related to Special Immigrant Juvenile Status.[113]

An alien is eligible for classification as a special immigrant juvenile status of the Immigration Act if the alien meets all of the following criteria:

- Is under 21 years of age.

- Is unmarried.

- Has been declared dependent on a juvenile court located in the United States[114] in accordance with state law governing such declarations of

---

[107] 42 U.S.C. § 674(d)(1).

[108] 42 U.S.C. § 674(d)(2).

[109] 42 U.S.C. § 674(3).

[110] *Id.*

[111] 42 U.S.C. § 674(d)(4).

[112] *See* § 8.6.1, Temporary Assistance for Needy Families (TANF).

[113] Immigration Act of 1990, Pub. L. No. 101-649, § 153; 8 U.S.C. § 1101(a)(27).

[114] 8 U.S.C. § 1101(a)(27)(J)(i).

dependency, while the alien was in the United States and under the jurisdiction of the court.

- Has been deemed eligible by the juvenile court for long-term foster care due to abuse, neglect or abandonment.[115]

- Continues to be dependent on the juvenile court and eligible for long-term foster care, such declaration, dependency or eligibility not having been vacated, terminated, or otherwise ended.

- Has been the subject of judicial proceedings or administrative proceedings authorized or recognized by the juvenile court in which it has been determined that it would not be in the alien's best interest to be returned to the country of nationality or last habitual residence of the beneficiary or his or her parent or parents.[116]

Except that—
(I) no juvenile court has jurisdiction to determine the custody status or placement of an alien in the actual or constructive custody of the Attorney General unless the Attorney General specifically consents to such jurisdiction; and
(II) no natural parent or prior adoptive parent of any alien provided special immigrant status under this subparagraph shall thereafter, by virtue of such parentage, be accorded any right, privilege, or status under this Act. . .[117]

§ 8.4.6 The Foster Care Independence Act (Chafee)

The Foster Care Independence Act (also known as "The Chafee Foster Care Independence Program" or "Chafee Act") was signed into law in December 1999.[118] The Chafee Act amends certain provisions of Title IV-E and the Medicaid program and is intended to assist older youth in the foster care system to transition out of foster care and into independence as young adults.[119] The Congressional findings that support the Chafee Act reaffirm that state agencies have an obligation to make reasonable efforts to obtain adoptive homes for older foster children who are free for adoption, but also recognize that "some older children will continue to live in foster care."[120] Congress also recognized a number of the challenges faced by young persons aging out of the foster care system. These include "high rates of homelessness, non-marital childbearing,

---

[115] 8 U.S.C. § 1101(a)(27)(J)(i).

[116] 8 U.S.C. § 1101(a)(27)(J)(ii).

[117] 8 U.S.C. § 1101(a)(27)(J)(iii).

[118] Pub. L. No. 106-169.

[119] *See* 42 U.S.C. §§ 671, 677, 1396a.

[120] *See* Pub. L. No. 106-169, § 101.

poverty, delinquent or criminal behavior; they are also the target of crime and physical assaults."[121] The primary goal of the Chafee Act is to increase flexibility in the use of funds to develop programs to meet the needs of this subgroup of the foster care population.

In order to address these problems, and to prepare youth to transition into independence, the Chafee Act:

- Establishes an improved independent living program, known as the John H. Chafee Foster Care Independence Program.[122]

- Allows states to provide Medicaid coverage to young adults between the ages of 18 and 21 who were in foster care on their eighteenth birthday.[123]

- Increases the minimum amount of assets from $1,000 to $10,000 that a youth in foster care may have and still be eligible for foster care funded by Title IV-E.[124]

- Requires states to ensure that foster parents are prepared, both initially and on a continuing basis, to care for children placed with them.[125]

- Authorizes increased funds for adoption incentive payments to the states to assist in finding permanent placements for children in foster care.[126]

States may apply for funding to support their youth initiatives and, when doing so, must submit a five-year plan for implementation.[127] In addition to meeting the technical requirements of the Chafee Act set out in 42 U.S.C. § 677, the state must provide a 20 percent match for the funds. When a state receives federal funds under the Chafee Act, the state has two years to spend the money on programming. Each state must ensure that each political subdivision within the state has access to these transitional services.

States receiving Chafee Act funds must establish an array of services aimed at meeting the needs of youth of various ages and at various stages of independence. States must establish objective eligibility standards for receipt of Chafee Act services. The state may use Chafee Act funds to assist young adults ages 18 to 21 who have or who will age out of foster care,[128] and may use as much as 30 percent of these funds to pay room and board for these youth.

---

[121] Pub. L. No. 106-169, § 1. *See generally* MARTHA SHIRK & GARY STANGLER, ON THEIR OWN: WHAT HAPPENS TO KIDS WHEN THEY AGE OUT OF THE FOSTER CARE SYSTEM (2004). Helpful information about older children in foster care and issues relating to aging out is available from the Jim Casey Youth Opportunities Initiative Web site: http://www.jimcaseyyouth.org.

[122] 42 U.S.C. § 677.

[123] 42 U.S.C. § 1396a.

[124] 42 U.S.C. § 672(a).

[125] 42 U.S.C. § 671(a)(24).

[126] 42 U.S.C. § 673b.

[127] 42 U.S.C. § 677(b).

[128] Some states permit youth to remain in foster care beyond their eighteenth birthday.

In addition to services directed at youth, the Chafee Act provides that some of the funds must be used to train foster parents, group home staff, and caseworkers in addressing the needs of older children and youth. As with the other federal funding statutes, the Chafee Act contains penalty provisions if the state misuses the funds.

Each state should have in place a program to aide youth transitioning from foster care to independence. The reader should seek out his or her state's plan and become familiar with its specifics.

§ 8.5 Other Relevant Federal and Uniform Statutes

In addition to the various federal child welfare legislation just described, there are several other federal statutes that have an impact on the practice of child welfare law. This section provides an introduction to these statutes.

§ 8.5.1 The Uniform Child Custody Jurisdiction and Enforcement Act

The Uniform Child Custody and Jurisdiction and Enforcement Act (UCCJEA) is an updated version of the Uniform Child Custody Jurisdiction Act (UCCJA). While not a federal law, every state has enacted some version of either the UCCJA or the UCCJEA. The UCCJA was enacted in 1968 and had as its intent the establishment of uniform rules regarding jurisdiction over child custody decisions.[129] In 1997, the UCCJA was updated to clarify questions raised by the enactment in 1980 of the Parental Kidnapping Prevention Act. These statutes become important when a parent with custody of a child takes the child from one state to another and becomes involved with the child protection system in the subsequent state. For example, imagine a case in which Mr. and Mrs. Smith are married in California. Mrs. Smith gives birth to Sally. When Sally is five years old, Mr. and Mrs. Smith divorce in California. Mrs. Smith, who is awarded primary custody of Sally, is allowed to move with Sally to New York. In New York, when Sally is seven years old, Mrs. Smith becomes involved with an abusive boyfriend, drugs, and the excessive use of alcohol, which causes Sally's mom to leave Sally alone for days at a time. When Sally tells a school teacher what is happening at her home, the school authorities report their concern to child protection authorities.

In general, the UCCJA and the UCCJEA establish a child's "home state" as the jurisdiction with authority to make determinations regarding custody of a child. In our case example, California is Sally's "home state." California had jurisdiction and properly resolved the custody dispute between Sally's parents. Under the UCCJA and the UCCJEA, California retains jurisdiction to make custody determinations regarding Sally. New York, however, has "emergency"

---

[129] *See generally* JOHN DEWITT GREGORY ET AL., UNDERSTANDING FAMILY LAW 426-435 (2001).

jurisdiction over Sally because her health and safety are impaired by her mother's inability to provide a fit home environment for Sally. Under the UCCJA or UCCJEA, New York has "emergency" jurisdiction to enter orders that are necessary to protect and provide for Sally.[130]

§ 8.5.2 The Parental Kidnapping Prevention Act

Despite the efforts of the uniform law—then just the UCCJA—to resolve jurisdictional disputes, there continued to be struggles regarding which of two states' courts had jurisdiction over child custody actions. In 1980 Congress responded to these concerns by enacting the Parental Kidnapping Prevention Act (PKPA),[131] which is intended to "specify which types of custody decrees must be afforded full faith and credit, as well as the circumstances that would allow states to modify an outstanding custody degree of another state."[132] The PKPA establishes a federal standard for giving effect to child custody orders. If a child custody order has been issued by a court with proper jurisdiction under state law, the PKPA ensures that that order will be entitled to full faith and credit in another state.

Regarding child maltreatment, the PKPA provides that a state court has jurisdiction if state law grants that court jurisdiction over child maltreatment cases and "the child is physically present in such state and (i) the child has been abandoned, or (ii) it is necessary in an emergency to protect the child because the child, a sibling, or parent of the child has been subjected to or threatened with mistreatment or abuse."[133]

Returning briefly to our example involving Sally and her parents, while the California court's order would generally be entitled to full faith and credit under PKPA, the PKPA would permit the New York court to take steps to protect Sally from parental maltreatment. The California court, however, retains jurisdiction to modify its original custody order.[134]

The PKPA contains no requirement that the New York court notify either Sally's father or the California court of its protective actions regarding Sally. The UCCJA and UCCJEA, however, contain mechanisms for the New York court to notify the father in California and for the New York court to communicate with the California court.[135]

---

[130] For a more detailed discussion of the application of the UCCJA and the UCCJEA to interstate child protective proceedings, *see* § 11.4.5.

[131] 28 U.S.C. § 1738A.

[132] JOHN DEWITT GREGORY ET AL., UNDERSTANDING FAMILY LAW n. 109 at 435 (2001).

[133] 28 U.S.C. § 1738A(c)(2)(C).

[134] 28 U.S.C. § 1738A(f).

[135] *See, e.g.*, Section 108 of the UCCJEA (notice to party outside of the state); Section 110 of the UCCJEA (communicate with court with prior jurisdiction).

When child welfare proceedings trigger concerns regarding these uniform jurisdictional acts or the PKPA, these issues must be carefully analyzed and the requirements of the relevant statutes adhered to.

§ 8.5.3 Accessing Substance Abuse Treatment Records

According to a report issued by the DHHS in 1999, "alcohol and other drug abuse is recognized as a major contributing factor to child neglect and abuse and as one of the key barriers to family reunification."[136] While the numbers of families involved in the child welfare system that are impacted by substance abuse is unclear, estimates suggest that between one-third and two-thirds of the cases in the child welfare system are complicated by substance abuse. What is certainly clear is that a substantial number of families who come to the attention of child welfare authorities are so impacted.[137] Because of the high correlation between involvement in the child welfare system and substance abuse, obtaining records of a parent's substance abuse treatment is an issue that child welfare attorneys must confront at some point.

The provision of substance abuse treatment is heavily subsidized, either directly through subsidies that support treatment programs or indirectly though publicly funded medical insurance, such as Medicaid, that pays for treatment for individuals in need of these services. Federal law provides a broad grant of confidentiality protection for records relating to "any program or activity relating to substance abuse education, prevention, training, treatment, rehabilitation, or research which is conducted, regulated, or directly or indirectly assisted by any department or agency of the United States."[138] After establishing the confidentiality of these records, the statute provides a broad grant of authority to the Secretary of the DHHS to establish regulations implementing the statute.[139]

The statute provides an exception for treatment providers to report suspected child abuse or neglect.[140] Once the report of suspected child maltreatment has been made, the federal regulations implementing the statute make clear that the substance abuse treatment program may not provide additional information, such as diagnosis or prognosis, without the consent of the person receiving the treatment or a court order.[141]

An individual who receives substance abuse treatment may consent to the release of his or her records. For a recipient's consent to be valid, it must meet

---

[136] U.S. Dep't of Health and Human Servs., Blending Perspectives and Building Common Ground: A Report to Congress on Substance Abuse and Child Protection 4 (1999), available on the Children's Bureau's Web site at http://www.acf.hhs.gov/programs/cb.

[137] *Id.*

[138] 42 U.S.C. § 290dd-2(a).

[139] *Id.*

[140] 42 U.S.C. § 290dd-2(e).

[141] *See* 42 C.F.R. §§ 2.1 and 2.67.

numerous technical requirements.[142] Regardless of whether an individual consents to the release of the substance abuse treatment records, a court of competent jurisdiction may order the records released.[143] However, a court may order the records released only after application by a party seeking the release and a showing of "good cause" for the release.[144] The statute provides that "[i]n assessing good cause the court shall weigh the public interest and the need for disclosure against the injury to the patient, to the physician-patient relationship, and to the treatment services."[145]

A number of courts have considered the release of substance abuse treatment records in the child welfare context.[146]

§ 8.5.4 Health Insurance Portability and Accountability Act of 1996 (HIPAA)

Congress, recognizing that the advances in electronic technology could erode the privacy of health information, incorporated into HIPAA[147] federal privacy protections for individually identifiable health information. Under the HIPAA Privacy Rule, a provider (or other "covered entity") may not use or disclose protected health information except: (1) as the Privacy Rule permits or requires; or (2) as the individual who is the subject of the health information (or the individual's personal representative) authorizes in writing. In a section entitled "Effect on State Law," HIPAA establishes that its provisions override state law. The statute then goes on to delineate a number of exceptions to this general rule. One exception that is specifically addressed relates to child maltreatment. That provision provides: "Nothing in this part [42 USCS §§ 1320d et seq.] shall be construed to invalidate or limit the authority, power, or procedures established under any law providing for the reporting of . . . child abuse . . . or public health investigation or intervention."[148] Thus, HIPAA should not prevent reports of suspected maltreatment as mandated by state law from being made nor prevent access to information necessary to respond to alleged child maltreatment.

---

[142] 42 C.F.R. § 2.31.

[143] 42 U.S.C. § 290dd-2(b)(2)(c).

[144] *Id.*

[145] *Id.*

[146] *See, e.g., State v. Harger*, 804 S.W. 2d 35 (Mo. Ct. App. 1991); *In re Baby X*, 97 Mich. App. 111, 293 N.W. 2d 736 (1980) (public's interest in protection of child out weighs parent's interest in confidentiality of records); *In re B.S.*, 163 Vt. 445, 659 A.2d 1137 (1995) (family court erred in ordering the release of substance abuse treatment records).

[147] Pub. L. No. 104-191; 42 U.S.C. § 1320d.

[148] 42 U.S.C. § 1320d-7(b).

§ 8.5.5 Americans with Disabilities Act of 1990 (ADA)

The Americans with Disabilities Act of 1990 (ADA)[149] was enacted to elim-inate discrimination against persons with mental or physical disabilities and to require public entities to make reasonable accommodation for disabled per-sons.[150] Most courts considering the issue have determined that the ADA neither provides a defense to nor creates special obligations in a dependency or parental rights termination proceeding because those proceedings are not a "service, pro-gram, or activity" within the meaning of the ADA.[151]

Broadly, the ADA requires covered entities to make "reasonable accom-modations" to permit individuals with disabilities to participate in and derive the benefit of employment, public accommodations, and the like. The ADA applies to discrimination in employment, in public accommodations, and in programs and services provided by state and local governments.[152] In general, there are two concerns for practitioners of child welfare law regarding the ADA. First, the ADA's protective provisions apply to children and protect them from discrimi-nation based on their disabilities. Thus, for example, a childcare center must make an individualized determination as to whether a particular child's disability should be accommodated by the program.[153] Because the ADA protects children in a number of circumstances, children's lawyers should become familiar with its provisions and use it when necessary to assure that clients' needs are met.

The second reason for concern is the application of the ADA to efforts pro-vided by state child welfare agencies to reunify families. State courts have split regarding whether the ADA applies to efforts made by state agencies to reuni-fy children with their natural parents after a finding of child abuse and neglect. Some state courts have determined that the ADA does not apply to reunifica-tion efforts.[154] Other courts have held that the ADA does apply at least in some form to the provision of services to parents and children in an effort to reunify.[155] When courts have held that the ADA applies in the child welfare context, they have typically found that the "reasonable accommodation" requirements of the ADA are satisfied if the state has met its burden to make "reasonable efforts"

---

[149] Pub. L. No. 101-336; 42 U.S.C. §§ 12101 through 12213.

[150] 42 U.S.C. § 12101(b).

[151] For example, *see In re B.S.*, 166 Vt. 345, 693 A.2d 716 (1997); *Adoption of Gregory*, 434 Mass. 117, 747 N.E.2d 120 (2001).

[152] 42 U.S.C. §§ 12101 through 12213.

[153] *See* U.S. DEPT. OF JUSTICE, CIVIL RIGHTS DIV., COMMONLY ASKED QUESTIONS ABOUT CHILD CARE CENTERS AND THE AMERICANS WITH DISABILITIES ACT, *available at* http://www.usdoj.gov/crt/ada/childq&a.htm.

[154] *See, e.g., State v. Raymond C.* (In re Torrance P.), 187 Wis. 2d 10, 522 N.W.2d 243 (1994); *Stone v. Daviess County Div. of Children & Family Servs.*, 656 N.E.2d 824 (Ind. Ct. App. 1995); *In re Karrlo K.*, 40 Conn. App. 73, 668 A.2d 1353 (1996).

[155] *See, e.g., In re Terry*, 610 N.W.2d 563 (Mich. Ct. App. 2000).

as required by the federal child welfare funding legislation.[156] The ADA does not provide a defense to a termination of parental rights action.[157] However, disabled parents involved in child welfare proceedings have the right to reasonable access to the courts, including physical access to the courthouse and provision of court interpreters where necessary.

Counsel should be aware of the ADA's potential applicability to child protection proceedings and should carefully consider its provisions, as well as the relevant case law, in determining how to proceed.

§ 8.5.6 Individuals with Disabilities Education Act (IDEA)

The Individuals with Disabilities Education Act (IDEA)[158] provides funding to states to ensure that all children, regardless of disability, have the right to free, appropriate public education. Parents or "surrogate parents" (often the child's foster parent, CASA, or specially trained adult appointed by the court for children in care) are entitled to participate in meetings concerning the child's eligibility for and participation in special education programs.[159] If the child qualifies, the school must provide an Individualized Education Program (IEP), which must be reviewed periodically.[160] The parent or surrogate parent has a right to participate in the formulation of the IEP and may present independent expert or multidisciplinary evidence at the IEP meeting. The IEP must state specifically how the child's disability affects his or her educational performance and must include specific, measurable goals and objectives and the services to be provided to remedy or accommodate the child's deficiencies.[161] There is an administrative review procedure, which includes a due process hearing and an administrative appeal, and, ultimately, provision for court review and attorney fees.

In general, the act favors mainstreaming children in their local schools and regular classrooms to the maximum extent that is appropriate, and requires that schools provide related services needed to enable that student to achieve educational goals. Where necessary, however, school districts can be required to pay even for residential private schools if the district cannot otherwise meet the child's educational needs.

Once approved, the IEP is implemented, and then it is revised, as needed, by the IEP team. The school is not permitted to change the child's placement,

---

[156] *See, e.g., In re C.M.*, 526 N.W.2d 562 (Iowa Ct. App. 1994); *J.T. v. Arkansas Dep't. of Human Servs.*, 329 Ark. 243, 947 S.W.2d 761 (1997); *Robinson v. Department of Social & Health Servs., (In re A.J.R.)*, 78 Wn. App. 222, 896 P.2d 1298 (1995); *In re Angel B.*, 659 A.2d 277 (Me. Sup. Ct. 1995).

[157] *See People v. T.B.*, 12 P.3d 1221 (Colo. App. 2000); *In re Terry*, 610 N.W.2d 563 (Mich. Ct. App. 2000).

[158] 20 U.S.C. §§ 1400 through 1487.

[159] 20 U.S.C. § 1415(b).

[160] 20 U.S.C. § 1401(14); 20 U.S.C. § 1414(d).

[161] 20 U.S.C. § 1414(d)(1)(A)(i).

except for a limited time for specified reasons (*e.g.*, up to 45-day removal due to a student's possession of drugs or weapons), without an approved revision in the IEP, unless the behavior that led to the removal was unrelated to the disability; in that case, regular school disciplinary rules and procedures apply.

IDEA also provides special education programs for qualified preschool children, including services even to infants.

§ 8.5.7 Education for Homeless Children and Youths Act

The Education for Homeless Children and Youths Act[162] provides that homeless children and youth be given a free and appropriate public education and that they be permitted to remain in their schools despite not having a residential address within the district. The Act also prohibits segregation of homeless children and youth in the school.[163] For purposes of the Act, the definition of "homeless children and youths" explicitly include those who "are living in motels, hotels, trailer parks, or camping grounds due to the lack of alternative adequate accommodations; are living in emergency or transitional shelters; are abandoned in hospitals; or are awaiting foster care placement" and "children and youths who are living in cars, parks, public spaces, abandoned buildings, substandard housing, bus or train stations, or similar settings."[164]

Schools are not permitted to require proof of residency, provision of birth or medical or school records, or proof of guardianship in order to admit homeless youth to school.[165] Students must be given full access to school enrollment (including pre-school, school lunch and breakfast, after-school programs, etc.) pending the school obtaining any records.[166] To the extent feasible and unless that is contrary to the wishes of the child's parent or guardian, a homeless child is entitled to remain in his or her "school of origin," the school he or she attended when permanently housed or the one in which the child was last enrolled so long as the child remains homeless.[167] This provision would apply, for example, to a child who disrupts from a foster home while that child is in a shelter awaiting further placement. The student is entitled to receive transportation to and from school. Instead of attending the "school of origin," the custodial parent or guardian may elect to have the homeless child attend any public school that other children living in the same attendance area may attend.

---

[162] 42 U.S.C. §§ 11431 through 11435.

[163] 42 U.S.C. § 11432(e)(3).

[164] 42 U.S.C. § 11434a(2)(B).

[165] *See* 42 U.S.C. § 11432(g)(1)(H).

[166] 42 U.S.C. § 11432(g)(3)(C)(i).

[167] 42 U.S.C. § 11432(g)(3)(A), 11432(g)(1)(J)(iii).

§ 8.5.8 Children's Health Act of 2000

The Children's Health Act of 2000[168] included new provisions regarding the rights of residents of federally assisted hospitals and other health care facilities to be free from physical or mental abuse, corporal punishment, and any restraints or involuntary seclusions imposed for purposes of discipline or convenience.[169] The Act also included new provisions regarding the rights of children and youth in federally assisted non-medical community-based facilities for children and youth, tightly circumscribing the use of physical restraints and seclusion.[170]

§ 8.5.9 Family Education Rights and Privacy Act of 1974 (FERPA)

The Family Education Rights and Privacy Act of 1974 (FERPA)[171] provides that federal education funding will be provided to state educational agencies only if they comply with certain privacy and access rights regarding educational records. Under the Act, absent a court order providing otherwise, parents have the right to inspect and review their minor children's education records and to challenge errors in the records.

However, information covered by FERPA is discoverable for child welfare legal cases. FERPA permits the release of education records pursuant to state law, including court orders and subpoenas. It provides, in part:

(b) Release of education records; parental consent requirement; exceptions; compliance with judicial orders and subpoenas. . . .

(1) No funds shall be made available under any applicable program to any educational agency or institution which has a policy or practice of permitting the release of educational records . . . of students without the written consent of their parents to any individual, agency, or organization, other than to the following—

* * *

(E) State and local officials or authorities to whom such information is specifically allowed to be reported or disclosed pursuant to State statute adopted—

* * *

(ii) after November 19, 1974, if—

* * *

(II) the officials and authorities to whom such information is disclosed certify in writing to the educational agency or institution that the informa-

---

[168] Pub. L. No. 106-310; 42 U.S.C. § 290jj.

[169] 42 U.S.C. § 290ii.

[170] 42 U.S.C. § 290jj.

[171] Pub. L. No. 93-380; 20 U.S.C. § 1232g.

tion will not be disclosed to any other party except
as provided under State law without the prior written consent of the parent or the student.[172]

Moreover, FERPA requires that school reports be released pursuant to either a
court's order or subpoena, although the parent and child must be notified that
the order or subpoena has been issued.[173] Thus, FERPA provides no barrier to
counsel obtaining access to a child's educational records, although it mandates,
as a contingency to receiving federal funding, that certain procedures be followed.[174]

§ 8.6 Current Federal Funding for Other Supports for Children and Families

There are a number of other federal programs that are not exclusively—or
even primarily—designed to serve abused or neglected children and their families, but that may be available, at least in part, to do so. Some are federal programs through which qualifying individuals may request particular assistance
from the local, state, or federal agency (*e.g.*, Temporary Assistance for Needy
Families, Medicaid, and Food Stamps). Others are federal block grants to states
for particular types of services; states establish services of the specified types,
and families may request assistance from state or local agencies (*e.g.*, Social
Services Block Grants and the Maternal and Child Health Block Grant). Some
of these federal programs include at least some amount of direct funding for
child welfare purposes (*e.g.*, TANF and SSBG); others are supports generally
available to assist categories of children and families, with some children and
families who are involved in the child welfare system included in those categories (*e.g.*, Food Stamps, Child Care, and Title I Education for the
Disadvantaged). Some, such as Foster Care and Adoption Assistance, are open-
ended entitlements, meaning that federal funding automatically expands or contracts each year to provide the defined benefit for all eligible persons (*e.g.*,
Medicaid and Food Stamps); most programs are funded at a specified level, not
directly dependent on the level of need (*e.g.*, TANF and SSBG).

The following are the significant federal programs that support assistance for
qualifying individuals—and include substantial child welfare services funding.

---

[172] 20 U.S.C. § 1232g(b)(1)(E).

[173] 20 U.S.C. § 1232g(b)(2)(B).

[174] *See Gonzaga Univ. v. Doe*, 536 U.S. 273 (2002) (addressing a case in which plaintiff asserted
that FERPA granted a private cause of action for release of educational records pursuant to
state law to a professional licensing board).

§ 8.6.1 Temporary Assistance for Needy Families (TANF)

Temporary Assistance for Needy Families (TANF)[175] is a block grant to states created in 1996 as the successor to the open-ended entitlement program called Aid to Families with Dependent Children (AFDC). Funded at $16.5 billion in Fiscal Year 2004, TANF funds time-limited (up to 5 years) financial assistance[176] to more than 2 million low-income families with children. Assistance is contingent on participants meeting work-hour requirements, and TANF also provides some work supports to participants (*e.g.*, training, child care, transportation). Most families who are TANF beneficiaries consist of children residing with their parents, but more than 12 percent of families who are TANF beneficiaries are children residing with grandparents or other non-parent relatives,[177] some of whom are providing care for the children after their removal from parents' care because of child abuse or neglect. In fact, TANF is a significant source of funding for child welfare services; according to the Urban Institute,[178] more than $1.7 billion in TANF funds are used for child welfare services, including out-of-home placements (*e.g.*, the kinship care situations described above), adoption, and other services. In addition, a portion (up to 10 percent) of TANF funds may be transferred by states to the Social Services Block Grant (Title XX), which also funds many child welfare services.

§ 8.6.2 Medicaid

Medicaid[179] was enacted in 1965, in the same legislation[180] that created the Medicare program, which ensures health care for senior citizens. Medicaid is an entitlement program targeted at low-income individuals, although income eligibility levels, services covered, and reimbursements to providers vary somewhat from state to state. In fiscal year 2004, federal Medicaid costs were over $180 billion. Over half of the more than 44 million people enrolled in Medicaid are under the age of 19 (including over 760,000 children in foster care), although only 16 percent of federal Medicaid expenditures are for children (those in foster care and other children) due to their far lower costs of care compared to costs for senior citizens and the disabled.

---

[175] Pub. L. No. 104-193; Social Security Act, Title IV-A; 42 U.S.C. §§ 601 through 619.

[176] In 2002, average monthly benefits ranged from $154 per month in South Carolina to $631 per month in Alaska. HOUSE COMM. ON WAYS AND MEANS, 2004 GREEN BOOK 7-36, tbl.7-32 (Pub. 108-6, 2004), *available at* http://waysandmeans.house.gov/media/pdf/greenbook2003/Section7.pdf.

[177] *Id.* at 7-91 to 7-92 & tbl.7-32.

[178] THE URBAN INST., THE COST OF PROTECTING VULNERABLE CHILDREN III: WHAT FACTORS AFFECT STATES' FISCAL DECISIONS?, Occasional Paper No. 61, at 18 tbl.4 (2002).

[179] Social Security Act, Title XIX; 42 U.S.C. §§ 1396 through 1396v.

[180] Pub. L. No. 89-97.

Eligibility

States are required to cover pregnant women and children under age 6 with family incomes below 133 percent of poverty,[181] and children over age 5 and under age 19 in families below the poverty line. States have the option to also cover pregnant women and infants under 1 year of age whose family income is between 133 and 185 percent of poverty (36 states do so). States must provide Medicaid to recipients of Title IV-E foster care and adoption assistance under age 18, and have the option (under the Chafee Act) to extend Medicaid coverage to former foster care recipients aged 18, 19, or 20. States also have the option of covering certain other young people under age 21, and states often use that option to cover children in state-sponsored foster care and children who are institutionalized. States are precluded from imposing cost-sharing on services for children under 18 or services related to pregnancy.

Benefits

Medicaid includes both mandatory services (*e.g.*, hospitalization, lab and x-ray fees, family planning and pregnancy-related services, family nurse practitioners, and physicians' services), and optional services (*e.g.*, eyeglasses, prescription drugs, dental care, and case management). In addition, children under age 21 are entitled to receive preventative care through "Early and Periodic Screening, Diagnosis and Treatment" (EPSDT), including comprehensive physical exams, immunizations, lead screening, vision and dental services, and other health care to address any conditions identified through the exams. About half of the children who receive Medicaid services receive them through managed care.[182]

According to the Urban Institute, Medicaid provides $781 million in child welfare services (beyond routine medical services), such as targeted case management and rehabilitative services.[183]

§ 8.6.3 State Children's Health Insurance Program (SCHIP)

In 1997, Congress established the State Children's Health Insurance Program (SCHIP)[184] under a new Title XXI of the Social Security Act. Unlike Medicaid, SCHIP is not an open-ended entitlement for qualifying individuals. SCHIP provides approximately $5 billion in federal funding to states, and states

---

[181] For 2003, the federal poverty threshold for a single parent with two children was $14,824 in annual income, for two parents with two children it is $18,660, and for a single parent with three children it was $18,725.

[182] HOUSE COMM. ON WAYS AND MEANS, 2004 GREEN BOOK, at 15-MEDICAID-33 to 15-MEDICAID-39 & tbl.15-MEDICAID-8 (Pub. 108-6, 2004), *available at* http://waysandmeans.house.gov/media/pdf/greenbook2003/MEDICAID.pdf.

[183] THE URBAN INST., THE COST OF PROTECTING VULNERABLE CHILDREN III: WHAT FACTORS AFFECT STATES' FISCAL DECISIONS?, Occasional Paper No. 61, at 18 tbl.4 (2002).

[184] Pub. L. No. 105-33; Social Security Act, Title XXI; 42 U.S.C. §§ 1397aa through 1397f.

may cover children under age 19 in families above Medicaid income eligibility but below a specified income level; about half of the states have established an upper income limit of 200 percent of poverty, with the rest of the states evenly split between those with higher income limits and those with lower income limits. In designing their SCHIP programs, states may expand their Medicaid program, create a new separate state insurance program, or combine the two approaches. States that choose to expand Medicaid to new eligibles under SCHIP must provide the full range of mandatory services as well as optional services specified in their state Medicaid plans. SCHIP enrollment is 5.3 million children, including 4 million in separate state programs and 1.3 million in Medicaid expansions.[185]

§ 8.6.4 Supplemental Security Income (SSI)

Supplemental Security Income (SSI)[186] is a means-tested federally administered income assistance entitlement program established in 1972. In 2002, it provided $34.6 billion for monthly cash payments[187] to 6.8 million qualifying needy individuals who are aged, blind, or disabled, more than 914,000 of whom were children, some of whom were in foster care.

SSI supports more than $73 million in funding for children in out-of-home placements. States have an incentive to ensure SSI funding for eligible children in foster care, since SSI is fully federally funded—there is no required state match, as there is for IV-E foster care and Medicaid.[188]

Eligibility

To qualify for SSI, children under 18 must have "a medically determinable physical or mental impairment which results in marked and severe functional limitations, and which can be expected to result in death or which has lasted or can be expected to last for a continuous period of not less than 12 months."[189]

§ 8.6.5 Other Federally Sponsored Assistance

Other federally sponsored assistance may be available to help qualifying children and families, including those in the child welfare system. Some of these assistance programs are listed below. In appropriate cases, attorneys in child welfare cases should take necessary actions to ensure that relevant services and

---

[185] HOUSE COMM. ON WAYS AND MEANS, 2004 GREEN BOOK 15-SCHIP-9 & tbl.15-SCHIP-1 (Pub. 108-6, 2004), *available at* http://waysandmeans.house.gov/media/pdf/greenbook2003/SCHIP.pdf.

[186] Pub. L. No. 92-603; Social Security Act, Title XVI; 42 U.S.C. §§ 1381 through 1383(d).

[187] The monthly federal benefit rate for individuals was $552 in 2003. HOUSE COMM. ON WAYS AND MEANS, 2004 GREEN BOOK 3-3 (Pub. 108-6, 2004), *available at* http://waysandmeans. house.gov/media/pdf/greenbook2003/Section3.pdf.

[188] THE URBAN INST., THE COST OF PROTECTING VULNERABLE CHILDREN III: WHAT FACTORS AFFECT STATES' FISCAL DECISIONS?, Occasional Paper No. 61, at 18 tbl.4 (2002).

[189] HOUSE COMM. ON WAYS AND MEANS, 2004 GREEN BOOK 3-1 to 3-70 (Pub. 108-6, 2004).

supports (for children and for their parents or other caretakers) and relevant placements for children—including those services and placements supported through the federal funding streams discussed in this chapter—are provided.

Nutrition Assistance Programs

Nutrition assistance programs include:

- Food Stamps,[190] which is a means-tested entitlement that enabled 8.2 million low-income households to receive over $18 billion in nutritional support in 2002—on average, just over $180 monthly per household.

- The Special Supplemental Nutrition Program for Women, Infants, and Children (WIC),[191] which is a non-entitlement program that in 2002 provided $4.5 billion in federal nutrition support—food, nutrition education, and service referrals—to about 7.5 million low-income pregnant women and children up to age 5 each month.

- Child Nutrition Programs,[192] which include School Lunch ($6.8 billion in fiscal year 2004), School Breakfast ($1.8 billion in fiscal year 2004), Special Milk ($14 million in fiscal year 2004), Child/Adult Care Food ($2 billion in fiscal year 2004), and Summer Food ($281 million in fiscal year 2004).

Section 8 Housing Assistance

Section 8 Housing Assistance[193] is a non-entitlement program providing $19.3 billion in rental assistance so 3 million low-income eligible families can afford decent housing.

Child Care and Development Block Grant (CCDBG)

The Child Care and Development Block Grant (CCDBG),[194] provided $4.8 billion in fiscal year 2004 for child care assistance to low-income working parents of nearly 3.2 million children under age 13.

Head Start

Head Start[195] is a non-entitlement program established in 1965, which provided $6.8 billion in fiscal year 2004 to support quality early childhood education opportunities and comprehensive services for over 900,000 low-income children

---

[190] The Food Stamps program was established in 1977 by Pub. L. No. 88-525; 7 U.S.C. §§ 2011 through 2036.

[191] 42 U.S.C. § 1786.

[192] 42 U.S.C. §§ 1751 through 1790.

[193] 42 U.S.C. §§ 1437 through 13664.

[194] 42 U.S.C. § 9858.

[195] 42 U.S.C. §§ 9831 through 9843a.

to ensure they are ready for kindergarten and prepared to succeed in school and life.

Post-Secondary Education Loans, Grants, and Work-Study

Higher Education Act (Title IV) post-secondary education loans, grants, and work-study[196] provided $14 billion in fiscal year 2004 for student financial aid, including:

- Federal "Pell Grants."

- Federal "Ford Direct Loans."

- Three Campus-Based Programs that include the Federal "Perkins Loan," the Federal Supplemental Educational Opportunity Grant, and Federal Work-Study.

- Federally guaranteed loans from private lenders (federal "Stafford Loans" to students and federal "PLUS loans" to parents).

Block Grants to States and Localities

A number of federal block grants to states and localities support state and local programs that may serve abused or neglected children and their families, such as:

- Social Services Block Grants to states (SSBG):[197] Of the $1.7 billion available for a wide variety of state social services expenditures, approximately $260 million is used for child protective services, foster care services, and adoption services for more than 1.8 million children.[198] Additional SSBG funds serve abused and neglected children, as well (*e.g.*, case management, counseling, home-based, independent living, prevention and intervention services), for a total of $900 million (over half) of SSBG funding spent on child welfare services.[199]

- Maternal and Child Health Block Grant[200] (funded at $730 million for fiscal year 2004).

- Substance Abuse and Mental Health Services Grants[201] (funded at $3.2 billion in fiscal year 2004).

---

[196] 20 U.S.C. §§ 1070 through 1087-2; 42 U.S.C. §§ 2751 through 2756b.

[197] Social Security Act, Title XX; 42 U.S.C. §§ 1397 through 1397f.

[198] ADMIN. FOR CHILDREN & FAMILIES, U.S. DEP'T OF HEALTH AND HUMAN SERVS., SSBG 2002: HELPING STATES SERVE THE NEEDS OF AMERICA'S FAMILIES, ADULTS AND CHILDREN (2002).

[199] THE URBAN INST., THE COST OF PROTECTING VULNERABLE CHILDREN III: WHAT FACTORS AFFECT STATES' FISCAL DECISIONS?, Occasional Paper No. 61, at 18 tbl.4 (2002).

[200] Social Security Act, Title V; 42 U.S.C. §§ 701 through 716.

[201] 42 U.S.C. §§ 300x-1 through 300x-9.

- Title I Education for the Disadvantaged[202] (funded at $14.4 billion in fiscal year 2004).

- Workforce Investment Act,[203] which provides for youth and adult employment assistance, including Job Corps (funded at $5.1 billion in fiscal year 2004).

- McKinney-Vento Homeless Assistance Act programs in the Department of Housing and Urban Development[204] ($1.26 billion for HUD Homeless Assistance, including Emergency Shelter Grants, Supportive Housing Program, Single Room Occupancy Dwellings Program, Shelter Plus Care Program), as well as the Runaway and Homeless Youth Act programs in the Department of Health and Human Services[205] ($105 million in fiscal year 2004 for Basic Centers, Transitional Living, and Street Outreach), and Education for Homeless Children and Youth[206] (funded at $60 million in fiscal year 2004).

- Juvenile Justice and Delinquency Prevention programs[207] (funded at $349 million in fiscal year 2004).

Other Federal Laws

Other federal laws that may be relevant include:

- The federal Child Support Enforcement Program[208] ($4.4 billion to assist states in locating noncustodial parents and including operating the Federal Parent Locator Service, establishing paternity, and enforcing support obligations of noncustodial parents).

- A variety of federal funding streams and statutory requirements under the Violence Against Women Act of 1994 (VAWA)[209] and the Victims of Trafficking and Violence Protection Act of 2000,[210] including a provision granting full faith and credit for domestic violence protective orders entered by state or tribal courts in compliance with the VAWA.

---

[203] 29 U.S.C. §§ 2801 through 2945.

[204] 42 U.S.C. § 11301.

[205] 42 U.S.C. §§ 5701 through 5785.

[206] 42 U.S.C. §§ 11431 through 11435.

[207] 42 U.S.C. §§ 5601 through 5785.

[208] Social Security Act, Title IV-D; 42 U.S.C. §§ 651 through 669b.

[209] Pub L. No. 103-322; 18 U.S.C. § 2265.

[210] Pub. L. No. 106-386.

§ 8.7 Sally's Case: Applying Selected Federal Funding Streams and Statutory Requirements

An at-risk (low-income, first-time, single) mom, during pregnancy, gets pre-natal and post-natal nurse home visits; the risk of child abuse/neglect is averted.	Title IV-B Promoting Safe and Stable Families funding and CAPTA Community-Based Prevention support this up-front prevention (prior to any report or suspicion of abuse/neglect).
Meanwhile, nearby, a teacher observes Sally, age 6, with black and blue marks on arms and swollen lip; her explanation of falling does not fit the injuries. Teacher calls hotline.	CAPTA requirement for mandatory reporting (and good faith immunity for reporters) of suspected child abuse/neglect by teachers, etc.
Child protective services worker receives report of suspected abuse, investigates, and substantiates abuse.	CAPTA state grants funding supports child protective services investigation of report.
Sally is removed from her mother's home; a petition of child abuse is filed in court, and the court appoints attorney/guardian ad litem.	CAPTA requirement for appointment of guardians ad litem for abused/neglected children who are the subject of court cases.
Sally is placed in foster care.	Title IV-E foster care pays for part of the costs of foster care (the state match pays for the rest). The agency also trains and licenses foster parents using IV-E funding, and conducts criminal background checks on the foster parents.
An initial hearing is held; attorney for Sally's mother argues that agency failed to make "reasonable efforts" to prevent Sally's placement in foster care.	Title IV-E foster care requirement that agency make "reasonable efforts" to prevent placement, while keeping safety of child the paramount consideration.
Sally's guardian ad litem investigates whether another state's court has exclusive continuing jurisdiction due to the divorce-related joint custody order entered where the family resided previously.	Parental Kidnapping Prevention Act determines court jurisdiction (all family members have since moved away from the state in which the joint custody order was issued; there is thus no continuing jurisdiction).

Sally's school performance begins to deteriorate; she cries often; the social worker refers her for therapy.	Medicaid covers the costs of weekly therapeutic treatment.
Meanwhile, the social worker's investigation determines that Sally's mother has a drug abuse problem.	Sally's mother receives drug abuse treatment through a program funded by the federal Substance Abuse block grant.
The social worker also develops contract with Sally's mother; Sally's mother promises to continue drug abuse treatment and anger management sessions.	Anger management sessions are supported through the Title XX Social Services Block Grant.
At an adjudication hearing, the court determines that Sally was abused, but that Sally may now be safely returned home, under protective supervision of agency.	Title IV-B Child Welfare Services supports in-home services for family.
Sally's mother drops out of drug treatment and anger management sessions; Sally arrives at school dirty, tired, and hungry; her mother hadn't come back after going out the day before; the agency places Sally with her grandmother.	Grandmother does not want to become licensed foster care provider; she gets TANF support to help with costs of caring for Sally ("kinship care").
Sally's grandmother is overwhelmed and thus unable to care for Sally for long; Sally's mother still hasn't completed drug treatment or anger management; Sally re-enters foster care.	IV-E foster care payments resume.
The court holds a disposition hearing; the agency's permanency goal is still to return Sally home.	Title XX and SAMHSA-funded services are again offered and partially completed by Sally's mother.
A year after Sally's placement, she remains in foster care (her mother keeps dropping out of drug treatment); the court holds a permanency planning hearing.	Title IV-E foster care requirement for such hearings.

Sally's mother stops all visits and treatment; the agency's permanency goal is changed to adoption; TPR is filed just before Sally has been in care 15 of the last 22 months.	Title IV-E foster care timeframe for such TPR filing.
Sally is placed in a preadoptive foster care home. TPR and adoption are finalized, and Sally is happy and well-adjusted in her safe, permanent home.	Title IV-E adoption assistance payments are provided, since Sally's emotional challenges make her a "special needs" child for purposes of adoption subsidies.

Chapter 9   CHILD WELFARE CONSTITUTIONAL CASE LAW

by Amanda George Donnelly[1] and Ann M. Haralambie[2]

The following U.S. Supreme Court cases form the constitutional parameters for the relationship between the state, parents, and children.

§ 9.1 Parent's Rights

§ 9.1.1 *Meyer v. Nebraska*

The Supreme Court, in *Meyer v. Nebraska*,[3] addressed a parent's right to control the education of his or her child. A parochial school teacher was criminally charged and convicted for teaching German to a ten-year-old child in violation of a statute prohibiting teaching in a language other than English or teaching a foreign language to children who had not completed the eighth grade. The Supreme Court held that the concept of liberty, as protected by the Fourteenth Amendment, denotes "not merely freedom from bodily restraint but also the right of the individual to contract, to engage in any of the common occupations of life, to acquire useful knowledge, to marry, establish a home and bring up children, to worship God according to the dictates of his own conscience, and generally to enjoy those privileges long recognized at common law as essential to the orderly pursuit of happiness by free men."[4]

The Court concluded that the statute was unconstitutional. It held that the teacher had a constitutionally protected liberty interest in teaching. Furthermore, the parents had a constitutionally protected liberty interest in educating their children. The Court noted that "[m]ere knowledge of the German language cannot reasonably be regarded as harmful. Heretofore it has been commonly looked upon as helpful and desirable. Plaintiff in error taught this language in school as part of his occupation. His right thus to teach and the right of parents to engage him so to instruct their children, we think, are within the liberty of the Amendment. . . . Latin, Greek, Hebrew are not proscribed; but German, French,

---

[1] Amanda George Donnelly, J.D., is Staff Attorney at the National Association of Counsel for Children (NACC).

[2] Ann M. Haralambie, J.D., is a certified family law specialist practicing in Tucson, Arizona. She is also an author and speaker in the fields of family and children's law.

Thank you to Frank Vandervort, J.D., Clinical Assistant Professor of Law at the Child Advocacy Law Clinic of the University of Michigan Law School for his assistance editing this chapter.

[3] 262 U.S. 390 (1923).

[4] *Id.* at 399.

Spanish, Italian, and every other alien speech are within the ban. Evidently the Legislature has attempted materially to interfere with the calling of modern language teachers, with the opportunities of pupils to acquire knowledge, and with the power of parents to control the education of their own."[5]

§ 9.1.2 *Pierce v. Society of Sisters*

In *Pierce v. Society of Sisters*,[6] the Supreme Court addressed a parent's right to decide the school his or her child attends. The constitutionality of a compulsory education law that required that children be educated in public schools was at question. A parochial school and a private school sought to enjoin the law, which prevented parents from sending children to their schools. The Supreme Court held that the statute was unconstitutional. It stated that although the state had the power to require children to attend school, it could not dictate which school a child attends.

The Oregon Compulsory Education Act required every child between the ages of 8 and 16 years to attend public schools. Oregon argued that the state had the authority to require children to attend schools, and that compulsory public school attendance did not deprive parents of their rights.

Private school representatives argued that the statute infringed on the rights of private and parochial schools, the freedom of private and parochial school teachers, the free choice of parents and guardians, and the rights of children. The schools contended that the sole intent of the statute was to end private and parochial schools, not to assimilate foreigners. They alleged that the power of the state to create public schools did not include the power to prevent the formation of other schools. The Court concluded that the law unreasonably infringed on a parent's right to direct the upbringing of children in his or her care.

§ 9.1.3 *Prince v. Massachusetts*

In *Prince v. Massachusetts*,[7] a woman who was the guardian of her niece was criminally convicted for violating child labor laws. She furnished her niece with Jehovah's Witness magazines, which the child then sold in the street. The Supreme Court explained that state law restricting child labor, which prohibited a child from distributing religious pamphlets, did not violate the parent's or guardian's First Amendment right to religious freedom.

The Court weighed the private interest in freedom of religion against society's interest in protecting the welfare of children. The court found that neither the rights of religion nor the rights of parenthood are beyond limitation. The court noted that each state had a wide range of power for limiting parental

---

[5] *Id.* at 400-401.

[6] 268 U.S. 510 (1925).

[7] 321 U.S. 158 (1944).

freedom, even in matters of conscience and religious conviction. The court also noted that the state has broader power to regulate the conduct of children than its power to regulate adult behavior. The legislative intent behind the child labor law was to prevent the negative effects of child employment and the possible harms inherent in street activities. Although the child's aunt accompanied her during the sales, the court concluded that this activity nonetheless violated the state law.

In addressing the appellant's equal protection argument, the Court rejected the assertion that the street was the Jehovah's Witness' temple. It held that there was no denial of equal protection since the state law excluded all children from selling items on the street, regardless of their religious affiliation.

§ 9.1.4 *Troxel v. Granville*

Troxel v. Granville[8] involved the constitutionality of Washington's third-party visitation statute. The statute provided that any person could petition the court for visitation rights at any time and that the court could grant visitation rights whenever visitation may serve the best interest of the child. The grandparents petitioned a Washington court for the right to visit their granddaughters. The children's mother agreed to grandparent visitation but wanted the visits to be limited to one day each month. The court granted the grandparent's request for visitation over the objections of the children's mother. The children's mother appealed the visitation order. The court of appeals reversed the lower court's order. The grandparent's appealed, and the Washington Supreme Court affirmed the appellate court's decision. The U.S. Supreme Court granted certiorari to consider the constitutionality of the Washington statute.

In a plurality opinion, the U.S. Supreme Court found that the statute violated the mother's due process liberty interest in the care, custody, and control of her children. The Court pointed out that the statute did not provide any deference to the parent's wishes and left the question of what was in the children's best interest solely to the judge. The Court reaffirmed the presumption that fit parents can make decision that are in the best interests of their children and affirmed the Washington Supreme Court's order. The Court noted that it was not holding that all nonparental visitation statutes violated the due process clause per se. The decision in this case was based on the breadth of the Washington statute.

Note: Parameters of Parents' Rights. Taken together, these early cases, *Meyer, Pierce,* and *Prince,* set the basic parameters of the relationship between parent and state. They establish the principle that parents have a fundamental liberty interest in directing the upbringing of their children, which is protected

---

[8]   530 U.S. 57 (2000).

by the Due Process Clause of the Fourteenth Amendment on which the state may infringe only for compelling reason and only insofar as that infringement is necessary to protect the state's interest. This basic framework has guided the courts' analysis of issues involving family life in a variety of circumstances, including matters pertaining to child welfare law.[9]

§ 9.2 Constitutional Rights of Children and Youth

§ 9.2.1 *In re Gault*

In this landmark case, *In re Gault*,[10] the Supreme Court declared that neither the Fourteenth Amendment nor the Bill of Rights is exclusively for adults. The Arizona juvenile court committed Gerald Gault, a 15-year-old delinquent, to the state industrial school until his 21st birthday. The court administered a typically informal proceeding. The proceeding took place in chambers where the judge questioned the juvenile. The alleged victim was not present, no witnesses were sworn, and no transcript was made of the proceeding. Gault was given no notice of charges, no counsel, no protection from self-incrimination, and no opportunity to confront and cross-examine his accuser. The juvenile court reasoned that because children had no right to liberty they could be denied due process. Furthermore, the juvenile court argued that the lack of procedural protection did not violate any rights because a child had none.

The Supreme Court held that the due process clause of the Fourteenth Amendment applied to delinquency adjudicatory proceedings. Specifically, the Court included:

- The right to notice of charges.

- The right to confrontation.

- The right to cross-examination.

- The prohibition against self-incrimination.

- The right to counsel.

Under *Gault*, youth accused of violating the law have essentially the same rights as adults and they are recognized as independent persons, not merely property of their parents.

---

[9]   *See, generally, Wisconsin v. Yoder*, 406 U.S. 205 (1972) (right of Amish parents to direct educational aspects of their children's upbringing pursuant to their religious convictions); *Moore v. East Cleveland*, 431 U.S. 494 (1977) (invalidating housing ordinance making it illegal for a grandchild to live in grandparent's home); *Troxel v. Granville*, 530 U.S. 57 (2000) (right of fit parent to determine grandparent visitation).

[10]   387 U.S. 1 (1967).

Note: It is important to recognize that Gault did not address the representation of children in abuse, neglect, and dependency proceedings. As of 2004, there does not exist a federal requirement for legal representation of children involved in dependency proceedings. The Child Abuse Prevention and Treatment Act (CAPTA)[11] requires that a "representative" be appointed to children involved in dependency proceedings. The CAPTA requirement, however, is not for an attorney representative. Therefore, many children are appointed lay representatives who can be court-appointed special advocates, lay guardians ad litem, or other volunteers. Advocates have argued for the establishment of Gault-like requirements for dependency proceedings. One such argument is contained in Jacob Smiles article, "A Child's Due Process Right to Legal Counsel in Abuse and Neglect Dependency Proceedings."[12] Mr. Smiles argues that the *Mathews v. Eldridge*[13] due process test, which is described below, can be used to assert a child's entitlement to legal counsel in dependency cases.

In *Mathews v. Eldridge*,[14] the U.S. Supreme Court applied a three-part test to determine whether a state action deprived a citizen of his due process rights. While this case does not deal with children's law, it is important because it outlined the factors the court must look at in determining whether due process rights have been violated. The Court, citing *Morrissey v. Brewer*, 408 U.S. 471, 481 (1972), stated that "[D]ue process is flexible and calls for such procedural protections as the particular situation demands."[15] To determine what the "situation demands," courts must weigh three factors: (1) "The private interest that will be affected;" (2) "The risk of an erroneous deprivation" of the private individual's interest "through the procedures used" and the probable benefits of additional procedural requirements; and (3) the Government's interest, including "fiscal and administrative burdens" that might result from additional procedural requirements.[16]

Recently, applying the three-part *Matthews* test to the question of whether a child has a due process right to legal counsel in neglect proceedings, the United States District Court for the Northern District of Georgia held that the Due Process Clause of the Georgia state constitution requires the appointment of legal counsel for a child when the state seeks to remove the child from parental custody.[17]

---

[11] 42 U.S.C. §§ 5101 through 5107.

[12] Jacob Smiles, *A Child's Due Process Right to Legal Counsel in Abuse and Neglect Dependency Proceedings*, 37 FAM. L.Q. 485 (Fall 2003).

[13] 424 U.S. 319 (1976).

[14] *Id.*

[15] *Id.* at 334.

[16] *Id.* at 335.

[17] *See Kenny A. v. Perdue*, 2005 U.S. Dist. Lexis 1891 (February 7, 2005).

§ 9.2.2 *Tinker v. Des Moines Independent Community School Dist.*

In *Tinker v. Des Moines Independent Community School Dist.*,[18] the Supreme Court held that students have a First Amendment right to wear arm bands in school to protest the Vietnam War. Justice Fortas, writing for the Court, wrote: "It can hardly be argued that either students or teachers shed their constitutional rights to freedom of speech or expression at the schoolhouse gate."[19] This case is most frequently cited for the proposition that a student's constitutional right to freedom of speech is of utmost importance and warrants protection.

The Court noted that students in and out of school are "persons" under the Constitution.[20] In order for a school to infringe on a student's First Amendment right to free speech, the school must demonstrate that it has a constitutionally sound reason for limiting the student's expression. In this case there was no evidence that the students' silent protest interfered with the school's work or with other students' interests. The Court concluded that students are entitled to freedom of expression.

§ 9.2.3 *Bellotti v. Baird*

In *Bellotti v. Baird*,[21] the Supreme Court held that pregnant girls cannot be required to obtain parental consent for an abortion without providing them a hearing as to their maturity to make the decision without anyone else's consent. The Massachusetts statute required that a minor received consent from both of her parents before she could have an abortion. If her parents refused to consent, she could obtain consent from a judicial order for good cause based on the judge's decision that an abortion was in her best interest. The Court concluded that the statute placed an undue burden on a minor's right to access abortion. It stated that every pregnant minor must be able to go directly to a court and request judicial consent for an abortion without being required to first consult her parents.

The court held that the statute was unconstitutional because it permitted a judge to withhold judicial authorization for an abortion even if the court found the minor to be mature and competent to make the decision. Additionally, the statute required parental consultation and notification, without affording the minor an opportunity to receive a judicial determination that she is mature enough to consent or that an abortion is in her best interests. Therefore, the court concluded that the statute created an undue burden on the right of minors to obtain an abortion.

In this case, the Supreme Court held that pregnant girls cannot be required to obtain parental consent for an abortion without providing them a hearing as

---

[18] 393 U.S. 503 (1969).

[19] *Id.* at 506.

[20] *Id.* at 511.

[21] 443 U.S. 622 (1979).

to their maturity to make the decision without anyone else's consent. The Massachusetts statute required a minor to receive consent from both of her parents before she could have an abortion. If her parents refused to consent, she could obtain consent from a judicial order for good cause based on the judge's decision that an abortion was in her best interest.

§ 9.2.4 *Wisconsin v. Yoder*

Wisconsin v. Yoder[22] involved a Wisconsin law that required children to attend school until age 16. Amish and Mennonite families in Wisconsin objected to the law because the period from the end of eighth grade to their adult baptism was very important for indoctrination into the Amish faith. The parents contended that if their children went to public high school the opportunity for religious education would be lost. The Court found for the Amish and Mennonite parents stating that the children continued to receive education at home and that the state's interest in using education to produce productive members of society was met by the vocational schooling the youth received from their parents. Therefore, the Court held that the Amish parents had the protection of the religious clause and their right to freedom of religion dominated the state's interests.

Justice Burger, writing for the Supreme Court, first pointed out that in "evaluating those claims we must be careful to determine whether the Amish religious faith and their mode of life are, as they claim, inseparable and interdependent. A way of life, however virtuous and admirable, may not be interposed as a barrier to reasonable state regulation of education if it is based on purely secular considerations; to have the protection of the Religion Clauses, the claims must be rooted in religious belief."[23] The Court concluded that "the record in this case abundantly supports the claim that the traditional way of life of the Amish is not merely a matter of personal preference, but one of deep religious conviction, shared by an organized group, and intimately related to daily living."[24] The Court detailed how the compulsory education law interfered with the Amish and Mennonite parents' right to free exercise of religion for their families and children and concluded that the compulsory education law violated their First Amendment rights.

In a famous dissent, Justice William O. Douglas noted that the wishes of the people most directly affected—two of the teenage students involved, Vernon Yutzy and Barbara Miller—were not considered. The students were not parties, nor were they consulted. Justice Douglas stated in part, "The Court's analysis assumes that the only interests at stake in the case are those of the Amish parents on the one hand, and those of the State on the other. The difficulty with this approach is that, despite the Court's claim, the parents are seeking to vindicate

---

[22] 406 U.S. 205 (1972).

[23] *Id.* at 215.

[24] *Id.* at 216.

not only their own free exercise claims, but also those of their high-school-age children."[25]

§ 9.2.5 *Parham v. J.R.*

Parham v. J.R.[26] was a class action brought by Georgia children who had been voluntarily committed to state mental health institutions. The Georgia District Court ruled in favor of the children finding that the state statutory scheme was unconstitutional because in did not protect the children's due process rights. The court held that minors who are going to be voluntarily committed are entitled to an adversary-type hearing before an impartial tribunal. The State appealed the decision to the U.S. Supreme Court. The Court concluded that the medical fact-finding process was consistent with due process guarantees.

The Court considered whether Georgia's procedures for voluntarily commitment of minors to state mental hospitals violated the children's Fourteenth Amendment due process rights. The state statute provided that for the voluntary commitment of a child there must be an application from the child's parent or guardian. The statute permitted any child who had been voluntarily committed for more than five days to be discharged at the request of his or her guardian. Additionally, it required the hospital superintendent to re-evaluate patients who were voluntarily committed and release them if they no longer need to be hospitalized.

The Court concluded that Georgia's practice satisfied due process requirements. It noted that children have a liberty interest in not being unnecessarily confined and an interest in not being erroneously labeled mentally ill. The Court, however, found that the law sufficiently protected the children's interests. Parents did not have absolute discretion to have their child committed. Furthermore, the medical fact-finders who admitted children had the authority to refuse to admit any patients, and they periodically reviewed continued commitment. The Court held that Georgia's statutory and administrative procedure for the voluntary commitment of children was not unconstitutional.

§ 9.3 Children Born Out of Wedlock/Right of Putative Fathers

§ 9.3.1 *Stanley v. Illinois*

Stanley v. Illinois[27] established rights for fathers whose children were born out of wedlock. The Illinois statute provided that children of unmarried fathers, upon the death of the mother, were declared dependents without any hearing on parental fitness and without proof of neglect, even though a hearing on parental

---

[25]   *Id.* at 241.

[26]   442 U.S. 584 (1979).

[27]   405 U.S. 645 (1972).

fitness and proof of neglect were required before the state assumed custody of children of married or divorced parents and unmarried mothers. The facts of this case are particularly compelling because the father and mother had lived together intermittently over 18 years, during which time their three children were born. Upon the mother's death, the state filed a dependency action, and the children were placed with court-appointed guardians. Nothing in the record indicated that the father was unfit or neglectful of his children in any way.

The state argued that most fathers of children born out of wedlock are unfit and that the statutory scheme appropriately served the needs of most children. The Supreme Court rejected this argument and found that parental unfitness must be established on the basis of individualized proof. The Court found it irrelevant that the father could have applied for adoption or for custody and control of his children, especially in light of the fact that he would not be afforded any priority and would bear the burden of proof that he should be permitted to serve as the children's guardian or adoptive parent. The Court concluded that the state's practice violated the Equal Protection Clause because parents are entitled to a hearing on their fitness before their children are removed. The Supreme Court held that under the Due Process Clause of the Fourteenth Amendment, all parents, including fathers of children born out of wedlock, are constitutionally entitled to a hearing on fitness before their children are removed from their custody in dependency proceedings.

§ 9.3.2 *Quilloin v. Walcott*

In *Quilloin v. Walcott*,[28] the U.S. Supreme Court considered whether the state of Georgia could constitutionally deny an unwed father the authority to object to the adoption of his child. The case involved a stepparent adoption of a child born out of wedlock, over the objection of the birth father. The child had lived with his mother since birth, and had never lived with his biological father. When the child was approximately 3 years old, his mother married another man. When the child was 11 years old, his mother consented to the child's adoption by her husband, and his biological father filed an adoption petition. The Georgia statute provided that only the mother's consent was required for the adoption of an illegitimate child. The biological father, however, could acquire veto authority over the adoption if he had legitimated the child. A child born in wedlock could not be adopted without the consent of each living parent who had not voluntarily surrendered rights of the child or been adjudicated unfit. The father in this case had not legitimated the child prior to the filing of the adoption petition. Using the "best interests of the child" standard, the trial court granted the stepparent adoption over the father's objection and denied the biological father's petition for legitimization, in which he sought visitation rights but not custody. The trial court did not find the father to be an unfit parent. The court did find

---

[28]   434 U.S. 246 (1978).

that, although the child had never been abandoned or deprived, the father had provided support only on an irregular basis.

The Supreme Court held that under the circumstances of the case, the father's substantive rights were not violated by application of a "best interests of the child" standard.[29] The biological father had never sought custody. For equal protection purposes, the Court found that the rights of a father who was never married to the mother are distinguishable from those of a separated or divorced father. The state, therefore, could permissibly give such a father less veto authority than it provides to a married father.

§ 9.3.3 *Caban v. Mohammed*

In *Caban v. Mohammed*,[30] the Supreme Court concluded that unwed fathers have the same rights to their children as unwed mothers. This case involved children born out of wedlock whose mother subsequently married and had the stepfather adopt the children over the birth father's objection. The biological father in this case was more involved in the children's lives than the father in *Quilloin*. The children's biological father was married to someone else, but he lived with their mother and held himself out as married to her for several years. During that time two children were born. He was named on the birth certificates and contributed to the children's support. After the parents separated, the mother took the children and married another man. During the next two years the father maintained contact with the children. When the children were four and six years old, their mother and her husband filed for a stepparent adoption. The birth father cross-petitioned for adoption. The surrogate court granted the stepparent adoption over the father's objection. The New York statutory and case law required the mother's consent for the adoption of children born out of wedlock but did not require the father's consent, even when his parental relationship was substantial. The father did have a right to notice and the opportunity to be heard, but he could prevent the termination of his parental rights only by showing that adoption was not in the best interests of the child.

The Supreme Court noted that this case demonstrated that an unwed father may have a relationship with his children fully comparable to that of the mother. The Court addressed the issue it had reserved in *Quilloin* and held that the New York statute unconstitutionally distinguished unwed parents according to their gender. The Court also found that the distinction did not bear a substantial relation to the state's interest in providing adoptive homes for illegitimate children. Therefore, the statute was unconstitutional under the Equal Protection Clause of the Fourteenth Amendment.

---

[29] *Id.* at 254.

[30] 441 U.S. 380 (1979).

§ 9.3.4 *Lehr v. Robertson*

Lehr v. Robertson[31] is the Supreme Court's most recent decision addressing the rights of fathers of children born out of wedlock. The father had lived with the mother prior to the child's birth and visited her in the hospital when the baby was born. His name, however, did not appear on the birth certificate. He did not live with the mother or child after the child's birth, never provided them with any financial support, never offered to marry the mother, and never registered on the state's putative father registry. The mother married another man eight months after the child's birth, and he filed a stepparent adoption petition when the child was two years old. The father was not given or entitled to notice of the adoption because he had not registered on the putative father's registry. The father learned of the adoption proceeding when he filed a paternity action and sought visitation. The Court noted that equal protection did not prevent a state from according parents separate legal rights when one parent had a continuous relationship with the child and the other parent had never established a relationship with the child.

The Supreme Court held that the New York statute did not violate the father's Fourteenth Amendment due process or equal protection rights by granting an adoption without notice to or consent by him. The statutory scheme provided him ample opportunity to put himself in a position of being entitled to receive notice, which he did not use. Justice Stevens summarized the varying constitutional protections given to fathers of various degrees of involvement with their children born out of wedlock:

> The difference between the developed parent-child relationship that was implicated in Stanley and Caban, and the potential relationship involved in Quilloin and this case, is both clear and significant. When an unwed father demonstrates a full commitment to the responsibilities of parenthood by '[coming] forward to participate in the rearing of his child," Caban, 441 U.S., at 392, his interest in personal contact with his child acquires substantial protection under the Due Process Clause. At that point it may be said that he "[acts] as a father toward his children." Id., at 389, n. 7. But the mere existence of a biological link does not merit equivalent constitutional protection. . . .

> The significance of the biological connection is that it offers the natural father an opportunity that no other male possesses to develop a relationship with his offspring. If he grasps that opportunity and accepts some measure of responsibility for the child's future, he may enjoy the blessings of the parent-child relationship and make uniquely valuable contributions to the child's development. If he fails to do so, the Federal

---

[31] 463 U.S. 248 (1983).

Constitution will not automatically compel a state to listen to his opinion of where the child's best interests lie. . . .

In this case, we are not assessing the constitutional adequacy of New
York's procedures for terminating a developed relationship. Appellant
has never had any significant custodial, personal, or financial relationship with Jessica, and he did not seek to establish a legal tie until after
she was two years old. We are concerned only with whether New York
has adequately protected his opportunity to form such a relationship.[32]

§ 9.3.5 *Michael H. v. Gerald D.*

Michael H. v. Gerald D.[33] addressed the constitutionality of Section 621 of
the California Evidence Code, which provided that "the issue of a wife cohabi-
tating with her husband, who is not impotent or sterile, is conclusively presumed
to be a child of the marriage."[34] Paternity tests established that Michael H. was
the biological father of Victoria D. Victoria's mother had lived with Michael H.
in an on-again, off-again manner and asserted that he was the child's father. At
the time of Victoria's birth, she was married to Gerald D., who was named as
Victoria's father on her birth certificate. Eventually, Victoria and her mother
went to live with Gerald D., and Michael H. filed an action to establish his paternity and visitation rights. The California courts denied his request, finding that
Section 621 of the California Evidence Code prevented a putative father from
establishing paternity and California law denied visitation requests by a putative
father against the wishes of the mother. Michael H. asserted on appeal to the
U.S. Supreme Court that Section 621 violated his substantive and procedural
due process rights.

Michael H. first contended that procedural due process prevented the state
from terminating his relationship with his child without permitting him an
opportunity to prove his paternity in an evidentiary hearing. The Supreme Court
rejected this argument. It found that the California legislature devised the
statute to prohibit paternity inquiries when a child was born to a married couple
to protect family privacy and integrity. Next, Michael H. argued that because he
had established a relationship with Victoria, as a matter of substantive due
process the state's interest in protecting marriage was insufficient to terminate
his relationship with his daughter. The Court also rejected this argument, and
concluded that in the history of the United States the relationship between a
putative father and his child has never been constitutionally protected. Finally,
the Court considered whether Victoria had a liberty interest in maintain a relationship with Michael H. and Gerald D. The Court rejected this claim and concluded that there is no historical support to recognize multiple fathers.

---

[32] *Id.* at 261-263 (citations omitted).

[33] 491 U.S. 110 (1989).

[34] *Id.* at 117.

§ 9.4 Termination of Parental Rights

§ 9.4.1 *Lassiter v. Dept. of Social Services*

Lassiter v. Dept. of Social Services[35] addressed whether states were constitutionally required to provide appointed counsel for indigent parents in termination of parental rights cases. In the present case, the child was removed from the mother's custody as an infant based on her failure to provide proper medical care. The mother was subsequently convicted of second degree murder and sentenced to 25 to 40 years incarceration. Three years after the child's initial removal, the county department of social services filed a petition to terminate the mother's parental rights. The petition was based on her lack of contact with the child, and the fact that she left the child in foster care without showing substantial progress, a positive response to the agency's efforts, or constructive planning for the child's future. The mother had retained counsel in order to seek invalidation of the criminal conviction, but she had failed to mention the termination proceeding to him. The agency arranged to have the mother transported to the termination hearing. The trial court found that the mother's failure to have counsel was without just cause. Further, she did not allege that she was indigent. After the trial court held that she was not entitled to court appointed counsel, Ms. Lassiter represented herself at the hearing.

In this case, the Court stressed, there were no allegations of abuse or neglect that might result in criminal prosecution, no expert witnesses were called, nor were there any substantively or procedurally difficult points of law. Additionally, the mother had previously failed to attend a custody hearing, she hadn't bothered to mention the case to her criminal attorney, and she had not evidenced much interest in the child after his removal. It did not appear that the presence of counsel would have made a determinative difference. While the Court held that the mother in this case was not constitutionally entitled to appointed counsel under the circumstances, it noted that there may be termination of parental rights cases in which the nature of the allegations and the evidence to be presented give rise to a due process right to the appointment of counsel. Moreover, the Court encouraged state courts to appoint counsel in termination cases, stating that a "wise public policy . . . may require that higher standards be adopted than those minimally tolerable under the Constitution. Informed opinion has clearly come to hold that an indigent parent is entitled to the assistance of appointed counsel not only in parental termination proceedings, but in dependency and neglect proceedings as well."[36]

---

[35] 452 U.S. 18 (1981).

[36] *Id.* at 33-34.

Despite the Court's holding in *Lassiter*, a number of state appellate courts have held that their state constitution demands that a parent alleged to be abusive or neglectful has the right to the appointment of counsel.[37]

§ 9.4.2 *Santosky v. Kramer*

A 5-4 majority of the Supreme Court held in *Santosky v. Kramer*[38] that under the due process clause of the Fourteenth Amendment, in state-initiated termination of parental rights cases, the state must prove its case by at least clear and convincing evidence. The Court ruled, therefore, that New York's statutory scheme, which required only proof by a preponderance of the evidence, was unconstitutional.

The Court discussed a parent's fundamental liberty interest in the care, custody, and management of his or her children. It noted that even those who have lost custody of their children or who are not model parents still retain an interest in maintaining their parental rights. The Court concluded that the state must provide parents with fundamentally fair procedures. The Court found that in termination of parental rights proceedings, "the private interest affected is commanding; the risk of error from using a preponderance standard is substantial; and the countervailing governmental interest favoring that standard is comparatively slight. Evaluation of the three *Eldridge* factors compels the conclusion that use of a 'fair preponderance of the evidence' standard in such proceedings is inconsistent with due process."[39] The Court found that a clear and convincing standard was necessary to protect a parent's due process rights.

§ 9.4.3 *M.L.B. v. S.L.J.*

In *M.L.B. v. S.L.J.*,[40] the Supreme Court held that when an indigent parent appeals the termination of his or her parental rights, the Fourteenth Amendment's Due Process Clause requires that he or she be provided "a record of sufficient completeness to permit proper appellate consideration of her claims" at public expense.[41] M.L.B. was the mother of two children, a boy and a girl. M.L.B.'s ex-husband, S.L.J., and his new wife sought to terminate M.L.B.'s parental rights so that S.L.J.'s new wife could adopt the children. The trial court found that "there had been a 'substantial erosion of the relationship between the natural mother, [M.L.B.], and the minor children' which has been caused 'at

---

[37] *See, e.g., In the Interest of D.B. and D.S.*, 385 So.2d 83 (Fla. 1980); *Reist v. Bay County Circuit Judge*, 396 Mich. 326, 241 N.W.2d 55 (Mich. 1976); *Danforth v. State Dep't of Health and Welfare*, 303 A.2d 794 (1973).

[38] 455 U.S. 745 (1982).

[39] *Id.* at 758.

[40] 519 U.S. 102 (1996).

[41] *Id.* at 106 (internal quotation marks omitted).

least in part by [M.L.B.'s] serious neglect, abuse, prolonged and unreasonable absence or unreasonable failure to visit or communicate with her minor children.'"[42] M.L.B. sought to appeal and paid a $100 filing fee. M.L.B. was unable to pay the additional $3253.36 fee for the production of the record necessary to prosecute the appeal. After examining a number of precedents in both the criminal and civil spheres regarding the appointment of counsel or the provision of transcripts at public expense and relating to the termination of parental rights, the court framed the precise question to be answered: "Does the Fourteenth Amendment require Mississippi to accord M.L.B. access to an appeal—available but for her inability to advance required costs—before she is forever branded unfit for affiliation with her children?"[43]

The majority observed that "termination decrees 'work a unique kind of depravation.' . . . In contrast to matters modifiable at the parties' will or based on changed circumstances, termination adjudications involve the awesome authority of the State 'to destroy permanently all legal recognition of the parental relationship.'. . . Our *Lassiter* and *Santosky* decisions, recognizing that parental termination decrees are among the most severe forms of state action . . . have not served as precedent in other areas. . . . We are therefore satisfied that the label 'civil' should not entice us to leave undisturbed the Mississippi courts' disposition of this case."[44] Because of the importance of the rights at stake for the parent, and the relatively minimal financial burden placed on the state if it is compelled to provide a court record at public expense, the court held that the State is required to provide an indigent parent enough of the record to permit appellate consideration of his or her case.

§ 9.5 Foster Parent Relationships

§ 9.5.1 *Smith v. Org. of Foster Families for Equality & Reform*

Smith v. Org. of Foster Families for Equality & Reform[45] was brought by foster parents and a foster parents' organization seeking declaratory and injunctive relief challenging procedures for removal of foster children from their foster homes. The applicable New York statutes and New York City regulations provided that the agency with custody of a foster child was required, except in emergencies, to notify the foster parents in writing ten days in advance of any removal of the child. If the foster parents objected to the child's removal, they could

---

[42] *Id.* at 108 (citations omitted).

[43] *Id.* at 119.

[44] *Id.* at 127.

[45] 431 U.S. 816 (1977).

[46] *Id.* at 830.

request a "conference" with the social services department to be held within ten days of the receipt of the request.[46] The foster parents had the right to be advised of the reasons for the removal, to appear with counsel, and to submit reasons why the child should not be removed. A written decision would be made within five days, and the removal would be stayed until the outcome of the conference. If the decision was to remove the child, the foster parents could appeal for a full administrative "fair hearing,"[47] the determination of which was subject to judicial review. If the child was being transferred to another foster home, but not if the child was being returned to his parents, the foster parents could also request a full trial-type hearing before the child's removal. Finally, if the child had been in foster care longer than 18 months, the foster parents were made parties to the proceeding and could request review of the child's status by the family court, which could result in a court order that the agency leave the child with the foster parents.

The foster parents contended that when a child has lived in a foster home for a year or more, the foster family becomes the true "psychological family" of the child, and the foster family acquires a Fourteenth Amendment liberty interest in maintaining that family unit, which requires a higher level of due process before a foster child is removed.[48] The trial court did not recognize such a right, and instead granted relief based on an independent right of the foster child to be heard before being "condemned to suffer grievous loss," namely, disruption of a stable foster placement.[49] On appeal, the state alleged that the trial court's analysis was not constitutionally sound.

The Court considered the alleged defect in the procedures—not affording the foster child an opportunity to participate in the removal proceeding. The Court pointed out that "nothing in the New York City procedure prevents consultation of the child's wishes, directly or through an adult intermediary. We assume, moreover, that some such consultation would be among the first steps that a rational factfinder, inquiring into the child's best interests, would pursue. Such consultation, however, does not require that the child or an appointed representative must be a party with full adversary powers in all preremoval hearings."[50] The Court then considered the private interests of the foster families, the risk of erroneous deprivation of that interest, and the state's interest. The Court reversed the lower court's decision. It concluded that foster parents' rights were sufficiently protected by the procedure provided. Foster families are given notice and an administrative hearing with judicial review before a foster child who has been in their home for over 18 months is removed.

---

[47] *Id.*

[48] *Id.* at 839.

[49] *Id.* at 840.

[50] *Id.* at 852.

§ 9.6 State Agency Duties

§ 9.6.1 *DeShaney v. Winnebago County Dept. of Social Services*

In *DeShaney v. Winnebago County Dept. of Social Services,*[51] the Court concluded that the state did not have a duty to act to protect a child that was not in the state's custody. This case involved a civil rights action under 42 U.S.C. §1983, filed on behalf of a severely abused child against social workers and local officials who had received complaints that he was being abused by his father and had reason to believe that he was abused. They initially removed the child for three days to evaluate him in a hospital, but he was returned to his father's care. The department provided voluntary services. The juvenile court dismissed the child protection case and returned the child to the custody of his father. The caseworker did not take action after a report from an emergency room physician, but made monthly visits to the child's home. During this time, she observed a number of suspicious injuries on the child's head and noticed that the father had not followed through with some of his voluntary agreements. She noted in the record these problems and her suspicion that the child was being abused but took no action to protect the child. The caseworker responded to the home two additional times following another report from the emergency room and was told that the child was too ill to see her. She took no further action. Finally, the child was beaten so severely that he suffered brain damage so severe that he is expected to spend the rest of his life confined to an institution for the profoundly retarded.

The Supreme Court considered whether the child's due process rights were violated by Child Protective Services when they failed to protect him from the abuse. The Court concluded that nothing in the language of the due process clause required the state to protect citizens from private actors. The Court stated that there is no "affirmative right to governmental aid, even where such aid may be necessary to secure life, liberty, or property interests of which the government itself may not deprive the individual."[52] The Court additionally concluded that if "the Due Process Clause does not require the State to provide its citizens with particular protective services, it follows that the State cannot be held liable under the Clause for injuries that could have been averted had it chosen to provide them."[53]

The Supreme Court rejected the argument that a "special relationship" existed between the agency and the child in this case.[54] The petitioner's argued the relationship existed because the State knew that the child faced a special

---

[51] 489 U.S. 189 (1989).

[52] *Id.* at 196.

[53] *Id.* at 196 to 197.

[54] *Id.* at 197.

danger of abuse at his father's hands, and specifically proclaimed, by word and by deed, its intention to protect him against that danger, thereby creating a duty to act reasonably. The Court found that such a duty would arise only where "the State by the affirmative exercise of its power so restrains an individual's liberty that it renders him unable to care for himself, and at the same time fails to provide for his basic human needs . . . . The affirmative duty to protect arises not from the State's knowledge of the individual's predicament or from its expressions of intent to help him, but from the limitation which it has imposed on his freedom to act on his own behalf."[55] The Court reasoned that the Fourteenth Amendment does not require a state agency to protect citizens from private conduct that is not attributable to the agency's employees. It concluded that because the child was not in the state's custody, there was no duty to act.

§ 9.6.2 *Youngberg v. Romeo*

The Court held, in *Youngberg v. Romeo*,[56] that a mentally retarded man who was involuntarily confined in a state institution had constitutionally protected liberty interests under the due process clause of the Fourteenth Amendment to reasonably safe conditions of confinement, freedom from unreasonable bodily restraints, and such minimally adequate training as reasonably might be required by these interests. This case involved a 33-year-old man who had the mental capacity of an 18-month-old child. He was involuntarily committed to a state institution. Shortly after his commitment, he sustained a number of injuries. His mother filed suit under 42 U.S.C. § 1983 on behalf of him against the institution officials. She alleged that his rights under the Eighth and Fourteenth Amendments were violated.

The Court concluded that when a person is institutionalized and dependent on the state, the state has a duty to provide certain services and care. The Court expanded the State's responsibilities to include: (1) providing patients with safe conditions; (2) freedom from restraint; and (3) adequately trained employees. The Court stated that the proper test to determine whether the State violated a patient's rights is to consider whether the State adequately protected those rights and whether the State exercised professional judgment.

Note: Significance of *DeShaney* and *Youngberg*. Taken together, *DeShaney* and *Youngberg* suggest a rule that while the State has no duty to intervene to protect a child from parental maltreatment, when the State does intervene and removes a child from his or her home, the federal civil rights statutes require that the child not be placed in a home that the state actors know or suspect may be abusive.[57]

---

[55] *Id.* at 200.

[56] 457 U.S. 307 (1982).

[57] *See, e.g., K.H. ex rel Murphy v. Morgan*, 914 F.2d 846 (7th Cir. 1990); *Lewis v. Anderson*, 308 F.3d 768 (7th Cir. 2002), *cert. den., sub nom Lewis v. Stolle*, 538 U.S. 908, 123 S.Ct. 1500 (2003).

§ 9.6.3 *Suter v. Artist M.*

Suter v. Artist M.[58] involved an action for injunctive and declaratory relief filed on behalf of children adjudicated dependent. The respondents sought to enforce the state agency's duty under the Adoption Assistance and Child Welfare Act (Adoption Act) and the state plan adopted pursuant to the Act to provide reasonable efforts to maintain an abused or neglected child in his home or return the child to his home from foster care. The Adoption Act provided the federal government with the authority to reduce or eliminate payments to a State on finding that the state's plan did not comply with the Act's requirements. The Court held that the Adoption Act did not create enforceable rights for dependent children.

The Adoption Act established a reimbursement program for certain expenses incurred by states in administering foster care and adoption services. The purpose behind the Adoption Act, according to the sponsor, Sen. Cranston, was ". . . to free up a little bit of money . . . so you will have an incentive to keep a family together."[59] In order for a State to receive federal reimbursement, they were required to use "reasonable efforts . . . to prevent or eliminate the need for removal of the child from his home, and . . . to make it possible for the child to return to his home . . . ."[60] The Court determined that, although the Adoption Act placed requirements on the States, the only requirement was that the States have a plan approved by the Secretary of Health and Human Services and that the plan called for reasonable efforts. The respondents, child beneficiaries of the Adoption Act, claimed that the state failed to make reasonable efforts to preserve and reunite families. Respondents argued that the "reasonable efforts" clause of the Adoption Act could be enforced through a Section 1983 action,[61] and applied the standard of *Cort v. Ash*[62] to find that the Act created an implied right of action entitling respondents to bring suit directly under the Act. Respondents' claim failed because they did not show that Congress intended to allow them a remedy.

The Supreme Court held that there was no private cause of action created under the Adoption Assistance and Child Welfare Act. The Court concluded

---

[58] 503 U.S. 347 (1992).

[59] *Id.* at 362 (citing 125 Cong. Rec. 29939 (1979) (remarks of Sen. Cranston, sponsor of the Act)).

[60] *Id.* at 351 (citing §§ 671(a)(3), (15)).

[61] 42 U.S.C. § 1983. *See id.* at 350 n.1 ("Section 1983 provides, in relevant part: 'Every person who, under color of any statute, ordinance, regulation, custom, or usage, of any State or Territory or the District of Columbia, subjects or causes to be subjected, any citizen of the United States or other person within the jurisdiction thereof to the deprivation of any rights, privileges, or immunities, secured by the Constitution and laws shall be liable to the party injured in an action at law, suit in equity, or other proper proceeding for redress.'").

[62] 422 U.S. 66, 78 (1975) (establishing four relevant factors through which respondents may demonstrate that Congress intended to create a private enforcement remedy where none is explicitly provided by statute). *See Suter v. Artist M.*, 503 U.S. 347, 363-364 n.16 (1992) ("As established in *Cort v. Ash*, . . . these factors are: 'First, is the plaintiff one of the class for whose

that "the 'reasonable efforts' language does not unambiguously confer an enforceable right upon the Act's beneficiaries. The term 'reasonable efforts' in this context is at least as plausibly read to impose only a rather generalized duty on the State, to be enforced not by private individuals, but by the Secretary in the manner previously discussed."[63]

Note: Following *Suter v. Artist M*, the Second Circuit Court of Appeals allowed certification of a class action lawsuit on behalf of children in New York City's child welfare system.[64] The D.C. Circuit Court of Appeals also permitted a class action lawsuit on behalf of foster children in the District of Columbia.[65] The Supreme Court's decision in *Suter v. Artist M*. was limited by statute in 1994 when Congress amended the Social Security Act.[66] The amendments did not, however, alter the Court's holding in Suter that Section 671(a)(15) is not enforceable in a private right of action.[67]

§ 9.7 Access to Child Protective Service's Records

§ 9.7.1 *Pennsylvania v. Ritchie*

In *Pennsylvania v. Ritchie*,[68] the Supreme Court considered a defendant's right to access the records of child protective services regarding the alleged victim. The defendant was charged with various counts of sexual assault against his daughter. During pretrial discovery he requested access to all of the Children and Youth Services (CYS) records related to the charges. The defendant argued that he was entitled to access to the records because they might contain the names of witness and other evidence. The trial judge did not examine the entire record, but refused to order disclosure. The defendant was convicted. On appeal, the Pennsylvania Supreme Court held that denying the defendant access

---

especial benefit the statute was enacted, that is, does the statute create a federal right in favor of the plaintiff? Second, is there any indication of legislative intent, explicit or implicit, either to create such a remedy or to deny one? Third, is it consistent with the underlying purposes of the legislative scheme to imply such a remedy for the plaintiff? And finally, is the cause of action one traditionally relegated to state law, in an area basically the concern of the States, so that it would be inappropriate to infer a cause of action based solely on federal law?'" (internal citations and emphasis omitted)). *But see Thompson v. Thompson*, 484 U.S. 174, 188-189 (1988) (Scalia, J., concurring with the holding that no private remedy will be implied in the absence of legislative intent but arguing that the *Cort v. Ash* analysis has been "effectively overruled" by subsequent case law).

63 *Suter v. Artist M.*, 503 U.S. 345, 363 (1992).

64 *See Marisol A. v. Giuliani*, 126 F.3d 372 (2d Cir. 1997).

65 *See LaShawn A. by Moore v. Kelly*, 990 F.2d 1319 (D.C. Cir. 1993).

66 42 U.S.C. §§ 1320a-2, 1320a-10.

67 *Dajour B. et al. v. City of New York et al.*, 00 Civ. 2044 (JGK), 2001 U.S. Dist. LEXIS 10251 (S.D.N.Y. July 23, 2001).

68 480 U.S. 39 (1987).

to CYS records violated the Confrontation and Compulsory Process Clauses and the Sixth Amendment.

The U.S. Supreme Court addressed the defendant's due process rights. The Court noted that the Compulsory process clause required the government to assist in getting witness to attend trial. It does not guarantee the right to favorable witnesses' identities, nor does it provide additional protections then the due process clause. Under due process principles, the government must share material evidence with the accused. In this case, the Pennsylvania statute provided that CYS records must be kept confidential unless there is a court order requiring disclosure. Therefore, the Court concluded that the accused is entitled to ask the trial court to review a CYS file and determine whether it has material information that should be disclosed.

§ 9.8 Social Security Benefits for Children in Foster Care

§ 9.8.1 *Washington State Dept. of Social and Health Services v. Guardianship Estate of Keffeler*

Washington State Dept. of Social and Health Services v. Guardianship Estate of Keffeler[69] was a class action on behalf of children in foster care who were receiving Social Security benefits that were being paid to the state as the representative payee. The children alleged that the state agency violated federal law by reimbursing itself for foster care expenditures from their Social Security benefits. The Supreme Court, in an opinion by Justice Souter, stated that "[a]lthough it is true that the State could not directly compel the beneficiary or any other representative payee to pay Social Security benefits over to the State, that fact does not render the appointment of a self-reimbursing representative payee at odds with the Commissioner's mandate to find that a beneficiary's 'interest . . . would be served' by the appointment."[70] The Court held that it was permissible for the agency to reimburse itself for the current costs of maintaining the children in foster care.

§ 9.9 Indian Child Welfare Act

§ 9.9.1 *Mississippi Band of Choctaw Indians v. Holyfield*

Mississippi Band of Choctaw Indians v. Holyfield[71] involved the attempt by unmarried Indian parents, who were enrolled members of the Mississippi Band of Choctaw Indians, to avoid tribal jurisdiction over the proposed adoption of

---

[69] 537 U.S. 371 (2003).

[70] *Id.* at 389.

[71] 490 U.S. 30 (1989).

their twin infants. Under the Indian Child Welfare Act (ICWA),[72] the tribe had exclusive jurisdiction over the adoption of children domiciled on the reservation. The mother left the reservation and gave birth to her children 200 miles away. Both parents voluntarily consented to the adoption by non-Indians, and the tribe was neither notified nor consulted about an appropriate adoptive placement for the children.

The tribe moved to vacate the adoption. It argued that under ICWA the tribal court had exclusive jurisdiction over the adoption of children who were eligible for enrollment in the tribe. The court rejected the tribe's argument and held that because the parents purposefully gave birth off of the reservation and independently arranged adoption by non-Indians, the tribe did not have jurisdiction. The tribe appealed the court's decision to the Mississippi Supreme Court, which affirmed the lower court's decision, finding that because the children were never domiciled on the tribe's reservation, ICWA did not apply, and the tribal court did not have jurisdiction. The U.S. Supreme Court granted plenary review to consider the issues presented.

The Supreme Court held that a federal definition of "domicile" would be applied to Indian Child Welfare Act cases. If the parents were domiciled on the reservation, their children were also domiciled on the reservation by operation of law, even though the children had never been physically present on the reservation. The Court pointed out that Congress intended ICWA to give tribes rights even in voluntary adoptions because of concerns going beyond the wishes of individual parents. The concerns included the long-term survival of the Indian tribes and the recurring developmental problems encountered during adolescence by Indian children raised in a white environment. Placement of Indian children in non-Indian homes was seen by Congress as depriving them of their tribal and cultural heritage. Based on the Congressional objectives, the Court noted that a domicile rule that permitted individual Indian parents to bypass ICWA requirements and avoid tribal jurisdiction would be contrary to the objective of the Act. It reversed the decision of the Mississippi Supreme Court and remanded the case to the tribal court.

§ 9.10 Children's Statements and Testimony

Editors' Note: *The following are criminal law cases and do not arise out of the dependency court context. They are included in this publication because of their importance to discussions of children's testimony. Many state courts have referenced these cases, and some state legislatures have essentially codified the holdings in child-witness statutes. For a fuller discussion of children as witnesses, see Chapter 15, particularly the Residual and Hearsay Exceptions (Section 15.6.2) and Hearsay and the Confrontation Clause (Section 15.6.3).*

---

[72] 25 U.S.C. §§ 1901 through 1963.

§ 9.10.1 *Crawford v. Washington*

In *Crawford v. Washington*,[73] the Supreme Court addressed the constitutionality of admitting testimonial hearsay statements of an unavailable witness in criminal proceedings. The Court overruled the precedent that hearsay statements could be admitted if there were sufficient indicia of reliability. The Court did not define what constituted "testimonial" hearsay. However, the Court defined the following as testimonial: prior testimony that the defendant was unable to cross examine grand jury testimony; affidavits and depositions; and statements made during formal police interrogations. It noted that hearsay falling within in a recognized exception is still admissible. Ultimately, the Court overruled *Ohio v. Roberts*.[74] Under *Ohio v. Roberts*, the Sixth Amendment right to confront witnesses against you did not bar admission of an unavailable witness's statement against a criminal defendant if the statement had "adequate 'indicia of reliability,'" "a test met when the evidence either fell within a "firmly rooted hearsay exception" or had "particularized guarantees of trustworthiness."[75] The Court concluded that in order to admit hearsay that is testimonial the Sixth Amendment requires that the witness is unavailable and that the defendant had the prior opportunity to cross-examine the witness.

Please note that *Crawford v. Washington* does not apply to civil dependency and neglect cases for the same reasons that the Sixth Amendment confrontation clause is not invoked in civil proceedings. Although the decision does not apply to civil child welfare cases, it may impact the prosecution of criminal child abuse cases. Prosecutors may no longer be able to admit child hearsay statements when the child is not available to testify.

§ 9.10.2 *Coy v. Iowa*

In *Coy v. Iowa*,[76] the Supreme Court affirmed a defendant's right to confront witness against him in child sexual abuse cases. The case involved an Iowa statute that permitted the trial judge to place a screen between the criminal defendant and the victims during their testimony in child sexual abuse cases. The procedure allowed the witnesses to avoid looking at the defendant. The statute did not require any individualized findings before the court could use this special procedure.

The defendant was charged with two counts of child sexual assault. At trial the judge permitted the use of a screen to shield the witness from the defendant. The defendant objected to the screen, and argued that it violated his Sixth Amendment right to confront witnesses and his due process rights because the

---

[73] 541 U.S. 36 (2004).

[74] 448 U.S. 56 (1980).

[75] *Id.* at 66.

[76] 487 U.S. 1012 (1988).

procedure made him appear guilty. The trial court rejected the defendant's claims. The jury convicted the defendant, and he appealed to the Iowa Supreme Court. The court affirmed the defendant's conviction and found that since the ability to cross examine the witness was not impaired by the screen, the practice did not violate the confrontation clause. The defendant appealed the decision to the U.S. Supreme Court.

The Supreme Court held that putting a screen between the defendant and the alleged victims was an unconstitutional denial of the defendant's Sixth Amendment right to confront witnesses against him. The Court noted that the statute adopted by Iowa did not require individualized findings that the practice shielded the child from additional trauma. Furthermore, the practice was not firmly rooted in national jurisprudence. The Court concluded that the practice was an obvious violation of the defendant's right to confront witnesses against him. It reversed the Iowa Supreme Court's decision and remanded the case.

Note: For a discussion of the Supreme Court's decision that a defendant's right to face-to-face confrontation is not absolute, please see Section 9.10.4, *Maryland v. Craig.*

§ 9.10.3 *White v. Illinois*

In *White v. Illinois*[77] the Supreme Court held that the prosecution was not required to produce a four-year-old victim of a sexual assault at trial. Additionally, there is no requirement to have the trial court find that the victim was unavailable for testimony before the out-of-court statements of the child could be admitted under the traditional spontaneous declaration and medical examination exceptions to the hearsay rule. The Court held that the confrontation clause did not require that the declarant be produced at trial or found unavailable before out-of-court statement could be admitted into evidence. Statements by the child's babysitter, the child's mother, the police officer who interviewed the child, and emergency room personnel concerning the four-year-old child's report of sexual assault had substantive probative value that could not be duplicated simply by having victim testify in court. Therefore, the confrontation clause did not require proof that the victim was unavailable for testimony before her out-of-court statements could be admitted as spontaneous declarations and statements made for medical treatment.

§ 9.10.4 *Maryland v. Craig*

The Supreme Court, in *Maryland v. Craig,*[78] upheld the practice of permitting child witnesses to testify via closed circuit television. This case involved a

---

[77]   502 U.S. 346 (1992).

[78]   497 U.S. 836 (1990).

procedure that allowed the victim of child sexual abuse to testify in the defendant's criminal case without looking at the defendant. The testimony was provided by the use of a one-way closed circuit television. The defendant challenged the procedure alleging that it violated his Sixth Amendment right to confront witnesses. The U.S. Supreme Court concluded that the constitutional right to confrontation is not absolute but is subject to a state's legitimate interests.

The confrontation clause's primary purpose is to ensure the reliability of evidence by subjecting the evidence to the adversary process. A face-to-face confrontation is only one part of the confrontation right. The right may be satisfied without a physical confrontation in order to further public policy, and when the reliability of the testimony is otherwise assured. Maryland's public policy interest in protecting children was sufficiently important to justify the use of one-way closed circuit television as long the state showed that testifying would cause the children serious emotional distress.

The Court noted that Maryland's statute preserved the elements of the confrontation clause: the child had to be found competent to testify, the defendant had the opportunity to cross-examine the witness, and the defendant, judge, and jury could view the witnesses' demeanor. It concluded that the state's interest in protecting child witnesses may outweigh the defendant's right to face-to-face confrontation. The Court held that closed circuit television (or similar techniques) may be used to help a child testify when there is a finding that it will prevent the child from suffering trauma while testifying in open court.

Note: In 1990, Congress enacted the Comprehensive Crime Control Act,[79] which permits federal courts to order two-way closed circuit testimony in federal child abuse cases.

§ 9.10.5 *Idaho v. Wright*

Idaho v. Wright[80] involved the admissibility of one child sexual abuse victim's statements about her sister's sexual abuse under the residual hearsay exception in a criminal proceeding. The defendant was charged with molesting two sisters, ages 5½ and 2½. The younger child had reluctantly answered the pediatrician's questions about her own abuse, but had spontaneously volunteered information about her sister's abuse. The trial court determined that the younger girl was not capable of testifying. The pediatrician, who had extensive experience in child abuse cases, testified about the statements the child made to him. The defendant was convicted of abusing both children. He appealed his conviction with respect to the younger child. On appeal, the defendant alleged that the trial court erred by admitting the doctor's testimony about the child's statements

---

[79] Comprehensive Crime Control Act of 1990, Pub.L.No. 101-647, 18 U.S.C. § 3509.
[80] 497 U.S. 805 (1990).

under the residual hearsay exception. The Iowa Supreme Court affirmed the defendant's conviction. The children's mother was also convicted for her part in the abuse. She appealed her conviction on the grounds that the doctor's testimony about her daughter's statements violated her rights under the confrontation clause. The Iowa Supreme Court agreed and reversed her convictions. The court held that the testimony violated the confrontation clause because the interview did not have sufficient procedural safeguards. The U.S. Supreme Court granted certiorari and affirmed.

For a hearsay statement to be admitted under the residual hearsay exception, the declarant must be unavailable, and there must be sufficient indicia of reliability. The court looks at the totality of the circumstances to determine whether the child was most likely telling the truth when the statement was made. The court concluded by looking at the totality of the circumstances surrounding the child's statements that there were no particularized guarantees of the trustworthiness of her statements. It noted the trial court's finding that the statement lacked trustworthiness because the doctor was under the belief the children had been abused when he was questioning them. Furthermore, the doctor's interview was not recorded, and leading questions were used. The court determined that evidence corroborating the truth of the child's out of court statement could not be used to support the determination of whether there were particularized guarantees of trustworthiness. The court held that the admission of the younger child's hearsay statements violated the defendant's Sixth Amendment confrontation clause rights and affirmed the Iowa Supreme Court's order.

§ 9.11 Parent's Right against Self-incrimination in Child Protection Cases

§ 9.11.1 *Baltimore City Dept. of Social Services v. Bouknight*

Baltimore City Dept. of Social Services v. Bouknight[81] involved a juvenile court order for a mother to produce her child, who was the subject of a child welfare proceeding. The child was initially removed from the mother's home as an infant based on physical abuse, including fractures. After being adjudicated a child in need of services, the child was returned to his mother, subject to the court's ongoing protective supervision. Eight months later, the mother had failed to comply with nearly all of the conditions of the protective order. Both the child welfare agency and law enforcement were unable to locate the child. Therefore, court ordered the child to be removed again. However, the mother refused to produce the child or reveal where he could be found, invoking her Fifth Amendment privilege against self-incrimination. She believed that production of the child would amount to an admission of her physical control over the child.

---

[81] 493 U.S. 549 (1990).

The court and agency were concerned that the child might be dead. The juvenile court ordered that the mother jailed for contempt until she complied with the order by producing the child or revealing his exact whereabouts. The mother appealed the juvenile court's order. The court of appeals vacated the juvenile court contempt order and found it was unconstitutional because it compelled testimony or production that could be incriminating. The Supreme Court granted certiorari and reversed the court of appeals.

The Supreme Court held that a mother who is the custodian of a child pursuant to a court order may not invoke the Fifth Amendment privilege against self-incrimination to resist an order of the juvenile court to produce the child. The court cited previous cases that established that the Fifth Amendment cannot be invoked to resist cooperation with the state when the state's purpose does not involve enforcing criminal laws. The court compared the juvenile court's order to government orders compelling individuals to produce records. It concluded that the mother could not invoke the privilege against self-incrimination because the child was a ward of the state, she accepted custody of him subject to conditions set by the juvenile court, and the state had concerns about the child's well-being. The court noted that the foregoing circumstances lessened the parent's right to invoke the Fifth Amendment privilege.

III. THE CHILD WELFARE LEGAL PROCESS

Chapter 10 A CHILD'S JOURNEY THROUGH THE CHILD WELFARE SYSTEM*

by Sue Badeau, Sarah Gesiriech, Ann M. Haralambie, Amanda George Donnelly, and Donald N. Duquette[1]

§ 10.1 Introduction

While 542,000 children were in foster care on September 30, 2001, 805,000 spent some time in care over the course of that year.[2]

Children in care in 2001 had been in foster care for an average of 33 months. More than 17 percent (91,217) of the children had been in care for five or more years.[3]

Once a child is known to the child welfare agency, the child and his or her family become subject to a series of decisions made by judges, caseworkers, legal representatives, and others, all of whom have an important role to play. A child may encounter dozens of other new adults, including foster parents, counselors, and doctors.

---

* Portions of this chapter appeared originally as *A Child's Journey*, Copyright 2003 by The Pew Commission on Children in Foster Care by Sue Badeau and Sarah Gesiriech. Those portions are adapted and reprinted with permission of the Pew Commission.

[1] Sue Badeau is the Deputy Director of the Pew Commission on Children in Foster Care. She has been a child welfare professional for over 22 years and was a Public Policy Fellow in the U.S. Senate in 1999.

Sarah Gesiriech is the Special Assistant to the Deputy Director of the U.S. Department of Health and Human Services. Previously she worked as the Associate Director at the Domestic Policy Council for the White House.

Ann M. Haralambie, J.D., is a certified family law specialist practicing in Tucson, Arizona. She is also an author and speaker in the fields of family and children's law.

Amanda George Donnelly, J.D., is a Staff Attorney at the National Association of Counsel for Children (NACC).

Donald N. Duquette, J.D., is Clinical Professor of Law and Director of the Child Advocacy Law Clinic of the University of Michigan Law School. He is also a member of the National Association of Counsel for Children (NACC) Board of Directors.

[2] U.S. Department of Health and Human Services, Children's Bureau, *The AFCARS Report* #8 (March 2003). *Available at* www.acf.dhhs.gov/programs/cb/publications/afcars/report8.htm.

[3] *Id.*

Most children (60 percent) enter foster care when removed from their homes by a child protective agency because of abuse or neglect, or both. Others (17 percent) enter care because of the absence of their parents, resulting from illness, death, disability, or other problems. Some children enter care because of delinquent behavior (10 percent) or because they have committed a juvenile status offense (5 percent), such as running away or truancy. Roughly 5 percent of children enter care because of a disability.[4] For many, it represents their only access to disability services, for example, mental health care for a child with severe emotional disturbance. In these rare instances, in states that allow such placements, a child is placed in foster care voluntarily at the request of the child's parents.

Foster care is intended to provide a safe temporary home to a child until the child can be reunited safely with his or her parent or parents or adopted. However, being removed from home and placed in foster care is traumatic for a child, and the period of time a child may spend in care can be filled with uncertainty and change.[5]

A child in foster care is affected by a myriad of decisions established by federal and state laws designed to help the child. At each decision point, action or inaction can profoundly influence the child's current circumstances and future prospects. The discussion that follows highlights typical decision points on a child's journey through foster care. Although the format is based on federal and common state law and practice, it is only a model. Laws vary across states, as do the capacity and practices of child welfare agencies and courts to manage their caseloads. These factors can and often do create delays that complicate a child's journey through the child welfare system and often extend the child's time there.

---

[4] Karen Spar, Specialist in Social Legislation, Domestic Social Policy Division, Congressional Research Library, Library of Congress, Testimony before the Subcommittee on Human Resources, July 20, 1999. The figures in this paragraph represent Fiscal Year 1994 data.

[5] *Id.*

A Child's Journey through the Child Welfare System

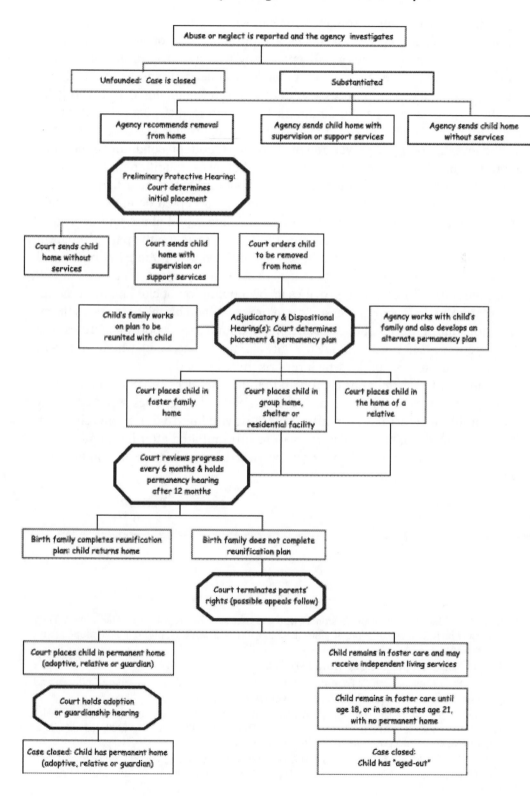

§ 10.2 Reporting Child Maltreatment

The child's journey through foster care usually begins when a mandated reporter[6] or concerned citizen makes a report of abuse or neglect to a state agency. For example, a doctor delivers a baby who has drugs in his or her system; a neighbor notices bruises on a child; a toddler is found abandoned in a public place; or a teacher notices a student who is unclean, unfed, or severely ill.

In 1974, Congress passed landmark legislation in the federal Child Abuse Prevention and Treatment Act (CAPTA).[7] The Act provided states with funding for the investigation and prevention of child maltreatment, conditioned on states adopting mandatory reporting laws. The Act also conditioned funding on reporter immunity, confidentiality, and the appointment of guardians ad litem for children. Although there is no one commonly accepted definition of "child abuse and neglect," the federal government defines child abuse and neglect in CAPTA as, at minimum, "any recent act or failure to act on the part of a parent or caretaker which results in death, serious physical or emotional harm, sexual abuse or exploitation; or an act or failure to act which presents an imminent risk of serious harm."[8] Each state provides its own definition of child maltreatment.[9] Abuse is often defined by states as "harm or threatened harm" or "serious threat or serious harm" to a child. All states have mandatory reporting statutes, but there are some differences among the various states concerning who must report and the circumstances under which reports must be made.

The U.S. Department of Health and Human Services (HHS) estimates that in 2001 (the last year for which data is available), CPS agencies received nearly three million referrals of maltreatment involving five million children. Approximately 903,000 of these cases were substantiated after investigation.[10]

The following types of abuse and neglect occurred (some in combination with others):

Type of Abuse	Percentage
Neglect	59.2%
Physical Abuse	18.6%

---

[6] State laws identify certain professionals who are mandated to report suspected abuse. They generally include medical professionals, teachers, daycare workers, photo lab developers, and law enforcement.

[7] Pub. L. No. 93-273; 42 U.S.C. § 5101 (2003).

[8] Child Abuse Prevention and Treatment Act (CAPTA), as amended by Keeping Children and Families Safe Act of 2003, 42 U.S.C. § 5106(g) (2003).

[9] *See* Nat'l Clearinghouse on Child Abuse and Neglect Information, 2003 Mandatory Reporters of Child Abuse and Neglect and Reporting Procedures (2003), *available at* http://nccanch.acf.hhs.gov/general/legal/statutes/manda.pdf.

[10] U.S. Department of Health and Human Services, Administration on Children, Youth and Families, Child Maltreatment 2001, p. 21 (Washington, DC: U.S. Government Printing Office 2003).

Sexual Abuse	9.6%
Emotional/Psychological maltreatment	6.8%
Other (abandonment, congenital drug addiction)	19.5%[11]

The ages of the victims ranged as follows:

Age	Percentage
Birth to 3 years	27.7%
4-7	24.1%
8-11	22.8%
12-15	19.5%
16-21 or unknown	6.0%[12]

More than half (56.5 percent) of substantiated reports were made by professionals, including teachers, law enforcement officers, and physicians. The remaining 43.5 percent were made by family members, neighbors, and other members of the community.[13]

The majority of the victims were maltreated by a parent (birth, adoptive, or step). The breakdown is as follows:

Relationship to the Child	Percentage
Mothers (acting alone or with a non-parent)	46.9%
Fathers (acting alone or with a non-parent)	18.7%
Mother and Father	19.3%
Non-parent	11.9%
Unknown	3.1%[14]

In 2001, an estimated 1,300 children died from abuse or neglect. Eighteen of these deaths (1.5 percent) occurred while a child was under the custody or supervision of the child welfare agency.[15]

§ 10.3 Reporting by Professionals

Typically, professionals who deal with children are required to report suspicion of abuse. If they fail to do so, they may suffer criminal or civil penalties. Under some statutes, professionals are required to report suspicion of abuse if the suspicion originates from the professional's observation or examination of

---

[11] *Id.* at 21. The percentages total more than 100 percent of victims because children may have been victims of more than one type of maltreatment.

[12] *Id.* at 23.

[13] *Id.* at 3, 7.

[14] *Id.* at 43, 45.

[15] *Id.* at 51, 55.

the child (as opposed to merely hearing about the abuse from a person other than the child). Doctors, nurses, teachers, psychologists, and daycare workers who have a reasonable *suspicion* of abuse generally must make a report, even if they would not be in a position to testify that they held a professional opinion that abuse had occurred. In other words, it is the duty of child protective services or law enforcement to investigate suspected abuse. It is not the reporter's obligation to conduct an investigation. Tort liability may lie against a mandated reporter who delays making a report because he or she has not determined whether, in fact, the child's injuries were caused by abuse. Similarly, the obligation to report is personal to the mandated reporter and may not be discharged by reporting to an administrative supervisor who decides not to report.

Professional privileges for confidential communications are generally abrogated by the mandatory reporting laws. However, in some states a few privileges remain and excuse an otherwise mandated reporter from making a report if the source of the suspicion is a privileged communication. In Nevada and Ohio, for example, attorneys and clergy are mandated reporters. Both states, however, have exceptions for privileged communications between attorney and client, and between clergy and penitent.[16] If the abuse is disclosed during a privileged conversation, these specific mandated reporters are not required to report it.

§ 10.4 Reporting by Nonprofessionals

Any person *may* report cases of suspected child abuse or neglect. But in some states family members or neighbors *must* report suspicions of child maltreatment. In 2003, eighteen states required all citizens, regardless of their profession, to report suspected child maltreatment.[17] Additionally, some states require any individual who has contact with children to report suspected child abuse or neglect. For example, Arizona requires all parents and anyone responsible for the treatment or care of a child to report suspected child abuse or neglect.[18] Most states require the reporter to have reasonable cause to suspect child maltreatment.

§ 10.4.1 Good Faith: Immunity from Civil Liability

Even if a person is not mandated to make a report, discretionary reports may be made, even anonymously. In most cases, the reporter is entitled to immunity from civil suit by the parents based on the report, so long as the report was made in good faith.

---

[16] *Id.* at 16, 19.

[17] *Id.* at 1.

[18] *Id.* at 4.

§ 10.4.2 Liability for Making False or Malicious Report

Many states now provide specifically for tort liability against people making malicious reports. The California penal code addresses liability for persons making false reports; the statute provides in part:

> No mandated reporter shall be civilly or criminally liable for any report required or authorized by this article . . . Any other person reporting a known or suspected instance of child abuse or neglect shall not incur civil or criminal liability as a result of any report authorized by this article unless it can be proven that a false report was made and the person knew that the report was false or was made with reckless disregard of the truth or falsity of the report, and any person who makes a report of child abuse or neglect known to be false or with reckless disregard of the truth or falsity of the report is liable for any damages caused . . .[19]

Similarly, the Idaho Code states that any person who reports suspected child abuse or neglect in bad faith or with malice is not provided immunity for reporting.[20]

§ 10.5 Investigating Child Maltreatment

Once a report of maltreatment has been made, the CPS agency investigates whether abuse or neglect has occurred and assesses the risks to the child. According to the National Child Abuse and Neglect Data System, a total of 2.6 million referrals to child protective services, involving 4.5 million children, were made in 2002.[21] Child protective services received more than 50,000 referrals alleging child abuse or neglect on a weekly basis.[22] Approximately one-third of reports made to child protective services are "screened out" and not investigated. The remainder of the referrals were either investigated by CPS to determine if a child was maltreated or assessed for risk of maltreatment. Of the reports that were investigated, 26.8 percent resulted in a substantiated report of child maltreatment.[23]

§ 10.5.1 Time Frame

Once a report is made, child protective services or law enforcement must investigate within a specific period of time unless the facts alleged would not

---

[19] CAL. PENAL CODE § 11172(a) (2004).

[20] IDAHO CODE § 16-1620 (2004).

[21] CHILDREN'S BUREAU, U.S. DEP'T OF HEALTH AND HUMAN SERVS., CHILD MALTREATMENT 2002, at 5 (Washington, D.C.: U.S. Government Printing Office 2004), *available at* http://www.acf.dhhs.gov/programs/cb/publications/cm02/cm02.pdf.

[22] *Id.* at 5.

[23] *Id.* at 7.

constitute abuse or neglect under the requisite state statutes. Most states designate reports as high or low priority and respond accordingly.[24] High-priority reports of child maltreatment are generally investigated within 1 to 24 hours of the report. Child protective services agencies respond to lower-priority reports of abuse between 24 hours and 14 days of the report.[25] Given limited funding for child protective services, there is always some degree of triage involved, and rarely are all required investigations performed in a timely manner or at all. Other cases are investigated in only a cursory manner.

§ 10.5.2 Risk Assessment

Initially, child protective services must assess the situation to determine if the child has been maltreated or if the child is at a substantial risk of maltreatment.[26] Most states use risk assessment models designed to structure decision making, predict future harm, aid in resource management by identifying service needs for children and families, and facilitate communication between the agency and community.[27] The assessment may include a visit to the family home and interviews with the family and persons outside the family. The family may help identify services that may be needed to better care for their child, such as parenting skills training or addiction services.[28]

> *The majority of children entered foster care because of neglect, often the result of inadequate housing, poor child care, or insufficient food or medical care.*
>
> *A substantial percentage of parents with children in foster care have substance abuse treatment needs.*[29]

Agencies analyze the risk assessment information and evaluate the situation of the child and family, their strengths and resources, and community services. Child protective services then determines whether there is sufficient and believable information to confirm maltreatment and assigns significance to the risks and family strengths. Additional risk assessment criteria are considered in cases

---

[24] *Id.*

[25] *Id.* (citing CHILDREN'S BUREAU, U.S. DEP'T OF HEALTH AND HUMAN SERVS., NATIONAL STUDY OF CHILD PROTECTIVE SERVICES SYSTEMS AND REFORM EFFORTS: REVIEW OF STATE CPS POLICY (Washington, D.C: U.S. Government Printing Office 2003), *available at* http://aspe.hhs.gov/search/hsp/CPS-status03/.

[26] DIANE DEPANFILIS & MARSHA K. SALUS, U.S. DEP'T OF HEALTH AND HUMAN SERVS., CHILD PROTECTIVE SERVICES: A GUIDE FOR CASEWORKERS 25-26 (2003), *available at* http://nccanch.acf.hhs.gov/pubs/usermanuals/cps/cps.pdf.

[27] *Id.* at 43-45 (internal citations omitted).

[28] The Oklahoma Department of Human Services, *The Child Welfare Journey*, *available at* http://www.okdhs.org/cfsd/howtos/CW/Index.html.

[29] Child Welfare League of America, Behavioral Health Division, *Alcohol and Other Drugs: About the Program*, *available at* http://www.cwla.org/programs/bhd/aod.htm.

involving substance abusing families, families where partner abuse is an issue, and families with unique cultural backgrounds.[30] Child protective services then evaluates the child's safety.

§ 10.5.3 Safety Assessment

The Adoption and Safe Families Act requires states to provide safe environments for children in birth families, out-of-home care, and adoptive homes. The risk of child maltreatment and the safety of a child are two separate inquiries. Safety assessment requires the caseworker to make two determinations. First, when the caseworker initially meets with the family, he or she must determine if the child is currently in danger. Then, at the end of the initial assessment, the caseworker must consider the following factors:

- Whether the child will be safe in the home without further involvement by child protective services.

- Under what circumstances the case could be moved to community partners.

- Whether home-based services are necessary to protect the child.

- Ultimately, whether the child needs to be placed in out-of-home care.

Child protective services uses the findings of the risk assessment to determine the child's safety at the conclusion of the initial assessment.[31]

§ 10.5.4 Investigating Evidence of Child Maltreatment

Child protective services also considers whether the harm to the child constitutes child maltreatment and whether there is sufficient evidence to support a case of child maltreatment.[32] For example, a thorough investigation of a report involving physical abuse includes collecting information about the injury and photographing the child as soon as possible.[33] Additionally the investigator should interview the child and possible witnesses, including siblings, neighbors, teachers, caregivers, and medical personnel. It is crucial that the investigation is well documented; legally it is very important to be able to trace what exactly was asked during interviews.[34] The child's medical records, school or daycare records, and family history should also be reviewed.[35]

---

[30] *Id.*

[31] *Id.*

[32] *Id.* (internal citations omitted).

[33] Many state statutes permit photographing children as part of an investigation into child maltreatment. *See* FLA. STAT. § 39.301(19) (2003); ARIZ. REV. STAT. § 13-3620(I) (2004).

[34] JOHN E.B. MYERS, LEGAL ISSUES IN CHILD ABUSE AND NEGLECT PRACTICE 166 (2d ed.) (Thousand Oaks, CA: Sage 1998).

[35] *See generally* OFFICE OF JUVENILE JUSTICE AND DELINQUENCY PREVENTION, U.S. DEP'T OF JUST., PORTABLE GUIDES TO INVESTIGATING CHILD ABUSE (1996-1998).

If the investigation reveals problems that do not pose an immediate danger to the child, and if the family will cooperate with services, the agency might refer the family to voluntary services without filing a court action. The family might agree to an informal period of out-of-home placement of the child with a relative, friend, or foster home. The agency might require the parents to file a written contract covering this arrangement. If the parent does not cooperate with the voluntary services or does not remedy the problem, the agency might choose to pursue court action.

§ 10.5.5 Interpreting Labels of "Founded" or "Unfounded" on Agency Reports

Attorneys involved in child welfare cases must understand the limitations of investigations in some circumstances and not assume that reports labeled "unfounded," "unsubstantiated," or otherwise closed without a finding of abuse or neglect mean that there was an affirmative determination that no abuse or neglect occurred. Many child protective services agencies are limited to two choices (such as "founded" and "unfounded") and are not permitted to indicate varying degrees of suspicion. In some agencies, reports are designated "unfounded" if the family cannot be located. Sometimes, even with a good investigation, a report may be labeled "unfounded" because there is simply insufficient evidence to prove what the investigator feels was real abuse. Sometimes a series of "unfounded" reports reflects a malicious or hypervigilant reporter. Often it reflects limitations of proof, limitations of time or experience of the investigator, or children and families unwilling to speak honestly. Attorneys need to look carefully at the facts of each case without making assumptions based on the labels assigned to reports.

§ 10.5.6 Emergency Protective Custody

Some states provide that child protective services or law enforcement may take a child into emergency protective custody for an investigative period without the parent's consent or a court order. When a child is taken into emergency protective custody, there must be a judicial review of the state's action within a specified amount of time, generally between 48 and 96 hours. For example, in Florida, a law enforcement officer or a social worker may take a child into custody without a court order if he or she has probable cause to believe the child has been abused or is in imminent danger of injury.[36] The child's parents must be notified immediately and there must be a shelter hearing within 24 hours of removal.[37] State legislatures are challenged with striking a balance between pro-

---

[36] FLA. STAT. § 39.401 (2003).

[37] FLA. STAT. § 39.402 (2003).

viding law enforcement and child protective services with the authority to protect children, on the one hand, and safeguarding the rights of parents, on the other.

In most states, child protective services or law enforcement may enter a home without a search warrant if they believe a child is in imminent danger. In Utah, however, the state legislature passed a bill in 2002 that required state workers to obtain a court-ordered warrant before they take a child into protective custody.[38] The law was changed in response to citizens' concerns about the lack of due process in the state's child welfare laws, which previously allowed the state to take custody of a child if they had substantial cause to believe the child was at risk.[39] Additionally, many states provide statutory authority for social services, law enforcement, or school personnel to conduct an initial interview with a child at school without giving the child's parents prior notice.[40]

§ 10.6 Initiating Court Action

Every child welfare case begins with either the filing of a petition or an emergency removal. The case then proceeds to a detention hearing to determine whether the child should be removed from his or her home or returned if he or she was previously removed. The case then proceeds through these procedural steps:

- The adjudicatory (fact-finding) hearing.

- The disposition hearing.

- A series of periodic review hearings and permanency hearings.

- A termination of parental rights hearing.

A child welfare case can be dismissed at any time during the case process, and appeals can be made at different stages throughout the life of the case.

If the investigator determines that court action is necessary, the agency will file a petition. Many states restrict the ability to file dependency petitions to the state or county agency. Sometimes a private child welfare agency is given standing to file. In some states, designated private individuals may file. In a few states, any person having a legitimate interest in the child may file a petition; in those states, even if the agency's investigation is closed without the filing of a petition, a concerned adult may nevertheless seek court intervention. Local law determines whether such actions are filed in juvenile court, family court, probate court, or other courts. For purposes of this chapter, we will refer to the relevant court generically as "juvenile court."

---

[38] UTAH CODE ANN. § 62A-4a-202.1 (2000).

[39] Charles G. Wentworth, Recent Legislative Developments, *Taking Minor Into Protective Custody Without Warrant*, 2003 UTAH L. REV. 803 (2003).

[40] ME. REV. STAT. ANN. tit. 22, § 4021(3) (2003).

§ 10.7 Emergency Removal/Detention

In most cases, the temporary custody order is obtained *ex parte*. Usually, all that is required is a *prima facie* showing that the child is likely to be in danger of imminent harm. In some jurisdictions, the *prima facie* showing may be established by hearsay, written declarations, or other procedures short of a full evidentiary hearing. If a child is placed in temporary custody, the parents and, arguably, the child are entitled to an expedited hearing to review custody. This may be called an "emergency hearing," "shelter care hearing," or "preliminary hearing" and is typically held 24 to 72 hours after an emergency removal of the child. Some courts use mediation, family group conferencing, family group decision-making, or other procedures to attempt to work out temporary orders involving placement, access, and pretrial services to address the family's problems.[41] The temporary custody hearing may also address other temporary orders, such as establishing initial services to be provided to the parents and children, visitation if the child is not returned to the parent, and the designation of financial responsibility for the child.

The court may provide third parties, such as relatives, limited party status. For example, the court may permit a relative who desires to be a placement for the child to appear at the temporary custody hearing and to participate on the issue of placement. Full intervening party status might be granted under certain circumstances.

If the child is placed in a shelter, the state's statute may require interim review hearings of temporary custody until the child is placed in a foster home or other more long-term placement. In such cases, the agency is required to make reasonable efforts to find a more appropriate placement for the child.[42]

The agency has a duty to make reasonable efforts to prevent or eliminate the need for removal of the child from the home, except under certain circumstances.[43] The agency must be prepared to explain to the court what efforts it has made, why the child must be removed, or why reasonable efforts were not required under the statutory criteria.[44] The agency must develop a case plan for the child within 60 days of the child's removal from home.[45] The parents have a right to be involved in developing the case plan.[46] Once a child is removed, the agency has a duty to make "reasonable efforts" to maintain the family unit and make it possible for the child to return home safely.[47]

---

[41] For a further discussion of alternative dispute resolution, *see* Chapter 16, Non-Adversarial Case Resolution.

[42] 45 C.F.R. § 1356.21(b).

[43] 45 C.F.R. § 1356.21(b)(3).

[44] 45 C.F.R. § 1356.21(b)(3).

[45] 45 C.F.R. § 1356.21(g)(2).

[46] 45 C.F.R. § 1356.21(g)(1).

[47] 45 C.F.R. § 1356.21(b).

The court's determination at a temporary custody hearing is non-appealable, but it may be reviewed by filing for an extraordinary writ. Child placement decisions are time-sensitive for children, and extraordinary writs are an appropriate means for reviewing a temporary custody order or order denying temporary custody.

§ 10.8 Pretrial Discovery and Motion Practice

Child welfare law includes trial practice, and child welfare law specialists should be excellent trial lawyers. Because many courts schedule only short hearings in child welfare cases, it is particularly important to be well prepared, well organized, efficient, and compelling in presenting evidence and cross-examining witnesses.

In most states, the state rules of civil procedure apply to child welfare cases. In some states, there are additional juvenile court rules or local rules. In states that follow the Federal Rules of Civil Procedure, parties to child welfare cases may have an affirmative duty to provide disclosure.[48] In addition, discovery should be available, at least with respect to the adjudicatory dependency or termination hearings. Children's attorneys, as well as agency attorneys and parent's attorneys, should avail themselves of discovery techniques when appropriate. Appointed counsel may or may not be given funds with which to conduct discovery. In such cases, while it may not be possible to take depositions, the attorney can still use less costly methods of discovery, such as requests for admission, requests for production of documents, and interrogatories. Requests for admission are particularly helpful in narrowing the contested trial issues. Where discovery is permitted after adjudication, interrogatories can be used to clarify expectations and to monitor the compliance and progress of all parties with rehabilitative services.

Attorneys for each of the parties should develop a trial strategy, plan and prepare witnesses and exhibits, and present a cogent, efficient case.[49]

§ 10.9 Adjudication

The court at the dependency trial determines whether or not the facts alleged have been proven true by a preponderance of the evidence, and whether the case meets the statutory requirements for a dependency adjudication under state law. Under the federal Child Abuse Prevention and Treatment Act (CAPTA),[50] the court must provide representation for the child by an attorney

---

[48] FED. R. CIV. P. 26.

[49] *See* Chapter 22, Trial Advocacy, for in-depth treatment of trial practice issues.

[50] Child Abuse Prevention and Treatment Act (CAPTA), 42 U.S.C. § 5106a(b)(2)(A)(xiii). For a more detailed discussion of CAPTA, *see* Chapter 8, Federal Child Welfare Law and Policy: Understanding the Federal Law and Funding Process.

or guardian ad litem. Various states have different requirements for who provides such representation and the role of that person. Although not required as a matter of federal constitutional law, most states appoint attorneys for indigent parents.[51]

State law determines how quickly the adjudicatory hearing must be held. If the child is placed out-of-home, the hearing may be accelerated. The hearing may have to be completed in as little as 60 days from the date of filing the petition.[52]

The petitioner has the burden of proving the abuse or neglect by a preponderance of the evidence.[53] A heightened standard of proof is not required because dependency cases balance the interests of the child as well as those of the parents and the state or county. While a parent's criminal conviction for abuse or neglect involving the same facts may establish the grounds for dependency, acquittal on the criminal charges is not relevant because of the heightened criminal standard of proof and the different statutory requirements for the juvenile court proceeding.

§ 10.10 Disposition

If the child is adjudicated dependent, the court may enter dispositional orders at the same time as the adjudication, or it may set a separate dispositional hearing. The child may be adjudicated dependent but permitted to remain in the home, under the supervision of the agency and court. The dispositional hearing will determine: (1) the child's custodial placement; (2) terms of contact between child and parent if the child is not placed in the home; and (3) services to be provided to both the parent and child. If the child is an "Indian child"[54] within the meaning of the Indian Child Welfare Act (ICWA),[55] the court must observe the placement priorities set forth in the federal law.[56] The tribe may approve deviations from the placement preferences, and the court may alter the preferences for good cause shown, as construed by the applicable federal standards.[57]

---

[51] *See Lassiter v. Dept. of Soc. Servs.*, 452 U.S. 18, 30 (1981).

[52] *See* NATIONAL COUNCIL OF JUVENILE AND FAMILY COURT JUDGES, RESOURCE GUIDELINES: IMPROVING COURT PRACTICE IN CHILD ABUSE & NEGLECT CASES (Reno, NV 1995) for a discussion of adjudication timelines.

[53] *See, e.g., In re Redmon*, 460 So. 2d 1317 (Ala. Civ. App. 1984) (proof beyond a reasonable doubt not necessary); *People in Interest of P.*, 654 P.2d 312 (Colo. 1982); *In re Sabrina M.*, 460 A.2d 1009 (Me. 1983); *In re Tammie Z.*, 66 N.Y.2d 1, 484 N.E.2d 1038, 494 N.Y.S.2d 686 (1985); *Wright v. Arlington County Dept of Social Servs*, 388 S.E.2d 477(Va. Ct. App. 1990); *In re Chubb*, 46 Wash. App. 530, 731 P.2d 537 (1987). *See also* 17B A.R.S. JUV. CT. RULES OF PROC. R. 17 (2004); N.J. STAT. ANN § 9:6-8.46(b); A.C.A. § 9-27-325(h) (2004); COLO. REV. STAT. § 19-3-505(1) (2004).

[54] For the definition of "Indian child," *see* 25 U.S.C. § 1903(4).

[55] 25 U.S.C. §§ 1901 through 1963. For a more detailed discussion of ICWA, *see* Chapter 8, Federal Child Welfare Law and Policy: Understanding the Federal Law and Funding Process.

[56] 25 U.S.C. § 1915 (2004).

[57] 25 U.S.C. § 1915(a) (2004).

The permanency plan for the family should be specified. In 2001, the case goals of 541,998 children in state custody were:

Case Goal	Percentage (number)
Mothers Reunify with Parent(s) or Principal Caretaker(s)	44% (241,051)
Adoption	22% (116,653)
Case Plan Goal Not Yet Established	11% (62,014)
Long Term Foster Care	8% (45,792)
Emancipation	6% (32,309)
Live with Other Relative(s)	5% (26,555)
Guardianship	3% (17,624)[58]

In 2001, the placement settings for children in state custody were:

Placement Setting	Percentage (number)
Foster Family Home	48% (260,384)
Relative foster home	24% (130,869)
Institution	10% (56,509)
Group Home	8% (43,084)
Pre-Adoptive Home	4% (20,289)
Trial Home Visit	3% (16,685)
Runaway	2% (9,112)
Supervised Independent Living	1% (5,068)[59]

Placement of the child is reevaluated at disposition and remains an essential and ongoing concern of the case. Placement at home may be risky for a child, but out-of-home placement carries its own hazards. More than 20 percent of children in foster care will move at least three times, and in some cases they move seven or more times.[60] Children move for many reasons, including attrition and lack of training or support for foster families, lack of resources to address a child's special needs, or because the child's behavior may be difficult for some foster parents to manage. Lawyers for all the parties are well advised to see placement "through the eyes of the child." If the child is removed from his or her home, the child is separated from his or her parents and may be separated from siblings, as well. The child will meet new temporary "parents" and adjust to their lifestyle and house rules. Foster parents may have their own children or other foster children in their homes. The child may have to attend a new school,

---

[58] U.S. Department of Health and Human Services, Children's Bureau, *The AFCARS Report #8* (March 2003), *available at* www.acf.dhhs.gov/programs/cb/publications/afcars/report8.htm.

[59] *Id.*

[60] Kathy Barbell & Madelyn Freundlich, *Foster Care Today* (Washington, DC: Casey Family Programs 2001), pp. 3-4. These figures were based on 1994 data from the U.S. House of Representatives, 2000.

leaving old friends behind and adjusting to a new teacher, new classmates, and new rules. The emotional adjustments will differ for children placed with relatives or placed in their own neighborhood. The child will have to make these adjustments each time he or she is moved.

Federal law recognizes a preference for placement with relatives.[61] However, the regulations clarify that health and safety are the paramount considerations when any placement decision is made regarding a child in foster care, including care with a relative.[62] Generally, relatives do not receive foster care payments unless they are licensed foster care providers.

Although the total number of licensed family foster homes in the United States is not known, in 1998, 38 states reported a total of 133,503 homes.[63] Unfortunately, turnover among foster parents is high; 30 to 50 percent leave the system every year.[64] Foster parents receive stipends to cover room and board, child care, and clothing. They may also receive Medicaid coverage for the children in their care.

In some jurisdictions, mediation, family group conferencing, or family group decision making are available to assist the parties in reaching a dispositional agreement. The best dispositional orders are clear and specific in outlining the terms of placement, and in setting forth the specific expectations of all the parties.

§ 10.11 Case Plans

At any time the child is removed from the parent's home, federal law requires that the agency develop a case plan within a reasonable time, not to exceed 60 days.[65] All of the parties are entitled to participate in developing the case plan.[66] The case plan should outline the responsibilities of each party, including what services the agency will provide and what is expected of the parents and child. Any party may suggest alternate services, different visitation, participation of the child in ongoing activities, or different time lines.[67] The goals and objectives of the case plan and the services provided should reflect the

---

[61] 42 U.S.C. § 671(a)(18).

[62] Children's Defense Fund, Child Welfare and Mental Health Division, *The Adoption and Safe Families Act (ASFA) Basics* (Spring 2000), *available at* http://www.childrensdefense.org /child-welfare/adoption/asfa_basics.asp; Title IV-E Foster Care Eligibility Reviews and Child and Family Services State Plan Reviews, 65 FED. REG. 4020-01 (January 25, 2000), pp. 4032-4033.

[63] U.S. Department of Health and Human Services, Administration for Children & Families, National Clearinghouse on Child Abuse and Neglect Information, *Foster Care National Statistics* (April 2001).

[64] University of Tennessee Family Foster Care Project, *Foster Family Forum*, Issue 1 (July 2002), *available at* http://utcmhsrc.csw.utk.edu/caseyproject/newsletters/Newsletter%20July%2002.pdf.

[65] 45 C.F.R. § 1356.21(g)(2).

[66] 45 C.F.R. § 1356.21(g)(1).

[67] 45 C.F.R. § 1356.21(g)(1)

court's findings and the statutory bases for the dependency adjudication. The services should be designed to remedy or address the problems identified and should include realistic time lines by which each party is expected to be responsible for meeting the goals and objectives. The case plan should build on the strengths and resources of the parents, child, and family. The case plan should address both the reasonable needs of the child and the deficits of the parents.[68] The child's needs are broader than those merely designed to return the child home or find an alternative permanency plan—addressing the child's needs means responding to the child's educational, extracurricular, and associational needs. The more specific and objectively measurable the case plan is, the easier it will be for the parties to determine when and whether each party is in compliance. Such specificity also assists the court in determining whether the agency has made reasonable efforts toward achieving the case plan, and whether the parents have made reasonable efforts at compliance.

Concurrent planning is permitted.[69] Therefore, even if the plan is return to the child to his or her parent, the agency may also prepare for a different plan in the event that the reunification does not occur. For example, if it appears that the agency must provide reasonable efforts to reunify the family, but reunification seems unlikely, the agency might choose to place the child in a foster-adoptive home so that if the plan changes to termination of parental rights, the child's foster parents would adopt the child. Such concurrent planning increases the likelihood that the child will not have to move if the permanency plan changes.

§ 10.12 Review Hearings

Review hearings must be held every six months from the previous hearing until the child is adopted or until an alternate permanent plan has been effectuated.[70] Some states hold review hearings quarterly or even more frequently. Federal law permits review hearings to be conducted by the court or an administrative body (including a citizen review panel). But state law may specify that review hearings must be heard by the court. Notice of the review hearings must be provided not only to the parties, but also to foster parents, fost-adopt parents, and relative caretakers, who are entitled to be heard at review hearings even though they are not parties.[71] In some states, review hearings may include hearsay reports, so long as the caseworker providing the report is available for cross-examination. One particular type of review hearing, the permanency planning hearing, is discussed separately below.

---

[68] 45 C.F.R. § 1356.21(g)(3). *See also* Adoption and Safe Families Act of 1997, Pub. L. No. 105-89.

[69] 45 C.F.R. § 1356.21(b)(4).

[70] 25 C.F.R. § 20.510.

[71] 45 C.F.R. § 1356.21(o).

In a review hearing, the court needs to be able to determine from the evidence whether the child is safe, whether additional or different steps must be made to ensure the child's safety, or whether the child may now be safely returned to the parent. The court needs to be able to determine whether the parent has achieved the case plan objectives, and if so, whether there should be changes to the child's placement or visitation, or whether there need to be changes in the services offered. If the parent has not yet achieved any of the case plan objectives, the court needs to be able to determine whether there should be changes in the objectives, changes in the services, or changes in the case plan or whether the parent should be given more time to achieve the objectives. The case review must also set a target date for the child's return home, adoption, or other permanent placement.[72]

As well as reviewing the parent's progress, the court will review whether the agency has provided timely and appropriate services. Unless the case circumstances fall within an exception, the agency has a continuing duty to make reasonable efforts to prevent the need for removal of the child from the home or to reunify the child with the family if the child has been removed.[73] At each review hearing, the court must make specific findings concerning whether the child continues to be dependent and whether the agency is making reasonable efforts to reunify the family or pursue another approved permanency plan. The court will review the appropriateness of the current case plan and order appropriate changes or additions to the case plan.

§ 10.13 Permanency Hearings

The Adoption and Safe Families Act (ASFA)[74] requires that the court must hold a permanency planning hearing within 12 months from the time the child enters foster care.[75] If the court determines that the agency is not required to make any or further reasonable efforts at reunification, the permanency hearing must be held within 30 days of that determination.[76]

There are a variety of permanency plans other than simply the choice between return to parent and termination of parental rights followed by adoption. For example, in some cases an appropriate plan could be permanent guardianship or independent living. Some children are best served by maintaining the legal parent-child relationship even if they are not permitted to have visitation.

---

[72] U.S. Department of Health and Human Services, National Clearinghouse on Child Abuse and Neglect Information, *Overview of the Civil Child Protective Court Process* (1992), *available at* http://nccanch.acf.hhs.gov/pubs/usermanuals/courts/courtsd.cfm (last visited March 30, 2005).

[73] 42 U.S.C. § 671(a)(15)(B).

[74] The Adoption and Safe Families Act of 1997 (ASFA), Pub. L. No. 105-89.

[75] 42 U.S.C. § 675(5)(C).

[76] 42 U.S.C. § 671(a)(15)(E)(i).

It is important that permanency plans be made thoughtfully, based on an individualized assessment of the particular child's needs and family circumstances, rather than on generalized philosophical positions. The agency must propose a permanency plan, but the parents and child should also develop and advocate an appropriate plan.

Under some circumstances, the court might extend foster care for an additional period to continue reunification efforts. This is particularly likely when there have been defects in the services offered by the agency. For example, the agency may not have been diligent in obtaining appropriate services, or long waiting lists may have precluded a parent from participating in a service identified in the case plan, despite the parent's best efforts. If the parent has been diligent in participating in the case plan and is making good progress but is not yet ready to assume custody of the child, and if reunification is in the child's best interests, the court may continue the child in foster care. However, under ASFA, maintaining reunification as a permanent plan for more than 12 months after the child's removal is less likely than it used to be.

A court may choose from among several permanency options for the child. In 2001, 263,000 children exited foster care in the following ways:

Outcomes for Children Exiting Foster Care	Percentage (number)
Reunification with Parent/Primary Caretaker	57% (148,606)
Living with Other Relative(s)	10% (26,084)
Adoption	18% (46,668)
Guardianship	3% (8,969)
Emancipation	7% (19,008)
Transfer to Another Agency	3% (7,918)
Runaway	2% (5,219)
Death of Child[77]	less than 1% (528)[78]

If the parents are successful with the court-ordered treatment plan, the child is reunited with his or her parents, and the case is closed.

In 2001, more than 57 percent (148,606) of children in out-of-home care were reunited with their families.[79]

However, other studies have noted that approximately 33 percent of children who were reunified with their families re-entered foster care within

---

[77] These deaths resulted from all causes, including accidental and natural. Only 18 deaths resulted from abuse.

[78] U.S. Department of Health and Human Services, Children's Bureau, *The AFCARS Report #8* (March 2003), *available at* www.acf.dhhs.gov/programs/cb/publications/afcars/ report8.htm.

[79] *Id.*

three years.[80] *And, approximately 17 percent of children who entered fos-ter care had been in foster care before.*[81]

§ 10.14 Termination of Parental Rights

If a parent fails to comply with the reunification plan, the child welfare agency will petition the court to terminate the parents' rights to the child. At any point during the court process, a parent may seek to voluntarily relinquish his or her parental rights.[82] When the parents' rights are terminated, a permanent plan for the child will be created.[83]

Federal law requires states to initiate Termination of Parental Rights (TPR) proceedings for: (1) children who have been in foster care for 15 of the most recent 22 months; (2) infants determined to be abandoned; (3) cases in which a parent has killed another of his/her children; or (4) certain other egregious situations. States may opt not to initiate TPR if: (1) the child is in a relative's care; (2) the child welfare agency has documented a compelling reason that TPR would not be in the child's best interest; or (3) the state has not provided necessary services to the family.[84]

In 2001, the living parents of more than 65,000 children had their parental rights terminated.[85]

As a matter of federal constitutional law, the petition must prove the grounds for termination by clear and convincing evidence.[86] Typically, the petitioner must also prove by a preponderance of the evidence that termination is in the best interests of the child. Even if the parent's actions or inactions constitute statutory grounds for termination, the child's circumstances may be such that maintaining the legal parent-child relationship promotes the child's best inter-

---

[80] U.S. General Accounting Office, *FOSTER CARE Recent Legislation Helps States Focus on Finding Permanent Homes for Children, But Long-Standing Barriers Remain* (GAC-02-585) (Washington, DC: U.S. Government Printing Office 2002), p. 10.

[81] U.S. Department of Health and Human Services, Administration for Children & Families, National Clearinghouse on Child Abuse and Neglect Information, *Foster Care National Statistics* (April 2001), (2000b).

[82] The Oklahoma Department of Human Services, *The Child Welfare Journey*, *available at* http://www.okdhs.org/cfsd/howtos/CW/Index.html.

[83] *Id.*

[84] 42 U.S.C. § 675(1)(5)(E). In the case of an abandoned child, regulations require States to initiate TPR within 60 days of a court determination of abandonment and in the case of a child whose parent has been convicted of a felony specified in the law 60 days of a court determination that reasonable efforts to reunite are not required.

[85] U.S. Department of Health and Human Services, Children's Bureau, *The AFCARS Report #8* (March 2003), *available at* www.acf.dhhs.gov/programs/cb/publications/afcars/ report8.htm.

[86] *See Santosky v. Kramer*, 455 U.S. 745, 747-749 (1982).

ests. With the accelerated time lines provided by ASFA, agencies are moving more quickly to termination. For some children, however, termination does not result in the child having a permanent home. Older children in particular may drift from group home to group home or be placed in correctional facilities or residential treatment centers, as "legal orphans" in the de facto permanent guardianship of the state.

If the case falls within the federal Indian Child Welfare Act (ICWA),[87] then notice must also be provided to the child's Indian tribe or Native Alaskan Village.[88] The tribe or village may have the right to have the case transferred to tribal court.[89] If the case proceeds in state court, the tribe or village has the right to participate in the state proceeding.[90] The standard of proof, at least for the required ICWA findings, is proof beyond a reasonable doubt; this is true even when applied to the non-Indian parent of an Indian child.[91] ICWA also requires that certain findings be supported by expert testimony.[92]

§ 10.15 Post-Termination Review Hearings

When a child is not immediately adopted, so long as the court maintains jurisdiction over the child, review hearings will continue, even after termination of parental rights. Post-termination reviews are like regular review hearings, with some additional features. Family reunification is no longer a goal, but the court must still ensure that adequate services are provided to the child and that a realistic placement plan is aggressively pursued.[93] Continuation of sibling and other familial relationships may also be an appropriate part of the case plan. Because the child is a "legal orphan," having no legal parent, the court and agency or other legal guardian have a particularly important role to play in the child's life, especially in preparing the child for independence.

§ 10.16 Achieving Permanence for the Child

Options for legal permanence for the child are discussed in Chapter 17, Establishing Legal Permanence for the Child.

---

[87] 25 U.S.C. §§ 1901 through 1963. For a more detailed discussion of ICWA, *see* Chapter 8, Federal Child Welfare Law and Policy: Understanding the Federal Law and Funding Process.

[88] 25 U.S.C. § 1912(a) (2004).

[89] 25 U.S.C. § 1911(b) (2004).

[90] 25 U.S.C. § 1911(c) (2004).

[91] 25 U.S.C. § 1912(f) (2004).

[92] 25 U.S.C. § 1912(f) (2004).

[93] NATIONAL COUNCIL OF JUVENILE AND FAMILY COURT JUDGES, RESOURCE GUIDELINES: IMPROVING COURT PRACTICE IN CHILD ABUSE & NEGLECT CASES, 94 (Reno, NV 1995).

Chapter 11   DEPENDENCY COURT JURISDICTION AND INTERSTATE AND INTERNATIONAL PROCEEDINGS

by Ann M. Haralambie[1]

§ 11.1 Jurisdiction of the Dependency Court and Collateral Courts

Some states have specialized trial courts, and child welfare proceedings may be heard in family, juvenile, or probate courts. States differ on whether such proceedings come within the jurisdictional requirements of the Uniform Child Custody Jurisdiction Act (UCCJA) or its more recent version: the Uniform Child Custody Jurisdiction and Enforcement Act (UCCJEA).[2] In states that do include dependency actions under those uniform acts, the child's presence in the state will not be sufficient to assure the court's jurisdiction, at least not beyond initial temporary orders. If the child's habitual residence is in a different country that is a signatory to the Hague Convention on the International Aspects of Civil Child Abduction,[3] the juvenile court may not be able to make more than provisional orders concerning the child.

Notice must be provided to a person who has custody of the child, and in many states notice must also be provided to noncustodial parents, persons standing in *loco parentis*, and putative fathers of children born out of wedlock. Persons who have court-ordered visitation may also be entitled to notice. If the case falls within the federal Indian Child Welfare Act (ICWA),[4] then notice must also be provided to the child's Indian tribe or Native Alaskan Village. The tribe or village may have the right to have the case transferred to tribal court. If the case proceeds in state court, the tribe or village has the right to participate in the state proceeding.

§ 11.2 Causes of Action

Grounds for child welfare cases are prescribed by state law. Such grounds must be pled according to the statutory requirements. Grounds may include physical abuse, sexual abuse, neglect, emotional abuse, and abandonment. The

---

[1]   Ann M. Haralambie, J.D., is a certified family law specialist practicing in Tucson, Arizona. She is also an author and speaker in the fields of family and children's law.

[2]   *See* discussions at §§ 11.4.4, 11.4.5.

[3]   *See* discussion at § 11.5.1.

[4]   Indian Child Welfare Act of 1978 (ICWA), 25 U.S.C. § 1903(4). For a discussion of ICWA, *see* Chapter 8, Federal Child Welfare Law and Policy: Understanding the Federal Law and Funding Process.

statute may define components of the various types of abuse of neglect. For example, a state might require that emotional abuse be supported by expert evidence establishing that the child carries certain diagnoses and that the diagnosed condition must have been caused by the acts or omissions of the parent. Many states require the pleading of specific facts adequate to support each ground alleged. It is important to ensure the adequacy and completeness of the petition under state law.

§ 11.3 Party Status and Standing

In some states, only the governmental child welfare agency may file child welfare proceedings. Other states allow private agencies to file. Still other states permit adults with a certain relationship to the child to file, and some states permit filing by any person with a legitimate interest in the child, including filing by the child himself or herself. States that permit actions to be initiated by private parties may apply additional procedural requirements for such actions. Actions filed by a person without standing are subject to dismissal.

Once a case has been properly filed, state law will provide who has standing as a party. Some parties, such as the legal parents, guardians, or other third party custodians, automatically have party status and may be mandatory parties who must be joined to the action. Where paternity has not been established legally, the putative father may or may not need to be included as a party. In many states, the child is also given automatic party status. Other persons may become parties through mandatory or permissive intervention.

Grandparents or other third parties may already have court-ordered visitation rights when the child welfare proceeding is initiated, in which case they should be provided notice of the child welfare case. In some states, persons with court-ordered visitation rights have an explicit right to notice. This right to notice, however, does not necessarily afford the third party the status of a party to the child welfare action. Permissive intervention may be appropriate in such cases.

Sometimes intervening parties become full parties to the action. Some intervening parties may be permitted to participate for only a limited purpose, such as to be considered on the issue of placement. Grandparents and other relatives or family friends may be permitted to intervene to offer themselves as a potential placement or to seek visitation. In post-adjudication dependency cases, foster parents may be permitted to intervene on the issues of placement, visitation, and services for the child.

Petitioners must ensure that all mandatory parties have been properly joined and served. For children born out of wedlock, state law may require an inquiry into paternity and the joinder of any putative father. In other states, a putative father who has not established paternity or registered on a putative father registry is not entitled to participate as a party until paternity has been established. Where the child is an Indian child within the meaning of the Indian Child Welfare Act (ICWA), the child's tribe or tribes must be given notice and will be entitled to intervene as a party in any proceeding covered by the Act.

§ 11.4 Interstate Proceedings

§ 11.4.1 Interstate Compact on the Placement of Children (ICPC)

The Interstate Compact on the Placement of Children (ICPC)[5] has been adopted by all 50 states, the District of Columbia, and the U.S. Virgin Islands. The ICPC establishes uniform legal and administrative procedures governing the interstate placement of children. Every jurisdiction has a Compact Administrator. Notice of a proposed placement is initiated by filing a specific form with the Compact Administrators of both states. Prior to the child being placed in the other jurisdiction, the Compact Administrators in both jurisdictions must approve the interstate placements of children covered by the ICPC. The requirements of the Compact apply to interstate placements arranged by courts, agencies, and private persons other than parents, stepparents, grandparents, adult siblings, aunts, uncles, and guardians for the purpose of placing the child with any such relative or non-agency guardian. The ICPC also applies to the interstate placement of a dependent child with his or her parent.

The sending state retains jurisdiction after the child's interstate placement, and it also retains legal and financial responsibility for the child in the other state. The receiving state conducts a pre-placement home study to determine the appropriateness of the proposed placement and provides post-placement supervision, including making reports to the sending state.

§ 11.4.2 Interstate Compact on Adoption and Medical Assistance (ICAMA)

The Interstate Compact on Adoption and Medical Assistance (ICAMA)[6] addresses the need for assistance with special needs adoptions. At least 44 states have adopted the ICAMA. The ICAMA provides for the "establishment and maintenance of suitable substantive guarantees and workable procedures for interstate cooperation and payments to assist with the necessary costs of child maintenance, the procurement of services, and the provision of medical assistance."[7]

§ 11.4.3 Interstate Compact on Mental Health (ICMH)

The Interstate Compact on Mental Health (ICMH) applies to patients who are transferred from a public psychiatric facility in one state to the same kind of facility in another state. At least 44 states have adopted the ICMH.

---

[5] The Interstate Compact on the Placement of Children is *available at* http://icpc.aphsa.org/documents/Guidebook_2002.pdf.

[6] The Interstate Compact on Adoption and Medical Assistance, *available at* http://aaicama.aphsa.org/Compacts/ICAMA.pdf.

[7] *Id.* at § 1(d).

§ 11.4.4 Uniform Child Custody Jurisdiction Act (UCCJA)

The Uniform Child Custody Jurisdiction Act (UCCJA)[8] was the first uniform act to address interstate custody jurisdiction. Prior to the Uniform Child Custody Jurisdiction and Enforcement Act, all 50 states had enacted the UCCJA. The intent of the UCCJA was to provide that only one state at a time could have jurisdiction to make or modify a custody or visitation order. There are four bases by which states may acquire jurisdiction over custody and visitation determinations: home state, significant connections, emergency, and a default basis when no other state has jurisdiction. Personal jurisdiction is neither necessary nor sufficient for UCCJA subject matter jurisdiction. Orders that comply with the UCCJA are entitled to full faith and credit in other states.

Courts are directed to communicate with one another when there are proceedings pending in different states simultaneously to determine which state is more appropriate to hear the matter. The parties are also required, in their first pleading, to provide information on previous or pending custody actions, as well as information on the child's residence for the preceding five years, to assist courts in determining whether UCCJA jurisdiction exists.

A party may offer the testimony of witnesses, including parties and the child, by deposition or otherwise in another state, or the court on its own motion may request testimony to be taken in another state in such manner and under such terms as the court may prescribe.

§ 11.4.5 Uniform Child Custody Jurisdiction and Enforcement Act (UCCJEA)

The Uniform Child Custody Jurisdiction and Enforcement Act (UCCJEA)[9] supercedes the UCCJA. It resolved the ambiguities in the UCCJA and made explicit in the UCCJEA the requirements of the federal Parental Kidnapping Prevention Act (PKPA).[10] At least 39 states have adopted the UCCJEA.[11] Personal jurisdiction is neither necessary nor sufficient for UCCJEA subject matter jurisdiction. The UCCJEA provides for jurisdiction for a state when: (1) the state is a home state; (2) the state has significant connections; (3) other states

---

[8]   9(1A) U.L.A. 271 (1999), *available at* http://www.law.upenn.edu/bll/ulc/fnact99/1920_69/uccja68.pdf.

[9]   9(1A) U.L.A. 657 (1997), *available at* http://www.law.upenn.edu/bll/ulc/fnact99/1990s/uccjea97.pdf.

[10] 28 U.S.C. § 1738A.

[11] As of 2004 the following states have adopted the UCCJEA: Alabama, Alaska, Arizona, Arkansas, California, Colorado, Connecticut, Delaware, District of Columbia, Florida, Georgia, Hawaii, Idaho, Illinois, Iowa, Kansas, Kentucky, Maine, Maryland, Michigan, Minnesota, Mississippi, Montana, Nebraska, Nevada, New Mexico, New York, North Carolina, North Dakota, Oklahoma, Oregon, Pennsylvania, Rhode Island, Tennessee, Texas, Utah, Virginia, Washington and West Virginia. *See* National Conference of Commissioners on Uniform State Laws. This information is *available at* http://www.nccusl.org/nccusl/uniformact_factsheets/uniformacts-fs-uccjea.asp.

with higher priority have declined jurisdiction in favor of the state; or (4) there is no state that fulfills the other jurisdictional requirements. The home state is the state in which a child lived with a parent or a person acting as a parent for at least six consecutive months immediately before the commencement of a child custody proceeding. The UCCJEA prioritizes home state above the other jurisdictional bases, in conformity to the Parental Kidnapping Prevention Act (PKPA).[12] If there is a home state, in the absence of the home state's declination of jurisdiction, another state may not assume jurisdiction based on the child's best interests. If there is no home state, or if the home state has declined to exercise jurisdiction in favor of another court because it is a more appropriate forum, that state may exercise significant connections jurisdiction if: (1) both the child and at least one parent, or person acting as a parent, have a significant connection with the state other than mere physical presence; and (2) substantial evidence is available in the state concerning the child's care, protection, training, and personal relationships.

A court that exercised jurisdiction consistent with the UCCJEA retains exclusive, continuing jurisdiction over the determination until that court determines that either: (1) neither the child, parents, nor person acting as a parent have a significant connection with the state and that substantial evidence is no longer available in the state concerning the child's care, protection, training, and personal relationships; or (2) the child, parents, or person acting as a parent do not presently reside in the state. Alternatively, a court with continuing jurisdiction may decline to exercise its jurisdiction in favor of another court that it finds to be more appropriate. Except for temporary orders made in an emergency, a court may not exercise modification jurisdiction so long as another state has exclusive continuing jurisdiction and has not declined to exercise its superior jurisdiction.

The UCCJEA provides for inter-court communication and specifies more clearly than the UCCJA how such communications should be handled. The court may permit the parties to participate in the communications, but if they do not participate, they must be given the opportunity to present facts and legal arguments prior to a decision being made on jurisdiction. A record must be made of substantive communications.

The UCCJEA also provides for taking the testimony of witnesses, including parties and the child, by deposition or otherwise in another state, or in a manner that the court prescribes. Out-of-state testimony may also be offered by telephone, audiovisual means, or other electronic means before a designated court or at another location in that state. A court may request the court of another state to do any of the following:

- Hold an evidentiary hearing.

---

[12] 28 U.S.C. § 1738A.

- Produce or give evidence pursuant to the procedures of that state.

- Order a custody evaluation.

- Have a person appear with or without the child.

- Transmit a certified copy of the transcript or evaluation.

Orders that comply with the UCCJEA are entitled to full faith and credit in other states and must be enforced. UCCJEA enforcement actions are expedited procedures. Generally, a hearing must be held on the next judicial day after service of an order directing the respondent to appear (with or without the child), unless that date is impossible, in which case the hearing must be held on the first judicial day possible.

§ 11.4.6 Uniform Child Witness Testimony by Alternative Methods Act (UCWTAMA)

The UCWTAMA[13] sets forth methods for taking the testimony of child witnesses for circumstances in which *all* of the following do not occur: the child testifies in person in an open forum, in the presence and full view of the finder of fact and presiding officer; and all of the parties are allowed to be present, to participate, and to view and be viewed by the child. However, if an alternate method is permitted, the parties must still be provided as full and fair opportunity for examination or cross-examination of the child witness as would otherwise be available if an alternate method were not used. The Act allows states to adopt a cutoff age for "child," suggesting that the Act applies to children under 13. Different procedures apply for civil and criminal or delinquency proceedings. In noncriminal proceedings, the Act does not preclude the use of other recognized state procedures for taking the testimony of a child by an alternative method, such as in-chambers interviews, or by accepted discovery means, such as a deposition.

The Act provides that the court "shall order the hearing upon motion of a party, a child witness, or an individual determined by the presiding officer to have sufficient standing to act on behalf of the child." A child's attorney or guardian ad litem would be considered to have sufficient standing to make the application on behalf of a child, even where the child was not a party to the action. The hearing to determine whether to allow a child witness to testify by an alternative method "must be conducted on the record after reasonable notice to all parties, any nonparty movant, and any other person the presiding officer specifies. The child's presence is not required at the hearing unless ordered by the presiding officer. In conducting the hearing, the presiding officer is not bound by rules of evidence, except the rules of privilege."[14]

---

[13] The Uniform Child Witness Testimony by Alternative Methods Act is *available at* http://www.law.upenn.edu/bll/ulc/ucwtbama/2002act.pdf.

[14] *Id.* at § 4(b).

In a criminal/delinquency case, an alternate method of testifying that is not in an open forum in the presence and full view of the finder of fact is permitted only if the court finds by clear and convincing evidence that the child would suffer "serious emotional trauma that would substantially impair the child's ability to communicate with the finder of fact if required to testify in the open forum."[15] In a criminal/delinquency case, the child may testify other than face-to-face with the defendant if the court finds by clear and convincing evidence that the child would suffer "serious emotional trauma that would substantially impair the child's ability to communicate with the finder of fact if required to be confronted face-to-face by the defendant." In a noncriminal case, an alternate method of testifying is permitted if the court finds by a preponderance of the evidence that allowing the child to testify by an alternative method "is necessary to serve the best interests of the child or enable the child to communicate with the finder of fact,"[16] with the court to consider all of the following factors:

- The nature of the proceeding.
- The age and maturity of the child.
- The relationship of the child to the parties in the proceeding.
- The nature and degree of emotional trauma that the child may suffer in testifying.
- Any other relevant factor.

If the threshold finding is made, then the court must determine whether to permit the particular child witness to testify by alternate means. In making its determination, the court must consider each of the following:

- Alternative methods reasonably available.
- Available means for protecting the interests of or reducing emotional trauma to the child without resort to an alternative method.
- The nature of the case.
- The relative rights of the parties.
- The importance of the proposed testimony of the child.
- The nature and degree of emotional trauma that the child may suffer if an alternative method is not used.
- Any other relevant factor.

In order to allow for new technologies and innovations, the Act does not define what types of alternate methods of testimony are appropriate. Currently,

---

[15] *Id.* at § 5(a)(1).

[16] *Id.* at § 5(b).

states use such methods as live closed-circuit television where the witness is in another room, screens or other rearranged rooms that shield the child from the adult party, and videotaped testimony. In its order permitting an alternate method of testimony, the court must state the findings of fact and conclusions of law that support the determination. The court order must:

- Specify the method by which the child is to testify.

- List any individual or category of individuals allowed to be in, or required to be excluded from, the presence of the child during the testimony.

- State any special conditions necessary to facilitate a party's right to examine or cross-examine the child.

- State any condition or limitation on the participation of individuals present during the testimony of the child.

- State any other condition necessary for taking or presenting the testimony.

The method ordered "must be no more restrictive of the rights of the parties than is necessary under the circumstances to serve the purposes of the order."[17]

As of the completion of this book, the UCWTAMA had been adopted by Idaho, Nevada, Oklahoma, and Pennsylvania.[18]

§ 11.5 International Proceedings

Several international conventions impact parties involved in child welfare proceedings. Applicants for specialty certification should become directly familiar with at least the following conventions and the enabling federal legislation, as well as the relevant case law, and not merely rely on this short summary.

§ 11.5.1 Hague Convention on the International Aspects of Civil Child Abduction (Hague Convention on Child Abduction)

The Hague Convention on Child Abduction and its implementing legislation, the International Child Abduction Remedies Act (ICARA),[19] came into force in the United States in April 1988. The Convention provides civil procedures and remedies for obtaining the return of a child who has been wrongfully removed from, or retained in a country other than, the "state of habitual residence." The Convention addresses only *which* country has the right to make orders regarding custody and does not address the substantive custody issues.

---

[17] *Id.* at § 7(c).

[18] *See* NAT'L CONFERENCE OF COMM'RS ON UNIF. STATE LAWS, A FEW FACTS ABOUT THE UNIFORM CHILD WITNESS TESTIMONY BY ALTERNATIVE METHODS ACT (2002), *available at* http://www.nccusl.org/Update/uniformact_factsheets/uniformacts-fs-ucwtbama.asp.

[19] Pub. L. No. 100-300, 102 Stat.437 (codified as amended at 42 U.S.C. §§ 11601 through 11610 (1988)).

The U.S. State Department is the designated "Central Authority" for the United States, and the Bureau of Consular Affairs, Office of Children's Issues, has primary responsibility for implementing the Convention. The State Department has contracted with the National Center for Missing and Exploited Children (NCMEC) to provide services. The Convention applies between the United States and original participating countries and countries who subsequently acceded to the Convention and whose accessions have been accepted by the United States. A list of countries, with the dates on which the Convention became effective, may be found on the Web site of the U.S. Department of State.[20] The wrongful removal or retention must have occurred after the effective date.

In general, the Convention requires that a child who was habitually resident in one country, but who was wrongfully removed to or retained in another country while the non-abducting parent was exercising custodial rights, must be returned to the country of habitual residence. The Convention can also be used to assist parents in exercising their access rights in another country. Most countries (but not the United States) provide legal counsel for aggrieved parents. However, NCMEC has a referral panel, which includes the availability of some pro bono counsel. In the United States, applications under the Convention may be filed in state or federal court, or both.

The remedy of return may be lost if the aggrieved custodian does not file an application under the Convention within one year. There are also limited defenses to return even when application has been timely filed. A court may deny return of a child to the habitual residence if the person, institution, or other body having the care of the person of the child was not actually exercising the custody rights at the time of removal or retention, or had consented to or subsequently acquiesced in the removal or retention. Most courts have held that the exercise of access rights only is not sufficient to constitute the exercise of custody rights. Access rights are also protected by the Convention, but to a lesser extent that does not involve return of the child to the country of habitual residence. There is a "maturity" exception to return, but the Convention does not give any guidance with respect to how old a child must be before his or her wishes are considered as a part of the exception.

A defense to return that may arise in a child welfare context is the Article 13(b) exception for "grave risk" of physical or psychological harm to the child or of placing an intolerable situation. This defense requires more than showing that the child has been abused in the country of habitual residence. Most courts construe the exception very narrowly and require that a showing that the courts in the country of habitual residence are unable or unwilling to provide proper protection for the child pending the substantive hearing.

---

[20] *See* http://travel.state.gov/family/adoption/convention/convention_461.html .

A free Internet research tool is the International Child Abduction Database (INCADAT), which contains leading international case law under the Convention.[21]

§ 11.5.2 Hague Convention on Protection of Children and Co-operation in Respect of Intercountry Adoption (Hague Convention on Intercountry Adoption)

The Hague Convention on Intercountry Adoption and its implementing legislation, the Intercountry Adoption Act of 2000 (IAA),[22] came into force in the United States in October 2000. Federal regulations will be promulgated to further govern adoptions under the Convention and the IAA. The U.S. State Department is the designated "Central Authority" for the United States, and the Bureau of Consular Affairs, Office of Children's Issues, will have primary responsibility. The Convention applies to the adoption of children between the United States and the other signatory countries. The Convention provides that adoptions must take place in the best interests of the child and prevent the abduction, sale, or traffic in children. Participating countries must regulate agencies and individuals who are involved in intercountry adoptions between the participating countries. Only competent bodies may be accredited. Authorities in the country of origin must verify that the child has been legally made free for adoption and that all necessary consents have been freely given in writing and not withdrawn. The Convention provides that:

- Consents to adoption may not be induced by payment or compensation in kind.

- Mothers may not consent until after the child is born.

- Children are to be counseled concerning the effects of adoption (having regard to the child's age and maturity).

- Consideration must be given to the child's wishes and opinions.

- No one shall derive improper financial or other gain from an activity related to an intercountry adoption.

- Only costs and expenses, including reasonable professional fees of persons involved in the adoption, may be charged or paid.

- Directors, administrators, and employees of bodies involved in an adoption shall not receive remuneration that is unreasonably high in relation to services rendered.

---

[21] *See* http://www.incadat.com. The search form in English *is available* at http://212.206.44.26/index.cfm?fuseaction=convtext.showDetail&lng=1.

[22] Pub. L. No. 106-279.

- The authorities in the receiving country must ensure that the adoptive parents are qualified to adopt the child and have been counseled as necessary.

- The Central Authorities of both countries must take all necessary steps to secure permission for the child to leave the country of origin and to enter and permanently reside in the receiving country.

The Convention prohibits contact between prospective adoptive parents and birth parents or other caretakers until certain prerequisites have been met, unless it is a relative adoption or the contact complies with conditions established by the competent authority in the country of origin. The Central Authority of the country of origin must provide the receiving country with a report including information about the child's identity, adoptability, background, social environment, family history, medical history, and any special needs of the child and must give due consideration to the child's upbringing, ethnic, religious, and cultural background. If there is a probationary period, the Central Authorities of both countries are required to keep each other informed about the progress of the adoption. If the adoptive placement disrupts or is no longer in the child's best interests after the child is in the receiving country, the Central Authority of the receiving country is required to take steps to protect the child, including removing the child from the prospective adoptive parents and arranging alternate adoptive or foster care in consultation with the Central Authority of the country of origin. The Central Authority of the country of origin must be informed in advance of any adoption by another family. As a last resort, the child may need to be returned to the country of origin.

The Immigration and Nationality Act was amended to provide that children may be qualified to receive immigrant visas either because of their Convention adoption abroad or their placement abroad with U.S. prospective adoptive parents for Convention adoption in the United States.[23]

§ 11.5.3 United Nations Protocol to Prevent, Suppress and Punish Trafficking in Persons, Especially Women and Children, supplementing the United Nations Convention against Transnational Organized Crime

The United Nations Protocol to Prevent, Suppress and Punish Trafficking in Persons, and its implementing legislation, the Trafficking Victims Protection Act of 2000 (TVPA),[24] came into force in the United States in October 2000.

The Protocol defines "trafficking in persons" as "the recruitment, transportation, transfer, harbouring or receipt of persons, by means of the threat or use of force or other forms of coercion, of abduction, of fraud, of deception, of

---

[23] 8 U.S.C. § 1154.

[24] Pub. L. No. 106-386.

the abuse of power or of a position of vulnerability or of the giving or receiving of payments or benefits to achieve the consent of a person having control over another person, for the purpose of exploitation. Exploitation shall include, at a minimum, the exploitation of the prostitution of others or other forms of sexual exploitation, forced labour or services, slavery or practices similar to slavery, servitude or the removal of organs." The consent of a victim of trafficking is irrelevant under the Protocol. When the victim is a child (a person under the age of 18), the "recruitment, transportation, transfer, harbouring or receipt of a child for the purpose of exploitation shall be considered "trafficking in persons" even if this does not involve" any of the prohibited means.

The protocol provides that to the extent permitted by domestic law, the privacy and identity of victims of trafficking in persons should be protected, including by making legal proceedings relating to such trafficking confidential. The Protocol recommends that the participating countries "consider implementing measures to provide for the physical, psychological and social recovery of victims of trafficking in persons," including "[c]ounselling and information, in particular as regards their legal rights, in a language that the victims of trafficking in persons can understand."

Pursuant to the Protocol, the U.S. Department of Justice has issued regulations for a "T visa," which will enable certain trafficking victims to live and work legally in the United States for three years while their cases are investigated and prosecuted. The Department of Health and Human Services can provide certification letters to permit victims of trafficking to become eligible to apply for federal and certain state benefits to the same extent as refugees.

Commercial sex trafficking of children is considered to be a severe form of trafficking in persons under TVPA.[25]

---

[25] 22 U.S.C. § 7102(8)(A).

Chapter 12   COLLATERAL PROCEEDINGS

Part 12A: DELINQUENCY

by Ann M. Haralambie[1]

The NACC believes that federal, state, and local law must mandate that independent attorneys be appointed to represent the interests of children in all child welfare proceedings. In addition to child welfare proceedings, many children and youth who are subject to child welfare proceedings may become involved in collateral proceedings. It is critical that the child's attorney become informed about and involved in collateral proceedings affecting his or her client. Children's attorneys play a critical role in empowering children and ensuring that children's views are heard in legal proceedings that affect their lives. The following is a discussion of collateral proceedings commonly encountered by children's attorneys.

§ 12A.1 Delinquency and Status Offenses

Many children involved in the child welfare system are also involved in the delinquency system. Often such children are "dually adjudicated," meaning that they have been found to be both dependent and delinquent. Changes in foster placements and placement in a shelter or group home setting may make it more likely that a dependent child will engage in delinquent behavior or be reported to police for infractions committed in the living environment that parents would not have reported to the police. Services available through the child's dependency case plan may address the underlying causes of the child's delinquent behavior. The fact that the child has a caseworker and services provided in the child welfare proceeding may make a prosecutor more willing to allow the child to participate in diversion programs to avoid a delinquency adjudication.[2]

Some courts have specific protocols for dealing with dually adjudicated children. In some jurisdictions, the same judge hears both the dependency and delinquency cases. In a few courts, the hearings in both cases are held jointly, with a coordinated disposition. Where such coordinated systems are not used, the case plan and services provided for in the dependency court may conflict with the terms of probation, incarceration, or parole of the juvenile from the delinquency court. The child may have different attorneys in each proceeding, in which case the attorney in the child welfare case should coordinate with the

---

[1]   Ann M. Haralambie, J.D., is a certified family law specialist practicing in Tucson, Arizona. She is also an author and speaker in the fields of family and children's law.

[2]   For examples of such diversion programs, *see, e.g.,* CAL. PENAL CODE § 1000.5 (Deering 2004); COLO. REV. STAT. § 19-2-303 (2004); MINN. STAT. ANN. § 388.24 (2003); OR. REV. STAT. § 419C.225 (2003).

delinquency attorney. Resources that would benefit the child may be more readily available in one proceeding than the other, often because of different funding streams and "slots" or "beds" allocated to juvenile justice cases.

If the child is adjudicated delinquent, information from the child welfare proceeding will be very important to the disposition. Therefore, it is important to ensure that the defense attorney and probation officer have that information available and that the court considers it. Evaluations and reports prepared in child welfare cases are often broader in time and scope and more comprehensive than those that are prepared specifically for delinquency dispositions. Caseworkers and other professionals involved in the child welfare proceeding may be called to testify in the dispositional hearing. Foster parents and other care providers may also testify, although in some cases they may be the victims in the delinquency proceeding. Even if the two cases are not directly coordinated, it is often helpful to have joint staffing to determine what resources each system can bring to address the child's needs.

It is also important for the dependency court, caseworker, and attorneys to be kept apprised of the delinquency proceedings. It may be possible for copies of hearing notices, pleadings, and orders to be sent to the participants in both cases if the cases are not otherwise consolidated or coordinated.

If the child is sent to a secure facility as a part of the delinquency case, it is important to make arrangements for appropriate services to be continued to address the dependency case plan and the needs identified through the child welfare proceeding.

Part 12B: CRIMINAL PROCEEDINGS

by Ann M. Haralambie[3]

§ 12B.1 Interface Between Civil Child Protection and Criminal Prosecution

More serious forms of child abuse, neglect, and abandonment also constitute crimes under state and, sometimes, federal law. Some prosecutors choose not to prosecute cases that are being handled in the child welfare system. Sometimes cases are pursued in both forums, either simultaneously or seriatim. Parents' attorneys may be hesitant to have a parent participate in services or testify in the child welfare case because of admissions that might be used in the criminal trial. Therefore, parents' attorneys often prefer that the criminal proceeding take place first so that their clients can fully participate in the child welfare proceeding. However, the clock on the various statutory time limits discussed

---

[3]   Ann M. Haralambie, J.D., is a certified family law specialist practicing in Tucson, Arizona. She is also an author and speaker in the fields of family and children's law.

in Chapter 8 does not stop running while the criminal process plays itself out. Therefore, a parent who does not move forward with the child welfare proceedings in a timely manner may end up at a termination hearing without having had the benefit to demonstrate compliance with a reunification plan.

In some cases, the prosecutor may be willing to agree not to use admissions concerning the charged crime that are made in therapy or as part of other reunification services because the prosecutor believes that involving the defendant in such services minimizes damage to the child. This is particularly true with regard to "apology sessions" in which the parent apologizes to the child and takes full responsibility for the maltreatment. However, in the absence of an agreement, evidence developed in the child welfare proceeding is generally available to the prosecutor in the criminal proceeding.

A criminal conviction for the abuse or neglect alleged in the dependency or termination petition, because it is made based on proof beyond a reasonable doubt, can be used to establish the abuse or neglect in the child welfare proceeding. The reverse is not true because of the difference in the burden of proof. Further, abuse or neglect sufficient to sustain a finding of dependency or termination may not fulfill the statutory elements of the crime.

The federal Children's Justice Act (CJA)[4] provides grants to states to improve the investigation, prosecution, and judicial handling of cases of child abuse and neglect, particularly child sexual abuse and exploitation. Among the programs qualifying for funding are establishing or enhancing child advocacy centers and other multidisciplinary programs to serve child victims and their families in order to minimize trauma. Funds may also be used to support the enactment of laws to improve systems response, including allowing the admission of indirect testimony of children into evidence, making the courtroom setting less intimidating to children, increasing the penalties for sexual offenses against children, requiring mandatory sentencing, shortening the trial process, and permitting victims to make statements prior to sentencing.

Every state has a statutory victims' bill of rights.[5] Child victims may also be entitled to some or all of these rights, which may include the right:

- To be notified of all criminal proceedings.

- To be kept apprised of the status of the defendant (including the release of the defendant from jail and the conditions of release or notice of escape).

- To confidentiality of the victim's address.

---

[4] Children's Justice Act, 100 Stat. 903 (1986), 42 U.S.C. § 5101 (2004). *See also* CHILDREN'S BUREAU, U.S. DEP'T OF HEALTH & HUMAN SERVS., CHILDREN'S JUSTICE ACT FACT SHEET (2004), *available at* http://www.acf.hhs.gov/programs/cb/publications/cjafact.htm.

[5] *See, e.g.,* GA. CODE ANN. § 17-17-1 (2004); TENN. CODE ANN. § 40-38-101 (2004); MISS. CODE. ANN. § 99-43-1 (2004); R.I. GEN. LAWS § 12-28-1 (2004).

- To be present at certain criminal proceedings.

- To be consulted before a case is dismissed or a plea agreement entered.

- To refuse to be interviewed by defense counsel or to have an advocate present during any interview by defense counsel.

- To a separate waiting area.

- To make a statement at sentencing or various pre- and post-trial release proceedings.

- To obtain restitution after the defendant is convicted.

Children may be required to exercise these rights though a legal guardian or guardian ad litem. In some states, the prosecutor may exercise the child victim's rights on behalf of the child.

In addition to providing victims' rights by statute, at least 32 states[6] have adopted constitutional amendments to their constitutions concerning victims' rights. Congress is considering legislation to provide a constitutional amendment that would establish a federal victims' bill of rights, at least with respect to violent crimes. Most of these bills of rights apply only to victims of adult perpetrators and not to victims of juvenile offenders who are being prosecuted in juvenile courts.

Children who are victims often end up being interviewed or testifying in conjunction with the criminal case. It is not always clear who has standing to assist the child through the process by asserting any rights the child may have, including asserting the child's privilege and confidential interests in his or her records. A parent, particularly a non-offending parent whose parental rights have not been terminated, may be able to assert the child's rights. The agency that has legal custody pursuant to the child welfare proceeding may have the right and duty to protect the child's interests in the criminal proceeding. The child's attorney or guardian ad litem may have standing to assert the child's rights. It might be necessary or prudent for the respective parties and their counsel to seek a judicial determination in the dependency case concerning who may and may not act on behalf of the child in the criminal proceeding. Where more than one person or entity has that right, such as the agency and the child's attorney, some effort should be made to coordinate a unified approach if possible.

Many states provide various accommodations for child witnesses, such as permitting the child to be accompanied by a support person or to have special procedures for taking the child's testimony. Whichever adult is assisting the child

---

[6] Alabama, Alaska, Arizona, California, Colorado, Connecticut, Florida, Idaho, Illinois, Indiana, Kansas, Louisiana, Maryland, Michigan, Mississippi, Missouri, Montana, Nebraska, Nevada, New Jersey, New Mexico, North Carolina, Ohio, Oklahoma, Rhode Island, South Carolina, Tennessee, Texas, Utah, Virginia, Washington, and Wisconsin; a similar amendment in Oregon has been repealed. VICTIMS' RIGHTS CONSTITUTIONAL AMENDMENTS (2004), *available at* http://www.ojp.usdoj.gov/ovc/ncvrw/1999/amend.htm.

through the criminal process should inquire about the availability of any such procedures.[7]

§ 12B.2 The Child's Attorney or Guardian Ad Litem in the Criminal Case

A few states provide for appointed attorneys or guardians ad litem to represent children who are witnesses in criminal cases.[8] If the child is represented by an attorney or guardian ad litem in the child welfare proceeding, that person is often the one appointed in the criminal case. The attorney may be required to affirmatively seek the appointment from the judge in the criminal case. In addition to helping with preparing the child to testify, the attorney may be permitted to address the issue of sentencing, especially where the defendant is the child's parent. Many child victims are ambivalent about the abuser and feel guilty that their testimony has helped to convict the parent. The child may feel guilty because the prosecution of the abuser has resulted in financial detriment to the family and the *de facto* break-up the family. In some cases, it may be appropriate to advocate for a work-release sentence that permits the defendant to earn money during the workday while spending nights and weekends in jail.

The guardian ad litem in the criminal case can assist in minimizing the number of duplicate interviews and evaluations of the child. The prosecutor may not be aware of all of the information already gathered in the child welfare process. Some jurisdictions have joint child abuse investigations, including requiring that all child interviews be conducted at child advocacy centers where both the prosecutor (or law enforcement) and child protective services worker funnel their questions to one forensic interviewer, who is often on the other side of a one-way mirror in a room with the child. However, even in those situations, the prosecutor may not be kept informed of new information developed in the child welfare case. The guardian ad litem can ensure that the prosecutor is aware of such information on an on-going basis. In particular, the guardian ad litem can inform the prosecutor of any special needs the child might have with respect to testifying or sentencing. The guardian ad litem can assist in scheduling the child's interviews or testimony at times convenient to the child and any support person who will be accompanying the child.

Child witnesses are often attacked as being incompetent to testify, confused, or testifying based on contaminated memories. The guardian ad litem can assist in supporting the child's credibility by ensuring that the child is well prepared to testify, perhaps with therapeutic support.

---

[7] *See* Chapter 15, Children in Court.

[8] *See, e.g.,* VT. STAT. ANN. tit. 15, § 594 (2004); N.Y. SURR. CT. PROC. ACT § 1722 (Consol. 2004).

§ 12B.3 Protective Orders

All states have statutes providing for domestic violence protection orders.[9] Children who have been victims of child abuse or exposed to domestic violence are proper beneficiaries of those protective orders. The Violence Against Women Act (VAWA)[10] provides for full faith and credit for domestic violence protective orders that are entered by state or tribal courts in compliance with the Act. Therefore, it is important that any protective order issued comply with the requirements of VAWA.

In addition to domestic violence protective orders, the child's attorney can seek discovery protective orders, if appropriate, to maintain the privacy of the child's school, medical, and counseling records, as well as records generated within the child welfare proceeding. These records might be sought by both the prosecution and defense, and the child has a privacy interest in the records regardless of who is seeking them. The attorney can ask either that the records remain entirely confidential or that they be submitted to the criminal court judge for *in camera* inspection and redaction. Further, the attorney can request an order prohibiting further dissemination of released records.

Part 12C: DIVORCE, CHILD CUSTODY, AND VISITATION PROCEEDINGS

by Ann M. Haralambie[11]

§ 12C.1 Staying Together or Divorcing

For some parents, the decision either to stay in an abusive home or to leave is problematic. When child protective services workers investigate a family, they are concerned not only about an active abuser, but also about a parent who fails to protect the children from the abuse. However, when a non-abusive parent who has never been involved with the child welfare system leaves the abuser, files for divorce, and alleges child abuse by the abusive parent, the fact that the parties are involved in custody litigation may cause the professionals involved to view the protective parent's allegations with skepticism. While custody litigation may in fact spawn some false allegations of abuse and exaggerated reports, it is

---

[9] *See* Chapter 12, Part D, Domestic Violence, for a discussion of domestic violence orders of protection.

[10] The Violence Against Women Act (VAWA), 42 U.S.C. § 3796gg, Title IV of the Violent Crime Control and Law Enforcement Act of 1994, Pub. L. No. 103-322. *See* The Office on Violence Against Women Online Resources, *available at* http://www.vaw.umn.edu/library/.

[11] Ann M. Haralambie, J.D., is a certified family law specialist practicing in Tucson, Arizona. She is also an author and speaker in the fields of family and children's law.

also true that good parenting may compel separation and divorce from an abuser. So a non-abusing parent may land in a no-win situation, where he or she is criticized as a bad parent for staying in the marriage, but disbelieved after leaving. The ultimate penalty for not being believed about abuse by the other parent is the loss of custody to the abuser. This is particularly likely to happen with respect to allegations of child sexual abuse.[12] The American Psychological Association's Presidential Task Force on Violence and the Family found that batterers are twice as likely to seek custody than non-batterers.[13] So it should come as no surprise that domestic violence, child abuse, and neglect may be issues in divorce, paternity, and custody cases as well as in post-decree modification actions. Many legal and mental health professionals become very frustrated at what have come to be called "high conflict divorce cases." Johnston and Campbell found that in approximately 75 percent of intractable custody conflicts there is a history of domestic violence.[14] Bancroft and Silverman suggest that "many of the characteristics that [Johnston and Campbell] consider to be inherent to 'high-conflict divorce' may actually be the dynamics of domestic violence."[15] Therefore, they believe that the assumption that high-conflict divorces are the result of both parents' inappropriate behaviors may be incorrect, and that one parent's abuse may actually be the cause of the intractability in many cases.

The time of separation and divorce can be particularly dangerous for victims of domestic violence.[16] Bancroft and Silverman write:

> In fact, we observe that many batterers' motivation to intimidate their victims through the children *increases* when the couple separates, because of the loss of other ways to exert control. In addition, the batterer's partner is no longer present to monitor his behavior toward the children. If there is litigation involving custody or visitation, her reports of physical abuse of the children by him may be dismissed by the courts as a divorce tactic, which may leave him feeling free to behave with impunity.[17]

---

[12] *See, e.g.,* JOHN E. B. MYERS, A MOTHER'S NIGHTMARE–INCEST: A PRACTICAL GUIDE FOR PARENTS AND PROFESSIONALS (1997).

[13] *See* REPORT OF THE AMERICAN PSYCHOLOGICAL ASSOCIATION PRESIDENTIAL TASK FORCE ON VIOLENCE AND THE FAMILY (1996).

[14] *See* JANET R. JOHNSTON & LINDA E. G. CAMPBELL, IMPASSES OF DIVORCE: THE DYNAMICS AND RESOLUTION OF FAMILY CONFLICT (Free Press 1988).

[15] *See* LUNDY BANCROFT & JAY G. SILVERMAN, THE BATTERER AS PARENT: ADDRESSING THE IMPACT OF DOMESTIC VIOLENCE ON FAMILY DYNAMICS 131 (Sage Publications, 2002).

[16] *See, e.g.,* Jennifer L. Hardesty, *Separation Assault in the Context of Postdivorce Parenting: An Integrative Review of the Literature*, 8 VIOLENCE AGAINST WOMEN 597 (2002); Martha Mahoney, *Legal Images of Battered Women: Redefining the Issue of Separation*, 90 MICH. L. REV. 1 (1999).

[17] *See* LUNDY BANCROFT & JAY G. SILVERMAN, THE BATTERER AS PARENT: ADDRESSING THE IMPACT OF DOMESTIC VIOLENCE ON FAMILY DYNAMICS 44 (Sage Publications, 2002).

The failure to accurately determine whether abuse has occurred places children in greater danger during and after the divorce than before the divorce for several reasons. Children are obviously in danger when they are being abused within the secrecy of their family life. Abuse is reported with the goal of obtaining protection for the children and rehabilitation of the parents where appropriate. When a parent attempts to obtain the protection of the child welfare and judicial system, but the courts do not believe that abuse has occurred, the would-be protector has no place else to turn. Each subsequent attempt to get help may be viewed as vindictiveness, paranoia, hypervigilance, or attempts to "alienate" the child from the other parent. Parents may actually be ordered not to make any further CPS reports or to first have a report screened by some other professional, even if such orders put parents who are mandated reporters at risk of violating mandatory reporting laws. Self-help may be dealt with even more severely. A parent who flees with the child risks not only a contempt citation, but also loss of custody and criminal prosecution for custodial interference. If that parent takes the child across state lines, the matter becomes a federal criminal offense. The resources of local law enforcement, the FBI, and the National Center for Missing and Exploited Children are available to assist the left-behind (abusive) parent in obtaining return of the child and punishment of the protective parent. A child whose protective parent is incarcerated for attempting to protect the child and who is placed in the full-time custody of the abuser is being taught a disturbing lesson: seeking help for the abuse makes the situation much worse, not better.

Family court judges may tend to be more skeptical about child abuse allegations than juvenile or criminal court judges, who daily see parties who have committed violence or other abusive acts.[18] They are used to hearing litigants exaggerate trivial events that were accepted during the marriage but that take on the characterization of unacceptable abuse during the divorce trial. In addition to exaggerations, some divorce litigants lie outright in order to gain an advantage or punish the other parent. It is within this context that many domestic relations judges view allegations of child abuse. This same perspective holds true for some custody evaluators as well. These biases are particularly evident in child sexual abuse cases.[19] Even child protective services investigators tend to be more skeptical of abuse allegations made in the context of divorce proceedings, even

---

[18] *See generally* ANN M. HARALAMBIE, CHILD SEXUAL ABUSE IN CIVIL CASES: A GUIDE TO CUSTODY AND TORT ACTIONS ch. 2 (American Bar Association, 1999).

[19] *See generally* THE BACKLASH: CHILD PROTECTION UNDER FIRE (John E. B. Myers ed., Sage Publications 1994); BILLIE WRIGHT DZIECH & CHARLES B. SCHUDSON, ON TRIAL: AMERICA'S COURTS AND THEIR TREATMENT OF SEXUALLY ABUSED CHILDREN (Beacon Press 1989); DAVID HECHLER, THE BATTLE AND THE BACKLASH: THE CHILD SEXUAL ABUSE WAR (Lexington Books 1988).

where the parent making the allegations asserts that he or she left the marriage as a response to the abuse.[20]

§ 12C.2 Child Welfare and Family Court Interaction

Family law attorneys may advise divorce litigants to make CPS reports when they suspect the other parent is abusing the child. In fact, parents are mandated reporters in many states. However, CPS investigators often complain that divorce litigants are trying to use them in the divorce case as a weapon to gain an advantage over the other party. With child welfare systems under increasing budgetary crises, investigation priorities tend to favor putting resources into families where neither party is willing to protect the child. A parent who recognizes the danger and is seeking family court assistance in protecting the child is not high on the list of cases to investigate. Further, as mentioned above, many CPS workers are skeptical of reports made in the context of a divorce case, believing many such allegations to be either fabricated or wildly exaggerated. This is particularly true when no allegations had been received before the initiation of the divorce action or post-decree litigation. Parents who lack the financial resources to obtain private evaluations, especially in jurisdictions where the family court does not have its own social service investigators, may have little hope of an expert investigation into allegations of abuse unless CPS conducts the investigation. However, CPS investigations into allegations arising during litigation may not be as thorough or objective as investigations done while the family was still together.

In many cases, there is inadequate coordination between the child welfare and family court systems and a lack of understanding of the implications of the findings of each. For example, most CPS investigators are required to label the results of an investigation in a very restrictive way (either "founded" or "unfounded," "substantiated" or "unsubstantiated") rather than along a continuum of confidence that abuse did or did not occur. Many custody evaluators, attorneys, and judges in the family court system construe "unfounded" or "unsubstantiated" findings as indications by CPS that the accused parent did not abuse the child. This undercuts the credibility of the protective parent, even where the initial report was made by a third party and not by that parent. Future allegations of abuse are likely to be met with increased skepticism based on the

---

[20] For example, one small study in Boulder, Colorado, looked at eighteen cases of sexual abuse allegations arising in family court custody litigation. Seventeen of the reports were deemed by the Sexual Abuse Team to be unfounded (the one "founded" allegation was admitted by the perpetrator). The same CPS workers reviewed the cases again, with no additional information, using an improved validation protocol and reclassified an additional seven as substantiated (having even overlooked physical evidence in two of the cases). The CPS workers admitted that they viewed allegations in a custody dispute context with greater skepticism. *See* J. Melbourne McGraw & Holly A. Smith, *Child Sexual Abuse Allegations Amidst Divorce and Custody Proceedings: Refining the Validation Process*, 1 J. CHILD SEXUAL ABUSE 49 (1992).

assumptions that: (1) CPS determined that the allegations lacked merit; and (2) if the child were deemed to be in danger, the child welfare agency would have sought judicial relief. However, where there is a parent willing and able to take protective action, the child welfare system generally does not intervene, and the dependency statute generally requires that a petition be filed only where there is not a parent protecting the child, even where abuse has occurred. Therefore, even if a CPS investigator believed that one parent was abusing the child, if the other parent has initiated a divorce and sought orders to protect the child, the CPS investigation is likely to be closed without taking any further action. The assumption is made that the child will be adequately protected in the family law case. The various professionals and judges involved in the family court case, however, may not understand that the allegations were credited by the neutral investigators.

Similarly, when family courts have addressed abuse allegations and found inadequate evidence to prove them or even that they were maliciously made, CPS investigators may assume that the allegations were thoroughly investigated by the family court and will be even more skeptical of future allegations made. In fact, the professionals involved in the family court case may not be experienced in investigating and litigating child abuse claims. Many custody evaluators do not have special training in the abuse field, and most family law attorneys do not routinely practice in juvenile courts or otherwise have experience dealing with abuse cases. Further, multidisciplinary evaluations are rare in family court. Therefore, whether the family court finds that abuse did or did not occur, child welfare professionals should not assume that the finding was based on a thorough, appropriate investigation into the merits of the case.

Failure to appreciate the weaknesses and biases of both the child welfare and family court systems can result in failure to protect a child from abuse. Therefore, in either arena, it is important for there to be an individualized determination of the underlying allegations and not merely an assumption that the decision has already been made.

§ 12C.3 Coordinating Legal Proceedings

Ideally, all legal proceedings affecting the same family will be heard by the same judge. Although this "one-family one-judge" principle is reflected in policy recommendations[21] and in some state laws,[22] it is not universal. When proceedings are pending in both juvenile and family court, juvenile court proceedings

---

[21] *See* PERMANENCY PLANNING FOR CHILDREN DEP'T, NAT'L COUNCIL FOR JUVENILE AND FAMILY CRT. JUDGES, RESOURCE GUIDELINES: IMPROVING COURT PRACTICE IN CHILD ABUSE & NEGLECT CASES (1995). There are 25 courts currently participating in the NCJFCJ national Child Victims Act Model Courts Project, including juvenile and family courts from Alexandria, VA; Buffalo, NY; Charlotte, NC; Chicago, IL; Cincinnati, OH; Des Moines, IA; El Paso, TX; Honolulu, HI; Indianapolis, IN; Los Angeles, CA; Louisville, KY; Miami, FL; Nashville, TN; New Orleans, LA; New York City, NY; Newark, NJ; Omaha, NE; Portland, OR; Reno, NV; Salt Lake City, UT; San Jose, CA; Toledo, OH; Tucson, AZ; Washington, DC; and the Tribal Court in Zuni, NM. *Id.*

are given priority in dealing with custody and visitation issues. Therefore, if a divorce or post-divorce proceeding occurs while the case is in juvenile court, the family court generally loses jurisdiction to address the custody and visitation issues. In some states, there are agreements or protocols for dealing with simultaneous proceedings. Sometimes the cases are consolidated for hearing in one court or the other. In some states, juvenile courts may enter "exit orders" that allow dismissal or termination of the child welfare proceeding in favor of final resolution in the family court, with the exit orders acting as a bridge to protect the child until the family court enters its final orders. Applicants for certification should understand the local law concerning simultaneous proceedings.

Where there is a choice of forum, juvenile courts are often better equipped to deal with the substantive analysis of the abuse-related allegations. In addition, the child is more likely to have independent representation in a child welfare proceeding than in the family court proceeding. Further, juvenile courts generally have greater access to resources to protect the child and rehabilitate the family than the family court. However, child welfare proceedings are generally more intrusive into family life than family court proceedings and may stigmatize families in a way that family court proceedings do not. A careful analysis should be made in comparing which forum will best meet the client's needs.

Part 12D: DOMESTIC VIOLENCE

by Ann M. Haralambie[23]

§ 12D.1 Domestic Violence

Child abuse is a particular type of domestic violence. Children who are exposed to domestic violence in their homes, even if they are not the targets of that abuse, also suffer harm by being in that environment.[24] In 1999, the National Council of Juvenile and Family Court Judges issued its report, EFFECTIVE INTERVENTION IN DOMESTIC VIOLENCE & CHILD MALTREATMENT CASES: GUIDELINES FOR POLICY AND PRACTICE. Among the Council's recommendations were that "[j]uvenile courts must collaborate with other courts" and that "[w]hen courts and agencies exchange information concerning family members, the safety and privacy concerns of all parties must be balanced carefully with the

---

[22] *E.g.*, California, Illinois, Kentucky, and New Hampshire. *See* CAROL R. FLANGO ET AL., HOW ARE COURTS COORDINATING FAMILY CASES? (1999), *available at* http://www.ncsconline.org/WC/Publications/Res_SCtFam_CtCoordFamCasesPub.pdf.

[23] Ann M. Haralambie, J.D., is a certified family law specialist practicing in Tucson, Arizona. She is also an author and speaker in the fields of family and children's law.

[24] *See, e.g.*, Carolyn Copps Hartley, *The Co-occurrence of Child Maltreatment and Domestic Violence: Examining Both Neglect and Child Physical Abuse*, 7 CHILD MALTREATMENT 349 (2002).

need for access to . . . information."[25] Judges in child welfare cases may be particularly open to requests for coordination with other courts addressing domestic violence in the family involved in the child welfare proceeding.

In some child welfare cases, aside from parallel criminal cases addressing the abuse or neglect of the child, there may be separate domestic violence proceedings filed against the abuser. These may be criminal prosecutions or civil proceedings for protection orders. The child may or may not be a victim or a witness in these proceedings. States differ on whether children can be included within the protections of a civil protection order, especially where the child's parent, but not the child, was a victim of the domestic violence. Many states permit children[26] or parties acting on their behalf[27] to seek orders of protection, especially where the child was a victim of the domestic violence. In most states, courts hearing civil protection order cases have expressed or implied authority to enter orders affecting custody. However, while a court may restrict contact more than an existing juvenile court order, a civil protection order generally cannot change custody or increase contact beyond what is permitted by an existing order in a child welfare proceeding. If the civil order of protection attempts to do so, the child welfare order generally takes precedence. In practice, law enforcement officers are likely to look at and enforce the most recent order, so it is important to obtain a new order reconciling any inconsistencies.

In states where different courts have jurisdiction to issue civil protection orders, some courts may not be able to include orders curtailing contact between the defendant and his or her children. If those provisions are desired, but the action has been filed in a court without adequate jurisdiction, it may be possible to transfer the case to a court that can grant full relief. It may also be possible to consolidate the civil protection case with the child welfare case.

In criminal cases, release orders or conditions of probation may regulate or prohibit contact between the offender and the child. If part of the child's case plan involves therapeutic or other contact with the offender, the criminal court's orders may conflict with the orders or plans in the child welfare case. Parties in both cases need to be made aware of the relevant orders existing in the other case. Ideally, the criminal court will be aware of the existing orders and case plan before entering its own orders. If possible, sentencing orders should coordinate

---

[25] NAT'L COUNCIL OF JUVENILE AND FAMILY COURT JUDGES, EFFECTIVE INTERVENTION IN DOMESTIC VIOLENCE & CHILD MALTREATMENT CASES: GUIDELINES FOR POLICY AND PRACTICE 91-92 (1999), *available at* http://www.thegreenbook.info/documents/greenbook.pdf.

[26] *E.g.*, California, Connecticut, District of Columbia, Minnesota, Nevada, New Hampshire, New Jersey, New Mexico, North Dakota, Oklahoma, Oregon, Rhode Island, South Dakota, Tennessee, Utah, and Washington.

[27] *E.g.*, Alabama, Alaska, Arizona, Arkansas, California, Colorado, Delaware, Georgia, Hawaii, Idaho, Illinois, Indiana, Iowa, Kansas, Kentucky, Louisiana, Maine, Maryland, Minnesota, Mississippi, Montana, North Carolina, Ohio, Oklahoma, Pennsylvania, South Carolina, Texas, Vermont, and Washington.

with the child welfare case plan. The probation officer, prosecutor, and defense attorney should be provided with relevant information from the child welfare proceeding. The criminal justice system may have access to different resources than the juvenile court that can be used in sentencing in furtherance of the case plan. Criminal courts are often willing to carve out exceptions for contact that is undertaken pursuant to the juvenile court's orders or required by attendance at court hearings at which the victim will also be present.

Similarly, civil protection orders may carve out exceptions to no-contact orders to permit contact allowed by the juvenile court. The child's attorney or caseworker may be able to provide an affidavit or other information to be included in the petition to support the need for issuance of a protective order. Many civil protection orders are obtained *ex parte*, and the issuing judge may even be unaware of the child welfare proceeding, unaware that an agency has legal custody of the child, or unaware that orders regarding custody and access may already exist. Some states[28] permit appointment of an attorney for the child in a civil protection order case, and if the judge is aware that the child is represented in the child welfare proceeding, that attorney may be permitted to represent the child in the civil protection order case as well.

Defendants have a right to object to the civil protection order, and if they do so, information concerning the child welfare proceeding may be presented at that hearing. An application to modify the order may also be brought based on the needs of the case plan. In some jurisdictions, the child, guardian ad litem, or child welfare agency may be permitted to intervene to address the need for more or less contact in furtherance of the child's needs or to suggest how the limitations on contact might be structured.

The attorneys and the court hearing the child welfare proceeding should be made aware of the existence of any civil domestic violence proceedings and should be notified when orders of protection are issued, modified, dismissed, or expire in order to be sure that appropriate orders are in place at all times.

Part 12E: GUARDIANSHIPS

by Ann M. Haralambie[29]

§ 12E.1 Guardianships

Aside from guardianships that may be granted within the child welfare proceeding, there may also be guardianship actions heard by probate and other

---

[28] *E.g.*, Alaska, California, Indiana, Massachusetts, Missouri, Montana, New Hampshire, North Dakota, and Washington.

[29] Ann M. Haralambie, J.D., is a certified family law specialist practicing in Tucson, Arizona. She is also an author and speaker in the fields of family and children's law.

courts. If a collateral guardianship proceeding is pending at the same time as a child welfare proceeding, it is important to ensure that both courts are aware of the other proceeding. Typically, only the child welfare system has the ability to provide comprehensive services to the child and family. Further, only the child welfare court is likely to be able to provide independent representation for the parties. If the child's attorney in the child welfare proceeding becomes aware of the collateral guardianship proceeding, that attorney may be able to intervene in the guardianship on behalf of the child.[30]

Part 12F: IMMIGRATION–REPRESENTING CHILDREN WHO ARE NOT UNITED STATES CITIZENS

by Katherine Brady[31]

§ 12F.1 Introduction

Martha's parents brought her illegally into the United States when she was six years old. Soon after, both parents began to abuse her severely. When Martha was eleven, a court terminated her parents' rights and placed her in a foster care group home. Martha blossomed in her relatively stable life, completed high school as an A-student, and was accepted into a local state college. A few months before Martha's eighteenth birthday, however, her caseworker realized that Martha was an undocumented immigrant. To her horror, the worker realized that Martha would not be able to attend college or obtain lawful employment. If immigration authorities ever discovered Martha, she could be deported to her home country, where she had no one.

The happy ending to this true story is that a representative discovered information about Special Immigrant Juvenile Status (SIJS). SIJS is a federal law that permits immigrant children who are juvenile court dependents to apply for lawful permanent residency (a "green card"). As a lawful permanent resident, the child is eligible for in-state tuition in most state universities, can work legally, and can remain in the United States permanently and apply for U.S. citizenship, if desired, in five years. In Martha's case, although a few months before her eighteenth birthday was a dangerously late time to begin the application process, she was granted a green card under SIJS and went on to have a successful college experience.

---

[30] For a more thorough discussion of guardianship, *see* Chapter 17, Establishing Legal Permanency for the Child.

[31] Katherine Brady, J.D., is a staff attorney at the Immigration Legal Resource Center in San Francisco, California and the author of several manuals and articles about immigration law. She is the director of the ILRC National Project on Immigrant Children.

Applying for SIJS for an immigrant child is a life-saving gift and one of the most important benefits a representative can obtain for the child. Tragically, many caseworkers, attorneys, and judicial staff are not aware of the existence of the SIJS application. As a result, each year thousands of eligible children are not advised to make the application, and forever lose the chance to apply when they leave the dependency system. This article sets out the basic requirements for SIJS in a question and answer format. It also provides information about *free technical assistance and materials* that are available to anyone assisting a child with this application.

§ 12F.1.1 What is Special Immigrant Juvenile Status?

Special immigrant juvenile status is a way for a juvenile court dependent, generally in permanent placement, to become a lawful permanent resident of the United States.[32]

§ 12F.1.2 What are the Benefits and Risks of Applying?

A successful applicant will become a lawful permanent resident, with the right to remain lawfully in the United States, work legally, qualify for in-state tuition at college, and in five years apply for U.S. citizenship. If the application is denied, however, the child might be deported. This is why it is so important to take advantage of the free technical assistance to screen cases and help with applications.

§ 12F.1.3 What are the Requirements for Special Immigrant Juvenile Status?

A juvenile court in the United States must have declared the child a court dependent, or legally committed the child to a state agency or department. The court must have found that, due to abuse, neglect or abandonment, parental reunification is not possible and also that it is not in the child's best interest to be returned to the home country. The child should proceed or have proceeded to long-term foster care, adoption, or guardianship.[33]

§ 12F.1.4 What is the Procedure for Applying?

The child, a social worker, or an attorney can complete the application, which will be submitted to the Immigration and Naturalization Service (INS).[34] The child must complete INS forms, obtain a special medical exam, and provide

---

[32] *See* 8 U.S.C. § 1101(a)(27)(J) and the federal regulation at 8 C.F.R. § 204.11.

[33] 8 U.S.C. § 1101(a)(27)(J).

[34] 8 C.F.R. § 204.11(b).

fingerprints, a photograph, and proof of age.[35] The application must include an order from a dependency court making the findings set out above.[36] The application costs a few hundred dollars in fees, but a fee waiver is available. The INS will grant the applicant employment authorization as soon as the application is filed, and schedule a date for the SIJS interview in the future. The INS generally will decide the case at the SIJS interview.

§ 12F.1.5 When Must the Child Apply and How Long Does the Process Take?

It might take from 6 to 18 months ore more after submitting the application to get an SIJS interview. It is critical to apply for SIJS as soon as possible, so that the case may be resolved while the child still is a juvenile court dependent. If the court ends jurisdiction before the interview, current INS policy is to deny the SIJS application.

§ 12F.1.6 What Cases Carry a Risk of Being Denied?

An applicant might be required to file a waiver or might face potential denial if the applicant:

- Is HIV positive.

- Has been deported in the past.

- Has a juvenile delinquency or adult criminal record.

- Is almost at the point of leaving dependency.

- Could be diagnosed as having a mental condition posing a threat to self or others.

Applicants should not apply without first obtaining expert assistance and evaluation.

§ 12F.1.7 Technical Assistance for SIJS

The Immigrant Legal Resource Center (ILRC) is a nonprofit legal center with expertise in laws affecting immigrant children. It offers free telephone consultation, a free SIJS manual, updates on new developments, and in some areas free training. Contact the ILRC attorney of the day by telephone (415) 255-9499, ext. 6263, fax (415) 255-9792, e-mail at aod@ilrc.org, or mail at 1663 Mission St., Suite 602, San Francisco CA 94103. State that you are calling about SIJS or another issue facing an immigrant child in dependency.

---

[35] For the proof of age requirement, *see* 8 C.F.R. § 204.11(d)(1).

[36] 8 C.F.R. § 204.11(d)(2).

Part 12G: ADVOCACY FOR FOSTER YOUTH IN MENTAL HEALTH COMMITMENT PROCEEDINGS

by Bernard P. Perlmutter[37] *and Carolyn S. Salisbury*[38]

§ 12G.1 Introduction

"Karina," a former foster care client of the University of Miami School of Law's Children & Youth Law Clinic, submitted the following comments to the Florida Supreme Court in 2002 on proposed Florida Rule of Juvenile Procedure 8.350 governing the commitment of dependent children to psychiatric facilities:

> I was placed in several treatment facilities over the years I was in foster care. . . I wish I would have had a lawyer during all the years I was kept in locked facilities. I think it would have made a big difference. I don't think that I would have been abused like I was if I would have had a lawyer. I don't think I would have even been in locked facilities as long as I was if I would have had a lawyer. If I hadn't finally gotten a lawyer, DCF would have kept me in a locked facility until I turned 18, and I never would have learned to live outside of a facility. . . .

> I think it's very important for a foster child to have a hearing before DCF sends them to a facility so they can talk to the judge. After I got my attorney, she made sure that I got a hearing and that I went to court. I was able to speak to the judge, and my lawyer told the judge why I shouldn't be placed in a facility. The judge said that I didn't need to be put in another facility. . . Also, I think it's very important for every foster child in a facility to have a lawyer. If a child doesn't have a lawyer, then there's no one to stand up for what the child wants. This makes a child lose hope, which is how I felt for a long time.[39]

This chapter provides an overview of the legal framework governing the commitment of children like Karina to psychiatric residential treatment programs or facilities, the research on the effectiveness of residential treatment for emotionally disturbed children, the therapeutic jurisprudence considerations pertinent to the representation of children committed to these facilities, the

---

[37] Bernard P. Perlmutter, J.D., is Director and Clinical Instructor of Law at the Children & Youth Law Clinic, an in-house legal clinic at the University of Miami School of Law. He is also a Clinical Fellow at the law school's Center for Ethics and Public Service.

[38] Carolyn S. Salisbury, J.D., is Associate Director and Instructor of Law at the Children & Youth Law Clinic at the University of Miami School of Law. She teaches classes in Children and the Law, Public Interest Advocacy and Ethics, Community Justice and Ethics, and Legal Research and Writing. She also serves as Co-Director of the law school's Public Interest Law Summer Program.

[39] *See* Karina's Comments, Appendix to University of Miami School of Law Children & Youth Law Clinic Comments, in *In Re Fla. R. Juv. P. 8.350* (filed February 15, 2002).

ethical responsibilities of lawyers who represent these children, and the roles performed by attorneys both before and after a child's commitment to a psychiatric facility.

§ 12G.2 Background

There has been growing skepticism about the effectiveness, necessity, and cost benefit value of the psychiatric commitment of emotionally disturbed or behaviorally disordered children and adolescents in state care like our client Karina. In recent years, advocates have voiced and documented their concerns about the overuse and misuse of mental hospitals and residential treatment centers to institutionalize "troublesome youth" diagnosed with relatively mild adolescent disorders such as "conduct disorder," "oppositional defiant disorder," and "adolescent adjustment reaction."[40] While some children who have serious psychiatric disorders may need such care, many other children are institutionalized in psychiatric facilities for a wide variety of typical teenage behaviors including running away, aggression, opposition to parental values and rules, engaging in sexual activity, or antisocial behavior.

Nationally, a review of data from several states has indicated that at least 40 percent of children and youth committed to psychiatric institutions are inappropriately placed.[41] Also, studies of the psychiatric commitment of adolescents have shown that fewer than one-third of those children admitted for inpatient mental health treatment were diagnosed as having severe or acute mental disorders of the type typically associated with such admissions (such as psychotic, serious depressive, or organic disorders).[42] Disturbingly, "the rising rates of psychiatric admission of children and adolescents reflect an increasing use of hospitalization to manage a population for whom such intervention is typically inappropriate: 'troublesome' youth who do not suffer from severe mental disorders."[43]

Erroneous placement in a residential treatment facility can have an extremely harmful and traumatic impact on a child:

A recent review of psychological research concluded that certain degrees of freedom of movement, association, and communication are critical to the psychological well-being of children and adolescents. Mental hospitalization may entail substantial periods of isolation, particularly in the

---

[40] *See, e.g.,* Lois A. Weithorn, Note, *Mental Hospitalization of Troublesome Youth: An Analysis of Skyrocketing Admission Rates,* 40 STAN. L. REV. 773, 788-792 (1988).

[41] *Id.* at 784 n.72 (*quoting* J. KNITZER, UNCLAIMED CHILDREN: THE FAILURE OF PUBLIC RESPONSIBILITY TO CHILDREN AND ADOLESCENTS IN NEED OF MENTAL HEALTH SERVICES 46 (1982)). Inappropriateness was judged on the basis of "factors such as whether the 'children could have been served as outpatients' or in day treatment, and whether the severity of the children's diagnoses warranted inpatient treatment." *Id.*

[42] *Id.* at 788.

[43] *Id.* at 773-774.

case of recalcitrant children and adolescents, and may be characterized by involuntary administration of heavy doses of psychotropic medication (that is, medication used to alter psychological functioning), invasions of privacy, and social pressure to conform behavior to certain norms. . . .Certain aspects of mental hospitalization can be extremely frightening for some children. Children who are not seriously emotionally disturbed may be greatly upset by exposure to children who are.[44]

Many of the "troublesome" youth who are committed to psychiatric institutions are children who have been abused, abandoned, or neglected and placed in state foster care: "[A] very large proportion of children in mental hospitals and other residential treatment facilities are wards of the state . . . Once children are placed in state custody, a new set of problems emerge. Social service placements often are far from children's families and therefore, promote an institutional climate. Children find themselves amid a slow bureaucracy in which they are stuck in restrictive settings for long periods of time without effective recourse."[45]

Children who are committed to psychiatric institutions remain there indefinitely. In fact, once hospitalized, juvenile psychiatric patients remain in the institution approximately twice as long as do adults.[46] Additionally, foster children who are in state custody remain institutionalized for longer periods of time.[47]

§ 12G.3 The Legal Framework

§ 12G.3.1 *Parham v. J.R.*

In 1979, the United States Supreme Court decided *Parham v. J.R.*,[48] a widely criticized decision in which the Court ruled that the Fourteenth Amendment to the United States Constitution does not require a court hearing prior to parents or the state committing a child to a psychiatric hospital. The *Parham* court set forth the minimum due process that is required under the federal constitution when a child is committed to a psychiatric facility.

In *Parham*, the Court established that "[i]t is not disputed that a child, in common with adults, has a substantial liberty interest in not being confined

---

[44] *Id.* at 797 (citations omitted).

[45] GARY B. MELTON ET AL., NO PLACE TO GO: THE CIVIL COMMITMENT OF MINORS 15-16 (1998) (citations omitted). "[A]t least 40% of children and youth in state hospitals could have been treated in less restrictive settings, *by the states' own admission*. This is true of residential treatment facilities as well." *Id.* at 37 (*citing* J. KNITZER, UNCLAIMED CHILDREN: THE FAILURE OF PUBLIC RESPONSIBILITY TO CHILDREN AND ADOLESCENTS IN NEED OF MENTAL HEALTH SERVICES 46 (1982)).

[46] Lois A. Weithorn, Note, *Mental Hospitalization of Troublesome Youth: An Analysis of Skyrocketing Admission Rates*, 40 STAN. L. REV. 773, 789 (1988).

[47] GARY B. MELTON ET AL., NO PLACE TO GO: THE CIVIL COMMITMENT OF MINORS 16 (1998).

[48] 442 U.S. 584 (1979).

unnecessarily for medical treatment and that the state's involvement in the commitment decision constitutes state action under the Fourteenth Amendment."[49] Accordingly, the Court "assume[d] that a child has a protectable interest not only in being free of unnecessary bodily restraints but also in not being labeled erroneously by some persons because of an improper decision by the state hospital superintendent."[50]

Under the Georgia statute challenged in *Parham*, a parent or guardian could admit a child for "observation and diagnosis."[51] The statute governing voluntary admissions further provided that if the superintendent of the hospital found "evidence of mental illness" and that the child was "suitable for treatment" in the hospital, the child could be admitted "for such period and under such conditions as may be authorized by law."[52] Although one of the plaintiffs in *Parham* had been voluntarily admitted to the mental hospital by his parents, the lead named plaintiff, J.R., was "declared a neglected child" and removed from his parents' care by the county. As a ward of the State of Georgia, J.R. had been admitted to the mental institution by the Georgia Department of Family and Children Services.[53]

The Court first discussed whether the procedure used by the State of Georgia violated due process when the child's parent admitted the child to the state mental hospital.[54] The Court determined that precedents permit parents to retain a substantial—if not the dominant—role in the decision, absent a finding of neglect or abuse, and that the traditional presumption that the parents act in the best interests of their child should apply. The Court also stated, however, that the child's rights and the nature of the commitment decision are such that parents cannot always have absolute and unreviewable discretion to decide whether to have a child institutionalized. The Court concluded that parents retain plenary authority to seek such care for their children, subject to a physician's independent examination and medical judgment.[55] In addition, the Court recognized that the State has "a significant interest in confining the use of its costly mental health facilities to cases of genuine need."[56]

Answering the question, "What process protects adequately the child's constitutional rights?" the Court concluded that the risk of error inherent in the parental decision to have a child institutionalized for mental health care is sufficiently great that some kind of inquiry should be made by a "neutral factfinder"

---

[49] *Id.* at 600.

[50] *Id.* at 601.

[51] *Id.* at 591.

[52] *Id.* at 590-591.

[53] *See id.*

[54] *Id.* at 589-617.

[55] *Id.* at 604.

[56] *Id.* at 604-605.

to determine whether the "statutory requirements for admission are satisfied."[57] That inquiry must carefully probe the child's background using all available sources, including, but not limited to, parents, schools, and other social agencies. The review must also include an interview with the child. It is necessary that the decision-maker have the authority to refuse to admit any child who does not satisfy the medical standards for admission. Finally, it is necessary that the child's continuing need for commitment be reviewed periodically by a similarly independent procedure.[58]

The Court next considered what process is due when the child is a ward of the state.[59] The Court indicated that when a child is in the custody of the state due to the parent's abuse or neglect, the state has a statutory duty to consider the best interests of the child with regard to commitment.[60] Although the majority recognized that "what process is due varies somewhat when the state, rather than a natural parent, makes the request for commitment," the Court concluded that "the differences in the two situations do not justify requiring different procedures at the time of the child's initial admission to the hospital."[61] However, the Court determined that "[i]t is possible that the procedures required in reviewing a ward's need for continuing care should be different from those used to review the need of a child with natural parents."[62]

Thus, the United States Supreme Court in *Parham* set forth three minimum due process requirements that must be provided when a child is committed: (1) an inquiry by a neutral factfinder, which is not required to be in the form of a judicial inquiry; (2) the inquiry must probe the child's background using all available resources; and (3) there must be periodic review by a neutral factfinder.[63] These minimum standards apply whether the child has been admitted by the state as the guardian of its ward or by a natural parent.[64]

---

[57] *Id.* at 606.

[58] *Id.* at 606-607 (emphasis added) (citations omitted).

[59] *See id.* at 617-621.

[60] *See id.* at 618-619.

[61] *Id.* at 617-618. Justice Brennan, joined by Justices Marshall and Stevens, strongly dissented on the issue of what procedures are constitutionally required when the child is a ward of the state. *See id.* at 636-639 (Brennan, J., concurring in part and dissenting in part). Justice Brennan wrote that "there is no justification for denying children committed by their social workers the prior hearings that the Constitution typically requires." *Id.* at 637. In addition, he observed that the social worker-child relationship is not deserving of the deference accorded the parent-child relationship, and that when a child is already in state custody, pre-hospitalization hearings will not prevent children from receiving needed care. *See id.* at 637-638.

[62] *Id.* at 619. The Court directed the district court to consider this issue on remand. *Id.*

[63] *Id.* at 606.

[64] *See id.* at 618-619. Although some would argue that U.S. Supreme Court cases regarding the scope of procedural due process protections in delinquency proceedings should accord minors facing civil commitment greater due process (*see, e.g., In re Gault*, 387 U.S. 1 (1967); *Kent v. United States*, 383 U.S. 541 (1966)), these decisions are not helpful because they were issued prior to the Court's ruling in *Parham*.

The *Parham* decision has been widely criticized for not mandating that children be provided with judicial due process safeguards prior to their commitment to psychiatric facilities,[65] as well as for relying on faulty assumptions about adolescent decision making.[66] When the Court decided *Parham* in 1979, the Court relied on an *amicus curiae* brief submitted by the American Psychiatric Association that argued against providing judicial hearings prior to the minor's commitment. However, both the American Psychiatric Association and the American Psychological Association now strongly support judicial due process for adolescent minors facing psychiatric institutionalization, particularly when the minor is a ward of the state. Both associations have drafted model state commitment statutes or approved guidelines for minors facing commitment to psychiatric facilities that provide the youth with substantial judicial due process prior to commitment.[67]

---

[65] As one commentator has noted, "[n]o modern U.S. Supreme Court civil case dealing with the rights of the mentally handicapped has been criticized as consistently or as thoroughly as [has] been *Parham*." MICHAEL L. PERLIN, MENTAL DISABILITY LAW 3.72, at 428 (1989). *See also* Ira C. Lupu, *Mediating Institutions: Beyond the Public/Private Distinction: The Separation of Powers and the Protection of Children*, 61 U. CHI. L. REV. 1317 (1994) (discussing *Parham* and the mechanism for distributing decision-making authority over children); Bernard P. Perlmutter & Carolyn S. Salisbury, *"Please Let Me Be Heard": The Right of a Florida Foster Child to Due Process Prior to Being Committed to a Long-Term, Locked Psychiatric Institution*, 25 NOVA L. REV. 725, 731-737 (2001) (summarizing research on residential treatment of "troublesome" youth in the wake of *Parham*); Lois A. Weithorn, *Mental Hospitalization of Troublesome Youth: An Analysis of Skyrocketing Admission Rates*, 40 STAN. L. REV. 773, 826 (1988) (criticizing *Parham* as tolerating the inappropriate use of inpatient facilities, the result of "a combination of factors, including laissez-faire judicial policies, insurance coverage favoring inpatient treatment, the rise of corporate medicine, a mental health establishment willing to assume control over troublesome youth, and the symbolic appeal of a medical perspective on deviance").

[66] In *Parham*, Justice Burger stated that "[m]ost children, even in adolescence, simply are not able to make sound judgments concerning many decisions, including their need for medical care or treatment." *Parham*, 442 U.S. at 603. However, this dicta by the Supreme Court is one of a number of outmoded "assumptions" that the Court relied upon in its ruling. Indeed, the social science research now indicates that, at least in their reasoning about treatment decisions, adolescents are indistinguishable from adults. In a leading research study, clinical psychologists "presented hypothetical dilemmas about medical and psychological treatment decisions to nine, fourteen, eighteen, and twenty-one-year olds. The responses of the fourteen-year-olds could not be differentiated from those of the adult groups, according to any of the major standards of competency: evidence of choice; reasonable outcome or choice; reasonable decision making process; understanding the facts." *See* Gary B. Melton, *Toward "Personhood" for Adolescents: Autonomy and Privacy as Values in Public Policy*, 38 AM. PSYCHOL. 99 (1983). This empirical evidence indicates that "[t]here seems to be ample basis for reversal of current presumptions in favor of a view of adolescents as autonomous persons possessed of independent interests regarding liberty and privacy. Accordingly, psychologists should actively involve minors in decision making about treatment and research, and policy-makers should begin their analyses of issues involving adolescents with respect for their autonomy and privacy." *Id.*

[67] In 1981, two years after *Parham*, the American Psychiatric Association approved a set of guidelines for the psychiatric hospitalization of minors. The guidelines, prepared by the Association's Task Force on the Commitment of Minors, guarantee children over the age of 16

§ 12G.3.2 State Laws

The *Parham* Court noted that states are free to provide additional due process safeguards for minors in mental health commitment proceedings.[68] State law varies widely in this area, and therefore children's attorneys need to familiarize themselves with the applicable case law and legislation in their states. Several state supreme courts have granted minors greater due process protections in mental health commitment proceedings.[69] In addition to state case law, legislation regulating minors' psychiatric commitment also varies by state:

---

the right to contest an involuntary admission to a psychiatric facility, the right to an involuntary commitment hearing, and the right to counsel at the involuntary commitment hearing. At the involuntary commitment hearing, the child through the child's appointed counsel has the right to cross examine witnesses favoring commitment and the right to present testimony and evidence in opposition to commitment and/or in favor of less structured alternatives. In addition to these protections, the party seeking to commit the child against the child's will has the burden of showing the court by clear and convincing evidence that: (a) the child has a mental disorder; (b) the child is in need of treatment or care available at the institution to which involuntary commitment is sought; and (c) no less structured means are likely to be as effective in providing such treatment or care. If the court, after hearing the evidence presented, commits the child to a psychiatric program, the duration of the initial commitment cannot exceed 45 days, with the next commitment for 90 days, and subsequent commitments of 6 months. *See* GUIDELINES FOR THE PSYCHIATRIC HOSPITALIZATION OF MINORS, § 4(C), AMERICAN PSYCHIATRIC ASSOCIATION OFFICIAL ACTION, 139 AM. J. PSYCHIATRY 971-974 (1982).

More recently, the American Psychological Association's Division of Child, Youth, and Family Services endorsed guidelines that provide significant judicial due process to youth facing psychiatric commitment. *See* GARY B. MELTON ET AL., NO PLACE TO GO: THE CIVIL COMMITMENT OF MINORS 17 (1998) (citing A MODEL ACT FOR THE MENTAL HEALTH TREATMENT OF MINORS, AMERICAN PSYCHOLOGICAL ASSOCIATION, § 108). Both the guidelines by the American Psychological Association and the American Psychiatric Association apply even where the parent is seeking the youth's commitment.

[68] *Parham v. J.R.*, 442 U.S. 584, 607 (1979).

[69] *See, e.g., In re Roger S.*, 569 P.2d 1286 (Cal. 1977) (holding that no interest of the State sufficiently outweighs the liberty interest of a mature minor over age 14 to independently exercise his right to due process in a commitment to a mental hospital); *In re P.F., Jr. v. Walsh*, 648 P.2d 1067 (Colo. 1982) (holding that a minor has a substantial and protectable liberty interest in being free from the physical restraints attendant to commitment in a psychiatric hospital); *Amendment to Rules of Juvenile Procedure, Fla. R. Juv. P.* 8.350, 804 So. 2d 1206 (Fla. 2001), 842 So. 2d 763 (Fla. 2003) (adopting rule of court that provides a dependent child with an attorney and a pre-commitment hearing if the state seeks to involuntarily commit the child to a psychiatric facility); *M.W. v. Davis*, 756 So.2d 90, 107-108 (Fla. 2000) (holding that "[a]n order approving the placement of a fifteen-year-old dependent child in a locked residential facility against the wishes of that child deprives the child of liberty" and directing the promulgation of a court rule that provides a dependent child "a meaningful opportunity to be heard" in psychiatric commitment proceedings); *In re Commitment of N.N.*, 679 A.2d 1174 (N.J. 1996) (holding that even though the state has an interest in ensuring the mental health of its children, that interest is not sufficiently compelling to justify infringement upon a child's due process and liberty rights and ruling that a minor who is in need of intensive institutional psychiatric therapy may not be committed without a finding based on clear and convincing evidence that the minor without such care is a danger to others or self); *State of Wash. ex rel. T.B. v. C.P.C. Fairfax Hosp.*, 918 P.2d 497 (Wash. 1996) (granting a 15-year-old mentally ill minor's petition for writ of habeas corpus on the ground that the involuntary incarceration of the minor in a mental hospital against her will violated Washington state law and the minor's constitutional right to liberty).

State legislation governing the admission of minors to psychiatric facilities can be classified into four general categories. One category includes states which merely abide by the informal admission process authorized in *Parham*. Other states go beyond the minimal requirements mandated in *Parham* by imposing additional pre-admission procedures. For example, some states require that consent be obtained from older children, while a few others implement a pre-admission review hearing. A third category is composed of several states which require some form of post-admission review procedure. A fourth classification includes those states which simply prohibit the voluntary psychiatric hospitalization by parents or other third parties.[70]

Since laws governing minors' psychiatric commitment vary widely among states, it is important for children's attorneys to familiarize themselves with the relevant law in their respective jurisdictions.

§ 12G.3.3 Provisions Governing Psychiatric Commitment of Foster Children

Some states also have specific case law, legislation, or court rules regulating the psychiatric commitment of children in foster care,[71] and children's attorneys need to familiarize themselves with these provisions. Additionally, even in the absence of specific state law in this area, children's attorneys can use federal and state foster care law to protect the interests of their foster child clients who face commitment to psychiatric facilities.

Under federal law, if a court has decided that a child cannot return home, then the court must also decide whether the state's proposed placement is the least restrictive, most family-like setting for the child and whether it is in as close proximity as possible to the parents' home.[72] Using foster care judicial review provisions, the child's attorney can argue that placement in a psychiatric facility

---

[70] Dennis E. Cichon, *Developing a Mental Health Code for Minors*, 13 T.M. COOLEY L. REV. 529, 561-562 (1996). For a survey of state legislation in effect at the time of the article's publication, *see id.* at 561-569. *See also* Jan C. Costello, *"The Trouble is They're Growing, The Trouble is They're Grown": Therapeutic Jurisprudence and Adolescents' Participation in Mental Health Care Decisions*, 29 OHIO N.U. L. REV. 607 (2003) (surveying legislation in California, Illinois, and Ohio); Gary B. Sutnick, Comment, *"Reasonable Efforts" Revisited: Reforming Federal Financing of Children's Mental Health Services*, 68 N.Y.U. L. REV. 136, 149-154 (1993) (surveying select state legislation); Alexander V. Tsesis, *Protecting Children Against Unnecessary Institutionalization*, 39 S. TEX. L. REV. 995, 1019-1021 (1998) (surveying select state legislation).

[71] *See, e.g.*, ARIZ. REV. STAT. § 36-518 (2004); CAL. WELF. & INST. CODE § 6552 (2004); CONN. GEN. STAT. ANN. § 17a-79 (2004); FLA. R. JUV. P. 8.350 (2004); OKLA. STAT. tit. 43A, § 5-503 (2004); TEX. HEALTH & SAFETY CODE § 572.001 (2004). *See also In re E.*, 538 P.2d 231 (Cal. 1975); *Amendment to Rules of Juvenile Procedure, Fla. R. Juv. P.* 8.350, 804 So. 2d 1206 (Fla. 2001), 842 So. 2d 763 (Fla. 2003); *M.W. v. Davis*, 756 So. 2d 90 (Fla. 2000); *In re Commitment of N.N.*, 679 A.2d 1174 (N.J. 1996).

[72] *See* 42 U.S.C. § 675(5)(A).

is not the least restrictive, most family-like setting for the child. Usually, such placements are also not in close proximity to the home of the child's family.

Additionally, federal law mandates that states must have a court-approved case plan for each foster child, which specifies tasks for each party, as well as the type of placement for the child.[73] Placements can range from a foster home, to kinship care, to institutional placement in a residential treatment center or psychiatric facility. Once case plans are adopted by the court, amendments do not need to receive court approval. Thus, if the state seeks to change a child's placement to commit the child to a psychiatric facility, the child's attorney can argue that this change in the type of placement for the child can only be accomplished through court approval amending the child's case plan, after notice and the opportunity to be heard.

Children's attorneys should carefully examine their states' laws governing foster care judicial review proceedings and foster care case plans to develop arguments for providing foster children with judicial safeguards prior to the state committing the children to psychiatric facilities. Additionally, for children who have already been committed, children's attorneys should examine their states' laws regarding petitions for writs of habeas corpus to challenge the legality of their clients' commitments to these facilities.

§ 12G.4 Therapeutic Jurisprudence Considerations

Prior to undertaking representation of a child in mental health commitment proceedings, it is important for children's attorneys to familiarize themselves with the therapeutic jurisprudence literature demonstrating the therapeutic and psychological benefits of ensuring that the child is provided with meaningful due process. Therapeutic jurisprudence is an interdisciplinary field of legal scholarship that seeks to "reshape legal rules and practices in ways that minimize their antitherapeutic effects and maximize their potential to enhance the emotional well-being of the individual and society."[74] Therapeutic jurisprudence recognizes that people are more satisfied with and comply more with the outcome of legal proceedings when they perceive those proceedings to be fair and have an

---

[73] *See* 42 U.S.C. § 675(1) (requiring that the case plan include "[a] description of the type of home or institution in which a child is to be placed, including a discussion of the safety and appropriateness of the placement").

[74] Bruce J. Winick & Ginger Lerner-Wren, *Do Juveniles Facing Civil Commitment Have a Right to Counsel?: A Therapeutic Jurisprudence Brief*, 71 U. CIN. L. REV. 115, 115 (2002). *See also* Jan C. Costello, *Why Have Hearings for Kids if You're not Going to Listen?: A Therapeutic Jurisprudence Approach to Mental Disability Proceedings for Minors*, 71 U. CIN. L. REV. 19 (2002); Bernard P. Perlmutter & Carolyn S. Salisbury, *"Please Let Me Be Heard": The Right of a Florida Foster Child to Due Process Prior to Being Committed to a Long-Term, Locked Psychiatric Institution*, 25 NOVA L. REV. 725 (2001) (proposing application of principles of therapeutic jurisprudence to civil commitment hearings for foster children).

opportunity to participate in them.[75] Research on civil commitment hearings conducted by social psychologists and therapeutic jurisprudence scholars strongly favors procedures that "increase patients' perceptions of fairness, participation, and dignity."[76] Therapeutic jurisprudence research has shown that providing a minor with judicial due process in the context of mental health commitment enhances therapeutic and psychological benefits for the minor.

A number of research studies have found that providing adversarial proceedings produces positive psychological benefits for children. Research indicates that "having some control over the process (a form of control inherent in a truly adversarial system) is likely to enhance a child's sense of perceived justice . . . and perhaps decrease resistance to treatment if it ultimately is ordered."[77] Significant clinical evidence exists showing a greater likelihood of the treatment succeeding when adolescents participate in the decision to begin treatment.[78]

A research study found considerable benefits resulted from allowing adolescents to have judicial hearings prior to their commitment if they objected to hospitalization.[79] The researchers reported that hospital staff believed giving adolescents a hearing if they objected to hospitalization was "helpful to children" for the following reasons:

- The procedure gave the child the opportunity to tell how the child felt and to express his or her objection.

- The procedure made the child (and the family) confront the issue of whether or not the child really needed or wanted to be hospitalized.

- The procedure made the child feel that he or she had been treated fairly; if the child objected, the child would have an impartial hearing.

- The procedure afforded the child some measure of control over his or her own destiny.

- The procedure was a step in the patient's involvement in planning for his own care.

---

[75] *See* Bruce J. Winick & Ginger Lerner-Wren, *Do Juveniles Facing Civil Commitment Have a Right to Counsel?: A Therapeutic Jurisprudence Brief*, 71 U. CIN. L. REV. 115 (2002).

[76] Bruce Winick, *Therapeutic Jurisprudence and the Civil Commitment Hearing*, 10 J. CONTEMP. LEGAL ISSUES 37, 60 (1999).

[77] GARY B. MELTON ET AL., NO PLACE TO GO: THE CIVIL COMMITMENT OF MINORS 139-141 (1998).

[78] *See* Rochelle T. Bastien & Howard S. Adelman, *Noncompulsory Versus Legally Mandated Placement, Perceived Choice, and Response to Treatment Among Adolescents*, 52 J. CONSULTING & CLINICAL PSYCHOL. 171, 177 (1984).

[79] Alan Meisel & L.H. Roth, *The Child's Right to Object to Hospitalization: Some Empirical Data*, 4 J. OF PSYCHIATRY & L. 377 (1976).

- The judge could only release the child if the child did not need to be hospitalized.[80]

The therapeutic jurisprudence literature also recognizes the vital role of the child's attorney as a zealous advocate for the child's wishes in psychiatric commitment proceedings:

> The attorney is the primary vehicle for effectuating the juvenile's participatory interests. Both the American Psychological Association and the American Psychiatric Association have recognized the therapeutic importance of having a juvenile represented by an attorney in their Model Act and Guidelines. Without representation [by an attorney] who is professionally bound to articulate the juvenile's wishes and preferences, juveniles will not experience the sense of voice and participation in the proceedings that are essential to their having a positive response to the outcome of the hearing.[81]

Additionally, for both therapeutic and due process reasons, the child's attorney should seek to ensure that the court safeguards the child's right to assert the psychotherapist-patient privilege. Asserting the privilege gives the child a voice and validation in the legal process and assures the integrity of the psychotherapist-patient relationship. Denying the child the right to assert the privilege can have profound anti-therapeutic consequences. The psychotherapist-patient privilege serves an important public interest by facilitating the provision of appropriate treatment for individuals suffering from mental or emotional problems. Foster children in particular, many of whom suffer for severe emotional disorders, must be given the assurance that they can trust their therapists with private disclosures, should be encouraged to seek mental health treatment, and must be able to establish clear boundaries of privacy within the framework of the psychotherapist relationship in order for treatment to succeed. Respect for confidentiality rights is particularly crucial for such children. It allows them to exert some measure of control over their world, and the ability to develop a degree of trust in those around them.[82]

---

[80] *Id.* at 384-385. *See also In re Gault*, 387 U.S. 1, 27 (1967) (observing that studies have shown that "the appearance as well as the actuality of fairness, impartiality and orderliness—in short, the essentials of due process—may be a more impressive and more therapeutic attitude so far as the juvenile is concerned").

[81] Bruce J. Winick & Ginger Lerner Wren, *Essay: In the Supreme Court of Florida, Amendment to the Rules of Juvenile Procedure Fla. R. Juv. P.* 8.350, 71 U. Cin. L. Rev. 119, 124-125 (2002) (internal citations omitted).

[82] *See generally S.C. v. GAL.*, 845 So. 2d 953 (Fla. Dist. Ct. App. 2003); David R. Katner, *Confidentiality and Juvenile Mental Health Records in Dependency Proceedings*, 12 Wm. & Mary Bill Rts. J. 511 (2004).

§ 12G.5 Ethical Role and Responsibilities of the Child's Attorney

Attorneys who represent children in mental health commitment proceedings have special obligations and challenges:

> For lawyers/advocates to provide effective legal representation they must be familiar with the client's legal rights under state and federal statutes and constitutions. They must have a clear understanding of their professional role and their unique duty to identify and pursue the client's *legal interests* and avoid functioning as a guardian ad litem or therapist. They must be comfortable with the language and concepts of mental health culture and be able to use them in communicating with mental health professionals and the court consistent with the client's *legal* interests. By skillful and zealous representation they must seek to empower the child client and to help fashion for him or her a future filled with possibilities.[83]

A lawyer who serves as the child's attorney has a very different role from a guardian ad litem or an attorney who represents a guardian ad litem. Thus, prior to undertaking representation of a child client, it is of utmost importance for the child's attorney to understand his or her unique role in the context of representing a child facing commitment to a mental health facility.

Rule 1.14 of the AMERICAN BAR ASSOCIATION MODEL RULES OF PROFESSIONAL CONDUCT mandates that attorneys who represent children and other clients with disabilities shall, as far as reasonably possible, "maintain a normal client-lawyer relationship with the client." The Comment to the rule further states that "children as young as 5 or 6 years of age, and certainly those of 10 or 12, are regarded as having opinions that are entitled to weight in legal proceedings concerning their custody."

Additionally, in 1996, the American Bar Association promulgated STANDARDS OF PRACTICE FOR LAWYERS WHO REPRESENT CHILDREN IN ABUSE AND NEGLECT CASES, in order to clarify attorneys' ethical obligations in dependency proceedings. STANDARD A-1 states: "The term 'child's attorney' means a lawyer who provides legal services for a child and who owes the same duties of undivided loyalty, confidentiality, and competent representation to the child as is due an adult client."[84] The Commentary to STANDARD A-1 adds that, "[t]o ensure that the child's independent voice is heard, the child's attorney must advocate the child's articulated position. Consequently, the child's attorney owes

---

[83] Jan C. Costello, *Representing Children in Mental Disability Proceedings*, 1 J. CTR. CHILD. & CTS. 101, 120 (1999).

[84] ABA STANDARDS OF PRACTICE FOR LAWYERS WHO REPRESENT CHILDREN IN ABUSE AND NEGLECT CASES (1996), *available at* http://www.abanet.org/child/repstandwhole.pdf.

traditional duties to the child as client consistent with ER 1.14(a) of the Model Rules of Professional Conduct."[85] STANDARD B-4 further mandates: "The child's attorney should elicit the child's preferences in a developmentally appropriate manner, advise the child, and provide guidance. The child's attorney should represent the child's expressed preferences and follow the child's direction throughout the course of litigation."

The lawyer who serves as the child's attorney in mental health commitment proceedings owes several important responsibilities to the child client. Prior to an initial commitment hearing, at the initial hearing, and at subsequent review hearings (if the child is committed), the child's attorney performs three critical responsibilities at each stage of the proceedings: (1) client counseling, (2) mediation and negotiation, and (3) zealous advocacy. The ABA STANDARDS OF PRACTICE FOR LAWYERS WHO REPRESENT CHILDREN IN ABUSE AND NEGLECT CASES provide a lodestar to understand how the attorney's responsibilities should be fulfilled in representing the child facing commitment to these facilities.[86]

§ 12G.5.1 Lawyer as Counselor

First, the child's lawyer must provide client-centered counseling to the child.[87] ABA Standard B-4, Commentary, addresses this responsibility as follows:

> The lawyer has a duty to explain to the child in a developmentally appropriate way such information as will assist the child in having maximum input in determination of the particular position at issue. The lawyer should inform the child of the relevant facts and applicable laws and the ramifications of taking various positions, which may include the impact of such decisions on other family members or on future legal positions. The lawyer may express an opinion concerning the likelihood of the court

---

[85] *Id.*

[86] *Id.* The ABA ABUSE AND NEGLECT STANDARDS FOR LAWYERS WHO REPRESENT CHILDREN IN ABUSE AND NEGLECT CASES were adopted in 1996 and build on the ABA JUVENILE JUSTICE STANDARDS RELATING TO COUNSEL FOR PRIVATE PARTIES, promulgated by the ABA Institute of Judicial Administration Joint Commission on Juvenile Justice in 1979.

[87] For discussions of the concept of client-centered counseling, which is based on deference to client autonomy and is designed to foster client decision making, *see* DAVID A. BINDER ET AL., LAWYERS AS COUNSELORS: A CLIENT-CENTERED APPROACH 8-13 (2d ed. 2004) (describing the hallmarks of client-centered counseling and integrating client-centered counseling into the interviewing and counseling process). *See also* ROBERT M. BASTRESS & JOSEPH D. HARBAUGH, INTERVIEWING, COUNSELING, & NEGOTIATING SKILLS FOR EFFECTIVE REPRESENTATION 334-338 (1990); Robert D. Dinerstein, *Client-Centered Counseling: Reappraisal and Refinement*, 32 ARIZ. L. REV. 501 (1990). For a discussion of the therapeutic (client-centered therapy, or Rogerian) derivations of this legal counseling model, which are based on the premise that individuals can achieve full potential or self-actualization when facilitated by a helping, empathic, and nonjudgmental person, *see* Bruce J. Winick, *Client Denial and Resistance in the Advance Directive Context: Reflections on How Attorneys Can Identify and Deal With a Psycholegal Soft Spot*, 4 PSYCHOL. PUB. POL'Y & LAW 901, 916-917 (1998).

or other parties accepting particular positions. The lawyer may inform the child of an expert's recommendations germane to the issue. . . .

On the one hand, the lawyer has a duty to ensure that the child client is given the information necessary to make an informed decision, including advice and guidance. On the other hand, a lawyer has a duty not to over-bear the will of the child. While the lawyer may attempt to persuade the child to accept a particular position, the lawyer may not advocate a position contrary to the child's expressed position except as provided by these Abuse and Neglect Standards or the Code of Professional Responsibility.

In proceedings involving a child's commitment to a psychiatric facility, the lawyer's client-counseling role is essential. To properly fulfill the client-counseling role, it is important for the attorney to become familiar with the child's background and special needs and to show special sensitivity to the child client. In a developmentally appropriate manner, "[t]he lawyer should first provide the client with the information necessary for an informed decision. After providing this information, the lawyer/advocate's task is to assist the client in reaching a decision. This means helping the client identify goals and weigh the pros and cons of the proposed course of action, answering the client's questions, and expressing a professional opinion on the practical effect of the client's decision. The lawyer's role is to facilitate the client's decision, not make it for the client."[88]

The child's lawyer needs to provide the child with an honest legal assessment of his or her case, a legal opinion as to whether the merits of the case are strong, and legal advice as to the chances of prevailing. If the merits of the child's case are not strong, then the lawyer may counsel the child that it may be in his or her best interests to waive the commitment hearing and voluntarily consent to placement. If the child wants to contest commitment, then the child's lawyer needs to proceed to engage in negotiation, mediation, and zealous advocacy on the child's behalf.

§ 12G.5.2 Lawyer as Negotiator and Mediator

In addition to client counseling, the attorney serves an important role through the use of skills in negotiation and mediation with the state and other parties to explore and consider less restrictive alternatives to residential commitment. Indeed, "only the dependent child's own attorney can give meaning to the child's right to be heard by allowing the child to actively participate in such procedures as negotiating alternatives with the GAL and the Department."[89] The Commentary to ABA Standards C-6 states that "[p]articularly in contentious

---

[88] Jan C. Costello *Representing Children in Mental Disability Proceedings*, 1 J. Ctr. Child. & Cts. 101, 108 (1999).

[89] *In Re Fla. R. Juv. P.* 8.350, 804 So. 2d 1206, 1209 (Fla. 2001), 842 So. 2d 763 (Fla. 2003).

cases, the child's attorney may effectively assist negotiations of the parties and their lawyers by focusing on the needs of the child."[90]

While ethically bound to advocate for the child's expressed wishes, children's lawyers should be prepared to interact with guardians ad litem, social workers, therapists, and other professionals who follow a best interests standard. "Because the best interests standard is prevalent in the child client's interactions with legal, medical, mental health, and social work institutions, the attorney cannot carry out effective representation without developing a sophisticated, principled understanding of the best interests of each client."[91]

In some cases, it may be possible to avoid the child's commitment if the child's attorney is able to mediate and negotiate community-based treatment alternatives that would be in the child's best interests. For example, in some cases, the child's attorney could help a treatment team to prepare a treatment plan that may involve placement in a therapeutic foster home (a foster home with fewer children and specially-trained foster parents), outpatient therapy, and enrollment in a special education school program. The child's attorney can play a vital role in negotiating treatment alternatives to commitment, as well as counseling the child to cooperate with these treatment alternatives.

Additionally, if commitment of the child seems inevitable or imminent, the child may be more likely to voluntarily agree to the commitment and waive a hearing, after consulting with counsel, if the lawyer mediates and negotiates concerns that are important to the child and asserts the child's legal rights. For many dependent children, it will be important to them to be placed in a residential treatment center or hospital that is as close as possible to their community. Additionally, it will also be important to many dependent children to have regularly scheduled visitations and phone contact with their parents or siblings, or both. The child's attorney can play a critical role in such issues as negotiating the frequency and duration of familial contact, ascertaining who will provide transportation for visits, and establishing whether the contact will be supervised or unsupervised.

§ 12G.5.3 Lawyer as Zealous Advocate

Finally, the attorney for the child serves a vital advocacy role. The Commentary to ABA Standard B-1 emphasizes that: "The child's attorney should not be merely a fact-finder, but rather, should zealously advocate a position on behalf of the child. . . In furtherance of that advocacy, the child's

---

[90] ABA Standards of Practice for Lawyers Who Represent Children in Abuse and Neglect Cases (1996).

[91] Jean Koh Peters, *The Roles and Content of Best Interests in Client-Directed Lawyering for Children in Child Protective Proceedings*, 64 Fordham L. Rev. 1505, 1565 (1996).

attorney must be adequately prepared prior to hearings. The lawyer's presence at and active participation in all hearings is absolutely critical."[92]

If the child objects to commitment, then the child's attorney has an important duty to represent the child at the hearings and present and rebut evidence to zealously contest the child's commitment. If the child agrees to commitment, then the attorney still has an important responsibility to ensure that the agreed order includes terms protecting the child's legal rights, including the general location of placement, the terms of family visitation, and other terms that the child's attorney achieved through negotiations with the parties.

If the child ultimately is committed to a facility, the role of the child's lawyer to provide zealous advocacy at review hearings is as important as at the initial commitment hearing, as many dependent children are forced to endure prolonged stays in residential treatment. ABA Standard D-13 provides that: "The child's attorney should seek to ensure continued representation of the child at all further hearings, including at administrative or judicial actions that result in changes to the child's placement or services, so long as the court maintains its jurisdiction."[93] Thus, not only does the child's attorney have vital roles of client counseling, mediation, negotiation, and zealous advocacy at the initial commitment hearing, but the child's attorney also fulfills these roles at the subsequent review hearings if the child is committed to a mental health facility.

§ 12G.6 Protection of Children's Rights Within Residential Treatment Centers and Hospitals

If the child is committed to a treatment facility, the child's attorney also has an important responsibility to help safeguard the child's rights while the child is in the facility. This requires the child's attorney to develop an understanding of children's psychiatric facilities and the laws governing the facilities.

---

[92] ABA Standards of Practice for Lawyers Who Represent Children in Abuse and Neglect Cases (1996). *See also* Bruce Winick, *Therapeutic Jurisprudence and the Civil Commitment Hearing*, 10 J. Contemp. Legal Issues 37, 42-43 (1999) ("Lawyers in commitment hearings who take the paternalistic or best interest approach serve their clients inadequately in a number of respects. They often defer to the expert witness, performing little or no cross-examination. They frequently fail even to meet with the client prior to the hearing, or to perform any investigation of the facts that are alleged to justify the client's need for hospitalization. Many fail to controvert the allegation that the patient is mentally ill. They fail to explore alternatives to hospitalization or to obtain benefits for their clients that might avoid its necessity. Some attorneys play largely a clerical role, treating their function as just being 'to look through the paperwork to make sure it is in order, and thus give the false impression that the client has had the benefit of legal representation.' These lawyers 'roll over' in the hearing, deferring to the expert and even stipulating to the hospital's allegations and waiving the client's right to testify." (Citations omitted)).

[93] ABA Standards of Practice for Lawyers Who Represent Children in Abuse and Neglect Cases (1996).

Children's residential treatment centers and hospitals generally use behavioral modification techniques and employ a "level" and/or "point" system. Under the level/point system, the children gain or lose privileges and receive rewards or punishments, depending on how many points they accumulate in a day and what level they are on in the program. This system varies depending on the facility. Some facilities use the system to determine discretionary privileges like the child's bedtime, whether the child can have snacks, or whether the child can watch television or listen to a radio. However, some facilities attempt to use the level/point system not just to deny discretionary privileges, but also to deny basic legal rights, and this is an area that the child's attorney needs to be prepared to address.

For example, some facilities may attempt to prohibit the child from having any communication, including communication with the child's family, state caseworker, guardian ad litem, or attorney, and even including the ability to contact the state Abuse Registry, unless the child is on a suitably high behavioral level of the program or has acquired "enough" points to be able to exercise certain privileges. However, such communication bans are illegal. Children cannot be denied communication with their families or their advocates as punishment because they do not have enough points or are not on a high enough level. A particular communication (for example, with a family member) may only be denied if it is determined by the court or treatment team to be harmful to the child. Additionally, contact with a particular family member would be denied if the court has ordered no contact as part of the dependency proceeding.

Some facilities also use the point/level system to determine whether the child is shackled with wrist and ankle restraints when transported to court or other hearings. Other facilities use the point/level system to determine whether children are allowed to wear their own clothing or whether they must wear hospital gowns and whether or not they are allowed to keep personal items. Like other mental health patients, children have the right to be transported without restraints and the right to wear their own clothing and to maintain their own personal items, unless there have been individual clinical determinations made about patient safety that bear directly on restraints, clothing and personal items. Children cannot be forced to wear hospital gowns, to be transported in restraints, or to be denied their personal effects as punishment because they do not have enough points or are not on a high enough level. These can only occur if it they are for the safety of the child.

Further, concerns may arise regarding the administration of psychotropic medications to children in residential treatment centers. While some psychotropic drugs can be beneficial for a child, serious concerns have been expressed nationally regarding overmedication of foster children with psychotropic drugs, resulting in severe side effects for the children.[94] Therefore, it is

---

[94] *See, e.g.*, Maggie Brandow, Note, *A Spoonful of Sugar Won't Help This Medicine Go Down: Psychotropic Drugs for Abused and Neglected Children*, 72 S. CAL. L. REV. 1151 (1999).

important for the child's attorney to represent the child's interests when the facility seeks to administer psychotropic drugs to the child. Additionally, throughout the child's commitment to a facility, the child's attorney must be vigilant to ensure that the child is not being overmedicated or inappropriately medicated with psychotropic drugs.

Concerns may arise regarding the use of restraint and seclusion in the facility. It is important for the child's attorney to review the child's clinical record, which must be maintained by every mental health facility. Among other documents, the child's clinical record contains notes regarding the facility's use of restraints, seclusion, and psychotropic drugs. In addition to maintaining regular contact with the child, every attorney who represents a child in a residential treatment center or hospital needs to regularly review the child's clinical record to ensure that the child is receiving appropriate treatment and that the child's rights are being protected.

§ 12G.7 Advocacy for Other Legal Entitlements and Services for the Child

Finally, the child's attorney has a vital role in advocating for the child's legal entitlements and needed services. In order to fully represent the child, the child's attorney should ensure that the child is receiving all services to which the child is entitled under the law. ABA STANDARD C-4 states that: "Consistent with the child's wishes, the child's attorney should seek appropriate services (by court order if necessary) to access entitlements, to protect the child's interests and to implement a service plan."[95] Additionally, specifically regarding a child with special needs, ABA STANDARD C-5 states that: "Consistent with the child's wishes, the child's attorney should assure that a child with special needs receives appropriate services to address physical, mental, or developmental disabilities."[96] These services should include Independent Living services and skills training pursuant to the federal Foster Care Independence Act of 1999, which created the John H. Chafee Foster Care Independence Program,[97] and special education and related services under the federal Individuals With Disabilities in Education Act (IDEA) and Section 504 of the Rehabilitation Act of 1973.[98]

Many foster youth with mental health needs or other disabilities are not provided with mandated independent living services or skills training to meet their special needs. Attorneys for foster youth with disabilities should zealously

---

[95] ABA STANDARDS OF PRACTICE FOR LAWYERS WHO REPRESENT CHILDREN IN ABUSE AND NEGLECT CASES (1996).

[96] *Id.*

[97] Pub. L. No. 106-169, 113 Stat. 1822 (1999) (codified at 42 U.S.C. § 677) (John H. Chafee Foster Care Independence Program, referred to here as Chafee Program or Act).

[98] *See* Individuals With Disabilities Education Act ("IDEA"), 20 U.S.C. §§ 1400 through 1491, and Section 504 of the Rehabilitation Act (Section 504), 29 U.S.C. § 794.

advocate for youth to be provided with the full range of independent living services to which they are legally entitled under the Chafee Act.[99] Youth with disabilities may need additional and specialized programming to help them achieve independence, and state child welfare agencies must provide developmentally appropriate independent living services.[100]

Additionally, many foster youth with disabilities are in special education programs, and attorneys who represent these youth should ensure that appropriate educational services are coordinated with the youth's school. Pursuant to the Individuals with Disabilities Education Act (IDEA), every youth in a special education program must have an Individualized Education Plan (IEP).[101] For adolescent youth, the IEP must contain educational transition services to help the youth make the transition to adulthood.[102] Attorneys for these youth should advocate to ensure that the state child welfare agency coordinates its independent living plan for the youth with the school's IEP for the youth. Additionally, the child's lawyer can sometimes use the IDEA to advocate for the child's placement in a less restrictive residential or educational setting.[103]

Further, attorneys for foster children committed to facilities should ensure that the client is provided with all independent living services that children outside of facilities receive. Title II of the Americans with Disabilities Act (ADA) of 1990[104] provides that "no qualified individual with a disability shall, by reason of such disability, be excluded from participation in or be denied the benefits of the services, programs, or activities of a public entity, or be subjected to discrimination by any such entity."[105] A public entity is defined under the ADA to include "any State or local government" and "any department, agency, special purpose district, or other instrumentality of a State or States or local government."[106] States are subject to the ADA and, in providing services to foster children, are required under the law to make "reasonable accommodations" for children with disabilities.

The ADA defines a "qualified individual with a disability" as "an individual with a disability who, with or without reasonable modifications to rules, policies, or practices, the removal of architectural, communication, or transportation

---

[99] *See* 42 U.S.C. § 677.

[100] *See* JUVENILE LAW CTR., DEPENDENT YOUTH AGING OUT OF FOSTER CARE IN PENNSYLVANIA: A JUDICIAL GUIDE 29 (3d ed. 2003), *available at* http://www.jlc.org/Resources/pdfs/agingout judgesguidePA.pdf.

[101] *See* 20 U.S.C. § 1414.

[102] 20 U.S.C. § 1414(d)(1)(i)(VIII).

[103] Federal education law requires schools to ensure that "[t]o the maximum extent appropriate, children with disabilities . . . are educated with children who are not disabled." 20 U.S.C. § 1412(a) (5). *See also* 34 C.F.R. § 300.550(b) (2); 34 C.F.R. § 104.33(a).

[104] 42 U. S. C. §§ 12201 through 12213.

[105] 42 U.S.C. § 12132.

[106] 42 U.S.C. § 12131.

barriers, or the provision of auxiliary aids and services, meets the essential eligibility requirements for the receipt of services or the participation in programs or activities provide by a public entity."[107] The Foster Care Independence Act also "makes clear that Independent Living services . . . must be provided for youth 'at various stages of independence,' including those youth with disabilities."[108]

It is especially important for lawyers who represent children in these facilities to pay attention to adolescent youth with special needs, as they are at increased risk "for several of the least desirable outcomes such as poverty, early or unintended pregnancy and becoming a victim of sexual assault" in comparison to their non-special-needs peers.[109] State independent living programs must develop and provide services "in ways that address the multiple needs and learning styles of participants,"[110] and lawyers representing foster children in psychiatric facilities have special obligations to ensure that their clients in particular are provided independent living services and training so that they have the resources to live on their own after their discharge from these facilities and from foster care.

§ 12G.8 Conclusion

By giving voice to the child's wishes, protecting the child's legal rights, and advocating the child's articulated position in all mental health commitment proceedings, the child's attorney fills a vital role. As Professor Jan Costello, an expert on the representation of children in mental health proceedings, has concluded:

> Ultimately, the most therapeutic thing a lawyer can do is to empower the child client. That means treating the client with respect and building trust, trying to understand and communicate effectively with him or her, and resisting the temptation to coerce the client's compliance. It means encouraging others involved with the child, including parents, mental health professionals, and court personnel, to behave the same way. It means maximizing the client's understanding of and participation in legal or treatment proceedings by informing, listening, counseling, assisting in decision making, and expressing the client's unique individual perspective

---

[107] 42 U.S.C. § 12131(2).

[108] *See* Juvenile Law Ctr., Dependent Youth Aging Out of Foster Care In Pennsylvania: A Judicial Guide 29-30 (3d ed. 2003). *See also Olmstead v. L.C.,* 527 U.S. 581 (1999) (mentally disabled institutionalized patients entitled to services that will enable them to develop skills to survive in community-based settings).

[109] Susan H. Badeau et al., Frequently Asked Questions II: About the Foster Care Independence Act of 1999 and The John H. Chafee Foster Care Independence Program 24 (2000), *available at* http://www.nrcys.ou.edu/nrcyd/programs/programspdfs/faq2_final.pdf.

[110] *Id.* at 25.

to the decision-maker. It means working to identify not just the legal issues involved in the immediate proceeding but also those that may be pursued in the future by or on behalf of the client. Finally, it means affirming to the client and to the outside world the inherent value of the child. In a system of law, the idea of rights, and the recognition that an individual has a right to something, is all but synonymous with a recognition that the person is worthy of respect. . . The assistance of a lawyer advocate affirms both the importance of the right and of the person.[111]

Part 12H: EDUCATIONAL ADVOCACY*

by Kathleen McNaught[112]

§ 12H.1 Introduction

Of the more than 500,000 children in foster care, approximately 30-40% are receiving special education services.[113] Many others may need these services, but have not been identified. Still others have been identified inappropriately. As an advocate in the child welfare system, you need to know how the special education system works and understand the benefits and services that can be accessed for children in foster care. By understanding the federal Individuals with Disabilities Education Act (IDEA),[114] which governs the special education

---

[111] Jan C. Costello, *Representing Children in Mental Disability Proceedings*, 1 J. Ctr. Child. & Cts. 101, 116 (1999).

* Copyright *2004* by *American Bar Association Center on Children and the Law.* Reprinted by permission. For further information contact:

Lisa Waxler
ABA Center on Children and the Law
740 15th Street NW
Washington DC 20005
202-662-1743
WaxlerL@staff.abanet.org

Original Appeared in July 2004 issue of ABA Child Law & Practice, Vol. 23, No. 5 published by the ABA Center on Children and the Law. *See* Learning Curves: Education Advocacy for Children in Foster Care (ABA 2004).

Editor's Note: Nonsubstantive changes have been made to the text and formatting to reflect the style of this publication. Section numbers have also been added to reflect the style of this publication.

[112] Kathleen McNaught, J.D., is a staff attorney at the ABA Center on Children and the Law in Washington D.C.

[113] Wingerden, Claire. *Education Issue Brief: Improving Special Education for Children with Disabilities in Foster Care.* Seattle, Washington: Casey Family Programs, June 2002.

[114] For more information about basic legal rights under IDEA and other federal laws related to education, *see* McNaught, Kathleen. "Education Law Primer for Child Welfare Professionals." *ABA Child Law* Practice 22 (1 & 2), 1.

process, you can help the child welfare system provide education services for children with disabilities.

This article answers common questions about how the special education process works and the issues that arise for children in the foster care system. It also provides tips on navigating the special education system and ensuring the process benefits children in foster care. The questions and answers are listed in order of how issues may arise in each step of the special education process.

§ 12H.2 Preliminary Steps

§ 12H.2.1 What Signs Should I Look for That a Child Needs Special Education Services?

While some children in foster care may have apparent disabilities (*e.g.*, orthopedic impairments or blindness), other disabilities are not easy to identify. For less obvious disabilities, such as learning impairments and speech and language issues, look for subtle signs of problems. In addition to obtaining information about family medical history, watch for signs that the child is having school difficulties, such as:

- poor grades

- delays in academic achievements or developmental milestones

- lack of interest in school

- refusal to attend school

- behavior problems at school and at home

If you observe these signs, get professional opinions about their causes. While not all children who show one or more of these signs will qualify for special education services, without your follow through a child with possible needs may never be identified. Children in the child welfare system often already have counselors or therapists who may supply information that will help identify causes of concerning behaviors.

§ 12H.2.2 What Do I Do if I Suspect a Child Needs Special Education Services, But is Not Yet Identified?

You have two options:

1. Conduct an independent investigation. Before getting the school involved, especially if you have concerns that the school may move too slowly (or too quickly) to identify the child as needing special education services without a legitimate basis, consider an intermediate step. Over- and under-identifying children in foster care as needing special education services are problems. Therefore, before involving the school, find out if someone outside the school system has already conducted a thorough evaluation.

Consider seeking a thorough evaluation, or additional evaluations, of the child by a clinician familiar with educational disabilities. You will have to determine what types of evaluations are needed, which may require outside expert assistance. For example, in addition to educational testing, you may want a physical health evaluation or a neurological evaluation by a medical doctor, or a psychological or psychosocial evaluation by a clinical psychologist, or some combination of these and other evaluations. The child welfare agency would need to pay for these evaluations,[115] either voluntarily or perhaps through an order from the child welfare judge instructing the child welfare agency to arrange and pay for them.

Consider arranging an in-school observation of the child in the classroom; the school system should allow a qualified individual to conduct such an observation. Review the evaluation reports, and all information from other professionals involved with the child, to determine whether enough documentation establishes the need to move forward with a request for special education services. Be sure to review the legal definitions for the various disabilities under IDEA, and consult other professionals who know about special education practice to determine if the documented evidence supports your request for special education services.

This type of strategy has three benefits. One, it allows you to have a good idea of your desired outcome when you contact the school system to seek services. In other words, when you get aboard the special education train, you already know where you want it to stop. Two, if appropriate outside evaluations can be accessed more quickly by the child welfare agency, this may speed the identification process. Three, it arms you with good evaluative materials to combat the school system, should it not agree with your assessment. This could save time later.

A disadvantage to this strategy is that it may delay getting the ball rolling with the school system, as the school will still have the right to review your evaluations and conduct its own independent evaluations. The school will still be entitled to the same period of time to conduct these additional evaluations as they would have to conduct all of the evaluations. While one goal of this strategy is to save time, there is no guarantee that it will. Also, the child welfare system in this scenario is responsible for the cost of the original evaluation.

If you choose this option, inform the school in writing that you have conducted outside evaluations of the child that you want the school to review, and that you believe the child needs special education services. If you plan to do an in-school observation, call the school in advance to arrange a suitable time to

---

[115] The reason the evaluation would not be at the school's expense is because of the strategic decision to pursue the evaluation without involving the school system. Schools would be responsible for the expense of the evaluation if they were requested to conduct the evaluation, or an additional independent educational evaluation (IEE).

observe the student. Remember, in this situation the school has the right to review your evaluation and conduct its own independent evaluations.

2. Make a formal, written request to the school for a full evaluation of the child. This second option puts the responsibility for obtaining evaluations of the child solely on the school system. This is appropriate for situations when there are no resources to pursue outside evaluations, or when parties involved are comfortable using the evaluation services offered by the school. Put another way, these are situations where you are comfortable getting on the special education train without knowing where it is going to stop.

With this option, your first action needs to be a written request to the school to evaluate the child. Consult your state law to determine who is permitted to make such a request; most states permit any advocate to do so. This request should be in writing to clearly document your actions. Consider using certified mail to have official receipts of your correspondence. Keep copies of every document you send the school for your records. This documentation may be needed later if you need to challenge the school system for failing to complete the evaluation process promptly.

§ 12H.3 Education Decision Makers

§ 12H.3.1 How Do I Determine Who Can Act as the Parent or if a Surrogate Parent is Needed?

Usually any advocate can request a referral for evaluation of special education needs of a child in foster care. Only the parent or surrogate, however, can consent to the evaluation or reevaluation of the child and ultimately to the services put in place for the child. Therefore, when consents for evaluations need to be signed, it must be determined if a parent is available or if a surrogate needs to be appointed. The parent or the surrogate is the key decision maker for all IDEA-related issues, including services and placement, so clarity at the beginning of the process is critical.

The IDEA statute requires states to establish procedural safeguards to ensure children with disabilities receive a free and appropriate public education (FAPE). The law specifically requires procedures to be in place when:

- "the parents of the child are not known,

- the agency cannot, after reasonable efforts locate the parents, or

- the child is a ward of the State."[116]

These procedures need to include the assignment of an individual as the surrogate when needed.[117]

---

[116] 20 U.S.C. § 1415(b)(2).

[117] *Id.*

To determine the need for a surrogate you must review the IDEA regulation; it defines parent as a:

- "natural or adoptive parent of the child;

- a guardian, but not the state if the child is a ward of the state;

- a person acting in the place of a parent (such as a grandparent or step-parent with whom the child lives, or a person who is legally responsible for the child's welfare);

- or a surrogate parent..."[118]

Based on the four prongs of this definition, you can argue under the second and third prong that guardians and relative caretakers or anyone with legal custody of a child (other than the state) have the same rights as a parent under IDEA. In some states foster parents are considered the parents under this third prong and do not need to be appointed as surrogates (see next section). It may be wise to get a court order to memorialize this legal arrangement.

Children in foster care without a person fitting the first three prongs of the definition of parent above will need a surrogate parent. A surrogate parent sits in the shoes of the parents and makes decisions about special education services for the child. Federal law leaves the specific process of appointing a surrogate up to states. Consult state law, regulations, and policies to find out how your state appoints a surrogate when one is needed for a child in foster care.

§ 12H.3.2 Who Can Be Appointed as a Surrogate for a Child in Foster Care?

Some states require anyone acting as the parent (people that fit under the third prong) to be officially appointed as a surrogate parent (under the forth prong), to make their role as the education decision maker even clearer. Be sure to consult your state law to determine the best way for these individuals to have the authority to be the child's decision maker.

Some jurisdictions permit foster parents, child advocates, CASAs, and guardians ad litem to be appointed as surrogates, while others believe this would be a conflict of interest.[119] Federal law is clear that a surrogate parent cannot be an employee of the state education agency, the lead education agency, or any other agency that is involved in the education or care of the child.[120] Therefore, child welfare agency personnel, including caseworkers, cannot be the surrogate parent for a child in foster care.

---

[118] 34 C.F.R. § 300.20(a).

[119] *E.g., see* CAL. GOV. CODE § 7579.5: When appointing a surrogate parent, the local educational agency shall, as a first preference, select a relative caretaker, foster parent, or court-appointed special advocate, if any of these individuals exists and is willing and able to serve.

[120] 34 C.F.R. § 300.515(c)(2)(i).

It is important that a child in foster care have a person who knows about the child's needs to make educational decisions. If this cannot be the parent, guardian, or person acting in place of the parent, the next best option is to have a surrogate appointed who has some knowledge of the child. This may be the foster parent, a relative, a court appointed special advocate (CASA), a child's attorney or guardian ad litem, or some other person involved in the child's life. The appropriateness of the individual will differ from state to state, and even from case to case. Preferably, the individual will understand the special education process, or at least be willing to learn and work with someone who can guide them through the process. For example, a relative may agree to be the surrogate, with assurances that the child's attorney will attend meetings and help advocate for the child.

If there is no clear individual in the child's life available to be appointed as the surrogate, a surrogate will be appointed for the child. Specific procedures, such as who makes such appointments, may differ depending on state law, but often the school system is responsible for appointing surrogates. Because the appointed surrogate will not know the child, and may not have any experience with the child welfare system or what it means for a child to be in foster care, this is the least desirable option. An advocate's role in this situation is to educate the surrogate on the foster care system, and the child's specific needs and situation.

§ 12H.3.3 How Can a Foster Parent Be the Education Decision Maker?

The federal IDEA regulations state that foster parents may act as the parent, if:

- the "natural parent's authority to make educational decisions on the child's behalf has been extinguished under state law"; and

- the foster parent:

    o "has an ongoing, long-term parental relationship with the child,

    o is willing to make educational decisions under the act, and

    o has no interest that would conflict with the interests of the child."[121]

This regulation raises some questions. First, does "act as the parent" mean that foster parents must be appointed as surrogates, or is an official surrogate appointment unnecessary when a foster parent meets the above outlined criterion? States vary on this issue; some have foster parents appointed as surrogates and others have foster parents act as the parent (prong 3) without a formal appointment.

---

[121] 34 C.F.R. § 300.20.

Second, what does "extinguished under state law" mean? Certainly a termination of parental rights (TPR) would end the parent's rights to make educational decisions. You should consult your state laws to determine if education decision-making rights of a parent of a child in foster care end before a TPR ruling. For example, Maryland allows by statute "limited guardianship" for educational decisions to be given to the agency or an individual as early as the dispositional hearing when a parent is "unavailable, unwilling, or unable to consent to services that are in the best interest of the child."[122] If your state statute is unclear, a court may need to determine what factors to consider when deciding to strip a parent of education decision-making authority.

Another interpretation of the federal regulations could be that foster parents may "act as the parent" (prong 3) when decision making authority has been extinguished (*i.e.*, termination of parental rights), but before that time, foster parents may be appointed as surrogates.[123]

Finally, what would be "an interest that would conflict with the interests of the child?" Arguably, foster parents have some emotional and monetary interest in keeping a child in their care. What if foster parents, acting as surrogate parents, had to decide if a child was to be placed in a residential setting, meaning the child would be removed from her home? Would the foster parents' emotional bond with the child, or their need for foster care payments, affect their ability to make the best decisions for the child? Or, would a foster parent, who is perhaps burned out, agree to a residential placement for a child even though the child could be maintained in the community with appropriate services? Most foster parents do have the best interests of the child at heart and would not act in their own self-interest, but this does not change the issue of the appearance of, or the potential for, conflict.

§ 12H.4 Special Education Process

§ 12H.4.1 When Should an Eligibility Meeting Occur and What Should Happen at the Meeting to Determine Eligibility for Special Education Services?

IDEA states that the school system has a "reasonable period of time" after the evaluation request to complete the evaluations and meet as a team with the parent to determine whether the child is eligible for special education services. Many states specify a time limit for this process. For example, Maryland says this process must be completed in 90 days.[124]

---

[122] MD. CODE ANN., Courts and Judicial Proceedings §3-819(c)1(ii) (Supp. 2003).

[123] *E.g., see* Nevada Department of Education. "The Appointment of Surrogate Parents for Students with Disabilities." February 2000.

[124] COMAR: MD. REGS. § 13A.05.01.06A.

IDEA specifies that the parent is entitled to a copy of any evaluation conducted by the school. While IDEA does not specify a timeframe for providing a parent a copy, advocates should argue for parents to receive copies of these evaluations before the eligibility meeting. That way, parents and surrogates can consult other professionals involved with the child to review the evaluations. Be aware, that some school psychologists will not release a report without the opportunity to review the report with the parent in person. Another reality is that often reports are not completed until right before the eligibility meeting. A parent or surrogate needs to consider whether having the evaluations in advance is worth the possible delay in holding the eligibility meeting.

If the parent or surrogate disagrees with the school's evaluation, the parent may request, in writing, an independent educational evaluation (IEE) be conducted at the school's expense. The school may either agree to this second evaluation or take the case to a due process hearing to establish whether the school's original evaluation is sufficient. (For more information on due process hearings, see discussion below).

The meeting to determine eligibility must include the parent or surrogate and a team of qualified professionals. Often the team consists of the individualized education program (IEP) team members (see discussion below). Look to your state law to determine if you have more specific requirements regarding required participants at the eligibility determination meeting. Other advocates should seek an invitation to the meeting from the parent or surrogate or the school. (see further discussion below).

At the eligibility meeting, parents must be provided a copy of the written policies (known as procedural safeguards) related to their rights under IDEA. IDEA requires schools to provide these safeguards, at minimum, when the child is referred for an evaluation, when parents are notified of an IEP meeting, when the child is being reevaluated, and when the parent is registering a complaint.[125]

At this eligibility meeting, the team should review the existing evaluations, including any information provided by the parents, and any current classroom-based assessments and teacher observations. Based on this information, the team must determine:

- whether the child has a disability as defined under IDEA;

- the present levels of performance and educational needs of the child;

- whether the child needs special education and related services.

Your role as an advocate for the child is to participate in the process as much as possible to ensure these IDEA-dictated procedures are being followed. For example, are the right individuals present? Have procedural safeguards been provided? Has the parent or surrogate reviewed the procedural safeguards and

---

[125] 20 U.S.C. § 1415(d).

do they understand them? Are evaluations appropriate and being reviewed? Is the eligibility decision truly a team decision? Bring a copy of the IDEA definitions (and a list from your state code or regulation if they differ) and ensure that the team is using the criteria outlined in the definition of each disability.

§ 12H.4.2 Who is Part of the Individualized Education Program (IEP) Team?

Once eligibility has been determined, an IEP must be developed. The IEP team develops and revises the IEPs, and often is the same team that makes decisions about eligibility. Federal law requires that the IEP team include:

- parents
- regular education teacher
- special education teacher
- school system representative who is qualified to provide instruction for children with disabilities, and knows about the general curriculum and the availability of resources (*e.g.*, principal, vice principal, school administrator)
- an individual who can interpret the instructional implications of evaluation results (*e.g.*, school psychologist, speech and language therapist)
- at the discretion of the parent or the school system, other individuals with knowledge or expertise about the child, including related services personnel
- the child, if appropriate[126]

If you, as the advocate, are the parent or surrogate, then you are part of the IEP team. However, what about other advocates not appointed to that role? The school must invite a representative of any other agency that is likely to be responsible for providing or paying for transition services when transition planning is being discussed at an IEP meeting (which must happen by the child's 14th birthday, if not sooner).[127] This will likely mean that child welfare agency personnel must be included in these IEP meetings for older youth (more on transition planning below).

Participating at the IEP meeting is also possible through two avenues: the discretion of the parent (or surrogate parent) or the discretion of the school system. When the parent is still making educational decisions, and the parent has a good relationship with you, the parent may request your presence at the IEP meeting. Likewise, if the parent surrogate knows about the child welfare case,

---

[126] 34 C.F.R. § 300.344.

[127] 34 C.F.R. § 300.344(b)(3).

it is likely the surrogate would invite the other child advocates to the school meetings.

Problems arise when there is either an uncooperative parent who still retains education decision-making rights, or a surrogate parent who is unaware of, or uninterested in involving, child welfare advocates. A solution to both situations is to be invited to the team by the school. Best practice would dictate that schools should involve any child welfare advocates who have contact with the child and play a role in the child's life. You may need to establish a relationship with school personnel, and convince them that your presence at the IEP team meetings is necessary to achieve good educational planning for the child. In this way, even if you lack legal decision-making authority, you can still play a role advocating for the child's educational needs.

§ 12H.4.3 What is an Individualized Education Program (IEP) and How Should it Be Developed?

Once a child is found in need of special education services, IDEA requires that an IEP be developed within 30 days.[128] An IEP is a written plan outlining the child's needs and how the school must address those needs. It must be detailed and child specific, and when implemented, should result in the child making meaningful educational progress. When the parent or other education decision maker signs the IEP, she agrees to everything it contains.

The IEP must be developed with input from all team members, including the parent or surrogate. Be wary when an IEP is prepared before an IEP meeting and merely presented to the parent or surrogate for signature. This is not to say that school staff cannot suggest some provisions for the IEP, as long as they are presented to the parent or surrogate in that manner, explained fully, the parent or surrogate can comment on the provisions, and there is an opportunity to discuss and add or delete provisions as necessary.

Key IEP elements include:

- *The child's present levels of educational performance:* This information is needed to measure how much progress a child is making as a result of the IEP services.

- *Measurable annual goals, including benchmarks or short-term objectives:* This section spells out reasonable expectations for progress for the child in the coming year. In the IEP document, the team specifies broad educational goals for the child, with more specific short-term objectives. For example, a broad goal could be improving written language, while the short-term objective could be "given a topic, write a persuasive paragraph." These goals and objectives must be measurable (*e.g.*, by evaluations, reviewing student work, or observation) and must specify what

---

[128] 34 C.F.R. § 300.343 (b)(2).

level of mastery is expected (*e.g.*, 80% accuracy). The goals must also specify who is responsible for monitoring this progress (*e.g.*, classroom teacher).

- *The special education and related services and supplementary aids and services, program modifications, and staff supports to be provided:* Based on the goals and objectives established for the child, the team then determines what services will help the child achieve these goals. These include any related services. The IEP must specify when the services will begin, and the anticipated frequency, location, and duration of the services and modifications. For example, a child may receive one hour per day, five days a week of specialized instruction in a special education classroom to work on writing skills. The child may also need one hour per week of occupational therapy as a related service.

- *Statement of transition services:* This portion of the IEP requires:

  ○ By age 14: The team must address what instruction will assist the child prepare for transition.[129]

  ○ By age 16: The IEP must a state what transition services the child needs, and specify interagency responsibilities or needed linkages.[130]

- Be aware of the kinds of transition services available under IDEA for a child with a disability. All child welfare advocates need to ensure the transition planning happening as part of a child's IEP is coordinated with the youth's transition planning in the child welfare system.

- *Whether the child qualifies for extended school year (ESY) services:* Qualifying for ESY services depends on several factors; among them: whether a child with a disability would regress significantly over the summer break, and how much time it will take a child to regain skills learned the previous year.[131] If a child qualifies, the child is entitled to school services over the summer.

- *The recommended placement for the child:* The team must determine where the services will be provided. There is a continuum of placement options, from a regular education classroom with minimal supports to a residential treatment facility. The services identified in the IEP must be provided in the least restrictive environment (LRE). In some cases, the local school may not be able to recommend a placement, other than

---

[129] 34 C.F.R. § 300.437(b)(1)(i).

[130] 34 C.F.R. § 300.347(b)(2).

[131] For an in-depth discussion of ESY, *see Extended School Year Services Under IDEA*, available for purchase from http://www.napas.org/I-6/pub%20awareness%20mat%20home.htm.

specify that it cannot provide the services. In these cases, the placement decision may occur at a separate meeting involving additional school system officials, and sometimes at a central school system office.

§ 12H.4.4 How Should I Prepare for an IEP Meeting?

Before the Meeting

- Think about what you would like to see the child accomplish in the coming year. Consider listing the child's strengths, needs, and interests and your major concerns about his education.[132]

- Collect and bring any documentation describing the child's disability, behaviors, and school progress (*e.g.*, evaluations, child's schoolwork examples).

- Review materials you have collected and any materials the school has sent you. If the school has not given you any advance materials, request a copy of the record that will be discussed at the meeting. Review the evaluations and determine if you agree with the conclusions, or if the described behavior in the evaluation matches what you know of the child.

- If you are an attorney, make sure you notify the school that you will be attending the meeting. The school will then have the right to have a school attorney present at the meeting.

At the Meeting

- *Participating at the meeting:* Share your knowledge about the child and carefully listen to what others say about the child to be able to respond appropriately. If you do not understand something, ask for clarification.

- *Tape recording:* In many states, parents and their advocates have a right to tape record IEP meetings, as long as they notify the school beforehand and the school allows the meeting to be taped. Frequently, the school will record the meeting as well. Since many people attend these meetings, much information is given orally and conversations are often intense. Therefore, taping is a great way to document everything said by the team.

---

[132] For more information on planning for an IEP meeting, *see Planning Your Child's Individualized Education Program: Some Suggestions to Consider*. Minneapolis, MN: Families and Advocates Partnership for Education, Pacer Center Inc., Sept. 2001, *available at* http://www.fape.org/pubs/FAPE-25%20Planning%20Your%20Childs%20IEP.pdf.

- *Signing the IEP:* If you are the parent or the parent surrogate, and are asked at the end of the meeting to sign the IEP consenting to everything it contains, be sure you understand fully what you are being asked to approve. You are permitted to delay signing for a reasonable period, to take the document home to review outside of the sometimes pressure-filled meeting room, or to consult with other professionals involved with the child. If the parent or surrogate does not agree with the IEP, she should not sign. Note that if this is the initial IEP, services cannot begin for the child until the IEP is signed. If this is a revised IEP, the school must provide services according to the old IEP until a new IEP is agreed to and signed.

- *Copies and follow up:* Make sure you are given a copy of the notes and all documents from the meeting. If anyone at the meeting has promised to provide additional information to you, be sure to follow up with that team member, preferably in writing.

§ 12H.5 Monitoring and Implementation

§ 12H.5.1 What Do I Do if I Suspect a Child is Identified with the Wrong Disability?

It is critical that a child receiving special education services be correctly identified with the appropriate disability. Keep in mind that a child's identified disability will guide the services the school arranges for that child. However, once identified to receive special education services, the child will be eligible to receive any services the IEP team finds are needed.[133] You may encounter cases where a child in foster care already has an IEP, but upon reviewing the information in that document it becomes clear, or you suspect, that the child's disability has been misidentified and the child has other needs not addressed in the IEP. In these cases, additional services can be added by the IEP team without further evaluations, however you may still want to make a written request to the school system for a meeting either to review the IEP or to reevaluate the child's disability. This is also true for a child who may have multiple disabilities, but has only been identified with one.

If you feel a child who is receiving special education services may not need those services, request an IEP meeting to reevaluate the child. If the reevaluation finds the child does not have, or no longer has, a disability, the child will be discharged from special education.

---

[133] This means that if a child is identified with a learning disability and also has some behavior problems, even though the behaviors don't rise to the level of an additional ED. identification, the child's IEP can include goals and objectives or services to address the behavior issues.

§ 12H.5.2 How Should I Monitor the Student's Progress and the Implementation of the IEP?

- After an IEP is in place, monitor how the services are working for the child. Review assignments and tests that the child brings home.

- Find out what the child thinks about the new services, whether they are helpful, and what, if anything, needs to be changed.

- Communicate regularly with the child's teachers through phone calls, e-mails, or progress reports.

- A parent or surrogate can request an IEP meeting any time if there is reason to believe the IEP is not being implemented appropriately or if something needs to be added or changed. At a minimum, IDEA requires an annual review of the IEP to review achievement of past goals and establish goals and services for the coming year.

- Reevaluation: IDEA requires that a child with a disability be reevaluated at least every three years.[134] However, it also states that a reevaluation shall be conducted whenever conditions warrant, or if the child's parent or teacher requests one.[135] Parents and surrogates should not hesitate to request a reevaluation of a child if they feel it is warranted.

- Discharge from special education: IDEA provides that the school system cannot decide that a child is no longer eligible for special education services without first evaluating the child.[136] This protects the child from being terminated from special education erroneously, and requires that termination be based on a thorough evaluation of the child.

§ 12H.5.3 What If I Do Not Agree with the Decision Reached by the IEP Team?

If the parent or surrogate does not agree with the decisions made by the team regarding identification, services, or placement, she should not sign the IEP. The parent or surrogate has three options: mediation, due process hearing, and state board of education complaints.

Mediation and/or a due process hearing should be seen as the last straw in advocating the needs of the child. For example, if an IEP meeting has gotten heated, an interim strategy may be to reconvene the meeting in a few days to see if resolution can be reached short of mediation and due process. At times, mediation and/or a due process hearing may be needed.

---

[134] 20 U.S.C. § 1414 (a)(2).

[135] 20 U.S.C. § 1414(a)(2)(A).

[136] 20 U.S.C. § 1414 (c)(5); 34 C.F.R. § 300.534 (c)(1).

Mediation must be provided, at a minimum, whenever a due process hearing is requested. Often states permit mediation to be requested without scheduling a due process hearing. Mediation is voluntary and cannot be used to deny or delay a parent's right to a hearing. A qualified and impartial mediator must conduct the mediation, and the school bears the cost of the mediation. All information shared in mediation is confidential and cannot be used in a later due process hearing. If agreement can be reached during mediation, the terms of the agreement must be documented in writing.

A *due process hearing* is a trial-like administrative proceeding, where evidence and witnesses are presented and cross-examined. A hearing officer presides over the hearing and issues a written ruling in the case. A successful result at a due process hearing may involve obtaining appropriate services or placement for a child, and also can involve receiving compensatory services (services to make up for the school's error or failures) and money to recoup costs and attorney expenses.

Due process hearings can be complicated. If you do not have experience pursuing these kinds of hearings, proceed with caution. Parents and surrogate parents may appear unrepresented, however that is often unwise, as these hearings can involve long and intense conflicts. School systems are frequently represented by attorneys with expertise in this area of law. An attorney without experience handling due process cases should ask an experienced education attorney for assistance, to co-counsel, or even handle the case.

Another method of noting a disagreement is to file an *IDEA complaint with your state* department of education. The advantages of this type of complaint over a due process proceeding are that it is less time intensive and stressful, and it resolves issues in a less adversarial manner. This type of complaint can be effective for procedural violations or clear-cut issues (*e.g.*, were the appropriate team members present at the child's IEP meeting?). Problems with this type of complaint are that states vary in the quality of their investigations and decision making, and this method may not effectively resolve quality issues (*e.g.*, is this speech language therapy adequately meeting the child's needs?).

§ 12H.6 Conclusion

You can help link children in foster care to special education services and ensure those services are meeting their needs. Understanding the IDEA and what services are available to children in the foster care system is critical to navigating the special education process. With child welfare systems struggling to provide all children in care with the services they need, failing to access services under IDEA is wasting an important source of education assistance for these children.

Chapter 13 CONFIDENTIALITY OF JUVENILE COURT PROCEEDINGS AND RECORDS

by Amanda George Donnelly [1]

§ 13.1 Introduction

Confidentiality of juvenile court proceedings and records is a cornerstone of the juvenile dependency court process. The longstanding assumption is that maintaining the confidentiality of juvenile court proceedings protects the youth involved. Similar analysis is applied to the value of maintaining confidentiality of juvenile court records. Recently, internal and external critics have suggested that the secrecy created by closed courts is not healthy and is not the most conducive to good outcomes. Many states are debating the potential benefits of opening juvenile court proceedings and records. In the Child Abuse Prevention and Treatment Act (CAPTA) amendments of 2003, Congress provided a State with the flexibility to allow public access to court proceedings that determine child abuse and neglect, as long as policies ensure the safety and well-being of the child, parents, and families. [2]

§ 13.2 Historical Background

Historically, the Supreme Court has enforced the public's First Amendment right to access, requiring open court proceedings unless a court orders otherwise. The Court applied a two-prong analysis to determine whether criminal proceedings should be open, considering the history of access to a proceeding, and the function of the proceeding. [3] The rationale behind the Court's decision to open proceedings included the importance of increased public understanding and confidence in the judicial process. [4] In *Globe Newspaper Co. v. Superior Court*, [5] the Supreme Court rejected the Massachusetts Supreme Court's decision to close a sex offense trial during the testimony of minor victims. The court ruled

---

[1] Amanda George Donnelly, J.D., is a staff attorney at the National Association of Counsel for Children (NACC).

[2] Child Abuse Prevention and Treatment Act (CAPTA), as amended by The Keeping Children and Families Safe Act of 2003, 42 U.S.C. § 5106a (b)(2)(D).

[3] *Richmond Newspaper, Inc. v. Virginia*, 448 U.S. 555 (1980) (plurality opinion) (recognizing right of access to criminal trials through the First and Fourteenth Amendments, Burger, C. J., joined by White and Stevens, J.J.; Brennan, J., joined by Marshal, J., concurring; Stewart, J., concurring; Blackmun, J., concurring and finding additional Sixth Amendment grounds; and Rehnquist, J., dissenting (Powell, J., did not participate in the decision)).

[4] *See* Heidi S. Schellhas, *Children in the Law Issue: Contributors Open Child Protection Proceedings in Minnesota*, 26 Wm. Mitchell L. Rev. 631, 642 (2000).

[5] *Globe Newspaper Co. v. Superior Court*, 457 U.S. 596 (1982).

that closing a criminal proceeding, even for a limited amount of time, violated the First Amendment.[6]

Family law matters have traditionally been viewed as private proceedings. Family courts exist nationwide to provide privacy and a less adversarial atmosphere. Confidentiality restrictions in child welfare proceedings exist to protect children and families from public exposure of the intimate details of their lives.[7] Many states, however, are questioning the value of closed child welfare proceedings and considering the potential benefits of open proceedings.

§ 13.3 Benefits of Open Court Proceedings

Advocates for opening child welfare proceedings argue that an open system will increase public awareness and accountability.[8] Others argue that open proceedings will motivate the public to improve the child welfare system.[9] Additionally, some view open proceedings as an opportunity to receive more accurate information in child protection proceedings by allowing families, friends, and neighbors to participate as witnesses.[10]

When a state is determining whether it should open child welfare proceedings, it must consider the confidentiality requirements of federal mandates. All states receiving federal grants under the Child Abuse Prevention and Treatment Act (CAPTA) must provide "methods to preserve the confidentiality of all records in order to protect the rights of the child and the child's parents or guardians."[11] The statute does provide exceptions for access to people who are subject to the reports, government entities, or agencies involved in child protection, child abuse citizen review panels, child fatality review panels, a grand jury or a court, and other entities authorized to receive the information by State statute. In the 2003 CAPTA amendments, a new provision was added which *requires* States to disclose confidential information to a government entity that needs the information to carry out its responsibilities to protect children.[12] Additionally, the Social Security Act requires states to provide safeguards to prevent the use or disclosure of information about children receiving Title IV-E

---

[6] *See* Heidi S. Schellhas, *Children in the Law Issue: Contributors Open Child Protection Proceedings in Minnesota*, 26 WM. MITCHELL L. REV. 631, 644 (2000).

[7] *See* MARK SOLER ET AL., GLASS WALLS: CONFIDENTIALITY PROVISIONS AND INTERAGENCY COLLABORATIONS (San Francisco, CA: Youth Law Center, 1993).

[8] EVERY CHILD MATTERS & THE LEGACY FAMILY INST., BALANCING ACCOUNTABILITY AND CONFIDENTIALITY IN CHILD WELFARE: SOURCEBOOK, at II-36 (2003).

[9] Barbara White Stack, *Few Problems, Benefits in Open Proceedings*, PITTSBURGH POST-GAZETTE, Sept. 30, 2001, *available at* http://www.post-gazette.com/regionstate/20010930 minn0930p8.asp.

[10] Heidi S. Schellhas, *Contributors Open Child Protection Proceedings in Minnesota*, 26 WM. MITCHELL L. REV. 631, 666 (2000).

[11] CAPTA, as amended, 42 U.S.C. § 5106a (b)(2)(A)(viii) (2003).

[12] *Id.*

adoption and foster care assistance.[13] Records maintained under titles IV-B and IV-E of the Act are subject to the confidentiality provisions in 45 C.F.R. 205.50.

Likewise, providing access to records in child welfare proceedings requires consideration of other federal requirements, specifically the Health Insurance Portability and Accountability Act (HIPAA).[14] Title II of HIPAA was enacted in April 2003 to provide security and privacy of patient health data.[15] The privacy provisions apply to any "covered entity," which is any program or entity that provides health care, bills for health care, or electronically transmits information related to health care or billing.[16] Patients must be given written notice of their privacy rights, and programs must receive permission from patients before disclosing information from their records. HIPAA specified that health care providers suspecting child maltreatment must still report it. The privacy provisions, however, impact accessing information regarding parent's treatment in dependency cases. To access personal health information from a health care or other "covered entity" (*e.g.,* treatment provider), one must obtain consent from the patient or a court order for disclosure.

The Minnesota Supreme Court Foster Care Task Force conducted a three-year pilot project mandating open proceedings and records for neglect and termination of parental rights proceedings.[17] Minnesota's pilot project permitted access to all documents, except those restricted by rules; Social Services and GAL files were not open, and Judges could issue protective orders to keep any file closed. The National Center for State Courts evaluated Minnesota's project and concluded that "no devastating downsides or remarkable benefits" resulted from open proceedings.[18] In 2002, the Minnesota Supreme Court ordered dependency court proceedings presumptively open.[19]

---

[13] Social Security Act, § 671(a)(8).

[14] Health Insurance Portability and Accountability Act as Amended in 2003, 45 C.F.R. § 160 (2003). *See also* Rae Ann Steinly, *HIPAA: What States Should Know*, 2002 American Public Human Services Association, *cited in* EVERY CHILD MATTERS & THE LEGACY FAMILY INST., BALANCING ACCOUNTABILITY AND CONFIDENTIALITY IN CHILD WELFARE: SOURCEBOOK (2003).

[15] Health Insurance Portability and Accountability Act, 45 C.F.R. § 164 (2003).

[16] *See* Howard Davidson, *The Impact of HIPAA On Child Abuse and Neglect Cases, cited in* EVERY CHILD MATTERS & THE LEGACY FAMILY INST., BALANCING ACCOUNTABILITY AND CONFIDENTIALITY IN CHILD WELFARE: SOURCEBOOK, at VII-I (2003) ("Disclosure of child abuse/neglect related information is addressed in three sections of the HIPAA regulations—Sections 160.203, 164.502(g)(5), and 164.512.").

[17] *See* FRED. L. CHEESMAN, MINN. SUPREME COURT STATE COURT ADMIN'R'S OFFICE, KEY FINDINGS FROM THE EVALUATION OF OPEN HEARINGS AND COURT RECORDS IN JUVENILE PROTECTION MATTERS: FINAL REPORT (2001).

[18] Barbara White Stack, *Few Problems, Benefits in Open Proceedings*, PITTSBURGH POST-GAZETTE, Sept. 30, 2001, *available at* http://www.post-gazette.com/regionstate/20010930 minn0930p8.asp.

[19] State of Minn. Supreme Court File No. C2-95-1476, "Order Mandating Public Access to Hearings and Records in Juvenile Protection Matters" (Dec. 26, 2001).

State statues or court rules dictate access to proceedings and records in most jurisdictions. Currently, 22 states have some variation of open proceedings.[20] Each state with presumptively open proceedings has a provision to close the courtroom when it is determined to be in the best interest of the child involved.[21] A number of states have statutory regulations providing for presumptively closed proceedings with judicial discretion to open them.[22] Many jurisdictions, however, have clung to the principle of closed proceedings.[23]

§ 13.4 Arguments Against Open Court Proceedings

Opponents of open proceedings argue that open dependency proceedings could psychologically harm the children involved. A finding of the psychological analysis, developmental victimology, indicates that in sexual abuse cases a child's psychological distress is increased by self-blame for the abuse. Public exposure and the public's reaction to abuse appear to increase the child's self-blame, which impacts the duration and severity of the child's psychological trauma.[24]

Additionally, opponents of open proceedings are concerned about the potential negative impact of open proceedings on the child welfare system. Advocates of closed proceedings note the risk for a decrease in admitting to allegations because the admissions would be made public. They are also concerned that open proceedings may cause more contested hearings and requests for closed hearings, resulting in increased costs and delayed placement of children.[25]

Critics of open proceedings doubt the value of the media's access to dependency proceedings. Many child advocates fear that the media will exploit children involved in dependency proceedings.[26] They argue that the media feeds on sensationalism and will likely expose identifying information of children involved.

---

[20] Sara VanMeter, *Public Access to Juvenile Dependency Proceedings in Washington State: An Important Piece of the Permanency Puzzle*, 27 SEATTLE U. L. REV. 859, 862 (summarizing Jonathan Martin, *Push on to Open Child Court Hearings*, SPOKESMAN REV., July 21, 2002, at B1).

[21] Lynne Tucker, *Open or Closed: A Survey of the Opinions and the Reality of Opening Juvenile Court Dependency Proceedings*, Barton Child Law and Policy Clinic at Emory University (Nov. 2000), *available at* http://www.childwelfare.net/activities/interns/2000summer/OpenCourts/.

[22] KAY FARLEY, PUBLIC ACCESS TO CHILD ABUSE AND NEGLECT PROCEEDINGS 3-4 (Nat'l Ctr. for State Courts Issue Brief No. 5, 2003).

[23] *See* DIONNE MAXWELL ET AL., TO OPEN OR NOT TO OPEN: THE ISSUE OF PUBLIC ACCESS IN CHILD PROTECTION HEARINGS (NCJFCJ Technical Assistance Brief, 2004).

[24] *See* William Patton, *An Empirical Rebuttal to the Open Juvenile Dependency Court Reform Movement* (forthcoming Fall 2004).

[25] William Patton, *Pandora's Box: Opening Child Protection Cases to the Press and Public*, 27 W. ST. U. L. REV. 181, 186-186 (1999/2000).

[26] Informal survey conducted on the NACC Listserv, March 2003.

The media rarely report on dependency proceedings, and when they do they are under no ethical duty to withhold identifying information.[27]

§ 13.5 The NACC's Position

Although there may be benefits to opening child welfare proceedings, it is still debatable whether the potential safeguards of an open system outweigh the interests of protecting children's privacy and mental health. The following is the NACC's position on the confidentiality of juvenile court proceedings and records as of October 29, 2004:

> After weighing the pros and cons of confidentiality in juvenile court, the NACC concludes that neither absolute confidentiality nor total opening of juvenile court records and proceedings would be appropriate. Rather, the presumption of confidentiality should remain, with the exception that judges should be allowed—on a case-by-case basis, after articulating findings that there would not be harm to the child, after an opportunity to be heard by child's counsel, to open up proceedings and records to members of the media, researchers, and others with a bona fide interest in reporting on the juvenile court system (and related service systems) to the public. Such an opening up of proceedings and records, however, should only occur on the condition that the identity of any reporter of neglect/abuse, and the names, addresses, telephone numbers, photographs or other identifying information of the children and families in question NOT be made public in any way. In addition, the judge should be allowed to exclude the media and any other observers from child victim/witness testimony, and/or to provide for child victim/witness testimony via video or closed circuit television, and the judge may choose to close all or part of the proceeding. Since case law has clearly established that publication, by the media, of lawfully-obtained truthful information can not be restricted or punished, adequate safeguards would have to be adopted prior to opening proceedings or records to the media: redaction of identifying information from records, and prohibition of photography in the courtroom and refraining from using full names or other identifying information in proceedings viewed by the media. Finally, identifying records of adjudication of juvenile delinquency should be made available to juvenile and criminal courts and law enforcement officials, to ensure appropriate decision making with regard to subsequent delinquent or criminal offenses; such information shall not, however, be disseminated beyond those courts and law enforcement officials. Certain child protection records may be

---

[27] *See* William Patton, *An Empirical Rebuttal to the Open Juvenile Dependency Court Reform Movement* (to be published in April 2005 in the Suffolk University Law Review).

released subject to a Ritchie-type (*Pennsylvania v. Ritchie*, 480 US 39 (1987)) in camera inspection.

This position ensures that the major benefits of confidentiality are retained (see above), while the major benefits of opening juvenile court records and proceedings are also realized—especially the benefits of promoting accountability in the system, and promoting public under-standing of the system. There are too many problems in the current child protection and juvenile justice systems—most notably, inadequate placements and services, and unjustifiable delays—to allow these sys-tems to continue to operate outside the light of public scrutiny. The needs of each child and family in the system must be met in order to lessen their likelihood of re-entering the system. However, those needs are less likely to be met if the proceedings and records were fully opened to the public, for the reasons listed above. The NACC position is, therefore, to take a "middle ground" position, which allows for inte-gration of the best elements of a fully confidential system and a fully open system. The NACC supports efforts to study the impacts of release of information regarding children's cases on the children and families in question and on improvements in the system. The NACC supports independent evaluations of court systems to help ensure accountability (modeled after the federal general accounting office or state legislative auditors offices.)[28]

---

[28] *See* NAT'L ASS'N OF COUNSEL FOR CHILDREN, CONFIDENTIALITY OF JUVENILE COURT PROCEEDINGS AND RECORDS, (NACC Policy Papers, adopted April 25, 1998), *available at* http://www.naccchildlaw.org/policy/policy_papers.html.

Chapter 14   SPECIAL EVIDENTIARY ISSUES

by John E.B. Myers[1]

§ 14.1 Selected Evidence Issues

This chapter discusses the following evidence issues: expert testimony, use of syndrome evidence, and privilege.

§ 14.2 Expert Testimony

Expert testimony from mental health and medical experts plays an important role in child maltreatment litigation.

§ 14.2.1 Qualifications to Testify as Expert Witness

To qualify as an expert, a witness must possess sufficient "knowledge, skill, experience, training, or education."[2] Unless a medical or mental health professional is clearly unqualified, deficiencies in qualifications go to the weight accorded the expert's testimony rather than admissibility.[3] A professional need not be the foremost authority on child maltreatment, nor must the witness understand every aspect of the subject. In *State v. Best*,[4] defendant challenged the qualifications of two physicians. One was an orthopedic surgeon and the other a radiologist. The orthopedic surgeon testified that the victim's fractured arm was probably the result of child abuse. The radiologist testified that the twisting force required to produce the fracture could not have resulted from getting an arm caught in crib bars. Defendant claimed that the surgeon was not qualified in the area of child abuse and that the radiologist was not qualified on the force needed to produce a fracture. The South Dakota Supreme Court rejected both challenges, noting that experts do not have to be expert in every aspect of a subject.

In *Deese v. State*,[5] the victim died of Shaken Baby Syndrome. The prosecution's expert was a pediatrician specializing in pediatric emergency medicine. Although not a pathologist, the doctor was qualified to offer an opinion on the cause of the child's death. The Maryland Court of Appeals wrote, "Assuming,

---

[1] John E.B. Myers, J.D., is Professor of Law at University of the Pacific, McGeorge School of Law.

[2] FED. R. EVID. 702.

[3] *See* FED. R. EVID. 702, Commentary ("Courts have not required a party to show that the witness is an outstanding expert, or to show that the witness is well-known or respected in the field; these are generally questions of weight.").

[4] 232 N.W.2d 447 (1975).

[5] 786 A.2d 751 (2001).

arguendo, that the most relevant field of expertise was forensic pathology, as distinct from pediatrics and pediatric emergency medicine, previous decisions have affirmed a trial court's admission of expert testimony when the expert, although not a specialist in the field having the most sharply focused relevancy to the issue at hand, nevertheless could assist the jury in light of the witness's 'formal education, professional training, personal observations, and actual experience.'"[6]

Many pediatricians, radiologists, pathologists, emergency room physicians, psychiatrists, psychologists, and social workers possess the training and experience required to testify as experts.

§ 14.2.2 Bases for Expert Opinion

Under the Federal Rules of Evidence, expert witnesses may base their testimony on a broad range of facts and data.[7] An expert may state an opinion without specifying the factual basis for the opinion.[8] As a practical matter, however, experts nearly always provide the factual data on which testimony is based. This information may precede or follow the expert's opinion.

In many child abuse and neglect cases, the expert has firsthand knowledge of the child because the expert examined or treated the child. Firsthand knowledge is not always required, however, and in the right circumstances, an expert may render an opinion without personally examining the child. For example, an expert may base an opinion on review of records. In *State v. Moyer*,[9] defendant argued that expert testimony should be excluded because the doctor had not personally examined the child. The doctor reviewed records and photographs of the child. The court rejected defendant's argument, writing, "We find no requirement and do not consider it imperative that the doctor actually examine the child. [The doctor] was an expert, he understood the [battered child] syndrome and he knew what factors to look for. He had sufficient evidence before him from which he could formulate his expert opinion."[10]

Experts may base opinions on information that is not admissible in evidence, provided such information is "of a type reasonably relied upon by experts in the particular field in forming opinions or inferences upon the subject."[11] For example, a doctor evaluating the possibility of physical abuse may consider the caretaker's prior violence toward the child.[12] Although the caretaker's violent history may be character evidence, the doctor's reliance on character is clinically

---

[6] *Id.* at 756 (citations omitted).

[7] *See* FED. R. EVID. 703.

[8] *See* FED. R. EVID. 705.

[9] 727 P.2d 31 (Ariz. Ct. App. 1986).

[10] *Id.* at 34.

[11] FED. R. EVID. 703.

[12] *See People v. Gordon*, 738 P.2d 404, 406 (Colo. Ct. App. 1987) (noting expert considered defendant's "prior violent behavior toward the child").

appropriate. Expert testimony may be based in part on hearsay. Written hearsay includes medical and psychological records, consultation reports, and documents prepared by police and social services agencies. Verbal hearsay plays an important role in diagnosis. The patient's history—which lies at the heart of diagnosis—is hearsay. With children, the history is often provided by a parent or caretaker. A doctor or therapist acts properly when the professional bases court testimony partly on a medical history.

Although an expert's opinion may be based on inadmissible evidence, Rule 703 of the Federal Rule of Evidence provides, "Facts or data that are otherwise inadmissible shall not be disclosed to the jury by the proponent of the opinion or inference unless the court determines that their probative value in assisting the jury to evaluate the expert's opinion substantially outweighs their prejudicial effect."

§ 14.3 Syndrome Evidence

Expert testimony describing syndrome evidence is often admitted in child maltreatment litigation, including testimony on Battered Child Syndrome, Shaken Baby Syndrome, Munchausen Syndrome by Proxy, Child Sexual Abuse Accommodation Syndrome, and Posttraumatic Stress Disorder. These and additional syndromes are addressed below, following a discussion of the use and abuse of syndrome evidence.

Dorland's Medical Dictionary defines syndrome as "a set of symptoms which occur together."[13] The word "syndrome" is not the only term that is used to describe concurring symptoms. The word "profile" is occasionally found in the literature describing a set of symptoms, characteristics, or behaviors. The American Psychiatric Association's *Diagnostic and Statistical Manual of Mental Disorders*[14] uses the word "disorder" rather than "syndrome," but it acknowledges that "Each of the mental disorders is conceptualized as a clinically significant behavioral or psychological syndrome or pattern."[15]

Many diseases and some syndromes share the feature of diagnostic value. That is, many diseases and some syndromes point with varying degrees of certainty to a particular cause or etiology. The clinician reasons backward as follows: "In my patient I observe symptoms A, B, and C. These symptoms comprise Disease X or Syndrome Y. From the presence of Disease X or Syndrome Y, I reason backward to the cause or etiology of the symptoms." The ability to reason backward from symptoms to etiology is diagnostic value.

With diseases, the relationship between symptoms and etiology is often clear. Thus, many diseases have high diagnostic value. The same is true for some

---

[13] Dorland's Illustrated Medical Dictionary 1632 (28th ed. 1994).

[14] Am. Psychiatric Ass'n, Diagnostic and Statistical Manual of Mental Disorders, Text Revision (4th ed. 2000).

[15] *Id.*

syndromes, that is, the relationship between the symptoms comprising the syndrome and the etiology is clear. With many syndromes, however, the relationship between symptoms and etiology is unclear or unknown. When it is not possible to reason backward from symptoms to etiology, the syndrome or disease lacks diagnostic value.

Nearly all of the psychological syndromes that find their way into child maltreatment litigation lack diagnostic value. In other words, nearly all psychological syndromes are nondiagnostic. One cannot reason backward from the syndrome to its etiology.

Focusing for the moment on syndromes that do have diagnostic value, it is important to understand that diagnostic value varies from syndrome to syndrome. Syndromes with diagnostic value are on a continuum of diagnostic certainty. Some diagnostic syndromes point with greater certainty to their etiology than others. Two syndromes that are used in litigation illustrate the continuum of diagnostic certainty: Battered Child Syndrome and Rape Trauma Syndrome. A child with Battered Child Syndrome is very likely to have suffered nonaccidental injury. Battered Child Syndrome points convincingly to abuse. The doctor can reason backward from symptoms to cause. Battered Child Syndrome has high diagnostic value.

Compare the high diagnostic value of Battered Child Syndrome with the decidedly low diagnostic value of Rape Trauma Syndrome. Rape Trauma Syndrome consists of symptoms and behaviors that are caused by a broad range of events including, but not limited to, rape. Rape Trauma Syndrome may have no diagnostic value at all. Even if the Syndrome has some diagnostic value, it is low, which accounts for the fact that nearly all courts hold that Rape Trauma Syndrome is not admissible to prove lack of consent.

Lawyers and judges sometimes fail to appreciate that some syndromes have diagnostic value and others do not. As stated above, many syndromes do not point with *any* degree of certainty to a particular cause. The term "nondiagnostic syndrome" is useful to describe syndromes that have no diagnostic value. To repeat, nearly all of the psychological syndromes used in court are nondiagnostic.

A further example will nail down the distinction between diagnostic and nondiagnostic syndromes. Compare two syndromes—one nondiagnostic, the other diagnostic. The nondiagnostic syndrome is Child Sexual Abuse Accommodation Syndrome (CSAAS), which appeared in the literature in 1983.[16] Psychiatrist Roland Summit coined the term CSAAS to describe how children react (accommodate) to ongoing sexual abuse. Children "learn to accept the situation and to survive. There is no way out, no place to run. The healthy, normal, emotionally resilient child will learn to accommodate to the

---

[16] Roland C. Summit, *The Child Sexual Abuse Accommodation Syndrome*, 7 CHILD ABUSE & NEGLECT 177-193 (1983).

reality of continuing sexual abuse."[17] Summit described five aspects of CSAAS: (1) secrecy, (2) helplessness, (3) entrapment and accommodation, (4) delayed, conflicted, and unconvincing disclosure, and (5) retraction or recantation.

CSAAS is nondiagnostic because one cannot reason backward from CSAAS to sexual abuse. The fact that a child demonstrates one or more aspects of CSAAS does not provide substantive evidence of sexual abuse. For example, the fact that a child delayed reporting and then recanted is hardly evidence of abuse. Summit observed, "The accommodation syndrome is neither an illness nor a diagnosis, and it can't be used to measure whether or not a child has been sexually abused."[18] CSAAS was not designed to prove that abuse occurred. Rather, CSAAS was intended to explain how children who are abused react to their maltreatment.

Contrast CSAAS, which lacks diagnostic value, to Battered Child Syndrome, which has high diagnostic value. Battered Child Syndrome points decisively to physical abuse. With Battered Child Syndrome, we reason backward from the presence of certain injuries to the cause of the injuries.

To sum up, the common feature of nondiagnostic syndromes is that they do not point with any certainty to a cause. The cause must be ascertained through other means. The purpose of nondiagnostic syndromes is *not* to establish cause, but to describe reactions to *known* causes. When evidence of a syndrome is offered, the first step is to determine whether the syndrome is diagnostic or nondiagnostic. Determining whether a syndrome is diagnostic is essentially a question of logical relevance, that is, does the presence of certain symptoms have any tendency to make the existence of a particular etiology more probable? If the answer is yes, the syndrome is diagnostic. If it is not possible to draw a logical inference from symptoms to etiology, the syndrome is nondiagnostic. If the syndrome is nondiagnostic, it should not be used to establish the etiology of a person's symptoms.

When a new syndrome or a syndrome of dubious scientific merit is offered, a *Frye* or *Daubert* hearing is an ideal venue to test the validity and reliability of the syndrome. A *Frye* or *Daubert* hearing allows inquiry into whether the syndrome is diagnostic or nondiagnostic. If nondiagnostic, care can be taken to ensure that the syndrome is not used as substantive evidence. If the syndrome is diagnostic, the hearing affords an opportunity to locate the syndrome along the continuum of diagnostic certainty.

§ 14.3.1 Battered Child Syndrome

Expert testimony on Battered Child Syndrome is frequently offered to prove nonaccidental injury. The term Battered Child Syndrome was coined in

---

[17] *Id.* at 184.

[18] Mary B. Meinig, *Profile of Roland Summit*, 1 VIOLENCE UPDATE 6, 6 (1991).

1962 by pediatrician Henry Kempe and his colleagues.[19] Kempe described the syndrome:

> The battered-child syndrome may occur at any age, but, in general the affected children are younger than 3 years. In some instances the clinical manifestations are limited to those resulting from a single episode of trauma, but more often the child's general health is below par, and he shows evidence of neglect including poor skin hygiene, multiple soft tissue injuries, and malnutrition. One often obtains a history of previous episodes suggestive of parental neglect or trauma. A marked discrepancy between clinical findings and historical data as supplied by the parents is a major diagnostic feature of the battered-child syndrome. . . . Subdural hematoma, with or without fracture of the skull . . . is an extremely frequent finding even in the absence of fractures of the long bones. . . . The characteristic distribution of these multiple fractures and the observation that the lesions are in different stages of healing are of additional value in making the diagnosis.[20]

Not all battered children have injuries in different stages of healing. Kempe noted, for example, that abusive injury sometimes results from "a single episode of trauma." Moreover, many child abuse fatalities lack a pattern of repeated injury.

Battered Child Syndrome is an accepted medical diagnosis. Pediatrician David Chadwick and his colleagues wrote, "Diagnosis of classical 'battered children' who are presented for care with multiple injuries in differing stages of healing is relatively simple for experienced physicians."[21] Expert testimony on Battered Child Syndrome is routinely approved.[22] As the U.S. Supreme Court observed in *Estelle v. McGuire*,[23] the "syndrome exists when a child has sustained repeated and/or serious injuries by nonaccidental means. . . . [E]vidence demonstrating battered child syndrome helps to prove that the child died at the hands of another and not by falling off a couch, for example; it also tends to establish that the 'other,' whoever it may be, inflicted the injuries intentionally."[24]

A finding of nonaccidental injury can be premised partially or entirely on expert testimony on Battered Child Syndrome. The Battered Child Syndrome is not novel scientific evidence, and is not subject to *Frye* or *Daubert*.

---

[19] C. Henry Kempe et al., *The Battered-Child Syndrome*, 181 JAMA 17-24 (1962).

[20] *Id.* at 17-18, *cited in United States v. Boise*, 916 F.2d 497, 503 n.14 (9th Cir. 1990).

[21] David L. Chadwick et al., *Deaths from Falls in Children: How Far Is Fatal?*, 31 J. TRAUMA 1353, 1354 (1991).

[22] *See United States v. Boise*, 916 F.2d 497, 503 (9th Cir. 1990); Milton Roberts, Annotation, *Admissibility of Expert Medical Testimony on Battered Child Syndrome*, 98 A.L.R.3d 306 (1980).

[23] 502 U.S. 62 (1991).

[24] 502 U.S. at 66, 68.

§ 14.3.2 Battering Parent Syndrome

There is no personality profile of a "typical" child abuser. Thus, there is no Battering Parent Syndrome or Battering Parent Profile that can determine whether someone abused a child. In the few instances where prosecutors offered expert testimony on a purported Battering Parent Syndrome or Battering Parent Profile, courts rejected the evidence.[25]

§ 14.3.3 Munchausen Syndrome by Proxy

Munchausen Syndrome in *adults* is "a condition characterized by habitual presentation for hospital treatment of an apparent acute illness, the patient giving a plausible and dramatic history, all of which is false."[26] English pediatrician Sir Roy Meadow coined the term Munchausen Syndrome by Proxy in 1977 to describe adults who use a child as the vehicle for fabricated illness or injury.[27] Pediatrician Donna Rosenberg defined Munchausen Syndrome by Proxy as "illness in a child [that] is persistently and secretly simulated (lied about or faked) and/or produced by a parent or someone who is *in loco parentis*, and the child repeatedly presented for medical assessment and care."[28] The Iowa Supreme Court described the Syndrome as "a form of child abuse in which a parent repeatedly presents their child for unnecessary medical treatments by simulating or producing symptoms in the child."[29]

The prevalence of Munchausen Syndrome by Proxy is unknown, although it appears to be uncommon. Mothers are the most frequent perpetrators of the Syndrome. Boys and girls are victimized in roughly equal numbers. Most victims are babies or toddlers.

There is no psychological test that detects Munchausen Syndrome by Proxy. Nor is there a personality profile that describes the "typical" perpetrator of this bizarre form of child abuse. Psychiatrist Herbert Schreier wrote, "The primary

---

[25] *See State v. Maule*, 667 P.2d 96 (Wash. Ct. App. 1983) (finding it reversible error to permit testimony in statutory rape case that majority of child abuse cases involved male parent figure, with biological parents in the majority); *State v. Steward*, 660 P.2d 278, 280 (Wash. Ct. App. 1983) (finding it reversible error to admit "expert" testimony in a second degree murder prosecution of a babysitting boyfriend that "serious injuries to children were often inflicted by either live-in or babysitting boyfriends."). *See also* Gregory G. Sarno, Annotation, *Admissibility at Criminal Prosecution of Expert Testimony on Battering Parent Syndrome*, 43 A.L.R.4th 1203 (1986).

[26] DORLAND'S ILLUSTRATED MEDICAL DICTIONARY 1635 (28th ed. 1994).

[27] *See* Roy Meadow, *Munchausen Syndrome by Proxy: The Hinterland of Child Abuse*, 2 LANCET 343-345 (1977); Roy Meadow, *False Allegations of Abuse and Munchausen Syndrome by Proxy*, 68 ARCHIVES DISEASES CHILDHOOD 444 (1993) (describing 14 children in 7 families where allegations of child abuse were fabricated by parent as part of syndrome).

[28] Donna Andrea Rosenberg, *Munchausen Syndrome by Proxy, in* CHILD ABUSE: MEDICAL DIAGNOSIS AND MANAGEMENT 363, 363 (2d ed., Robert M. Reece & Stephen Ludwig eds.) (Philadelphia: Lippincott, Williams & Wilkins 2001).

[29] *Geringer v. Iowa Dep't of Human Servs.*, 521 N.W.2d 730, 730-731 (Iowa 1994).

motivation seems to be an intense need for attention from, and manipulation of, powerful professionals, most frequently, but not exclusively a physician."[30]

Munchausen Syndrome by Proxy manifests itself in many ways, including smothering, poisoning, injecting contaminants into the child (*e.g.*, drugs, saliva, salt, urine, feces), inducing fever, inducing vomiting, fabricating symptoms, and in other ways.

For survivors of Munchausen Syndrome by Proxy, there may be long-lasting psychological and physical sequelae. The efficacy of psychotherapy for perpetrators of Munchausen Syndrome by Proxy is an open question. Therapy may work for parents who admit they have a problem.

When Munchausen Syndrome by Proxy occurs, the child is at risk of serious injury or death, and removing the child from the custody of the suspected offender is typically the only way to ensure safety. Moreover, separating the child from the suspect, and documenting that the child's symptoms abate following separation, is often the best way to confirm the diagnosis of Munchausen Syndrome by Proxy. For children in the hospital, covert video surveillance can be life saving, and is often the only way to catch the abuser in the act.

Expert testimony is necessary to prove Munchausen Syndrome by Proxy, and courts allow such testimony.[31] In *People v. Phillips*,[32] for example, the California Court of Appeal approved expert psychiatric testimony on the syndrome to establish the defendant's motive to poison her baby by putting large amounts of salt in the baby's food.

Munchausen Syndrome by Proxy is an accepted diagnosis. In *State v. Hocevar*,[33] where a mother was accused of poisoning her young child, and two of her other children died of smothering, the court noted that:

> The expert testimony regarding MSBP is neither novel nor scientific. The term "Munchausen Syndrome By Proxy" has appeared in medical literature since at least 1977. . . .While this Court has not previously addressed the admissibility of MSBP evidence, other courts have considered such evidence since 1981. . . . A Westlaw search reveals that the term "Munchausen Syndrome by Proxy" has appeared in over forty state and federal cases since then. Thus testimony regarding MSBP is not novel to the field of pediatrics or law.[34]

---

[30] Herbert Schreier, *Munchausen by Proxy Defined*, 110 PEDIATRICS 985, 985 (2002).

[31] *See People v. Phillips*, 175 Cal. Rptr. 703 (Cal. Ct. App. 1981); *In re Colin R.*, 493 A.2d 1083 (Md. Ct. App. 1985); *State v. Hocevar*, 7 P.3d 329 (Mont. 2000) (suggesting Munchausen Syndrome by Proxy is beyond the ken of jurors).

[32] 175 Cal. Rptr. 703 (1981).

[33] 7 P.3d 329, 342 (Mont. 2000).

[34] *Id.* (citations omitted).

Courts hold that expert testimony on the Syndrome is either not subject to analysis under *Frye* or *Daubert*, or that is passes muster.[35] In *Reid v. State*,[36] defendant was charged with murdering her infant child. The prosecution offered expert testimony on Munchausen Syndrome by Proxy. The Texas Court of Appeals provided a thorough analysis of the scientific reliability of expert testimony on the Syndrome, concluding, "the trial court did not err in determining the scientific reliability of MSBP testimony."[37]

§ 14.3.4 Shaken Baby Syndrome

The average infant spends two to three hours a day crying. Frustrated caretakers sometimes grasp young children by the shoulders or under the arms and shake them. Violent shaking can cause direct injury to brain tissue. Babies are particularly susceptible to such injury because they have weak neck muscles and because the infant brain is not as solid as the brain in older children and adults.

Neurological damage caused by shaking is called Shaken Baby Syndrome, Whiplash Shaken Infant Syndrome, or Shake-Impact Syndrome. Many experts believe that shaking alone—without impact on a hard surface—can cause Shaken Baby Syndrome, with resultant severe injury or death. Other experts believe that in most cases of Shaken Baby Syndrome, the damage results from a combination of violent shaking plus impact, as when the out-of-control adult shakes the baby and slams it down on a surface. Whatever the precise mechanism of injury, it is clear that this form of child abuse causes enormous damage, often resulting in death.

Although not all physicians agree with Shaken Baby Syndrome, the Syndrome is an accepted medical diagnosis. The Syndrome is not novel, and is not subject to *Frye* or *Daubert*.[38] Courts routinely approve expert testimony on Shaken Baby Syndrome.[39]

Shaking can cause bleeding in the eye, especially retinal hemorrhages. Quite a few babies are born with retinal hemorrhages, although birth-related retinal hemorrhages disappear within a few weeks. Although retinal hemorrhages are not diagnostic of abusive head injury, retinal hemorrhages are seen much more frequently with inflicted head injury than with accidental head injury.

There is some disagreement over whether cardiopulmonary resuscitation can cause retinal hemorrhages. Byard and Cohle wrote in 2004, "More recent

---

[35] *See id.*

[36] 964 S.W.2d 723 (Tex. App. 1998).

[37] *Id.* at 729.

[38] *See People v. Martinez*, 74 P.3d 316, 323 (Colo. 2003) ("we assume, as it is not in dispute, that the scientific principles of shaken-impact syndrome and subdural hematomas resulting from extreme accidents are reasonably reliable."); State v. McClary, 541 A.2d 96, 102 (1988) (stating shaken baby syndrome is generally accepted by medical science).

[39] *See United States v. Vallo*, 238 F.3d 1242 (10th Cir. 2001); *Steggall v. State*, 8 S.W.3d 538 (Ark. 2000); *People v. Malfavon*, 125 Cal. Rptr. 2d 618 (Ct. App. 2002) (involving fatal shaking of a seven-month-old infant); *People v. Dunaway*, 88 P.3d 619 (Colo. 2004).

studies have supported the concept that retinal hemorrhages occur rarely, if ever, from cardiopulmonary resuscitation."[40]

§ 14.3.5 Posttraumatic Stress Disorder

Posttraumatic Stress Disorder (PTSD) is a psychiatric diagnosis describing the reaction some people experience to extreme trauma, including rape and sexual assault. The American Psychiatric Association observed that PTSD "may be especially severe or long lasting when the stressor is of human design (*e.g.*, torture, rape)."[41] PTSD is a well-established diagnosis. The diagnostic Criteria for PTSD are set forth in the fourth edition of the American Psychiatric Association's *Diagnostic and Statistical Manual of Mental Disorders* (DSM IV TR):

A. The person has been exposed to a traumatic event in which both of the following were present: (1) the person experienced, witnessed, or was confronted with an event or events that involved actual or threatened death or serious injury, or a threat to the physical integrity of self or others; (2) the person's response involved intense fear, helplessness, or horror. Note: In children, this may be expressed instead by disorganized or agitated behavior.

B. The traumatic event is persistently reexperienced in one (or more) of the following ways: (1) recurrent and intrusive distressing recollections of the event, including images, thoughts, or perceptions. Note: In young children, repetitive play may occur in which themes or aspects of the trauma are expressed. (2) recurrent distressing dreams of the event. Note: In children, there may be frightening dreams without recognizable content. (3) acting or feeling as if the traumatic event were recurring (includes a sense of reliving the experience, illusions, hallucinations, and dissociative flashback episodes, including those that occur on awakening or when intoxicated.) Note: In young children, trauma-specific reenactment may occur. (4) intense psychological distress at exposure to internal or external cues that symbolize or resemble an aspect of the traumatic event. (5) physiological reactivity on exposure to internal or external cues that symbolize or resemble an aspect of the traumatic event.

C. Persistent avoidance of stimuli associated with the trauma and numbing of general responsiveness (not present before the trauma), as indicated by three (or more) of the following: (1) efforts to avoid thoughts, feelings, or conversations associated with the trauma; (2) efforts to avoid

---

[40] Roger W. Byard & Stephen D. Cohle, *Homicide and Suicide, in* SUDDEN DEATH IN INFANCY, CHILDHOOD, AND ADOLESCENCE 77, 142 (2d ed., Roger W. Byard ed.) (Cambridge, UK: Cambridge University Press, 2004).

[41] AM. PSYCHIATRIC ASS'N, DIAGNOSTIC AND STATISTICAL MANUAL OF MENTAL DISORDERS, TEXT REVISION 464 (4th ed. 2000).

activities, places, or people that arouse recollections of the trauma; (3) inability to recall an important aspect of the trauma; (4) markedly diminished interest or participation in significant activities; (5) feeling of detachment or estrangement from others; (6) restricted range of affect (e.g., unable to have loving feelings) (7) sense of a foreshortened future (e.g., does not expect to have a career, marriage, children, or a normal life span).

D. Persistent symptoms of increased arousal (not present before the trauma), as indicated by two (or more) of the following: (1) difficulty falling or staying asleep; (2) irritability or outbursts of anger; (3) difficulty concentrating; (4) hypervigilance; (5) exaggerated startle response.

E. Duration of the disturbance (symptoms in Criteria B, C, and D) is more than 1 month.

F. The disturbance causes clinically significant distress or impairment in social, occupational, or other important areas of functioning.

Children experience PTSD. "For children, sexually traumatic events may include developmentally inappropriate sexual experiences without threatened or actual violence or injury."[42] As the DSM IV TR criteria explain, the symptoms displayed by young children differ in some respects from those observed in adolescents and adults. The *Diagnostic and Statistical Manual of Mental Disorders* states, "In younger children, distressing dreams of the event may, within several weeks, change into generalized nightmares of monsters, of rescuing others, or of threats to self or others. Young children usually do not have the sense that they are reliving the past; rather, the reliving of the trauma may occur through repetitive play . . . . Children may also exhibit various physical symptoms, such as stomachaches and headaches."[43]

§ 14.3.6 Posttraumatic Stress Disorder in Litigation

Individuals with PTSD resort to the courts in search of money damages, workers' compensation, and government benefits. There are thousands of civil PTSD cases. The present focus is limited to the use of PTSD in proving rape, sexual assault, and child abuse. In the context of such litigation, the question is whether a diagnosis of PTSD has probative value. In other words, is PTSD a diagnostic syndrome? Upon reading the diagnostic criteria for PTSD, one quickly sees a roadblock to using PTSD as diagnostic of trauma. The criteria for PTSD presuppose a traumatic event. That is, to reach a diagnosis of PTSD, the clinician must accept the fact that the patient has experienced a traumatic event. Yet, if the diagnosis depends on acknowledging a traumatic event, how can the

---

[42] *Id.*

[43] *Id.* at 466.

diagnosis prove the event? The circularity of such reasoning is obvious. Given the definitional requirements of PTSD, a diagnosis of PTSD has little probative value as substantive evidence of trauma.

If the diagnostic label PTSD has little probative value in proving trauma, what about the symptoms that make up PTSD? Do the symptoms themselves have a tendency to prove trauma? To be diagnosed with PTSD, an individual must experience intense fear, helplessness, or horror. The traumatic event must be persistently reexperienced (*e.g.*, recurrent dreams, distress when thinking about the trauma), and the person must avoid stimuli associated with the trauma. Additionally, there must be symptoms of increased arousal (*e.g.*, difficulty sleeping, hypervigilance). PTSD symptoms can indicate that something traumatic occurred.

Symptoms of PTSD can take on probative value when independent evidence establishes the date of onset for the symptoms, and when the symptoms represent a marked departure from the individual's long-established behavior. Consider, for example, a sixth grade student who claims she was raped in a park near her school on March 1, 2004. Evidence establishes that prior to March 1 the girl was high functioning, self-confident, happy, outgoing, and not inordinately fearful. After March 1, however, she routinely expressed intense fear of men, feelings of helplessness, nightmares in which she is assaulted, intense distress whenever she approaches the park where she says she was attacked, difficulty concentrating on schoolwork, and a steep downturn in academic performance. All these are symptoms of PTSD, and when their sudden onset is considered in conjunction with the girl's prior behavior, the symptoms have considerable probative force. Although the symptoms are not specific for rape, the symptoms have a tendency to prove trauma at the relevant time.

In sum, because of the circularity issue discussed above, a diagnosis of PTSD has little probative value in itself. The symptoms of PTSD, standing alone, say little about the timing and cause of the symptoms. When PTSD symptoms are considered with other evidence, however, the symptoms can assume probative force.

Several courts recognize that a diagnosis of PTSD does not prove trauma. In *Hutton v. State*,[44] the Maryland Court of Appeals wrote:

> [D]etermining from the symptoms that PTSD is the proper diagnosis ordinarily does not answer the question of what traumatic event caused it; the symptoms, in other words, are not reliable identifiers of the specific cause of the disorder. . . . The literature concludes that a PTSD diagnosis is essentially a therapeutic aid, rather than a tool for the detection of sexual abuse . . . . Because causes other than sexual abuse may trigger PTSD—the traumatic event being unable to be verified objectively, its

---

[44] 663 A.2d 1289 (Md. 1995).

occurrence must necessarily be assumed—a diagnosis of PTSD does not reliably prove the nature of the stressor.[45]

Similarly, the Louisiana Supreme Court wrote in *State v. Chauvin*:[46]

[T]he psychiatric procedures used in developing the diagnosis of PTSD are designed for therapeutic purposes and are not reliable as fact-finding tools to determine whether sexual abuse has in fact occurred. . . . [T]he potential for prejudice looms large because the jury may accord too much weight to expert opinions stating medical conclusions which were drawn from diagnostic methods having limited merit as fact-finding devices. . . . [W]e find expert testimony of PTSD is inadmissible for the purpose of substantively proving that sexual abuse occurred.[47]

The court added, "Although PTSD is widely accepted among professionals as an anxiety disorder attributable to some type of trauma, it has not been proven to be a reliable indicator that sexual abuse is the trauma underlying the disorder or that sexual abuse has even occurred."[48] The Louisiana court ruled that expert testimony on PTSD offered as substantive evidence of abuse did not "pass the *Daubert* threshold test of reliability."[49]

Illinois, by statute, makes evidence of PTSD admissible.[50]

§ 14.3.7 Acute Distress Disorder

In addition to PTSD, the *Diagnostic and Statistical Manual of Mental Disorders* contains the closely related diagnosis of Acute Distress Disorder. "The essential feature of Acute Stress Disorder is the development of characteristic anxiety, dissociative, and other symptoms that occurs within 1 month after exposure to an extreme traumatic stressor."[51] The *Diagnostic and Statistical Manual of Mental Disorders* provides, "Acute Stress Disorder is distinguished from Posttraumatic Stress Disorder because the symptom pattern in Acute Stress Disorder must occur within 4 weeks of the traumatic event and resolve within that 4-week period. If the symptoms persist for more than 1 month and meet criteria for Posttraumatic Stress Disorder, the diagnosis is changed from Acute Stress Disorder to Posttraumatic Stress Disorder."[52]

---

[45] *Id.* at 1294-1295 (citations omitted).

[46] 846 So.2d 697 (La. 2003).

[47] *Id.* at 707-708 (citations omitted).

[48] *Id.* at 707.

[49] *Id.* at 708.

[50] 725 ILL. COMP. STAT. 5/115-7.2 provides, "In a prosecution for an illegal sexual act perpetrated upon a victim . . . testimony by an expert, qualified by the court relating to any recognized and accepted form of post-traumatic stress syndrome shall be admissible as evidence."

[51] AM. PSYCHIATRIC ASS'N, DIAGNOSTIC AND STATISTICAL MANUAL OF MENTAL DISORDERS, TEXT REVISION 469 (4th ed. 2000).

[52] *Id.* at 467.

§ 14.3.8 Child Sexual Abuse Accommodation Syndrome

As discussed above, Child Sexual Abuse Accommodation Syndrome (CSAAS) was described in 1983 by psychiatrist Roland Summit.[53] Summit described five characteristics observed in many sexually abused children, particularly incest victims:

- Secrecy.

- Helplessness.

- Entrapment and accommodation.

- Delayed, conflicted, and unconvincing disclosure.

- Retraction.

Summit's purpose in describing CSAAS was to provide a "common language" for professionals working to protect sexually abused children. Summit did not intend CSAAS as a device to detect sexual abuse.

CSAAS is a nondiagnostic syndrome. The Indiana Supreme Court observed in *Steward v. State*[54] that CSAAS "was not intended as a diagnostic device and does not detect sexual abuse."[55] The syndrome assumes that abuse has occurred and helps explain the child's reaction to it. The Mississippi Supreme Court noted in *Hall v. State*[56] that the accommodation syndrome "was not meant to be used as a diagnostic device to show that abuse had, in fact, occurred. . . . Thus, any attempt to show that a child had been abused because he exhibits some signals of CSAAS is an improper usage of Dr. Summit's theory."[57]

CSAAS has a role to play in child sexual abuse litigation, but not as substantive evidence of abuse. Expert testimony on CSAAS is admissible to rehabilitate a child's credibility following impeachment focused on delayed reporting, inconsistency, or recantation. Such rehabilitation is appropriate because jurors may not understand that delayed reporting, recantation, and inconsistency are relatively common among sexually abused children.

§ 14.3.9 Parental Alienation Syndrome

In contested child custody litigation, one parent sometimes alienates the children from the other parent. Psychiatrist Richard Gardner coined the term Parental Alienation Syndrome (PAS) to describe this phenomenon.[58] Gardner

---

[53] Roland C. Summit, *The Child Sexual Abuse Accommodation Syndrome*, 7 CHILD ABUSE & NEGLECT 177-193 (1983).

[54] 652 N.E.2d 490 (Ind. 1995).

[55] *Id.* at 493.

[56] 611 So.2d 915 (Miss. 1992).

[57] *Id.* at 919 (citations omitted).

[58] RICHARD A. GARDNER, THE PARENTAL ALIENATION SYNDROME: A GUIDE FOR MENTAL HEALTH AND LEGAL PROFESSIONALS (Cresskill, NJ: Creative Therapeutics 1992).

defined PAS as follows: "In this disorder we see not only programming ('brain-washing') of the child by one parent to denigrate the other parent, but self-created contributions by the child in support of the preferred parent's campaign of denigration against the non-preferred parent."[59]

Gardner pointed out that if the child was abused, the child *should* feel alienated from the abuser. Gardner wrote, "When bona fide abuse does exist, then the child's responding hostility is warranted and the concept of the parental alienation syndrome is *not* applicable."[60] One finds occasional reference to PAS is reported decisions, primarily custody cases.[61]

PAS is nondiagnostic.[62] Kathleen Faller wrote, "Because the parental alienation syndrome is a nondiagnostic syndrome, it is only useful for mental health professionals in explaining the symptom presentation if they know from other information that an abuse allegation is a deliberately made, false accusation. The syndrome cannot be used to decide whether the child has been sexually abused. As a consequence, it is of little probative value to courts making decisions about the presence or absence of sexual abuse."[63] Because PAS is nondiagnostic, it sheds no light on whether allegations of abuse are true or false. Any use of PAS for diagnostic purposes is a misuse of the syndrome that does not pass muster under *Frye* or *Daubert*.[64]

PAS has been criticized.[65] The American Psychological Association wrote, "There are no data to support the phenomenon called parental alienation

---

[59] *Id.* at xv.

[60] *Id.* at xviii.

[61] *See Pearson v. Pearson*, 5 P.3d 239 (Alaska 2000); *In re Paternity of V.A.M.C.*, 768 N.E.2d 990 (Ind. Ct. App. 2002); *Ellis v. Ellis*, 840 So.2d 806 (Miss. Ct. App 2003) (involving child custody and visitation dispute).

[62] *See* Kathleen Coulborn Faller, *The Parental Alienation Syndrome: What Is It and What Data Support It?*, 3 CHILD MALTREATMENT 100, 111 (1998).

[63] *Id.*

[64] *See C.J.L. v. M.W.B.*, 879 So.2d 1169, 1178 (Ala. Civ. App. 2003) ("Although we might, if faced squarely with the question whether evidence concerning an actual diagnosis of PAS was admissible under *Frye*'s 'general acceptance' test, be inclined to agree with the mother and find that PAS had not been generally accepted in the scientific community, we do not need to make that decision in this case."); *People v. Sullivan*, 2003 WL 1785921 (Cal. Ct. App. 2003) (not officially published) (finding no need for expert testimony that in contested custody cases parents sometimes alienate children; this is within the ken of the jury); *People v. Fortin*, 289 A.D.2d 590, 590 (N.Y. App. Div. 2001) ("The County Court was correct in determining that the defendant failed in his burden of demonstrating that 'Parental Alienation Syndrome' was generally accepted in the relevant scientific communities. In making that determination, the County Court properly considered that the defendant's sole witness at the *Frye* hearing [Dr. Richard Gardner] had a significant financial interest in having his theory accepted." (internal citations omitted)); *Zafran v. Zafran*, 740 N.Y.S.2d 596 (N.Y. Sup. Ct. 2002) (granting *Frye* hearing on PAS).

[65] *See* Carol S. Bruch, *Parental Alienation Syndrome and Parental Alienation: Getting It Wrong in Child Custody Cases*, 35 FAM. L.Q. 527-552 (2001).

syndrome."[66] Carol Bruch wrote, "PAS as developed and purveyed by Richard Gardner has neither a logical nor a scientific basis. It is rejected by responsible social scientists and lacks solid grounding in psychological theory or research."[67] Kathleen Faller stated, "A fundamental flaw in the syndrome, as described by Gardner is that it fails to take into account alternative explanations for the child's and mother's behavior, including the veracity of the allegations or that the mother has made an honest mistake."[68]

§ 14.4 Evidentiary Privileges and Confidentiality

The evidentiary privileges protecting confidential communications apply to children as well as adults. Thus, the privileges of attorney-client, physician-patient, psychotherapist-client, and other evidentiary privileges apply to children.

The person entitled to assert a privilege is the "holder" of the privilege. A child may be the holder, and if the child possesses sufficient maturity, the child may assert or waive privileges after receiving advice from counsel. In at least one state, California, a child's attorney, as well as the child, is a holder of the psycho-therapist-client, the physician-patient, and the clergyman-penitent privileges.[69]

In the normal case, parents exercise privileges on behalf of their children. However, when a parent has a conflict of interest with the child, however, or is accused of harming the child, someone other than the parent should be responsible for the child's privileges.[70]

Privileges are waived in several ways. When the privilege holder is competent to do so, the hold is entitled to waive or assert a privilege. Waiver may occur when the privilege holder's mental or physical condition is in issue in litigation. In *In re Daniel C.H.*,[71] the California Court of Appeals considered a juvenile court dependency proceeding in which a father allegedly molested his son. The father sought access to the child's privileged communications with a therapist. To overcome the privilege, the father argued that by disclosing the sexual abuse, the child placed his mental condition in issue, waiving the psychotherapist-client privilege. Rejecting this argument, the Court of Appeals wrote, "Daniel did not 'tender' his mental state here by complaining of the acts of his father."[72]

---

[66] Am. Psychol. Ass'n, Violence and the Family 40 (1996).

[67] Carol S. Bruch, *Parental Alienation Syndrome and Parental Alienation: Getting It Wrong in Child Custody Cases*, 35 Fam. L.Q. 527, 550 (2001).

[68] Kathleen Coulborn Faller, *The Parental Alienation Syndrome: What Is It and What Data Support It?*, 3 Child Maltreatment 100, 112 (1998).

[69] Cal. Welf. & Inst. Code § 317(f).

[70] *See State v. Hunt*, 406 P.2d 208, 220 (Ariz. Ct. App. 1965); *In re Daniel C.H.*, 269 Cal. Rptr. 624, 631-632 (Cal. Ct. App. 1990) (finding, in juvenile court dependency proceeding, father accused of abuse had no right to child's therapy records; proper to allow child's attorney to assert child's privilege).

[71] 269 Cal. Rptr. 624 (Cal. Ct. App. 1990).

[72] *Id.* at 631.

Most states have one or both of the two spousal privileges: (1) the spousal testimonial privilege, which allows one spouse to refuse to testify against the other, and (2) the spousal confidential communications privilege, which protects confidential communications between married persons form disclosure. Neither of these privilege is likely to play a role in child abuse and neglect litigation because the privileges do not apply when one spouse is accused of committing a crime or offense against the other spouse or against the children of the marriage.

Chapter 15   CHILDREN IN COURT

by John E. B. Myers[1]

§ 15.1 Introduction

This chapter discusses children as witnesses and hearsay declarants. The following topics are addressed: suggestibility, testimonial competence, impact on children of testifying, techniques to help children testify, hearsay, and whether children should be in court during hearings.

§ 15.2 Suggestibility

This section summarizes findings of suggestibility research that are relevant to the investigation and litigation of child abuse.

§ 15.2.1 Age and Suggestibility

There is no simple relationship between age and suggestibility.[2] Thus, it is incorrect to say that a 4-year-old is invariably more suggestible than a 40-year-old. Suggestibility on a particular occasion depends on a host of situational, developmental, and personality factors, including the type of event, how well it is remembered, the type of information sought by the interviewer (*e.g.*, central details versus peripheral details), the way the interview is conducted and the language used, whether or not the questioner intimidates the subject, and a host of other influences before and during the interview.

As a group, young children, particularly children under age six, are more suggestible than older children and adults.[3] By the time children near adoles-

---

[1]   John E.B. Myers, J.D., is Professor of Law at University of the Pacific, McGeorge School of Law.

[2]   *See* MEMORY AND SUGGESTIBILITY IN THE FORENSIC INTERVIEW (Mitchell L. Eisen et al. eds.) (Mahwah, NJ: Lawrence Erlbaum Associates 2002); Gail S. Goodman & Beth M. Schwartz-Kenny, *Why Knowing a Child's Age is Not Enough: Influences of Cognitive, Social, and Emotional Factors on Children's Testimony, in* CHILDREN AS WITNESSES 15, 22 (Helen Dent & Rhona Flin eds.) (West Sussex: John Wiley & Sons 1992).

[3]   *See* Maggie Bruck et al., *I Hardly Cried When I Got My Shot!: Influencing Children's Reports About a Visit to Their Pediatrician*, 66 CHILD DEV. 193-208 (1995); Stephen J. Ceci & Mary Lyn Crotteau Huffman, *How Suggestible Are Preschool Children? Cognitive and Social Factors*, 36 J. AM. ACAD. OF CHILD & ADOLESCENT PSYCHIATRY 948-958 (1997); Jodi A. Quas et al., *Questioning the Child Witness: What Can We Conclude From the Research Thus Far?*, 1 TRAUMA, VIOLENCE & ABUSE 223, 225 (2000) ("Across studies of children's memory and suggestibility, the most consistent and robust predictor of differences in children's performance is age. Older children generally remember more than younger children do, and older children are

cence, most approach adult levels of suggestibility.[4] This is not to say, of course, that older children are not suggestible. The point is that with older children and adolescents, concerns about suggestibility are less acute.

Despite the fact that young children as a group are at increased risk of being misled by suggestive questions, preschoolers are not invariably suggestible.[5] Children can resist suggestive questions.[6] Stephen Ceci and his colleagues wrote, "when the adults who have access to preschool children do not attempt to usurp their memories through repeated suggestions over long intervals, even very young children do very well."[7] Gary Melton and his colleagues added, "Age does have some relation to suggestibility, but probably less than often has been assumed."[8] Jodi Quas and her colleagues wrote, "Although young children can be misled to report inaccurate information about their experiences, they are more resistant to false suggestions about negative and abuse-related activities than false suggestions about other never-experienced activities."[9]

---

less susceptible to false suggestion. However, young children still can and do remember their experiences."); Karen J. Saywitz, *Developmental Underpinnings of Children's Testimony, in* CHILDREN'S TESTIMONY: A HANDBOOK OF PSYCHOLOGICAL RESEARCH AND FORENSIC PRACTICE 3, 11 (Helen L. Westcott et al. eds.) (West Sussex, England: John Wiley & Sons 2002) ("Younger children (especially 3-5-year-olds) are much more suggestible than older children and older children are much less suggestible than younger ones."). *See also In re G.B.*, 838 A.2d 529, 530 n.1 (2004) ("children in the three- to four-year-old age group are most vulnerable to suggestions by the questioner").

[4] *See* Karen J. Saywitz & Lynn Snyder, *Improving Children's Testimony with Preparation, in* Gail S. Goodman & Bette L. Bottoms, CHILD VICTIMS, CHILD WITNESSES: UNDERSTANDING AND IMPROVING TESTIMONY (New York: Guilford Press 1993).

[5] *See* Gail S. Goodman et al., *Nearly Four Years After an Event: Children's Eyewitness Memory and Adults' Perceptions of Children's Accuracy*, 28 CHILD ABUSE & NEGLECT 849-884 (2002).

[6] *See* Elisa Krackow & Steven Jay Lynn, *Is There Touch in the Game of Twister? The Effects of Innocuous Touch and Suggestive Questions on Children's Eyewitness Memory*, 27 LAW & HUM. BEH. 589, 592 (2003) ("Studies of abused and nonabused children's responses to both stressful and nonstressful events have indicated that for the most part preschool children do not falsely assent to questions that imply they were touched."); Jodi A. Quas et al., *Individual Differences in Children's and Adults' Suggestibility and False Event Memory*, 9 LEARNING AND INDIVIDUAL DIFFERENCES 359-390 (1997).

[7] Stephen J. Ceci & Mary Lyn Crotteau Huffman, *How Suggestible Are Preschool Children? Cognitive and Social Factors*, 36 J. AM. ACAD. CHILD & ADOLESCENT PSYCHIATRY 948, 957 (1997) (original emphasis omitted).

[8] Gary B. Melton et al., *Empirical Research on Child Maltreatment and the Law*, 24 J. CLINICAL CHILD PSYCHOL. 47, 59 (1995).

[9] Jodi A. Quas et al., *Individual Differences in Children's and Adults' Suggestibility and False Event Memory*, 9 LEARNING & INDIVIDUAL DIFFERENCES 359, 362 (1997).

§ 15.2.2 Questioning by Authority Figures; The Social Demands of Interviews

Children are sometimes more suggestible when questioned by an authority figure.[10] Moreover, young children, particularly preschoolers, appear less able than older children to withstand the social demands of the interview.[11] Thus, because they find it difficult to "stand their ground" in the face of suggestive questions, young children are at greater risk of going along with the adult's suggestions.[12]

§ 15.2.3 Central Details vs. Peripheral Details

Children, like adults, are more likely to be suggestible about peripheral details of events than about central, salient, memorable details.[13] Child abuse is typically salient, and a child who is questioned about abuse may be less suggestible than a child questioned about an innocuous event.[14] Gail Goodman and Karen Saywitz wrote, "Children, similar to adults, are more likely to give incorrect reports and to be more suggestible about peripheral information than about more salient, memorable information. Abusive genital contact is likely to be a fairly salient event for a child, and therefore children are likely to be less suggestible about such actions."[15]

---

[10] *See* Michael E. Lamb et al., *Factors Influencing the Reliability and Validity of Statements Made by Young Victims of Sexual Maltreatment*, 15 J. APPLIED DEVELOPMENTAL PSYCHOL. 255, 265 (1994) ("Misleading or suggestive questioning can manipulate both young and old witnesses. Such questions are most likely to be influential when the memory is not rich or recent, when the questions themselves are so complicated that the witness is confused, and when the interviewer appears to have such authority or status that the witness feels compelled to accept his or her implied construction of events.").

[11] *See* William S. Cassel et al., *Developmental Patterns of Eyewitness Responses to Repeated and Increasingly Suggestive Questions*, 61 J. EXPERIMENTAL PSYCHOL. 116-133 (1996).

[12] *See* Gary B. Melton et al., *Empirical Research on Child Maltreatment and the Law*, 24 J. CLINICAL CHILD PSYCHOL. 47-77 (1995).

[13] *See* Michael E. Lamb et al., *Factors Influencing the Reliability and Validity of Statements Made by Young Victims of Sexual Maltreatment*, 15 J. APPLIED DEVELOPMENTAL PSYCHOL. 255, 264 (1994) ("there is agreement that suggestions are less likely to be effective when they pertain to central or salient details"); Gary B. Melton et al., *Empirical Research on Child Maltreatment and the Law*, 24 J. OF CLINICAL CHILD PSYCHOL. 47, 59 (1995) ("Generally, children are more resistant to suggestion about salient actions than peripheral details, including abuse-related events like physical assault or removal of clothes.").

[14] Gary B. Melton et al., *Empirical Research on Child Maltreatment and the Law*, 24 J. OF CLINICAL CHILD PSYCHOL. 47, 59 (1995) ("Generally, children are more resistant to suggestion about salient actions than peripheral details, including abuse-related events like physical assault or removal of clothes.").

[15] Gail S. Goodman & Karen J. Saywitz, *Memories of Abuse: Interviewing Children When Sexual Victimization is Suspected*, 3 CHILD AND ADOLESCENT PSYCHIATRIC CLINICS OF NORTH AMERICA 645, at 648 (1994).

§ 15.2.4 Ambiguous Body Touch

The touching involved in sexual abuse is sometimes ambiguous. For example, touching a young child's genitals may be entirely proper caretaking or a felony, depending on the intention of the adult. Young children may be particularly suggestible regarding acts that are ambiguous, especially when they are questioned by a biased interviewer.[16] A child who is unsure how to interpret an event—"good touch" or "bad touch"—may go along with an adult's interpretation.[17]

Although children may go along with suggestive questions about the *meaning* of ambiguous events, children are likely to be less suggestible regarding the facts they observed.[18] Thus, although a child might be led astray about the interpretation of an ambiguous event, the child is likely to be accurate about what happened.

§ 15.2.5 Participant vs. Bystander

Participating in an event, as opposed to watching from the sidelines, sometimes lowers suggestibility, probably because the participant has a stronger memory for the event.[19] Ann Tobey and Gail Goodman observed, "Participation can both strengthen children's recollections of an event and their ability to resist suggestion."[20]

§ 15.2.6 Negative Stereotypes and Accusatory Atmosphere

Interviewers should avoid creating an atmosphere that is accusatory regarding a particular person.[21] Nor should interviewers describe individuals in terms

---

[16] *See* William C. Thompson et al., *What Did the Janitor Do? Suggestive Interviewing and the Accuracy of Children's Accounts*, 21 L. & HUM. BEHAV. 405-426 (1997).

[17] *See* Karen J. Saywitz, *Developmental Underpinnings of Children's Testimony*, in CHILDREN'S TESTIMONY: A HANDBOOK OF PSYCHOLOGICAL RESEARCH AND FORENSIC PRACTICE 3, 9-10 (Helen L. Westcott et al. eds., 2002) ("One reason for heightened suggestibility is that young children are particularly deferential to adults' beliefs. Adults may convey their view of events to children through the question they ask, the comments they make, and through their demeanor. At an early age children recognize adults' superior knowledge base.").

[18] *See* Gail S. Goodman & Alison Clarke-Stewart, *Suggestibility in Children's Testimony: Implications for Sexual Abuse Investigations,* in THE SUGGESTIBILITY OF CHILDREN'S RECOLLECTIONS: IMPLICATIONS FOR EYEWITNESS TESTIMONY 92-105 (John Doris ed.) (Washington, D.C.: American Psychological Association 1991).

[19] *See* Gail S. Goodman et al., *Children's Concerns and Memory: Issues of Ecological Validity in the Study of Children's Eyewitness Testimony,* in KNOWING AND REMEMBERING IN YOUNG CHILDREN 249-284 (Robyn Fivush & Judith A. Hudson eds.) (New York: Cambridge University Press 1990).

[20] Ann E. Tobey & Gail S. Goodman, *Children's Eyewitness Memory: Effects of Participation and Forensic Context*, 16 CHILD ABUSE & NEGLECT 779, 792 (1992).

[21] For examples of how not to interview children, see *State v. Michaels*, 642 A.2d 1372, 1385, 1391 (1994) (presenting appendix to court's opinion containing portions of several interviews).

of negative stereotypes. Negative stereotypes and an accusatory atmosphere cause some interviewees—children and adults—to be suggestible regarding the object of the unflattering commentary.[22]

Ann Tobey and Gail Goodman examined the effect on non-abused four-year-old children of questioning by a police officer.[23] The children in the study played with a research assistant who was described to the children as a "baby sitter." Eleven days later, the children were interviewed about the experience. Some of the children were interviewed in a neutral fashion by a research assistant, while other children were interviewed by a police officer who said, "I am very concerned that something bad might have happened the last time that you were here. I think that the babysitter you saw here last time might have done some bad things, and I am trying to find out what happened the last time you were here when you played with the babysitter." Questioning by the police officer had a deleterious impact on some children's accuracy, although "only two children in the police condition seemed to be decisively misled by the police officer's suggestion that the babysitter may have done some bad things."[24]

Michelle Leichtman and Stephen Ceci designed an experiment to highlight the dangers of negative stereotypes during interviews of young children.[25] In this study, one group of preschool children was told on several occasions about a man named Sam Stone, who, according to the story, was very clumsy. Thus, the children were inculcated with a stereotype of a clumsy Sam Stone. Other children in the study did not receive this stereotyping information. Some time later, Sam Stone visited the children's preschool classroom. He stayed about two minutes, but did nothing clumsy or unusual. Following Sam Stone's uneventful visit to the classroom, the children in both groups were interviewed once a week for four successive weeks—some with leading questions—about Sam Stone's visit. The leading questions contained an implication that Sam ripped a book and soiled a teddy bear. Finally, at a fifth interview, the researchers examined the impact of leading questions on the children who had been told that Sam Stone was clumsy. Children who received the stereotyping message about Sam were more likely than other children to provide inaccurate information in response to leading questions. Leichtman and Ceci's study underscores the importance of avoiding interview practices that stereotype possible perpetrators.

---

[22] *See* Michelle D. Leichtman & Stephen J. Ceci, *The Effects of Stereotypes and Suggestions on Preschoolers' Reports*, 31 DEVELOPMENTAL PSYCHOL. 568-578 (1995).

[23] Ann E. Tobey & Gail S. Goodman, *Children's Eyewitness Memory: Effects of Participation and Forensic Context*, 16 CHILD ABUSE & NEGLECT 779-796 (1992).

[24] *Id.* at 790.

[25] *See* Michelle D. Leichtman & Stephen J. Ceci, *The Effects of Stereotypes and Suggestions on Preschoolers' Reports*, 31 DEVELOPMENTAL PSYCHOL. 568-578 (1995).

It is generally inappropriate for an interviewer to tell a child what others said about the suspect or the facts under investigation.[26] John Shaw and his colleagues used the term "co-witness information" to describe the situation in which interviewers tell interviewees what others said. Describing their research on "co-witness information," Shaw wrote, "As expected, co-witness information had an immediate impact on the accuracy of the participant-witness' memory reports. In all three experiments, when participants received incorrect information about co-witnesses' responses to a question just before they provided their own response to that same question, the participants were more likely to give the same incorrect responses as the co-witness (or co-witnesses) than they were if they received no co-witness information."[27]

§ 15.2.7 Lowering Suggestibility

Interviewers can lower children's suggestibility.[28] Children can be instructed to pay close attention and to report only what "really happened." Children can be informed that some questions may be difficult to understand, and that the child should not guess or make up answers. Helen Dent advises telling children that the interviewer does not know what happened, and that the child is free to say "I don't know."[29]

Karen Saywitz and her colleagues suggest that children be given instructions such as these: "There may be some questions that you do not know the answers to. That's okay. Nobody can remember everything. If you don't know the answer to a question, then tell me 'I don't know,' but do not make anything up. It is very important to tell me only what you really remember. Only what really happened." "If you do not want to answer some of the questions, you don't have to. That's okay. Tell me 'I don't want to answer that question.'" "If you don't know what something I ask you means, tell me 'I don't understand' or 'I don't know what you mean.' Tell me to say it in new words." "I may ask you some questions more than one time. Sometimes I forget that I already asked you that question. You don't have to change your answer, just tell me what you remember the best you can."[30] Statements like these are helpful during interviews. At trial,

---

[26] *See* John S. Shaw III et al., *Co-Witness Information Can Have Immediate Effects on Eyewitness Memory Reports*, 21 L. & HUM. BEHAV. 503-523 (1997).

[27] *Id.* at 516.

[28] *See* Kathy Pezdek & Jeolle Greene, *Testing Eyewitness Memory: Developing a Measure that is More Resistant to Suggestibility*, 17 L. & HUM. BEHAV. 361-369 (1993); Amye Warren et al., *Inducing Resistance to Suggestibility in Children*, 15 L. & HUM. BEHAV. 273-285 (1991).

[29] Helen R. Dent, *Experimental Studies of Interviewing Child Witnesses, in* THE SUGGESTIBILITY OF CHILDREN'S RECOLLECTIONS: IMPLICATIONS FOR EYEWITNESS TESTIMONY 138-146 (John Doris ed.) (Washington, D.C.: American Psychological Association 1991).

[30] Karen J. Saywitz et al., *Effects of Cognitive Interviewing and Practice on Children's Recall Performance*, 77 J. APPLIED PSYCHOL. 744-756 (1992).

however, an attorney should not tell a child, "If you don't want to answer, you don't have to."[31]

§ 15.3 Testimonial Competence

To testify, a child must possess:

* The capacity to observe.

* Sufficient intelligence.

* Adequate memory.

* Ability to communicate.

* Awareness of the difference between truth and falsehood.

* An appreciation of the obligation to tell the truth in court.[32]

A child of any age who possesses these characteristics may testify. There is no minimum age below which children are automatically disqualified as witnesses.

Rule 601 of the Federal Rules of Evidence provides, "Every person is competent to be a witness except as otherwise provided in these rules."[33] A majority of states have adopted the Federal Rules, including Rule 601. In states that have not adopted the Federal Rules, evidence codes generally provide that competence is presumed. Thus, California Evidence Code Section 700 provides that "every person, irrespective of age, is qualified to be a witness."[34] New York Criminal Procedure Law Section 60.20 states that "[a]ny person may be a witness in a criminal proceeding."[35] A small number of states (*e.g.*, Missouri) retain the older view that children below a specified age (*e.g.*, 10 or 12) are presumed incompetent until the contrary is established.[36] In Federal Court, Section 3509(c) of Title 18 provides: "A child is presumed to be competent."[37] Despite Rule 601's pronouncement that "every person is competent to be a witness," trial judges have authority to hold competency examinations when legitimate questions arise about testimonial competence.

---

[31] *See In re Pers. Restraint Petition of Grasso*, 84 P.3d 859 (Wash. 2004).

[32] *See Walters v. McCormick*, 108 F.3d 1165 (9th Cir. 1997); *State v. Pham*, 75 Wash. App. 626, 879 P.2d 321 (1994) ("The age of the child is not determinative of his or her capacity as a witness").

[33] FED. R. EVID. 601.

[34] CAL. EVID. CODE § 700.

[35] N.Y. CRIM. PROC. LAW § 60.20.

[36] MO. REV. STAT. § 491.060(2) (2004); PA. STAT. ANN. tit. 42 § 5911.

[37] 18 U.S.C. § 3509(c)(2).

§ 15.3.1 Capacity to Observe

To testify, a child must have the physical and mental capacity to observe. Courts sometimes refer to this as the ability to receive correct impressions by the senses.[38] Children's observational capacity develops rapidly during the first year of life, and the capacity to observe almost never poses a barrier to testimony.

§ 15.3.2 Memory

Children have good memory capacity, and the capability to recall events should almost never pose a barrier to testimonial competence. Whether a child's memory for particular events is accurate is a matter of credibility, not testimonial competence.[39]

§ 15.3.3 Capacity to Communicate

To be competent as a witness, a child must be able to communicate so as to be understood. In nearly all cases, children possess the capacity to communicate.

§ 15.3.4 Intelligence

To testify, a witness must possess a threshold level of intelligence. Normal intelligence is not required for testimonial competence, and children with below-average intelligence may testify if they possess the ability to observe, recollect, and relate in a manner that assists the trier of fact.[40]

§ 15.3.5 Understanding the Difference Between Truth and Falsehood

To testify, a child must understand the difference between truth and falsehood.[41] The child need not comprehend the finer points of truth and falsity, nor must the child understand the concept of perjury.[42] The child may articulate the necessary understanding in childlike terms. The fact that a child makes mistakes

---

[38] *See State v. Earl*, 252 Neb. 127, 560 N.W.2d 491 (1997); *State v. Segerberg*, 131 Conn. 546, 41 A.2d 101, 102 (1945) ("The principle…is that the child shall be sufficiently mature to receive correct impressions by her senses…"); *State v. Guy*, 227 Neb. 610, 419 N.W.2d 152, 155 (1988) (trial court must determine whether child is sufficiently mature to receive correct impressions by senses).

[39] *See* Robyn Fivush & Jennifer R. Shukat, *Content, Consistency, and Coherence of Early Autobiographical Recall, in* MEMORY AND TESTIMONY IN THE CHILD WITNESS 5-23 (Maria S. Zaragoza et al. eds., 1995) (Thousand Oaks, CA: Sage Publications). *See also United States v. Frederick*, 78 F. 3d 1370 (9th Cir. 1996).

[40] *See United States v. Benn*, 476 F.2d 1127 (D.C. Cir. 1972).

[41] Bett N. Gordon et al., *Remembering Activities Performed Versus Those Imagined: Implications for Testimony of Children with Mental Retardation*, 23 J. OF CLINICAL CHILD PSYCHOL. 239, 248 (1994).

[42] *See Ricketts v. State*, 488 A.2d 856, 857 (Del. 1985) (six-year-old who did not understand concept of perjury, but knew difference between truth and falsehood, was found competent to testify).

or is to some degree inconsistent does not render the child incompetent.[43] When judges and attorneys use developmentally appropriate methods to question children, most youngsters demonstrate the necessary understanding.

Although children understand the difference between truth and lies, judges and attorneys are sometimes not very good at eliciting children's understanding. Three techniques are commonly employed to question children about truth and falsehood. First, the adult may ask the child to define the truth and a lie. For example, the adult might ask, "What is the truth?" Although a young child probably understands the difference, the child may not be able to define truth and lies. Thus, it is generally advisable to avoid asking young children questions like, "What is the truth?" or "What is a lie?" Many young children find it difficult to generate examples of truthful statements and lies. Second, judges and attorneys sometimes ask young children to explain the difference between the truth and a lie. Explaining the difference between things presupposes understanding of the word "difference." Moreover, even if a child understands the word "difference," explaining the difference between truth and lies is linguistically and cognitively challenging. Although many children perform well on this task, others who know the difference between truth and falsehood stumble over providing a self-generated explanation. The third approach to questioning young children about truth and lies is more closely attuned to children's developmental capabilities. Rather than ask the child to define truth and lie, or to explain the difference, the adult provides simple examples of lies and truthful statements, and asks the child to identify them. Children as young as three perform well on this task. Thus, the adult might say, "Sally, if I told you this pen is blue, would that be the truth or a lie?" or "Billy, take a look at the shirt I'm wearing. If I said this shirt is green, would that be the truth or a lie?"

§ 15.3.6 Duty to Testify Truthfully

To testify, a child must understand the duty to tell the truth in court.[44] Children as young as three and four comprehend the duty to tell the truth. For young children, telling the truth means reporting what they saw. If the judge is concerned about a child's understanding of the obligation to testify truthfully, the judge may instruct the child.[45]

In addition to understanding the obligation to tell the truth, a child must realize that untruthful testimony can result in punishment.[46] By age three or four,

---

[43] *See People v. Norfleet,* 142 Mich. App. 745, 371 N.W.2d 438 (1985); *State v. Ybarra,* 24 N.M. 413, 174 P.212, 214 (1918); *State v. Pettis,* 488 A.2d 704, 706 (R.I. 1985).

[44] *See Richardson v. State,* 33 Ark. App. 128, 803 S.W.2d 557 (1991); *Hester v. State,* 187 Ga. App. 873, 371 S.E.2d 684, 685 (1988); *Hodges v. State,* 524 N.E.2d 774, 780 (Ind. 1988).

[45] *See Hester v. State,* 187 Ga. App. 873, 371 S.E.2d 684, 685 (1988).

[46] 2 JOHN H. WIGMORE, EVIDENCE IN TRIALS AT COMMON LAW § 506, at 513.

children understand they can be punished for lying. It is not necessary that the child understand or believe in divine punishment for false swearing. Nor must the child comprehend the concept of perjury. The anticipated punishment may come from any source, including God, the judge, or a parent, and the child may describe the punishment in childlike terms.[47]

§ 15.3.7 Burden of Proof Regarding Testimonial Competence

In jurisdictions where "every person is competent to be a witness,"[48] the party challenging a child's competence has the burden of establishing incompetence.[49] The opponent of a child's testimony must make timely objection.[50] Failure to object constitutes a waiver unless permitting the child to testify was plain error.[51] In the small number of jurisdictions where children below a specified age are presumed incompetent, the proponent of a child below the specified age has the burden of rebutting the presumption.[52]

§ 15.3.8 Oath or Affirmation

To testify, a witness must take a religious oath or a secular affirmation. The oath or affirmation is "calculated to awaken the witness' conscience and impress the witness' mind with the duty" to tell the truth.[53] A judge may question a child to ascertain the child's understanding of the oath.[54] A child need not define the word "oath." Most children are unable to define "oath" until adolescence. A childlike understanding of the oath and the consequences of untruthful testimony are permissible.[55] No particular form of words is required for an oath.[56] The judge or clerk may simplify the language of the oath, and may take the time to

---

[47] *See. State v. Dunn*, 731 S.W.2d 297, 301 (Mo. Ct. App. 1987); *State v. Higginbottom*, 312 N.C. 760, 324 S.E.2d 834, 839 (1985).

[48] FED. R. EVID. 601.

[49] *See Mitchell v. State*, 473 So. 2d. 591, 596 (Ala. Crim. App. 1985); *Richardson v. State*, 33 Ark. App. 128, 803 S.W.2d 557, 559 (1991). *See also* 18 U.S.C. § 3509(c)(3) (in federal court, party opposing child's competency must file written motion and offer proof of incompetency).

[50] FED. R. EVID. 103(a)(1); *see also* 81 AM. JUR. 2D WITNESSES § 134, at 175-176 (1976).

[51] FED. R. EVID 103(d); *see also People v. Burton*, 55 Cal. 2d 328, 359 P.2d 433, 11 Cal. Rptr. 65 (1961); *State v Gordon*, 316 N.C. 497, 342 S.E.2d 509, 511-512 (1986).

[52] *See, e.g.,* PA. STAT. ANN. tit. 42 § 5911; *see* COLO. REV. STAT. § 13-90-106(b) and MO. ANN. STAT. § 491.060(2) (children under the age of ten who appear incapable of receiving just impressions and relating them truly are incompetent except in child abuse cases, in which all child victims are competent).

[53] FED. R. EVID. 603.

[54] 6 JOHN H. WIGMORE, EVIDENCE IN TRIALS AT COMMON LAW § 1821, at 406.

[55] *See Huggins v. State*, 184 Ga. App. 540, 362 S.E.2d 120 (1987); *In re Ralph D.*, 557 N.Y.S.2d 1003, 1005 (App. Div. 1990).

[56] *See* CAL. EVID. CODE § 710; COLO. REV. STAT. § 13-90-117.5 (1990).

ensure complete understanding.[57] Several states have statutes allowing children to testify without an oath.[58]

An affirmation is a secular undertaking to testify truthfully. As with an oath, an affirmation may take any form calculated to awaken the child's conscience and impress the child with the duty to tell the truth.[59]

§ 15.4 The Effects of Testifying on Children: Psychological Research

Psychologists began studying the effects of testifying on children in the 1980s. Based on the empirical work to date, "no agreement has been reached as to whether the effect of testimony on children is positive or negative."[60] Desmond Runyan and his colleagues found that for some children, testifying in juvenile court is a positive experience.[61] Runyan concluded that juvenile court "testimony may improve the child's sense of control and treat the sense of powerlessness induced by the abuse." Gail Goodman and her colleagues followed 218 children during the two years it took their sexual abuse cases to progress through Denver, Colorado's criminal justice system.[62] Of the children who testified, "On average, the short-term effects on the children's behavioral adjustments, as reported by their caretakers, were more harmful than helpful. In contrast, by the time the cases were resolved, the behavioral adjustment of most, but not all, children who testified was similar to that of children who did not take the stand. The general course for these children, as for the control children, was gradual improvement." Debra Whitcomb and her colleagues reviewed research up to 1994 and wrote, "Virtually all of the children improved emotionally, regardless of their experiences in court. At worst, testifying may impede the improvement process for some children; at best, it may enhance their recovery."[63]

§ 15.5 While Children are on the Witness Stand

Certain factors help children cope with testifying. These are discussed below.

---

[57] *See State v. Dwyer*, 149 Wis. 2d 850, 440 N.W.2d 344, 347 (1989); *In re R.R.*, 79 N.J. 97, 398 A.2d 76, 83 (1979).

[58] FLA. STAT. ANN. § 90.605(2); N.Y. CRIM. PROC. LAW § 60.20.

[59] FED. R. EVID. 603.

[60] *See* Comm. on Psychosocial Aspects of Child & Family Health, Am. Acad. of Pediatrics, *The Child in Court: A Subject Review*, 104 PEDIATRICS 1145, 1146 (1999).

[61] Desmond K. Runyan et al., *Impact of Legal Intervention on Sexually Abused Children*, 113 J. PEDIATRICS 647, 652 (1988).

[62] Gail S. Goodman et al., *Testifying in Criminal Court*, 57 MONOGRAPHS SOC'Y FOR RES. CHILD DEV. 1–141 (1992).

[63] U.S. DEP'T OF JUSTICE, DEBRA WHITCOMB ET AL., THE EMOTIONAL EFFECTS OF TESTIFYING ON SEXUALLY ABUSED CHILDREN 5 (Research in Brief NCJ 146414, 1994).

§ 15.5.1 Emotional Support

Children who have emotional support are more likely to cope well with testifying than children lacking such support. Children benefit from the supportive presence of a non-offending parent, loved one, or victim advocate. Children who are emotionally supported while testifying are often better able to cope with the stress of facing the accused. On direct examination, emotionally supported children may be better able to answer questions than children lacking support. During cross-examination, emotionally supported children tend to provide more consistent testimony. In sum, emotional support helps children testify.

§ 15.5.2 Preparing Children to Testify

Preparing children to testify lowers their stress, increases their capacity to answer questions, and helps them understand the nature and seriousness of the proceeding.

§ 15.5.3 Scheduling a Young Child's Testimony

Young children perform best when they are rested. Up to age five, many children nap in the afternoon. A young child's testimony should be scheduled to accommodate naptime. Testifying in the morning is a good solution for many young children. With school-age children, it is usually best to schedule testimony during school hours. Few children are dismayed at the prospect of missing a little school. More importantly, a child who testifies following a full school day is tired and has spent the day worrying about going to court. It is better to take the child's testimony early in the day.

§ 15.5.4 Leading on Direct

Traditional practice restricts leading questions on direct examination. Rule 611(c) of the Federal Rules of Evidence provides, "Leading questions should not be used on the direct examination of a witness except as may be necessary to develop the witness' testimony."[64] Courts allow leading on direct regarding preliminary and undisputed matters (*e.g.*, name, address, relationship to the events or parties). Leading is often permitted to introduce new topics or to rekindle memory. The judge may allow leading questions on embarrassing topics. Judges routinely permit leading questions during the direct examination of children who experience difficulty testifying due to fear, timidity, embarrassment, confusion, or reluctance. The better practice is to begin with nonleading questions and to move to leading questions if the child is unable to proceed.

---

[64] FED. R. EVID. 611(c).

§ 15.5.5 Testimonial Aids

Many children can show what they cannot tell, and children may use dolls or other props to help them testify. Anatomical dolls are helpful to illustrate penetration. It is not necessary that a child be completely unable to testify before using a testimonial aid. The question is whether the aid will assist the child to describe events.

§ 15.5.6 Allowing a Child Witness a Comfort Item

Many children derive comfort from a favorite toy, stuffed animal, or blanket, and children should be permitted to bring their particular favorite with them to the witness stand.

§ 15.5.7 Recesses During Child's Testimony

Judges have discretion to recess the proceedings during a child's testimony, and should do so when a child shows signs of fatigue, loss of concentration, or unmanageable stress. It is not sufficient to tell a child, "If you want a break, just ask." Children will not take the initiative to request a recess. Moreover, young children have difficulty monitoring their own needs. A five-year-old is more likely to stop answering questions or cry than to ask for a rest. Responsibility falls on the court and counsel to monitor the child's needs.

Recesses during direct examination pose few problems. Interruptions during cross-examination are another matter, although it is during cross-examination that children often are most uncomfortable and in need of rest. The court has authority to recess the proceedings at reasonable intervals during cross-examination.[65] To avoid the complainant that recesses interfere with cross-examination, the court may inform counsel ahead of time that recesses will occur at regular intervals, for example, every 20 minutes.

§ 15.6 Hearsay

Hearsay is important in child abuse litigation for three reasons:

- The child's out-of-court statements are often powerful evidence of abuse.

- In many cases, the importance of the child's out-of-court statements is magnified by a paucity of physical evidence and eyewitnesses.

- Although most children have the capacity to testify, some children are ineffective witnesses, and some cannot take the stand at all.

---

[65] *See State v. Hillman*, 613 So.2d 1053, 1058-1059 (La. Ct. App. 1993).

§ 15.6.1 Hearsay Defined

Rule 801(c) of the Federal Rules of Evidence defines hearsay as "a statement, other than one made by the declarant while testifying at the trial or hearing, offered in evidence to prove the truth of the matter asserted."[66] For hearsay purposes, a "statement" is an oral or written assertion or nonverbal conduct that is intended as an assertion.[67] A child makes an assertion when the child speaks, writes, acts, or fails to act with the intent to express some fact or opinion. Nonverbal conduct intended as an assertion is hearsay when offered to prove the matter asserted.[68] Suppose, for example, that a physician who is examining a child for possible sexual abuse asks, "Did anyone touch you in your private parts?" The child nods her head up and down. This nonverbal conduct is the equivalent of words and is hearsay when offered to prove that the child was touched.

An out-of-court statement is hearsay only if it is offered to prove the truth of the matter asserted. If a statement is offered for some other purpose, it is not hearsay. Suppose a four-year-old makes the following out-of-court statement, "Daddy's private was hard, and white pee came out that tasted really yucky." If this disturbing statement is offered for the truth of the matter asserted, it is hearsay. If the child's statement meets the requirements of an exception to the hearsay rule, the statement is admissible for the truth. Even if the statement does not fall within an exception, it may be admissible if it is relevant for some purpose other than proving the truth of the matter asserted. The child's statement demonstrates sexual knowledge one would not expect in a four-year-old, and developmentally unusual sexual knowledge can constitute circumstantial evidence of sexual abuse. Offered to prove sexual knowledge, the statement is not hearsay because it is not offered for the truth. A second non-hearsay use of a child's out-of-court statement is to establish the timing and circumstances in which a child reported abuse. Third, a child's out-of-court statement may reveal knowledge of a place, person, or thing that the child could not know unless the child had prior contact with the place, person, or thing. Finally, children's out-of-court statements are sometimes offered to establish why the police or social services began an investigation. The problem with the latter use of out-of-court statements is that, in most circumstances, the reason for the investigation is irrelevant.

§ 15.6.2 Exceptions to the Hearsay Rule

Although there are many exceptions to the hearsay rule, only a handful play a day-to-day role in child abuse and neglect litigation. Relevant exceptions are briefly described below.

---

[66] FED. R. EVID. 801(c).

[67] FED. R. EVID. 801(c).

[68] *See State v. Hall*, 946 P.2d 712 (Utah Ct. App. 1997); MUELLER & KIRKPATRICK, FEDERAL EVIDENCE § 369 (2d ed. 1995) (Rochester, N.Y.: Lawyers Cooperative); *see also State v. Egger*, 8 Neb. App. 740, 601 N.W.2d 785 (1999).

Prior Inconsistent Statements

A witness's testimony may be impeached with evidence that the witness told a different story prior to testifying.[69] When a prior inconsistent statement is used solely to impeach, it is not offered for the truth of the matter asserted, and is not hearsay.[70] A prior inconsistent statement that is offered both to impeach and for the truth is hearsay.[71]

Under the Federal Rules of Evidence, prior inconsistent statements are generally admissible to impeach. However, only a limited class of prior inconsistent statements are admissible for the truth as well as to impeach. Under Federal Rule 801(d)(1)(A), only prior inconsistent statements that were "given under oath subject to the penalty of perjury at a trial, hearing, or other proceeding, or in a deposition"[72] are admissible for the truth of the matter asserted. In some states, all or nearly all prior inconsistent statements are admissible for the truth of the matter asserted as well as to impeach.[73]

Prior Consistent Statements

Prior consistent statements that are admitted solely to rehabilitate a witness's credibility are not offered for the truth, and are not hearsay.[74] When a prior consistent statement is offered for the truth as well as to rehabilitate, it is hearsay. States have hearsay exceptions for prior consistent statements. Rule 801(d)(1)(B) of the Federal Rules of Evidence governs admissibility of prior consistent statements offered for the truth in federal court, and provides: "A statement is not hearsay if . . . [t]he declarant testifies at the trial or hearing and is subject to cross-examination concerning the statement, and the statement is . . . consistent with the declarant's testimony and is offered to rebut an express or implied charge against the declarant of recent fabrication or improper influence or motive."[75]

---

[69] *State v. Gomez*, 131 N.M. 118, 33 P.3d 669 (Ct. App. 2001). *See United States v. Hale*, 422 U.S. 171, 176 (1975) ("a basic rule of evidence provides that prior inconsistent statements may be used to impeach the credibility of a witness"); *Commonwealth v. Brown*, 538 Pa. 410, 648 A.2d 1177, 1185 (1994).

[70] *State v. Patterson*, 742 So.2d 50 (La. Ct. App. 1999) (discussion of foundation for impeachment with prior inconsistent statement); *State v. Wood*, 126 Idaho 241, 880 P.2d 771, 778 (Ct. App. 1994).

[71] *See People v. Sambo*, 197 Ill. App. 3d 574, 554 N.E.2d 1080, 1086 (1990); *State v. Mancine*, 124 N.J. 232, 590 A.2d 1107 (1991).

[72] FED. R. EVID. 801(d)(1)(A).

[73] *See* CAL. EVID. CODE § 1235 (West); 725 ILL. COMP. STAT. 5/115-10.1; N.J. R. EVID. 803(a)(1). *See also State v. Borrelli*, 227 Conn. 153, 629 A.2d 1105 (1993).

[74] MCCORMICK ON EVIDENCE § 49, at 118 (Edward W. Leary ed., 1984) (St. Paul, Minn.: West).

[75] FED. R. EVID. 801(d)(1)(B).

To gain admission as a prior consistent statement, an out-of-court statement must be consistent with trial testimony. The prior statement does not have to be identical to trial testimony. Some children disclose abuse gradually, revealing additional details over time. A child's trial testimony may contain more, less, or slightly different information than out-of-court disclosures. If the gist of the child's out-of-court statements is consistent with the child's trial testimony, the out-of-court statements are consistent.

Rehabilitation with prior consistent statements must await impeachment. The following modes of impeachment can open the door for rehabilitation with prior consistent statements.

Charge of Fabrication

An express or implied assertion that a witness's testimony is fabricated paves the way for rehabilitation with prior consistent statements. When the witness is a child, the cross-examiner may suggest that the child was coached during questioning by parents, police, social workers, or an attorney.

When the cross-examiner asserts fabrication, the majority rule is that prior consistent statements are admissible only if they were uttered before the motive or pressure to fabricate arose.[76] The logic of the "prior to motive" rule is that consistent statements uttered before there was a motive to fabricate have rehabilitative value, while statements uttered after the motive to fabricate arose lack rehabilitative value. Sometimes it is difficult to tell when an alleged improper influence or motive to fabricate arose. When the impeaching attorney concentrates heavily on fabrication, the need for rehabilitation increases, and courts are more likely to admit prior consistent statements despite uncertainty regarding when the influence or motive arose.

Impeachment by Contradiction

Impeachment by contradiction sometimes triggers rehabilitation with prior consistent statements, especially when the cross-examiner implies fabrication.

Impeachment by Evidence of Untruthful Character

Most authorities hold that impeachment that attacks a witness's character for truthfulness (*e.g.*, impeachment by conviction (Rule 609))[77] or specific acts of

---

[76] *See Tome v. United States*, 513 U.S. 150, 156, 115 S.Ct. 696, 700 (1995) ("The prevailing common-law rule for more than a century before adoption of the Federal Rules of Evidence was that a prior consistent statement introduced to rebut a charge of recent fabrication or improper influence or motive was admissible if the statement had been made before the alleged fabrication, influence, or motive came into being, but it was inadmissible if made afterwards."); *Noel v. Commonwealth*, 76 S.W.3d 923, 928 (Ky. 2002); *Commonwealth v. Cruz*, 53 Mass. App. Ct. 393, 759 N.E.2d 723 (2001).

[77] FED. R. EVID. 609.

untruthfulness (Rule 608(b))[78] does not trigger rehabilitation with prior consistent statements.[79]

Impeachment with Prior Inconsistent Statements

Impeachment by a prior inconsistent statement sometimes amounts to a charge of fabrication, triggering rehabilitation with prior consistent statements.

Impeachment Charging Lapse of Memory

The cross-examiner sometimes hopes to undermine a child's testimony by implying that the child's memory is faulty. The impeaching attorney emphasizes inconsistencies between the child's trial testimony and earlier statements on the theory that the earlier statements were accurate and the child's memory faded in the interim. Faced with such impeachment, courts often admit prior consistent statements uttered close in time to the event, when the child's memory was fresh.[80]

Present Sense Impressions

Rule 803(1) of the Federal Rules of Evidence creates a hearsay exception for "[a] statement describing or explaining an event or condition made while the declarant was perceiving the event or condition, or immediately thereafter."[81] The present sense impression exception has three requirements:

- The declarant must perceive an event or condition. The event need not be startling or shocking, and the declarant need not be a participant in the event.

- The statement must describe or explain the perceived event.[82]

- The statement must be made while the declarant was perceiving the event or condition, or immediately afterwards.[83]

---

[78] Fed. R. Evid. 608(b).

[79] *See* McCormick on Evidence § 49, at 118 (Edward W. Leary ed., 1984) (St. Paul, Minn.: West); Mueller & Kirkpatrick, Federal Evidence § 406, at 186-187 (2d ed. 1995) (Rochester, N.Y.: Lawyers Cooperative).

[80] *State v. Bakken*, 604 N.W.2d 106 (Minn. Ct. App. 2000); *Applebaum v. American Export Isbrandsten Lines*, 472 F.2d 56, 61-62 (2d Cir. 1972); *United States v. Keller*, 145 F. Supp. 692, 697 (D.N.J. 1956); *State v. Bruggeman*, 161 Ariz. 508, 779 P.2d 823, 825 (Ct. App. 1989).

[81] Fed. R. Evid. 803(1).

[82] *See United States v. Portsmouth Paving Corp.*, 694 F.2d 312, 323 (4th Cir. 1982) ("We perceive events with our ears as much as with our eyes...").

[83] Mueller & Kirkpatrick, Federal Evidence § 434, at 387 (2d ed. 1995) (Rochester, N.Y.: Lawyers Cooperative).

The time element is strict. A statement made during the event qualifies.[84] Difficulty arises when the statement is uttered shortly after the event. A few moments delay between the event and the statement should not disqualify a statement as a present sense impression. When delay extends into minutes, however, the statement is not a present sense impression.[85]

Excited Utterances

The excited utterance exception is codified at Rule 803(2) of the Federal Rules of Evidence,[86] and provides that the hearsay rule does not exclude statements relating to a startling event made while the declarant was under the stress of excitement caused by the event. The rationale for the excited utterance exception is that statements made under the stress of a startling event are unlikely to be the product of conscious reflection or fabrication.

The excited utterance exception has three requirements:

- There must be a startling or exciting event.

- The out-of-court statement must relate to the event.

- The statement must be made while the child is under the stress of excitement induced by the event.[87]

To determine whether the child was under the stress of excitement when the statement was made, courts consider the following factors: spontaneity of the statement, nature of the event, type of questions used to elicit the statement, how much time elapsed between the startling event and the child's statement, the child's emotional and physical condition when the statement was made (*e.g.*, child crying, physically injured, or in pain), the words spoken that may indicate excitement, pressured or hurried speech that may indicate excitement, and the child's age.[88]

---

[84] *Territory of Guam v. Ignacio*, 10 F.3d 608 (9th Cir. 1993) (three-year-old's statement during bath that her vaginal area hurt was admissible as present sense impression); *State v. Perry*, 95 N.M. 179, 619 P.2d 855 (Ct. App. 1980) (rape of adult took place in motel room; declarant in neighboring room heard victim scream and called motel office to complain about noise; declarant's statement to manager was admitted as present sense impression); *Walton v. Elftman*, 64 Ohio Misc. 45, 410 N.E.2d 1282, 1286 (1980) (in an auto accident case, where a child riding in one car involved "exclaimed at about the time of the impact, 'The blue car could not stop'" the child's exclamation was properly admitted as present sense impression).

[85] *See Hilyer v. Howat Concrete Co.*, 578 F.2d 422, 426 n.7 (D.C. Cir. 1978) (delay of 15 to 45 minutes too long); *Tucker v. State*, 264 Ark. 890, 575 S.W.2d 684, 685 (1979).

[86] FED. R. EVID. 803(2).

[87] FED. R. EVID. 803(2). *See also* MUELLER & KIRKPATRICK, FEDERAL EVIDENCE § 435, at 390 (2d ed. 1995) (Rochester, N.Y.: Lawyers Cooperative).

[88] *Barnett v. State*, 757 So. 2d 323 (Miss. Ct. App. 2000). *See United States v. Renville*, 779 F.2d 430, 440 (8th Cir. 1985); *People v. Hackney*, 183 Mich. App. 516, 455 N.W.2d 358, 362 (1990).

Fresh Complaint of Rape or Sexual Abuse

In rape and sexual assault prosecutions, it has long been the law that when the victim testifies, her fresh complaint of rape or sexual assault is admissible to support her credibility.[89] With the exception of Tennessee,[90] the fresh complaint doctrine applies when the victim is a child. The fresh complaint doctrine is not found in the Federal Rules of Evidence or in most state evidence codes, although several states have statutes codifying the doctrine.

The fresh complaint doctrine is based on the idea that evidence of the victim's complaint is needed to forestall jurors from improperly discounting the victim's trial testimony. Some jurors believe that a victim of rape or sexual assault will naturally report the crime shortly after it occurs. Unless such jurors are informed that the victim spoke out promptly, these jurors may infer that no report was made and, since no report was made, no crime occurred.

Although a fresh complaint is an out-of-court statement, it is not hearsay. The report is not admitted for the truth, but to corroborate the victim's testimony. A few decisions and statutes define fresh complaint evidence as hearsay within an exception.[91]

Fresh complaint evidence is admissible during the state's case-in-chief. As a general rule, the victim must testify before a fresh complaint is admissible. Impeachment is not a condition precedent to admission of the victim's fresh complaint. Under the traditional view, evidence of fresh complaint is limited to the statement of complaint. Details are not admissible. The court may permit more than one fresh complaint witness. As the name suggests, the fresh complaint doctrine requires a complaint to be made promptly.[92] A complaint satisfies this requirement if it is made within a reasonable time. Delay in reporting may be explained.[93]

---

[89] *See* Russel M. Coombs, *Reforming New Jersey Evidence Law on Fresh Complaint of Rape*, 25 RUT. LJ 699 (1994); Michael H. Graham, *The Cry of Rape: The Prompt Complaint Doctrine and the Federal Rules of Evidence*, 19 WILLAMETTE L. REV. 489-512 (1983). *See also State v. Dabkowski*, 199 Conn. 193, 506 A.2d 118 (1986).

[90] *Ruff v. State*, 978 S.W.2d 95 (Tenn. 1998); *State v. Speck*, 944 S.W.2d 598 (Tenn. 1997).

[91] *State v. Joel H.*, 755 A.2d 520 (Me. 2000). *See Commonwealth v. Bailey*, 370 Mass. 388, 348 N.E.2d 746 (1976); *State v. Sanders*, 691 S.W.2d 566, 568 (Tenn. Crim. App. 1984) (statements by five-year-old victim "were admissible under the fresh complaint exception to the hearsay rule"); OR. EVID. CODE 803(18a); LOUISIANA CODE EVID. 801(D)(1)(d).

[92] *See People v. Baggett*, 185 Ill. App. 3d 1007, 541 N.E. 2d 1266, 1273 (1989); *Commonwealth v. Lamontagne*, 42 Mass. App. 213, 675 N.E.2d 1169 (1997); *Commonwealth v. Swain*, 36 Mass. App. Ct. 433, 632 N.E.2d 848 (1994).

[93] *Brown v. Commonwealth*, 37 Va. App. 169, 554 S.E.2d 711 (2001) (two-year delay in reporting was not unreasonable given the circumstances of this case); *Folse v. Folse*, 738 So. 2d 1040 (La. 1999); *State v. Marshall*, 246 Conn. 799, 717 A.2d 1224 (1998).

Diagnosis or Treatment Exception

Certain hearsay statements that are made for purposes of obtaining a diagnosis or treatment are admissible under Federal Rule of Evidence 803(4) and similar state rules. The rationale for the diagnosis or treatment exception is that statements to secure diagnosis or treatment are reliable because the declarant has an incentive to be truthful with the doctor or nurse.

Do young children understand the importance of telling the truth to the doctor or nurse? Psychologists have studied children's understanding of illness, medical care, and the role of medical professionals. As one would expect, children's understanding follows a developmental progression.[94] In general, the understanding of older children about illness and its causes is more complex than that of younger children. Yet, even some very young children have the capacity to meet the medical hearsay exception. Assessment of children's understanding should proceed case-by-case.

Not everything that is said to a doctor or nurse is admissible under the medical diagnosis or treatment exception. The exception reaches only statements that are "pertinent" to diagnosis or treatment. Any information that assists a professional in reaching diagnostic or treatment decisions is pertinent. The exception includes statements describing past as well as present symptoms. Thus, the patient's medical history is admissible under the exception. The exception also embraces the patient's description of the cause of illness or injury. In child abuse litigation, most courts hold that a child's statement identifying the perpetrator can be pertinent to diagnosis or treatment, and admissible under the exception. Most courts admit selected statements to mental health professionals.

Residual and Child Hearsay Exceptions

The Rule 807 of the Federal Rules of Evidence contains an exception[95] for reliable hearsay that does not fall within one of the traditional exceptions. This is the so-called residual or catch-all exception. Of states that have adopted the Federal Rules, a majority has a version of the residual exception. In addition to a residual exception, most states have a special catch-all exception for children's hearsay in child abuse cases.

When hearsay is offered under a residual or child hearsay exception, the primary issue usually is whether the hearsay is sufficiently reliable. In criminal

[94] *See* Janice L. Genevro, Carol J. Andreassen, & Marc H. Bornstein, *Young Children's Understanding of Routine Medical Care and Strategies for Coping with Stressful Medical Experiences*, in CHILD DEVELOPMENT AND BEHAVIORAL PEDIATRICS 59-83 (Marc H. Bornstein & Janice L. Genervo eds., 1996) (Mahwah, N.J.: Lawrence Erlbaum). *See also* Pamela M. Kato, Thomas D. Lyon, & Christina Rasco, *Reasoning About Moral Aspects of Illness and Treatment by Preschoolers Who Are Healthy or Who Have Chronic Illness*, 19 DEVELOPMENTAL AND BEHAV. PEDIATRICS 68 (1998).

[95] FED. R. EVID. 807.

cases, the starting place for analysis of reliability is the U.S. Supreme Court's decision in *Idaho v. Wright*.[96] In that case, the Supreme Court ruled that under the Confrontation Clause of the Sixth Amendment, reliability is assessed in light of "the totality of the circumstances." Yet, the Court divided this totality into two categories: (1) circumstances "that surround the making of the statement and that render the declarant particularly worthy of belief;" and (2) circumstances that corroborate the statement but do not surround it. The Court ruled that the Confrontation Clause allows judges assessing reliability to consider circumstances that surround the statement, but forbids consideration of corroborating evidence such as medical or physical evidence of abuse, the defendant's opportunity to commit the offense, or the testimony of another witness identifying the defendant as the perpetrator.

In civil litigation, including dependency cases in juvenile court, the Sixth Amendment Confrontation Clause does not apply. One can argue that *Idaho v. Wright*'s[97] distinction between immediately surrounding factors and corroborating factors is inapplicable in civil cases, and that the court may consider all factors shedding light on reliability, including corroborating factors.

A judge evaluating the reliability of hearsay offered under a residual or child hearsay exception considers the following factors:

- Whether the child was testimonially competent when the statement was uttered. The fact that a child possessed or lacked the competence to testify *at the time* an out-of-court statement was uttered may impact reliability.

- Whether the child is testimonially competent at the time of trial. The fact that a child lacks testimonial competence at trial may or may not impact the reliability of the child's out-of-court statements. One must ask *why* the child is incompetent to testify at trial. If the child lacks the ability to distinguish truth from lies, this incapacity may or may not have existed when the out-of-court statement was made. On the other hand, if the only reason the child cannot testify is fear of the defendant, then the child's lack of testimonial competence has no bearing on the reliability of out-of-court statements.

- The more spontaneous a statement, the less likely it was a product of fabrication.

- The reliability of an out-of-court statement may be influenced by the type of questions used to elicit the statement. When questions are leading, the possibility exists that the questioner influenced the statement.

---

[96] 497 U.S. 805 (1990).
[97] 497 U.S. 805 (1990).

- Reliability may be enhanced when a child's out-of-court statements are consistent.

- Young children lack the experience required to fabricate detailed accounts of sex acts. A four-year-old cannot describe fellatio, including ejaculation, unless the child has experienced fellatio or witnessed it. Naturally, care must be taken to rule out innocent explanations for a child's developmentally unusual sexual knowledge.

- Evidence that a child had or lacked a motive to fabricate impacts reliability. The motivation of adults is also relevant.[98]

In addition to the foregoing factors, the following factors may corroborate a child's statement:

- A child's statement may be corroborated by medical, laboratory, scientific, or physical evidence.[99]

- When a child's behavior changes in a way that corroborates the child's hearsay description of abuse, it may be appropriate to place increased confidence in the hearsay.[100]

- In some cases, a young child's developmentally unusual sexual knowledge surrounds the child's out-of-court statement and may be considered in assessing reliability.[101] In other cases, the child's developmentally unusual sexual knowledge corroborates the child's statement.[102]

The fact that the defendant had the opportunity to commit the act described in a child's statement may increase the reliability of the statement.[103]

§ 15.6.3 Hearsay and the Confrontation Clause

The hearsay rule and the Confrontation Clause of the Sixth Amendment share the goal of excluding unreliable evidence. In criminal trials, when a declarant testifies at trial and is subject to cross-examination, the Confrontation Clause

---

[98] *See* Daniel B. Lord, Note, *Determining Reliability Factors in Child Hearsay Statements: Wright and Its Progeny Confront the Psychological Research*, 79 IOWA L. REV. 1149 (1994); Gilles Renaud, *A Thematic Review of "Principled Hearsay" in Child Sex Abuse Cases*, 37 CRIM. LQ. 277 (1995). *See also United States v. Harrison*, 296 F.3d 994 (10th Cir. 2002); *State v. Peterson*, 557 N.W.2d 389 (S.D. 1996).

[99] *Morgan v. Foretich*, 846 F.2d 941 (4th Cir. 1988).

[100] *See State v. Robinson*, 153 Ariz. 191, 735 P.2d 801 (1987); *State v. Ritchey*, 107 Ariz. 552, 490 P.2d 558 (1971); *People v. Bowers*, 801 P.2d 511 (Colo. 1990).

[101] *See People v. Bowers*, 801 P.2d 511 (Colo. 1990).

[102] *See In re Stephen "GG,"* 279 A.D.2d 651, 719 N.Y.S. 2d 167 (2001); *In re Nicole V.*, 71 N.Y.2d 112, 518 N.E.2d 914 (1987).

[103] *See State v. Bellotti*, 383 N.W.2d 308 (Minn. Ct. App. 1986); *State v. Booth*, 124 Ore. App. 282, 862 P.2d 518 (1993).

is satisfied and raises no barrier to hearsay. When the declarant does not testify at trial, admission of hearsay against the defendant in a criminal trial is governed by *Crawford v. Washington*.[104] Under *Crawford*, if the hearsay is "testimonial," it is inadmissible unless the defendant had a prior opportunity to cross-examine the declarant. If the hearsay is not testimonial, admissibility is governed the principles laid down in *Ohio v. Roberts*.[105]

In *Crawford*, the Supreme Court did not provide a definitive definition of "testimonial." But the Court did provide the following examples of testimonial hearsay:

- A formal declaration made for the purpose of proving a fact.

- Prior testimony (including grand jury testimony) that the defendant had no opportunity to cross-examine.

- An affidavit.

- A statement by a person in police custody in response to formal police interrogation.

- Hearsay statements that the declarant would reasonably expect to be used in later court proceedings.

The Court's principal concern in *Crawford* was limiting the admissibility of hearsay generated by government officials with an eye toward prosecution.

In *Crawford*, the Court provided the following example of nontestimonial statements: off-hand, casual remarks to friends or family members. Thus, a child's hearsay statements to parents, babysitters, teachers, or friends are nontestimonial.

Crawford v. Washington is a Sixth Amendment decision, and does not apply in civil litigation. Thus, *Crawford*'s limitations on the admissibility of hearsay should not apply in juvenile court protective proceedings.

§ 15.7 Should Children Attend Court Hearings?

An issue that divides judges and attorneys in juvenile court protective proceedings is whether the child should attend court hearings. Obviously, if the child is scheduled to testify, the child must attend. But what of the numerous hearings where the child's testimony is not required? Reasonable minds differ on whether children should attend such hearings.

Those who believe children should attend all or most hearings point out that the case is about the child—the child's future is at stake—and the child should be present when decisions are made. Having the child present is a mark of respect for the child. Children often have useful information to contribute,

---

[104] 541 U.S. 36 (2004).

[105] 448 U.S. 56 (1980), *overruled by Crawford v. Washington*, 541 U.S. 36 (2004).

regardless of whether they are scheduled to testify. When a child is present in the courtroom, the hearing comes alive. The hearing is no longer about a stack of papers—it is about a living, breathing child whose presence in the courtroom focuses the attention of the professionals. Having the child in court ensures that the hearing is treated with the seriousness and respect it deserves.

Those who believe children generally do not need to attend hearings point out that many hearings are perfunctory, lasting only a few minutes and accomplishing important but routine matters. Children have little or nothing to add to such proceedings. Yet, requiring the child's attendance disrupts the child's routine, including school attendance, as well as the routines of foster parents, social workers, and others. At some hearings, sensitive information is discussed that the child should *not* hear. For example, does a child benefit when unflattering information is disclosed about the child's parents. Is it wise for a child to be present when a psychotherapist discusses the child's mental health problems?

As with many controversial issues, there may be a middle ground when it comes to children's attendance at court hearings. When a child is old enough to understand and contribute to proceedings, the child's presence is generally warranted for the reasons discussed above. If the child's attorney, the judge, or another professional believes the child's attendance at a particular hearing is contraindicated, the adult can raise the issue before the hearing. As for young children, attendance at hearings may have little utility in the run of cases.

§ 15.7.1 Children's Presence in their Court Proceedings: NACC Policy

The *NACC Recommendations for Representation of Children in Abuse and Neglect Cases*[106] provides as follows in section III, A, 6:

> Children need to be involved as litigants in the entire litigation process, including any post disposition, termination of parental rights, and adoption proceedings. The system of representation must recognize the child as a party to the litigation and must include the child in all phases of the litigation, including the opportunity to participate in arguments and jury selection where applicable, offer exhibits, call witnesses, examine and cross examine witnesses and engage in motions and discovery processes. The child must also be given notice of all proceedings and copies of all pleadings.

> **Comment:** The child should be physically present early in the proceedings, so as to allow all parties and their representatives the opportunity to become acquainted with the child as an individual. Although the child's presence may not be required at every court hearing, it should not

---

[106] This publication is provided in Appendix A-1.

be waived by the representative, unless the child has already been introduced to the court and his/her presence is not required by law, custom, or practice in that jurisdiction. Every child should be notified through counsel of every court hearing, every agency meeting, and every case conference or negotiation among the various professionals involved in the case and the child's attorney should be notified concerning any change in the child's welfare, placement, education, or status. Every child should be considered a party to the litigation, and should therefore, be entitled to any and all benefits under the law granted to any other party. Every child should have access to sufficient information to allow his/her representative to provide competent representation including the child's representative having access to social services, psychiatric, psychological, drug and alcohol, medical, law enforcement, school and other records relevant to the case, and opportunity for interviewing child welfare caseworkers, foster parents and other caretakers, school personnel, health professionals, law enforcement, and other persons with relevant information. This access may require the representative to file motions for discovery, subpoenas, subpoenas duces tecum, depositions and interrogatories, according to the discovery mechanisms available in the jurisdiction. Every child should have the opportunity to present his/her witnesses in the court proceedings. This requires the representative to investigate facts, identify and communicate with witnesses, and issue subpoenas to ensure that witnesses appear in court.

Chapter 16   NON-ADVERSARIAL CASE RESOLUTION

by Donald N. Duquette[1]

§ 16.1 Introduction

Professionals who work with children and parents have become increasingly dissatisfied with the customary reliance on the traditional adversarial system in resolving family-related disputes, including cases involving children's protection, placement, and permanent care. The power struggle in contested cases and hearings relating to child welfare may foster hostility among the parties and dissipate money, energy, and attention that could otherwise be used to solve problems cooperatively. Parties may become polarized, open communication may be discouraged, and there may be little investment in information sharing and joint problem solving. Children may suffer when adversarial tensions escalate and ameliorative services are delayed.

The adversarial system is essential and well-suited to resolving conflicts, however, when differences regarding the true facts of a child abuse or neglect case, or the differing views of the proper response to a family's problems related to child protection, are irreconcilable. Nonetheless, most child abuse and neglect cases are resolved through informal settlement negotiations. Unfortunately, these settlements are often quickly made in courthouse hallways where the interests of all parties may not be carefully or fully considered. Hastily made agreements or stipulations made immediately prior to a hearing can do a disservice to both children and their families.

Courts traditionally encourage resolution of contested matters through pretrial hearings and party negotiations that narrow the issues in contention. These court-based approaches to avoid lengthy and contested case proceedings, including pretrial case settlement and case status conferences, are commonly used and often authorized by statute or court rule. Non-Adversarial Case Resolution (NACR)[2] has become an accepted alternative to the traditional adversarial

---

[1]   Donald N. Duquette, J.D., is Clinical Professor of Law and Director of the Child Advocacy Law Clinic of the University of Michigan Law School. He is also a member of the National Association of Counsel for Children (NACC) Board of Directors.

[2]   Howard Davidson, Director of the American Bar Association Center for Children and the Law, deserves credit for coining the term, *Non-adversarial Case Resolution (NACR)* as it applies to the child welfare law context. In the *Guidelines* project, Howard was chair of the subcommittee developing policy recommendations for the use of alternative dispute resolution mechanisms in child protection and foster care legal cases. The use of this name reflects the hope of many that perhaps someday in the future non-adversarial case resolution will become

processes of the courts. It has also been widely adopted to resolve conflicts within government agencies and elsewhere. Surveys of court improvement projects indicate that one of the most popular reforms identified by the states is the use of alternative forms of dispute resolution.[3] Non-adversarial case resolution programs now exist in a number of states, and the popularity of these programs seems to be growing. A lawyer practicing in child welfare is increasingly likely to either want to refer a case to a NACR program or to be ordered into NACR by the court. This chapter is intended to orient a lawyer to the most common forms of NACR in the United States today, prepare him or her to participate competently in that structure, and to encourage more widespread use of these promising alternatives.

Two forms of NACR are in common use among the states and have considerable potential for improving decision making in the courts. Those are mediation and family group conferencing. A related practice, relinquishment counseling, is often a component of both mediation and family group conferencing.

§ 16.2 Mediation

§ 16.2.1 Definition

"Mediation in the child welfare context is well established in many jurisdictions. It is commonly defined as 'an intervention into a dispute or negotiation by an acceptable, impartial and neutral third party who has no authoritative decision-making power but who assists the disputing parties in voluntarily reaching their own mutually acceptable settlement of disputed issues in a non-adversarial setting.'"[4] Mediation is widely used today in domestic relations custody disputes between parents, and it is increasingly found in many juvenile delinquency, juvenile status offender, and child welfare proceedings.[5] Mediation in the child welfare context has existed in Los Angeles and Orange Counties in California and in Connecticut since the mid-1980s. Child welfare mediation programs now exist in some form in a number of states, including: Alaska, Arizona,

---

widespread enough so as not to be considered the *alternative* dispute resolution, but rather the more commonplace means of conflict resolution. *See* CHILDREN'S BUREAU, U.S. DEP'T OF HEALTH & HUMAN SERVS., ADOPTION 2002: THE PRESIDENT'S INITIATIVE ON ADOPTION AND FOSTER CARE, GUIDELINES FOR PUBLIC POLICY AND STATE LEGISLATION GOVERNING PERMANENCE FOR CHILDREN (1999), *available at* http://www.acf.hhs.gov/programs/cb/publications/adopt02/.

[3]   *See* NAT'L COUNCIL OF JUVENILE & FAMILY COURT JUDGES, SUMMARIES OF TWENTY-FIVE STATE COURT IMPROVEMENT ASSESSMENT REPORTS (1998).

[4]   CHILDREN'S BUREAU, U.S. DEP'T OF HEALTH & HUMAN SERVS., ADOPTION 2002: THE PRESIDENT'S INITIATIVE ON ADOPTION AND FOSTER CARE, GUIDELINES FOR PUBLIC POLICY AND STATE LEGISLATION GOVERNING PERMANENCE FOR CHILDREN, at V-2 (1999).

[5]   *Id.* at V-2 to V-3.

Arkansas, California, Colorado, Connecticut, Florida, Iowa, Massachusetts, Michigan, New Jersey, Ohio, Oregon, Utah, Wisconsin, Texas, and the District of Columbia.[6] In addition, several states, including Arizona, California, Colorado, Delaware, and Florida, have state legislation authorizing the use of mediation in cases related to child welfare.[7]

§ 16.2.2 Philosophy and Principles

The adversarial process in child abuse and neglect cases can sometimes break down communications and create hostility, divisiveness, and rigid position-taking between participants, most notably between the parents and the child protective agency or the child's attorney. Mediation, on the other hand, brings all significant case participants together in a non-adversarial and problem-solving setting.[8] Mediation in child welfare cases typically has several central characteristics:

- Always focuses on preserving the safety and best interests of the children (and the safety of all family members), while simultaneously attempting to validate the concerns, points of view, feelings, and resources of all participants, especially family members.

- Involves discussions facilitated by one or more neutral, highly skilled and trained third-party mediators, involving all relevant case participants and attorneys at some point during the mediation.

- May occur at any stage in the history of the case. Typically the earlier it occurs once the most significant case information is available, the better.

- Can be used to resolve a broad range of disposition and post-disposition issues, as well as certain jurisdictional issues.

- Serves to orient and educate family members, clarify issues, facilitate exchange of the most current case information, and creatively intervene to resolve roadblocks to case resolution.

- Should be confidential with exceptions limited to new reports of suspected child abuse and neglect, and threats to harm self or others.

- Usually results in agreements that become part of the court record and, if approved by the court, are entered as fully enforceable court orders.

---

[6] KATHLEEN STACK, NAT'L RES. CTR. FOR FOSTER CARE & PERMANENCY PLANNING, INFORMATION PACKET: CHILD WELFARE MEDIATION 2 (2003), *available at* http://www.hunter.cuny.edu/socwork/nrcfcpp/downloads/child-welfare-mediation.pdf.

[7] CHILDREN'S BUREAU, U.S. DEP'T OF HEALTH & HUMAN SERVS., ADOPTION 2002: THE PRESIDENT'S INITIATIVE ON ADOPTION AND FOSTER CARE, GUIDELINES FOR PUBLIC POLICY AND STATE LEGISLATION GOVERNING PERMANENCE FOR CHILDREN (1999).

[8] L. P. Edwards & S. Baron, *Alternatives to Contested Litigation in Child Abuse and Neglect Cases*, 33 FAM. & CONCILIATION CTS. REV. 275-285 (1995).

- Seeks to leave family members with an experience of having been significant, respected, and understood participants in the court process, with an investment in accepting and complying with the terms of the resolution or decisions of the court.

- Serves to reduce the degree of animosity held by family members toward "the system" and focuses the family's energy instead on child protection and parenting-related issues.[9]

§ 16.2.3 The Mediation Process

A child welfare lawyer, representing a child, parent, or child welfare agency, is very likely to have a case in mediation or to participate in mediation, either as a mediator or as a legal representative of one of the parties. The first stage in the process is to determine whether a particular case is suitable for mediation. Although mediation is successful in a large *number* of cases and in many *types* of cases, not every case is suitable. Your case may be referred for voluntary mediation or court-ordered into mediation. Once the case is selected for mediation, the parties are identified and the session is scheduled. The mediation steps are fairly simple, but the process itself can be complex. The nomenclature and outline may vary by local practice or depending on the unique variables of the case or the personalities of the individuals involved. The following anatomy is expanded from Beer and Stief, *The Mediator's Handbook*.[10] A typical mediation will be structured as follows:

Opening Statement

Mediations are held in a neutral place at a time convenient to the parties. Commonly, there are two mediators who open the session with a welcome and an explanation of the process. The mediators generally explain that they, the mediators, have no power to mandate a settlement but rather they are neutral facilitators who are charged with helping the parties to come to an agreement if possible.

Uninterrupted Time

Sometimes this is called the "opening statement." Each person takes a turn speaking while everyone else listens. The statement is generally open-ended in

---

[9] NAT'L COUNCIL OF JUVENILE & FAMILY COURT JUDGES, RESOURCE GUIDELINES: IMPROVING COURT PRACTICE IN CHILD ABUSE AND NEGLECT CASES 133-138 (1995).

[10] J. BEER & E. STIEF, THE MEDIATOR'S HANDBOOK (3d ed.), developed by the Friends Conflict Resolution Programs. Copyright 1997 by New Society Publishing Company. Reprinted by permission. For further information contact:

New Society Publishers
PO Box 189
Gabriola, BC VOR 1XO
Canada

response to a question like, "Tell us why you are here today." Typically the party, not the lawyer, speaks about anything that is relevant to the situation. Very commonly a mediator repeats back what the party has said in a neutral summary that reiterates the essential points—and communicates that the party has been respectfully heard.

The Exchange

Then the arguing and discussion begin. People commonly accuse each other and attempt to straighten out the other person on the facts. They explain why they are upset and make demands. The hostility and emotions come to the surface and are expressed. The mediators keep the discussion in bounds, making sure that each person is heard and each is protected. The mediators do not try to determine the truth or who is at fault. Rather, they listen for what matters to people and for possible areas of agreement. Sometimes the Exchange brings about a "turning point" of reconciliation.

Separate Meetings

Separate meetings, or caucuses, can occur at any time during the mediation and they have many uses, including checking out a person's concerns, confronting unhelpful behavior, or helping people think through their options. Typically the caucuses are confidential so that the mediator cannot share information obtained there without permission of the party. In some cases a shuttle diplomacy, with the mediators conveying information or options and offers, may help facilitate settlement.

Setting the Agenda

Once information is drawn out and hopefully heard by all sides, discussion turns to identifying the needs and interests of the parties, identifying and framing the issues, and setting and organizing the agenda for the remainder of the session.

Building the Agreement

The parties then work through each issue on the agenda, generating options, expanding options, and then weighing, adjusting, and testing the alternatives to craft a workable, mutually satisfactory solution.

Writing the Agreement and Closing

If the parties are able to settle their differences, the mediators write a formal agreement containing those decisions. Everyone present signs and takes a copy home. The mediators review what has been accomplished, remind people of next steps, congratulate them on their accomplishment, and wish them well.[11]

---

[11] *Id.* at 4-5.

§ 16.3 Family Group Conferencing

Family Group Conference (FGC) is a fairly new form of NACR that focuses on engaging the extended family in planning for a child and does not necessarily involve the mediating of disputes. It is a promising NACR model that has been recently imported to the U.S. from New Zealand. A Family Group Conference, whether it takes the form of Family Group Decision Making or a Family Unity Meeting, is characterized as a family-focused, strengths-oriented, and community-based process where parents, extended family members, and others come together to collectively make key decisions for children involved in the child welfare system.[12] Family Group Conference is often administered by the child welfare agency as authorized by Oregon statute. FGC could also be a form of court-approved NACR as described by Lowry.[13]

§ 16.3.1 Philosophy and Principles

The following principles and values characterize Family Group Conferences:

- Children are best raised in families.

- The primary responsibility for the care of children rests with their families, who should be respected, supported, and protected.

- Family groups can make safe decisions for their own children. Families have strengths and can change.

- Family groups are experts on themselves. Families have wisdom and solutions that are workable for them.

- The essence of family empowerment is the belief in self-determination: Those we help have a right and need to be free in making their own decisions and choices.[14]

§ 16.3.2 Structure of Family Group Conferencing

The Family Group Conference process comprises four main parts. The first is the referral, in which a coordinator or gatekeeper decides whether to hold a conference. The second is the preparation and planning. The third is the confer-

---

[12] Lisa Merkel-Holguin, Putting Families Back into the Child Protection Partnership: Family Group Decision-Making (American Humane Association, Summer 1996).

[13] *See* Jolene M. Lowry, *Family Group Conferences as a Form of Court Approved Alternative Dispute Resolution in Child Abuse and Neglect Cases,* 31 U. Mich. J.L. Reform 57 (1997).

[14] *Id.* at 66. *See also* Elizabeth Cole, *Key Policy Decisions in Implementing Family Group Conferences: Observations Drawn from the New Zealand Model, in* Mark Hardin, Family Group Conferences in Child Abuse and Neglect Cases: Learning from the Experience in New Zealand (ABA Center on Children and the Law, 1996).

ence itself, which is generally divided into four stages of welcome, information sharing, family meeting, and decision. The fourth is writing, distribution, and implementation of the plan.[15]

There are two primary differences between the Family Group Decision Making (FGDM) and Family Unity models (FUM). FGDM discourages the practice of excluding any family members from the meeting, while the FUM permits parents to veto the participation of any family member, a practice that provides parents with more control over the process and with whom information will be shared. The second major difference is that the FUM model allows professionals and support persons to be present during the family discussion, while a key tenet of FGDM is that families, once briefed by the professionals, must have a private family meeting without the presence of any nonfamily persons.

The Oregon Revised Statutes authorize family group conferences, which are generically referred to as "family decision-making meetings."[16] Kansas legislation authorizes a "conference of relatives," which is described in the statute as "a conference of the child's grandparents, aunts, uncles, siblings, cousins and other relatives determined...to have a potential interest in determining a placement which is in the best interests of the child."[17] Family Group Conferences are also being held in Santa Clara County, California, Grand Rapids, Michigan, and other jurisdictions.

§ 16.4 Voluntary Relinquishment Counseling

Voluntary relinquishment counseling is an underutilized child welfare NACR that should receive special attention. It may be employed as part of mediation or Family Group Conferencing, or it may occur separate from these mechanisms. Many professionals believe that it would be helpful for parents and children alike if parental counseling concerning the voluntary relinquishment of parental rights were readily available. Voluntary relinquishment can be more humane than contested termination proceedings by avoiding some trauma to parent and child. It can also avoid delay. In many cases, voluntary relinquishment of parental rights is preferable to contested termination because it reduces the financial, emotional, and time costs.

The use of NACR in the voluntary relinquishment process may also *add civil liberty protections* to the birth parents when compared with more common methods of working with birth parents on parental rights termination issues. By

---

[15] Jolene M. Lowry, *Family Group Conferences as a Form of Court Approved Alternative Dispute Resolution in Child Abuse and Neglect Cases,* 31 U. MICH. J.L. REFORM 57, 66-76 (1997); LISA MERKEL-HOLGUIN, PUTTING FAMILIES BACK INTO THE CHILD PROTECTION PARTNERSHIP: FAMILY GROUP DECISION-MAKING 5-7 (American Humane Association, Summer 1996).

[16] OR. REV. STAT. §§ 417.365 through 417.375.

[17] KAN. STAT. ANN. § 38-1559 (2003).

participating in NACR, parents may be more likely to feel that those within the "system" are consciously protecting their rights, rather than simply coercing them to "give up" their rights to their child. Also, where voluntary relinquishments are not made within the court, making them within a NACR process could provide protections to parents that are similar to those that should be provided to parents within more formal termination of parental rights proceedings. Parents should be aware of the possibility of voluntary relinquishment at all stages of the court process.

Voluntary relinquishment will be more attractive if options for permanency, such as cooperative adoption or adoption with contact, are available under state law.[18] Some parents will be more willing to relinquish parental rights if they can ensure that their child will be adopted by someone of whom they approve. Subject to the court finding that it is in the best interests of a child, some states permit parents involved in child protection proceedings to voluntarily relinquish their child for adoption by specified persons to the same extent that so-called direct-consent adoptions are permitted for other birth parents. Relinquishment under state law is generally of two types. In one type, often called surrender, the agency determines who the adoptive parents will be subject to court approval. The other type involves direct or specific consent, in which the parents are allowed to relinquish the child to a designated individual, also with court approval.[19]

An amicable relationship between the birth parent and the new parent is also more likely under these circumstances. Further, if more contested terminations of parental rights could be converted into voluntary relinquishments, states would save considerable time and expense. Some voluntary relinquishment programs have involved elements of mediation, including the possibility of formal agreements concerning future contact between the birth parent and child. In such processes, parents' legal rights should be carefully protected. Parents should be legally represented, even though their lawyer might not participate in each stage of the relinquishment counseling or mediation.

§ 16.5 Uses of NACR in Child Welfare Cases

NACR techniques can be used in various ways and at various times in a child welfare case. Both mediation and Family Group Conferences can be used:

- To resolve conflicts between *child welfare agencies and parents* concerning proposed case plans and final case resolutions, to help divert cases from the court system, and to work out disputes over a child's supervision,

---

[18] Options for legal permanency are discussed in Chapter 17, Establishing Legal Permanence for the Child.

[19] *See* JOAN H. HOLLINGER ET AL., ADOPTION LAW AND PRACTICE (Matthew Bender & Co., Inc. 1988).

placement, visitation, family reunification, and permanent plans for the child (*e.g.*, mediated relinquishment of parental rights or guardianship, as well as facilitation of cooperative adoption agreements where appropriate and permitted by law).

- To increase intrafamilial involvement among *parents, relatives, and other extended (kinship) family members* in fashioning case resolutions and improving cooperation and coordination with government child protection and child welfare authorities.[20] Proponents of NACR in child welfare cases have seen it used successfully to help expedite adoptions and guardianships for severely abused or neglected children.

Mediation can be used:

- To resolve conflicts among substitute care providers, foster care caseworkers and case reviewers, and children's court-appointed advocates about the needs of children during periods of substitute care.

- To resolve matters more promptly as part of the court process among the various attorneys and other advocates, caseworkers, therapists, other involved professionals, and the parents and other family members in child protection judicial proceedings. Mandatory case mediation facilitated by a trained independent mediator can help focus attention on collaborative problem solving on behalf of the child.[21]

Confidentiality is an essential component of NACR. The confidentiality provisions are intended to promote the free and unreserved discussion and sharing of information. Statements made in the NACR process should be treated as if they were statements made in the course of settlement discussions. Even when there is only partial agreement on the issues, the substance of the NACR discussion should not be used in the court process. When mediation is unsuccessful, neither the mediators nor other participants in the process should testify against any party in court nor should any product of the mediation be used in court, including whether in the mediator's opinion one party cooperated or failed to cooperate.[22]

As a corollary to confidentiality and also to ensure free and open discussion, sharing of information with all the participants is important. Information about the child and family can be shared, as appropriate, with members of the extended family during the NACR process, but the people who receive such information

---

[20] CHILDREN'S BUREAU, U.S. DEP'T OF HEALTH & HUMAN SERVS., ADOPTION 2002: THE PRESIDENT'S INITIATIVE ON ADOPTION AND FOSTER CARE, GUIDELINES FOR PUBLIC POLICY AND STATE LEGISLATION GOVERNING PERMANENCE FOR CHILDREN, at Ch. V (1999).

[21] *Id.*

[22] NAT'L COUNCIL OF JUVENILE & FAMILY COURT JUDGES, RESOURCE GUIDELINES: IMPROVING COURT PRACTICE IN CHILD ABUSE AND NEGLECT CASES 137 (1995).

have a duty to treat it in confidence. Relevant information about the child, parents, and other family members is likely to be known only to certain individuals directly involved in child welfare agency or court actions related to the child. Ideally, the persons affected would voluntarily release such information for purposes of NACR, but the voluntary cooperation may not be forthcoming, especially when the court mandates NACR. If information about the child, parents, and other family members is withheld, the type of shared decision making that is critical to successful NACR may be impossible.

On occasion, and where appropriate, children will be involved in the process, especially if they are older and reasonably mature. Exposure of children to NACR can help them recognize that their immediate families and relatives are truly interested in their welfare and that their own concerns are taken seriously.

The NACR process must not be delayed by strategic litigation concerns. The permanency timelines of Federal and State law must be met and delays in the formal process avoided. For example, in cases involving the abuse or neglect of a child, in which criminal charges are pending against a parent/party, mediation should not be delayed because the related criminal matter has not yet been resolved.[23]

Typically, any interested person is authorized to request NACR in a child welfare case. To avoid trivial issues taking up valuable time within NACR, court or agency gatekeepers or facilitators of these processes generally explain the ground rules to participants and indicate how matters inappropriate for resolution within NACR can be separately addressed. Because a Family Group Conference is more logistically complex and time consuming than mediation, the gatekeepers may be more cautious in convening the FGC. Some important questions must be addressed in any NACR program implementation. For example, do the parents have the right to consent, or opt out of, the convening of a Mediation or Family Group Conference process? Who should be considered "family members" or other "interested persons" and therefore invited to participate? Should the coordinator or facilitator of the process have authority to exclude certain family members, such as those believed to be intimidating the child or other family members? Should there be mandatory timetables for convening and completing the NACR process?

To assure that all parties consider it an objective process, some authorities recommend that mediators be independent of the child welfare agency or the judge, even though the child welfare and court system must coordinate in the execution of these processes to ensure NACR is effectively implemented.[24]

---

[23] CHILDREN'S BUREAU, U.S. DEP'T OF HEALTH & HUMAN SERVS., ADOPTION 2002: THE PRESIDENT'S INITIATIVE ON ADOPTION AND FOSTER CARE, GUIDELINES FOR PUBLIC POLICY AND STATE LEGISLATION GOVERNING PERMANENCE FOR CHILDREN (1999).

[24] *Id.* at V-11.

Some also recommend that certification standards for NACR staff be established. NACR personnel should be trained in dispute resolution generally and on issues relevant to the child welfare NACR process. The training should include information on the following:

- Child abuse and neglect.

- Child development.

- Domestic violence and its impact on children.

- Substance abuse.

- Family functioning and family systems.

- Power imbalance concerns in mediating child welfare cases.

- Working with diverse communities.

- Access to community resources.

Because these are highly transferable skills, many in the community may want to be trained as mediators. All trainees should be monitored by more experienced NACR experts. Trainees should observe others in action.[25]

§ 16.6 Effectiveness of NACR

Evaluations of mediation programs have demonstrated that a variety of models proved effective, mediation can produce settlements at all *stages* of cases, and that all *types* of cases can be settled in mediation. Some argue that certain cases, such as domestic violence or child sexual abuse, are not appropriate for mediation, but Toennes found no evidence to support blanket screening out of certain types of cases.[26] There is also widespread support for mediating both jurisdictional and dispositional case issues, although time constraints pose problems in doing both. Parents report that mediation gave them a place to be "heard" and to better understand what was required of them.[27]

Agreements produced in mediation were similar to outcomes promulgated by judges. The former were more likely, however, to include detailed visitation plans for children in out-of-home placement, to address communication problems between family members or between the family and the child welfare

---

[25] *Id.*

[26] Nancy Thoennes, *An Evaluation of Child Protection Mediation in Five California Courts*, 35 FAM. & CONCILIATION CTS. REV. 184-195 (1997).

[27] NANCY THOENNES & J. PEARSON, MEDIATION IN FIVE CALIFORNIA DEPENDENCY COURTS: A CROSS-SITE COMPARISON (Report to the California State Legislature, Denver, Colorado Center for Policy Research (1995)); Nancy Thoennes, *An Evaluation of Child Protection Mediation in Five California Courts*, 35 FAM. & CONCILIATION CTS. REV. 184-195 (1997).

agency, and to result in parents specifically acknowledging the need for services. Mediated contested cases were also less likely than non-mediated contested cases to result in later contested hearings. Mediated settlements enjoy greater compliance by parents at least in the short run.[28]

Both mediation and Family Group Conferences are alternatives to traditional adversarial litigation case approaches, and help divert children and families from the child welfare and court system while engaging parents in a non-threatening situation. NACR may enable parents who have been inappropriately denying or minimizing the impact of the children's abuse or neglect to safely acknowledge responsibility for the mistreatment and to willingly accept help. Within the NACR process, parents can be given choices of methods to solve the problems they and their children face. The informal and participatory setting of NACR can facilitate this problem-solving approach. Everyone benefits if disputes can be resolved earlier in the process when a child has been identified as abused or neglected.

The advantages to using NACR in child welfare cases include:

- Sharing of responsibility for child protection beyond the child welfare agency and the courts to include the child's immediate family, the child's extended family, and the child's community.

- Empowering parents in the decision-making process related to their children.

- Helping assure that, in addition to parents, others with a strong interest in abused and neglected children are heard within the process of intervention.

- Facilitating parental compliance with agency case plans.

- Avoiding conflicts and delay, especially those harmful to children, which are associated with the adversarial process.

- Reducing crowded judicial case dockets.

- Circumventing the need for expensive, lengthy contested trials and case review hearings.

Additionally, family members often feel more comfortable raising the cultural, ethnic, or religious needs of the child in the more informal NACR process.

Several unique factors should be considered whenever NACR is considered for a matter involving child welfare. First, those involved with the process must remember that the safety of children must never be compromised or endangered through the use of any non-adversarial case approaches. Second, parents who participate in the NACR process must be competently represented in order to

---

[28] *Id.*

compensate for the potential power imbalance that can exist when government is intervening in a family's life. Third, NACR, if done properly within child welfare proceedings, may provide a beneficial process—but it will not be inexpensive. Programs must have adequate funding for properly trained mediators or family-group facilitators who can resolve cases in a timely manner.

§ 16.7 Compromising Child Safety or Well-Being

The principal goal of NACR in the child welfare context is to assure the safety and protection of children through resolution of disputes without having to rely on the traditional adversarial court process. At the same time, the process should assure that the parents' legal rights are properly protected. There should be no compromise on protection of parental rights.

NACR should also focus on child well-being and permanency, family empowerment, and community involvement in the process. NACR should not delay the resolution of cases nor create additional trauma for the child and family. NACR should empower parents and promote shared responsibility with the extended family and community to serve the best interests of the child effectively and more promptly.[29]

The greatest fear among critics of NACR in these cases is that child safety will be compromised or sacrificed during the process. Proponents and critics of such processes agree that child safety must never be sacrificed in the interests of reaching agreement or as part of any "plea bargains." Concerns about children being endangered through the use of NACR can be alleviated in several ways:

- NACR must assure that the child's "voice" is clearly heard within the process, either through the child, by the child's legal representative, or both.

- NACR must permit the child's representative, the convenor/facilitator/mediator, or others to veto any agreements reached through the process that compromise the child's safety or welfare.

- NACR should provide for an independent review of any mediated agreements, stipulations, or settlements by judges and child welfare agency supervisors.

- NACR should structure more frequent involvement by protective family members during the mediation processes and within mediated agreements.

---

[29] CHILDREN'S BUREAU, U.S. DEP'T OF HEALTH & HUMAN SERVS., ADOPTION 2002: THE PRESIDENT'S INITIATIVE ON ADOPTION AND FOSTER CARE, GUIDELINES FOR PUBLIC POLICY AND STATE LEGISLATION GOVERNING PERMANENCE FOR CHILDREN, at V-8 (1999).

- NACR should be initiated promptly, and ideally a decision should be reached within 30 days of its initiation; in emergency situations, it should be completed even sooner.

- The NACR process should clarify how any agreement will be enforced and what will happen if the agreement fails.

- In addition to being ever conscious about the child safety issues in mediating case resolutions, those involved within the NACR process must constantly think about how the process, and its outcomes, will promote permanency for the child.

§ 16.8 Conclusion

Non-adversarial case resolution approaches are increasingly used throughout the child protection process—both before and after court intervention becomes necessary. NACR, while not inexpensive, is generally more expeditious and efficient than traditional litigation and can often resolve disputes without the hostile overtones characteristic of the court's adversarial process. When children are endangered, their extended families may provide invaluable resources to help fashion safe and permanent case resolutions.

NACR in the child welfare context can be structured to involve the parents and the child's extended family in responsible planning and decision making for the child. Use of various forms of NACR can provide clients with the opportunity to vent, disagree and be heard, and to understand the points of view of others. Typically, the earlier in the process that NACR is implemented, the greater its chance for success.

Different forms of NACR can be useful at any stage of state intervention to facilitate the well being of children—from the initial identification of abuse and neglect through the final permanent placement of a child. Child welfare lawyers must understand the process and make judgments about whether and how NACR will serve the interests of their clients.

Chapter 17   ESTABLISHING LEGAL PERMANENCE FOR THE CHILD*

by Donald N. Duquette[1]

§ 17.1 Introduction

This chapter is intended to identify options for legal permanency that state law and the federal Adoption and Safe Families Act (ASFA) commonly recognize to better serve children in foster care. Ideally, the child will ultimately return safely to his or her home of origin. But when a return home is not possible, the child welfare legal process should result in a safe and legally secure alternative permanent placement for the child. The emphasis on legally secure permanent placement is meant to provide the child with psychological stability and a sense of belonging, and limit the likelihood of future disruption of the parent-child relationship. All state laws authorize adoption of children, but traditional adoption does not meet the needs of all children in public foster care. Attorneys representing children, parents, or the government agency may seek other legal options for permanent and legally secure placement. Some authorities recommend that these options be broad enough to serve the needs of all children in care who are not able to return to their home of origin; options could include adoption, adoption with contact, permanent guardianship, stand-by guardianship, and "another planned permanent living arrangement" (APPLA) such as permanent long-term foster care.[2]

For children who cannot be reared by one or both of their birth parents, adoption, by relatives or non-relatives is the preferred option for a permanent legal placement. By providing children with a new family, adoption is most likely to ensure protection, stability, nurturing, and familial relationships that will last throughout their lives. Alternatives to adoption discussed here, such as permanent guardianship, are generally appropriate only when adoption has been thoroughly explored and found unsuitable to meet the needs of a particular child.

---

* This chapter is adapted from the work of Principal Authors Donald N. Duquette and Mark Hardin in CHILDREN'S BUREAU, U.S. DEP'T OF HEALTH & HUMAN SERVS., ADOPTION 2002: THE PRESIDENT'S INITIATIVE ON ADOPTION AND FOSTER CARE, GUIDELINES FOR PUBLIC POLICY AND STATE LEGISLATION GOVERNING PERMANENCE FOR CHILDREN (1999), *available at* http://www.acf.hhs.gov/programs/cb/publications/adopt02/02final.htm.

[1] Donald N. Duquette, J.D., is Clinical Professor of Law and Director of the Child Advocacy Law Clinic of the University of Michigan Law School. He is also a member of the National Association of Counsel for Children (NACC) Board of Directors.

[2] CHILDREN'S BUREAU, U.S. DEP'T OF HEALTH & HUMAN SERVS., ADOPTION 2002: THE PRESIDENT'S INITIATIVE ON ADOPTION AND FOSTER CARE, GUIDELINES FOR PUBLIC POLICY AND STATE LEGISLATION GOVERNING PERMANENCE FOR CHILDREN (1999); CECILIA FIERMONTE & JENNIFER RENNE, MAKING IT PERMANENT: REASONABLE EFFORTS TO FINALIZE PERMANENCY PLANS FOR FOSTER CHILDREN (ABA Center on Children and the Law, 2002).

A certain priority among these options for permanency is generally accepted and reflects a preference for permanent placement of foster children with relatives that is expressed in federal and most state laws: (1) safe reunification with the biological parents or a suitable member of the family of origin; (2) adoption; and (3) permanent guardianship. Long-term foster care is generally disfavored but may be appropriate for some children, particularly older children who have a connection with their biological families.

This hierarchy of preference is not inflexible and requires individualized judgments based on the circumstances of each individual child. For example, if a child is psychologically attached to a relative and has been living for an extended time with that relative, but the relative cannot or will not adopt, a permanent guardianship with that relative may be preferable to moving the child to a recruited adoptive family. On the other hand, a relative with no established relationship with the child who offers to become a child's caretaker late in the court process may not be as appropriate for adoption as foster parents who have cared for the child for some time and who wish to adopt.

§ 17.2 Principles for Permanency Options

The President's Initiative on Adoption and Foster Care, *Guidelines for Public Policy and State Legislation Governing Permanence for Children* recommend the following principles in identifying options for permanence:

Principles. We recommend that State law reflect the following principles:

a) The most preferred permanent placement for a child is safe and permanent reunification with the birth parent or extended family of origin.

b) For children who cannot be reared by their birth parents or within their extended family of origin, adoption is the preferred permanent placement.

c) If adoption is not appropriate for a child unable to return home safely, State law should establish other legally sanctioned permanent placements including permanent guardianships.

d) A permanent placement includes the following characteristics:
    i. It is legally intended to be permanent—both to last throughout the child's minority and to establish family relationships that will last for the child's lifetime.
    ii. It is legally secure from modification.
    iii. The permanent caregiver has the same legal responsibility for the child as a birth parent.
    iv. The State no longer has legal custody of the child and the permanent caregiver is not subject to continuing State supervision.

e) State law should establish several legal options for permanent placement, including legal guardianship or planned permanent living arrangements. In addition, State law should permit agreed upon legally protected contacts between the child and members of the child's birth family or other significant persons, so long as the permanent placement option is based on the child's best interests and ensures the stability and security of the placement.

f) A decision to place a child permanently should comply with the letter and spirit of the Multiethnic Placement Act of 1994 as amended (42 U.S.C. 5115a *et seq.*) and with the Indian Child Welfare Act (ICWA) (25 U.S.C. 1901 *et. seq.*).

g) State law should authorize the court that handled the child protection action to approve an option for permanent placement and to exercise jurisdiction over any post placement matters.[3]

§ 17.3 Adoption

Adoption, the legal and permanent transfer of all parental rights and responsibilities to the adoptive parents, remains the placement of choice when a child cannot be returned to his or her birth family because it gives the child a new, permanent, legal family with the same legal standing and protection as a family created through birth. An adopted individual is entitled to inherit from and through the adoptive parents and is treated as the child of the adoptive parents for purposes of social security, insurance, retirement, pension, and all other public and private benefit programs. Conversely, adoptive parents acquire rights to inherit from and through the adopted child. Adoption thus provides, for the most part, the same autonomy, security, and durability of family relationships that children experience in their families of birth. Children, adoptive parents, birth parents, and the general public also understand and are familiar with this type of legal relationship. Children may be adopted by relatives, step-parents, foster parents, or persons previously unrelated or unknown to them.[4]

§ 17.3.1 Adoption Subsidies

Adoption subsidies play an important role in achieving permanency for children. The agency's reasonable efforts to finalize a permanency plan should include informing caregivers about adoption subsidies and securing them when appropriate. For many children, adoption assistance can make adoption possible.[5]

---

[3] CHILDREN'S BUREAU, U.S. DEP'T OF HEALTH & HUMAN SERVS., ADOPTION 2002: THE PRESIDENT'S INITIATIVE ON ADOPTION AND FOSTER CARE, GUIDELINES FOR PUBLIC POLICY AND STATE LEGISLATION GOVERNING PERMANENCE FOR CHILDREN, at II-2 (1999).

[4] For a useful guide for state legislatures regarding adoption from foster care, *see* STEVE CHRISTIAN & LISA EKMAN, A PLACE TO CALL HOME: ADOPTION AND GUARDIANSHIP FOR CHILDREN IN FOSTER CARE (National Conference of State Legislatures, 2000).

[5] For a more thorough, detailed explanation of adoption assistance agreements, please *see* Chapter 9, *Adoption Assistance for Children with Special Needs, in* ADOPTION LAW AND PRACTICE (Joan Hollinger ed., 2001). In New York, for example, subsidies are provided in over 80 percent of the adoptions that occur through the child welfare agency. *Id.*

Denial of the subsidy or an insufficient subsidy can be a barrier to permanency. In many states, adoption assistance can include regular monthly cash payments, Medicaid, social services to the family, and nonrecurring adoption expenses. The federal government and the state share the costs of adoption assistance for those children who meet federal eligibility requirements. For children who do not meet federal eligibility requirements, some states will pay the entire cost of the subsidy. Most states will also provide Medicaid.[6] For children who qualify, federal adoption assistance is an entitlement. The ABA Center on Children and the Law report that an agency may not refuse assistance if the child is eligible, and eligibility requires that the child meet the following four criteria:[7]

(1) The child was eligible, before adoption, for assistance under one of two programs:

    (a) Foster care or adoption assistance under Title IV-E. The child (or the child's birth family) must have been eligible to receive federal AFDC. Even though AFDC was discontinued in 1996, a child's eligibility for Title IV-E is based on the states' AFDC eligibility standards as of July 16, 1996.[8]

    (b) Supplemental Security Income (SSI), a program for low-income people with disabilities.[9]

(2) The child has special needs as defined by the state's definition of special needs.[10] Special needs may include certain medical, emotional, mental health conditions; and membership in a minority, sibling, or age group.[11]

(3) The child could not be placed for adoption without a subsidy. In other words, a "reasonable, but unsuccessful, effort has been made to place the child with appropriate adoptive parents [without providing any assistance]."[12] This requirement can be waived if the child already has a significant relationship or significant emotional ties with the caregiver.[13]

(4) There has been a judicial determination that the child cannot or should not be returned home. Obviously, if the child's parents' rights have been terminated, this requirement is satisfied.

States may not impose additional eligibility criteria for federal assistance beyond what is required by federal law.

---

[6] Debra Ratterman Baker, *Adoption Assistance: A Legal Primer*, 19 ABA CHILD LAW & PRACTICE 97 (2000).

[7] *Id.*

[8] 42 U.S.C. § 673(a)(2)(A), (B).

[9] 42 U.S.C. §§ 673(a)(2)(A)(ii), 673(a)(2)(B)(iii).

[10] 42 U.S.C. § 673(a)(2)(C).

[11] *See* 42 U.S.C. § 673(c)(2)(A). Agencies and courts have traditionally referred to these children as "hard to place." The more common current term is "special needs."

[12] 42 U.S.C. § 673(c)(2)(A), 673(c)(2)(B).

[13] 42 U.S.C. § 673(c)(2)(B).

§ 17.3.2 Post-Adoption Contact

Post-adoption contact between the child and the birth parents, siblings, or other people who are psychologically important to the child may serve the long-term interests of a child and is often arranged. Commonly, the adoptive parents, whether kin or non-kin, recognize that certain people are important to the child and that it is important for the child to maintain contact with them. Purely voluntary, "open adoptions" occur in all states, where the adoptive parents freely and voluntarily permit or even encourage contact with the child's natural networks. No force of law or court order requires that such contact occur, and the adoptive parents may end such arrangements at will.

State Laws

At least 18 states have enacted "open" or "cooperative" adoption laws that provide some mechanism for approval and enforcement of post-adoption agreements.[14] Annette Appel reports:

> Though variable in specifics, these statutes are nearly identical in several respects: first, by definition, none permit a court to grant an adoption with contact unless the adoptive parents agree; second, each statute indicates who must approve of the agreement in order for it to be enforceable later; third, all but one (West Virginia) require the agreement to be in writing, either as a written contract, relinquishment, or court order; fourth, all of the statutes explicitly, or through court interpretation, provide for enforcement of the agreements unless there are grounds not to enforce or there are grounds to modify; finally, no statutes permit vacation of the adoption or withdrawal of relinquishment as a sanction for breach or modification of the agreement or order.

While most States make contact between the child and his or her natural networks available to all adoptees,[15] some state laws limit such post-adoption contact to children who have been in foster care.[16] California limits post-adoption contact to children adopted by relatives[17] while Indiana limits it to children

---

[14] *E.g.*, Arizona, California, Connecticut, Florida, Indiana, Louisiana, Massachusetts, Minnesota, Montana, Nebraska, New Mexico, New York, Oregon, Rhode Island, South Dakota, Vermont, Washington, and West Virginia. Annette R. Appell, *Survey of State Utilization of Adoption with Contact,* ADOPTION Q., Vol. 6(4), at 75 (2003), *available at* http://www.haworthpress.com/store/product.asp?sku=J145.

[15] *E.g.*, Minnesota (MINN. STAT. ANN. § 259.58 (West 1997)); Montana (MONT. CODE ANN. § 42-5-301 (1997)); New Mexico (N.M. STAT. ANN. § 32A-5-35 (Michie 1978 & Supp. 1994)); Oregon (OR. REV. STAT. § 109.305 (1993)); South Dakota (S.D. CODIFIED LAWS § 25-6-17 (Michie 1997)); Washington (WASH. REV. CODE § 26.33.295 (Supp. 1994)); West Virginia (W. VA. CODE § 48-22-704 (2001)).

[16] *See, e.g.*, NEB. REV. STAT. §§ 43-162 to 164; N.Y. SOC. SERV. LAW § 383-c (McKinney 1992 & Supp.).

[17] CAL. R. OF COURT 5.400(b) (2003) (formerly CAL. FAM. CODE § 8714.7 (renumbered 2003)).

age two and over.[18] Other States simply acknowledge that post-adoption contact can occur (*e.g.*, Ohio)[19] or prohibit the court from forbidding such contact (*e.g.*, Missouri).[20] At least one State (Florida) permits the court that is terminating parental rights to order post-termination contact to be reviewed upon the adoption of the child.[21] This may be a useful mechanism when: (1) the child has a need for post-termination or post-adoption contact; and (2) the adoptive parents have not been identified at the time of termination of parental rights; and (3) the birth parents will not be present at the adoption.

Benefits and Pitfalls

Many foster children have psychological connections to their birth families, siblings, and other significant persons, such as foster parents, so that it would be in the child's interest to maintain some sort of contact even after adoption. The child may need to know and understand his or her ethnic background and heritage. There may be a need to share medical information and health histories. Preservation of an emotional tie may be beneficial to the child. Continued contact may relieve an older child's guilt or concerns about the birth parent. Contact may help the child come to terms with his or her past. A connection with a biological parent may be a positive, yet limited, influence, and may prevent the child from running away or disrupting a new placement when the child desires continuing ties. Continued contact may avoid the trauma of contested and prolonged termination of parental rights proceedings. Children generally benefit from contact with siblings. These needs may be recognized and agreed to by the new parents and approved by the court. The contact could be as simple as exchanging photos each year without any physical contact, but the arrangements could leave a door open for future relationships *when helpful to the child*.

Birth parents, when given a chance, can be tremendous resources in planning for their children, and their participation can have positive outcomes for adoption. For many years, certain adoption agencies have placed children in adoptions where birth parents and adoptive parents voluntarily maintain contact and exchange information. This happens with infant adoption, direct consent adoption, and in adoptions within the extended family. These "cooperative adoption" arrangements are often negotiated in the context of an adoption of older children, especially children with special needs, who have been in foster care before being placed for adoption. In appropriate situations, even where child protection proceedings have been initiated, state law and the parties to a child protection proceeding could encourage birth parents' involvement in planning for relinquishment of parental rights and adoption of the child.

---

[18] IND. CODE ANN § 31-19-16-2 (1997).

[19] OHIO REV. CODE ANN. § 3107.62.

[20] MO. REV. STAT. § 453.080(4).

[21] FLA. STAT. ANN. § 39.811(7)(b) and § 63.0427.

On the other hand, there may be pitfalls to maintaining ties between birth parents and their children after children are placed into new permanent homes. For example, birth parents might only reluctantly accept the new placement and may later try to disrupt or undermine it. The child may be fearful or resistant to continuing contacts. The determination of whether an individual child needs a permanent placement with ongoing birth parent-child contacts or contacts with siblings or members of the extended family is a subtle and sophisticated task. Each case is unique and demands thoughtful and expert consideration. Any post-adoption contact agreement must be voluntary, whether the court ratifies it or not. In some cases, however, there are no court orders and final discretion is left to the adoptive parents, while in other cases contact agreements are ratified by the court and become legally enforceable.

Elements of a Successful Post-Adoption Contact Agreement

Adoption with contact will be most successful when all of the parties to the contact agree on each of the following points:

- That the contact should occur.
- What type of contact should occur.
- How or where the contact will occur.
- How frequently the contact will occur.

Post-adoption contact agreements should be flexible enough to accommodate the changing needs and abilities of all the parties, particularly the child. The parties could agree simply that the adoptive parents will keep the birth parents informed about the child through voice, written, photographic, or videographic communication. Or the parties could agree to face to face visitation. Or they could agree to any combination of the two simultaneously or chronologically. The important issue is that the parties are comfortable with the agreement.

Determining Whether Post-Adoption Contact is Appropriate

To determine whether post-adoption contact is warranted, the primary concern is whether it will meet the child's needs, interests, and desires, not the needs and interests of the adults involved without necessarily benefiting the child. "Adoption with contact" will likely promote settlement of some termination of parental rights cases. The court, however, should not allow adoption with contact merely because it is a convenient settlement option for parents facing a strong termination of parental rights case. Nor should it be allowed merely because it is more expeditious and convenient for an agency that is unwilling to put time and energy into a difficult termination of parental rights case. "Adoption with contact" must serve the best interests of the child.

Post-adoption contact, particularly between the child and birth parents, may be contraindicated under certain circumstances. Contact should not be allowed if the child is fearful of the parent or fearful that he or she will be removed from the adoptive home and returned to the parent. It may be contraindicated when the child has had many placements and does not have strong ties to the parent, or where there is evidence that post-adoption contact will undermine the integrity and security of the adoptive relationship.

Enforcing the Agreement

Some experts recommend against any post-adoption legally enforceable rights of contact between a child and members of his or her family of origin, particularly with those against whom there was an adjudication or stipulation of child abuse or neglect. The belief is that contact between the adoptive and biological families, if contact occurs at all, should remain entirely voluntary with no enforceability by the court. An enforceable right of contact, even when based on initial agreement among the parties, may erode the exclusive rights and prerogatives of the adopting parents. In this view, the government should not continue to be involved in the lives of families once an adoption is approved because adoptive families are entitled to as much autonomy as any other legally-recognized family. One precedent for this view is the Uniform Adoption Act,[22] which was proposed to the States by the National Conference of Commissioners on Uniform State Laws (NCCUSL) and approved by the American Bar Association. In the Uniform Adoption Act, post-adoption visitation arrangements between adoptive parents and birth parents or other members of the child's biological family are permitted; however, they are not enforceable by the court except in the context of adoption of a child by a stepparent.

The *Guidelines for Public Policy and State Legislation Governing Permanence for Children*[23] recommend that clarity within the statutes is important to give guidance to the court and parties and to diminish the likelihood of future litigation. States must strike a balance between enabling parties to change orders and making such actions so accessible that the parties will be in court unnecessarily. The *Guidelines* propose that only a party to the agreement may move to enforce it. Typically, the parties to the agreement will be the child, adoptive parent(s), and biological parent(s); in some cases, however, the parties to the agreement could include siblings, grandparents or other relatives, foster parents, or any other significant person in the child's life. Only a person who is accepted by the court as a party to the post-adoption contact agreement at the time of the signing of the agreement or entering the agreement into the court record should be able to move to enforce the agreement. Many of the existing post-adoption contact statutes provide that the contact can be modified or terminated only (1) when the parties agree or circumstances have changed and (2) it is in the child's

---

[22] *See* UNIF. ADOPTION ACT, 9 U.L.A. 1 (Supp. 1998).

[23] CHILDREN'S BUREAU, U.S. DEP'T OF HEALTH & HUMAN SERVS., ADOPTION 2002: THE PRESIDENT'S INITIATIVE ON ADOPTION AND FOSTER CARE, GUIDELINES FOR PUBLIC POLICY AND STATE LEGISLATION GOVERNING PERMANENCE FOR CHILDREN (1999).

best interests. This standard strikes an appropriate balance because it does not permit frivolous actions and protects the best interests of the child.[24]

§ 17.4 Permanent Guardianship

A legally secure permanent guardianship, particularly with subsidy, could provide an appropriate permanent plan for those children whose return home or adoption is not appropriate or possible. Children in permanent guardianship would not require ongoing court or agency supervision. Parental rights might not be terminated, but the custodial rights of the parents would be transferred to the guardians. Unfortunately, although a number of distinct legal categories of custody and guardianship are available under state law, most are easily revoked and provide inadequate legal protections for the guardian or custodian as well as inadequate permanence for the child.[25] The forms of guardianship available in most states are too legally vulnerable to provide the permanency that are required, and only a few states have subsidized guardianship.[26]

The Adoption and Safe Families Act of 1997 (ASFA) allows the court, during a permanency hearing, to consider both adoption and legal guardianship as permanent placements.[27] Permanent guardianships under state law are not necessarily consistent with the Federal definition of legal guardianship in ASFA:

> The term "legal guardianship" means a judicially created relationship between child and caretaker which is intended to be permanent and self-sustaining as evidenced by the transfer to the caretaker of the following parental rights with respect to the child: protection, education, care and control of the person, custody of the person, and decision making. The term "legal guardian" means the caretaker in such a relationship.[28]

The Adoption 2002 *Guidelines for Public Policy and State Legislation Governing Permanence for Children* recommend that because the goal of permanent guardianship is to create a permanent *family* for the child, guardians for this purpose should be adult individuals or couples, rather than public or private agencies. Once a permanent guardianship is established, there need not be any ongoing court review or agency supervision of the guardianship. The only exception is that the court could retain jurisdiction, just as it would in child custody

---

[24] *Id.* at II-8.

[25] *See* STEVE CHRISTIAN & LISA EKMAN, A PLACE TO CALL HOME: ADOPTION AND GUARDIANSHIP FOR CHILDREN IN FOSTER CARE (National Conference of State Legislatures, 2000); Mark Hardin, *Legal Placement Options to Achieve Permanence for Children in Foster Care, in* FOSTER CHILDREN IN THE COURTS 128, 150-170 (Mark Hardin ed., 1983).

[26] CHILDREN'S DEFENSE FUND, SUBSIDIZED GUARDIANSHIP (2004); Mark F. Testa, *Subsidized Guardianship: Testing An Idea Whose Time Has Finally Come*, 26 SOC. WORK RES. 145 (2002).

[27] Adoption and Safe Families Act of 1997, Pub. Law No. 105-89, § 302 amending 42 U.S.C. § 675(5)(C).

[28] ASFA, Pub. Law No. 105-89, § 101(b), 42 U.S.C. § 675(7).

determinations following divorce, to consider any subsequent motions to modify or terminate the guardianship or enforce orders of child support.[29]

In some jurisdictions, the judge handling the child protection proceeding has the authority to order a guardianship. An efficient legal process should address the whole needs of the child consistent with the principle of one child, one judge. In States where guardianship requires a separate proceeding in another court, there are formidable procedural barriers and guardianship is sometimes avoided when it is most appropriate for the child and family. California, Michigan, and Rhode Island, among other States, authorize courts to hear child protection cases to order guardianship.

The permanent guardian would exercise full rights and responsibilities concerning the child, including the obligation to support the child. Birth parents could retain an obligation to contribute to the support of a child to the extent of their financial abilities if ordered to do so by the court. Courts could enter standing orders for support as part of the guardianship order, as appropriate in the circumstances. The court may reserve certain contact to the parents in the decree of permanent guardianship, including rights of visitation with the birth parents, siblings, and extended family. The court decree of permanent guardianship divests the birth parents or prior adoptive parents of legal custody and guardianship but does not terminate their parental rights. Thus, the decree of permanent guardianship differs from an adoption in that it does not affect a child's inheritance rights or rights to other government benefits (*e.g.*, social security in certain cases) from and through the birth parents.[30] In fact, one legally significant difference between adoption with contact and permanent guardianship can be the survival of financial rights and benefits from the parents.

Permanent guardianship achieves a legally protected permanency but without terminating parental rights. Some legal theorists distinguish between three levels of parental rights:

- Custody (to have physical possession and responsibility for daily care).

- Guardianship (the right to make the important decisions for the child).

- Residual rights (connection to the biological extended family, rights of inheritance, and the possibility of regaining custody or guardianship, should one lose them temporarily).

Termination of parental rights generally terminates all legal relation between the child and the extended biological family, whose legal connection is derived from the parents' rights, so that the child is no longer related and becomes a legal

---

[29] *See* Chapter II of CHILDREN'S BUREAU, U.S. DEP'T OF HEALTH & HUMAN SERVS., ADOPTION 2002: THE PRESIDENT'S INITIATIVE ON ADOPTION AND FOSTER CARE, GUIDELINES FOR PUBLIC POLICY AND STATE LEGISLATION GOVERNING PERMANENCE FOR CHILDREN (1999).

[30] Mark Hardin, *Legal Placement Options to Achieve Permanence for Children in Foster Care*, in FOSTER CHILDREN IN THE COURTS 128, 171-173 (Mark Hardin ed., 1983).

stranger to them. (Similarly, in adoption the child acquires a new set of parents and a new extended family.) In a permanent guardianship the child remains legally related for inheritance purposes and may receive government and other benefits from the biological mother and father and the extended biological family. Should the permanent guardianship be terminated, for example, by death or disability of the guardian, the parents and extended family members retain their legal relationship with the child. They could have a right to be notified and attempt to show the court that the guardianship should be terminated completely, restoring the rights of the parent or parents, or that the court should appoint another relative as successor guardian for the child.

Obviously this legal status is not for every child. Adoption probably remains the preferred permanent placement for children who cannot be reunited with their biological parents. But permanent guardianship may serve some children very well. The judgment as to when this status is in the best interests of the child is legally and psychologically complex and should be made on a case-specific basis.

Because a permanent guardianship is legally secure and very difficult to set aside, fairness, particularly to the parents, warrants application of strict standards. Permanent guardianship is not a status to be entered into lightly. State law should require that the court make a record in support of the guardianship including, where applicable, the fact that prior to the permanent guardianship the child was in State custody as the result of parental abuse or neglect and the parents were not able to resume care. Developing a sound legal record in support of the permanent guardianship protects the status from challenges except on the grounds cited below.

Permanent guardianship may be based on the consent of the parties if a factual basis for the guardianship is preserved on the record. All parties need not consent to a permanent guardianship, however, and the court may order permanent guardianship following a contested hearing.

In Washington, for instance, a form of guardianship may be ordered after proofs equivalent to those required for termination of parental rights.[31]

The court must also find that the proposed guardian is suitable. In cases where the child has been living with the guardian, the quality of care will help establish this suitability, along with a careful home study and criminal and other background checks. In cases where the child has not been living with the guardian, the agency and court might rely entirely on the home study and background check, or the court might delay a permanent decision until the child has been in the home for a trial period.

When an adult individual or couple has permanent legal guardianship of a child, the legal position of the guardian should be as secure as that of a typical birth parent or adoptive parent. That is, it should not be possible to remove the

---

[31] WASH. REV. CODE § 13.34.230.

child from the guardian unless it is shown that continuing placement in the home is detrimental to the child. If there is a report of child abuse or neglect, the child protection agency will have to provide the same evidence and proof that would be required against a biological parent.[32]

Another way in which federal law affects legal permanent placement options is through the availability of federal matching funds. Through the Federal Adoption Assistance program,[33] persons who adopt eligible foster children with special needs are able to obtain federally matched payments to enable them to financially afford to care for children with special needs. There are no equivalent federally matched payments for children covered by legal guardianships. Under the Title IVE Demonstration Authority, several states are testing legal guardianship as a permanency provision for children for whom the agency cannot locate adoptive parents.[34] States with waivers to permit subsidized guardianships include Oregon and Illinois; a program in Delaware ended in 2002, with children currently enrolled in the program supported through State funds.[35] In addition, a number of other states provide guardianship subsidies using primarily state funds. Among these states are Alaska (for Native Americans), Connecticut, Hawaii, Idaho, Kansas, Massachusetts, Nebraska, North Dakota, and Wyoming.[36]

In calculating the cost of subsidized guardianships, it is important to take into account the savings from reduced administrative costs. That is, when children are moved from foster care into a subsidized permanent guardianship with an adult individual or couple, the state no longer has to pay for the administrative and court costs (staff time and other expenses) related to monitoring and overseeing the child and foster home placement. Consider the large number of public employees who are no longer required to supervise the child's life. They include judges, lawyers for the state, child advocates, parents' attorneys, court clerks, bailiffs, caseworkers, supervisors, agency administrators, and more.

---

[32] For recommendations for a state statute providing for permanent guardianship, *see* CHILDREN'S BUREAU, U.S. DEP'T OF HEALTH & HUMAN SERVS., ADOPTION 2002: THE PRESIDENT'S INITIATIVE ON ADOPTION AND FOSTER CARE, GUIDELINES FOR PUBLIC POLICY AND STATE LEGISLATION GOVERNING PERMANENCE FOR CHILDREN, at II-9 (1999).

[33] 42 U.S.C. § 673.

[34] For a description of the program, see Children's Bureau, U.S. Dep't of Health & Human Servs., *Children Find Permanence in Subsidized Guardianship*, Vol. 5, No. 10, CHILD. BUREAU EXPRESS (Dec. 2004/Jan. 2005), *available at* http://cbexpress.acf.hhs.gov/articles.cfm?issue_id=2004-12&article_id=895.

[35] *See* Children's Defense Fund, *States' Subsidized Guardianship Laws at a Glance*, at tbl. IV, 16-17 (2004), *available at* http://www.childrensdefense.org/childwelfare/kinshipcare/guardianship_laws.pdf.

[36] *See id. See also* MARIANNE TAKAS, KINSHIP CARE AND FAMILY PRESERVATION: OPTIONS FOR STATES IN LEGAL AND POLICY DEVELOPMENT (ABA Center on Children and the Law, 1994); MERYL SCHWARTZ, REINVENTING GUARDIANSHIP: SUBSIDIZED GUARDIANSHIP, CO-GUARDIANS AND CHILD WELFARE (Vera Inst. of Justice, New York, 1993).

Children benefit because guardianship provides more stability than long-term foster care and removes the stigma of being a foster child.

§ 17.5 Standby Guardianship

Standby guardianship is a legal mechanism that transfers decision making for children in those circumstances where a custodial parent suffering from a chronic or terminal illness is able to designate a person to care for the child during the time the parent is unable to care for the child or upon the parent's death.

With respect to Standby Guardianship, ASFA contains the following language:

SEC. 403 SENSE OF CONGRESS REGARDING STANDBY GUARDIANS

It is the sense of Congress that the States should have in effect laws and procedures that permit any parent who is chronically ill or near death, without surrendering parental rights, to designate a standby guardian for the parent's minor children, whose authority would take effect upon:

1) the death of the parent,
2) the mental incapacity of the parent, or
3) the physical debilitation and consent of the parent.

A parent can arrange for Standby Guardianship without immediately ending his or her parental rights. If the parent dies, the Standby Guardian can become guardian and also should have the option of applying for adoption. Standby Guardianship may be an appropriate option where parents are terminally ill (*e.g.*, with cancer or HIV/AIDS) or when they suffer from a disease or disorder that will become incapacitating. Standby Guardianship allows terminally ill parents to choose who will become their child's guardian. It allows the parent to develop a practical plan for transition of responsibilities. It allows the identified guardian to take over the parental functions when the birth parent dies or becomes incapacitated.[37] At least 19 states have enacted Standby Guardianship laws.[38] The National Conference of Commissioners on Uniform State Laws proposes a standby guardianship in its Uniform Guardianship and Protective Proceedings Act (1997), Section 202(b). Thus, there has now been significant experience with Standby Guardianship as a legal option for permanence.

---

[37] New York was one of the first States to enact Standby Guardianship. *See* N.Y. SURR. CT. PROC. ACT § 1726.

[38] *See* NAT'L ADOPTION INFORMATION CLEARINGHOUSE, 2003 ADOPTION STATE STATUTE SERIES STATUTE-AT-A-GLANCE: STANDBY GUARDIANSHIP (2003), *available at* http://naic.acf.hhs.gov/general/legal/statutes/guardianship.pdf. *See also*, Y. SAMERSON, CHOICES FOR TERMINALLY ILL PARENTS: A GUIDE FOR STATE LAWMAKERS (American Bar Association, 1997).

California allows for "joint guardianship" for terminally ill parents, which is similar but not identical to Standby Guardianship.[39] Joint guardianship allows the parent and guardian to have decision-making authority for the child at the same time, while the parent is still alive and not yet incapacitated. It also allows the surviving joint guardian to automatically take over upon the parent's death or incapacity without confirmation by the court. Eliminating the requirement of court confirmation following the triggering event may create a smoother shift of authority than many Standby Guardianship procedures. New York's Standby Guardianship statute, however, permits immediate commencement of the guardian's authority without court confirmation if the parent provides written consent that is filed with the court within 90 days.[40]

§ 17.6 Another Planned Permanent Living Arrangement

"Another planned permanent living arrangement" (or APPLA) is recognized as a permanency option under the Adoption and Safe Families Act (ASFA), but it is the least favored of the permanency options.[41] APPLA, defined as "any permanent living arrangement not enumerated in the statute," is intended to be *planned* and *permanent*.[42] The ABA Center on Children and the Law notes that the preferred permanency plans involve a specific adult or couple (not an organization), who will be in charge of the youngster and likely live with him or her. They give these examples of APPLAs:

- A 14 year-old child, Angela, is in a residential treatment facility. She spends some weekends and holidays with a family friend, Mrs. S., who she has known for years. Mrs. S. is unwilling to adopt Angela because she is concerned that the adoption subsidy would not adequately address Angela's significant mental health needs. Mrs. S. is open to the idea of adopting Angela after she turns 18, and possibly being the representative payee for Angela's SSI benefits. In addition to addressing her mental health needs, Angela's permanency plan would include a structure of regular visitation with Mrs. S., and would include Mrs. S. in Angela's treatment and therapy, as appropriate.

- A 16-year-old boy, Robert, lives in a supervised apartment and is receiving independent living services. He stays with his aunt and uncle every other weekend. They are unwilling to allow him to live there full time

---

[39] CALIF. PROB. CODE § 2105.

[40] N.Y. SURR. CT. PROC. ACT § 1726(3)(e)(iii).

[41] The material in this section is adapted from Jennifer Renne, *Reasonable Efforts to Finalize a Permanency Plan for "Another Planned Permanent Living Arrangement,"* 21 ABA CHILD LAW & PRAC. 33, 38-42 (ABA Center on Children & the Law, 2002), *available at* http://www.abanet.org/child/clp/.

[42] *Id.*

because they have three children under age 9. Robert has also had problems with drugs in the past, and they are concerned that he will be a negative influence on their young children. They do help him with school issues, and are in the process of helping him fill out applications for college. Robert's permanency plan would not only include the independent living services he needs, but would also address issues between him and his aunt and uncle so that those relationships are strengthened and nurtured.

- Termination of parental rights is not being pursued for an 8-year-old Native American child because the agency doesn't think they can meet the burden of proving beyond a reasonable doubt that continued custody of the child by the parent is likely to result in serious emotional or physical damage to the child. Consistent with tribal custom, the tribe has placed the child with a (nonrelative) tribe member who has agreed to be responsible for the child, and with whom the child will reside on a permanent basis.

- A sibling group, ages 6, 9, and 14 have been in foster care with Mr. and Mrs. J. for three years. They visit regularly with their biological mother, and the agency is not pursuing termination of parental rights. The children are bonded with Mr. and Mrs. J. who have committed to caring for the children on a permanent basis. This APPLA could be approved as "permanent foster care with Mr. and Mrs. J."[43]

Long-term foster care is the least desirable option among the permanent placement options when a foster child cannot safely return home. ASFA and its regulations explicitly discourage long-term foster care as an APPLA. The preamble to the ASFA Regulations explains, "Far too many children are given the permanency goal of long-term foster care, which is not a permanent living situation for a child."[44] Foster care is generally not stable and may be disrupted, leading to frequent moves for the child and instability. Emancipation is also discouraged as an alternative permanent placement.

Nonetheless, some youth will not be adopted and a long-term placement with a specific foster family may be in their long-range best interests. Each decision must be individualized and focus on the context and needs of a particular child. ASFA permits a long-term foster placement as an APPLA option if the agency demonstrates a "compelling reason" to the court. "If the agency concludes, after considering reunification, adoption, legal guardianship, or relative placement, that the most appropriate permanency plan is an APPLA, the agency must document to the court the compelling reasons for the alternate plan."[45]

---

[43] *Id.*

[44] *See id.*

[45] *Id.* (original emphasis omitted).

The regulations give three examples of a compelling reason for establishing an APPLA as a permanency plan:

(1) an older teen who specifically requests that emancipation be established as his or her permanency plan;

(2) the case of a parent and child who have a significant bond but the parent is unable to care for the child because of an emotional or physical disability and the child's foster parents have committed to raising the child to the age of majority and to facilitate visitation with the disabled parent; or

(3) the Tribe has identified another planned permanent living arrangement for the child.[46]

Children in planned long-term living arrangements should continue to receive assistance from the state agency and supervision of the court, including continuing access to an attorney for the child. All should exercise great caution to support the family and child to prevent disruption of the placement.

Decisions resulting in permanent or long-term living arrangements should be based on a thorough assessment of the child's needs *and* the family's capacity to meet those needs *currently and into the child's future*. Simply meeting state licensing standards is not sufficient. A home study or an evaluation of the family, a written agreement between the agency and the family, the child's consent, and a statement of the family's intent to parent the child into adulthood should also be required. These materials should be discussed, developed, and agreed to by all parties, including the child, the surrogate parents, and the agency. Some states use a "permanent foster family agreement" (PFFA) to structure these arrangements.[47] Such agreements should be based on a thorough assessment of the family's capacity to meet the ongoing, lifelong developmental needs of the child.

§ 17.7 Re-establishing Parental Rights After Termination

The permanency planning philosophy of America sometimes results in termination of parental rights where the child is not adopted; adoption is disrupted or the child does not settle into some alternative permanent placement. The tight timelines of permanency planning and aggressive termination of parental rights have been criticized for not allowing enough individualized decision making and for creating a certain number of "legal orphans." Guggenheim observes:

> Modern reforms aimed at helping families in need have resulted in creating the highest number of unnatural orphans in the history of the United States. . . .Now is the time to re-examine a child protection system that relies on foster care as the most prominent child protection

---

[46] 45 C.F.R. § 1356.21 (h)(3)(i), (ii), & (iii).

[47] *See, e.g.*, MICH. COMP. LAWS § 712A.13a(h).

mechanism and that also creates more legal orphans than it appears to have the capacity to place in permanent, adoptive homes.[48]

Sometimes, after parental rights are severed and after a youth has been in foster care for some time, the situation changes—the child is older, there may have been unsuccessful or disrupted placements, and the parent's ability to provide for the child has improved. Youth occasionally vote with their feet and run from foster care to be with their extended family, including the parents whose parental rights were previously terminated. It sometimes happens that a reunification with the parent, even after all this history, is indeed in the interests of the child. With the passage of time and change of circumstances a legal, as well as a physical, reunification may be appropriate for the child.

Some state laws permit restoration of parental rights in those circumstances.[49] In other states parents may apply to adopt the child or to become the legal guardians of the child. Although restoration of parental rights is certainly not a common occurrence, it may serve the interests of a child and we should be open to that possibility.

---

[48] Martin Guggenheim, *The Effects of Recent Trends to Accelerate the Termination of Parental Rights of Children in Foster Care: An Empirical Analysis in Two States*, 29 FAM. L.Q. 121, 140 (1995).

[49] *See, e.g.*, MICH. COMP. LAWS § 712A.20.

Chapter 18   CHILD WELFARE APPELLATE LAW AND PRACTICE

by Donna Furth[1]

§ 18.1 Introduction

It's always best to win at trial, of course. If your opponent files an appeal, the reviewing court must presume that the trial court's decision is correct.[2] However, if you lose at trial, you should at least consider seeking relief in the appellate courts.

Even if you win at trial, you have a duty to take a position in any appeal filed by another party. If you represent the child, for example, ABA Standards advise that you "take a position in any appeal filed by the parent, agency, or other party."[3] Moreover, "[I]f the child's interests are affected by the issues raised in the appeal, the lawyer should seek an appointment on appeal or seek appointment of appellate counsel to represent the child's position in the appeal."[4]

This chapter is intended as a primer on the appellate process; however, appeals are creatures of statute. You must be familiar with the statutes and rules of court governing appeals in your jurisdiction. You should also know the availability of writ relief and the unique role of extraordinary writs in child welfare cases. An argument can be made that an appeal, in which delay seems inherent, is always an inadequate remedy for an appellant in a child welfare case.[5]

---

[1]   Donna Furth, J.D., is a member of the Board of Directors of the National Association of Counsel for Children (NACC), a member of the NACC Certification Project Advisory Board, and an officer of the Northern California Association of Counsel for Children. She practices child welfare law, with an emphasis on appellate matters, and teaches at the University of San Francisco School of Law.

[2]   LINDA D. ELROD, CHILD CUSTODY PRACTICE AND PROCEDURE § 14:01, at 14 (2004).

[3]   AMERICAN BAR ASSOCIATION STANDARDS OF PRACTICE FOR LAWYERS WHO REPRESENT CHILDREN IN ABUSE AND NEGLECT CASES Standard F-3 (1996) ("The child's attorney should participate in an appeal filed by another party unless discharged."). This standard was adopted by the National Association of Counsel for Children (NACC). *See* ABA STANDARDS (NACC REVISED VERSION) (2001), *available at* http://www.naccchildlaw.org/documents/abastandardsnaccrevised.doc (last visited January 21, 2005).

[4]   AMERICAN BAR ASSOCIATION STANDARDS OF PRACTICE FOR LAWYERS WHO REPRESENT CHILDREN IN ABUSE AND NEGLECT CASES Standard F-3 cmt. (1996).

[5]   *See, e.g., In re Pablo D.*, 79 Cal. Rptr. 2d 247, 248 (Cal. Ct. App. 1998) ("We bewail the waste of time this appeal has caused, for this court, the parents, and, most importantly, for Pablo. If counsel had sought traditional writ relief immediately following the 12-month review hearing, any error could have been dealt with in a timely and effective manner."); *In re Micah S.*, 243 Cal. Rptr. 756, 761 (Cal. Ct. App. 1988) (every delay in an appeal from an order terminating parental rights "*is purchased at the expense of the person who is in law and morality the primary object of judicial solicitude, namely the child.*").

§ 18.2 Initial Considerations

§ 18.2.1 Is the Order Appealable?

The Final Judgment Rule

The general rule in most jurisdictions and the federal courts is that only final judgments are reviewable on appeal "with the substance of any prior order which remains significant at the end of the trial being reviewable along with the judgment."[6] A decision is final if it "ends the litigation on the merits and leaves nothing for the trial court to do except execute the judgment."[7]

Nonetheless, all states recognize that barring all appeals from nonfinal orders would be unfair in many instances and is not required for effective judicial administration. Hence, there are many exceptions to the finality rule.

Collateral Final Orders

Collateral final orders are immediately appealable in most jurisdictions and in the federal courts. A collateral final order conclusively resolves an issue completely separate from the merits of an action that would otherwise not be reviewable on appeal from the final judgment. "Under the collateral order exception to the finality rule, an order is immediately appealable if: (1) it is separable from and collateral to the main cause of action; (2) the right involved is too important to be denied review; and (3) the question presented is such that, if review is postponed until final judgment in the case, the claimed right will be irreparably lost."[8] An order denying a motion to intervene is one example.

Interlocutory Orders Appealable by Statute

Interlocutory orders are appealable by statute in all jurisdictions. For example:

- New York allows appeals as of right from any interlocutory order that "involves some parts of the merits" or "affects a substantial right."[9] Commentaries to the statute conclude that "almost anything can be appealed to New York's intermediate appellate court," the Appellate Division.[10]

---

6   Robert L. Stern, Appellate Practice In The United States § 4.1, at 77 (2d ed. 1989) (citing F. James & G. Hazard, Civil Procedure, §§ 12.41 to 12.42 (3d ed. 1985) and other treatises).

7   Ruggero J. Aldisert, Winning On Appeal § 4.3.1, at 45 (2d ed. 2003) (citing *Van Cauwenberghe v. Biard*, 486 U.S. 517, 521 (1988)).

8   Linda D. Elrod, Child Custody Practice And Procedure § 14:03, at 14-5 (2004 Cum. Supp.).

9   N.Y. C.P.L.R. 5701(a)(2)(iv), (v) (McKinney 2004).

10   Robert L. Stern, Appellate Practice In The United States § 4.2, at 79 (2d ed. 1989).

- In Massachusetts, "temporary appellate relief from interlocutory orders" may be sought in "single justice" appeals," often heard in fewer than 30 days.[11]

- Minnesota Rule 103.03 contains a long list of appealable orders and judgments and is not the exclusive basis for appellate jurisdiction.[12]

- California makes the dispositional order in a dependency case the appealable "judgment" and every post-dispositional order directly appealable as an "order after judgment," including rulings on discovery and visitation.[13]

Interlocutory Orders Reviewable as a Matter of Discretion

In the federal system and some states, trial courts have discretion to authorize interlocutory review in accord with standards prescribed by the trial court in the first instance and then by the reviewing court, or by the reviewing court alone.[14] These standards, although variously phrased, relate in general to the urgency of immediate review, whether it will expedite the litigation, and the importance of the questions to be decided.[15]

---

[11] MASS. GEN. LAWS ANN. ch. 231, § 118 (West 2004) ("A party aggrieved by an interlocutory order of a trial court justice in the superior court department . . . and family court department may file, within thirty days of the entry of such order, a petition in the appropriate appellate court seeking relief from such order. A single justice of the appellate court may, in his discretion, grant the same relief as an appellate court is authorized to grant pending an appeal . . . ."). *See also* John H. Henn, *Civil Interlocutory Appellate Review under G.L.M. c. 231, §118 and G.L.M. c. 211, § 3*, 81 MASS. L. REV. 24, 25 (1996) ("Once the petition is timely filed, the single justice has a duty to consider it. In this sense, therefore, any and all interlocutory orders can be 'appealed.' With respect to interlocutory 'appellate relief,' however, the single justice is given broad discretion in deciding whether or not to grant it. The single justice has extensive power to grant relief; whether he or she will do so is an entirely different matter.").

[12] MINN. R.103.03 (West 2004). *See* Advisory Committee Comments to Rule 103.03, 1998 Amendments (2004 Electronic Update) ("While Rule 103.03 contains a nearly exhaustive list of appealable orders and judgments, it is not the exclusive basis for appellate jurisdiction. *See In re State & Regents Bldg., Asbestos Cases*, 435 N.W.2d 521 (Minn. 1989); *Anderson v. City of Hopkins*, 393 N.W.2d 363 (Minn. 1986.) In these and other cases, the Minnesota Supreme Court has recognized that there are certain instances in which an appeal may be allowed as a matter of right even though the ground for that appeal is not found in the provisions of Rule 103.03.").

[13] CAL. WELF. & INST. CODE § 395 (West 2004); *In re Daniel K.*, 71 Cal. Rptr. 2d 764, 768 (Cal. Ct. App. 1998) ("Juvenile dependency law does not abide by the normal prohibition against interlocutory appeals.").

[14] ROBERT L. STERN, APPELLATE PRACTICE IN THE UNITED STATES § 4.5(a), at 84 n.29 (2d ed. 1989) (identifying the states as Alabama (to the supreme court in cases within its "original appellate jurisdiction"), Idaho, Illinois, Kansas, Michigan, New Mexico, Pennsylvania, Rhode Island, Tennessee, Vermont, and Colorado).

[15] *Id.* § 4.5(a), at 83-84 ("The most common provision for appeals from nonfinal orders appears in the Federal Interlocutory Appeals Act of 1958 (28 U.S.C. § 1292(b)), and similar statutes or rules of a number of states. Section 1292(b) permits interlocutory appeal when the district judge entering an interlocutory order certifies 'that such order involves a controlling question

§ 18.2.2 What are the Time Limits?

Time Limit for Filing Notice of Appeal

The appealing party typically has 20 to 30 days from "the date judgment is rendered" to file a notice of appeal. The date judgment is rendered may be the oral pronouncement of the ruling, the filing of the judgment by the clerk of the court, or the service of the judgment on the parties to the matter. The time for filing may be extended by certain post-trial motions. For the permissible period in your jurisdiction and its proper calculation, check local statutes and court rules.

Notice of Appeal Vests Jurisdiction in Appellate Court

A timely notice of appeal vests jurisdiction in the appellate court. Hence, a late-filed appeal is subject to dismissal.[16] The court is without jurisdiction to consider it. As a result, if you do not file a timely notice of appeal from an appealable order, the issues determined by the order are *res judicata*. They may not be raised on appeal from a subsequent order. Nor will writ review generally be available if errors could have been, but were not, raised on a timely appeal.[17]

§ 18.2.3 Does Your Client Have Standing?

The appellant must be a party of record who is aggrieved by the judgment: that is, he or she must be a party to the lower court proceeding whose interests are directly, substantially and injuriously affected by the judgment.[18] An appellant is not permitted to urge errors that affect only another party who does not appeal.[19] However, if the interests of two parties interweave, either party has

---

of law as to which there is substantial ground for difference of opinion and that an immediate appeal from the order may materially advance the ultimate termination of the litigation.' The appellant must file a petition for leave to appeal in the court of appeals within 10 days after the trial court's certificate explaining why the standards for interlocutory review have been met and why the appeal should be heard. Adverse parties have seven days to answer.").

[16] LINDA D. ELROD, CHILD CUSTODY PRACTICE AND PROCEDURE § 14:07, at 14-8 to 14-10 (2004) (citing cases from Alabama, California, Kansas, Louisiana, Missouri, Ohio, Rhode Island, Tennessee, and Texas).

[17] *See, e.g.,* Adoption of Alexander S., 750 P.2d 778, 783 (Cal. 1988) (a writ "'cannot serve as a substitute for an appeal, and . . . the writ will not lie where the claimed errors could have been, but were not, raised upon a timely appeal from a judgment'" (internal citations omitted)).

[18] JON B. EISENBERG ET AL., CALIFORNIA PRACTICE GUIDE: CIVIL APPEALS AND WRITS §§ 2:270 to 2:271, at 2-124 to 2-125 (2004); *In re Dependency of J.W.H.*, 24 P.3d 1105, 1108 (Wash. Ct. App. 2001) ("An aggrieved party is one who is a party to the action and whose property, pecuniary or personal rights are directly and substantially affected by the lower court's judgment."), *rev'd on other grounds by* 57 P.3d 266 (Wash. 2002).

[19] *See, e.g., In re Gary P.,* 46 Cal. Rptr. 2d 929, 930 (Cal. Ct. App. 1995) (finding that parents whose rights have been terminated lack standing to appeal the termination order on the ground that the order severs the children's ties with their grandmother).

standing to raise issues that have an impact on the related interests.[20] An appeal filed by a party without standing is subject to dismissal, standing to appeal being jurisdictional.[21]

An aggrieved nonparty may seek party status by filing a motion to intervene. If the motion is denied, he or she has standing to seek writ review or may be granted leave to appeal in an appropriate case.[22]

§ 18.2.4 Was the Error Preserved?

Issues not raised at trial are generally waived for purposes of appeal. The rationale is that it is unfair to the trial judge and the adverse party for an appellate court to reverse for an error that could have been corrected in the proceedings below.[23] Hence, "preserve the issue for appeal by making the proper contemporaneous objection or motion . . . and be certain that the record reflects that the objection or motion had been made and that the trial court adversely ruled on it."[24]

Under federal rules, the erroneous admission of evidence is preserved by a timely and proper objection or motion to strike, setting forth the specific ground for the objection or motion; the erroneous exclusion of evidence is preserved by an offer of proof.[25] "Once the court makes a definitive ruling on the record admitting or excluding evidence, either at or before trial, a party need not renew an objection or offer of proof to preserve a claim of error for appeal."[26] All state appellate courts recognize exceptions to these rules, of course. Hence, check the case law in your jurisdiction.[27]

---

[20] *See, e.g., In re Patricia E.*, 219 Cal. Rptr. 783, 786 (Cal. Ct. App. 1985) (finding that parent has standing to appeal based on the minor's right to counsel and noting, "[a]t stake in a dependency proceeding is both the child's welfare and the parent-child relationship. The two considerations are intertwined" (internal citations omitted)), *overruled on other grounds in In re Celine R.*, 71 P.3d 787, 797 (Cal. 2003).

[21] *Marsh v. Mountain Zephyr, Inc.*, 50 Cal. Rptr. 2d 493, 496-497 (Cal. Ct. App. 1996).

[22] *See, e.g., Cesar V. v. Super. Ct.*, 111 Cal. Rptr. 2d 243, 251-252 (Cal. Ct. App. 2001) (ruling that grandmother who was not a party to the lower court proceeding held sufficiently aggrieved to seek writ review of the order denying placement in her home); *In re M.K.*, 636 A.2d 198, 200-201 (Pa. Super. Ct. 1994) (ruling that mother's boyfriend had standing to appeal dependency adjudication based on finding that he sexually abused the child).

[23] "An appellate court will ordinarily not consider procedural defects or erroneous rulings . . . where an objection could have been but was not presented to the trial court by some appropriate method." *Doers v. Golden Gate Bridge, Highway & Transp. Dist.*, 588 P.2d 1261, 1262-63 & n.1 (Cal. 1979); *In re Dakota S.*, 102 Cal. Rptr. 2d 196, 201 (Cal. Ct. App. 2000) (citing *Doers*).

[24] RUGGERO J. ALDISERT, WINNING ON APPEAL § 5.1, at 56 (2d ed. 2003).

[25] FED. R. EVID. 103(a)(1), (2).

[26] FED. R. EVID 103(a)(2).

[27] In California, for example, a challenge to sufficiency of the evidence is not waived by failure to object at trial. The fact that counsel suffered a conflict of interest is not waived if the trial court knew or should have known of the conflict. A pure question of law may be raised for the first time on appeal and, in many cases, an issue of first impression or an issue on which the law was uncertain at time of trial. Lack of objection by a family member does not waive the tribe's right

§ 18.2.5 What is the Standard of Review?

The reviewing court does not reweigh the evidence presented in the trial court. Rather it reviews the record under standards of review determined by the nature of the issue raised. Findings of fact, for example, will not be set aside unless they are clearly erroneous, not supported by substantial evidence, or indisputably wrong. Thus, the standard of review determines the likelihood of reversal.

Findings of Fact

Findings of fact are reviewed under a deferential standard, such as the "clearly erroneous" or "substantial evidence" standard. A finding is clearly erroneous when:

> "although there is evidence to support it, the reviewing court on the entire evidence is left with the definite and firm conviction that a mistake has been committed." This standard plainly does not entitle a reviewing court to reverse the finding of the trier of fact simply because it is convinced that it would have decided the case differently. . . . If the district court's account of the evidence is plausible in light of the record viewed in its entirety, the court of appeals may not reverse it even though convinced that had it been sitting as the trier of fact, it would have weighed the evidence differently. Where there are two permissible views of the evidence, the factfinder's choice between them cannot be clearly erroneous.[28]

A comparable standard, controlling in a few states, is the substantial evidence standard, under which the reviewing court will not reweigh the evidence, evaluate the credibility of witnesses, resolve evidentiary conflicts, or otherwise substitute its findings for those of the trial court. Rather, the reviewing court will draw all reasonable inferences in support of the trial court's findings (applying a presumption of correctness) and affirm the order if it is supported by substantial

---

to notice under the Indian Children Welfare Act of 1978. California courts are split on whether challenges to the court's subject matter jurisdiction may be raised at any time. *Cf. In re Alysha S.*, 58 Cal. Rptr. 2d 494 (Cal. Ct. App. 1996) (refusing to apply waiver rule to bar claim that lower court lacked subject matter jurisdiction) *with In re Shelley J.*, 79 Cal. Rptr. 2d 922, 923 (Cal. Ct. App. 1998) (finding that claim that dependency petition failed to state a cause of action was waived by appellant's failure to raise it in juvenile court and stating that "*Alysha S.* was wrongly decided on that point."). For comprehensive discussion, *see* MALVINA E.J. ABBOTT ET AL., CALIFORNIA JUVENILE DEPENDENCY PRACTICE §§ 10.28 to 10.36, at 499-503 (2004).

[28] *Anderson v. City of Bessemer City*, 470 U.S. 564, 573-574 (1985) (internal citations omitted).

evidence, even if other evidence supports a contrary conclusion. This is the standard for reviewing questions of fact regardless of the standard of proof at trial.[29]

Discretionary Decisions

Discretionary decisions are reviewed under the "abuse of discretion" standard. This comparably deferential standard is applicable in more than 30 states for custody and placement decisions.[30] It is also applicable to rulings on admission of evidence. Under this standard, "the appellate court will not substitute its judgment and discretion for that of the trial court except where the record reflects a clear abuse of discretion. Some courts use the term 'manifest' abuse of discretion. And abuse of discretion implies a perversity of will that no reasonable person viewing the facts could have decided the way the judge did."[31] Thus, the jurisdictional findings of a juvenile court are reviewed under a standard such as substantial evidence, while the ultimate placement decision is reviewed for abuse of discretion.[32]

Issues of Law

Issues of law are reviewed "*de novo*." Pure issues of law, including questions of statutory interpretation, are reviewed independently (*de novo*) by the appellate court. No deference is given to the trial court's determination. The reviewing court "'makes an original appraisal of all the evidence to decide whether or not it believes' the outcome should have been different."[33] Chances for reversal are most favorable under this standard.

---

[29] *See, e.g., In re Angelia P.*, 623 P.2d 198,207 (Cal. 1981) (noting "the [appellate] court must review the whole record in the light most favorable to the judgment below to determine whether it discloses substantial evidence–that is, evidence which is reasonable, credible, and of solid value–such that a reasonable trier of fact could find [that termination of parental rights is appropriate based on clear and convincing evidence]" (alteration in original) (citations omitted)).

[30] LINDA D. ELROD, CHILD CUSTODY PRACTICE AND PROCEDURE § 14:27, at 14-34 to 14-35 (2004) (citing cases from Alaska, Nebraska, New York, Pennsylvania, South Carolina, Connecticut, Minnesota, Wyoming, Alabama, Illinois, Indiana, Louisiana, Missouri, Montana, New Mexico, Rhode Island, Maryland, and Michigan).

[31] LINDA D. ELROD, CHILD CUSTODY PRACTICE AND PROCEDURE.§ 14.27 at 14-34 to 14-37 (citing cases from Alaska, Indiana, Missouri, Nebraska, Pennsylvania, South Dakota, and Kansas). *See, e.g., In re Stephanie M.*, 867 P.2d 706, 718-19 (Cal. 1994) ("[W]hen a court has made a custody determination in a dependency proceeding, 'a reviewing court will not disturb that decision unless the trial court has exceeded the limits of legal discretion by making an arbitrary, capricious, or patently absurd determination. . . . The appropriate test for abuse of discretion is whether the trial court exceeded the bounds of reason. When two or more inferences can reasonably be deduced from the facts, the reviewing court has no authority to substitute its decision for that of the trial court.'" (internal citations omitted)).

[32] JON B. EISENBERG ET AL., CALIFORNIA PRACTICE GUIDE: CIVIL APPEALS AND WRITS §§ 8:130, 8:130(a), at 8-72 to 8-73 (2004).

[33] *In re George T.*, 93 P.3d 1007, 1015 (Cal. 2004) (quoting *Bose Corp. v. Consumers Union of United States, Inc.*, 466 U.S. 485, 514, n. 31 (1984)).

Mixed Questions of Law and Fact

Mixed questions of law and fact are reviewed under the clearly erroneous or *de novo* standard, depending on whether the issue is primarily factual or legal. "If the pertinent inquiry requires application of experience with human affairs, the question is predominantly factual and its determination is reviewed under the substantial-evidence [or clearly erroneous] test. If, by contrast, the inquiry requires a critical consideration, in a factual context, of legal principles and their underlying values, the question is predominantly legal and its determination is reviewed independently."[34]

§ 18.2.6 Was the Error Prejudicial?

The fact that an error occurred will not result in reversal of the judgment unless the error was prejudicial (as opposed to harmless). In other words, the appealing party must first prove error, and then show the error was prejudicial.

The Test of Prejudice

The test of prejudice in most civil cases is whether, but for the error, it is more probable than not that the result would have been more favorable to the appealing party. Thus if the trial judge committed an error, but there is substantial evidence to support the judgment in spite of the error, the appellate court will let the decision stand.[35]

Federal Constitutional Errors

Federal constitutional errors are evaluated under the *Chapman* test, *i.e.,* reversal is required if the error is not shown to be harmless beyond a reasonable doubt.[36] Although this standard is usually applied in criminal cases, it has also been applied in dependency cases raising constitutional issues.[37]

Errors that are Reversible Per Se

"These are structural defects in the constitution of the trial mechanism, which defy analysis by 'harmless error' standards. The entire conduct of the trial

---

[34] *Crocker Nat'l. Bank v. City & County of San Francisco*, 782 P.2d 278, 281 (Cal. 1989).

[35] *See* LINDA D. ELROD, CHILD CUSTODY PRACTICE AND PROCEDURE § 14:31, at 14-50 to 14-51 (2004) (citing cases from Florida, Indiana, Minnesota, Nebraska, North Dakota, Vermont, Wisconsin, and Wyoming). *See also People v. Watson*, 299 P.2d 243, 254 (Cal. 1956)) (appellate court will not reverse unless it is of the opinion, after examining the entire record, including the evidence, that "it is reasonably probable that a result more favorable to the appealing party would have been reached in the absence of the error"); *Goldman v. Logue*, 461 So. 2d 469 (La. Ct. App. 1984) (judge erred in interviewing the minor in chambers, but since judge did not rely on the interview and all findings of fact were supported by the evidence, decision was upheld).

[36] *Chapman v. California*, 386 U.S. 18, 24 (1967).

[37] *See In re Stacy T.*, 61 Cal. Rptr. 2d 319, 321 (Cal. Ct. App. 1997); *In re Dolly D.*, 48 Cal. Rptr. 2d 691, 695-696 (Cal. Ct. App. 1995); *In re Amy M.*, 283 Cal. Rptr. 788, 799 (Cal. Ct. App. 1991).

from beginning to end is obviously affected by the absence of counsel for a criminal defendant, just as it is by the presence on the bench of a judge who is not impartial."[38] Almost all reversible per se errors arise in criminal cases.[39]

Factors in Evaluating Prejudice

The factors to weigh in evaluating prejudice include:

- *Seriousness of the error.* Some errors are so material that they prevent the judge from properly considering the case. Others are obviously trivial.

- *Weight of the evidence.* An error is not prejudicial if the evidence could not support a judgment in appellant's favor.

- *Number of errors.* In some cases, the sheer number of errors establishes prejudice.

- *Independent basis for decision.* An error is not prejudicial if the judgment can be sustained on a theory untainted by the error.

- *Whether effect of the error cured.* The effect of improperly admitted evidence can be cured by striking the evidence, for example.

§ 18.3 Stay Requests

§ 18.3.1 Effect of Filing an Appeal—Execution of the Judgment Not Always Stayed

Filing an appeal does not automatically stay execution of the judgment.[40] Hence, a critical step in the appellate process may be seeking to stay the judgment being appealed. Failure to do so may result in the very harm that the appellant is seeking to avoid. Thus, ABA Standards provide that if a child client wishes to appeal the order and the appeal has merit, "the lawyer should take all steps necessary to perfect the appeal and seek appropriate *temporary orders or extraordinary writs necessary to protect the interests of the child during the pendency of the appeal.*"[41]

---

[38] *Arizona v. Fulminante*, 499 U.S. 279, 309 (1991) (Rehnquist, J., delivering opinion of the Court as to Part II).

[39] Such errors include the total deprivation of the right to counsel at a criminal trial, a judge who was not impartial, unlawful exclusion of members of the defendant's race from a grand jury, denial of the right to self-representation at trial, and denial of a public trial. *Id.* at 309-310. *But see In re Andres G.*, 75 Cal. Rptr. 2d 285, 288 (Cal. Ct. App. 1998) (holding act in excess of jurisdiction which violated comprehensive statutory scheme and offended public policy reversible per se).

[40] A few states do grant an automatic 10-day stay upon entry of most judgments. LINDA D. ELROD, CHILD CUSTODY PRACTICE AND PROCEDURE § 14:14, at 14-15 (1996) (citing KAN. STAT. ANN. § 60-262(a)).

[41] AMERICAN BAR ASSOCIATION STANDARDS OF PRACTICE FOR LAWYERS WHO REPRESENT CHILDREN IN ABUSE AND NEGLECT CASES Standard F-1 (1996) (emphasis added).

§ 18.3.2 Making the Request for a Stay

A request for a stay must be made in the trial court and, if denied, in the appellate court.[42] "There is no right to a stay or supersedeas. Stays are discretionary with the court and difficult to obtain. In some states the lawyer must convince the reviewing court that the applicant will suffer injustice and irreparable harm from the trial court's order."[43]

§ 18.3.3 Factors Considered in Ruling on a Stay Request

Whether the court will grant a stay in a child welfare case depends on the potential for harm to the children in the current situation and the probable merits of the appeal. "If the child will not be harmed by the present custodial arrangement, the court may be willing to grant the stay to allow the child to remain in as stable a situation as possible pending the determination of the appeal."[44] Elrod sets out the following factors that courts consider in ruling on stay requests:

- The likelihood of hardship or harm to the child if the stay is denied.

- Whether the appeal has probable merit and is taken in good faith.

- The harm, if any, to the nonmoving party if a stay is granted.

- Other equitable considerations.[45]

An appellate court will also consider whether the petitioner has exhausted his or her trial court remedies, although this requirement may be excused if petitioner shows that seeking a stay in the lower court would have been futile, there was no time to seek a stay in the lower court, or that seeking a stay in the trial court would have mooted any subsequent effort to seek the stay in the appellate court.

---

[42] In California, the petitioner seeks a writ of supersedeas to preserve the jurisdiction of the appellate court pending review on appeal and a ruling on the merits. *See* JON B. EISENBERG ET AL., CALIFORNIA PRACTICE GUIDE: CIVIL APPEALS AND WRITS §§ 7:288 to 7:323, at 7.56 to 7.62.2 (2004). In Guardianship of Simpson, for example, the paternal grandparent/guardians appealed the order granting O.J. Simpson custody of his children, but did not seek a stay of the order. The appellate court noted with disapproval that the guardians' "failure to request a writ [of supersedeas] resulted in Simpson having custody during the pendency of this appeal." 79 Cal. Rptr. 2d 389, 395 (Cal. Ct. App. 1998).

[43] LINDA D. ELROD, CHILD CUSTODY PRACTICE AND PROCEDURE § 14:14, at 14-24 (2004).

[44] *Id.* § 14:14 at 14-24 (citing *Sanchez v. Sanchez*, 178 Cal. App. 2d 810 (1st Dist. 1960), opinion vacated, 55 Cal. 2d 118 (1961)).

[45] *Id.*, § 14:14 at 14-25 (citing *Alpers v. Alpers*, 111 N.M. 467, 806 P.2d 1057 (Ct. App. 1990)).

§ 18.4 Procedural Sequence on Appeal

§ 18.4.1 In General

Most states have a two-tiered court system modeled on the federal courts and follow procedures that mirror those in the federal system. Cases are appealed as a matter of right to lower or intermediate appellate courts, which in most jurisdictions are called the "court of appeals" or the "court of appeal."[46] Intermediate courts are "courts of error," designed to determine if a lower court erred and if its ruling must be reversed or modified.

Appeals to the highest or supreme court are discretionary, *i.e.*, granted only by permission of the court. These are "courts of review," whose principal purpose is to adjudicate important questions of law and resolve conflicts between the intermediate courts.[47] Thus most cases come to supreme courts through petitions for review filed by the losing party in the court of appeal.[48]

§ 18.4.2 Appeals of Right

Notice of Appeal

To perfect an appeal of right to the intermediate appellate court, the appealing party must file a notice of appeal within the time limits prescribed by statute or court rule. This notice is filed with the clerk of the trial court and, in many states, sent to the court to which the appeal is taken. The notice must identify the appealing party or parties, the court to which the appeal is taken, the order or judgment being appealed, and the relief sought. It must also be served in most jurisdictions on opposing parties.

As noted above, a timely notice of appeal vests jurisdiction in the appellate court. Hence, a late-filed appeal is subject to dismissal.

The Appellate Record

After filing the notice of appeal, counsel for the appellant must ensure that the appellate record is prepared by the clerk of the trial court and transmitted to the appellate court. Except for rare exceptional circumstances, which are discussed below, the appellate court may not consider matters outside the appellate

---

[46] ROBERT L. STERN, APPELLATE PRACTICE IN THE UNITED STATES § 6.1, at 135 (2d ed. 1989) (noting that in New York and Maryland, the highest court is the Court of Appeal. In Massachusetts and Maine, it is the Supreme Judicial Court, and in West Virginia, the Supreme Court of Appeals).

[47] Twelve states have only one appellate court, a supreme court; however, they contain less than seven percent of the population of the United States. *Id.* § 6.1, at 135.

[48] The principal document filed (which is both a prayer and a brief) may also be called a "petition for application for certiorari" or "certification", "a petition for leave to appeal" or "to allow or permit an appeal or a hearing." *Id.* § 6.7(a) at 151.

record; hence a complete record is essential to a successful appeal.[49] "Some states require both the record and an appendix; others require one or the other. Generally speaking, you must file a copy of the judgment appealed from and the entire trial court record. Requirements for appendices vary: some require a table of contents, relevant docket entries, the judgment of the trial court or any intermediate court of appeals, the trial court opinion, the jury instructions, and other pertinent portions of the pleadings and transcript."[50] The required components of the appellate record are usually set forth in the rules of court.

Appellant's Opening Brief

State courts do not follow a uniform briefing system, but most states require that appellant's opening brief include the following:

Cover Page, Table of Contents, and Table of Authorities. The cover page is used by the clerk's office and the court to identify the brief. It is therefore important that it comply with the pertinent rules of court.[51] The table of contents provides an outline of the legal argument, often phrased in declarative sentences ("The lower court abused its discretion in denying appellant's request that . . . ."). The table of authorities separately lists the cases, constitutions, statutes, court rules, and other authorities cited in the brief, along with the pages on which they are cited.

Introduction. This critical opening section is a concise overview of the nature of the action, the relief sought, the judgment or order appealed from, and the issues to be decided. It may also set forth what the holding should be. Indeed, one senior jurist advises: "You are not writing a mystery novel, so you should immediately tell the reader that the butler did it. In some cases, you may want to state the holding in the very first sentence."[52]

Statements of the Case, the Issues, and the Facts. A statement of the case is the procedural history of the case, accompanied by citations to the record. A statement of the facts—which is generally separate from the statement of the case—provides the court with a narrative statement of the facts pertinent to the issues being raised. This statement too must be accompanied by citations to the record. The statement of the issues succinctly phrases the issues to be decided by the court, often as questions.

Memorandum of Points and Authorities. The legal argument is divided into the sections identified in the table of contents. Each section includes an explana-

---

[49] LINDA D. ELROD, CHILD CUSTODY PRACTICE AND PROCEDURE § 14:13, at 14-21 (2004).

[50] RUGGERO J. ALDISERT, WINNING ON APPEAL § 6.7, at 82-83 (2d ed. 2003).

[51] *See, e.g.,* FED. R. APP. P. 32(a)(2): The front covers of the briefs must contain: (1) the name of the court and the number of the case; (2) the title of the case (see Rule 12(a)); (3) the nature of the proceeding in the court (*e.g.,* Appeal, Petition for Review) and the name of the court, agency, or board below; (4) the title of the document (e.g., Brief for Appellant, Appendix); and (5) the names and addresses of counsel representing the party for whom the brief is filed.

[52] Arthur Gilbert, *Notes to Myself,* 16 CAL. LITIG. 45 (2003).

tion of the lower court's ruling, your objection to it, the standard of review for that issue, an exposition of the pertinent law, and the application of the law to the facts of your case.

Conclusion. The conclusion is an opportunity to summarize the argument, reiterate the precise relief sought, and add a broader perspective on the issues raised.

Appellee's Brief

Appellee's brief follows the same format as appellant's opening brief, but addresses every point raised by appellant to demonstrate that it lacks legal merit. It presents the facts, the legal issues, and the discussion from "a perspective of *affirmance*, casting the case in a manner that shows reversal is not warranted."[53] Appellee is entitled to the benefit of the prejudicial error rule; hence, he or she will generally urge that any error was harmless. "More judgments are affirmed on the ground of 'harmless error' than on any other ground."[54]

Appellant's Reply

Some jurisdictions permit appellant to file a reply to appellee's assertions. This is not an opportunity to raise new issues, however. Permitting the appellant to raise a new issue in the reply would deprive the appellee of an opportunity to counter the argument or require the effort and delay of an additional brief. Thus, reply briefs are effectively organized by paraphrasing the appellant's premise and the appellee's answer, then explaining why the appellee's answer is incorrect, misplaced, or irrelevant.

Oral Argument

Appeals are generally won or lost on the briefs. Nonetheless, oral argument is the only opportunity for a dialogue between the parties and the justices who will decide the case. There is no requirement that parties actually exercise the right to oral argument, of course; however "appellant's waiver may project an image that the appeal is unimportant or hopeless."[55] Thus, under the Performance Standards promulgated by the Committee for Public Counsel Services in Massachusetts, attorneys in child welfare appeals may not waive argument without the express approval of the client and the co-director of the appointment agency.[56]

---

[53] JON B. EISENBERG ET AL., CALIFORNIA PRACTICE GUIDE: CIVIL APPEALS AND WRITS § 9:68, at 9-21 (2004).

[54] MYRON MOSKOWITZ, WINNING AN APPEAL 47 (3d ed. 1995).

[55] *Id.,* § 10:28, at 10-7.

[56] MASS. COMM. FOR PUBLIC COUNSEL SERVS., PERFORMANCE STANDARDS GOVERNING THE REPRESENTATION OF CLIENTS IN CHILD WELFARE APPEALS Standard 11 (revised 11/16/99), *available at* http://www.mass.gov/cpcs/manuals/pcmanual/MANUALChap4Civil.pdf, at 43.

The chance of obtaining oral argument in state appellate courts varies widely. Some courts clearly favor argument, while others clearly disfavor it.[57] The trend in both state and federal appellate courts is to dispense with oral argument.[58]

§ 18.4.3 Discretionary Appeals

Review of the decision of the intermediate appellate court is generally sought by filing a petition for discretionary review in the state's highest court, usually within 30 days of the decision below.[59] The factors considered by most courts are "the public importance or significance of the case or the questions raised, the existence of conflict with decisions of other courts of the same rank (immediately below the supreme court) or of the supreme court of the state or the United States, and the extent of error or injustice in the result reached by the court below."[60] Thus, a petition seeking discretionary review should focus on the importance of the issues presented, rather than the error of the lower court. A good way to achieve that goal is to recruit uninvolved third parties or organizations to file *amicus* letters and briefs in support of granting review.[61]

§ 18.5 The Problem of Post-Judgment Events

The appellate court reviews the correctness of a judgment as of the time of its rendition, on a record of matters that were before the trial court and factual determinations made by the lower court. Thus, in a normal situation, an attempt by counsel to rely on facts outside the appellate record will be deemed improper.[62]

---

[57] RUGGERO J. ALDISERT, WINNING ON APPEAL § 1.4, at 16 (2d ed. 2003) (citing percentages of cases argued from 2001 to 2002 in Iowa (49.5%), Mississippi (69.3%), New York (98.7%), North Carolina (98.9%), Oregon (95.5%), Pennsylvania (89.0%), Rhode Island (14.5%), Texas Supreme Court (74.5%), and Vermont (66.5%)).

[58] ROBERT L. STERN, APPELLATE PRACTICE IN THE UNITED STATES § 13.1, at 368 n.17 (2d ed. 1989) (citing Colorado Supreme Court Rule 34; Delaware Rule 16; Florida Rule of Appellate Procedure 9.320; Hawaii Rules 601-10; Iowa Supreme Court Rule 6, Rule of Appellate Procedure 21; Kansas Rule 7.02; Louisiana Court of Appeals Rule 11.4, Supreme Court Rule VIII, Section 5; New Jersey Rule 2:11-1(b); and Oklahoma Court of Appeals Rule 3.7, Criminal Appeals Rule 3.8). The Florida Committee Note elaborates: "There is no right to oral argument. It is contemplated that oral argument will be granted only when the court believes its consideration of the issues raised would be enhanced." Florida Rule of Appellate Procedure 9.320.

[59] *Id.*, § 6.7(b), at 154-55 (citing applicable rules from various jurisdictions).

[60] *Id.*, § 6.7(c) at 156-59 (citing grounds for granting review in numerous jurisdictions).

[61] Kent L. Richards, *Taming the Odds: Increasing the Chances of Getting Relief from the Supreme Court*, 5 CAL. LITIG. 3, 8 (1992).

[62] ROBERT L. STERN, APPELLATE PRACTICE IN THE UNITED STATES § 10.12 at 276 (2d ed. 1989) (citing ABA STANDARDS RELATING TO THE ADMINISTRATION OF CRIMINAL JUSTICE, Compilation 98, 135-136 (1974)).

Nonetheless, if the appeal is mooted by subsequent events, it is subject to dismissal. Counsel is required to inform the appellate court of any such event.[63] There are also instances in which the post-judgment events undermine the basis of the judgment. Such circumstances arise all too frequently in dependency cases. A reviewing court "cannot simply unwind a juvenile case and presume that circumstances cannot have changed in the interim. They always do."[64]

Although normal rules precluding consideration of new evidence on appeal apply in juvenile dependency cases, there are two things you can do when post-judgment events moot the appeal or undermine the basis of the judgment: (1) request judicial notice; and (2) ask the appellate court to exercise its discretion to take additional evidence.

§ 18.5.1 Judicial Notice

Judicial notice is a well-settled exception to the general rule. "The taking of judicial notice of a fact outside of the record is part of the inherent power and function of every court, whether a trial or appellate tribunal."[65] A judicially-noticeable fact is one "not subject to reasonable dispute in that it is either (1) generally known within the territorial jurisdiction of the trial court or (2) capable of accurate and ready determination by resort to sources whose accuracy cannot reasonably be questioned."[66]

It is particularly useful to ask the court to take judicial notice of court records where (as in some dependency cases) part of the case is on appeal and another part is going forward in the trial court. The limits are that a court may take judicial notice of the *existence* of court records and documents, but may not take judicial notice of the *truth of matters asserted* except those asserted in orders, conclusions of law, findings of fact, and judgments.[67]

Note that judicial notice is taken of "adjudicative facts," which are those relevant to that particular case.[68] A court is not unrestricted in taking notice of "legislative facts," which are "those which have relevance to legal reasoning and the

---

[63] *Fusari v. Steinberg*, 419 U.S. 379, 391 (1975) (Burger, C.J., concurring) ("[C]ounsel have a continuing duty to inform the Court of any development which may conceivably affect an outcome."). If the appeal is moot but raises important questions, counsel may still ask the court to exercise its discretion to reach the merits. *See In re Raymond G.*, 281 Cal. Rptr. 625, 627 (Cal. Ct. App. 1991) ("Although [the issues at detention are] technically moot, the standard applicable to emergency removal of minors needs to be addressed because it is an issue capable of repetition yet evading review.").

[64] *In re Isayah C.*, 13 Cal. Rptr. 3d 198 (Cal. Ct. App. 2004) (internal citations omitted).

[65] ROBERT L. STERN, APPELLATE PRACTICE IN THE UNITED STATES § 10.12(a), at 276 (2d ed. 1989).

[66] FED. R. EVID. 201(b).

[67] *See, e.g., Williams v. Wraxall*, 39 Cal. Rptr. 2d 658, 663 n.7 (Cal. Ct. App. 1995).

[68] FED. R. EVID. 201(a).

lawmaking process, whether in the formulation of a legal principle or ruling by a judge or court or in the enactment of a legislative body."[69] Thus, Louis Brandeis devoted most of his brief in *Muller v. Oregon*,[70] to scientific writings demonstrating that overly long working hours were detrimental to women's health. The Supreme Court relied on this material by taking "judicial cognizance of all matters of general knowledge" to uphold an Oregon law fixing maximum working hours for women.[71]

§ 18.5.2 Request that Additional Evidence Be Taken

At least one state permits a reviewing court in a non-jury case to take additional evidence concerning facts occurring prior to the decision of the appeal and to make independent factual determinations.[72] This power is exercised sparingly—in most instances, to the end that the judgment be affirmed and the litigation terminated.[73] Thus, it has been exercised to establish the occurrence of an event rendering the appeal moot, to correct a clerical error, and to supply a missing factual determination that is necessary for affirmance.[74]

The propriety of receiving post-judgment evidence as a basis for reversing an order terminating parental rights that was unassailable in the trial court was recently addressed by California's highest court: "In a juvenile dependency appeal from an order terminating parental rights, may the Court of Appeal receive and consider post-judgment evidence that was never before the juvenile court, and rely on such evidence outside the record on appeal to reverse the judgment? The general answer is no, although in the rare and compelling case an exception may be warranted."[75] The court has yet to identify the "rare and compelling" case in which an exception will be warranted, although it did note that it had recognized one such exception in an earlier case.[76]

---

[69] ROBERT L. STERN, APPELLATE PRACTICE IN THE UNITED STATES § 10.12(a), at 277 (2d ed. 1989) (quoting Advisory Committee Note to FED. R. EVID. 201(a)).

[70] 208 U.S. 421 (1908).

[71] ROBERT L. STERN, APPELLATE PRACTICE IN THE UNITED STATES § 10.12(b), at 279 (2d ed. 1989) (quoting *Muller v. Oregon*, 208 U.S. 412, 421 (1908)).

[72] CAL. CODE CIV. PROC. § 909 (West 2004).

[73] JON B. EISENBERG ET AL., CALIFORNIA PRACTICE GUIDE: CIVIL APPEALS AND WRITS § 5:168, at 5-44.7 (2004).

[74] *Id.* § 5:172, at 5-44.9.

[75] *In re Zeth S.*, 73 P.3d 541,543 (Cal. 2003).

[76] *See In re Elise K.*, 654 P.2d 253 (Cal. 1982) (reviewing court accepted stipulation reversing order terminating parental rights based on post-judgment evidence that child was unadoptable); *In re Zeth S.*, 73 P.3d 541, 553 n.11 (Cal. 2003) ("*Elise K.* . . . serves as precedent for the proposition that where postjudgment evidence stands to completely undermine the legal underpinnings of the juvenile court's judgment under review, and all parties recognize as much and express a willingness to stipulate to reversal of the juvenile court's judgment, an appellate court acts within its discretion in accepting such a stipulation and reversing the judgment.").

§ 18.6 Extraordinary Writs

§ 18.6.1 Appellate vs. Original Jurisdiction

All state and federal appellate courts review the decisions of lower courts, *i.e.,* they exercise appellate jurisdiction. They also have original jurisdiction in certain instances, including original jurisdiction to issue writs—most commonly extraordinary writs of mandamus, prohibition, certiorari and habeas corpus. They have this ancillary, discretionary authority by explicit constitutional provision or statute or "as a matter of history and common law even in the absence of explicit constitutional or statutory language. Both supreme and intermediate appellate courts have such power."[77]

It should be noted that writ petitions "almost invariably follow proceedings in a lower court to which the petitioner for the writ is objecting. Indeed, the appellate court would usually dismiss the application if relief available below had not first been sought."[78] In this sense, the appellate court, in reviewing a writ petition, is in substance exercising its appellate jurisdiction.

§ 18.6.2 How Writs are Different from Appeals

Extraordinary Nature of Writ Relief

Unlike an appeal, which is heard as a matter of right, relief by means of writ is deemed "*extraordinary,* equitable and *completely discretionary.* Thus, even if a trial court ruling is incorrect, the appellate court is not required to grant an immediate writ petition; it may instead leave review of the issue to await an appeal from the final judgment."[79] As the United States Supreme Court has observed, writs "'are drastic and extraordinary remedies' to be 'reserved for really extraordinary causes,' in which 'appeal is a clearly inadequate remedy.'"[80] Thus, although "the *power* of the courts to grant extraordinary writs is very broad, [it] . . . is exercised very narrowly."[81] In short, most writ petitions are denied.

---

[77] ROBERT L. STERN, APPELLATE PRACTICE IN THE UNITED STATES § 1.4, at 9 (2d ed. 1989). *See also* 20 AM. JUR. 2D *Courts* § 72 ("[I]n certain cases a court functioning primarily as an appellate court ... exercises original jurisdiction. They may be authorized by constitutional provision, or by statute. Original jurisdiction may also be derived from a court's inherent powers.").

[78] ROBERT L. STERN, APPELLATE PRACTICE IN THE UNITED STATES § 1.4, at 10 (2d ed. 1989) (citing *Marbury v. Madison,* 5 U.S. (1 Cranch) 137 (1803) (noting United States Supreme Court lacks constitutional authority to issue writs when it is not in substance acting in an appellate capacity)).

[79] JON B. EISENBERG ET AL., CALIFORNIA PRACTICE GUIDE: CIVIL APPEALS AND WRITS § 15:1.2, at 15-1 (2004).

[80] ROBERT L. STERN ET AL., SUPREME COURT PRACTICE 582 (8th ed. 2002) (quoting *Ex Parte Fahey,* 332 U.S. 258, 259-60 (1947); *Will v. United States,* 389 U.S. 90, 106-107 (1967)).

[81] *Id.*

Writ Review May Supplement, But Not Substitute for, an Appeal

The writ petition is often an effort to obtain review of an unappealable order, *i.e.,* to obtain interlocutory review.

- In California, for example, "'the writ is ordinarily allowed whenever the question presented is either of great practical importance in a particular case,' as when great hardship would result to the petitioner if he could not appeal until after the final judgment, or 'of general importance as a matter of procedural law.'"[82]

- In Missouri, statutes permit interlocutory appeals in only a few situations; however, the appellate courts grant writs "when the result will be 'attractive,' which presumably means fair and just."[83]

- "Other states, such as Arizona, Pennsylvania, Tennessee, Vermont and Washington, accomplish the same result by abolishing the writs, at least by name, and establishing a new remedy for reviewing otherwise unappealable orders previously reviewable by writ or under one of the more modern procedures permitting review of interlocutory orders."[84]

Nonetheless, as noted, a writ "cannot serve as a substitute for an appeal, and . . . the writ will not lie where the claimed errors could have been, but were not, raised on a timely appeal from a judgment."[85]

Parties in a Writ Proceeding

The parties in a traditional writ proceeding are the petitioner, the respondent, and the real party in interest. The petitioner is the person seeking relief—someone who is beneficially interested, but who is not always a party to the lower court proceeding. The respondent is the lower court whose action is being challenged, generally a nominal party whose judgment is defended by those who prevailed in the lower court, the real parties in interest.[86] Under federal rules, all parties other than the petitioner are respondents. The real party in interest is the party who prevailed in the lower court who will oppose granting the relief sought by the petitioner. For example, in *J.A.R. v. Superior Court (E.C.G. and D.R., Real Parties in Interest)*, the parties are as follows:[87]

---

[82] ROBERT L. STERN, APPELLATE PRACTICE IN THE UNITED STATES § 4.7 at 97 (2d ed. 1989) (quoting E. JAMES & G. HAZARD, CIVIL PROCEDURE § 12.11 (3d ed. 1985)).

[83] *Id.* (quoting Dennis J. Tuchler, *Discretionary Interlocutory Review in Missouri: Judicial Abuse of the Writ?*, 40 MO. L. REV. 577 (1975)).

[84] *Id.*

[85] *Adoption of Alexander S.*, 750 P.2d 778 (Cal. 1988) (internal citations omitted).

[86] ROBERT L. STERN, APPELLATE PRACTICE IN THE UNITED STATES § 4.7 at 98 (2d ed. 1989) (citing DEL. R. 43, PA. R. 1513 to 1516).

[87] 877 P.2d 1323 (Ariz. Ct. App. 1994).

- J.A.R. is a 7-year-old petitioner who filed a motion to intervene in his parents' custody battle over him.

- The respondent is the Maricopa County Superior Court and the judge of that court, who denied J.A.R.'s motion to intervene.

- E.C.G. and D.R., Real Parties in Interest, are J.A.R.'s parents, the parties in the lower court proceeding.

Types of Traditional Writs

The major traditional ("prerogative" or "remedial") writs are mandamus, prohibition, certiorari, and habeas corpus. A writ of mandamus (or mandate) lies to compel the respondent court to perform a duty that the law requires. It will not usually issue to control the exercise of discretion.

A writ of prohibition issues to restrain a threatened judicial act in excess of jurisdiction. "The concept of 'jurisdiction' within the context of prohibition is broad. It refers to fundamental 'subject matter' and 'personal' jurisdiction, as well as the power to act in a particular manner. Thus, the writ lies to restrain the exercise of any unauthorized power even though the respondent court has jurisdiction over the subject matter and the parties."[88]

Mandate is a prayer for an affirmative order; prohibition, for a negative one. Since most issues can be framed either affirmatively or negatively, the distinction between mandate and prohibition is now blurred. Appellate practitioners commonly title a writ petition, "Petition for Writ of Mandate, Prohibition, or Other Appropriate Relief." Most courts characterize the relief granted as mandamus.[89]

The common law writ of certiorari issues to correct a completed, nonappealable judicial act in excess of jurisdiction (*e.g.,* a civil contempt adjudication). This writ is rarely used in dependency cases and is beyond the scope of this publication. Nonetheless, it should be noted that the discretionary writ of certiorari issued by the United States Supreme Court and other supreme courts is a statutory writ, derived from, but not to be confused with, the common law writ of certiorari.[90]

A writ of habeas corpus is used to secure the release of persons held unlawfully in custody.[91] This writ has a constitutional as well as a common law

---

[88] JON B. EISENBERG ET AL., CALIFORNIA PRACTICE GUIDE: CIVIL APPEALS AND WRITS § 15:57, at 15-32.2 to 15-33 (emphases omitted) (2004).

[89] ROBERT L. STERN, APPELLATE PRACTICE IN THE UNITED STATES § 4.7 at 95.

[90] *Id.*

[91] See, *e.g.,* 28 U.S.C. § 2241(a) ("[w]rits of habeas corpus may be granted by the Supreme Court, any justice thereof, the district courts and any circuit judge within their respective jurisdictions.")

foundation, and "a history uniquely its own of which its use in appellate courts, now also based upon statutes and court rules, is an inseparable part."[92]

Writs Abolished in Some States

Some states have abolished traditional writs and created a new remedy for reviewing otherwise unappealable orders. In Arizona, that remedy is called a "special action"; in Washington, "discretionary review"; and in Tennessee, "application for extraordinary appeal."[93] In Vermont, "a complaint showing that no adequate remedy is otherwise available may be filed in the Supreme Court or with a justice thereof."[94] New York has also adopted a special action rule merging the three remedies, and Colorado has to a considerable extent done the same.[95] "The effect of such provisions is to eliminate the historical, often technical, restrictions on the use of particular writs, and either to leave the court with unfettered discretion to do what seems right, as in Arizona, or to substitute general standards which concentrate on the practical reasons why allowing review before termination of a case is reasonable in the circumstances."[96]

Statutory Writs Distinguished from Traditional Writs

All jurisdictions have statutes authorizing the review of particular rulings by writ. These so-called "statutory writs" are not an independent kind of writ. The term simply refers to particular situations in which review by a common law writ (mandate, prohibition or certiorari) is expressly authorized by statute.[97]

The differences are that traditional writs are subject to equitable deadlines; an unreasonable delay in seeking relief may bar relief on the ground of laches. The deadlines for filing statutory writs are usually set forth in the statute itself and are often jurisdictional. Traditional writs require a showing of inadequate remedy at law and irreparable injury, while the required showing for statutory writs is set forth in the pertinent statute. A statutory writ petition may also be the exclusive method of obtaining appellate review. In that event, failure to seek the writ waives the right to review of the ruling in a subsequent appeal.

---

[92] *Id.* In California, for example, a writ of habeas corpus is used to support a claim of ineffective assistance of counsel where the basis for the claim lies outside the record in a pending appeal. *See, e.g., In re Darlice C.*, 129 Cal. Rptr. 2d 472, 475 (Cal. Ct. App. 2003).

[93] ROBERT L. STERN, APPELLATE PRACTICE IN THE UNITED STATES § 4.7, at 97-98 (2d ed, 1989). For models of the Arizona legislation, *see*, for example, 17B ARIZ. REV. STATS., SPECIAL ACTIONS, R. PROC. 1(a) (West 2002) ("Relief previously obtained against a body, officer, or person by writs of certiorari, mandamus, or prohibition in the trial or appellant courts shall be obtained in an action under this Rule . . . .") and State Bar Committee Note (citing N.Y. C.P.L.R. § 7801 (McKinney 1964) and COLO. R. CIV. P. 106 (1964) as models for the legislation).

[94] ROBERT L. STERN, APPELLATE PRACTICE IN THE UNITED STATES § 4.7, at 98 (2d ed., 1989).

[95] *Id.* at 97-98.

[96] *Id.* at 98.

[97] For example, appellate review of an order setting a hearing to select and implement a permanent plan for a dependent child in California must be sought by statutory writ. *See* CAL. WELF. & INST. CODE § 366.26 (l) (West 2004).

§ 18.6.3 Procedure in Traditional Writ Proceeding

The Petition

The petition to a reviewing court for issuance of any common law writ within its original jurisdiction is both an original pleading and a legal memorandum. It is generally required to conform as far as possible to the rules applicable to briefs on appeal. It should include:

- *An introduction* setting forth the nature of the case, the issues presented, why extraordinary relief is warranted, and the basis for any stay request.

- *A statement of facts* presented either as a narrative or, in the historical manner, as enumerated allegations of ultimate fact—including allegations identifying the parties, setting forth the facts of the case, the action taken by the lower court, and allegations showing the basis for writ relief (inadequate remedy at law and irreparable harm if writ denied). Statements in the petition must be followed by citations to the writ record, the "record" being the exhibits assembled by petitioner and attached to the petition or filed under separate cover.

- *Prayer* identifying the relief sought, namely, an alternative or peremptory writ, or both; and whether petitioner seeks a stay. The prayer also typically includes a request that the court grant "whatever further relief the Court deems just and proper."

- *Memorandum of points and authorities,* such as that in an opening brief.

- *Proof of service* on the respondent trial court and any real parties in interest (respondents under the federal rules).[98]

- *Exhibits* creating a record adequate to review the claims made, generally including: (1) the order or judgment from which relief is sought; (2) all documents submitted in support of and in opposition to petitioner's position; (3) all documents needed to understand the case and the ruling; and (4) transcripts of the proceedings in the lower court.

The Reviewing Court's Alternatives

Appellate courts are generally afforded maximum flexibility in responding to petitions for writs of mandate and prohibition on their individual basis; however, when an appellate court receives such a petition, it has three basic alternatives, each of which sets in motion its own procedural sequence.

1. Petition Appears Facially Without Merit. If the petition appears facially without merit, the court may deny it summarily, before or after receiving prelim-

---

[98] *See* Fed. R. App. P. 21(a)(1).

inary or formal opposition. The usual reason for a summary denial is failure to provide the court with a record sufficient to review the claims made.[99]

2. Petition Makes a Prima Facie Case for Relief. If the petition makes a prima facie case for relief, the court may request the filing of briefs or a formal answer, set the case for oral argument, and dispose of the matter in whatever manner seems appropriate.[100] In traditional writ terminology, it may issue an "alternative writ," which commands the respondent to comply with the prayer of the petition or, in the alternative, to show cause why it should not be ordered to do so. This is an order to the real party in interest to file an answer to the petition, called in formal writ terminology a "return."[101] If the court determines after briefing, and perhaps argument, that the petitioner is entitled to relief, it will discharge the alternative writ and issue a "peremptory writ" requiring the performance of the act sought to be enforced.

3. Petitioner is Entitled to Relief Based on the Petition. If petitioner is entitled to relief based on the petition, the court may grant a peremptory writ in the first instance, generally after having given notice to opposing parties of its intent to do so.[102] This relief is granted "only when petitioner's entitlement to relief is so obvious that no purpose could reasonably be served by plenary consideration of the issue—for example, when such entitlement is conceded or when there has been clear error under well-settled principles of law and undisputed facts—or when there is an unusual urgency requiring acceleration of the normal process."[103]

§ 18.7 Conclusion

In most states, the case law in child welfare is relatively undeveloped. The burden is on those of us who practice in this area to bring adverse judicial decisions and questions of first impression to the attention of appellate courts—for the benefit of individual clients and the child welfare system as a whole.

---

[99] Hon. J. Anthony Kline, Address at San Francisco Bar Association, *Puttin' on the Writs* (San Francisco, March 27, 2001).

[100] ROBERT L. STERN, APPELLATE PRACTICE IN THE UNITED STATES § 4.7, at 98 (2d ed., 1989).

[101] *See, e.g.,* FED. R. APP. P. 21 (b)(1): "The court may deny the petition without an answer. Otherwise, it must order the respondent, if any, to answer within a fixed time." The answer may consist of admissions, denials and affirmative defenses. Any allegation not denied is deemed admitted. The answer must also allege any facts omitted from the petition and include a memorandum of points and authorities. SORGEN ET AL., CALIFORNIA CIVIL WRIT PRACTICE § 8.10, at 307 (3d ed. 2004). A formal return consists of a response to the formal allegations of the petition in the form of a verified answer, a demurrer, or both. The most commonly asserted basis for a demurrer is failure of the petition to state facts that constitute a cause of action. "This failure in effect raises all prerequisites for the writ being sought." *Id.* § 8.5, at 305-306.

[102] One state court has held that "a peremptory writ may be issued ex parte and does not require notice or that the defendant be given an opportunity to show cause why he or she has not done as commanded." 52 AM. JUR. 2d *Peremptory Writ* § 418 (citing *State ex rel. Shepherd v. Neb. Equal Opportunity Comm'n,* 557 N.W. 2d 684 (Neb. 1997)).

[103] *Ng. v. Super. Ct.,* 840 P.2d 961, 964 (Cal. 1992).

IV. THE ROLE AND DUTIES OF LEGAL COUNSEL IN CHILD WELFARE PROCEEDINGS

Chapter 19   REPRESENTING THE STATE OR WELFARE AGENCY: THE ROLE AND DUTIES OF AGENCY COUNSEL

Part 19A: ABA Agency Attorney Standards*

© 2004 American Bar Association

Standards of Practice for Lawyers Representing Child Welfare Agencies
August 2004

Introduction

The purpose of these standards is to improve the quality of child welfare agency representation and uniformity of practice throughout the country. Many agency attorneys who read these standards may recognize their practice in this document. The standards are meant to improve practice, but also to be realistically attainable by individual jurisdictions. The standards were written with the help of a committee of practicing agency attorneys and child welfare professionals from different jurisdictions in the country. With their help, the standards were written with the difficulties of day-to-day practice in mind, but also with the goal of raising the quality of representation as much as possible. While local adjustments may be necessary to incorporate these standards into practice, jurisdictions should strive to meet the fundamental principles and spirit of the standards.

The standards are divided into the following five categories:
  A. Definitions
  B. Role of the Agency Attorney, including a list of the Basic Obligations
  C. Fulfilling the Obligations
  D. Ethical and Practice Considerations
  E. Administrative Responsibilities, including a list of the Basic Obligations of an Agency Attorney Manager

Section B and E-1 contain lists of the standards for agency attorneys and agency attorney managers for quick reference. These standards are explained in more detail in the rest of the document. Within sections C, D, and E there are "black letter" standards, or requirements written in bold. Following the black letter are "actions." These actions provide additional discussion on how to fulfill the standard; implementing each standard requires the accompanying action. After the action is "commentary" or a discussion of why the standard is necessary and how it should be applied. In some instances, a standard did not need further explanation, so there is no action or commentary attached. A number of the standards relate to specific sections of the Model Rules of Professional Conduct, and the Model Rules are referenced in these standards.

Representing a child welfare agency is a difficult yet important job. There are many, sometimes conflicting, responsibilities. These standards are intended to help the agency attorney prioritize his or her duties and manage the practice in a way that will benefit the agency and ultimately the children and families for whom the agency provides services.

A. Definitions

A-1 <u>Agency</u>: The state or county child welfare agency that is charged with protecting and caring for children suspected or found to be abused or neglected and providing services to the child's family. The agency investigates reports of child abuse and neglect, provides preventative services to families and takes custody of children and oversees their placement in foster care. If a child is placed in foster care, the agency works with the family to reunite the child or achieve another permanency outcome for the child. The agency may also work with unruly children, status offenders, or delinquent children.

<u>Commentary</u>: When applying or adapting these standards locally, it is important to define this term in a jurisdiction-specific manner. There are a wide range of names for child welfare agencies such as the Department of Human Services (DHS), the Department of Social Services (DSS), Children Youth and Families.

A-2 <u>Agency Attorney</u>: An attorney who is an employee or contractor with the government who is charged with the responsibility of initiating proceedings on behalf of the government or the people to protect abused and neglected children.

<u>Commentary</u>: Defining this term in a jurisdiction-specific manner is critical. Everyone should be clear on which attorneys are covered by the practice standards and who the client is.

A-3 <u>Client</u>: A person or entity who employs an attorney or counselor to appear in court, advise, assist and defend in legal proceedings. The client is the entity to which the agency attorney is responsible.[1]

<u>Commentary</u>: State law varies concerning the agency attorney's client. Generally, it is either the child welfare agency itself, or "the people" in a prosecutorial model of representation. *See* section B-1 for further discussion. The attorney must understand who the client is and the parameters of the representation.

A-4 <u>Abuse and Neglect Proceedings</u>: A category of legal proceedings designed to protect maltreated or endangered children that is generally initiated by the government. This group of cases may involve such proceedings as abuse, neglect, dependency, or abandonment cases. It typically involves, among other things, adjudications, case reviews, permanency hearings, termination of parental rights, adoption, and, in some states, guardianship and custody. "Family Drug Courts" and other specialty dockets, if they handle dependency cases, should be included in this category.

<u>Commentary</u>: State law and procedure will dictate the names and types of cases that fall in this category. Many states use different terminology to describe these cases such as "child in need of assistance," "dependency," "abuse and neglect."

B. Role

B-1 <u>Models of Agency Attorney Representation</u>: There are two basic models of agency representation:

Agency Representation Model: Under this model, the agency attorney represents the agency as a legal entity, much the same as in-house counsel's role in representing a corporation.[2] The attorney could be an employee of the agency or of another governmental body, but the agency is clearly the defined client. Some of the benefits of this model include:

- reliance on agency's familiarity with a child and family in decision making;
- value placed on the agency's expertise in making decisions regarding the safety, permanency and well-being of children and on the lawyer's legal expertise on legal matters;
- consistent decision making and interpretation of laws;
- legal action supported by caseworker opinion, thus boosting caseworker credibility in court, for example, in deciding when to file an initial petition; and,
- the attorney is very familiar with the agency and its practices and policies.

One drawback to this model is that caseworkers may believe the attorney represents them personally rather than the agency as a whole. While in practice this may generally be true because the caseworker is the voice for the agency in court, the agency attorney must clearly communicate that he or she represents the agency as an entity and should use the conflict resolution system (refer to D-1 below) when the caseworker's opinion varies from agency policy or the attorney has reason to question the caseworker's decision.[3]

Prosecutorial Model: Under this model, an elected or appointed attorney (or the attorneys working for this individual), often a district attorney or county attorney, files petitions and appears in court on behalf of the agency, and represents the state or "the people" of the jurisdiction. This may mean the elected attorney may override the views of the agency in court. One positive aspect of this model is that the attorney may be more in tune with the wishes and beliefs of the community and how the community feels about handling child welfare cases. Concerns with this model include:

- the caseworker is often the only party in court without an attorney speaking for him or her;
- the caseworker's expertise may be ignored, as the attorney has the ultimate say;
- the attorney may be handling all the business for the community and therefore not be able to specialize in child welfare law;
- political agendas may play a large role in decision-making;
- the agency as a whole may not be getting legal advice on policy issues;
- the attorney's personal beliefs about issues such as permanency rather than caseworker expertise dictate what will happen for a child; and,
- potential conflicts of interest may arise, such as when the prosecutor is pursuing a delinquency petition against a child who is in the agency's custody.[4]

Commentary: No matter what model of representation, it is essential that the agency attorney and agency communicate clearly about which model applies. Each should understand who makes the ultimate decisions in different circumstances and there should be a method for resolving a decision making conflict, should it arise. In each model, there will be times when decision-making roles are unclear and open communication is essential. The agency attorney and agency should understand the attorney's role and responsibilities concerning advising and protecting the agency on liability issues. Additionally, no matter which representation model is used, the agency attorney must understand his or her role with respect to private agencies with whom the agency contracts. The most important issues are that children are safe, their needs are met, and their families are treated fairly.

The drafting committee of these standards recommends the agency representation model. However, state legislation may dictate what model each attorney must follow. States are cautioned against developing hybrid models which incorporate elements of both the agency model and the prosecution model of representation because of the inherent risks of conflict such hybrid models could create for attorneys. These standards apply to all agency attorneys, no matter what model they use for representation.

B-2 Basic Obligations: The agency attorney shall:

General[5]
1. Fully understand and comply with all relevant federal and state laws, regulations, policies, and rules;
2. Promote timely hearings and reduce case continuances;
3. Protect and promote the agency's credibility;

4.   Cooperate and communicate on a regular basis with other professionals and parties in a case, including the client/agency;[6]

Advise and Counsel[7]

5.   Counsel the client/agency about all legal matters related to individual cases as well as policy issues and periodically monitor cases;

Court Preparation[8]

6.   Develop a case theory and strategy to follow at hearings and negotiations;
7.   Prepare or help prepare the initial petition and all subsequent pleadings;
8.   Timely file all pleadings, motions, and briefs;
9.   Obtain all documents and information needed, including copies of all pleadings and relevant notices filed by other parties;
10. Participate in all depositions, negotiations, discovery, pretrial conferences, mediation sessions (when appropriate), and hearings;
11. Participate in settlement negotiations and attempt speedy resolution of the case, when appropriate;
12. Develop a case timeline and tickler system;
13. Subpoena and prepare all witnesses, including the client;
14. Ensure proper notice is provided to all parties and necessary caretakers;

Hearings

15. Attend and prepare for all hearings;
16. Prepare and make all appropriate motions and evidentiary objections;
17. Present case in chief, present and cross-examine witnesses, prepare and present exhibits;
18. In jurisdictions in which a jury trial is possible, participate in jury selection and drafting jury instructions;
19. Request the opportunity to make brief opening and closing arguments when appropriate;
20. Prepare or help prepare proposed findings of fact, conclusions of law and orders when they will be used in the court's decision;

Post Hearings/Appeals

21. Follow all court orders pertaining to the attorney for the client/agency;
22. Review court orders to ensure accuracy and clarity and review with agency when necessary;
23. Take reasonable steps to ensure the agency complies with court orders;
24. Consider and discuss with the agency the possibility of appeal;

25. If a decision is made to appeal, timely file the necessary post-hearing motions and the notice to appeal paperwork;
26. Request an expedited appeal, when feasible, and file all necessary paperwork while the appeal is pending;
27. Communicate the results of the appeal and its implications to the agency/client.

Commentary: This list is not comprehensive but includes key aspects of the agency attorney's role. The agency attorney has many tasks to perform. An initial section of any standards should define these responsibilities.

C. Fulfillment of Obligations

C-1 General:

1. Fully understand and comply with all relevant federal and state laws, regulations, policies and rules

Action: The following laws, at a minimum, are essential for the agency attorney to understand:

- Titles IV-B and IV-E of the Social Security Act, including the Adoption and Safe Families Act (ASFA), 42 U.S.C. §§ 620-679 and the ASFA Regulations, 45 C.F.R. Parts 1355, 1356, 1357
- Child Abuse Prevention Treatment Act (CAPTA), 42 U.S.C. §5101
- Indian Child Welfare Act (ICWA) 25 U.S.C. §§1901-1963, and the ICWA Regulations, 25 C.F.R. Part 23
- Multi-Ethnic Placement Act (MEPA), as amended by the Inter-Ethnic Adoption Provisions of 1996 (MEPA-IEP) 42 U.S.C. § 622 (b)(9) (1998), 42 U.S.C. § 671(a)(18) (1998), 42 U.S.C. §1996b (1998).
- Interstate Compact on Placement of Children (ICPC)
- Foster Care Independence Act of 1999, P.L. 106-169
- Individuals with Disabilities Education Act (IDEA), P.L. 91-230
- Family Education Rights Privacy Act (FERPA), 20 U.S.C. §1232g
- Health Insurance Portability and Accountability Act of 1996 (HIPPA), P. L., 104-192 §264, 42 U.S.C. §1320d-2 (in relevant part)
- All state laws, policies and procedures regarding child abuse and neglect
- State laws concerning privilege and confidentiality, public benefits, education, and disabilities
- State's Rules of Professional Responsibility or other relevant ethics standards

Commentary: The agency attorney, in most instances, files the initial petition with the court and has the burden of proof during court proceedings. Additionally, the agency attorney must advise caseworkers and agency administrators concerning the legality of actions and policies. To best perform these functions, the agency attorney should be an expert in all relevant laws.

2. Promote timely hearings and reduce case continuances

Action: The agency attorney must be prepared to move cases forward in a timely manner. The agency attorney should only request case continuances in extenuating circumstances. The agency attorney should oppose other parties' requests for continuances absent extenuating circumstances. The agency attorney must be thoroughly prepared for all hearings.

Commentary: Delay in cases slows permanency for children. The agency has a duty to ensure that children do not linger in foster care, and the agency attorney must assist the agency meet this duty. Requesting or agreeing to case continuances should be unusual rather than routine practice.

3. Protect and promote the agency's credibility

Action: The agency attorney should work with the agency to bring only appropriate cases to the court. The agency attorney should not file frivolous motions or appeals and should counsel caseworkers concerning the legitimacy of positions. The agency attorney should present cases to the court in a professional, knowledgeable manner. The agency attorney should ensure accurate testimony and correct any misstatements in the courtroom. The agency attorney should present a positive image of the agency at community functions and meetings. The agency attorney should be respectful of caseworkers in the courtroom and in the presence of other professionals and parties in a case.

Commentary: The agency must abide by confidentiality laws, and therefore must keep some information private. Without that information, the public may blame the agency on issues concerning controversial cases. Similarly, the agency may make unpopular decisions that it views are in the best interest of the children in the community. The agency attorney should do everything in his or her power to demonstrate the positive aspects of the agency. The agency attorney must thoroughly understand the attorney client confidentiality issue and work diligently to avoid divulging confidential information. The agency attorney should guide the agency to avoid steps that will make it look bad in court and the attorney should protect the caseworkers from humiliation by the judge or other attorneys.

4. Cooperate and communicate on a regular basis with other professionals and parties in a case, including the client/agency

Action: The agency attorney should have regularly scheduled opportunities to meet with caseworkers and other agency staff. Agency attorneys should treat everyone involved in a case with professional courtesy and should work with everyone to resolve conflict. The agency attorney should have open lines of communication with the prosecutor of related criminal matters. This can be important, for example, in ensuring that probation orders and disposition orders do not conflict, and, where appropriate, are mutually reinforcing (e.g., a visitation order in an abuse and neglect case should not contradict a stay away order from a criminal court).

Commentary: The agency attorney must have all relevant information to effectively try a case. This requires open and ongoing communication with caseworkers and other witnesses. The agency attorney is often the actual or perceived representative of the agency and should present him or herself in a professional manner when before the judge or meeting with other individuals involved in a case. The agency attorney should share relevant information from the case file with other parties in the case, when appropriate.

C-2 Advise and Counsel:

5. Counsel the client/agency about all legal matters related to individual cases as well as policy issues and periodically monitor cases

Action: The agency attorney must spend time with caseworkers to prepare individual cases and answer questions. The attorney should explain to the caseworker, in clear language, what is expected to happen before, during and after each hearing. The agency attorney should be available for in-person meetings, telephone calls, and when appropriate, to periodically monitor cases. The agency attorney is not the caseworker supervisor, but rather should monitor to ensure that legal barriers, such as notice and unresolved paternity, are removed. The agency attorney should attend major case staffings when appropriate. The attorney should be aware of any barriers the parents may have to participating in the proposed case plan, such as an inability to read or language barriers, and counsel the agency accordingly. The attorney should be available to agency administrative staff to advise on policy concerns or general issues facing the agency from the court or community.

Commentary: The agency attorney's job extends beyond the courtroom. The attorney should be a counselor as well as litigator. The agency attorney should be available to talk with caseworkers to prepare cases, to provide advice about ongoing concerns, and provide information about policy issues. Open lines of communication between attorneys and caseworkers help ensure caseworkers get answers to questions and attorneys get the information and documents they need. A major case staffing is one in which the attorney or caseworker believes the attorney will be needed to provide advice or one in which a major decision on legal steps or strategies will be decided. The attorney and agency may want to create a policy in advance concerning whether the agency attorney should routinely attend certain staffings, such as the development of an initial case plan, a case plan in which the goal will be changed to adoption, or when another major change is planned.

C-3 Court Preparation:

6. Develop a case theory and strategy to follow at hearings and negotiations

Action: At the beginning of the case, the agency attorney should try to project the future of the case and think through the steps that the caseworker and attorney will need to take to ensure the desired outcomes. In establishing the case theory and strategy, the agency attorney should think about concurrent planning, planning for reunification for the child as well as other permanency outcomes if needed. The legal steps the agency attorney takes at the beginning of a case lay the groundwork for strong case planning by the agency and positive outcomes for the child and family throughout the life of the case. The case theory and strategy should have some flexibility built in so that as the agency attorney receives additional facts and information, the theory and strategy can be amended.

Commentary: Each case has its own facts, and more importantly, concerns an individual child and family. The agency attorney should give each case his or her full attention. By creating a case theory and strategy, the attorney will ensure that he or she analyzes the case thoroughly and thinks through its intricacies to increase the chance that the agency will be well represented and the result will be the best possible outcome for the child.

7. Prepare or help prepare the initial petition and all subsequent pleadings

Action: The agency attorney should play a lead role in drafting a petition or at least editing and/or reviewing a draft before a petition is filed with court. Similarly, the attorney should review the affidavit and supporting documentation before filing.

Commentary: The initial petition, as well as later petitions, are influential legal documents. The petition controls admissibility of evidence and has a strong impact on the judge and other parties. In general, caseworkers are not trained to write legal documents. If the agency attorney does not draft the petition, or at least review and edit a petition that a caseworker drafts, the agency may miss an important opportunity to shape its case and lay a legal foundation. A legal assistant who works for the agency attorney may be the appropriate person to prepare initial drafts of petitions when attorneys are unable to do so. If the lawyer or legal assistant does draft the petition, it should be based on information the caseworker provides.

8. Timely file all pleadings, motions, and briefs

<u>Action</u>: The attorney must file petitions (including termination of parental rights petitions), motions, requests for discovery, and responses and answers to pleadings filed by other parties. These pleadings must be thorough, accurate and timely.

<u>Commentary</u>: The agency is generally the moving party in abuse and neglect proceedings. The motions and pleadings the agency attorney files frame the case and must, therefore, be complete and contain all relevant information.

9. Obtain all documents and information needed, including copies of all pleadings and relevant notices filed by other parties

<u>Action</u>: The agency attorney must ensure all relevant information is brought to the court's attention. To do so, the attorney should request notes and documents, when needed, from the caseworker. Further, the agency attorney should counsel the caseworker to make sure he or she obtains records that are needed, or may be needed for later hearings. For example, the casework file should include full mental health and substance abuse treatment records, histories for the children and parents, abuse and neglect reports with supporting materials about the investigation, education records, health records, birth certificates for the children, death certificates, affidavits of efforts to locate parents, and results of paternity tests. If the caseworker cannot obtain the necessary documents, the attorney may need to personally obtain them or request a court order so the agency may obtain what might otherwise be confidential documents.

<u>Commentary</u>: Strong exhibits and documentary evidence can make or break a case. Knowing what the documents contain is essential to fully prepare a case. Therefore, the agency attorney should ensure all necessary documents are available for preparation and court.

10. Participate in all depositions, negotiations, discovery, pretrial conferences, mediation sessions (when appropriate), and hearings

<u>Commentary</u>: Jurisdictions vary concerning pre-hearing activity. A great deal of information can be shared during the pre-trial stage of a case, and may help reduce conflict, and save court time and resources. Therefore, the agency attorney should be actively involved in this stage.

11. Participate in settlement negotiations and attempt speedy resolution of the case, when appropriate

<u>Action</u>: The agency attorney should participate in settlement negotiations to promptly resolve the case, keeping in mind the effect of continu-

ances and delays on the child. Agency attorneys should be trained in negotiation skills and be comfortable resolving cases outside a courtroom setting. However, the attorney must keep the agency's position in mind while negotiating. Certain things cannot be compromised (e.g., the child's safety, the key underlying facts of the case, or the assignment of culpability in abuse cases) and all parties should be aware of them. The attorney must communicate all settlement offers to the agency, and it is the agency's decision whether to settle. The attorney must be willing to try the case and not compromise on every point to avoid the hearing. The attorney should use mediation resources when available.

Commentary: Negotiation and mediation often result in a detailed agreement among parties of actions that must be taken by all participants. Generally, when agreements have been thoroughly discussed and negotiated all parties feel like they had a say in the decision and are, therefore, more willing to adhere to a plan. Negotiated settlements generally happen quicker than full hearings and therefore move a case along in a reasonable time period. The agency attorney should ensure that the court is notified of the settlement so it can adjust its calendar accordingly.

12. Develop a case timeline and tickler system

Action: At the beginning of a case, the agency attorney and caseworker should develop timelines that specify what actions should be taken and when. The attorney should keep federal and state laws in mind. For example, under the Adoption and Safe Families Act, the attorney will need to ensure that a permanency hearing occurs at 12 months and will need to file a termination of parental rights petition when the child has been in care for 15 of 22 months, unless certain exceptions apply. The attorney should know when the 15 month point is and whether any exceptions apply. If exceptions apply, the attorney should have a tickler system to revisit whether the exceptions continue to apply at future permanency hearings. Additionally, the agency attorney should develop a tickler system or a plan for remembering the timelines.

Commentary: Agency attorneys handle many cases at a time and must be organized to juggle them all. A good calendaring system, implemented at the beginning and used throughout each case, can help the attorneys better manage their cases. The agency attorney shares a responsibility with the agency for keeping deadlines in mind and moving a case forward.

13. Subpoena and prepare all witnesses, including the client

Action: The agency attorney should develop a witness list well before a hearing. The attorney should, when possible, call the potential witness to determine whether the witness can provide helpful testimony, and then, when appropriate, let them know a subpoena is on its way. The attorney should also ensure the subpoena is served. Attorneys should set aside time to prepare all witnesses in person before the hearing. Some witnesses may require written questions. These should be provided when needed. Additionally, the agency attorney should counsel the agency on its obligations when agency staff are served with subpoenas by opposing parties.

Commentary: Preparation is the key to successfully resolving a case, either in negotiation or trial. The attorney should plan as early as possible for the case and make arrangements accordingly. The agency attorney should consider working with other parties who share the agency's position (such as the child's representative) when creating a witness list, issuing subpoenas, and preparing witnesses. Doctors, nurses, teachers, therapists, and other potential witnesses have busy schedules and need advance warning about the date and time of the hearing. The agency attorney should do whatever possible to minimize the time a witness must spend in court, such as requesting a time certain hearing or arranging for the witness to testify on speakerphone from his or her office. Witnesses are often nervous about testifying in court. Attorneys should prepare them thoroughly so they feel comfortable with the process and the questions they will likely be asked. The agency attorney should know what the witness will say on the stand.

14. Ensure proper notice is provided to all parties and necessary caretakers

Action: The agency attorney should either send proper notice to parties and caretakers from the attorney office, or ensure that it is being done by the agency or court.

Commentary: ASFA requires that foster parents and relative caretakers receive notice of all review and permanency hearings. Parties to the case must receive notice of court hearings and motions filed with the court, such as TPR petitions. As the moving party in most proceedings, the agency has a duty to ensure this requirement is implemented properly. Since it is a legal obligation, the agency attorney should be directly involved. The agency attorney should ensure whoever is providing the notice provides it to noncustodial parents and any man who may have paternity rights to the child.

C-4 Hearings:

15. Attend and prepare for all hearings

Action: The agency attorney should attend and prepare for all hearings and participate in all telephone or other conferences with the court.

Commentary: If the agency is to be well represented, the agency attorney must be prepared and present in court. Even in jurisdictions in which the agency attorney represents the state, the attorney must be active in all stages of the court process to protect children and ensure their safety. In some jurisdictions a nonattorney representative from the agency appears in court on uncontested matters. In such a jurisdiction, there should be a system in place for a caseworker to request legal assistance before court, and an attorney should be available if the case becomes complicated. Even if the agency attorney has taken these precautions, it is possible that an unauthorized practice of law issue may arise from this practice.

16. Prepare and make all appropriate motions and evidentiary objections

Action: The agency attorney should make appropriate motions and evidentiary objections to advance the agency's position during the hearing. If necessary, the agency attorney should file briefs in support of the agency's position on evidentiary issues. The agency attorney should preserve legal issues for appeal.

Commentary: It is essential that agency attorneys understand the state's Rules of Evidence and all court rules and procedures. While there are many circumstances in which cases settle through alternative dispute resolution or during the pretrial phase of the case, agency attorneys must be comfortable zealously trying a case in court. To do so, the attorney must be willing and able to make appropriate motions, objections, and arguments.

17. Present case-in-chief, present and cross-examine witnesses, prepare and present exhibits

Action: The attorney must be able to coherently present witnesses to move his or her case forward. The witness must be prepared in advance and the attorney should know what evidence he or she expects to present through the witness. The attorney must also be skilled at cross-examining opposing parties' witnesses in an effective, but non-malicious, manner. The attorney must know how to offer documents, photos and physical objects into evidence.

Commentary: Because the agency is generally the moving party in most hearings, the burden is on the agency attorney to present a solid case with well-prepared witnesses and documentary evidence. The agency attorney must ensure that appropriate witnesses, e.g., caseworkers who are familiar with the entire case, are present in court and prepared to testify. Additionally, it is important that the agency attorney is comfortable cross-examining witnesses when the other parties present their cases.

18. In jurisdictions in which a jury trial is possible, participate in jury selection and drafting jury instructions

Commentary: Several jurisdictions around the country afford parties in child welfare cases the right to a jury trial at the adjudicatory or termination of parental rights stages. Agency attorneys in those jurisdictions should be skilled at choosing an appropriate jury, drafting jury instructions that are favorable to the agency's position, and trying the case before individuals who may not be familiar with child abuse and neglect issues.

19. Request the opportunity to make brief opening and closing arguments when appropriate

Action: When permitted by the judge, the agency attorney should make opening and closing arguments in the case to set the scene and ensure the judge understands the issues.

Commentary: In many child abuse and neglect proceedings, attorneys do not make opening and closing arguments. However, these arguments can help shape the way the judge views the case and therefore can help the attorney. Argument may be especially needed, for example, in complicated cases when information from expert witnesses should be highlighted for the judge, in hearings that take place over a number of days, or when there are several children and the agency is requesting different things for each of them.

20. Prepare or help prepare proposed findings of fact, conclusions of law, and orders when they will be used in the court's decision

Action: Proposed findings of fact, conclusions of law, and orders can be prepared before a hearing. When the judge is prepared to enter his or her ruling, the judge can use the proposed findings or amend them as appropriate. Once the order is made, the agency attorney should ensure a written order is entered and provided to the agency.

Commentary: By preparing the proposed findings of fact and conclusions of law, the agency attorney has the opportunity to frame the case and ruling for the judge. This may assure accurate orders are entered that meet federally mandated requirements, such as reasonable efforts findings. It may also result in orders that favor the agency, preserve appellate issues, and help the agency attorney clarify desired outcomes before a hearing begins. The agency attorney could provide the judge with the proposed findings and orders on a computer disk or electronically when the judge requests. When a judge prefers not to receive these proposed findings and orders, the agency attorney should not be required to provide them.

C-5 Post Hearings/Appeals:

21. Follow all court orders pertaining to the attorney for the client/agency

Commentary: There may be times the judge orders an agency attorney to do something, such as file a termination of parental rights petition by a certain date. The agency attorney must comply with such orders, or appeal them as appropriate.

22. Review court orders to ensure accuracy and clarity and review with agency when necessary

<u>Action</u>: After the hearing, the agency attorney and caseworker should each review the written order to ensure it reflects the court's verbal order. If the order is incorrect, the attorney should take whatever steps are necessary to correct it. If the order is correct but controversial, the caseworker is unhappy with it, or the caseworker has trouble understanding what is required, the agency attorney should review it with the caseworker and/or the caseworker's supervisor and potentially the agency's administrator and the attorney's supervisor. Follow whatever conflict resolution system is developed (see D-1 below). The agency attorney should counsel the agency to follow the order until a stay or other relief is secured.

23. Take reasonable steps to ensure the agency complies with court orders

<u>Action</u>: The agency attorney should monitor the agency's efforts to implement the order and answer any questions the caseworker may have about the agency's obligations under the order.

<u>Commentary</u>: Obligations 22 and 23 illustrate the importance of the agency attorney's role outside the courtroom. The attorney should help the agency understand and follow through with the court's orders to protect the agency, but more importantly to ensure the agency provides the best possible services for children and families as ordered by the court.

24. Consider and discuss with the agency the possibility of appeal

<u>Action</u>: The agency attorney should consider and discuss with the agency caseworker and supervisor the possibility of appeal when a court's ruling is contrary to the agency's position or interests. The decision to appeal should be a joint one between the attorney and agency staff and must have an appropriate legal basis.

<u>Commentary</u>: When discussing the possibility of an appeal, the attorney should explain both the positive and negative effects of an appeal, including the impact the appeal could have on the child's best interests. For instance, if a judge made a poor decision that could negatively impact the child's future and his or her chance at permanency, an appeal should be taken. Conversely, an appeal might unnecessarily delay a case or make "bad law" for future cases in which the agency participates. The agency attorney should not decide against an appeal because of concern about the trial judge's reaction. *See* section E-2, 10 for a discussion of appellate strategy.

25. If a decision is made to appeal, timely file the necessary post-hearing motions and the notice to appeal paperwork

Action: The agency attorney should carefully review his or her obligations in the state's Rules of Appellate Procedure. The attorney should timely file all paperwork, including requests for stays of the trial court order, transcript and case file. The appellate brief should be clear, concise and comprehensive and also timely filed. If arguments are scheduled, the attorney should be prepared, organized and direct. In jurisdictions in which a different attorney than the trial attorney handles the appeal, the agency attorney should identify issues that are appropriate for appeal and work with the new attorney on the appeal. As the attorney who handled the trial, the agency attorney may have insight beyond what the new attorney could get by reading the trial transcript.

Commentary: Appellate skills differ from the skills most agency attorneys use day-to-day. The agency attorney may wish to seek guidance from an experienced appellate advocate when drafting the brief and preparing for argument. An appeal can have a great deal of impact on the trial judge who heard the case and in trial courts throughout the state.

26. Request an expedited appeal, when feasible, and file all necessary paperwork while the appeal is pending

Action: If the state court allows, the attorney should always request an expedited appeal. In this request, the attorney should provide information about why the case should be expedited such as any special characteristics about the child and why delay would be personally harmful to this child. The request for an expedited appeal should always be considered.

Commentary: Appeals can delay the court process. Every effort should be made to move the child's case forward. The attorney should take great care during the appellate process to do so.

27. Communicate the results of the appeal and its implications to the client/agency

Action: The agency attorney should communicate the result and its implications to the agency. If, as a result of the appeal, the agency needs to take action in the case, it should be instructed to do so. If, as a result of the appeal, the attorney needs to file any motions with the trial court, the attorney should do so.

D. Ethical and Practice Considerations

D-1 Ensure a conflict resolution system is created

<u>Action</u>: The agency attorney and agency should jointly develop a conflict resolution system to cover attorney-caseworker conflict and conflicts among caseworkers.[9]

Key principles of the system should include: 1) the attorney and caseworker (or two caseworkers) should start with a face-to-face meeting to try to resolve the conflict; 2) if there is no resolution, the system should delineate how each should go up their respective chains of command; and 3) the system should set out examples of issues that are legal and those that are social work decisions, understanding that most issues will need to be resolved jointly. The system should incorporate timeframes for resolution so as not to delay a case. The agency attorney should prepare a caseworker before court so that conflicts do not surface in front of the judge.

<u>Commentary</u>: A conflict resolution system should be in place before conflict occurs. The attorneys and caseworkers should work as a team to reach the best outcomes for children and families.

D-2 Understand and comply with state and federal privacy and confidentiality laws

<u>Action</u>: The agency attorney must understand and comply with state and federal privacy and confidentiality laws, including releases of information and protective orders. The agency attorney should also develop protocols with the agency to help the agency access confidential information from external sources when needed for the case. Such methods might include obtaining court orders to access the necessary information.

<u>Commentary</u>: Because the child welfare system directly impacts the lives of children and families, there are numerous aspects of the system that are regulated by confidentiality laws and procedures. For example, the identity of the child, parents, and reporters, as well as treatment records and HIV status of any of the parties, must all be kept confidential. Additionally, the agency attorney should be aware of any HIPPA (medical records) or FERPA (education records) issues that arise. The agency attorney should thoroughly understand these laws to help the agency develop procedures, for example, concerning redacting confidential information from case files for discovery, and following them.

D-3 Initiate and maintain positive working relationships with other professionals in the child welfare system

<u>Action</u>: Because of the crucial role the agency attorney plays in the child welfare system, he or she should build relationships with the other professionals in the system. These include, but are not limited to:

- Judges
- Court staff
- Opposing counsel
- Child advocates, both attorney and nonattorney
- Criminal prosecutors
- CASAs
- Child Advocacy Centers
- Multidisciplinary Teams/Child Fatality Review Teams
- Key service providers
- Medical and mental health professionals
- School staff
- Other local child-centered organizations

<u>Commentary</u>: Maintaining positive relationships with other professionals will benefit the agency on individual cases as well as during times of reform. When these community members believe their opinion is valued and they are an integral part of the child welfare system as a whole, they will lend their support in different ways, such as when the agency seeks legislative support or buy-in for new projects.

D-4 **Play and active role in deciding whether the child should testify and/or be present in the courtroom during hearings**

<u>Action</u>: The agency attorney should consult with the caseworker and the child's attorney or GAL to decide whether the child should be present and/or testify at a hearing. It is important to consider the child's wishes, any possible effects of the testimony and the child's developmental ability to handle cross-examination. The agency attorney and child's attorney should decide together who will present the child's testimony. If the child is represented by an attorney (including an attorney serving as a guardian ad litem), the agency attorney may not speak with the child directly without the permission of the child's attorney, because the child is not his or her client.[10] Questions posed to the child should be clear and asked with the child's ability to understand in mind.[11] Consider requesting an *in camera* hearing, excluding the parents from the courtroom, or videotape for the child's testimony.

Even when the child is not testifying, there may be a benefit to having the child present in court.[12] For example, the child's presence may help the judge focus specifically on the child's needs, and the child may understand how the court makes its decisions. The basis of the decision concerning the child's presence in court should be any state law concerning the child's right to be in court and the child's safety, best interests, and emotional well-being. The agency attorney and caseworker, in coordination with the child's attorney or GAL, should consider whether being in court will be helpful to the child, whether he or she may want to be a part of the proceedings, and whether the child's presence will advance the position of the agency.

Commentary: Generally, the child should be present at substantive hearings because the proceeding concerns the child's life and the child's input must be considered. If the child can handle being in court, his or her presence is important because the judge and other parties should have the opportunity to become acquainted with the child as an individual.[13] This may have an important tactical impact on the case. For example, it is more difficult to continue a case when the judge actually sees the child getting bigger and older and remaining in foster care with no status change. However, if the child will be traumatized by the experience, he or she should not be present in court.

Deciding whether to call the child as a witness can be difficult. There could be a conflict between the caseworker's judgment and the agency attorney's recommendation on strategy to win a case. For example, in a sexual abuse case, the caseworker may believe it would be too difficult for the child to testify, whereas the attorney may think that without the child's testimony the judge would dismiss the case. In this type of situation, the attorney and caseworker should resolve the issue before court and may need to use the conflict resolution system as set forth in D-1 above. If the child is called to testify during the agency's case in chief, opposing parties and the judge may agree to allow the child's attorney to conduct the direct examination to make the child more comfortable. The judge may also agree to hear the child in chambers so the child does not have to testify in front of the parents. In a civil action there is no absolute right to confrontation and if the parents' attorneys are present to hear the child's testimony, generally the parents' rights are considered to be protected.

E. Administrative Responsibilities

E-1 Obligations of Agency Attorney Managers[14]

1. Clarify attorney roles and expectations;
2. Determine and set reasonable caseloads for agency attorneys;
3. Develop a system for the continuity of representation;
4. Provide agency attorneys with training and education opportunities;
5. Create a brief and forms bank;
6. Ensure the office has quality technical and support staff;
7. Develop and follow a hiring practice focused on hiring highly qualified candidates;
8. Develop and implement an attorney evaluation process;
9. Advocate for competitive salaries for staff attorneys;
10. Act as advisor, counselor and trainer for the agency;

11. Work actively with external entities to improve the child welfare system.

Commentary: In general, this section applies to attorneys in an organized office setting, not one attorney government law offices or solo practitioners.

E-2 Fulfilling Agency Attorney Manager Obligations

1. Clarify attorney roles and expectations

Action: The agency attorney manager, with the agency administration, should clearly set expectations for the agency attorneys. This may include:

- written job descriptions;
- responsibilities concerning work with the caseworkers; and
- protocols for assigning tasks and delineating timeframes.[15]

The agency attorney manager should ensure the agency attorneys perform their required tasks and ensure the agency understands and performs its roles.

Commentary: For agency attorneys to provide the best possible representation, both the attorneys and agency must understand their roles and responsibilities. There should be a collaborative approach. The agency attorney manager plays a key role in fostering this teamwork and clarifying each participant's obligations.

2. Determine and set reasonable caseloads for agency attorneys[16]

Action: An agency attorney manager should determine reasonable caseload levels for the agency attorneys and then monitor the attorneys to ensure the maximum is not exceeded. Consider a caseload/workload study, review written materials about such studies, or look into caseload sizes in similar counties to accurately determine the ideal caseload for attorneys in the office. Be sure to have a consistent definition of what a "case" is – a family or a child. When assessing the appropriate number of cases, remember to account for all agency attorney obligations, case difficulty, the time required to thoroughly prepare a case, support staff assistance, travel time, level of experience of attorneys, and available time (excluding vacation, holidays, sick leave, training and other non-case-related activity). If the agency attorney manager carries a caseload, the number of cases should reflect the time the individual spends on management duties.

Commentary: High caseload is considered one of the major barriers to quality representation and a source of high attorney turnover. It is essential to decide what a reasonable caseload is in your jurisdiction. How attorneys define cases and attorney obligations vary from place-to-place, but having a manageable caseload is crucial. One study found that a caseload of 40-50 active cases is reasonable, and a caseload of over 60 cases is unmanageable.[17] The standards drafting committee recommended a caseload of no more than 60.

3. Develop a system for the continuity of representation

Action: The agency attorney manager should develop a case assignment system that fosters ownership and involvement in the case by the agency attorney. The office can have a one-attorney: one-case (vertical representation) policy in which an attorney follows the case from initial filing through permanency and handles all aspects of the case. Alternatively, the cases may be assigned to a group of attorneys who handle all aspects of a case as a team and are all assigned to one judge or one group of caseworkers.

Commentary: Agency attorneys can provide the best representation for the agency, and therefore get the best results for children, when they know a case and are invested in its outcome. Additionally, having attorneys who are assigned to particular cases decreases delays because the attorney does not need to learn the case each time it is scheduled for court. Rather, the attorney has the opportunity to monitor action on the case between court hearings. This system also makes it easier for the agency attorney manager to track how cases are handled.

4. Provide agency attorneys with training and education opportunities

Action: The agency attorney manager must ensure that each agency attorney has the opportunity to participate in training and education programs. When a new agency attorney is hired, the agency attorney manager should assess that attorney's level of experience and readiness to handle cases. The agency attorney manager should develop an internal training program during which the new attorney will be paired with an experienced "attorney mentor" who will work with the new attorney. The new attorney should be required to: 1) observe each type of court proceeding (and mediation if available in the jurisdiction), 2) second-chair each type of proceeding, 3) try each type of case with the mentor second-chairing, and 4) try each type of proceeding on his or her own, with the mentor available to assist, before the attorney can begin handling cases alone.

Additionally, each attorney should be required to attend [fill in number of hours, at least 12] hours of training before beginning, and [at least 10 hours] of training every year after. Training should include general legal topics such as evidence and trial skills, and child welfare-specific topics, such as:
- Relevant State, Federal and Case Law, Procedures and Rules
- Agency Policies and Procedures
- Available Community Resources

- Legal Permanency Options
- Termination of Parental Rights Law
- Adoption Subsidies
- Child Development
- Child-Centered Communication
- Legal Ethics as it Relates to Agency Representation
- Negotiation Strategies and Techniques
- How Domestic Violence Impacts Children in the Child Welfare System
- Appellate Advocacy
- Immigration Law as it Relates to Child Welfare Cases
- Education Law as it Relates to Child Welfare Cases
- State and Federal Benefit Programs Affecting Children in Foster Care (e.g., SSI, SSA, Medicaid)
- Understanding Mental Illness
- Issues Arising from Substance Abuse
- Understanding the Impact of Out-of-Home Placement on Children
- Basic Principles of Attachment Theory
- Options for Presenting Children's Testimony
- Sexual Abuse
- Dynamics of Physical Abuse and Neglect and How To Prove It
  - ➤ Shaken Baby Syndrome
  - ➤ Broken Bones
  - ➤ Burns
  - ➤ Failure To Thrive

Commentary: Agency attorneys should be encouraged to learn as much as possible and participate in conferences and trainings to expand their understanding of developments in the child welfare field. While agency attorneys are often overworked and do not have extra time to attend conferences, the knowledge they gain will be invaluable. The philosophy of the office should stress the need for ongoing learning and professional growth. The agency attorney manager should require the attorneys to attend an achievable number of hours of training that will match the training needs of the attorneys. The agency, court and Court Improvement Program[18] may have training money available that the agency attorney manager may be able to access to defray costs of agency attorney training. Similarly, the agency attorney manager should reach out to the state and local bar associations, area law schools or local Child Law Institutes to learn about available education opportunities. Further, the agency attorney manager should ensure the attorneys have access to professional publications to stay current on the law and promising practices in child welfare.

5.   Create a brief and forms bank

<u>Action</u>: Develop standard briefs, memoranda of law and forms that attorneys can use, so they do not "reinvent the wheel" for each new project. For example, there could be sample discovery request forms, motions, notice of appeal, and even petitions. Similarly, memoranda of law and appellate briefs follow certain patterns that the attorney could copy and only have to fill in the specific facts of a case. These forms and briefs should be available on the computer and hard copy and should be maintained in a central location.

6.   Ensure the office has quality technical and support staff

<u>Action</u>: The agency attorney manager should advocate for high quality technical and staff support. The agency attorney must have adequate and operational equipment to do the high level job described in these standards. Additionally, quality staff support is essential. The office should employ qualified legal assistants and administrative assistants to help the agency attorney. The agency attorney manager should create detailed job descriptions for these staff members to be sure they are providing necessary assistance. For instance, a qualified legal assistant can do research, help draft petitions, schedule and help prepare witnesses and more.

<u>Commentary</u>: The agency attorney cannot do a good job when he or she spends a lot of time trying to get the copy machine to work. The attorney must at least have access to a good quality computer, voice mail, fax machine and copier to get the work done efficiently and with as little stress as possible. Also, by employing qualified staff, the attorney will be free to perform tasks essential to quality representation.

7.   Develop and follow a hiring practice focused on hiring highly qualified candidates

<u>Action</u>: The agency attorney manager should give a great deal of attention to hiring the best attorney possible. The agency attorney manager should form a hiring committee made up of managing and line agency attorneys and possibly an agency representative. Desired qualities of a new agency attorney should be determined, focusing on educational and professional achievements; experience and commitment to the child welfare field; interpersonal skills; diversity and the needs of the office; writing and verbal skills; and ability to handle pressure. Advertising the position widely will help draw in a wider group of candidates. The hiring committee should set clear criteria for screening candidates before interviews and should then conduct thorough interviews and post-interview discussions to choose the candidate with the best skills and strongest commitment. Reference checks should be done before making an offer.[19]

Commentary: Hiring high quality attorneys is essential to raising the level of representation and the level of services the agency receives. The agency attorney job is difficult. There are many tasks to complete in a short time. Since the agency attorneys often move the rest of the system, strong, committed attorneys can drastically improve the system.

8. Develop and implement an attorney evaluation process

Action: The agency attorney manager should develop an evaluation system that focuses on consistency, constructive criticism, and improvement. Some factors to evaluate include: moving cases to permanency in a timely manner; preparation and trial skills; ability to work with agency and other professionals; and ability to work as a team player. During the evaluation process, the agency attorney manager should consider observing the attorney in court, reviewing the attorney's files, talking with colleagues and agency representatives about the attorney's performance, having the attorney fill out a self evaluation, and meeting in person with the attorney. The evaluation should be based on information, which the agency attorney manager will need to collect.[20]

Commentary: A solid attorney evaluation process helps attorneys know what they should be working on, what management believes are priorities, what they are doing well and where they need improvement. If a positive process is created, the attorneys will feel supported in their positions and empowered to improve.

9. Advocate for competitive salaries for staff attorneys

Action: Agency attorney managers should advocate for salaries for the agency attorneys that are competitive with other government attorneys in the jurisdiction. To recruit and retain experienced attorneys, salaries must compare favorably with similarly situated attorneys.

Commentary: While resources are scarce, agency attorneys deserve to be paid a competitive wage. They will not be able to stay in their position nor be motivated to work harder without a reasonable salary. High attorney turnover may decrease when attorneys are paid well.

10. Act as advisor, counselor, and trainer for the agency[21]

Action: The agency attorney manager must ensure that the agency is receiving high quality representation both inside and outside the courtroom. No matter what model of representation, agency attorneys should be sure agency staff is fully informed about legal matters and fully prepared for court and policy decisions. The agency attorney manager should, therefore, develop protocols concerning such issues as:

- communication, such as regular office hours at the agency and timely responses by attorneys to agency telephone calls and emails;

- information sharing;
- conflict resolution;
- attorney-client work product and confidentiality issues; and
- dealing with media and high profile cases.

The agency attorney manager should be sure there is a system in place for reviewing all court orders and communicating the results with the agency.

The agency attorney manager should work with the agency to develop an overall strategy for appeals. It should identify the list of issues that will be most important and appropriate to appeal. It should include an internal system for bringing potential appeals to the agency attorneys and agency attorney manager's attention. The agency attorney manager should then be ready to pursue the strategy when appropriate cases arise.

The agency attorney manager should help prepare all federal reviews and implement any program improvement plans that result.

The agency attorney manager should ensure there is a process for agency legal training. As part of the process, the agency attorney manager could design materials, with samples, to help caseworkers prepare for court and provide testimony. Agency training could occur during formal, new hire training, at brown bag lunches or during after-hours courses. Topics could include, for example:

- overviews of state and federal laws;
- writing appropriate court reports and case plans;
- testifying in court;
- the trial and appellate court processes; and
- the need for and steps to complete acceptable searches for absent parents.

Commentary: Regardless of whether the agency attorney represents the agency or the state, the caseworkers often have the information needed to put together a strong case. Therefore, the attorneys and caseworkers must meet and communicate regularly. This could involve having office hours when the caseworkers can visit and ask questions or designating an attorney to take caseworkers' telephone calls. Similarly, the better the caseworkers and agency staff understand the law and legal process, the easier it is for them and the agency attorneys to do their jobs well. The agency attorney manager should be responsible for developing a system for training the agency staff as well as protocols to improve the working relationships between the agency and agency attorneys.

11. Work actively with external entities to improve the child welfare system

Action: The agency attorney manager should act as a liaison between the agency and outside entities involved in the child welfare system. For example, the agency attorney manager should meet regularly with the court and the state Court Improvement Program to improve issues concerning court administration. The agency attorney manager (or designee) should sit on all multidisciplinary committees charged with improving court functions or other aspects of the system. The agency attorney manager should be in regular contact with agencies, such as local hospitals or schools, that employ people who are frequently called as witnesses and who do work with the same population of children. Doing so can build strong relationships and improve the care the children receive from all of the involved agencies. The agency attorney manager should reach out to agencies such as law enforcement and treatment facilities that have information or documents often needed for litigation.

Commentary: The agency attorney manager should be visible in the community and provide a positive face for people to associate with the agency and agency attorney's office. The agency attorney manager should understand the many issues the agency faces and help resolve some of these through work with the court and other involved entities.

As mentioned above, the standards were drafted with the help of a committee. Many thanks to all of them for their time, expertise, and assistance in making these standards useful and practice focused. These members are:

Diane Bennett, Lead Deputy County Counsel, Santa Clara County, California

Bruce Boyer, Director and Clinical Professor Loyola University Chicago, and Chair, ABA Standing Committee on the Unmet Legal Needs of Children

Diane Garrity, Partner, Serra, Garrity & Masiowski, LLC and former General Counsel, New Mexico Children, Youth and Families Department

Marguerite Gualtieri, Child Advocate Staff Attorney Support Center for Child Advocates, and Co-chair of the ABA Section of Litigation Children's Rights Litigation Committee.

Connie Hickman Tanner, Director of Juvenile Courts, Arkansas

Virginia Peel, General Counsel Massachusetts Department of Social Services

Marvin Ventrell, Executive Director, National Association of Counsel for Children

Howard Davidson, Director, ABA Center on Children and the Law

Mark Hardin, Director of Child Welfare, ABA Center on Children and the Law

Cecilia Fiermonte, Assistant Director, ABA Center on Children and the Law

Kathleen McNaught, Assistant Director, ABA Center on Children and the Law

Moreen Murphy, Staff Director, ABA Standing Committee on the Unmet Legal Needs of Children

Thanks also to:

Jennifer Renne, Assistant Director, ABA Center on Children and the Law, for her expertise and assistance on issues involving ethics and the ABA Model Rules of Professional Conduct and

Claire Sandt, ABA Center on Children and the Law Editor, for her help in making these standards more clear and organized.

Endnotes

* The NACC Board of Directors adopted the ABA Agency Attorney Standards on April 16, 2005.

[1] Model Rules of Prof'l Conduct R. 1.13 (Organization as Client).

[2] Model Rule 1.13(Organization as Client).

[3] Model Rule 1.13(Organization as Client), cmt. 9&10.

[4] Renne, Jennifer. "Conflicts of Interest." *Child Law Practice* 2004 (not yet published).

[5] Model Rule 1.1 (Competence).

[6] Model Rule 1.4 (Communication).

[7] Model Rule 2.1 (Advisor).

[8] Model Rule 1.3 (Diligence).

[9] Model Rules 1.2 (Scope of Representation) and 1.13, cmt, 3.

[10] Model Rule 4.2 (Communication with Person Represented by Counsel).

[11] *American Bar Association Standards of Practice for Lawyers Who Represent Children in Abuse and Neglect Case.* D-5 – D-9. Washington, DC: 1996.

[12] NACC Recommendations for Representation of Children in Abuse and Neglect Cases. III A 6. Denver, CO: National Association of Counsel for Children , 2001.

[13] *Id.*

[14] Model Rule 5.1 (Responsibility of Partners, Managers and Supervisory Lawyers).

[15] Laver, Mimi. Chapter 8, "Agency Attorneys and Caseworkers: Working Well Together," *Foundations for Success Strengthening Your Agency Attorney Office.* Washington, DC: American Bar Association, 1999.

[16] Model Rules 1.1 (Competence) and 1.3 (Diligence)

[17] Segal, Ellen. *Evaluating and Improving Child Welfare Agency Legal Representation: Self Assessment Instrument and Commentary.* Washington, D.C.: ABA National Legal Resource Center for Child Advocacy and protection, 1990, 17.

[18] The Court Improvement Program (CIP) is a federal grant to each state's (as well as the District of Columbia and Puerto Rico) supreme court. The funds must be used to improve child abuse and neglect courts. States vary in how they allocate the dollars, but it typically involves training, benchbooks, pilot projects, model courts and information technology systems for the courts.

[19] Laver, Mimi. Chapter 2, "So You're Hiring? A Guide to Choosing the Best Candidate," *Foundations for Success Strengthening Your Agency Attorney Office.* Washington, DC: American Bar Association, 1999.

[20] Laver, Mimi. Chapter 4, "Getting the Most from Performance Evaluations," *Foundations for Success Strengthening Your Agency Attorney Office*. Washington, DC: American Bar Association, 1999.

[21] Model Rule 2.1 (Advisor).

Part 19B: Agency Attorneys and Caseworkers: Working Well Together*

by Mimi Laver[22]

§ 19B.1 Introduction

How often have you heard:

Agency Attorney:

"Those social workers are so 'touchy/ feely' they can't give the judge concrete facts?" or "The workers are always 'in the field,' where is that!?"

Child Welfare Agency Caseworker:

"Our agency attorneys are so arrogant and emotionally distant. . . ?" and "The attorneys care more about winning the case than about the kids?"

Attorney and Caseworker:

"They never return my call?" or "They just don't understand what I do. . . ?"

As an agency attorney representing the Department of Human Services in Philadelphia, I often heard these kinds of comments. At times I felt like a cruise director—trying to keep caseworkers and attorneys happy by coordinating their activities and helping them work together better. Sometimes, "cheerleading" about working as a team would improve life, but usually just for a little while. What we needed was some real effort and communication to improve our relationships.

If you also hear these gripes in the halls of your office, read on for a "beyond cheerleading" discussion of ways to ease the tensions in attorney-caseworker relationships and to form positive working teams. There's more to it than saying, "Let's all be friends . . ."

---

* This chapter has been adapted from MIMI LAVER, FOUNDATIONS FOR SUCCESS: STRENGTHENING YOUR AGENCY ATTORNEY OFFICE (ABA 1999). Copyright 1999, American Bar Association. All rights reserved. Reprinted with permission.

Editor's Note: Nonsubstantive changes have been made to the text and formatting to reflect the style of this publication. Section numbers have also been added to reflect the style of this publication.

[22] Mimi Laver, J.D., is Assistant Director of Child Welfare at the ABA Center on Children and the Law, Washington, D.C. She previously was a Deputy City Solicitor representing the Department of Human Services and the Department of Health in Philadelphia, Pennsylvania.

§ 19B.2 Roles of Attorneys and Social Workers

§ 19B.2.1 Defining the Client

As an agency attorney, it is important that you define your client. Many conflicts between attorneys and social workers stem from a misunderstanding of who the attorney represents. The models of agency representation vary by jurisdiction and should be defined by your state's law. Attorneys may be employed by local prosecutor's offices, state attorney general offices, local civil litigation offices, or the agency itself. Additionally, some agencies hire special prosecutors or contract attorneys.[23] If you are uncertain what your state legislation dictates, your state attorney general office should be able to advise.

Within each model, the view of who the client is differs. Some represent the agency as an entity, relying on the caseworker's opinions, but keeping the interests of the agency in mind at all times, and some, as in the prosecutor model, represent the "people." Each has its strengths and weaknesses.

If you represent the agency as an entity, as I did in my previous practice, there are two considerations. Sometimes the caseworkers feel the attorneys disregard their wishes, and do not represent them aggressively in court. What happens is the agency attorneys try to be mindful of agency policy, while listening to the individual caseworker's viewpoint. Sometimes the interests of the agency differ from those of individual caseworkers. Because the attorney represents the agency, not individual caseworkers, the attorney must defer to the agency.

The other concern is that if caseworkers make serious errors that conflict with agency policy and a contempt proceeding is held, the caseworkers' union attorney has to represent the caseworker, while the agency attorney represents the agency. In my experience, the benefits of this model outweighed the problems. We were able to consistently represent agency policy while advocating for the caseworkers' positions in court.

Several concerns about the prosecutor model make this method of representation particularly problematic. Often, the attorneys in these offices are new and choose to work in the prosecutor's office to practice criminal law. They rotate out of dependency cases quickly, and therefore never get proper training. As a result, the caseworkers often feel the representation is inadequate. Additionally, with this method the attorneys generally get the final word on whether a petition should be filed. This leaves the caseworker feeling as if his or her professional opinion is not considered. They may also fear that with attorneys making decisions about the caseworkers' clients, best social work practice will be ignored. The National Association of Social Workers (NASW) *Standards for Social Work Practice* in child protection set out: "The initiation of court

---

[23] Donald N. Duquette, *Lawyers' Roles in Child Protection*, in THE BATTERED CHILD (Mary Edna Helfer et al. eds., 5th ed.) (Chicago and London: The University of Chicago Press, 1997); Henry J. Plum, *Legal Representation of Agencies Presentation Outline*, June 15-17, 1998.

action is an agency team decision requiring legal counsel and legal representation."[24] In the prosecutor model of representation, the collaborative decision-making process can get lost and can cause tension between you and the caseworker.

No matter which model your jurisdiction uses, it is important for you to define your client.[25] Further, it is important for your client to understand the scope of your representation.

§ 19B.2.2 Remember Your Obligations

No matter who your client is, there are certain ethical obligations you have in your practice. You may need to communicate these rules to the caseworker from time to time. Your primary responsibility is as follows: "A lawyer shall provide competent representation to a client. Competent representation requires the legal knowledge, skill, thoroughness and preparation reasonably necessary for the representation."[26] Further, "In representing a client, a lawyer shall exercise independent professional judgment and render candid advice. In rendering advice, a lawyer may refer not only to law but to other considerations such as moral, economic, social and political factors, that may be relevant to the client's situation."[27] As an agency attorney, you will often be asked to act as an advisor. You must provide the best counsel possible and then allow your client to reach a decision.

Often, attorneys worry that if the caseworkers are making major decisions about a case, the attorneys will be forced to do something unethical. If you and the caseworker or supervisor disagree about a decision, you have an obligation to try to work out a solution that is comfortable for you and the client. You are bound by the Model Rules of Professional Conduct, however, and may not act in an unethical manner. Generally, if you and your client discuss the matter, you will be able to reach a mutually acceptable outcome.

§ 19B.2.3 Define Responsibilities

Decide which tasks you should handle and which should be handled by the caseworker. Decide what jobs should be shared. Deciding who has what responsibilities and sticking with it often causes tension in the attorney-caseworker relationship. Deciding together can make your team operate more smoothly.

---

[24] *NASW Standards for Social Work Practice in Child Protection.* Standard 21 (Washington, DC: NASW, 1997).

[25] *See* MODEL RULES OF PROF'L CONDUCT R. 1.13 and cmt. (1997) ("A lawyer employed or retained by an organization [including a governmental organization] represents the organization acting through its duly authorized constituents.")

[26] MODEL RULES OF PROF'L CONDUCT R. 1.1.

[27] MODEL RULES OF PROF'L CONDUCT R. 2.1.

Use the list in Section 19B.2.8 when deciding who should handle various duties. Your needs may be different and you may have additional tasks that should be considered when you and the caseworkers divide the workload.

You and the caseworkers should make your own list of jobs and openly discuss who should have primary responsibility for each. Consider creating protocols for some of the ongoing responsibilities you share. With the written protocol for termination petitions, for example, you, your staff, and the caseworker will have guidance about what jobs you must each complete and timeframes for completion.

§ 19B.2.4 Decide Who Calls the Shots

Once you have defined your responsibilities, you and the caseworkers need to decide who makes the decisions. Some will be fairly obvious. For example, if an issue clearly involves a legal strategy, you get to make the final decision.[28] Similarly, if the question concerns social work or family specific treatment, the caseworker, on behalf of the agency, calls the shots. Most questions though, are not so clearly defined. Your strong communication and teamwork will be needed to discuss the issue with the caseworker and try to resolve the issue in a manner that satisfies both of your goals.

Additionally, you will need to keep in mind the answer to the "who is my client?" question. Generally, your client will be the agency and not the caseworker. You and the agency administration should have a system in place to resolve conflicts between you and individual caseworkers. Sometimes just having a calm conversation with the caseworker and both of your supervisors can help. Sometimes the issue has systemic impact, and the head of the agency needs to make the decision. If a dispute resolution system is implemented before a major conflict, none of the players will be offended if the system is used.[29] There are times when you will need to talk with the caseworker's supervisor for clarification. This should not be viewed as "tattling" on the caseworker, but part of the process to improve and expand the team.

§ 19B.3 Need for Collaboration

As an agency attorney, you need good relationships with child welfare agency caseworkers to best serve children in the system. When you and the workers are busy complaining, your ability to work as a team and handle cases effectively and efficiently suffers. As a result, your cases may not be prepared

---

[28] *See* MODEL RULES OF PROF'L CONDUCT R. 1.2 and cmt.

[29] Donald N. Duquette, *Lawyers' Roles in Child Protection*, in THE BATTERED CHILD, 471-472 (Mary Edna Helfer et al. eds., 5th ed.) (Chicago and London: The University of Chicago Press, 1997). *See also* Gene D. Skarin, *The Role of the Child Protective Agency's Attorney in Family Court, in Practising Law Institute Criminal Law and Urban Problems* 171, March 1995, at 440-441.

thoroughly for court, your frustration about your job may increase, and the children on your caseload may remain in foster care longer than they should.

There are several characteristics of a strong working relationship: communication, mutual respect, trust, and teamwork.

§ 19B.3.1 Communication

Open communication is a basic element of any good relationship. It is no different when working with caseworkers. Communicating effectively requires returning phone calls promptly, asking questions, addressing differences of opinion, and making time to talk about cases. Caseworkers should expect this of you and you of them.

Work with the caseworkers to devise a workable communication system. Do you all have e-mail and are you using it? Is this a way to communicate that would save time and be reliable? Do you have an inter-office mail system? Are there mutually agreed upon times that you could be available to answer questions? Explore what, if any, complaints you each have about availability and level of communication and then, together, find ways to improve. When you are all communicating, there is less likelihood that you will arrive in court not knowing what the caseworker's position is or what needs to be done for the child.

§ 19B.3.2 Mutual Respect

Attorneys and caseworkers are both professionals with specific areas of expertise. You both have particular tasks to perform on all cases and are essential to a positive outcome in the case. Often, attorneys and caseworkers express that members of the other profession do not value their opinions and do not treat them courteously. When there is a lack of respect, incorrect assumptions about the other group emerge and add to negative feelings. It is essential that you each learn about the other's backgrounds and job responsibilities. With greater understanding of each other, an increased respect will grow.

§ 19B.3.3 Trust

In addition to respect, you and the caseworkers need to trust each other. If you are a new attorney it can be difficult to gain the trust of the caseworkers. The caseworkers may believe you do not know the answers to questions or are too new to advocate aggressively on their behalf. If you consistently provide good advice and perform well in court, the caseworkers will develop trust.

If you are an experienced attorney and have gained the caseworker's trust, keeping it requires that you are consistent and honest. When a trusting relationship exists, the caseworkers are more likely to call you with questions rather than acting first and then asking. Similarly, when you trust the caseworkers, you will have greater confidence in the cases you present in court.

§ 19B.3.4 Teamwork

Out of the communication, respect, and trust comes a sense of teamwork.[30] When you and the caseworker know what the other person has been doing on a case, know what the other person thinks about the case, and value the other person's viewpoint, the case will be its strongest and the child will benefit. Even if you and the caseworker do not agree about parts of the case, as a team you will be able to reach a mutually satisfactory decision. If you are functioning as a team, your representation will be its best and the caseworker's efforts for the family will be most effective.

§ 19B.4 Strengthening the Relationship

To improve the attorney-caseworker relationship, you need to talk and have more contact with each other. You and the caseworkers are probably overloaded in managing your day-to-day work, and the idea of trainings or group discussions may not be a pleasant one. However, taking time now will help improve the team for the long-term.

§ 19B.4.1 Informal Sessions

Find Shared Beliefs

Meet with caseworkers and agency administrators to eliminate existing barriers and identify common goals. You will probably all realize that you share the ideal of improving the lives of children in your community, and working through your differences may become easier with this understanding.

The NASW Standards for Social Work Practice in Child Protection delineate specific values that are central to improving the child welfare system and the lives of children and families. These include:

- Recognizing the dignity of the child.

- Commitment to the child's family.

- Promoting permanent and consistent care for children.

- Recognizing people's capacity to change.[31]

Child welfare attorneys generally share these ideals and the caseworkers need to know that.

---

[30] *See* Janet Weinstein, *And Never the Twain Shall Meet: The Best Interests of Children and the Adversary System*, 52 U. MIAMI L. REV. 79, 159 (October 1997).

[31] *NASW Standards for Social Work Practice in Child Protection*, Standard 2 and cmt.

Facilitate in Comfort

Ask a neutral person with experience controlling discussions to facilitate a series of sessions that allow participants to express concerns and work towards concrete remedies. If you do not have a person in your department with this kind of experience, consider contacting your local university's marketing department for referrals. Meet in a comfortable room. You and the caseworkers can alternate as hosts if your offices are not in the same place.

Be Concrete

These discussions may start as gripe-and-complaint sessions, but sometimes it is necessary for people to express their frustrations before being able to form positive resolutions. If complaining is permitted, the facilitator should set ground rules. For instance, names should not be used to bad mouth one another.

As an example of the need to be concrete, I remember an experience several years ago in Philadelphia. The caseworkers and attorneys in my office attempted to have some sessions focused on improving our relationships. The attorneys often found them frustrating because there was too much talking with too few concrete results. While we cared how the caseworkers felt about us and the court process, we were more interested in trying to "fix" the problems right away. Needless to say, we were unable to do so without also talking about our view of the system and really listening to what the caseworkers were sharing. Similarly, the process could not work without the caseworkers joining us in trying to think of practical ways to improve our relationships.

Understand Each Others' Languages

There needs to be an understanding that, in general, attorneys and social workers think about things differently. They do not always use the same language. Attorneys are taught and are generally good at "multi-tasking" while caseworkers concentrate on single tasks, such as working on specific goals with a family. Attorneys often look at things on a macro or system level, while caseworkers focus on the child or family level. Attorneys have good intuitive adversarial skills, while caseworkers have intuitive social skills. These social skills are necessary for good social work, but may not be useful when it comes to testifying in a courtroom where the adversarial skills come in handy. Additionally, attorneys are not trained in social work practice while in law school, and caseworkers learn very little about the law during their educations. The law is pervasive in the child welfare system, which may be frustrating for caseworkers who focus on helping a family.[32] To improve the relationships, attorneys and caseworkers must acknowledge these differences and try to learn each others' languages.

---

[32] Telephone interview with Melissa Mitchell, J.D., General Counsel, Franklin County Children Services, Columbus, Ohio based on her discussions with the in-house attorneys at Franklin County Children Services, July 14, 1998.

Share Basic Information

Often attorneys and caseworkers complain that the other group does not understand what they do or their roles. During discussion sessions you could talk about how you came to your positions and what your jobs entail. A caseworker could describe a home visit and the feelings that accompany removing a child from the home. You could discuss how you prepare for a contested hearing and the difficulties involved in getting attached to one of the children. Let the workers know that "lawyers have feelings too!"

Reach Outcomes

You are busy and so are the caseworkers, but try not to let the discussions end until you have realized some positive outcomes. Other areas in which protocols could help are:

- When attorneys should attend meetings between the caseworker and a family.

- The expected responsibilities of the attorneys and workers in preparing a solid case for court.

- Implementing an information system to inform everyone about changes in staff, law, and policy.

- How workers and attorneys will communicate: e-mail, written memos, telephone conferencing.

- What the dispute resolution system is and when it will be used.

If not all attorneys and caseworkers attend the sessions, develop a way to share the protocols and the other new approaches with the rest of the staff.

§ 19B.4.2 Interdisciplinary Training

In addition to informal sessions, it is helpful for you and the caseworkers to attend substantive trainings in areas that relate to both of your practices. By participating in training together, you will all have the same knowledge base. You will also benefit from spending time together outside the courtroom. While interdisciplinary training cannot resolve all of the issues between you and the caseworkers and it will not provide you will all of the strictly legal knowledge that you need, it is an excellent way for everyone to develop their skills and knowledge.

Topics to consider for training include:

- Invite a local judge to discuss court practice, the type of testimony he or she prefers, what should be included in a petition, and his or her view of how the court process relates to the child welfare system as a whole.

- Invite a local doctor or other medical expert to talk about the medical evidence that points to abuse, Munchausen Syndrome by Proxy, failure to thrive, and other medical issues that relate to child welfare. The discussion can also focus on the ethical decisions involved when a parent withholds medical treatment for religious reasons.

- Have a psychiatrist or psychologist discuss mental health diagnoses and the implications for parents and foster children who suffer from the disorders.

- Learn about the substance abuse programs available in your community and how they can be accessed for the children and their parents.[33]

§ 19B.4.3 Multidisciplinary Teams

In Washington, the agency attorneys and caseworkers have improved their relationships and their effectiveness in cases through two types of multidisciplinary meetings. First, for children, especially young children under three years of age, who have been in foster care for three months, the agency has a prognostic staffing meeting. An attorney attends, and the team reviews the case to determine whether a concurrent plan should be implemented. The caseworkers appreciate having the attorney attend and have found these meetings help reduce the time the child remains in foster care. Because the attorney knows the state legislation, he or she can advise as to whether the case is ready for a termination of parental rights petition or another permanent plan. Additionally, the attorneys and caseworkers are getting to know each other better, which improves their teamwork in all cases.

The courts in Washington also have initiated committees, which are made up of judges, agency attorneys, caseworkers or supervisors, and defense attorneys, to resolve procedural problems in the court. Through these committees, the court has reduced delays in cases, the participants have gained respect for each other, the judges have taken a positive leadership role, and all players work together to resolve the problems that affect the entire system.[34]

§ 19B.5 Conclusion

No matter what kind of relationship you have with the caseworkers in your agency, there is probably room for improvement. While it is not easy and may be frustrating, through increased communication and a focus on mutual respect you can work as a more effective team to benefit the children and families in your community.

---

[33] David J. Herring, *Interdisciplinary Training and Assessing Community Services Resources*, in AGENCY ATTORNEY TRAINING MANUAL: ACHIEVING TIMELY PERMANENCY FOR CHILDREN BY IMPLEMENTING THE PRIVATE MODEL OF LEGAL REPRESENTATION FOR THE STATE AGENCY IN CHILD ABUSE AND NEGLECT MATTERS (Pittsburgh: University of Pittsburgh Law School, 1992); *see also* Mimi Laver, *A Guide to Retaining Agency Attorneys*, 17 CHILD L. PRAC. 5, 73-75 (1998).

[34] Telephone interview with Linda Katz, MSW, adjunct faculty at the University of Washington School of Social Work, Seattle, Washington, July 14, 1998.

§ 19B.6 Sample Protocol for Termination Petitions[35]

Sample Protocol for Termination Petitions

Step 1. A recommendation is made by the permanency planning committee, legal unit, or supervisor that a termination petition be filed.

Step 2. Within **30 days** of Step 1, the caseworker will send a completed information packet with referral form to the legal unit.

Step 3. For a permanent neglect, mental illness or mental retardation case, within **30 days** of Step 2, the attorney will either draft a petition or request more information from the caseworker. The attorney will forward the draft petition or request for information to the caseworker.

For an abandonment case, within **15 days** of Step 2, the attorney will either draft a petition or request more information from the caseworker. The attorney will forward the draft petition or request for information to the caseworker.

Step 4. If additional information is requested, the caseworker shall return the petition or provide the information to the attorneys within **7 days**. Once the petition is returned, the attorney shall file the petition within **7 days**.

Step 5. After receiving the additional information, for a permanent neglect, mental illness or mental retardation case, the attorneys shall file the petition within **30 days**.

After receiving the additional information, for an abandonment case, the attorney shall file the petition within **15 days**.

Step 6. The attorney and caseworker shall meet at least **2 weeks** prior to the trial date to prepare for trial.

---

[35] *Source:* Albany County Permanency Planning Project, Attorney Caseworker Protocol for Termination Petitions. Developed by Anne Marie Lancour, J.D., Legal Training Director, ABA Center on Children and the Law. Washington, DC.

§ 19B.7 Sample Protocol for Dispute Resolution Between Agency Attorney and Caseworker

Sample Protocol for Dispute Resolution Between Agency Attorney and Caseworker

Step 1.   You and the caseworker thoroughly and calmly discuss the case or problem.

Step 2.   If you cannot resolve the problem, each of you go and discuss it with your supervisors. Pick a time to communicate again within two days.

Step 3.   Meet with your supervisors and determine whether you are taking the position of your agency. Try to work out other ways to view the issue. Find out when your supervisor is free to meet with the caseworker and supervisor if needed. This should be within one week, or sooner if the case is pending in court.

Step 4.   Keep the appointment to talk again and see if there has been a resolution.

Step 5.   If there was no resolution, pick a mutually convenient time for a meeting between you and the caseworker and your supervisors.

Step 6.   Have the meeting. Try to talk through the entire issue to reach an understanding.

Step 7.   If there is still no resolution, you will each need to go up your chain of command. If this is a policy issue, the head of your unit will need to discuss it with the head of the agency and find a reasonable position.

§ 19B.8 Attorney – Social Worker Responsibilities

RESPONSIBILITY	WHO SHOULD DO IT[36]
investigate report	caseworker
discuss facts with police, medical professionals, teachers	caseworker – may have discussions with attorney
prepare petition	legal assistant with information from caseworker and supervision of attorney
notify parties of hearing	law office by subpoena – if required caseworker
identify witnesses	caseworker gives information to attorney attorney after review of file
prepare witnesses	attorney – may have help from legal assistant
prepare child witness	attorney – may have caseworker present to emotionally support child; don't forget to collaborate with child's attorney or CASA
prepare exhibits for hearing	legal assistant and attorney caseworker should provide organized case file
other court preparation	attorney with conversations with caseworker
present case in court	attorney
enter into agreements with parents	parent's attorney should be present caseworker and/or attorney can work with parents and other should be included before final agreement
ongoing documentation	caseworker
attend meetings with family	caseworker and sometimes attorney
ongoing casework	caseworker

---

[36] Source: Robin Russel, *Role Perceptions of Attorneys and Caseworkers in Child Abuse Cases in Juvenile Court*, CHILD WELFARE Vol. 67, Number 3, May-June 1988, 205-216. *See also* DAVID J. HERRING, AGENCY ATTORNEY TRAINING MANUAL: ACHIEVING TIMELY PERMANENCY FOR CHILDREN BY IMPLEMENTING THE PRIVATE MODEL OF LEGAL REPRESENTATION FOR THE STATE AGENCY IN CHILD ABUSE AND NEGLECT MATTERS (Pittsburgh: University of Pittsburgh Law School, 1992); Gene D. Skarin, *The Role of the Child Protective Agency's Attorney in Family Court, in Practising Law Institute Criminal Law and Urban Problems* 171, March 1995, 431-468, 459-460.

Chapter 20 REPRESENTING PARENTS: THE ROLE AND DUTIES OF RESPONDENTS' COUNSEL

Part 20A: Representing Parents in Child Welfare Cases: A Basic Introduction for Attorneys*

*by Diane Boyd Rauber, Esq., with Lisa A. Granik, Esq.***
*Edited by Mimi R. Laver, Esq.****

§ 20A.1 Introduction

Representing parents in child protection cases is no easy task. In these cases, the rights of parents to raise their children is at stake.

Children are often removed from their homes amid allegations of abuse or neglect. The parent may face months of treatment or counseling and may be required to make major lifestyle changes before the safe return of the child is possible. Reunification may be an unrealistic goal, with termination of parental rights the ultimate result.

Recent federal and state legislation also affects the representation of parents in child protection cases. The most prominent is the Adoption and Safe Families Act (ASFA) of 1997, which was passed to reform the child welfare system. Intended to emphasize the safety, permanency, and well-being of children in foster care, ASFA tightens the timeframes within which efforts toward reunification can be achieved.

This booklet introduces you to the responsibilities and duties of attorneys who represent parents. It outlines the various proceedings in a case, addresses recent reforms, and refers to key state and federal laws. The final section cites books and articles that will help you learn more about the child welfare process.

Editor's Note: This chapter was originally printed in booklet form. Nonsubstantive changes have been made to the text and formatting to reflect the style of this publication. Section numbers have also been added to reflect the style of this publication. The bibliography and lists of other resources have been omitted.

** Diane Boyd Rauber, M.Ed., J.D., has co-authored or edited several ABA Center on Children and the Law publications, including the COURT IMPROVEMENT PROGRESS REPORTS, A JUDGE'S GUIDE: MAKING CHILD-CENTERED DECISIONS IN CUSTODY CASES and REPRESENTING PARENTS IN CHILD WELFARE CASES.

Lisa A. Granik, J.D., was a staff attorney at the ABA Center on Children and the Law and author of the First Edition of *Representing Parents in Child Welfare Cases: A Basic Introduction for Attorneys*.

*** Mimi Laver, J.D., is Assistant Director of Child Welfare at the ABA Center on Children and the Law, Washington, D.C. She previously was a Deputy City Solicitor representing the Department of Human Services and the Department of Health in Philadelphia, Pennsylvania.

This booklet is not intended as a substitute for a detailed practice manual, nor is it intended to give you a comprehensive knowledge of relevant law. Rather, this booklet is written for attorneys who are new to child protection cases and is designed to help you better understand your role as the parent's representative.

A note about variations in state law: Each state uses its own terms to describe the various hearings in child protection cases. While this booklet uses the most typical terminology, some of the hearings in your state may have other names. When reading about the court process, you will need to determine what the most nearly equivalent hearing is in your state.

While this booklet explains the essence of the court process in most states, you will need to learn the unique features of your own state statutes, court rules, agency policies, and local practice.

§ 20A.2 The Role of Parents' Counsel in Child Protection Proceedings

§ 20A.2.1 General Responsibilities of Parents' Attorneys

An attorney is required to provide competent representation to a client. "Competent representation requires the legal knowledge, skill, thoroughness and preparation reasonably necessary for the representation." *ABA Model Rules of Professional Conduct 1.1 (1999).*

An attorney also must act with reasonable diligence, as well as "with commitment and dedication to the interests of the client and with zeal in advocacy upon the client's behalf." *ABA Model Rules of Professional Conduct 1.3; Comment - Rule 1.3 (1999).*

Given the most serious potential outcome of a child protection matter—severance of the parent-child relationship—as the parent's attorney, you must recognize the ethical responsibilities of representation and you must be sensitive to the intense emotions involved. You must remember that the parent is your client, and the parent should make significant decisions as to the overall posture or the case.

You are responsible for apprising your client of alternatives, as well as of the ramifications and obligations surrounding each alternative. In addition, guide your client in making an informed decision about the posture of the case.

Tactical and strategic litigation decisions lie within your domain. For example, such decisions would include vigorously opposing delays when the child is out of parental custody—except in special circumstances, such as when a hearing is scheduled during a week in which a parent has been admitted to a mental hospital for a discrete short-term period. Part of your function as attorney is to challenge and test the child welfare agency's version of the facts, which may be based on an incomplete investigation or on unsupportable conclusions.

Although you must zealously represent the parent, experience shows that confrontational and obstructionist tactics often tend to be counterproductive to the parent's interests. Since the agency and the court wield enormous and continuing power over the life of the child and, therefore, the parent, it benefits your client when you are selective in deciding which issues to contest.

You should seek a productive working relationship with the agency whenever possible, especially at the early stages of the juvenile court process. Such a relationship may help:

- expedite the resolution of the case,

- minimize needlessly contentious relationships between the parents and agency caseworkers, and

- facilitate negotiated settlements that ensure the protection of the child without unnecessarily infringing on the family's integrity.

With the tightened timeframes under ASFA, in most cases, you should advise your client to cooperate and accept services immediately. In certain cases, however, cooperation may require potentially damaging admissions, *i.e.*, where a criminal case is pending or your client denies that the abuse ever occurred.

Although the American Bar Association (ABA) *Model Rules* do not state precisely what level of knowledge, skill, and preparation is necessary for a minimum level of competent representation, it is safe to say that before each factual hearing constituting a critical stage in the proceedings, among other things, you must:

- discuss the matter with your client sufficiently in advance to have time to investigate and prepare the case;

- conduct a thorough, independent investigation;

- conduct formal discovery, if needed;

- interview and subpoena necessary witnesses before the hearing;

- research any legal issues pertinent to the case; and

- continue with the case until it is specifically relieved.

As the result of court improvement efforts and other reforms, some jurisdictions have implemented specific standards addressing representation of parents and children in child protection cases. You should be familiar with any applicable standards in your jurisdiction.[1]

---

[1] For example, in 1996, the Oregon Board of Governors approved standards for attorneys handling criminal, delinquency, dependency, and civil commitment cases. *Indigent Defense Task Force Report: Principles and Standards for Counsel in Criminal, Delinquency, Dependency and Civil Commitment Cases.* Salem, Oregon: Oregon State Bar, 1996. The American Bar Association developed standards for attorneys representing children in child protection matters. ABA Family Law Section. *ABA Standards of Practice for Lawyers Who Represent Children in Abuse and Neglect Cases.* Washington, DC: American Bar Association, 1996.

In addition, you will need to determine whether the court adopts a formal or informal approach to child protection hearings. Courts adopting an informal approach either relax the rules of evidence or ignore them entirely, most notably in the admission of hearsay testimony. When it is in your client's interest, you must demand strict adherence to procedural and evidentiary rules.

Finally, the parent's attorney is not the advocate for the best interests of the child. That is the province of the agency, the guardian ad litem (GAL), and the court. *Your primary concern rests with the rights and interests of the parent and the preservation of the family unit.* Furthermore, even if the parent has done everything the agency has alleged, court and agency involvement may not be justified.

In the final analysis, if you work to ensure the integrity of the judicial process, you ultimately safeguard the interests of the child.

§ 20A.2.2 The Effect of the Adoption and Safe Families Act

When a child has been removed from the home due to allegations of abuse or neglect, federal and state legislation has been enacted that significantly shortens the time period for the parent to demonstrate that he or she has complied with the requirements set forth by the court and is ready for the return of the child.

You must be vigilant about the passage of time. Under the new mandates, every week is critical.

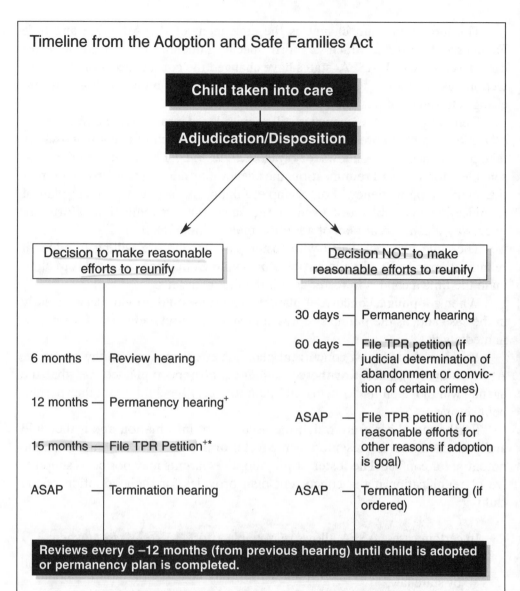

Timeline from the Adoption and Safe Families Act

Child taken into care

Adjudication/Disposition

Decision to make reasonable efforts to reunify | Decision NOT to make reasonable efforts to reunify

		30 days —	Permanency hearing
		60 days —	File TPR petition (if judicial determination of abandonment or conviction of certain crimes)
6 months —	Review hearing		
12 months —	Permanency hearing[+]	ASAP —	File TPR petition (if no reasonable efforts for other reasons if adoption is goal)
15 months —	File TPR Petition[+*]		
ASAP —	Termination hearing	ASAP —	Termination hearing (if ordered)

Reviews every 6 –12 months (from previous hearing) until child is adopted or permanency plan is completed.

+ When calculating when to have the permanency hearing or the 15 of 22 months, use the earlier of the date of adjudication OR 60 days after the child is removed from the home.

* Unless the child is being cared for by a relative, or compelling reasons not to TPR exist.

© 2000 ABA

Source: Laver, Mimi. "Implementing ASFA: A Challenge for Agency Attorneys." *Child Law Practice* 17, October 1998, 119.

The most important change is the enactment of the Adoption and Safe Families Act (ASFA),[2] which sets forth specific guidelines for children in foster care. To comply with ASFA, states have changed the court process of child protection cases. Therefore, it is important that you are familiar with any recent changes to state statutes and rules governing these cases.

Generally, while the agency is still required to demonstrate that *reasonable efforts* were made to preserve or reunify the family, the child's health and safety take precedence. ASFA allows for *concurrent planning, i.e.*, while providing reasonable efforts toward reunification, the agency may adopt a concurrent alternative plan for permanency.[3] For example, taking into account that the plan of reunification may not work even at the same time reunification efforts are underway, a concurrent plan of adoption may be implemented.

The child may be placed with foster parents who are willing to adopt if reunification fails. By already having a backup plan in place, the goal is to eliminate the time a child is in foster care if the first plan fails.

When adopting a concurrent plan, the agency should provide services early in the case and, as the parent's representative, you should advocate for services immediately.

You also should view concurrent planning efforts with a healthy suspicion. Always warn your client of the consequences of noncompliance, *i.e.*, that the agency will move on its "concurrent" plan to place the child in another permanent setting.

Furthermore, carefully weigh the accuracy of information about the child and your client that is presented by the foster or pre-adoptive parents, given the potential for conflict. The foster or pre-adoptive parents may not be as supportive of reunification if the concurrent plan provides for their adoption of the child.

In certain cases, ASFA allows reasonable efforts to be *bypassed* when:

- the parent has subjected the child to *aggravated circumstances* as defined by state law;

- the parent has been convicted of certain crimes, such as killing, attempting to kill, or committing a felony assault against another of his or her children; or

- the parent's rights to a sibling have been involuntarily terminated.

---

[2] Pub. L. No. 105-89, 111 Stat. 2115-22, 2125-36 (codified in scattered sections of 2 U.S.C. and 42. U.S.C.).

[3] For a detailed discussion of concurrent planning as contemplated under ASFA, *see* Weinberg, Anita, & Linda Katz. "Law and Social Work in Partnership for Permanency: The Adoption and Safe Families Act and the Role of Concurrent Planning." *Children's Legal Rights Journal* 18, fall 1998, 2.

The court's use of the bypass provision is discretionary and designed for extreme circumstances. It is important, however, to be aware of what circumstances the state deems to be "aggravated." You must be fully aware of any past circumstances that might cause the agency to argue for using the bypass provision.

Once there is a finding that reasonable efforts are not required, the court must hold a *permanency hearing* within 30 days. Even if the bypass provision is invoked, you may want to help the parent obtain the necessary services in an effort to convince the judge to reconsider the decision at the permanency hearing.

If a parent has participated in services during the interim period before the permanency hearing and is showing progress, the judge may be willing to reverse the prior decision and order that the agency make reasonable efforts to reunify.

Another change that affects many parents is the requirement that the court hold such a permanency hearing within 12 months:

- after the date of the first judicial finding that the child was subjected to abuse or neglect, or

- 60 days after removing the child from the custody of the parent, whichever date is earlier.

In other words, the permanency hearing must be held no later than 14 months after the date of removal. States can shorten this timeline, and some have a strict 12-month deadline after removal.

It is vital to explain to clients—particularly those who are familiar with the child welfare system—that the permanency hearing is not simply another foster care review hearing. Rather, as a result of this hearing, a decision is supposed to be reached as to a permanent placement for the child, *i.e.*, return home, adoption, legal guardianship, permanent placement with a ft and willing relative, or another planned permanent living arrangement.

At the permanency hearing, the court is permitted to direct the agency to file a termination of parental rights petition.

The permanency hearing requirement does not mean that a child's stay in foster care may never be extended. Such an extension, however, is less likely than before ASFA. Each state has or will design a process to consider when it may be in the child's best interest to extend foster care.

The bottom line is you must always be mindful of the 12- to 14-month deadline, and you will be required to provide more substantive reasons than in the past for arguing that foster care should be extended.

Finally, under ASFA, *a termination of parental rights* (TPR) *petition must be filed* and concurrent planning initiated to find an adoptive family for a child *if*

- the child has been in foster care for 15 of the past 22 months,

- the child is an infant that has been found by the court to be "abandoned," or

- the court determines that the parent has been convicted of certain crimes, such as those previously outlined.

The agency can opt not to file a TPR petition if

- the child is in the care of a relative (an option most states have accepted),

- the agency has documented compelling reasons why termination is not in the best interest of the child, or

- reasonable efforts were required to be made and the state did not provide the services it deemed necessary for reunification. For example, if there was a delay in the provision of services to the client, you may be able to argue that the agency should not file a TPR petition.

Some states have defined these criteria further in policies (agency manuals); therefore, you must determine if this is the case in your jurisdiction.

These new deadlines will have a particular impact on a client who has a chronic substance abuse problem or is mentally ill. For example, one of the biggest issues in many child welfare cases is the substance abuse of a parent. The chronic nature of substance abuse, coupled with the shortened timeframes contemplated under ASFA, presents a major challenge for attorneys representing parents.

Experts suggest that parents with a chronic substance abuse problem need at least one to two years to stabilize in recovery.[4] Given the propensity for relapses—especially early in recovery—and the limited availability of appropriate programs, it may be very difficult for a parent with a substance abuse problem to regain custody of a child within the 14-month period.

It is imperative, therefore, that you not wait for the agency to suggest appropriate services. You should immediately move to get services for the client and be creative in making suggestions for speedy, appropriate treatment.

Incarcerated parents are another group of parents that might be particularly affected by the shortened timelines. You must consider the timelines in light of the length of the prison term and the reason for the parent's incarceration. For example, if the parent is in jail because of a crime committed against the child, reunification efforts may be bypassed. In some states, length of incarceration alone may be a ground for termination of parental rights.[5]

If reunification efforts are not bypassed, you need to urge the caseworker to work with the incarcerated parent. Both you and the caseworker should contact the parent and the parent's prison social worker as soon as possible to determine what the parent wants.

Will the parent work toward reunification or would the parent prefer to surrender his or her rights? If the parent wants to work toward reunification,

---

[4] D'Aunno, Lisa & Gay Chisum. "Parental Substance Abuse and Permanency Decision Making: Measuring Progress in Substance Abuse Recovery." *Children's Legal Rights Journal* 18, fall 1998, 52, 53.

[5] Chiancone, Janet. "Children of Incarcerated Parents: What Lawyers Need to Know." *ABA Child Law Practice* 16, 1997, 33.

explore what services are available in prison and stress to your client the importance of participating in any appropriate services.

It is vital that your client keeps in contact with the agency caseworker and
the child through letters, phone calls, and small gifts to the child. If visits are possible, help to arrange them.

In addition, ask the parent if any relatives could be considered as placement
resources. If so, this option may be your client's best chance of avoiding the filing
of a termination petition after 15 of 22 months of the child's stay in foster care.

Remember that a parent's incarceration is likely to be scary and confusing
for a child, especially if the incarcerated parent was the custodial parent. It is
important for the parent to try to explain the situation in language the child can
understand. Frequent contact and visitation are also crucial. As the parent's
attorney, you can help facilitate an easier transition for your client, as well as for
the child.[6]

§ 20A.2.3 Pre-Trial Independent Investigation

An initial step in representing parents is a pretrial independent investigation. At this stage, you must take several steps:

- *Immediately contact the social welfare agency responsible for the child in
  care.* The agency should be able to provide information about the reasons for the child's supervision by the agency or removal from the home,
  as well as the agency's immediate plans for the child.[7] Early contact with
  the agency can help you influence the process to the greatest extent and
  potentially prevent removing the child from the home.

- *Contact the police or responsible law enforcement agency* and obtain a
  complete report of any incident leading to the removal.[8]

- *Interview any potential witnesses,* including school personnel, teachers,
  relatives, neighbors, friends, clergy, health care providers, counselors, or
  any other relevant individuals.[9]

- *Identify and confer in advance with the state's witnesses.* After determining which witnesses should appear in the initial hearing, prepare them
  and review their testimony well in advance.

- Since the document or report resulting from this investigation often
  becomes critical evidence in the case, *assert your right to review and*

---

[6] Craig, Ann Metcalf. "Meeting the Needs of Children of Incarcerated Mothers." *ABA Child
Law Practice* 17, 1998, 86.

[7] Wienerman, Gary T. "Improving Practice to Avoid Unnecessary Placements." In *Foster
Children in the Courts*. Edited by Mark Hardin. Boston: Butterworth, 1983, 4, 5.

[8] *Id.*

[9] *Id.*

scrutinize all contents of the child protection agency's case file as soon as possible and well before the court hearing.

Generally, the agency case file is the single most important written record which the attorney needs to review. You should be prepared to take any necessary steps to gain access to it. Then, you should determine if any records or casenotes in the custody of the caseworker have not been placed in the file and move to obtain those records as well.

Of course, other documents not in the case file may also be critical in some cases, such as medical and school records that the caseworker has not obtained. In seeking such documents, you should evaluate whether formal or informal discovery is needed. If formal discovery is needed, decide which techniques are appropriate (depositions, interrogatories, subpoenas duces tecum, etc.).

Be prepared to move for a copy of any written report before trial or to move for a continuance to ensure sufficient time to properly review the report.

§ 20A.2.4 Emergency Removal Hearing

Emergency proceedings are triggered when a child welfare agency worker or law enforcement officer decides that it is necessary to place a child in protective care before trial. Emergency placement is usually authorized by an ex parte order directing the placement of the child.

In extreme circumstances, the child may be placed first and a court order approving placement sought shortly thereafter. Whether or not an ex parte hearing is held, the parents are still entitled to a subsequent hearing within a short tune after the child is removed.

In nearly every jurisdiction, an informal emergency hearing (sometimes called the *shelter care* hearing) is automatically scheduled within a short time (pursuant to a statutory time limit) after placement.

Should the agency and court fail to comply with the statutorily mandated time period, you might argue for the immediate release of the child due to the failure to comply with the law.[10]

Be aware, however, that the court is not required to place a child in a highly dangerous situation even if the agency or court failed to comply with time periods set forth in the law.

At this emergency hearing, the court:

- reviews the decision to place the child,

- determines whether the child should be returned home before trial,

- decides what arrangements are needed for the child's care, and

- oversees the beginning of court proceedings.

---

[10] *Id.* at 6.

Among other things, the court also may address:

- whether relatives are available to help;
- whether the agency made reasonable efforts to avoid placement of the child;
- whether immediate services are warranted;
- whether appointing an attorney for the child, a GAL, or a Court Appointed Special Advocate (CASA) is appropriate or required; and
- under what terms visitation will be allowed.

The emergency hearing is often critical. Once a child is removed, it is easier for a judge to continue the placement.

If you are confronted with an emergency situation in which the child has already been removed from the home against the parent's wishes, you must act expeditiously to minimize the amount of time the child and parents are separated. *The longer the separation, the more difficult it often becomes to reunite the family.* In addition, for the entire time the family is separated, you should advocate for visitation and other ways to maintain parent-child contact.

In preparing for the emergency removal hearing, you must immediately determine both the agency's and your client's versions of the reasons for the child's removal. In addition, you must determine what the parent wants regarding the child's placement, frequency of visits, and communication with the child.

If the parent wishes to retain custody of the child, you must act quickly. Consider suggesting that the child be returned home while the parents accept agency support services for the problems that led to intervention, or have an acceptable relative or friend stay with the family. A court is less likely to order removal if the parents present a clear plan to address and eradicate the dangers the state alleges.

If the court determines that the child must be removed from the home, it may be appropriate to propose that a willing relative or friend take the child into their home pending the adjudication and disposition hearing.[11]

Alternatively, you may choose to raise such alternatives in a post-emergency hearing motion. This notification affords the agency the opportunity to investigate before the adjudication hearing. The court and agency therefore might be inclined to recommend placing the child with these individuals pending disposition.

Sometimes a child enters foster care as the result of domestic violence rather than strictly abuse or neglect.[12] In this case, the child welfare system may not be the best place for the family to receive the help it needs.

---

[11] *Id.* at 7.

[12] Chiancone, Janet. "Children: The Forgotten Victims of Domestic Violence." *ABA Child Law Practice*, 16, 1997, 65.

If you represent the parent who is the victim of violence—which is generally the mother—you may be able to assist her in getting a Civil Order of Protection or a Stay Away Order so the child could be returned to her. Separating a child from the parent should be a last resort, especially when the parent did not harm the child.

If you are unfamiliar with this area of the law, find out about the resources in the community and help your client take advantage of them. A legal clinic that specializes in this type of case or shelters for victims and their children may be available in your area. You may need to seek the assistance of an attorney who specializes in this type of law.

If you are involved in the case before the emergency hearing and your client opposes removal or seeks other relief not agreed to by the agency, you will have to quickly secure witnesses to appear at the emergency hearing. The emergency nature of the proceeding probably will not provide enough time for subpoenas, so you will need to secure desired witnesses by telephone.

Because the court must determine not only whether the child is in sufficient danger to justify sustained removal from his or her parents, but also whether the agency has made reasonable efforts to prevent placement, you should consider both these questions and work to ensure that the court record casts the parents in the most favorable light possible.

If the court finds that the agency has not made reasonable efforts to prevent placement, it may be more inclined to order the child's return.

If the emergency hearing occurred without notice to the parents or there was insufficient time to prepare, you should request a rehearing or short delay rather than risk an ineffective and potentially damaging defense.

Press for a hearing to be held quickly since the child is out of the home and momentum is building against reunification.

Any time before the adjudication, you should also be prepared to file any and all appropriate pretrial motions, including (but not limited to):

- motions for discovery,

- motions for psychological and other medical assessments,

- motions for protective or restraining orders,

- motions to strike or dismiss the petition,

- motions for change of placement, and

- motions to modify visitation.

§ 20A.2.5 Mediation and Alternative Dispute Resolution

As a result of court improvement efforts across the country and the mandates of ASFA, some jurisdictions are implementing alternative dispute resolution techniques, such as mediation and family group conferencing. As mediation becomes a part of many juvenile courts across the country, as the parent's attorney, you must learn to advocate for the client within that structure. In some courts, alternative dispute resolution techniques are being used throughout the course of the case.

If there is mediation,[13] you must *carefully consider the strategy to be employed.* Parents may be intimidated by the prospect of actively participating in a plan. Those who have been in the child welfare system for an extended period of time may distrust the process.

First and foremost, well before the initial mediation session, prepare your client for what to expect. Discuss the issues that will be considered as part of mediation. If a particular person's presence at the session will help your client, suggest that he or she attend.

One intended outcome of mediation is parent empowerment. Parents are included in the process and hopefully motivated to participate in a final plan.

An agreement reached through mediation, however, probably will result in your client's "giving up" something. Therefore, be sure your client is an active part of the case planning and is fully informed about any agreement. Be sure the agreement is complete and correct, and take the time necessary at the mediation session to clarify or confer with your client.

In many jurisdictions, any agreement must be approved by the court and may be made a part of the court order.

Finally, not all mediation results in an agreement. Even when an agreement is reached, it may require modification later. Understand any process for modification and explain it thoroughly to your client.

Another alternative dispute resolution technique gaining in popularity is family group conferencing (FGC) or family group decision making (FGDM). These techniques employ the family in making decisions about the child's placement, based on the underlying belief that involving extended families can achieve better results for children.[14]

While FGC and FGDM vary from place to place, the following is a common example:

> The social worker refers the case to a coordinator who determines if a FGC meeting should be held. The coordinator prepares for the meeting by contacting family members and other supportive individuals, determining who will be invited, describing the role of the FGC meeting, and arranging all aspects of the meeting.

---

[13] The information regarding mediation in this section was adapted from a recent article in *ABA Child Law Practice. See* Baker, Debra Ratterman. "Dependency Mediation Strategies for Parent's Attorneys." *ABA Child Law Practice* 18, 1999, 124-125.

[14] Merkel-Holguin, Lisa, et al., *Putting Families Back into the Child Protection Partnership: Family Group Decision Making, in 1997 National Roundtable Series on Family Group Decision Making: Summary of Proceedings.* Englewood, CO: American Humane Association, 1997, 34.

At the meeting, the professionals present factual information about the case to the assembled family members. The family members are then left in private to deliberate, considering whether or not the child was abused or neglected, and if so, what needs to happen to ensure the child's safety.[15]

Upon reaching a conclusion, the professionals meet with the Family members to consider their plan. If the agency and the family group cannot reach an agreement about the family's plan, the court will likely consider the case and determine the next step.[16]

The goal of the FGC is to empower the family and make the members part of any decision about the child's future.

§ 20A.2.6 Adjudication

Adjudication (sometimes called the *jurisdictional hearing, trial,* or *fact-finding hearing*) is the hearing in which the court determines if allegations of child maltreatment are sustained by the evidence and legally sufficient to justify state intervention against the family. Adjudication is the most formal stage in child protection cases and often the most familiar stage for attorneys.

As the attorney, you must pay careful attention to findings concerning maltreatment because, as explained below, the adjudication record often has impact beyond the adjudication itself.

First determine whether a legal basis for intervention exists and whether it is in your client's interest to contest.[17] Although you must contest if the parents choose, you also must inform the parent as to whether it is advisable. *The decision to contest depends on the chances of prevailing* and, if the parent is likely to lose, the impact on the relationship between the parent and the agency. It may be in the parent's best interest to negotiate the court's specific findings that the child was abused or neglected and consider accepting services from the agency through a negotiated settlement.

With the exception of termination proceedings, a contested adjudication is the most adversarial stage of the proceeding. If you plan to contest, do so vigorously. Vigorous action includes:

- forcing the state to adequately prove each element of its case;

- introducing suggested findings of fact, where appropriate;

---

[15] *Id.* at 5.

[16] *Id.* at 6.

[17] Wienerman, Gary T. "Improving Practice to Avoid Unnecessary Placements." In *Foster Children in the Courts.* Edited by Mark Hardin. Boston: Butterworth, 1983, 4, 12-14. This chapter addresses issues that a parent's attorney should consider when making the decision to contest and strategies to employ when that decision is made.

- raising objections to inadmissible evidence; and

- ensuring that all relevant issues are raised to preserve them for appeal.

Certain jurisdictions statutorily provide for specific findings of fact and conclusions of law. In some of these jurisdictions, the attorney's failure to request specific findings of fact is interpreted as a waiver of that right.

Although in most states hearsay evidence can be admitted at various stages of child welfare proceedings, it is generally not admissible at adjudication.[18] *It is crucial that you insist on adherence to the rules of evidence at the adjudication stage.*

The record at adjudication is vital to the entire process. If the court makes specific findings to explain the grounds for its judgment, the record will be clearer for appellate review. The record at adjudication should specify the precise nature of the allegations so that disposition and casework can focus on the specific problems precipitating the state's intervention.

A parent can sometimes refuse to cooperate with the agency on an issue not legally established at adjudication. A clear record may foreclose subsequent factual disputes or further evidence against the parent that might otherwise be admissible.

It is important to remember that, under ASFA, reunification efforts may be bypassed if the parent has been convicted of certain crimes against a child. If you are representing a parent on a matter relating to such a crime, carefully consider any plea that could result in a finding for bypass. If another attorney is representing your client on such a criminal matter, you may want to consult with him or her about the potential pitfalls of a plea.[19]

§ 20A.2.7 Disposition

At disposition, the court decides who shall have custody and control of the child and what steps are necessary to resolve the problems that caused state intervention. The questions addressed at disposition are therefore different from those asked at adjudication.

The issue is no longer whether the client abused the child, but what will happen next to the child; in other words, questions of placement, services, visits, and case plan. Inexperienced attorneys often overlook the disposition, which is frequently the most critical stage of the process.

Some states provide for the adjudication and disposition hearings to be held together, usually with disposition immediately following adjudication. Although separate hearings may delay the ultimate disposition, where it is not mandated, you should consider requesting that the disposition hearing be held at a later

---

[18] *Id.* at 12.

[19] Laver, Mimi. "Representing Parents Effectively Post-ASFA." *ABA Child Law Practice* 18,1999, 150.

date. In some cases, it is only after the court sustains a petition alleging maltreatment that the parents will accept the necessity of a long-term placement and discuss potential arrangements with the agency.

Be mindful of early service delivery—a delay in the disposition hearing should not delay services for your client. Prepare separately for each hearing, regardless of whether the hearings occur on different days, because different questions are at issue.

At the disposition hearing, courts often admit into evidence the caseworker's report. This report, prepared by the agency, summarizes the background of the case and makes a recommendation about disposition.[20]

Since the report is usually the agency's primary piece of evidence at disposition and often heavily influences the court's decision, you should insist on obtaining a copy of this report well before the hearing so that you can review the report and prepare for the hearing.

Some jurisdictions require that all parties receive a copy of the report no later than a specified time before the hearing. If you have not received this report by the specified time, you have a right to a continuance as a matter of due process so that you have adequate time to review the report and prepare for the hearing.

Always weigh the genuine need for a continuance against the running clock. You should also obtain a copy of any other pertinent report, *e.g.*, the report of the GAL or the Court Appointed Special Advocate (CASA).

The case plan, which may or may not be attached to the caseworker's report, typically sets forth the type of placement, visitation schedule, parental problems to be addressed, and services to be provided;

Under 45 C.F.R. § 1356.21(g), the case plan must be developed within a reasonable time, but no more than 60 days from the date of removal. These regulations require that the parents be involved in the process of developing the case plan, so insist that the caseworker comply with this requirement and provide you with a copy well before the hearing.

You need to prepare a response to the agency's proposal, and in particular, to negotiate or contest certain issues, if necessary. You can help ensure that the plan the agency and parents develop addresses the specific problems that necessitated state intervention. At this stage, a working relationship among the attorney, the parent, and the agency is especially important.

When reviewing the agency's plan and preparing for the hearing, consider the plausibility and logic of the plan in light of the proven allegations. Conduct discovery, if necessary, including questioning and preparing witnesses expected to testify on behalf of the parents. Experts may be needed to testify as to whether the agency's plan is workable, and if not, what alternatives are appropriate.

---

[20] Wienerman, Gary T. "Improving Practice to Avoid Unnecessary Placements." In *Foster Children in the Courts*. Edited by Mark Hardin. Boston: Butterworth, 1983, 4, 20.

The agency's plan may be limited by known resources. An initial review of services provided by the state and agency is crucial. Do not, however, feel restricted by these services. Rather, independently explore services to assist the parent, thoroughly understand quality resources in the community, and be creative in suggesting alternatives.

Try to get the advice of an independent social worker or other experts. Given the tight timelines within which to achieve permanency, you also should insist on the immediate start of all appropriate services.

Similarly, do not hesitate to suggest alternatives for both removal and visitation, and consider devising a modified version of the case plan. For example:

- How often should visits occur?

- Should visits be at home? Or should there be protective visits in the agency offices only?

- Should the visits be supervised?

To facilitate visitation, advocate for placement as close to home (or the parent) as possible.

If the child is or may be placed in foster care, when revising the plan, determine what type of placement is preferred. Whenever possible, attempt to locate a relative or family friend who gets along with the parent, is willing to take custody of the child, and is acceptable to the agency. Such a placement will likely help more smoothly facilitate visits.

If more than one child is involved, consider whether it is best and possible to keep the siblings together.

You should *ensure that the parties and the court concentrate on the most crucial issues causing state intervention.* Develop a plan on the record to address those issues.

Think about the disposition record in order to set a framework for review. The plan should address the issues raised at adjudication and should specify:

- what the parents are to do,

- what the agency is to do,

- what services are to be provided, and

- what the schedule should be for services.

Make sure the tasks and goals set forth for the parent are realistic and not designed to result in failure. Clear goals and the steps each party must take to accomplish those goals enable the court or agency to evaluate progress at later review hearings.

Additionally, a parent may gain significant advantage at a later date if he or she achieves the specified goals and the agency attempts to raise additional issues not addressed in the original plan.

Perhaps the most important advice you can give the parent is to adhere to the visitation schedule.[21] Advise the parent that if there is a legitimate reason for missing a visit, he or she should promptly notify all parties of the reason and promptly reschedule it. Regular visitation, especially where the parent behaves appropriately during the visit, may help sway a judge away from termination.

To ensure adherence to the case plan, frequently monitor the parent's progress and the services provided by the agency.

- Periodically call the parent and the caseworker.

- Be attentive to any problems that arise as the parties execute or fail to execute the plan.

- If aspects of the plan prove vague or unworkable, seek to modify the relevant prior orders.

§ 20A.2.8 Review Hearings

Review hearings refer to post-disposition proceedings where the court considers how the case is progressing. Such hearings are necessary for several reasons. Casework and services for the parent may be delayed, the child may be needlessly moved in foster care, or visitation may be insufficient.

The court will assess the performance of the parent and agency, as well as the status of the child's relationships. Furthermore, the court will determine the parent's progress in achieving case plan goals, as well as the agency's ability to provide promised services.

Determine whether any service providers view your client in a positive light or see progress in their program, and present that information to the court.

Vigilance at review is also important for the child. A child in foster care forms new relationships and ties to the biological family may weaken. If a child is moving between many placements, as often occurs, the child may lose the ability to form strong bonds with any family.

Timetables for foster care review can be governed by state statute and state or local court rules. Agency regulations or policy may require caseworkers to initiate review proceedings at particular intervals. In addition, federal law requires a review of children in foster care by either a court or an administrative body at least once every six months. 42 U.S.C. § 675(5)(B).

Under ASFA, foster parents, pre-adoptive parents, or relatives caring for the child must be given notice of and the opportunity to be heard at all review hearings. 42 U.S.C. § 675(5)(G). While this provision does not bestow party status on these individuals, you should inform the parent that these individuals will be given an opportunity to present their viewpoint to the court.

---

[21] *Id.* at 23-24.

Speak with any of these individuals before the hearing to prepare for their presentation. Since they are not parties to the case, there is no ethical problem in contacting them before the hearing. If their testimony helps your client, you may want to help them get to the hearing.

If your client has confidential issues to be discussed at the hearing—mental health problems, substance abuse, or HIV status—do not hesitate to move to have these individuals excused from the courtroom except while they address the court.

Before each review hearing, you should determine how the case has progressed since the last hearing.

- Read agency case records,

- Obtain the latest copy of the agency's case plan,

- Obtain the agency report and any other relevant reports, and

- Confer with your client.

Depending on changes in circumstances, you may request an update and revision of the plan in regard to the services provided by the agency. If caseworkers and agencies have not devoted sufficient time and energy to the case or have not provided the services mandated by court order, analyze recent case law regarding the power of the court to compel state agencies to provide services as required by law.

You also might work with the parent foster family, and agency to expand visits or to make them more frequent.

In some states, it can be tactically helpful to persuade the court to find that the agency has not made reasonable efforts to make it possible for the child to safely return home.

As with adjudication and disposition hearings, you should:

- identify areas of agreement and disagreement in the agency's (or other) reports,

- arrange for necessary witnesses and evidence, and

- inform the court of the estimated time of the hearing.

You will be most effective if you appear in court with a clear command of the facts and a proposed case plan that considers the changed circumstances.

At the hearing, *concentrate on creating a record that places the parent in the most favorable light possible.* While avoiding antagonism, emphasize any gaps in services and assistance to the parent. Focus on establishing a workable plan for the parents.

Depending on the circumstances and power of the court, you may request that the court order increased parental visitation and sibling contacts, strengthen the service obligations of the agency, and, if appropriate, return the child to the parent.

Where possible, try to use ASFA to your client's advantage. ASFA emphasizes the health and safety of the child. Therefore, if the client has completed enough of the case plan for the child to be safe, argue for the child's return.[22]

§ 20A.2.9 Permanency Hearings

After a child has been in foster care for an extended period of time or where a determination is made that no reunification efforts need to be made, a permanency hearing is held to determine the child's permanent placement.[23]

At a permanency hearing, the court will determine if the child can return home. If the child cannot return home, the court will decide if the child should be:

- placed for adoption,

- referred for legal guardianship,

- permanently placed with a fit-and-willing relative, or

- placed in another planned permanent living arrangement.

ASFA requires permanency hearings to be held, at the latest within 12-14 months of the child's removal from the home or within 30 days of a determination that no reunification efforts are necessary.

A permanency hearing is not just another review hearing. It is intended to truly resolve the issue of where the child's permanent home will be. The purpose of ASFA is to make it more difficult for courts and agencies to continue extending a child's placement in foster care with no plan for a permanent home.

You must impress upon the client the philosophy of ASFA and the reality that it entails. On one hand, not only does the client potentially have less time within which to improve his or her situation, the permanency hearing may result in a decision that will ultimately sever the parent-child relationship. For example, if the court decides that the child should be placed for adoption at the permanency hearing, the agency could be required to file for the termination of parental rights.

On the other hand, while the goal of the permanency hearing under ASFA is to reach a decision about a permanent placement, circumstances may arise where the court will extend the child's placement in foster care with the continued goal of reunification.

---

[22] Laver, Mimi. "Representing Parents Effectively Post-ASFA." *ABA Child Law Practice* 18,1999, 150.

[23] For a detailed description of permanency hearings, *see* Hardin, Mark "Improving Permanency Hearings: Sample Court Reports and Orders." Washington, DC: American Bar Association, 1999. This article, which does not address 30-day permanency hearings, can be ordered by calling (202) 662-1743.

The court may select this option if the parent and child continue to have a strong bond and the parent is making such significant progress that the child will likely be able to return home within a short period of time. Again, a solid record of visitation and cooperation with planned services will help the parent's argument for this option.

Therefore, if arguing for an extension of foster care with the continued goal of reunification, you should be prepared to set forth compelling reasons for this option. For example:

- document the substantial progress made by the client,

- state why the child cannot yet be returned to the home,

- specify if the agency has not provided all the services it promised in the case plan, and

- present a plan for the child's safe, early return home.

In addition, to strengthen your argument before the court, before the court hearing, try to convince the agency that this plan is appropriate.

§ 20A.2.10 Termination of Parental Rights

Most children in foster care are eventually returned home. However, when an agency regards the child's return home as unlikely or undesirable, it may seek to terminate parental rights in order to legally free the child for adoption. In some jurisdictions, termination is called *severance, guardianship with the power to consent to adoption* (granted to the child welfare agency), or *permanent commitment* of the child.[24]

Generally, a termination decree ends the duty of support, as well as the parent's right to visit, communicate, or have information about the child. In addition, the parent is no longer entitled to notice of further legal proceedings and is effectively denied further opportunity to regain custody. With the passage of ASFA, as noted before, termination of parental rights may be affected within a shorter period of time and more frequently than ever before.

If the agency is considering filing for termination and the parent is opposed, you should argue why the petition should not be filed. For example, you might argue that services have not been provided as specified in the case plan or that a committed relative may be prepared to provide a permanent home for the child, *e.g.*, through a permanent guardianship, without the necessity of termination.

In addition, consider arguing that there are compelling reasons why a termination petition should not be filed in your case. Understand that it is in the

---

[24] For a detailed discussion of termination and how to defend a termination petition, *see* Hewett, Carol. "Defending a Termination of Parental Rights Case." In *Foster Children in the Courts.* Edited by Mark Hardin. Boston: Butterworth, 1983, 229-263.

agency's discretion to file a termination petition and a compelling reason is not a defense for a parent.

However, making an argument that a compelling reason exists may persuade a judge in your client's favor. Some examples of compelling reasons include:

- a teenage child who is attached to his birth family and determines, after counseling, that he or she does not want to be adopted,

- a child with severe medical issues who cannot be placed with a family, or

- a child who is living with an individual who would accept guardianship but does not want to adopt.[25]

In light of the severity of the threat facing the client, you must engage in a vigorous and zealous defense, undiluted by any consideration of the client's working relationship with the agency. The essence of the parent's defense is that the child can eventually return home based on the history of state involvement with the family and/or that adoption is harmful or impractical for the child.

It is essential that you determine if the parent wants to contest termination. Voluntarily surrendering parental rights may be appropriate for some clients, yet many will be uncomfortable admitting that they want to surrender their rights.[26] Discuss this option honestly with your client and let your client reach his or her own conclusion.

You should also explain that voluntary surrender may save the parent's chance for the return of any other children in foster care or may protect the parent's rights with respect to any children that might be placed in care later.

Under ASFA, the agency has grounds to bypass reunification efforts if the parent's rights to a sibling were involuntarily terminated. Therefore, if the chances of winning the termination case appear very weak, voluntary surrender would prevent the agency from arguing for bypass of reunification efforts on this basis in the cases of any other children.[27]

It is important, however, to understand how your state defines *voluntary* termination. Some jurisdictions allow for the parent to "voluntarily" surrender up until the start of the termination hearing, while others might consider the parent's surrender to be "involuntary" as soon as the petition is filed.[28]

The first step in defending a termination of parental rights case is to *assemble a complete history of the case*. An initial interview with the client is critical, as virtually every aspect of a client's life can be of evidentiary significance.

---

[25] Laver, Mimi. "Representing Parents Effectively Post-ASFA." *ABA Child Law Practice* 18, 1999, 154-155.

[26] *Id.*

[27] *Id.*

[28] *Id.*

While you should never rely exclusively on the client's perception of the circumstances triggering agency and judicial intervention, the parent's motivation and explanation for his or her behavior may be a valuable source of rebuttal evidence.

Also *interview witnesses, friends, relatives, and the caseworker.* However, do not substitute an interview with the caseworker for the thorough inspection of agency records, court transcripts and files, and records from any other sources.

You should *obtain releases from your client* in order to acquire confidential documents, such as medical treatment, substance abuse treatment, employment, and welfare records.

In reconstructing the history of the case, *identify the bases of the original abuse or neglect allegations and carefully analyze the agency's efforts to work with your client.* While assessing the strength of the agency's case, you might explore the agency's amenability to a settlement proposal short of termination.

If a settlement is unlikely, *you must prepare for trial.* Because of the magnitude and finality of the decision at issue, you must use all available defenses and tactics to provide zealous representation.

The state is required to prove its case by clear and convincing evidence. Expert witnesses for the parent are often necessary to rebut the state's case. *Consider motions for expert evaluations* of, among other things:

- the child's relationship with the parent and with the foster parents,

- the child's response to continued contacts with the parent while in foster care, and

- the parent's capacity to care for the child.

In some situations, where the case for termination rests on mental disability or other specific diagnoses, expert opinion will be critical to the case.

If your client is indigent and unable to pay for these experts, check to see if your jurisdiction permits you to make a written motion asking the court to appoint an expert to testify on behalf of the parent. If your jurisdiction provides for such an appointment, *include a list of two or three proposed experts in the motion* to avoid the court making a potentially undesirable choice for you.

Besides contesting the legal grounds for termination, another basis to oppose termination exists. You may want to demonstrate that termination will not actually benefit the child. For example, you might assert that adoption is impractical and the child is likely to remain a "legal orphan."

You also might show that some other arrangement is best for the child. In some instances, legal guardianship could be a better solution and is permitted under 42 U.S.C. § 675(5)(C). Legal guardianship allows for a permanent placement with full responsibility for all decisions about the child given to the guardian.

Once the appointment is made, legal guardianship does not require state or court intervention and can allow a grandparent or other individual to care for a child without severing all parental contact. Such an arrangement might be best suited to an older child who does not wish to be adopted.

Planned permanent living arrangements, such as placement in a permanent foster home or some other well-considered permanent arrangement, is another option. 42 U.S.C. § 675(5)(C).

While considered the "least permanent" option under ASFA, it may be particularly appropriate for a disabled child who cannot live within a traditional family structure or for an older child who does not want to be adopted and does not have a guardianship option.

Planned permanent living arrangements may be used only when compelling reasons exist as to why the other permanency options would not be in the child's best interests.

As a settlement, you may want to explore the possibility of an open adoption arrangement. Determine whether your state allows for some form of open adoption, including informal visits or even enforceable visits.

§ 20A.2.11 Appeal

In determining whether to appeal an adjudication, disposition, review decision, or a decision to terminate parental rights, you must evaluate whether an appeal is in the parent's interest. Although serving as counsel to the parent includes pursuing an appeal when meritorious, you should consider other factors.

The primary factor to consider is that of time. Because appeals tend to drag on, tax (at the very least) the parents' emotional resources, and leave the family situation in continued disarray, it is not always a service to the parents to appeal.

However, if the appeal is meritorious, you should explore means of expediting it, possibly through a motion to expedite. In this motion, you might attach affidavits of experts outlining the damage to both the family and child if the appeal is not expedited.

You also should be aware that an increasing number of states are mandating expedited appeals in child abuse and neglect proceedings by statute or court rule.

If you are not skilled in appellate practice, you may want to consult with an experienced appellate practitioner before agreeing to continue or refer your client to another attorney for the appeal. If you do continue on appeal, you must strictly follow the Rules of Appellate Procedure.

Part 20B: Incarcerated Parents*

by Mimi Laver[29]

*A mother is incarcerated several hours from the courthouse and the child's
foster care placement. The father has told the caseworker he does not want to be
involved with the child. Ensuring speedy permanency for children is essential, yet
there are special considerations when working with a parent who is incarcerated.
What are these issues and what steps should be taken to ensure this family's case
is progressing appropriately?*

As an attorney or judge handling a case involving an incarcerated parent,
you have several key issues to address. Appellate decisions from around the
country offer some guidance on a parent's right to participate in a hearing, reasonable efforts for incarcerated parents, and the impact of incarceration on termination of parental rights. This article explores selected recent decisions and
case law trends and provides practice tips for lawyers and judges handling cases
like the one above.

§ 20B.1 Right to Participate

When a parent is in prison and a hearing will take place, what should you
do to include the parent in the court proceeding? Does the parent have an
absolute right to be in court or is it enough that he is represented during the
hearing? Should the parent be included by conference call, depositions, or given
the opportunity to review testimony with her attorney before the case moves
forward? Appellate courts around the country have been dealing with these and
similar questions.

In deciding whether incarcerated parents have a procedural due process
right in a hearing, many state courts follow the Supreme Court decision

---

Original Appeared in December 2001 issue of *ABA Child Law Practice*, Vol. 20 No. 10, pp.
145, published by the ABA Center on Children and the Law.

Editor's Note: Nonsubstantive changes have been made to the text and formatting to reflect the
style of this publication. Section numbers have also been added to reflect the style of this publication.

[29] Mimi Laver, J.D., is Assistant Director of Child Welfare at the ABA Center on Children and
the Law, Washington, D.C.

Matthews v. Eldridge[30] and cases following *Matthews*. *Matthews* set out a three-prong test in which a court must consider:

1. the private interest that will be impacted by the governmental action;

2. the risk of an erroneous deprivation of the private interest through the procedures used and the probative value, if any, of additional or substitute procedural safeguards; and

3. the opposing government interest and what the additional or substitute procedural requirement would entail.[31]

In balancing these factors, state courts have found a fundamental due process interest exists in a TPR hearing. Some courts have gone further to consider whether that due process right automatically means a parent must attend a hearing for the right to be protected. In *In re L.V. v. W.V.*,[32] the Supreme Court of Nebraska crafted the following considerations to help courts decide whether a parent should be at a TPR hearing, and if not, whether the parent's due process rights were protected:

- the delay resulting from prospective parental attendance;

- the need for a prompt disposition;

- the amount of time the proceeding has been pending before the juvenile court;

- the expense to the state of transporting the parent;

- the inconvenience or detriment to parties or witnesses;

- the potential danger or security risk posed by the parent's release from custody or confinement to attend the hearing;

- the reasonable availability of the parent's testimony through means other than attending the hearing; and

- the best interests of the parent's children.[33]

Based on these considerations, the *L.V.* court determined that because proper safeguards were used, the incarcerated father did not have a right to attend the termination hearing. Other state appellate courts have used the *L.V.* analysis to decide whether a parent received appropriate due process protec-

---

[30] 424 U.S. 319 (1976).

[31] *Id.* at 335.

[32] 482 N.W.2d 250 (Neb. 1992).

[33] *Id.* at 258-259.

tion.[34] Courts seem to agree that incarcerated parents lack an absolute right to attend a TPR hearing, but that they must have an opportunity to meaningfully participate in the hearing.[35] Most appellate courts leave the decision about the participation method to the trial court. It could include a parent:

- participating by phone using equipment that works;[36]

- submitting deposition testimony and having an opportunity to review the transcript of the state's case and submitting an affidavit in response;

- having the right to review the evidence presented against him, present evidence on his own behalf, and challenge the evidence presented;[37] or

- having adequate representation at the hearing with the opportunity to consult counsel about cross-examining witnesses.[38]

§ 20B.1.1 Practice Tips

Judges:

- Know whether your state appellate court or legislature has provided direction on how to protect a parent's due process rights.

- Avoid appellate delays (*e.g.*, do not allow an important hearing, such as a TPR hearing that involves an incarcerated parent, to go forward without the parent's meaningful participation).

- Be consistent from case to case when deciding what factors you will consider when deciding if participation is meaningful. This will help attorneys practicing in your courtroom be prepared to provide diligent representation for parents and help ensure fairness across cases.

- Remember, while speedy permanency is essential for the well-being of the child, protecting the parent's rights and ensuring an accurate and thorough judicial process is just as vital.

---

[34] *See In re Baby K*, 722 A.2d 470, 474 (N.H. 1998); *State ex rel. Children Youth and Families v. Ruth Anne E.*, 974 P.2d 164, 171 (N.M. 1999); *In re Involuntary Termination of the Parent Child Relationship of J.T., E.T. and R.T. v. Marion County Office of Family and Children*, 740 N.E.2d 1261 (Ind. Ct. App. 2000); *State ex rel. Jeanette H. v. Pancake*, 529 S.E.2d 865, 875-878 (W. Va. 2000).

[35] *See, e.g.,* Jamison v. Division of Family Servs., 768 A.2d 469 (Del. 2001) (unpublished decision).

[36] *See In re Baby K.*, 722 A.2d 470 (N.H. 1998) (due process not provided when incarcerated father could not hear witnesses over speaker phone and therefore did not have a fair opportunity to participate).

[37] *In re Ruth Anne E.*, 974 P.2d 164, 171-172 (N.M. 1999) (court provides alternatives concerning how to protect the parent's rights while being mindful of the child's need for finality).

[38] *See In re C.C.E.*, 540 S.E.2d 704 (Ga. Ct. App. 2000) (representation alone enough to protect incarcerated father's due process rights).

- Consider reviewing the systemic barriers to prisoners being brought to your court (*i.e.*, do the sheriffs resist transporting them, are prisoners in your court a lower priority than prisoners in other courts, are out-of-county/state writs not being handled correctly). Use your position to influence a change.

Parents' Attorneys:

- Object to any hearing proceeding without your client's participation and be prepared to argue reasons why the parent should be present.

- Find out if appearing in court could cause problems for the parent when she returns to prison, such as losing status and credit in certain programs for time away from prison, and discuss this issue with your client.[39]

- Know ahead of time what factors your judge will consider when deciding if participation is meaningful.

- Ensure an appropriate process has been developed to protect your client's rights by arguing the need for the parent's participation and assisting the court in making your client available.

- Make a record—if the process seems unfair, you will need a clear record for appeal.

Agency Attorneys:

- Attempt to have the incarcerated parent brought to court or ensure a process is in place before the hearing to allow the parent to participate in the proceeding.

- Understand your jurisdiction's requirements about adequate notice and provide the parent proper notice of the proceedings.

- Make a record of the reasons it is important to proceed immediately, even if the parent is not present, such as the importance of timely decision making for the child.

Children's Representatives:[40]

- Ensure proper protections are in place if testifying in front of the incarcerated parent would be difficult for the child.

---

[39] Telephone Interview with Carol Barnett, JD, San Jose, CA, February 23, 2001.

[40] Some jurisdictions have attorneys represent children as guardians ad litem (GALs) while others have the attorney act in a traditional attorney role, and still other jurisdictions use nonattorney GALs who cannot perform some of the tasks outlined in these tips. This article uses the term representative to include all these models.

- Advocate for the parent's presence in court if it will minimize delays for the child or support your case. The parent's presence may reduce the risk of appeal, and can make the trial move quicker than if parties need to conduct depositions or take extra time at trial when the parent is participating by phone.

- If the child will be present in court, prepare her in advance for what to expect and how she might feel when seeing the parent.

§ 20B.2 Reasonable Efforts

The child welfare agency's duty to provide reasonable efforts is complicated when the parent is incarcerated. In most cases, the child welfare agency must still provide the family necessary services to facilitate reunification or another permanency plan. The agency should explore with the incarcerated parent and prison social worker, if one exists, what services are accessible in prison. The parent may be able to participate in substance abuse treatment, parenting sessions, and job-related programs.

Even if no services exist at the prison, a parent can write or call the child if appropriate; write or call the agency to ask about the child; be actively involved in the child's health and education by participating, by phone, in any conferences and meetings about these issues; participate in hearings to the extent allowed by the court; and actively request visitation.

Visitation should be arranged when feasible and safe for the child because it helps maintain the attachment between parent and child and is an important indicator of whether a child will return to a parent.[41] The parent should be assisted in developing a placement plan while in prison and at the beginning of the case. If relatives can care for the child while the parent is in prison, that arrangement may be the best for the child and the whole family.[42] Parents have an obligation to be involved with their child and the child's care. Incarceration does not relieve the parent of the obligation; rather, the parent must comply with the services the agency and prison offer.[43] There are cases in which the agency is not

---

[41] *See In re Dylan T.*, 76 Cal. Rptr. 2d 684 (Ct. App. 1998) (incarcerated parent and child must be provided visitation unless there is a showing, by clear and convincing evidence, that visitation would be detrimental to child; see section on reasonable efforts not required for discussion of California's detriment standard).

[42] *See* Craig, Ann Metcalf. "Meeting the Needs of Children of Incarcerated Mothers." *Child Law Practice* 17(6), August 1998, 86-88 (discussion of importance of visitation and description of special mother/child visits at the Montgomery County, PA Correctional Facility).

[43] *Malone v. Arkansas Dep't of Human Servs.*, 30 S.W.3d 758, 762 (Ark. Ct. App. 2000) (incarceration does not end parental responsibility). *See also Johnson v. Ridgeway*, 2000 WL 794584 (Ark. Ct. App. 2000); *Michael J. v. Arizona Dep't. of Economic Security*, 995 P.2d 682 (Ariz. 2000).

required to make reasonable efforts to reunify the parent and child and this may be based on a parent's crime or incarceration. See below for more on this issue.

§ 20B.2.1 Practice Tips

Judges:

- Know what services are available to incarcerated parents in your state.

- Understand how far the appellate courts in your state have gone to set guidelines for level of parental responsibility.

- Be clear with all parties, from the beginning of the case on, that the agency must provide reasonable efforts and the parents must comply with them unless there has been a judicial decision that the agency is not required to provide reasonable efforts to reunify or a parent's rights have been terminated.

- Remember to strike a balance between ensuring reasonable efforts to parents and speeding permanence for children, while respecting the child's need for connection to his family.

Parents' Attorneys:

- Counsel your client to be involved.

- Request the agency to provide services to the parent.

- Request court orders for the services and visitation if needed.

- Talk to your client about relative placement and push the agency to investigate any potential family members.

- Find out if your state has any special programs for incarcerated parents to be placed with their children and advocate for a family placement.[44]

Agency Attorneys:

- Counsel the agency to provide any services possible, including visitation and regular communication between the parent and child when appropriate.

- If services are not available, counsel the agency to document the efforts they made to locate the services and the reasons they are not available.

- Advise the agency to work with the parent early to find kin to care for the child.

---

[44] Telephone Interview with Carol Barnett, JD, San Jose, CA, June 4, 2001.

- Encourage the agency to work with prison staff to develop family-friendly programs.

Children's Representatives:

- Evaluate the appropriateness of visitation and other parent-child contact by talking with the child, her therapist, foster mother, and other adults in her life.

- Request services and visitation from the agency and court if it is what is best for the child (or what the child wishes depending on your model of representation).

- Foster communication between the child and parent when appropriate. Ensure the child has the parent's address and phone number. Arrange times with the prison for the child to call the parent.

§ 20B.3 Reasonable Efforts Not Required

A court may determine that providing efforts to reunite a parent and child are not reasonable. The Adoption and Safe Families Act (ASFA)[45] categorizes some of these cases as aggravated circumstances and gives examples of these circumstances—when a child was abandoned, the victim of sexual abuse, or the victim of chronic abuse or torture.[46] States may legislate their own list of aggravated circumstances, and a number of states have gone beyond those set out in ASFA. Waiving reasonable efforts is a tool to move the child towards permanency early in a case and it may or may not lead to termination of parental rights and adoption.

Some states have defined incarceration as an aggravated circumstance. Length of incarceration is a factor in some states, while age of the child is a factor in others.[47] California, on the other hand, places emphasis on detriment to the child. The statute provides the following guidance to courts when deciding detriment: "the court shall consider the age of the child, the degree of parent-child bonding, the length of the sentence, the nature of the treatment, the nature of the crime or illness, the degree of detriment to the child if services are not offered and, for children 10 years of age or older, the child's attitude toward the

---

[45] The Adoption and Safe Families Act, Pub. L. No. 105-89, became law in November 1997. It amended the federal foster care law, Titles IV-B and IV-E of the Social Security Act.

[46] ASFA sets out two other categories of cases in which reasonable efforts may not be required – when a parent was convicted of certain crimes such as murder of one of the parent's children, and when the parent's rights to another child have been involuntarily terminated. ASFA § 101(a)(D), 42 U.S.C. § 671(a)(15)(D). This article will not discuss these types of cases in depth.

[47] *See, e.g.,* N.D. CENT. CODE § 27-20-02(3); 27-20-32.2 (1999) (must look at age of the child and length of sentence).

implementation of family reunification services, and any other appropriate factors."[48]

Some courts have reviewed cases in which the agency believed services should not be delivered. While incarceration may not be listed as a factor in the state statute, courts have gone beyond the state's enumerated list of aggravated circumstances to decide services are not needed if the services would be "futile" and the incarceration is "persistent and ongoing" and not a "temporary crisis" likely to dissipate in the near future.[49]

As ASFA implementation spreads in your area, expect to see more cases involving aggravated circumstances soon.

§ 20B.3.1 Practice Tips

Judges:

- Know what your state's statutes and case law say about incarceration as a reason to waive the agency's obligation to provide reasonable efforts.

- Find out if a general clause in the law gives you discretion when deciding whether making reasonable efforts would be effective or futile in reuniting the family.

- Remember this order generally means the parent and child will not be reunited. Carefully balance the age of the child and degree of attachment with the parent, the likelihood the parent will be released from prison and be able to care for the child in a reasonable period, the child's right to permanence, and the parent's rights to the child.

Parents' Attorneys:

- Be aware of any state statutes and case law addressing incarceration as a reason to waive reasonable efforts.

- Soon after your appointment, counsel your client about when reasonable efforts are not required and the likely consequences, including TPR. Find out whether your client wants to fight a no reunification services order.

- If your client wants to work towards reunification, find ways that your case differs from your state statute and any case law. For example, think

---

[48] CAL. WELF. & INST. CODE ANN. § 361.5(e)(1) (2001).

[49] *In re Adoption/Guardianship No. J970013*, 737 A.2d 604 (Md. Ct. Spec. App. 1999) *quoting In re Adoption/ Guardianship No. 10941*, 642 A.2d 201 (Md. 1994). *See also In re J.W. v. Williams*, 953 P.2d 104 (Wash. 1998) (court can look beyond enumerated list of aggravated circumstances to deny reasonable efforts if the remedial services would be futile).

about the length of the client's sentence, the child's age, the crime for which your client is serving time, and any existing attachments between your client and the child.

- Consider appealing a no reunification services decision.

Agency Attorneys:

- In appropriate cases, bring the no reunification services issue before the court as early in the case as possible. If the court finds the agency is not required to make reasonable efforts to reunify, ensure the case moves towards permanency, including filing a TPR if necessary, as quickly as possible.

- Be clear with the judge about how long the length of incarceration is expected to last.

- The child's developmental needs and relationship with the parent are key to the judge's ability to make a thoughtful decision. Ensure the caseworker has information about this, documents it well, and presents it to the court.

Children's Representatives:

- Work with the caseworker, foster parent or caretaker, the child's therapist, relatives and other people in the child's life to determine whether ending reunification services is in the child's best interests.

- Discuss this issue with the child to find out her position.

- Depending on your assessment of the case, collaborate with the agency attorney or parent's attorney to reach the best outcome for the child.

- If the court decides the agency need not make reunification efforts, ensure the agency makes and follows through on an appropriate permanency plan that includes necessary services for the child.

§ 20B.4 Termination of Parental Rights

Most case law involving incarcerated parents stems from termination of parental rights (TPR) cases. In addition to the right to participate line of cases, discussed above, frequently addressed issues include:

§ 20B.4.1 Incarceration as a Ground or Factor in TPR

Appellate courts largely agree that incarceration alone is not a ground for TPR. However, some courts have found incarceration is an element of abandonment of the child, and the TPR can be based on abandonment. In *Michael J. v.*

Arizona Dep't. of Economic Security,[50] the Arizona Supreme Court stated, "Imprisonment, per se, neither 'provides a legal defense to a claim of abandonment' nor alone justifies severance on the grounds of abandonment. Rather, incarceration is 'merely one factor to be considered in evaluating the father's ability to perform [his] parental obligations.'"[51] Many courts agree with the Michael J. court and terminate based on abandonment if the incarcerated parent does not communicate with the child or try to comply with the case plan.

Similarly, some courts have allowed the use of incarceration to demonstrate parental unfitness as a ground for termination. In *In re M.D.S.,*[52] the Kansas Court of Appeals considered a father's claim that incarceration prevented him from completing his case plan and should not be used as a factor in determining parental unfitness. The court rejected this claim and found the trial court properly terminated the father's rights. The court relied on the Kansas statute setting out factors for deciding a parent's fitness, including conviction of a felony and imprisonment.[53]

§ 20B.4.2 Length of Incarceration

A number of state legislatures and appellate courts have determined the length of a parent's incarceration is relevant to terminating parental rights. Some laws specify the exact number of years the parent must be incarcerated.[54] Other statutes are more general, requiring for example, the state show the incarceration will last a "substantial portion of the period of time before the child will attain the age of 18 years."[55]

Appellate courts usually consider length of incarceration as one factor in deciding a TPR, rather than basing the entire decision on this issue. A Colorado court, for example, terminated a mother's parental rights based on unfitness after considering the length of her incarceration and the length of her child's time in foster care.[56] The *Michael J.* court, on the other hand, thought it important to conduct a case-by-case analysis to determine if the "sentence…is of such

---

[50]   995 P.2d 682 (Ariz. 2000).

[51]   *Id.* at 686, *quoting In re Pima County Juvenile Action No. S-624*, 616 P.2d 948, 950 (Ariz. Ct. App. 1980). *See also W.T.J. v. E.W.R.*, 721 So. 2d 723 (Fla. 1998).

[52]   *In re M.D.S.*, 825 P.2d 1155 (Kan. Ct. App. 1992).

[53]   *See also* 13 DEL. C. § 1103(5)(a)(3) (one ground in termination statute allows TPR if parent is "incapable of discharging parental responsibilities due to extended or repeated incarceration…").

[54]   For example, Michigan (MICH. COMP. LAWS. ANN. § 712A.19b(3)(h)) and Illinois (750 ILCS § 50/1(D)(r)) law set out incarceration in excess of two years as the test. Until recently, in Arkansas (former ARK. CODE. ANN. § 9-27-341(2)(H)(ii)) a parent was required to be sentenced to a term of incarceration for 15 years for the state to demonstrate a "substantial period." In 2003, the 15-year requirement was removed from the statute.

[55]   FLA. STAT. ANN. § 39.806(1)(d)(1).

[56]   *In re M.H.*, 10 P.3d 713 (Colo. Ct. App. 2000).

a length that the child will be deprived of a normal home for a period of years."[57] This totality of the circumstances analysis seems a common way courts decide these types of cases.[58]

§ 20B.4.3 Nature of Crime

ASFA's implementing regulations require agencies to file a TPR petition within 60 days of a judicial determination that reasonable efforts to reunify the child and parent are not required because the parent was convicted of certain crimes.[59] While this does not necessarily make the type of crime a ground for termination, the 1996 amendments to the Child Abuse Prevention and Treatment Act (CAPTA) require these crimes be included in state legislation as TPR grounds.[60] Some states have expanded the list of crimes that are grounds for termination beyond the CAPTA crimes.[61] Expect to see more case law on this issue in the near future.

In analyzing the state statutory grounds for TPR, the Texas Court of Appeals reversed a TPR. The court found when deciding to terminate an imprisoned parent's rights, it is necessary to look at the expected length of sentence *and* whether the underlying conduct leading to the incarceration was the type from which child endangerment could be inferred.[62] In this case, the mother was convicted after writing bad checks and she did everything she could to comply with the case plan while in prison. When the parent is incarcerated for a nonviolent crime, or one not resulting from an act against a child, courts may be willing to consider facts favoring the parent.

---

[57] *Michael J. v. Arizona Dep't. of Economic Security*, 995 P.2d 682, 687 (Ariz. 2000) (court stated length of sentence should be one factor to consider in addition to nature of parent-child relationship, age of child, availability of another parent to provide care, and effect of parent's absence on child). *See also In re B.C. v. Deborah C.*, 15 P.3d 8 (Okla. Civ. App. 2000) (duration of incarceration and its detrimental effect on parent-child relationship is one factor to consider in TPR).

[58] *See, e.g., In re C.N.S.*, 545 S.E.2d 633 (Ga. Ct. App. 2001) (history of repeated incarcerations is a factor to support TPR and is evidence relevant to deciding that a child is presently without proper care and control).

[59] ASFA § 103(a)(3)(E), 42 U.S.C. § 671(a)(15)(D)(ii); 45 CFR § 1356.21(b)(3)(ii), (i)(iii) (enumerated crimes include: murder, voluntary manslaughter, or aiding, abetting, attempting, conspiring or soliciting to commit murder or voluntary manslaughter, of another child of the parent or felony assault that results in serious bodily injury to the child or another child of the parent).

[60] 42 U.S.C. § 5106a(b)(2)(A)(xvi), (xvii).

[61] *See, e.g.,* FLA. STAT. ANN. § 39.806(1)(d) (2001) (includes a finding that parent is a violent career criminal or sexual predator); IDAHO CODE § 16-2005(h) (2000) (includes murder of the other parent); OHIO REV. CODE ANN. § 2151.414(E)(7) (1999) (expands victims to any child in the household, not just a child of the parent).

[62] *In re D.T.*, 34 S.W.3d 625 (Tex. App. 2000) *analyzing* TEX. FAM. CODE ANN. § 161.001(D)(E)(N).

§ 20B.4.4 Practice Tips

Judges:

- Know if your state's TPR statute and case law identify factors to consider when terminating an incarcerated parent's rights;

- Determine if your state's case law gives you discretion to consider certain factors, such as length of sentence, when terminating a parent's rights.

- Don't forget to do a best interest analysis in reaching your decision in a TPR.

Parent's Attorneys:

- Know your state case law so you can distinguish your client's case.

- Conduct a thorough investigation. Find out what portion of a sentence a parent is likely to serve. Try to learn about the quality of your client's relationship with the child. Find out what efforts your client made to be in contact with the child from prison. Use these facts to argue against TPR if that is your client's wish.

- If your client is incarcerated for a crime unrelated to the child, or other children, establish this during the hearing.

- If your state statute allows and your client desires, negotiate for an open adoption agreement.

Agency Attorneys:

- Be prepared to prove several grounds for TPR, if possible. Don't rely just on the fact that the parent is incarcerated.

- Gather and present the court with information about the parent's criminal history, care of the child before incarceration, and attachment with the child.

- Consider referring the case to mediation, especially if relatives are willing to adopt.

- Depending on your state's statutory framework, consider filing a TPR motion soon after the child enters foster care. In some cases, you can bypass the no reasonable efforts decision process and proceed immediately to TPR.

Children's Representatives:

- Conduct a thorough investigation to ensure TPR is in the child's best interest and is what the child wants. Consider the child's relationship with the parent no matter what the sentence is or the nature of the parent's crime.

- If TPR is your position, help the agency attorney bring the case, or file your own TPR motion if allowed by your state's statute.

- If TPR is not appropriate, tell the caseworker and agency attorney your position and help the parent's counsel fight the motion, if one is filed.

- If your state statute allows, consider whether an open adoption is in the child's best interest, and if so, advocate for such an agreement.

§ 20B.5 Conclusion

Handling a case involving an incarcerated parent is complex and demanding, no matter whether you are the judge or one of the attorneys on the case. The resources available to the parent are often lacking, yet reunification when the parent is released is generally the appropriate permanency goal. Everyone needs to carefully balance the parent's rights with the child's right to permanency as well as her right to a relationship with her parent. More and more case law is emerging across the country addressing these dilemmas so be sure to keep up with trends to best serve the family in your case.

§ 20B.6 Programs

Chicago Legal Advocacy for Incarcerated Mothers (CLAIM) provides legal and educational services to help imprisoned mothers preserve their families. Through public advocacy, CLAIM promotes policies and programs to benefit families of imprisoned mothers.

Contact information: 220 South State Street, Suite 830, Chicago, IL 60604, (312) 332-5537, Web site: http://www.C-L-A-I-M.org.

The Community Prisoner Mother Program and the **Family Foundations Program** are projects of the California Department of Corrections Office of Community Resources, Women and Children Services Unit. These programs provide residential settings for women who are convicted of nonviolent crimes, generally drug offenses, and their young children. The women had to be the primary caretaker of their children and cannot have a history of child abuse. They are under 24 hour supervision and receive intensive services such as substance abuse treatment, parenting education, alcoholics anonymous, and child care. The staff also observes the interaction between the mother and child.

Contact information: David Robinson, Chief, Women and Children Services Unit, CA Department of Corrections, 1515 S Street, Room 400 South, Sacremento, CA 94283, (916) 327-7944, (916) 445-6029 (fax).

The Family and Corrections Network provides services for families of incarcerated individuals. Their Web site has an extensive list of links to legal services, agencies that assist family members, and foundations that support work relating to incarcerated parents.

Contact information: 32 Oak Grove Road, Palmyra, VA 22963, (804) 589-3036, (804) 589-6520 (fax), and e-mail: fcn@fcnetwork.org, Web site: www.fcnetwork.org.

The Incarcerated Mothers Law Project is a joint program of Volunteers of Legal Service and the Women's Prison Association. Through this program, pro bono attorneys provide legal education and direct representation to mothers who are incarcerated in New York city jails and two state prisons. Issues handled include custody, visitation and responsibilities toward children while incarcerated.

Contact information: Sara Effron, Assistant Director, 54 Greene Street, New York, NY 10013, (212) 966-4400, e-mail: volsprobono@worldnet.att.net.

Legal Services for Prisoners with Children (LSPC) advocates for the civil rights and empowerment of incarcerated parents, children, family members and people at risk for incarceration by responding to requests for information, trainings, technical assistance, litigation, community activism, and the development of more advocates. LSPC's focus is on women prisoners and their families, and it emphasizes that issues of race are central to any discussion of incarceration.

Contact information: 100 McAllister Street, San Francisco, CA 94102, (415)255-7036, Web site: www.prisonerswithchildren.org.

§ 20B.7 Literature

- Chiancone, Janet. "Children of Incarcerated Parents: What Lawyers Need to Know." *Child Law Practice* 16(3), May 1997, 33-34, 42-46. Available from the ABA Center on Children and the Law, 202/662-1743.

- Craig, Ann Metcalf. "Meeting the Needs of Children of Incarcerated Mothers." *Child Law Practice* 17(6), August 1998, 86-88. Available from the ABA Center on Children and the Law, 202/662-1743.

- Goodmark, Leigh. "Incarcerated Mothers" in *Keeping Kids Out of the System: Creative Legal Practice as a Community Child Protection Strategy*. Washington, D.C.: American Bar Association, 2001. This chapter discusses several legal services projects serving incarcerated mothers. Available from the Service Center, 888/285-2221.

- Mumola, Christopher J. "Incarcerated Parents and Their Children." *Bureau of Justice Statistics Special Report*. Washington, DC: U.S. Department of Justice Office of Justice Programs, August 2000. This report provides recent data on incarcerated parents with children. Available from the BJS Clearinghouse, 800/732-3277 (Order # NCJ 182335).

- Wright, Lois E. & Cynthia B. Seymour. *Working With Children and Families Separated by Incarceration: A Handbook for Child Welfare Agencies*. Washington, DC: CWLA Press, 2000. This handbook explains the special needs of children whose parents are in prison and suggests ways to improve child welfare policies and practices. Available by contacting Cynthia Seymour, 202/942-0270.

Part 20C: Representing a Parent with Diminished Capacity*

by Jennifer Renne[63]

§ 20C.1 Introduction

When representing a client with diminished capacity, it can be difficult for the lawyer to know when to defer to the client's wishes, and when to substitute his or her judgment for the client's. It can be hard to determine issues of client autonomy, control of litigation, and decision making with a fully functioning client, but what if there are questions about a client's capacity or ability to make decisions? This chapter focuses on representing clients with diminished capacity.

Many of our clients suffer from diminished capacity, defined as a client who is not fully functioning, whether as a result of substance abuse, age, or mental health issues. How a lawyer handles these delicate issues can profoundly impact the client-lawyer relationship. Effective advocacy, combined with empowering clients, can result in a more meaningful role for the lawyer and will positively affect case outcomes. The following case study shows the complexity and challenging nature of such representation. The chapter provides guidance by explaining lawyers' ethical duties under the relevant ethical rules. It also goes beyond the ethics rules to suggest practical ways child welfare lawyers can effectively represent clients with diminished capacity.

§ 20C.2 The Mason Case

Consider the following case from the view of the mother's lawyer. What is Marty Mason's capacity to make significant decisions about her life and her legal case? How is her lawyer to proceed under these circumstances?

Marty Mason, 19 years old, is the mother of newborn Cecily. Cecily, Marty's only child, was born drug-exposed to heroin. Marty had been living with a boyfriend, but he refused to allow either Marty or the baby to return to his apartment. He is not the father of the child, and the father of the child is unidentifiable. Marty had no other home for herself or the child. The agency filed a petition based on these facts.

When her lawyer interviewed her at court, Marty Mason seemed sullen, withdrawn, and depressed. She was nonresponsive throughout the interview.

---

* This chapter has been adapted with permission by Donald N. Duquette from Jennifer L. Renne, *Legal Ethics in Child Welfare Cases*, ABA Center on Children and the Law (2004).

[63] Jennifer Renne, J.D., is Assistant Director of Child Welfare at the ABA Center on Children and the Law in Washington, D.C.

Cecily's stay at the hospital was continued for medical reasons, and she was transferred to a foster home when she was medically ready. The following week, Marty stopped by her lawyer's office unannounced, and demanded to meet with her. Marty was excited, agitated, and insisted that Cecily shouldn't have been taken from her. They could both live with her friend, Marty said, who also had a baby. Because of her extreme mood change, her lawyer was puzzled and talked with her further. Marty warmed up to the lawyer and in the course of the interview, disclosed that she had used heroin the day of the first court hearing, but had not used that day. Marty said that she had used heroin regularly for over three years, since she was 16. Marty also said that she very much liked what heroin did for her. It settled her down and made her less jumpy. Her thoughts did not race around so much when she was on heroin.

At the next hearing, the baby Cecily was continued in foster care. Marty Mason was allowed supervised visits but was also required to participate in drug treatment, including regular screens. At the caseworker's request, the court ordered Marty to undergo a psychiatric evaluation. The psychiatrist diagnosed Marty with a psychotic disorder and prescribed anti-psychotic medication. Her intelligence was in the low normal range. Eventually, the court approved a case plan that continued drug treatment and psychiatric treatment. Marty's improvement in the first three months was quite dramatic. While taking her medication regularly, she was able to maintain herself off heroin. She did regular drops and participated fully in the drug treatment. Her psychiatrist reported a more stable mental condition. Marty's lawyer was struck by the momentous improvement in her mental alertness and mood. They talked about Marty's future plans concerning Cecily and Marty said she wanted to continue with her therapy and eventually get custody of Cecily—perhaps in six or nine months. Partly because of these improvements, an old rift between Marty and her mother, Adelaide, began to heal. Grandma Adelaide had essentially given up on her daughter after years of drug addiction and the devastating effects that had on the family. In the first three months of Cecily's life, Adelaide and Marty began visiting with one another, and Adelaide sometimes visited the child with Marty. At the end of the three-month period, Marty moved in with her mother and told her lawyer that if she couldn't get Cecily back, she wanted her mother to raise her.

Marty's lawyer had just started thinking she was witnessing a very welcome success story when Marty's situation deteriorated as suddenly and as dramatically as it had improved. Marty abruptly moved out of her mother's home and began living with a new boyfriend, leaving her anti-psychotic medication behind. She tested positive for heroin and cocaine and then stopped attending drug treatment altogether. She failed to appear for the six-month dispositional review hearing. Marty dropped out of contact with the caseworker, her mother, her lawyer, and her various treatment professionals, and she remained out of contact for over three months.

Finally, Marty's lawyer received word that Marty had been found wandering in the streets talking incoherently and had been committed to an inpatient psychiatric hospital, where she was receiving her anti-psychotic medication again. When Marty's lawyer finally was able to speak to her in the hospital, Marty was withdrawn and depressed. She said she had been using drugs during this time and supporting herself and her habit through prostitution. "I am in no position to take care of Cecily," she said. "I'm thinking I should give her up for adoption." Marty really likes the foster parents, whom she met at visits. They were better off financially and she thought they might be able to provide for her child better than she or her mother, who was also poor.

This was a difficult conversation for the lawyer for many reasons. Marty seemed confused, although she was not overtly psychotic. The lawyer never did determine what precipitated the sudden and dramatic decline. Marty simply said that all the pressures came crashing down on her. "I don't know what to do," she said. Marty's lawyer has had personal experiences with the child welfare system and feels personally that a child should stay with the biological parent if at all possible. The lawyer likes Marty and thinks she is a sympathetic figure and would present well in court. Personally, the lawyer would like to see Marty get herself together and work towards regaining custody.

The next hearing is a permanency planning hearing, and the lawyer told Marty that the court would make some important decisions about Cecily. The lawyer identified options for Marty that could include: (1) releasing her parental rights; (2) working to have the child placed with Grandmother Adelaide; or (3) working to get her back on track so Marty herself might be able to gain custody of the baby. Placement with Grandma Adelaide could be permanent or temporary. If it were temporary, it would give Marty even more time to get herself together. Her lawyer asked Marty what she would like to do. After seeming to listen to her options, Marty slumped in her chair and said, "I don't know. I'm really confused. Everything is so messed up. I really don't know what to do."

§ 20C.3 Model Rule 1.14: Representing a Client with Diminished Capacity

Model Rule 1.14,[64] amended in 2002, helps lawyers represent a client's wishes when capacity is an issue. Lawyers have been frustrated with the lack of guidance from the ethics rules. While lawyers still have much discretion (and sometimes confusion) in deciding how to best represent clients with diminished capacity, the amended Model Rule 1.14 provides more guidance.

§ 20C.3.1 Maintaining a Normal Client-Lawyer Relationship

The client-lawyer relationship assumes that the client, when properly advised and assisted, can make decisions about important matters. In other

---

[64] MR 1.14, Client With Diminished Capacity.

words, the presumption is that the client has capacity. The rule's first instruction is that when a client's capacity to make decisions is diminished, the lawyer shall, as far as reasonably possible, maintain a normal client-lawyer relationship.[65] Capacity may be diminished by a client's age, drug addiction, mental impairment, or for some other reason. A "normal client-lawyer relationship" means the lawyer owes duties of loyalty, confidentiality, diligence, conflict of interest, competence, communication, and advice. The duty of loyalty means that "a lawyer shall abide by a client's decisions concerning the objectives of representation, and that the client has the ultimate authority to determine the purposes to be served by legal representation."[66]

Maintaining a normal client-lawyer relationship requires communicating regularly. The commentary to the rules is clear that a client with diminished capacity often can understand, deliberate upon, and reach conclusions about matters affecting the client's well-being. It further explains that "children as young as five or six years of age, and certainly those of 10 or 12, are regarded as having opinions that are entitled to weight in legal proceedings concerning their custody."[67]

§ 20C.3.2 Assessing Client Capacity

In determining whether a client has capacity to make certain decisions, lawyers should know that they can have a strong influence on a client's decisions. Paternalistic tendencies can be problematic for even the most well-intentioned parents' and children's lawyers. Lawyers need to be aware of the power dynamics and other factors that influence the relationship and representation. In this case, the lawyer's personal views in favor of the biological connection could seriously affect the client's final decision. As perhaps the most influential person in the decision-making process, the lawyer must be very careful not to impose his or her attitude on the parent—whether it is a personal preference for placement with a biological parent or in favor of the grandparent or foster parent adoption. The lawyer's purely personal values must be recognized as such and held in check.

Just because a lawyer disagrees with a client's decision, or thinks what the client wants is not best for the client, does not mean the client lacks capacity to make decisions. A client's decision may result from many things—fear, lack of understanding, subjective interests—*not necessarily diminished capacity*. The lawyer should focus on the decision-making process, not whether he or she approves of the decision.

Factors to consider when assessing client capacity:

---

[65] MR 1.14(a).

[66] MR 1.2.

[67] MR 1.14, cmt. 1.

- *Cognitive ability.* In Marty Mason's case, her lawyer may need to talk to her therapist and psychiatrist to understand her cognitive ability since she has been diagnosed with a psychotic disorder.

- *Emotional and mental development and stability.* This often changes from one interview to the next, and can change dramatically as in Marty's case. For Marty's lawyer, consider the impact of Marty's drug use and psychiatric condition on her emotional and mental stability.

- *Ability to communicate.* When the case first came in, Marty could not communicate her feelings. Her ability to communicate first improved and then declined just as dramatically. Through time, medication, counseling, and other interventions, she may be able to communicate more effectively.

- *Ability to understand consequences.* Has the lawyer explained the case, including consequences of certain decisions, to help the client understand?[68] Marty, for example, might not understand the supports available to her or her mother.

- *Consistency of decisions.* Marty's feelings vary widely from hoping to get custody of her daughter herself, to hoping Grandmother Adelaide might be the best option, to wanting the current foster parents to adopt her.

- *Strength of wishes.* Marty Mason's feelings vary. She does not seem to know her own mind.

- *Opinions of others.* See the section below about considering bias when weighing this factor.

For children (in addition to above factors):

- Child's age (age alone is not dispositive).

- Child's developmental stage.

The amended Commentary to the Model Rules says that in determining the extent of the client's diminished capacity, the lawyer should consider and balance such factors as:

- The client's ability to articulate reasoning leading to a decision.

- Variability of state of mind.

- Ability to appreciate the consequences of a decision.

- The consistency of a decision with the known long-term commitments and values of the client.

---

[68] See also MR 1.4.

- In appropriate circumstances, the lawyer may seek guidance from an appropriate diagnostician.[69]

Marty's lawyer, for example, could consider that while Marty has articulated various goals at various times, she supports positions with reasons of different complexity and depth. For instance, if pressed to say why she would like the foster parents to adopt, Marty may simply say, "They seem like nice people." Her objections to her mother as Cecily's long-term caretaker may be based on a lifetime of experiences that she can recite. The lawyer could listen to and assess the reasoning behind the client's possible position.

Marty's lawyer also should consider Marty's mental health issues. At the outset of the case, Marty most likely lacked capacity to participate in decisions because she was under the influence of drugs. Subsequently, Marty's mental capacities improved when she stopped abusing substances and received treatment for her psychiatric disorder. Lawyers need to reassess capacity frequently because interventions such as therapy, medication, and substance abuse treatment can improve the client's level of functioning and ability to participate in the case.

The Model Rules also suggest that lawyers have a duty to maximize client capacities, so lawyers should always consider what interventions may increase capacity, as discussed in greater detail below. Parents' lawyers should take a proactive role in maximizing client capacities[70] and keep in mind their duties to advise the client under Model Rule 2.1.

§ 20C.3.3 Viewing Capacity as a Continuum

Even though a client has diminished capacity, the client may be able to understand, weigh, and reach conclusions about matters affecting his or her well-being.[71]

Increasingly, the law recognizes degrees of capacity. For example, the earlier version of Model Rule 1.14 was titled "Representing a Client with a Disability." The amended Model Rule 1.14 is titled "Representing a Client with a Diminished Capacity," implying that capacity is measured along a continuum, and is not an either/or prospect. Even when a client is impaired, he or she can participate in some decisions. In other words, a client may have capacity for some issues, but not others. In a recent Wisconsin case, the court held that there are different levels of capacity, and that a juvenile who has been declared incompetent to participate in the delinquency proceedings does not necessarily lack capacity to understand the sanctions in the "juvenile in need of protection and services" case.[72]

---

[69] MR 1.14, cmt. 6.

[70] MR 1.14, cmt. 5.

[71] MR 1.14, cmt. 1.

[72] *In re Eugene W.*, 641 N.W.2d 467 (Wis. Ct. App. 2002).

§ 20C.3.4 Taking Protective Action

Lawyers have always had the option of requesting a guardian or taking other protective action on behalf of a disabled client. However, the earlier version of the Model Rules offered little guidance on what "other protective action" meant. Therefore, the only form of protective action under the old rules was to ask that a guardian be appointed for the client, considered an extreme measure.

The amendments to Model Rule 1.14 add guidance regarding protective measures that may be taken short of requesting a guardian.[73] These include:

- Consulting family members.

- Consulting with professionals who can protect the client.

- Using a reconsideration period to clarify or improve circumstances.[74]

For example, if Marty comes to court on drugs and she cannot make certain decisions, her lawyer could ask to postpone the hearing (without disclosing the reasons) to give Marty time to improve her circumstances and her frame of mind (an example of maximizing client capacities). This may be an unsuccessful strategy, and the court may place limits on the number of continuances, but Marty's lawyer needs to attempt to maximize her capacity, and needs to protect his or her client.

Marty's lawyer could also consult family members or treating mental health professionals to help make decisions on Marty's behalf. For instance, the psychiatrist treating Marty may observe that releasing the child for adoption outside the family could indeed provide significant relief to Marty's mental health by relieving a huge stressor.

The Model Rules further provide that in taking any protective action, the lawyer should be guided by such factors as:

- *The client's wishes and values to the extent known.* For example, if Marty's mental health regresses again, her lawyer would make decisions based on wishes Marty expressed in the past.

- *The client's best interests and the goals of intruding into the client's decision-making autonomy to the least extent feasible.* The lawyer is not substituting his or her judgment for that of the client.

- *Maximizing client capacities.* Marty's lawyer might encourage drug rehabilitation and/or medication for Marty to improve her functioning and enhance her capacity to participate.

---

[73] MR 1.14(b).

[74] MR 1.14, cmt. 5.

- *Respecting the client's family and social connections.*[75] Marty's lawyer, for example, might be reluctant to provide Grandma Adelaide information that might damage the mother-daughter relationship, even if the lawyer thought Grandma Adelaide would be better off knowing Marty's situation.

When consulting family members or professionals involved with the case, the lawyer must keep the client's interests foremost in his or her mind. To the degree possible, a lawyer must look to the client to make decisions.

The lawyer should also be aware of any biases and misunderstandings that family members or others may have, and attempt to weigh these factors in determining the client's objectives. In representing Marty, for example, a lawyer would be aware of factors that may influence others' assessment of the case, such as:

- *Agency supervisor:* May want to free Cecily for adoption with the foster parents because of a personal allegiance to the foster parents and the pressure the agency is under to facilitate adoptions.

- *Grandma Adelaide:* May say she can't take Cecily, but not disclose that her reason is that she can't afford it. Perhaps she doesn't realize she would be eligible for a foster care or adoption subsidy.

- *Social worker:* Hasn't told Grandma Adelaide that she may be eligible for financial assistance and services if she agrees to take Cecily because the social worker does not want to place Cecily there.

Thus, under the Model Rules, the lawyer should speak to others who have an interest in the case to get their input on what Cecily wants. But the lawyer should be aware of any bias or misunderstanding that may impact Cecily's return home.

§ 20C.3.5 Appointing a Guardian

When a client's capacity is severely diminished and other less onerous protective actions are not successful, a lawyer can ask the court to appoint a guardian for the client.[76] While this is sometimes appropriate, it can traumatize the client[77] and undermine the client-lawyer relationship. In Marty Mason's case, her lawyer has been telling her for two years that she will advocate for what Marty wants. If the lawyer then asks to have a guardian appointed, and the guardian recommends that Marty be placed in a psychiatric hospital or agree to termination of her parental rights, this could upset Marty, who has trusted the lawyer to keep her word. It may cause clients to lose trust in the judicial process

---

[75] MR 1.14, cmt. 5.

[76] MR 1.14(b).

[77] MR 1.14, cmt. 7.

and not cooperate with the case plan. It also tips off the judge that the lawyer doesn't think the client can make his or her own decisions.

§ 20C.3.6 Maintaining Client Confidentiality

In taking protective action on behalf of a client, such as talking to Marty's family members, lawyers sometimes wonder how the confidentiality rules apply. The Model Rules clearly instruct the lawyer to keep client confidences, disclosing them only to protect the client's interests.[78] Lawyers can disclose information in order to perform their job responsibilities, *as long as the disclosure is in the client's best interests.* The commentary acknowledges that this is an *unavoidably difficult position.*[79] On one hand, the lawyer may need to disclose otherwise protected information to help make decisions for the impaired client. On the other hand, the lawyer is duty bound to maintain confidences.

Disclosing a client's condition could harm the client's interest.[80] For example, in representing Marty, the lawyer would not disclose that his or her client is on drugs. Sometimes simply revealing that the lawyer suspects a disability or diminished capacity violates the confidentiality rules. For example, the Wisconsin Supreme Court recently held that a lawyer violated privilege by testifying about his basic impressions, perceptions, and opinion on a client's competence to stand trial.[81] Therefore, given that Marty is behaving inconsistently, and her lawyer is unable to ascertain any of Marty's interests, it might be appropriate for her lawyer to discuss with Marty's psychiatrist her impressions of Marty's overall functioning. The psychiatrist could offer guidance on how to more effectively communicate with Marty. As the Model Rules acknowledge, this is an unavoidably difficult position because the lawyer might need to disclose otherwise protected information *for the purpose* of getting guidance on representation.[82]

§ 20C.3.7 Eliciting the Client's Position

When a lawyer has concluded that the client, although impaired, can understand certain issues and provide input on decisions, the lawyer should elicit

---

[78] MR 1.14(c).

[79] MR 1.14, cmt. 8.

[80] MR 1.14, cmt. 8.

[81] *State v. Meeks*, 666 N.W.2d 859 (Wis. 2003).

[82] Before the changes to the Model Rules, the ABA issued an ethics opinion on whether a lawyer who reasonably believes a client has abused prescription medication resulting in an inability to communicate or reach adequately informed decisions violates the MR 1.6 provision on confidentiality by discussing the client's condition with the client's physician. The opinion finds that such communication does not violate MR 1.6 because it is "impliedly authorized." The client cannot give consent, and it is not possible to seek the appointment of a guardian without disclosure to the court, and without such communication with the physician, the client risks serious harm. ABA Comm. on Ethics and Prof'l Responsibility, Informal Op. 89-1530 (1989).

the client's position in the case. The lawyer should explain the lawyer's role, *including what information the attorney may reveal about the client to protect the client's best interests.* It's important to establish this up front so the client doesn't later feel betrayed by his or her lawyer. Interviews with the client should take place where the client feels comfortable.

Lawyers should ask developmentally appropriate questions and provide advice and guidance without persuasion or manipulation that might influence a client's decision making. The lawyer should also be aware of verbal and nonverbal expressions and communications from the client. For example, Marty's lawyer can observe interactions between her and Grandmother Adelaide. Marty's lawyer can observe the way Marty interacts with her daughter. The lawyer can talk to social workers, a psychologist or therapist, family members, and any other person who might have insight into the client's feelings and preferences.

The key to representing parents is developing a good relationship. Getting to know the client helps the lawyer understand the case from the client's view. It empowers the client to participate in his or her case, and gives the client a sense that someone is advancing his or her interests.

§ 20C.3.8 Advocating in and out of Court

Once the lawyer has determined what the client wants, and whether the client suffers from diminished capacity, the lawyer must present his or her client's position in court. Many lawyers consider their job to be "the mouthpiece of the client," merely reiterating to the court what the client wants. Advocacy is more complicated. *Through creative problem solving and working with others in the case, lawyers should craft a solution so that what the client wants actually is in the client's best interest.*

The more the lawyer knows about the client, the more effective the representation. It's not about standing up in court and repeating what the client has said. It's about doing the legwork before the hearing, and finding out the family situation. The more prepared the lawyer is, the better the lawyer can explain to the client his or her options and the consequences of certain decisions. Let us work through one of the possible options available for Marty Mason and her daughter Cecily to demonstrate the important out-of-court advocacy that can be accomplished by Marty's lawyer. Assume Marty determines that what she really wants is for her mother, Grandmother Adelaide, to raise Cecily. Marty's lawyer's job then is to try and have other participants, and eventually the judge, see this outcome as in Cecily's best interest. Advocacy steps Marty's lawyer can take to have Cecily placed with her grandmother might include:

- Contacting Grandma Adelaide to find out if she is interested in the placement. If there are barriers or reservations in her mind, identify them and try to resolve them.

- Finding out if Grandma Adelaide knows she may be eligible to be licensed as a foster parent for Cecily and receive services to meet her needs. Finding out, too, if Grandma Adelaide knows about subsidized adoption and that she might be eligible.

- Determining if the agency has been in contact with Grandma Adelaide. Does state law provide a clear preference for relative placements? Tell the social worker that Grandma Adelaide might be willing to take Cecily if she gets some support and services.

- Telling the social worker that Marty Mason is willing to work for a permanent placement of Cecily with Grandma Adelaide.

- Exploring family counseling with Grandma Adelaide and Marty.

- Talking with Cecily's lawyer and the lawyer for the agency about the plan for permanent placement with Grandma Adelaide. Get their support, or identify their concerns and attempt to address them.

- Talking to Marty Mason regularly, keeping her informed, and finding out if her feelings have changed.

Marty's lawyer should seek to negotiate a strategy that can allow Cecily to be placed with her grandmother because this is what the client wants. Ensuring a safe and permanent placement also makes this outcome in Cecily's best interest. This aggressive problem-solving approach can be applied to whatever outcome is finally determined to be the client's position—regardless of whether the client suffers from a diminished capacity. The lawyer does not merely stand up in court and talk about her vision of success; the lawyer takes an assertive, problem-solving approach to make it happen.

These steps by Marty Mason's lawyer will also empower Marty to participate in case planning, which supports the lawyer's ultimate goal. Getting all players on board is key. Even if no agreement is reached before court, Marty's lawyer should come to court and present the plan to the judge, explain Marty's position, and why it might be best for the child and the entire family to be with Grandma Adelaide, instead of in foster care. Marty's lawyer should explain how Cecily can be placed safely with her grandmother, which includes addressing the relevant issues in the case. This is advocacy. The goal is to achieve a result for the client. Marty Mason is empowered knowing her lawyer is working for her, even if she has mixed feelings.

This type of advocacy also helps the judge make a best interest determination—the judge must understand the case from each party's perspective, not just what they want, but why they want it. The judge can consider other options presented by the lawyers who know the family dynamics and who have prepared solutions that enhance safety and support reunification.

§ 20C.4 Conclusion

Representing clients with diminished capacity takes the same hard work as representing a client where capacity is not an issue. Lawyers should begin with the premise that all clients have capacity to direct the representation. When a client's issues are so serious that the lawyer is concerned that the client cannot understand the proceedings or make reasoned decisions, the lawyer can look to the ethics rules for guidance. A poor decision by a client can result from fear, confusion, or other subjective concerns. The lawyer has a duty to explain matters to the client and maximize the client's decision-making ability.

Spending time with a client, talking to others about the case, being prepared, and knowing the case from the client's view are essential. The lawyer's job is not to repeat the client's position to the court, but to craft a solution so that what the client wants actually *is* in the best interest of the child. This doesn't mean trying to manipulate the client's desires, but rather working to provide services and creative solutions. This applies not only to lawyers for children, but parents' lawyers too, as many parent's lawyers merely state to the court the parent's position without attempting to craft the parent's position as one that will keep the child safe. When all parties are well represented, children and families are served by the system and outcomes improve.

Chapter 21   REPRESENTING CHILDREN AND YOUTH

Part 21A: The Role and Duties of the Child's Lawyer

by Donald N. Duquette[1] and Marvin Ventrell[2]

§ 21A.1 Introduction to the Representation of Children

Quality legal representation of all parties is essential to a high-functioning dependency court process.[3] Quality legal representation of children in particular is essential in obtaining good outcomes for children. An adversarial court process that depends on competing independent advocacy to provide information will not produce good outcomes for litigants who lack competent advocates. Dependency court decisions are as good as the information on which the decisions are based. In order to promote the welfare of children in dependency court, therefore, children must be provided with competent independent legal representation.

The role of the child's attorney is unique in American jurisprudence and not yet sufficiently defined by law or tradition. Although there is a growing consensus that children in dependency cases should have lawyers, there continues to be confusion and debate over the role and duties of the lawyer. At the outset, we recognize that children are not simply small adults, and that extending the traditional role of an attorney in the adult context to the representation of children will not necessarily serve the child client well. A lawyer representing a child has a client who may or may not be competent, and who may be competent for some decisions but not for others. Modifications to the lawyering role must, therefore, be made. The primary modification concerns the client's direction to the lawyer where a child is incapable or incompetent to make such decisions. With these modifications in place, the lawyer then participates in formulating the client's position and reporting that position to the court in a manner inconsistent with traditional adult representation. Such modifications, some argue, create a hybrid lawyer role that can diminish independent zealous advocacy. Crafting rules that blend the benefits of client autonomy and child protection have proved to be difficult.

---

[1]   Donald N. Duquette, J.D., is Clinical Professor of Law and Director of the Child Advocacy Law Clinic of the University of Michigan Law School. He is also a member of the National Association of Counsel for Children (NACC) Board of Directors.

[2]   Marvin Ventrell, J.D., is the President/CEO of the National Association of Counsel for Children (NACC).

[3]   ABA Center on Children and the Law, Court Improvement Progress Report (1998).

Yet progress has been made. Children have been represented in the child welfare cases for a relatively short time. In the 1970s, children were infrequently represented by counsel, but today children are nearly always represented under some model of lawyering.[4] Unlike delinquency law, which mandates independent legal counsel under *In re Gault*,[5] there is no such federal or constitutional mandate in dependency court.[6] Guidance comes primarily from the Federal Child Abuse Prevention and Treatment Act (CAPTA). As a condition for receiving Federal child abuse related funds, CAPTA requires that each state appoint a guardian ad litem for a child in every case involving an abused or neglected child that results in a judicial proceeding.[7] CAPTA permits the guardian ad litem to be an attorney or a lay advocate, or both. It also requires the guardian ad litem to obtain, first-hand, a clear understanding of the situation and needs of the child and make recommendations to the court concerning the best interests of the child.

CAPTA is a reasonable starting place but it is not a comprehensive model. The result of implementing CAPTA in the states, therefore, has been the creation of numerous—and oftentimes inconsistent and unclear—models of representation. It can be argued that no two models of child representation among the various U.S. jurisdictions are alike. Further, within jurisdictions, there is often considerable disagreement as to which model is used and what the role of the representative is within the model. This confusion has undoubtedly contributed to the poor quality of representation children frequently receive in our system.[8]

So what precisely are the role and duties of the child's lawyer in dependency cases? The lawyer must first look to state law for controlling authority. The role of the child's lawyer may be set forth in state statutes, case law, court rules, state's ethics codes, or appointment orders and contracts. In Colorado, for example, state statute mandates the appointment of a guardian ad litem and further requires that the GAL be an attorney.[9] The representation model is further defined by a body of case law, a supreme court directive, and the state ethics code.[10] Taken together, these authorities form what is generally called the

---

[4] For a discussion of the various models of child representation, see Appendix A-1, NACC RECOMMENDATIONS FOR REPRESENTATION OF CHILDREN IN ABUSE AND NEGLECT CASES, § IV.

[5] 387 U.S. 1 (1967).

[6] A few states have improved on the problem by determining that a child has a constitutional right to legal representation in child welfare proceedings. *See In re Jamie TT,* 599 N.Y.S.2d 892 (N.Y. App. Div. 1993).

[7] Child Abuse Prevention and Treatment Act (CAPTA), 42 U.S.C. § 5106a(b)(A)(xiii).

[8] *America's Children at Risk: A National Agenda for Legal Action,* 1993 REPORT OF THE ABA PRESIDENTIAL WORKING GROUP ON THE UNMET LEGAL NEEDS OF CHILDREN AND THEIR FAMILIES.

[9] COLO. REV. STAT. §§ 19-1-111(1), 19-1-103(59), 19-3-203(3).

[10] *See In re J.E.B.,* 854 P.2d 1372 (1973); Supreme Court of Colorado Directive 04-06, "Court Appointments Through the Office of the Child's Representative" (2004); Colorado Rules of Professional Conduct.

Attorney/GAL model, which requires the attorney to represent the child's best interests. It is the predominant model of dependency court legal representation throughout the states. A survey by the National Council of Juvenile and Family Court Judges determined that 40 states appoint counsel for children in child abuse and neglect cases. In 30 states, an "attorney-guardian-ad-litem" is typically appointed who serves a dual function of representing both the best interests and the wishes of the child. In the 10 other states that appoint counsel for a child, a guardian ad litem is appointed in addition to the attorney, so that the attorneys perform the single role of representing the child (*i.e.*, the child's wishes). In 10 states, the NCJFCJ reported that an attorney is usually *not* appointed for the child, but in nine of those States a non-attorney guardian ad litem is appointed for the child.[11]

Even with such guidance, the role of the child's lawyer presents unique difficulties. Moreover, some states offer very little guidance. Fortunately, there is a developing body of national authority to help guide the practitioner. By drawing on the authority of national ethics and practice standards, the dependency court child's attorney can fill in the gaps left by his or her state.

AUTHORITY FOR DEPENDENCY COURT LEGAL REPRESENTATION

- State Statute.
- Administrative Regulations.
- State Ethics Code.
- Case Law.
- State and Local Court Rule.
- Appointment Order.
- Appointment Contract with State Oversight Authority.
- State Standards of Practice or Guidelines.
- The Child Abuse Prevention and Treatment Act.
- NACC Recommendations for Representation of Children in Abuse and Neglect Cases.
- ABA Standards (and ABA / NACC Revised Version) of Practice for Lawyers Who Represent Children in Abuse and Neglect Cases.
- Department of Health and Human Services Guidelines for Public Policy and State Legislation Governing Permanence for Children.
- Treatises and Literature.

---

[11] SHIRLEY DOBBIN ET AL., NAT'L COUNCIL OF JUVENILE AND FAMILY COURT JUDGES, CHILD ABUSE AND NEGLECT CASES: REPRESENTATION AS A CRITICAL COMPONENT OF EFFECTIVE PRACTICE (1998).

§ 21A.2 Basic Lawyer Ethics: The Model Code and Model Rules

The starting place for the general rules of lawyer duties is the Model Code or Model Rules. Each state has adopted either the ABA Model Code of Professional Responsibility or Model Rules of Professional Conduct. The Model Code and Model Rules define the lawyer's basic responsibility of independent, competent, zealous advocacy.[12] These basic duties, including knowledge, skill, thoroughness, and preparation apply equally to lawyers representing children. No jurisdiction has created a blanket exception to the duty to abide by them for children's lawyers. Lawyers appointed to represent children, therefore, owe the same duties to the child client as he or she would to an adult client unless the state provides a specific exception, such as in the case of client confidentiality under some state's guardian ad litem provisions. Likewise, if one accepts that the duty to provide competent representation requires a lawyer to know his or her client, it would be a breach of the duty and a violation of the lawyer's ethics to fail to meet with your child client.

The American Bar Association's old Model Code of Professional Responsibility[13] did not provide any direct guidance for the attorney representing a child. The newer Model Rules of Professional Conduct[14] address the issue of dealing with a client under a disability. Rule 1.14(a) of the Model Rules provides: "When a client's ability to make adequately considered decisions is impaired, whether because of minority, mental disability or for some other reason, the lawyer shall, as far as reasonably possible, maintain a normal client-lawyer relationship with the client." The commentary to Rule 1.14 says: "Furthermore, to an increasing extent the law recognizes intermediate degrees of competence. For example, children as young as five or six years of age, and certainly those of ten or twelve, are regarded as having opinions that are entitled to weight in legal proceedings governing their custody." The default position, therefore, is for the child's lawyer to maintain as normal an attorney-client relationship as possible.

Rule 1.14(b) says: "A lawyer may seek the appointment of a guardian or take other protective action with respect to a client, only when the lawyer reasonably believes that the client cannot act in the client's own interest."

In August 2002, the American Bar Association adopted revised ethical rules with the "Ethics 2000" project.[15] The new Rule 1.14(a) of the Model Rules, now

---

[12] *See* MODEL RULES OF PROF'L CONDUCT Preamble, R. 1.1; MODEL CODE OF PROF'L RESPONSIBILITY EC 7-1; 7-12, DR 6-101.

[13] MODEL CODE OF PROF'L RESPONSIBILITY (American Bar Association 1969).

[14] MODEL RULES OF PROF'L CONDUCT (American Bar Association 1983).

[15] MODEL RULES OF PROF'L CONDUCT (2002).

referring to a client with *diminished capacity*, provides: "When a client's capacity to make adequately considered decisions in connection with a representation is diminished, whether because of minority, mental impairment or for some other reason, the lawyer shall, as far as reasonably possible, maintain a normal client-lawyer relationship with the client."

Rule 1.14(b) provides: "When the lawyer reasonably believes that the client has diminished capacity, is at risk of substantial physical, financial or other harm unless action is taken and cannot adequately act in the client's own interest, the lawyer may take reasonably necessary protective action, including consulting with individuals or entities that have the ability to take action to protect the client and, in appropriate cases, seeking the appointment of a guardian ad litem, conservator or guardian." The new Rule 1.14(b) gives the child's attorney broader guidance on what "other protective action" might be appropriate, including allowing consultation with other persons or entities. Further, the new Rule 1.14(b) provides more guidance regarding the previous trigger for acting ("only when the lawyer reasonably believes that the client cannot act in the client's own interest") to include situations in which the client "is at risk of substantial physical, financial or other harm unless action is taken and cannot adequately act in the client's own interest." This change reflects the Ethics 2000 loosening of the confidentiality rules under some circumstances.

The Comment to the new Rule 1.14 provides much greater guidance to the child's attorney wishing to take protective action on behalf of the child client:

[5] If a lawyer reasonably believes that a client is at risk of substantial physical, financial or other harm unless action is taken, and that a normal client-lawyer relationship cannot be maintained as provided in paragraph (a) because the client lacks sufficient capacity to communicate or to make adequately considered decisions in connection with the representation, then paragraph (b) permits the lawyer to take protective measures deemed necessary. Such measures could include: consulting with family members, using a reconsideration period to permit clarification or improvement of circumstances, using voluntary surrogate decision-making tools such as durable powers of attorney or consulting with support groups, professional services, adult-protective agencies or other individuals or entities that have the ability to protect the client. In taking any protective action, the lawyer should be guided by such factors as the wishes and values of the client to the extent known, the client's best interests and the goals of intruding into the client's decision-making autonomy to the least extent feasible, maximizing client capacities and respecting the client's family and social connections.

[6] In determining the extent of the client's diminished capacity, the lawyer should consider and balance such factors as: the client's ability to articulate reasoning leading to a decision, variability of state of mind and ability to appreciate consequences of a decision; the substantive fairness

of a decision; and the consistency of a decision with the known long-term commitments and values of the client. In appropriate circumstances, the lawyer may seek guidance from an appropriate diagnostician.

[7] If a legal representative has not been appointed, the lawyer should consider whether appointment of a guardian ad litem, conservator or guardian is necessary to protect the client's interests. Thus, if a client with diminished capacity has substantial property that should be sold for the client's benefit, effective completion of the transaction may require appointment of a legal representative. In addition, rules of procedure in litigation sometimes provide that minors or persons with diminished capacity must be represented by a guardian or next friend if they do not have a general guardian. In many circumstances, however, appointment of a legal representative may be more expensive or traumatic for the client than circumstances in fact require. Evaluation of such circumstances is a matter entrusted to the professional judgment of the lawyer. In considering alternatives, however, the lawyer should be aware of any law that requires the lawyer to advocate the least restrictive action on behalf of the client.

The new Comment 4 to Rule 1.14, modifying Comment 3 to Model Rule 1.14, provides that in "matters involving a minor, whether the lawyer should look to the parents as natural guardians may depend on the type of proceeding or matter in which the lawyer is representing the minor." In the child welfare context, it is likely that the child's attorney would not be looking to the parents for direction on the central questions of custody, although the parents could be helpful on collateral questions such as placement, education and health care.

§ 21A.3 The Best Interests vs. Expressed Wishes Conundrum

Although the new Model Rule 1.14 provides better guidance than before, neither the Model Code nor Model Rules were drafted specifically with child representation in mind. It has long been thought that the field would benefit from a comprehensive set of national standards specifically designed for the child's attorney. Producing those standards has proved difficult, largely because of the debate over the role of the child's attorney. Policy makers have differed in their views of whether the attorney should represent the best interests or expressed wishes of the child. The debate has received more than enough attention in the literature, yet it is necessary to understand the nature of the debate in order to move past it.

Should the lawyer for the child be guided by the child's expressed wishes or by the lawyers determination of what is in the best interests of the child? The competition between the two principle models has been called the dilemma of child advocacy.[16] The dilemma paradigm asks whether children's attorneys should advocate the expressed wishes (the client-directed model) or the best interests (the advocate-directed model) of the child.

Both the interests and wishes models are criticized. Proponents of traditional client-directed lawyering argue that children and youth benefit from the sense of empowerment that comes from a lawyer who works exclusively for the child rather than society's view of what is best for the child. Another objection is that best interests is a substituted judgment model that inappropriately substitutes the view a lawyer for that of the child while at the same time usurping the role of the court to make such determinations. With an infant or young child, the pure best interests approach fails to set out principles to guide the advocate's discretion in identifying the child's best interests.[17] The model has also resulted in what has come to be known as "relaxed advocacy," where attorneys feel free to ignore their traditional duties (such as seeing their client or filing motions) because they are appointed as a guardian ad litem.

Many critics of the best interests model have advocated for the traditional attorney model only to be criticized for endangering children's welfare by allowing children to determine their fate. The pure wishes or client-directed model is criticized where a child of limited capacity and poor judgment sets immature and even harmful goals for the outcome of the case. For example, the younger abused child commonly wants to return to the custody of the parent—even if it was that parent who caused the injuries. Child advocate lawyers say they do not wish to use their advocacy skills to put a child in continued danger.

Many also point out that "children are under tremendous pressure to misidentify and/or misarticulate their own interests because of pressure from their families, from the court process, and from the circumstances leading to the court process."[18] Haralambie notes that children's "wishes may be based on threats, bribes, and other questionable bases."[19] Buss interprets Perry as "suggesting that children's communications with their lawyers are hampered by, among other things, their difficulty in dealing with the emotional and social pressures connected with the proceeding, their feelings of guilt, their difficulty understanding and framing responses to lawyers' questions, and their lack of understanding of the court process."[20] Melton notes that "the necessity of making choices can be anxiety provoking for children."[21]

---

[16] ANN M. HARALAMBIE, THE CHILD'S ATTORNEY: A GUIDE TO REPRESENTING CHILDREN IN CUSTODY, ADOPTION, AND PROTECTION CASES (American Bar Association 1993).

[17] *See* Donald N. Duquette, *Legal Representation for Children In Protection Proceedings: Two Distinct Lawyer Roles Are Required*, 34 FAM. L.Q. 441 (Fall 2000).

[18] Emily Buss, *You're My What? The Problem of Children's Misperceptions of Their Lawyers' Roles*, 64 FORDHAM L. REV. 1699, 1702-1703 (1996) (citations omitted).

[19] *Id.* at 1703 n.9 (citations omitted).

[20] *Id.* (citations omitted).

[21] *Id.* at n.10 (citations omitted).

The pure client-directed model has another major flaw in that it does not give sufficient direction for the representation of the very young clients who may be nonverbal or lack the developmental capacity to make reasoned decisions and give guidance to the attorney.[22]

This wishes/best interests conundrum has tied the field in knots for over two decades, but experience and analysis are breaking the impasse.

§ 21A.4 The "Child's Attorney" Response

One response to the dilemma has been the creation of the "child's attorney" model of representation, which tends toward a client-directed approach. While state and federal statutes currently weigh in favor of a best interests approach, national policy advocates tend to favor a client-directed approach.[23] The model moves away from the substituted judgment, paternal guardian ad litem model and toward a more autonomous traditional attorney model that includes safeguards to protect autonomy, which may harm a child. This "child's attorney" model is found in each of the following events and literature:

- The December 1995 Fordham University School of Law Conference on Ethical Issues in the Legal Representation of Children, which resulted in a special law review issue by the same name.[24]

- The adoption in February 1996 of the *American Bar Association Standards of Practice for Lawyers Who Represent Children in Abuse and Neglect Cases.*[25]

- The publication of *Representing Children in Child Protective Proceedings: Ethical and Practical Dimensions* by Yale Clinical Law Professor Jean Koh Peters in 1997.[26]

- The Adoption in 1999 of the ABA (NACC Revised) *Standards of Practice for Lawyers Who Represent Children in Abuse and Neglect Cases.*

---

[22] Annette R. Appell, *Decontextualizing the Child Client: The Efficacy of the Attorney-Client Model for Very Young Children*, 64 FORDHAM L. REV. 1955, 1957.

[23] The representation of children in the dependency court has also evolved from the 1970's paternal model to the current tendency toward an independent child's attorney. *See, e.g.*, Brian G. Fraser, *Independent Representation for the Abused and Neglected Child: The Guardian Ad Litem*, 13 CAL. W. L. REV. 16 (1976); Ann M. Haralambie, *Current Trends in Children's Legal Representation*, 2 CHILD MALTREATMENT 193 (1997); Marvin R. Ventrell, *Rights & Duties: An Overview of the Attorney-Child Client Relationship*, 26 LOY. U. CHI. L.J. 259 (1995).

[24] Special Issue, *Ethical Issues in the Legal Representation of Children*, 64 FORDHAM L. REV. 1279 (1996).

[25] The ABA STANDARDS were adopted by the ABA February 5, 1996, and by the NACC (with reservation) on October 13, 1996. They are adapted and published with the permission of the ABA in the NACC DESKBOOK & DIRECTORY (3d ed. 1998).

[26] JEAN KOH PETERS, REPRESENTING CHILDREN IN CHILD PROTECTIVE PROCEEDINGS: ETHICAL AND PRACTICAL DIMENSIONS (Charlottesville, VA: LEXIS Law Publishing 1997).

Each of these sources rejects the notion that one must either represent the expressed wishes or best interests of the child.

§ 21A.4.1 The ABA Standards of Practice for Lawyers Who Represent Children in Abuse and Neglect Cases

The ABA Standards of Practice for Lawyers Who Represent Children in Abuse and Neglect Cases provide:

[t]he term "child's attorney" means a lawyer who provides legal services for a child and who owes the same duties of undivided loyalty, confidentiality, and competent representation to the child as is due an adult client. The child's attorney should elicit the child's preferences in a developmentally appropriate manner, advise the child, and provide guidance. The child's attorney should represent the child's expressed preferences and follow the child's direction throughout the course of litigation. To the extent that a child cannot express a preference, the child's attorney shall make a good faith effort to determine the child's wishes and advocate accordingly or request appointment of a guardian ad litem. To the extent that a child does not or will not express a preference about particular issues, the child's attorney should determine and advocate the child's legal interests. If the child's attorney determines that the child's expressed preference would be seriously injurious to the child (as opposed to merely being contrary to the lawyer's opinion of what would be in the child's interests), the lawyer may request appointment of a separate guardian ad litem and continue to represent the child's expressed preference, unless the child's position is prohibited by law or without any factual foundation.

§ 21A.4.2 The ABA (NACC Revised) Standards of Practice

The *ABA Standards* were adopted in 1996. The following year, the NACC adopted the standards with reservation as to Standard B-4. Standard B-4 is the client direction language of the standards, and some members of the NACC Board of Directors believed the *ABA Standards* gave too much autonomy to the child client and was unrealistic where young children were concerned. Subsequently, the NACC adopted its own revised version of the *ABA Standards* in the NACC's attempt to achieve a better balance of beneficence and autonomy within Standard B-4. The "Child's Attorney" model of the *ABA (NACC Revised) Standards of Practice* draws on the work of the Fordham Conference and Professor Peters. In essence, this child's attorney model places the attorney in the traditional role of zealous advocate but provides for an infusion of "protection" through the application of an objective best interests evaluation in limited situations. The model requires that the attorney assume the traditional role of zealous advocate and not GAL to avoid any propensity toward relaxed advocacy. At the same time, it recognizes that some children are not capable of directing their litigation, and that a degree of substituted judgment is unavoidable. In essence, where the ABA remained consistent with the client-directed attorney throughout, the NACC carved out a significant exception where the client cannot meaningfully participate in the formulation of his or her position. In such cases, the NACC's version calls for a GAL type substitution of judgment, but using objective criteria. Additionally, the NACC's version requires the attorney to request the appointment of a separate GAL, after unsuccessful attempts at counseling the child, when the child's wishes are considered to be potentially seriously injurious to the child.

§ 21A.5 The "Two Distinct Roles" Response

Another response calls for the creation of two distinct lawyer roles. This model suggests that it is a mistake to try to develop a single lawyer role for children in protection cases that attempts to accommodate developing capacities from infants to articulate teens. "We should adopt different standards for the different lawyer roles."[27] This model creates a bright line at age 12 or 14, and the court appoints a best interest lawyer for all the children younger than that age and a traditional attorney for the children over the strict age test. This avoids ad hoc, discretionary decision making, and makes it more likely that similarly situated children would receive the same level of advocacy for their stated preferences.[28] The state of Michigan has adopted this model.[29]

§ 21A.6 The "Duties" Response

No matter how the goals of the advocacy are determined, whether as directed by the child-client or as determined by a best interest of the child judgment of the lawyer, there is widespread agreement that the lawyer for the child should be an active and aggressive advocate. Few continue to argue that a lawyer representing a child client is absolved from the fundamental duties of thorough communication with the client or case investigation and preparation. While recognizing the difficulty of determining the goals of litigation in the face of a client of limited capacity, there is agreement that certain duties are fundamental.

§ 21A.6.1 NACC Recommendation for Representation of Children in Abuse and Neglect Cases

In an attempt to get past the best interests and expressed wishes debate, the NACC adopted the *NACC Recommendations for Representation of Children in*

---

[27] Donald N. Duquette, *Legal Representation of Children: Two Distinct Lawyer Roles are Required,* 34 FAM. L.Q. 441, 441 (Fall 2000).

[28] *Id.*

[29] *Id.* at 444.

Abuse and Neglect Cases in 2001.[30] The Recommendations encourage jurisdictions to avoid the wishes/interests debate and instead focus on providing fundamental services to child clients through a child's needs assessment. The NACC believes that, regardless of the role designation, attorneys should be able to provide competent independent legal representation by focusing on the following systemic safeguards, advocacy duties, and special advocacy issues.

A.   Systemic Safeguards

☐   1.   Children need competent, independent, and zealous attorneys. The system of representation must require the appointment of competent, independent, zealous attorneys for every child at every stage of the proceedings. The same attorney should represent the child for as long as the child is subject to the court's jurisdiction.

☐   2.   Children need attorneys with adequate time and resources. The system of representation must include reasonable caseload limits and at the same time provide adequate compensation for attorneys representing children.

☐   3.   Children need attorneys who understand their role and duties. The system of representation of children must be well defined by statute, bar standards, administrative guidelines, supreme court directive or other documents such that every attorney appointed for a child can understand his/her precise role and duties, and such that an attorney can be held accountable for performance of those duties.

☐   4.   Children need an opportunity to present their positions to the court through counsel. The system of representation must provide the child with an opportunity for his/her needs and wishes to be expressed to the court.

☐   5.   Children need confidential communication with their attorneys. The attorney has a duty to explain the extent of confidentiality in developmentally appropriate language.

☐   6.   Children need to be involved as litigants in the entire litigation process, including any post disposition, termination of parental rights, and adoption proceedings. The system of representation must recognize the child as a party to the litigation and must include the child in all phases of the litigation, including the opportunity to participate in arguments and jury selection where applicable, offer exhibits, call witnesses, examine and cross examine witnesses and

---

[30] For full text, *see* Appendix A-1, NACC RECOMMENDATIONS FOR REPRESENTATION OF CHILDREN IN ABUSE AND NEGLECT CASES.

engage in motions and discovery processes. The child must also be given notice of all proceedings and copies of all pleadings.

☐ 7.   Children need judicial review of adverse decisions. The system of representation must provide an opportunity to appeal an adverse ruling.

☐ 8.   Children need to be able to hold their attorneys accountable. The system of representation must provide recourse for ineffective assistance of counsel.

☐ 9.   Children need an attorney with a fair opportunity to be effective in the court system. The system of representation must include a court system that devotes adequate time and resources to cases.

B.   Advocacy Duties

☐ 1.   Children need attorneys who fully understand their cases. The attorney must perform a full and independent case investigation.

☐ 2.   Children need meaningful communication with their attorneys. The attorney must observe the child, and dependent upon the child's age and capabilities, interview the child. The attorney must engage in regular and meaningful communication with the child. Children need to participate in making decisions that affect their cases. The attorney has a duty to involve the child client in the process, whether under a client directed model or advocate directed model. The attorney has a duty to explain his/her role to the child in developmentally appropriate language.

☐ 3.   Children need loyal attorneys. The child's attorney is prohibited from representation that would constitute a conflict of interest.

☐ 4.   Children need the full benefit of legal counsel. The attorney must provide competent, independent and zealous representation for each client. The attorney must have adequate time and resources to devote to the child's case, and to understanding his/her role and duties, insuring confidentiality, and full active participation in all stages of the child's case.

C.   Advocacy Issues

☐ 1.   Children need permanence. The attorney must advocate for timely resolution and permanent resolution (absent compelling reasons to the contrary) of the case.

☐ 2.   Children need their immediate and basic needs met. The attorney must advocate for food, shelter, clothing, and safety, including a safe temporary placement where necessary and for educational, medical, mental health, and dental needs.

☐　　3.　　Children need family relationships. The attorney must advocate for continuation of appropriate familial relationships and family preservation services where appropriate.

☐　　4.　　Children need to be protected from unnecessary harm that can result from legal proceedings. The attorney must advocate for the utilization of court processes that minimize harm to the child, and make certain that the child is properly prepared and emotionally supported where the child is a witness.

§ 21A.6.2 The ABA Standards and NACC Revised ABA Standards Focus on Duties

Beyond the "child's attorney" role designation of the ABA Standards, the focus of the document is the basic obligations and required actions of the lawyer for the child that most policy makers support, regardless of their view of the dilemma. These obligations also appear in the NACC revised version of the standards and are consistent with the *NACC Recommendations* in Section 21A.6.1 above. They are also affirmed by the federal government in *Guidelines for Public Policy and State Legislation Governing Permanence for Children*.[31] The duties of the child's attorney, from the *ABA Standards*,[32] include:

. . .

B.   GENERAL AUTHORITY AND DUTIES

B-1.　Basic Obligations. The child's attorney should:

1. Obtain copies of all pleadings and relevant notices;

2. Participate in depositions, negotiations, discovery, pretrial conferences, and hearings;

3. Inform other parties and their representatives that he or she is representing the child and expects reasonable notification prior to case conferences, changes of placement, and other changes of circumstances affecting the child and the child's family;

4. Attempt to reduce case delays and ensure that the court recognizes the need to speedily promote permanency for the child;

5. Counsel the child concerning the subject matter of the litigation, the child's rights, the court system, the proceedings, the lawyer's role, and what to expect in the legal process;

---

[31] Adoption 2002: The President's Initiative on Adoption and Foster Care, Guidelines for Public Policy and State Legislation Governing Permanence for Children (1999).

[32] ABA Standards of Practice for Lawyers Representing a Child in Abuse and Neglect Cases (1996) (commentary ommitted).

6. Develop a theory and strategy of the case to implement at hearings, including factual and legal issues; and

7. Identify appropriate family and professional resources for the child.

. . .

C.   ACTIONS TO BE TAKEN

C-1. Meet With Child. Establishing and maintaining a relationship with a child is the foundation of representation. Therefore, irrespective of the child's age, the child's attorney should visit with the child prior to court hearings and when apprised of emergencies or significant events impacting on the child.

C-2. Investigate. To support the client's position, the child's attorney should conduct thorough, continuing, and independent investigations and discovery which may include, but should not be limited to:

1. Reviewing the child's social services, psychiatric, psychological, drug and alcohol, medical, law enforcement, school, and other records relevant to the case;

2. Reviewing the court files of the child and siblings, case-related records of the social service agency and other service providers;

3. Contacting lawyers for other parties and non-lawyer guardians ad litem or court-appointed special advocates (CASA) for background information;

4. Contacting and meeting with the parents/legal guardians/caretakers of the child, with permission of their lawyer;

5. Obtaining necessary authorizations for the release of information

6. Interviewing individuals involved with the child, including school personnel, child welfare case workers, foster parents and other caretakers, neighbors, relatives, school personnel, coaches, clergy, mental health professionals, physicians, law enforcement officers, and other potential witnesses.

7. Reviewing relevant photographs, video or audio tapes and other evidence; and

8. Attending treatment, placement, administrative hearings, and other proceedings involving legal issues, and school case conferences or staffings concerning the child as needed.

C-3. File Pleadings. The child's attorney should file petitions, motions, responses or objections as necessary to represent the child. Relief requested may include, but is not limited to:

1. A mental or physical examination of a party or the child;

2. A parenting, custody or visitation evaluation;

3. An increase, decrease, or termination of contact or visitation;

4. Restraining or enjoining a change of placement;

5. Contempt for non-compliance with a court order;

6. Termination of the parent-child relationship;

7. Child support;

8. A protective order concerning the child's privileged communications or tangible or intangible property;

9. Requesting services for child or family; and

10. Dismissal of petitions or motions.

C-4. Request Services. [Consistent with the child's wishes**], the child's attorney should seek appropriate services (by court order if necessary) to access entitlements, to protect the child's interests and to implement a service plan. These services may include, but not be limited to:

1. Family preservation-related prevention or reunification services;

2. Sibling and family visitation;

3. Child support;

4. Domestic violence prevention, intervention, and treatment;

5. Medical and mental health care;

6. Drug and alcohol treatment;

7. Parenting education;

8. Semi-independent and independent living services;

9. Long-term foster care;

10. Termination of parental rights action;

11. Adoption services;

12. Education;

13. Recreation or social services; and

14. Housing.

C-5. Child With Special Needs. Consistent with the child's wishes, the child's attorney should assure that a child with special needs receives appropriate services to address the physical, mental, or developmental disabilities. These services may include, but should not be limited to:

1. Special education and related services;

2. Supplemental security income (SSI) to help support needed services;

3. Therapeutic foster or group home care; and

4. Residential/in-patient and out-patient psychiatric treatment.

C-6. Negotiate Settlements. The child's attorney should participate in settlement negotiations to seek expeditious resolution of the case, keeping in mind the effect of continuances and delays on the child. The child's attorney should use suitable mediation resources.

D. HEARINGS

D-1. Court Appearances. The child's attorney should attend all hearings and participate in all telephone or other conferences with the court unless a particular hearing involves issues completely unrelated to the child.

D-2. Client Explanation. The child's attorney should explain to the client, in a developmentally appropriate manner, what is expected to happen before, during and after each hearing.

D-3. Motions and Objections. The child's attorney should make appropriate motions, including motions in limine and evidentiary objections, to advance the child's position at trial or during other hearings. If necessary, the child's attorney should file briefs in support of evidentiary issues. Further, during all hearings, the child's attorney should preserve legal issues for appeal, as appropriate.

D-4. Presentation of Evidence. The child's attorney should present and cross examine witnesses, offer exhibits, and provide independent evidence as necessary.

D-5. Child at Hearing. In most circumstances, the child should be present at significant court hearings, regardless of whether the child will testify.

D-6. Whether Child Should Testify. The child's attorney should decide whether to call the child as a witness. The decision should include consideration of the child's need or desire to testify, any repercussions of testifying, the necessity of the child's direct testimony, the availability of other evidence or hearsay exceptions which may substitute for direct testimony by the child, and the child's developmental ability to provide direct testimony and withstand possible cross-examination. Ultimately, the child's attorney is bound by the child's direction concerning testifying.

D-7. Child Witness. The child's attorney should prepare the child to testify. This should include familiarizing the child with the courtroom, court procedures, and what to expect during direct and cross-examination and ensuring that testifying will cause minimum harm to the child.

D-8. Questioning the Child. The child's attorney should seek to ensure that questions to the child are phrased in a syntactically and linguistically appropriate manner.

D-9. Challenges to Child's Testimony/Statements. The child's competency to testify, or the reliability of the child's testimony or out-of-court statements, may be called into question. The child's attorney should be familiar with the current law and empirical knowledge about children's competency, memory, and suggestibility and, where appropriate, attempt to establish the competency and reliability of the child.

D-10. Jury Selection. In those states in which a jury trial is possible, the child's attorney should participate in jury selection and drafting jury instructions.

D-11. Conclusion of Hearing. If appropriate, the child's attorney should make a closing argument, and provide proposed findings of fact and conclusions of law. The child's attorney should ensure that a written order is entered.

D-12. Expanded Scope of Representation. The child's attorney may request authority from the court to pursue issues on behalf of the child, administratively or judicially, even if those issues do not specifically arise from the court appointment. For example:

1. Child support;

2. Delinquency or status offender matters;

3. SSI and other public benefits;

4. Custody;

5. Guardianship;

6. Paternity;

7. Personal injury;

8. School/education issues, especially for a child with disabilities;

9. Mental health proceedings;

10. Termination of parental rights; and

11. Adoption.

D-13. Obligations After Disposition. The child's attorney should seek to ensure continued representation of the child at all further hearings, including at administrative or judicial actions that result in changes to the child's placement or services, so long as the court maintains its jurisdiction.

E. POST HEARING

E-1. Review of Court's Order. The child's attorney should review all written orders to ensure that they conform with the court's verbal orders and statutorily required findings and notices.

E-2. Communicate Order to Child. The child's attorney should discuss the order and its consequences with the child.

E-3. Implementation. The child's attorney should monitor the implementation of the court's orders and communicate to the responsible agency and, if necessary, the court, any non-compliance.

F. APPEAL

F-1. Decision to Appeal. The child's attorney should consider and discuss with the child, as developmentally appropriate, the possibility of an appeal. If after such consultation, the child wishes to appeal the order, and the appeal has merit, the lawyer should take all steps necessary to perfect the appeal and seek appropriate temporary orders or extraordinary writs necessary to protect the interests of the child during the pendency of the appeal.

F-2. Withdrawal. If the child's attorney determines that an appeal would be frivolous or that he or she lacks the necessary experience or expertise to handle the appeal, the lawyer should notify the court and seek to be discharged or replaced.

F-3. Participation in Appeal. The child's attorney should participate in an appeal filed by another party unless discharged.

F-4. Conclusion of Appeal. When the decision is received, the child's attorney should explain the outcome of the case to the child.

F-5. Cessation of Representation. The child's attorney should discuss the end of the legal representation and determine what contacts, if any, the child's attorney and the child will continue to have.

Whether the lawyer takes his or her direction from the child or makes a best interest judgment as to what the goals of the litigation should be, the above list of activities is what is expected of the lawyer in implementing the goals, once they are determined.

§ 21A.7 The Child's Wishes Are Always Relevant

The national authorities that have addressed the child preferences reflect a consensus on this issue, too.[33] Regardless of whether or not a child is competent to direct the attorney, and even if the role of the attorney is defined as other than purely client-directed, the wishes and preferences of the child are always relevant and should be communicated to the court unless limited by privilege. No matter what weight is given to the child's preferences in determining the goals of advocacy, the attorney should elicit the child's preferences in a developmentally appropriate manner, advise the child, and provide guidance. The child's attorney should communicate the child's wishes and preferences to the court. The lawyer also has a duty to explain to the child in a developmentally appropriate way information that will help the child have maximum input in the determination of the particular position at issue. According to the child's ability to understand, the lawyer should inform the child of the relevant facts, the applicable laws, and the ramifications of taking various positions, which may include the impact of such decisions on other family members or on future legal proceedings.

State law may provide authoritative guidance on how the stated wishes and preferences of the child are to be presented to the court, if at all. Maine provides an example:

> The guardian ad litem shall make the wishes of the child known to the court if the child has expressed his wishes, regardless of the recommendation of the guardian ad litem.[34]

Florida requires the guardian ad litem to file a written report that must include "a statement of the wishes of the child."[35]

In any event, the child's wishes are to be elicited and taken seriously. The lawyer is expected to play a counseling role, advising the child client of the risks and benefits of various options and, particularly, the likely consequences of the client's expressed choices. This discussion and counseling will, in many cases, produce agreement between client and lawyer about what they perceive to be in the client's best interests.

Assuming that the child's stated preferences are determined and elicited by the lawyer and communicated to the court, how much weight should the lawyer for the child attach to those stated preferences in determining the goals of the litigation? The vast majority of legal scholars and authorities who have

---

[33] These include the ABA STANDARDS; NACC STANDARDS OF PRACTICE; THE PRESIDENT'S INITIATIVE ON ADOPTION AND FOSTER CARE, GUIDELINES FOR PUBLIC POLICY AND STATE LEGISLATION GOVERNING PERMANENCE FOR CHILDREN; and the FORDHAM CONFERENCE ON ETHICAL ISSUES IN THE LEGAL REPRESENTATION OF CHILDREN.

[34] ME. REV. STAT. tit. 22, §4005(1)(e).

[35] FLA. STAT. § 39.465(2)(b).

addressed this issue recommend that a lawyer should take direction from his or her child client if the child is determined to have developed the cognitive capacity to engage in reasoned decision making. The national trend is in the direction of a more traditional lawyer role, giving more deference to the child's wishes and preferences, and turning to a more objective process for determining the child's position when that is required. Determining the decision-making capacity of any particular child and the weight to be given to that child's preferences remains a difficult and elusive question, however. The ABA Model Rules of Professional Responsibility, discussed above, especially the 2002 amendments, will provide some guidance. In the case of the very young child or the older child, the question of competence to instruct counsel may not be so difficult. If the client is an infant and cannot speak, the client cannot instruct counsel. If a client is a normally developed 15- or 16-year-old, however, he or she is quite likely to have clear and reasonable views as to the proper decisions to be made affecting his or her life that should be aggressively argued to the court. But determining capacity for the middle-years child, from 8 to 12 for instance, and the weight to be given to that child's preferences is perhaps the most difficult question in child advocacy today, and it does not yet have a clear answer.

The weight given to a child's stated wishes and preferences generally depend on the child's capacity, on his or her mental competence and maturity. But how should that capacity be assessed? Especially for the middle-years child, capacity is not an either-or proposition. Children mature at different rates and may be capable for some judgments and not for others. Professor Jean Koh Peters creates the image of a sliding scale or "dimmer switch" in which the child's capability is not an "on or off" phenomenon where a child is either capable of directing the lawyer or not.[36] "Competency, in this context, is a dimmer switch: the client can shed light on some aspects of the representation, even though she cannot participate in all of it."[37] A child's capacity, then, is a broader spectrum where children may be able to contribute various amounts to guide the representation if the lawyer properly incorporates the child's unique individuality.

State law and practice may incorporate the "dimmer switch" concept in authoritative directions to the lawyer. If the lawyer is appointed to represent the "best interests of the child," for instance, the statute may recognize the child's growing capacity. In Michigan, for example, the duties of the lawyer/GAL include:

(h) To make a determination regarding the child's best interests and advocate for those best interests according to the lawyer-guardian ad litem's understanding of those best interests, regardless of whether the lawyer- guardian ad litem's determination reflects the child's wishes. *The*

---

[36] JEAN KOH PETERS, REPRESENTING CHILDREN IN CHILD PROTECTIVE PROCEEDINGS 53-54 (1997).

[37] *Id.*

child's wishes are relevant to the lawyer-guardian ad litem's determination of the child's best interests, and the lawyer-guardian ad litem shall weigh the child's wishes according to the child's competence and maturity. Consistent with the law governing attorney-client privilege, the lawyer-guardian ad litem shall inform the court as to the child's wishes and preferences. (emphasis added)

Under Michigan law, the lawyer, when formulating a best interest goal, is to give increasing weight to the preferences of the child according to the child's age and maturity. At some point the best interests and wishes of the child merge, and the lawyer/GAL ends up representing the stated wishes of the child. If, however, a conflict remains between the child and the lawyer/GAL regarding the child's best interests, the lawyer/GAL should bring the matter to the court, which may appoint an attorney for the child who serves in addition to the lawyer/GAL.[38]

§ 21A.8 Conclusion

A child welfare legal system that serves and protects children must include independent legal counsel for all parties, including children. The practice of law for children has evolved over a relatively short period of time from a cottage age industry to a sophisticated legal specialty. That specialty includes new guidelines and standards of practice that guide the practitioner toward providing children with the full benefit of legal counsel. Despite some disagreement over the nuances of practice, there is widespread consensus on the primary duties of the child's lawyer. A national model of practice that serves the special needs of child clients has emerged.

---

[38] MICH. COMP. LAWS § 712A.17d(1)(h). Where there is a disagreement between the lawyer-guardian ad litem and the child as to the child's best interests, the lawyer is to bring the question before the court, and the court may appoint an attorney for the child who has the same duty of zealous representation as for an adult and serves in addition to the lawyer-guardian ad litem. MICH. COMP. LAWS § 712A.17d(2).

Part 21B: Developmentally Appropriate Lawyering*

by Ann M. Haralambie[39]

§ 21B.1 Introduction

In order to effectively represent a child, it is important to understand the child's developmental stage and competencies, as discussed in Chapter 4, The Impact of Maltreatment on Child Development. That understanding comes not only from reading records and consulting relevant parties and experts in the case, but also through spending time with the child. It is difficult to represent a child, either as an attorney or as a guardian ad litem, without developing a relationship with the child. It is only through talking and visiting with a child over a period of time that the child's special needs and interests may begin to emerge. Often this requires meeting with your child client under a variety of circumstances, both inside and outside of the child's home environment. Older children may be able to articulate their own needs quite accurately. Younger children may demonstrate their needs more through their behavior or emotions. Therapists and teachers are particularly helpful resources in assisting the attorney in interpreting the child's behaviors and statements.

§ 21B.2 Meeting With Your Child Client

By gathering background information from other sources first, the lawyer may be in a better position to evaluate what the child is saying to the lawyer or showing through behavior. Because of young children's short attention spans, they are generally not good sources for a detailed history. Nonetheless, meeting with the child is essential to building a relationship, and it may tell the attorney a great deal about the child and his or her environment and relationships with siblings, friends, and caretakers. It is important to strike a balance between having a safe, familiar adult nearby for the child's security and having the interview stifled by the presence of one of the parties. Children, unlike adults, are not used to talking to people they do not know well. The attorney must establish at least some level of relationship with the child before the child is likely to say anything at all that will be useful. Major adjustments are necessary in one's usual inter-

---

* Portions of this chapter are based on and adapted from a previous work by Ann M. Haralambie. The excerpts were previously published in The Child's Attorney: A Guide to Representing Children in Custody, Adoption, and Protection Cases, published by the American Bar Association, copyright 1993. All rights reserved. Reprinted by Permission.

[39] Ann M. Haralambie, J.D., is a certified family law specialist practicing in Tucson, Arizona. She is also an author and speaker in the fields of family and children's law.

viewing techniques when children are involved. A good start is to begin thinking about "talking to," rather than "interviewing," the child.

§ 21B.2.1 Choosing a Location

In many cases, having the child come to the office, sit in a big chair across a big desk, and discuss the case will not be productive. The child may feel ill at ease or intimidated. It is usually easier to build rapport with children on their own turf: at their house, in the school playground, or at the local ice cream or hamburger shop. A playroom, with child-sized furniture and toys, is a good location for interviewing children. Some attorneys get down on the floor to talk to the child. It is important that the attorney be comfortable, and if sitting on the floor is awkward, it will only appear condescending and phony to the child. Even without a play room, the child should be allowed some play at the beginning of the meeting.

A teenager may enjoy meeting the attorney in the office and may be able to speak openly there. The attorney should consider talking to teenagers on the phone before meeting them and asking them if they prefer to meet in the office or elsewhere. Teenagers may be insulted if they are treated as anything other than adults. It is important, therefore, to get a sense of how the child client feels before making assumptions about how and where to meet.

§ 21B.2.2 Communicating at the Child's Level

Many adults find it difficult to understand what attorneys are talking about. For children, the communication barriers can become immense. Children do not usually volunteer that they do not understand something, and they often give an answer whether or not they know what they were asked. It is important, therefore, for the attorney to understand how to talk to children at their own level. One excellent resource is Ann Graffam Walker's book, HANDBOOK ON QUESTIONING CHILDREN: A LINGUISTIC PERSPECTIVE,[40] which is brief enough to review before an attorney speaks to a child client. The book gives specific, practical guidance for every age group. Dr. Walker's general advice is:

- DO use simple, common, everyday English words and phrases. "Attorney," "Court," "deny," "subsequent," "take the witness stand," "at that point in time," and the like do not fall into that category.

- DO put names and places back in where pronouns once lived. Ask, "What did Albert say?" instead of "What did *he* say?" Ask, "Were there a lot of people in the kitchen?" instead of "Were there a lot of people there?"

- DO stay away from negatives. Phrase your questions positively, whenever possible.

---

[40] ANN GRAFFAM WALKER, HANDBOOK ON QUESTIONING CHILDREN: A LINGUISTIC PERSPECTIVE (2nd ed. American Bar Association 1999).

- DO use questions and comments that keep the number of ideas to a minimum. The younger the child, the smaller the number. One main idea is good.

- DO start your questions and comments off with the main idea. "Did the bell ring when you were eating?" instead of, "When you were eating, did the bell ring?"

- DO remember: this is a child. Children are not short adults. Try to listen to the proceedings with a child's ears. You might be surprised at what you hear.[41]

Dr. Walker's provides 18 principles for communicating with children, including the following:

- Language is shaped by experience.

- Language is not an all-or-nothing affair.

- Inconsistency in children's statements is normal.

- Children are very literal in their approach to language.

- Adult-like use of language does not necessarily reflect adult-like linguistic or cognitive capabilities.

- Young children in particular have difficulty attending to more than one or two things at once (including multi-part, multi-idea questions).

- Pausing is productive.

- Children will not necessarily tell you that they don't understand you.

- Framing is good (letting them know what the subject is and why you are asking the question).

- Children's responses to your questions are not necessarily answers to your questions.

- The ability to recite a list is not the same as the ability to understand its contents.

- Children are not born with the ability to give adult-like accounts of their personal experiences.

- Not all families talk to each other.

- Familiarity and culture matter.[42]

It behooves the attorney to prepare carefully in advance of talking to children when the purpose of the discussion is to obtain information from the child.

---

[41] *Id.* at 5-6.

[42] *Id.* at 9-24.

§ 21B.2.3 Establishing Rapport and Asking Questions

One way to begin to establish rapport with a child is to talk about mutual acquaintances or activities. Attorneys can talk to the child about things in their life, where they went on vacation, something their children or grandchildren used to do at the client's age, what activities they participate in, whatever might draw them into the child's sphere of experience. Anything that can build a bridge between the attorney and child, any common ground, can form the foundation of a relationship.

Children cannot be rushed. They are very inefficient interviewees. They quickly tire from answering a string of questions. They tend to ramble and jump from topic to topic as one comment reminds them of something else. They do not like to be brought back "on track" constantly, just when their answers were getting into interesting, if legally irrelevant, ground. It is all too easy for attorneys with rushed schedules to forget that children shut down under time constraints. Even if the attorney has made a list of questions to be asked, it is important not to be tied to the list. If the child's discussion goes in another direction, the attorney should follow the child's lead. One can always cover an important topic later, even if it is not in the order most helpful for note-taking.

§ 21B.2.4 Helping the Child Feel Comfortable

Many times children will speak about difficult topics more easily if they can hold on to a stuffed animal or doll or play with a toy while they talk. For many children, it is very uncomfortable to make eye contact while discussing very personal or painful things. It is easier for them to talk if they have the option of playing with a distracting toy. Sometimes the location itself can be the distraction: walking through the zoo or duck pond, playing at a park or playground, or visiting an amusement park. Some snack or juice should be available for the child to increase the child's comfort level during the interview if it is conducted at the attorney's office. Children who are hungry or thirsty or have to go to the bathroom will have even less concentration than normal.

§ 21B.2.5 Being Aware of Your Own Responses

It is preferable to allow children to say what they think is important in their own words, using questions only when necessary. The attorney should be aware of his or her own verbal and nonverbal responses. Nods, facial expressions, and filler comments such as "really?" and "wow!" may be interpreted as carrying a value judgment or other substantive reaction to the content of what the child has said. Surprise or an intended expression of sympathy, especially where a child has been abused or molested, may be interpreted as disgust or disapproval. Some animation and expression of interest is important for the development of a relationship, but the attorney should be very careful about what is being conveyed.

§ 21B.2.6 Explaining Your Role as Attorney

In addition to obtaining information from the child, the attorney should also convey information to the child. First, the attorney should explain who he or she is and what the attorney's role is in the case. Young children in particular are not likely to remember and may have been told erroneous information about the attorney's role by other people. The child should have a general understanding of the purpose of the interview. The child should be told something about confidentiality, if the attorney's role is protected by confidentiality. Basically, the child needs to know whether what he or she says to the attorney may be repeated to the child's parents, the judge, the social worker, the therapist, or anybody else. Children who are abused may be threatened with dire consequences if they reveal family secrets. When discussing such topics, confidentiality should be explained in a way that the child understands, and in a way that distinguishes it from the kind of "secret" cover-up of abuse that the parent has required.

§ 21B.2.7 Keeping Your Client Informed About the Case

The child's attorney is responsible for keeping the child informed about what is going on in the child's case, and the child's attorney must be available to explain the process to the child. It is extremely important that the child does not feel a sense of responsibility for the judge's decision. The child needs to understand that the judge, not the child, makes the final decision. The attorney should explain what will happen at different stages and that it may take "a long time" for a final decision to be made. If the attorney knows when the trial is set and how long the judge takes to render a decision, a time frame the child can relate to may be used, such as "after Christmas," "not until you're in second grade," or "before summer." Often the child does not need to know about the intricacies of the litigation, but a general idea of what will happen will ease the child's mind.

It is a mistake to think that a child will spontaneously ask questions that may be very pressing to the child. Some children will ask, but many will not. It is helpful to ask the child periodically whether he or she has any questions about why the attorney is there or about what is going on in court. The child should be given the opportunity to ask any final questions and should be encouraged to contact the attorney if any other questions arise. The child should be told how to get in touch with his or her attorney.

§ 21B.3 Determining the Child's Capacity

Determination of a client's capacity to make decisions with respect to each issue relevant to the representation is not an easy task, nor is it one for which most lawyers are trained. Further, unlike the concept of "competency" (a legal status that the client either possesses or does not), "capacity" occurs along a continuum; therefore, capacity can be "diminished" but still exist. The child's capacity to direct decisions involving the representation may change significantly during the period of representation. The attorney's inquiry must focus on the client's decision-making process, not the resulting decision. A child can have capacity to decide and still make an unwise decision. In such cases, the attorney is bound by the client's decision. The most specific guidance available for determining capacity comes from Comment 6 to the revised Model Rule 1.14:

> In determining the extent of the client's diminished capacity, the lawyer should consider and balance such factors as: the client's ability to articulate reasoning leading to a decision, variability of state of mind and ability to appreciate consequences of a decision; the substantive fairness of a decision; and the consistency of a decision with the known long-term commitments and values of the client. In appropriate circumstances, the lawyer may seek guidance from an appropriate diagnostician.

Young children who frequently change their minds about what they want may not demonstrate capacity to direct representation on those issues. Changes of mind, however, might come about because of changed circumstances, increased development, or deepening recognition of the alternatives. In such cases, the changeability can be understood within the decision-making process and can establish capacity. Because children are developing quickly and may also be receiving therapy, their capacity to direct representation on various issues may increase over the course of the representation, and the attorney should be vigilant to recognize this increased capacity.

§ 21B.4 The Lawyer's Duties

The lawyer has many duties to a child client, one of which is the duty to identify the child's permanency-related needs. The lawyer also has a duty to protect the child's important affiliations, property, records, and social history. Additionally, lawyers should advocate for therapeutically appropriate closure in cases where the child does not return home. These needs and interests may change based on the child's changing developmental needs.

§ 21B.4.1 Identifying Permanency Needs and Protecting Important Affiliations

The permanency needs of infants and very young children require that decisions be made comparatively quickly because of the way they experience time. Six months for a six-month-old child is his or her entire lifetime. A young child's need to form a secure attachment may be impaired by a delayed or ill-timed change of placement. At certain developmental stages, a change of placement—whether removal from a family, change to a different placement, or return home—is particularly problematic. When dealing with preschool-aged children, it is particularly important for the attorney to seek appropriate expert input on any decision to change the child's placement. Further, very young children who are separated from their parents but will likely return home need to have very frequent contact with their parents. Child welfare resources may not exist for daily visits, but attorneys should seek other potential supervisors to supplement agency-supervised visits where that is possible and appropriate. Where there are relatives or other people who have been close to the child and may be considered as placements, visitation may be appropriate for those persons, as well as the parents, to ensure the child's ongoing familiarity with them.

Older children are better able to tolerate longer separations and to understand adults' explanations of delays in the child welfare process. However, even older children generally need things to move more quickly than the system moves, and one task of the attorney is to ensure that things move along as quickly as possible. Older children also often have a wider range of people to whom they feel connected and a wider range of activities that are important to them. To the extent possible, these connections should be nurtured and continued unless they would specifically be detrimental to the child. As children become older, their peers and extra-curricular activities take on increased importance. Their sense of affiliation with their families may also increase, and many states require children of a certain age, typically 12, to consent to their adoption. An older child who does not want to be adopted, even if he or she will probably not be returned home, deserves to have that need for affiliation with his or her family of origin considered.

§ 21B.4.2 Maintaining the Child's, Property, Records, and Social History

Children in care often have nobody to maintain their social history, including their developmental milestones, photographs, important school papers and projects, and other documentary evidence of their progress through childhood. This early history can be preserved to some extent by preparing and maintaining "life books." Some child welfare agencies have programs for this, and some communities have volunteers who will compile records for the child's life book. These records should be accessible to the child and must be supplemented throughout the time the child is in care. Further, the information should be maintained in such a way that it is not lost as the child moves into different placements.

Older children need to have access to some discretionary money or allowance. They need to be able to participate in extracurricular activities, field trips, and functions such as school proms. Teenagers need to be given training in life skills that will prepare them for independence and financial autonomy, particularly if they will not be returned home or adopted.[43]

---

[43] For a discussion of Chafee Funds and transitional living services, *see* Chapter 8, Federal Child Welfare Law and Policy: Understanding the Federal Law and Funding Process.

§ 21B.4.3 Advocating for Appropriate Closure After Termination

When termination is ordered, the child may still have unfinished business. Even if there has not been visitation, the child may need to face the parent or otherwise deal with the finality of the termination. The child may need individualized therapeutic help to determine how to find closure and deal with any remaining issues of grief or anger. The attorney should consider getting current information on the parents' whereabouts in case the child wants to re-establish contact upon reaching adulthood. Similarly, the attorney should obtain any available information on how to contact relatives or other people who have been important while the child was in care. Even after adoption, children may have a desire to visit parents, siblings, other relatives, or other children with whom they have been in care. To the extent appropriate, the attorney may make arrangements to maintain these affiliations and associations.

Some states authorize legally enforceable "open adoptions" in which relatives and individuals with significant emotional ties to a child may have ongoing contact with the child even after an adoption.[44] In other states, informal agreements for this kind of contact are common, even where the agreements may not be legally enforceable.

Part 21C: Special Challenges for the Child's Lawyer: Conflict of Interest, Attorney-Client Privilege, Waiver of Rights, and Sibling Association

by Ann M. Haralambie[45]

§ 21C.1 Conflict of Interest

In addition to the typical situations involving conflict of interest, the representation of children may involve some particular circumstances worth considering separately. The first of these regards the representation of sibling groups.

§ 21C.1.1 Representation of Siblings

Representation of siblings does not, *per se,* create a conflict of interest. Possible conflicts may arise when the siblings want different outcomes in the case, such as wanting to live with different parents. If the reasons for the differences in preference do not undermine the other sibling's preference, there would

---

[44] *See* Chapter 17, Establishing Legal Permanence for the Child.

[45] Ann M. Haralambie, J.D., is a certified family law specialist practicing in Tucson, Arizona. She is also an author and speaker in the fields of family and children's law.

not appear to be a conflict. A more difficult situation arises when the siblings' differences go to issues that would affect each other. This may occur, for example, where the children take contrary positions with respect to whether or not there has been abuse or neglect. Similarly, siblings may all have witnessed domestic violence in the home, with some siblings wanting to testify about what they saw and the others denying that it happened in order to preserve the family or because of primary loyalty to the parents. In these cases, the attorney must carefully assess whether there is a conflict of interest that would preclude representing the siblings.

If the children are in counseling, a therapist may be able to assist the attorney in determining whether there is a conflict of interest. Sometimes the issues that are in conflict are areas being dealt with in therapy, and those conflicts may be resolved during the course of therapy. If the attorney is already appointed when the conflict arises, and there is no immediate need for the attorney to take a position on behalf of one or more of the children, the attorney may be able to wait until the therapy has reached a point where the conflict is resolved. However, an attorney who is not functioning as a guardian ad litem is probably not able to continue multiple representation of the siblings who retain such incompatible positions.

DR 5-105(A) of the American Bar Association's Model Code of Professional Responsibility prohibits employment if the attorney's "exercise of his professional judgment on behalf of a client will be or is likely to be adversely affected by the acceptance of the proffered employment, or if it would be likely to involve him in representing differing interests, except to the extent permitted by DR 5-105(C)." DR 5-105(C) permits an attorney to continue multiple representation "if it is obvious that he can adequately represent the interest of each and if each consents to the representation after full disclosure of the possible effect of such representation on the exercise of his independent professional judgment on behalf of each."

Rule 1.7 of the American Bar Association's Model Rules of Professional Conduct sets forth the general rule on conflicts of interest:

> (a)   A lawyer shall not represent a client if the representation of that client will be directly adverse to another client, unless:
>
>> (1)   the lawyer reasonably believes the representation will not adversely affect the relationship with the other client; and
>>
>> (2)   each client consents after consultation.
>
> (b)   A lawyer shall not represent a client if the representation of that client may be materially limited by the lawyer's responsibilities to another client or to a third person, or by the lawyer's own interests, unless:
>
>> (1)   the lawyer reasonably believes the representation will not be adversely affected; and

(2)   the client consents after consultation. When representation of multiple clients in a single matter is undertaken, the consultation shall include explanation of the implications of the common representation and the advantages and risks involved.

The 2002 modifications of the Model Rules rewrote Rule 1.7 to read:

(a)   Except as provided in paragraph (b), a lawyer shall not represent a client if the representation involves a concurrent conflict of interest. A concurrent conflict of interest exists if:

(1)   the representation of one client will be directly adverse to another client; or

(2)   there is a significant risk that the representation of one or more clients will be materially limited by the lawyer's responsibilities to another client, a former client or a third person or by a personal interest of the lawyer.

(b)   Notwithstanding the existence of a concurrent conflict of interest under paragraph (a), a lawyer may represent a client if:

(1)   the lawyer reasonably believes that the lawyer will be able to provide competent and diligent representation to each affected client;

(2)   the representation is not prohibited by law;

(3)   the representation does not involve the assertion of a claim by one client against another client represented by the lawyer in the same litigation or other proceeding before a tribunal; and

(4)   each affected client gives informed consent, confirmed in writing.

Under any set of American Bar Association ethics rules, the attorney is prohibited from providing more than direct advocacy against another client. Comment 1 to Model Rule 1.7 states that "[l]oyalty to a client is also impaired when a lawyer cannot consider, recommend or carry out an appropriate course of action for the client because of the lawyer's other responsibilities or interests. The conflict in effect forecloses alternatives that would otherwise be available to the client." Comment 1 to the revised Rule 1.7 provides that "[l]oyalty and independent judgment are essential elements in the lawyer's relationship to a client." Comment 6 to the revised Rule 1.7 provides that "a directly adverse conflict may arise when a lawyer is required to cross-examine a client who appears as a witness in a lawsuit involving another client, as when the testimony will be damaging to the client who is represented in the lawsuit."

Confidentiality

Confidentiality concerns, as well as compromised advocacy, also come into play with representation of multiple parties. Comment 31 to revised Rule 1.7

provides that "continued common representation will almost certainly be inadequate if one client asks the lawyer not to disclose to the other client information relevant to the common representation. This is so because the lawyer has an equal duty of loyalty to each client, and each client has the right to be informed of anything bearing on the representation that might affect that client's interests and the right to expect that the lawyer will use that information to that client's benefit."

Waiver

The attorney must be candid with the clients about the effect their differences may have on the attorney's ability to continue to represent them. In general, clients may waive conflicts of interest so long as they have full disclosure about the conflict and provide informed consent. The Comment 18 to the revised Rule 1.7 provides that informed consent "requires that each affected client be aware of the relevant circumstances and of the material and reasonably foreseeable ways that the conflict could have adverse effects on the interests of that client. . . . The information required depends on the nature of the conflict and the nature of the risks involved. When representation of multiple clients in a single matter is undertaken, the information must include the implications of the common representation, including possible effects on loyalty, confidentiality and the attorney-client privilege and the advantages and risks involved." Comment 19 provides that "when the lawyer represents different clients in related matters and one of the clients refuses to consent to the disclosure necessary to permit the other client to make an informed decision, the lawyer cannot properly ask the latter to consent." Older children may be able to appreciate the ethical dilemma of the attorney and may be competent to sign statements waiving the conflict. It is doubtful, however, that young children are competent to appreciate the conflict of interest sufficiently to waive it. If the children are in counseling, it is recommended that the therapist be consulted about the competence of the children to waive the conflict before the attorney relies on any such waiver. Children's legal competence to knowingly waive a potential or actual conflict of interest is problematic and presents unique questions of law and process, which are discussed below in Section 21C.2.

§ 21C.1.2 Payment of Attorney Fees by a Third Party

Another situation in which conflict of interest may arise is in cases where a third party pays the child's attorney fees. In some cases the court, state, or county may pay for the services of the child's attorney. Under such circumstances, it is understood that the attorney is an independent agent representing the child. Even when the court appoints an attorney for the child and orders that some other party, such as the child's parents, pay the fees, the third party payors generally understand that they have not retained the attorney and cannot direct the representation, especially if a fee award is not made until the end of the case. However, conflicts may arise when a third party privately retains an attorney to act on behalf of the child. It is not clear who has standing to retain an attorney for the child privately. Some courts have prohibited parents from retaining counsel to represent their children in custody or abuse cases because of the conflict between the parents' interests and the children's interests.

ER 1.8(f) of the Model Rules of Professional Conduct and DR 5-107(A)(1) of the Model Code of Professional Responsibility prohibit third-party payment unless the client consents after consultation, there is no interference with the attorney's independence of judgment or with the attorney-client relationship, and the confidentiality of client information is protected. The Comment to revised Rule 1.8 provides:

> [11] Lawyers are frequently asked to represent a client under circum-stances in which a third person will compensate the lawyer, in whole or in part. The third person might be a relative or friend, an indemnitor (such as a liability insurance company) or a co-client (such as a corpora-tion sued along with one or more of its employees). Because third-party payers frequently have interests that differ from those of the client, including interests in minimizing the amount spent on the representation and in learning how the representation is progressing, lawyers are pro-hibited from accepting or continuing such representations unless the lawyer determines that there will be no interference with the lawyer's independent professional judgment and there is informed consent from the client. See also Rule 5.4(c) (prohibiting interference with a lawyer's professional judgment by one who recommends, employs or pays the lawyer to render legal services for another).

> [12] Sometimes, it will be sufficient for the lawyer to obtain the client's informed consent regarding the fact of the payment and the identity of the third-party payer. If, however, the fee arrangement creates a conflict of interest for the lawyer, then the lawyer must comply with Rule. 1.7. The lawyer must also conform to the requirements of Rule 1.6 concern-ing confidentiality. Under Rule 1.7(a), a conflict of interest exists if there is significant risk that the lawyer's representation of the client will be materially limited by the lawyer's own interest in the fee arrangement or by the lawyer's responsibilities to the third-party payer (for example, when the third-party payer is a co-client). Under Rule 1.7(b), the lawyer may accept or continue the representation with the informed consent of each affected client, unless the conflict is nonconsentable under that paragraph. Under Rule 1.7(b), the informed consent must be confirmed in writing.

Again, the child's ability to provide an informed consent is problematic.[46]

---

[46] *See* the discussion of waiver in § 21C.3 below.

§ 21C.2 Attorney-Client Privilege

DR 4-101 of the Model Code of Professional Responsibility and ER 1.6(a) of the Model Rules of Professional Responsibility, including the 2002 revisions, provide for the confidentiality of attorney-client communications. While DR 4-101 protects only communications that occur directly between the attorney and client, ER 1.6(a) extends the confidentiality to all client information "relating to the representation." All states provide an evidentiary privilege for attorney-client communications. The attorney's role may determine whether a child's communications with the attorney are privileged. Where the attorney is appointed as legal counsel, communication should remain privileged. However, if the attorney is appointed as the child's guardian ad litem, this privilege may not apply.

Where allegations of abuse are raised during confidential communications between children and attorneys, the judge's right to be fully informed may conflict with the attorney-client relationship. When and how information about abuse should be presented creates a problem for a lawyer. State law may cover this issue. DR 5-102 of the Model Code of Professional Responsibility and ER 3.7 of the Model Rules of Professional Conduct discourage an attorney from acting as both a witness and an advocate. Mandatory child abuse reporting statutes may abrogate all privileges except the attorney-client privilege, and in some states, the attorney-client privilege may also be abrogated. An attorney acting as a guardian ad litem may not be covered by the privilege, depending on local law. Some state statutes specifically require a duty of confidence for the lawyer (*e.g.*, Michigan), while other states specifically eliminate the duty (*e.g.*, Alaska requires the attorney to report suspected child abuse and neglect).

Model Rule 1.6(b)(1) permitted revealing client confidences "to prevent the client from committing a criminal act that the lawyer believes is likely to result in imminent death or substantial bodily harm." This provision did not seem to directly permit the child's attorney to reveal confidences to prevent the child client from becoming the victim of such a crime at the hands of another. It would seem anomalous to permit disclosure of confidential information designed to protect a third party from harm at the client's hand but not to permit an attorney to reveal confidential information designed to protect the client from death or substantial bodily harm. The new Rule 1.6(b)(1) permits disclosure of client confidences "to prevent reasonably certain death or substantial bodily harm," without making reference to a crime or to harm to a third party. Comment 6 to the new Rule 1.6, amending Comment 9 to Model Rule 1.6, states that the new provision "recognizes the overriding value of life and physical integrity and permits disclosure reasonably necessary to prevent reasonably certain death or substantial bodily harm. Such harm is reasonably certain to occur if it will be suffered imminently or if there is a present and substantial threat that a person will suffer such harm at a later date if the lawyer fails to take action necessary to eliminate the threat." Unlike the Comment to the Model Rules, which discusses only the client who intends harm to a third person, the new Comment is broad enough to encompass harm to the client, as well as harm to a third person.

§ 21C.3 Waiver of Rights

Many of the ethical rules cited above require a knowing and informed waiver, sometimes in writing, of potential or actual conflicts of interest or privileged communications. Children are generally also entitled to the evidentiary benefits of other professional privileges, such as the physician-patient and psychotherapist-patient privileges. Generally, privileges may be asserted or waived by the holder of the privilege or that person's legal representative.

Who has the authority to exercise or waive such privileges on behalf of children? In a few states it is provided for by statute, case law, or court order. Generally, parents who have custodial rights can assert or waive these privileges; although, where the parents are in a legally adverse posture with the child, it is generally held that the parent should not be permitted to assert or waive the objection on behalf of the child over the child's objection. Where the child has an attorney or guardian ad litem, that person may be deemed the proper person to exercise the privilege on the child's behalf. Courts may even appoint a guardian ad litem for the purpose of deciding whether to assert or waive the child's privilege. Where the child is a ward of the court—that is, where the court already has formal authority over the child—the court itself may have the power to waive privileges. In some jurisdictions, a judge other than the judge hearing the case will consider and rule on whether the privilege should be waived. Since state laws on these issues are generally not well-developed, perhaps no one possesses the legal authority to enter a waiver on behalf of a child. In the potential conflict of interest situation, for example, the court may be in the odd position of having to appoint separate counsel for siblings for want of legal authority to enter a waiver.

Where local law permits children to waive conflicts and privileges, or where the law is not clear, the attorney must determine whether the child has the capacity to make an informed waiver. Functional capacity exists on a continuum, even for adults. Many factors contribute to whether a child has sufficient capacity to make a waiver with respect to a particular issue at a particular time, and there is no bright line test for determining capacity.

Children's capacity to waive rights has been considered most often in the context of juvenile delinquency cases. The United States Supreme Court has held that juveniles may have the capacity to waive their constitutional rights.[47] In

---

[47] *See, e.g., Fare v. Michael C.*, 442 U.S. 707 (1979) (finding that the totality-of-the-circumstances approach is adequate to determine whether there has been a waiver even where interrogation of juveniles is involved); *In re Gault*, 387 U.S. 1 (1967) ("We appreciate that special problems may arise with respect to waiver of the privilege by or on behalf of children, and that there may well be some differences in technique—but not in principle—depending upon the age of the child and the presence and competence of parents").

that context, mental health professionals[48] and some courts have found that children's actual capacity to waive rights has been overestimated. In assessing whether a child has capacity to waive constitutional rights, a crucial issue is the child's ability to appreciate the consequences of the waiver. It is at the developmental stage of formal operations, which begins around age 12, when the child develops the ability to appreciate consequences of decisions.[49] However, the protections offered by assertion of constitutional rights in a delinquency setting raise different concerns than the protections provided by ethical rules about conflict of interest of assertion of testimonial privileges. Further, the goals of juvenile justice and the child welfare system are different.

Children's capacity to give informed consent has also been considered in the context of medical or mental health treatment.[50] The United States Supreme Court,[51] as well as lower courts,[52] has adopted the doctrine of the "mature minor," who is permitted to make certain medical decisions without parental involvement. In obtaining informed consent on a child-friendly level, the medical or mental health professional will explain the consequences to the child. Similarly, the child's attorney must explain the likely or possible short- and long-term consequences of the child's direction. However, before the child has reached the stage of formal operations (and children in child welfare proceedings are often developmentally delayed or impaired), the child is not likely to have the capacity to appreciate the impact on his or her life of the consequences, even when the consequences have been explained.

Attorneys, by training, rarely have any specialized skills in judging a person's legal capacity. When undertaking such a task, it is easy to confuse capacity and

---

[48] *See, e.g.*, THOMAS GRISSO, JUVENILES' WAIVER OF RIGHTS: LEGAL AND PSYCHOLOGICAL COMPETENCE (1981); YOUTH ON TRIAL: A DEVELOPMENTAL PERSPECTIVE ON JUVENILE JUSTICE (Thomas Grisso & Robert G. Schwartz eds., 2000).

[49] *See, e.g.*, JEAN PAIGET & BARBEL INHELDER, THE PSYCHOLOGY OF THE CHILD (1969).

[50] For a survey of state laws on consent, *see* ABIGAIL ENGLISH & KIRSTEN E. KENNEY, STATE MINOR CONSENT LAWS (2nd ed. 2003). *See generally* Lois A. Weithorn & S.B. Campbell, *The Competency of Children and Adolescents to Make Informed Treatment Decisions*, 53 CHILD DEV. 1589 (1982).

[51] *See, e.g., City of Akron v. Akron Center for Reproductive Health, Inc.*, 462 U.S. 416, 439-440 (1983), (ruling that provision in ordinance prohibiting a physician from performing an abortion on a pregnant minor under the age of 15 unless he obtains "the informed written consent of one of her parents or her legal guardian" or unless the minor obtains "an order from a court having jurisdiction over her that the abortion be performed or induced" is unconstitutional because it makes a blanket determination that all minors under the age of 15 are too immature to make this decision or that an abortion never may be in the minor's best interests without parental approval), *overruled on other grounds by Planned Parenthood of Southeastern Pennsylvania v. Casey*, 505 U.S. 833 (1992).

[52] *See generally* Martin H. Harvey, *Adolescent Competency and the Refusal of Medical Treatment*, 13 HEALTH MATRIX: J OF L.-MED. 297 (2003).

wisdom. The fact that the child—or even an adult client—may make choices that the attorney disagrees with or that are foolish is not necessarily an indication that the child lacks capacity to make the choice. Further, the attorney may have a great deal of influence over how the child chooses to address waiver issues, with many children merely following the advice of the attorney. It is tempting to assume that because the child is following the attorney's advice, the child must possess adequate capacity to make the decision. Therefore, the determination of capacity should be made thoughtfully, based on consideration of many factors, perhaps with the input of other adults who know the child well or have specialized training in the field, such as teachers or mental health professionals. Comment 6 to revised Model Rule 1.14 provides:

> In determining the extent of the client's diminished capacity, the lawyer should consider and balance such factors as: the client's ability to articulate reasoning leading to a decision, variability of state of mind and ability to appreciate consequences of a decision; the substantive fairness of a decision; and the consistency of a decision with the known long-term commitments and values of the client. In appropriate circumstances, the lawyer may seek guidance from an appropriate diagnostician.

Most mental health professionals do not have adequate training to determine whether the child has adequate capacity to waive conflicts and privileges. That determination is very specialized. Child development experts may be aware of some means to assess the child's capacity, but as of the writing of this manual, there are no tests or batteries of tests that will provide a definitive answer. Whether or not a particular child can give informed consent to waive a particular right will remain a problem for future resolution.

§ 21C.4 Sibling Association

The child welfare system often attempts to place siblings together, but siblings are separated in many instances. They may not only be placed separately, but they may even be adopted by different families. For children who have been removed from home, their siblings may be the only continuity of family relationships they have. Siblings may represent the only people in their living circumstances who are not strangers, the only people with whom they share a history and memories, the only people who really understand what they have lived through and what they now miss. Of course, there are circumstances where sibling contact is not in the best interests of one or more of the siblings, and such contact might even be detrimental.

Maintaining sibling relations during any periods of separation may be very difficult, but unless there is a demonstrable reason for limiting contact, it is a valuable goal. Courts have been slow to recognize any constitutional right to sibling association.[53] Some states have statutes permitting sibling visitation. Where fit parents object to the visitation, there may be a constitutional challenge to a court's ordering visitation without affording some special weight to the parent's objection.[54] However, in child welfare cases, the courts are not generally dealing with "fit" parents. Therefore, the court may have greater latitude in ordering sibling visitation regardless of parental objection, especially when all of the involved children are in care. It is certainly appropriate to make ongoing sibling contact part of the family's case plan.

Because adoption creates a new legal family, it may be more difficult to provide any formal right to post-adoption sibling visitation. If such rights are to be secured, it is prudent to explore the possibility of an open adoption agreement providing explicitly for post-adoption contact with siblings. Even if no formal agreement is reached, it may be possible for the adoptive parents to allow ongoing contact on an informal basis. Children who at least know the new names and contact information for their siblings who were adopted by other families are in a better position to re-establish a relationship upon reaching majority.

Part 21D: Case Assessment and Planning

Colene Flynn Robinson[55]

§ 21D.1 Introduction

The complexities, fluctuating factual basis, and potentially subjective nature of child welfare cases require attorneys to engage in thoughtful, dynamic case analysis for every case. Case analysis includes developing a theory of the case, and then developing positions consistent with the theory of the case. An attorney should be prepared to answer the question "what is your theory of the case?" for each case, at each stage, for each child. This chapter describes how to analyze a case, develop an appropriate theory of the case, how to develop positions consistent with that theory, and what steps to take in litigation to present the theory of the case.

---

[53] *See generally* William Wesley Patton, *The Status of Siblings' Rights: A View into the New Millennium*, 51 DePaul L. Rev. 1 (2001).

[54] *See Troxel v. Granville*, 530 U.S. 57, 70 (2000) (addressing grandparent visitation).

[55] Colene Flynn Robinson, J.D., is a private practitioner representing children in Dependency Court in Denver, Colorado. From 2001 to 2004 she was Senior Staff Attorney at the National Association of Counsel for Children.

§ 21D.2 Investigate the Facts

Case analysis involves several steps, but it is always based on a thorough fact investigation. Children's advocates must independently gather facts for their cases, which includes:

- Talking to witnesses.

- Observing the scene.

- Reading reports.

- Talking to collateral sources, such as teachers, doctors, service providers, neighbors, family members, and respondents when possible.

Obtaining adequate discovery is a key part of investigating the facts. For example, relevant items of discovery might include school records, treatment provider records, drug toxicologies, mental health records, Department of Social Services records, criminal background information, health records, and requesting evaluations when necessary. Think creatively about discovery. For example, if a key element in a case is determining whether the respondent mother is still having contact with her incarcerated boyfriend, the prison's visitation and phone logs might be very helpful. Subpoenas are an enormous tool—use them to get records or talk to individuals to verify or expand on information you already have.

As a note of caution, it is imprudent to rely solely on the information the Department of Social Services provides: too often it is inaccurate or incomplete, and attorneys have an independent ethical obligation to conduct an investigation.[56]

§ 21D.3 Develop a Theory of the Case

First, what is a theory of the case? The theory of the case is your explanation of what has happened and why—it is the lawyer's "depiction of the child and her world, to convince the Powers that Be to honor the child's objectives."[57] The theory of the case should be a short, concise statement that addresses the positive and negative facts and concisely states how you want the case to be understood.

How is the theory of the case used? You present your theory of the case to the court to influence the court's decisions. In this section, an example domestic violence and sexual abuse case will be highlighted to illustrate how to analyze a case.

---

[56] For a more detailed discussion of investigation, *see* Chapter 21A, The Role and Duties of the Child's Lawyer.

[57] JEAN KOH PETERS, REPRESENTING CHILDREN IN CHILD PROTECTIVE PROCEEDINGS: ETHICAL AND PRACTICAL DIMENSIONS 147 (1997).

§ 21D.3.1 Preliminary Facts—A Sample Case

The guardian ad litem's (GAL)[58] client, Dorothy, is 5 years old. She has been sexually abused by her mother's live-in boyfriend, who also physically abuses Dorothy's mom, Sarah. The Department of Social Services has filed a neglect petition against Sarah for failing to protect Dorothy from the abuse by her boyfriend. The case has been filed in a jurisdiction where the GAL is charged with representing what is in the child's best interests, and not her stated wishes.

§ 21D.3.2 Focus Questions

Developing a theory of the case, and positions that support it, requires asking a series of basic focus questions. These questions, which are listed here and then discussed in greater detail below, are:

- What is the child advocate's role in the jurisdiction?

- What is the child's position?

- What is the permanency goal?

- At what stage is the case?

- What is the cause of action?

- What are the characteristics of the individual child?

- What will serve the child's well-being and maintain his or her safety?

- What other facts are relevant to the theory of the case or the position?

- Has the attorney's subjective bias influenced his or her decisions?

The Role of the Child's Advocate

Before you begin a case analysis, you must understand what your role is, what your ethical obligations are, and how they effect the development of your theory of the case. In some jurisdictions, the attorney is charged with representing what is in the child's best interests. In other jurisdictions, the attorney must advocate the child's wishes. Some jurisdictions use a combination of these approaches, and in some, the role of the child's advocate is unclear.[59] Your theory of the case must be consistent with whichever role is applicable in your jurisdiction.

---

[58] "Guardian ad litem" will be used in this chapter to generically refer to an attorney representing a child in a child welfare action.

[59] *See* Appendix A-1, NACC RECOMMENDATIONS FOR REPRESENTATION OF CHILDREN IN ABUSE AND NEGLECT CASES; APPENDIX A-2, AMERICAN BAR ASSOCIATION STANDARDS OF PRACTICE FOR LAWYERS WHO REPRESENT CHILDREN IN ABUSE AND NEGLECT CASES (NACC REVISED VERSION). *See also* ANN M. HARALAMBIE, THE CHILD'S ATTORNEY (American Bar Association 1993) (discussing in more detail the different roles of children's attorneys).

For GALs, their theory and position are impacted by what their role is. Attorneys who must represent what is in the child's best interests must take the child's position as their starting point, but analyze it to determine if it would serve the child's well-being. If not, they must modify the child's position until it does serve to protect the child's best interests, even if the result is contrary to what the child wants. For attorneys who represent a child's wishes, their theory is wholly consistent with the child's stated position.

Parties' roles in the case dictate their theory of the case. In the example case of domestic violence and sexual abuse, the mother's attorney's theory of the case may be: "This is a case about a loving mother who desperately wanted to leave an abusive relationship, but lacked the emotional and financial support to do so, and feared she or her child would be more severely hurt if she tried to leave. Now that she has the assistance of the Department of Social Services, she is able to leave the relationship safely." Yet the Department of Social Services attorney's theory might be: "This is a case about a mother who chose, and will continue to choose, her abusive boyfriend over her child's safety." The GAL's theory might be: "This is a case about a mother who loves her daughter but, due to emotional and physical abuse by her boyfriend, has been unable to protect her daughter and needs to prove over time that she can protect her child before reunification can happen."

In the example above, the GAL's position would probably change if he or she was representing the child's wishes, and not best interests, and her client did not think her mother had failed to keep her safe and wanted to return home immediately. In that case, the GAL's theory of the case would probably be the same as the mother's attorney.

Going further with the example case provides the details that illustrate how to develop a position consistent with the theory. The GAL's theory of the case is still: "This is a case about a mother who loves her daughter but, due to emotional and physical abuse by her boyfriend, has been unable to protect her daughter and needs to prove over time that she can protect her child before reunification can happen." Now, during the course of the litigation, the question of overnight visitation comes up, and the GAL needs to develop a position.

Determining the Child's Position

Part of your investigation includes speaking with your client, if he or she is old enough, to determine his or her position.[60] Each child has a position, so you must interview each child: do not assume that an older child speaks for his or her younger siblings. For children too young to express a thoughtful opinion, try to

---

[60] If the client is not old enough to speak with, the attorney still has an obligation to see the client and observe the client's interactions with family members and caregivers. *See* Appendix A-1, NACC Recommendations for Representation of Children in Abuse and Neglect Cases, Part III (B)(2), at 8, 9.

determine what you believe they would want, given the circumstances, their relationship and bond with other family members, and other developmental factors. This is not the same as what you believe is in their best interests: even though you may be charged with representing their best interests, at this stage in the analysis, you are only trying to determine what they would want, if they could form and articulate an opinion. The child's position is the starting point for determining what your position, as the advocate, will be.[61]

In our example case, Dorothy wants to have overnight visits with her mother, even though Sarah's boyfriend still lives with her. The GAL counsels Dorothy about the risks involved and alternatives, but Dorothy continues to state that her desire is to have overnight visits with her mom.

Once you have determined the child's position, you need to analyze his or her position given your role in the jurisdiction. If you are charged with representing what is in the child's best interests, then you test the child's position with that lens. The child's position influences what your theory of the case is, and what positions you will take. You should always present the child's position to the court, even if your position is different. After factoring in your role and the child's position, the GAL must examine the permanency goal.

Permanency Goal

Next, the GAL examines the permanency goal in the case. In many cases, your theory of the case is a statement of the permanency goal and the reasons for it. Even from the very beginning of a case, you must have an idea of what the permanency goal is and must take positions in the case which are consistent with that goal. As the case develops and the facts change, so may the permanency goal, and consequently your theory of the case. In this case, the permanency goal is reunification.

Stage of the Litigation

The next question is, "What stage of the case are you in?" Are you at the preliminary hearing stage, the fact-finding stage, or the termination of parental rights trial stage? Each stage will impact your position differently. If you are at the preliminary hearing stage, you may not know enough about the mother, or her ability to keep her boyfriend out of the house for one night, to know whether overnight visits are realistic. If you are at termination, overnight visits might be harder for Dorothy, if she is about to lose all contact with her mother.

---

[61] Your role as an attorney does not merely require you to just ask the child what her position is. No matter what role you play, your obligations as an attorney require you to counsel your client on the choices he or she is making, the ramifications of his or her decisions, and to provide your client with advice and guidance regarding that choice. *See generally* Appendix A-1, NACC RECOMMENDATIONS FOR REPRESENTATION OF CHILDREN IN ABUSE AND NEGLECT CASES.

Cause of Action

The causes of action in the case impact your position as well. Decisions about appropriate permanency goals and treatment plans depend entirely on the allegations in the petition and later on the court's findings. A position that drug testing must be a part of a treatment plan for someone in a case with no drug allegations or findings is obviously unsupportable.

The Characteristics of the Individual Child

The individual child and his or her strengths, weaknesses, and individual characteristics also impact your theory of the case. How old is your client? Is the child developmentally on track? What disabilities or medical needs, if any, does the child have? Has the child had previous experiences that impact your position? What strengths and skills does he or she have? Your position must be individually tailored to each child, considering many factors about that child's mental health, developmental abilities, and strengths and weaknesses.

In our example, Dorothy is five, and she is developmentally on target. She does not have any special educational, developmental, or medical needs. She is articulate and able to express her opinions and feelings to professionals involved in the case.

The Child's Safety and Well-being

The child's safety and well-being must also factor into your development of a theory of the case. Your role in the jurisdiction may complicate this analysis. A direct advocacy attorney at times may have a theory of the case that appears— and that may actually be—at odds with what some would consider to be best for the child's well-being. The attorney must understand what optimally provides the greatest well-being and safety for his or her client, and attempt to fashion a theory that addresses those factors and yet is consistent with the attorney's role.

In our example, the goal will be to protect Dorothy from further harm by Sarah's boyfriend.

Fact Analysis

Other facts will influence your position. In our example, the GAL has learned several things during the fact investigation that impact the question of overnight visits.

The GAL spoke with Dorothy's therapist and learned that it would be therapeutic for Dorothy to:

- Have experiences with her mother where her mother is able to be protective of her.

- Sleep safely in her own bed at home.

- Spend more time with her mother.

Overnight visits would potentially offer all of these benefits.

Now we take the position that overnight visits are appropriate and analyze that position with all the facts. Look at each fact and see if it supports the position or detracts from it. Looking first to the facts that do not support the GAL's position, it is obvious that the abuser's continuing presence in the home is dangerous for the client, and the GAL's position will have to account for this. Dorothy is also very young—only five years old—and does not have the skills necessary to protect herself, emotionally or physically.

One fact that supports the GAL's position is Dorothy's relationship with her therapist, who advocates for her and can provide help. Another is that Dorothy's mother wants overnight visits and is motivated to do what is necessary to obtain them.

How does the GAL address the bad facts? The boyfriend cannot be in the home, or Dorothy won't be safe. Dorothy's mother must agree to this, and the court and GAL must be confident that she will comply. One way to do that may be to have Dorothy's mother join Dorothy in therapy for several sessions, where the three of them can explore the possibility of overnight visits and the importance of keeping Dorothy safe, along with strategies for doing so. Perhaps the therapist and the mother can draft a safety contract that the mother signs. The therapist can also work with Dorothy regarding ways to keep herself safe.

The developing facts may also change a GAL's theory of the case. As the mother proves herself capable of protecting Dorothy, the GAL's theory might become: "This is a case about a loving mother who lacked the skills and resources to protect her child from an abusive boyfriend. But after receiving services and support, she has proven she can protect her child."

Now your position has grown through an analysis of all the facts. Like your theory of the case, your position should be about one sentence long, incorporate good and bad facts, and follow common sense. In the example, your position for visitation is: "Dorothy may have overnight visits with her mother provided that boyfriend is not present at any time, and if the mother signs a safety contract and cooperates with Dorothy's therapist, and if it continues to be therapeutically recommended."

Subjective Bias

At every stage, attorneys must check their position for any subjective bias they might unwittingly be imposing. While it would be impossible to eliminate our personal subjective biases, it is important to try to limit the role that cultural, racial, economic, gender, sexual orientation, age, or religious assumptions play in decision making.

By answering the above questions while developing your theory of the case, you account for and address the most important factors. A well-reasoned and well-presented theory of the case increases the likelihood of the court adopting recommendations that support it.

§ 21D.4 Litigation Strategy

Once you have developed a well-considered position, you must plan how and when to present your position to the court. Consider all the litigation options available: written motion, oral application during a regularly scheduled hearing, requesting a special hearing, a show cause order, or other practice options in your jurisdiction. Then consider what evidence you need to support your position. Will a signed safety contract be enough for the court? Should the therapist be available to answer the court's questions? Should you plan to put on the therapist as a witness? Should you call the boyfriend as a witness to discuss his treatment, his understanding of his culpability, his willingness to comply with the plans so that Dorothy can have an overnight visit with her mother? You must carefully consider the timing of the presentation of your position and how you present it in order to create the greatest chance of getting the order you want. These tactical decisions will obviously depend greatly on the practice in your area and the particular fact finder.

§ 21D.5 Conclusion

Your theory of the case guides your decision making and should point to your position on most of the questions that may come up in the life of the case. But your theory of the case is dynamic and adaptable, changing in course as new facts develop. A thorough analysis provides the foundation for your litigation preparation and assists you in examining witnesses, entering evidence, and making opening and closing arguments. A clear, well-examined theory of the case is more persuasive in court and greatly improves your effectiveness as an advocate.

§ 21D.6 Child Welfare Case Checklist

CHILD WELFARE CASE CHECKLIST

Developing a generic checklist for the work that needs to be done in each child welfare case is difficult. So much depends on the role of the attorney, local practice, the type of case, and all of the individual factors that dictate the appropriate course of action in a particular case. It is possible, however, to walk through the steps that should be considered in every case, and applied when appropriate. The checklist below does just that: ask these questions and follow these steps and know that you are thoroughly assessing the case and the litigation options before you.

Before getting to the checklist, however, it is important to note that the attorney should always focus on permanency, safety, and well-being for each client. When following the checklist, the attorney should place the questions and answers in the context of what permanency means for the child, what safety is required for the child, and whether the child's well-being is being served. Make sure you know the answers to those questions before proceeding at any stage. Also, in meeting ethical obligations and following standards of practice, the attorney must, at every stage, participate in the proceedings, advocate a position, and express the child's wishes to the court.

QUESTIONS

From the beginning of a case to the end, you should know the answers to these preliminary questions:

- [ ] When was the case filed?
- [ ] Who called in the report?
- [ ] What are the results of the Child Protective Services investigation?
- [ ] Does the family have any prior child welfare history?
- [ ] Has the child's father been identified?
- [ ] Are his whereabouts known?
- [ ] What is the father's role in the child's life, including legal status?
- [ ] If the child was removed from the home, why?
- [ ] Where is the child placed?
- [ ] When was the child placed there?
- [ ] What is the visitation plan for the parents?
- [ ] If siblings have been separated, why?
- [ ] What is the plan for reunifying the siblings?

☐ What is the visitation plan for the siblings?

☐ Will the child be staying in the current placement? Get contact information.

☐ Are there any other family members? Get contact information.

☐ Are other family members available as placement options?

☐ Where does the child go to school?

☐ What are the child's needs? (education, health care, etc)

☐ What services is the family currently receiving? Get contact information for service providers.

☐ Are there any other people in the child's life who play a significant role? (Babysitter, neighbor, family friend).

☐ What is the child's position?

☐ What is the social worker recommending, why, and what evidence or support is there?

☐ What is the parent's position, why, and what evidence or support is there?

☐ Does the child have Native American ancestry?

☐ If a criminal background check has been done on anyone involved in the case, what are the results?

ACTIONS

As soon as possible:

☐ Meet with clients and caregivers.

☐ Visit the family home, if possible and appropriate.? Interview respondents, if possible and appropriate.

☐ Speak with collateral sources, such as teachers, neighbors, family members.

☐ Obtain releases from respondents, if possible and appropriate, for drug or other treatment providers.

☐ Obtain discovery, including but not limited to Department of Social Services records, police reports, medical and school records, and witness statements.

At the temporary custody hearing:

☐ Advocate your position.

☐ Always apprise the court of the child's wishes, even if it is not your position.

☐ Present evidence when necessary.

☐ Request any necessary orders for discovery.

☐ Request any necessary orders for services for the parents.

☐ Request any necessary orders for services for the children.

☐ Request any necessary orders for visitation with parents, siblings, other family members, and important individuals.

☐ When necessary for compliance or enforcement, get orders even when everyone agrees to a service, etc. Present such requests as, for example, "upon consent of all parties, the child will receive a speech and language evaluation by one month from today."

☐ Request any orders necessary to ensure continuity of school and medical care.

☐ Request orders that children remain in the current placement home absent a court order or emergency, when necessary.

☐ Request an order that the attorney be notified prior to a client's change in placement.

☐ Clarify the court's orders and reduce them to writing, when necessary and appropriate.

After the preliminary hearing:

☐ Get a copy of the court's order.

☐ Make sure the social worker has a copy of court's order, along with any other collateral sources who need the information (get consent or a court order for disclosure).

☐ Monitor compliance with the court order.

☐ Visit clients to explain the court order and determine a position for adjudication.

Preparing for the adjudication:

☐ Investigate the facts.

☐ Investigate potential placement options, particularly kinship placements.

☐ Obtain discovery.

☐ Develop a theory of the case.

☐ Develop a litigation strategy.

☐ Interview the respondents, if possible and appropriate.

☐ Interview witnesses.

☐ Conduct depositions or send out interrogatories when appropriate.

☐ Subpoena witnesses.

☐ Order independent evaluations when necessary.

☐ Participate in pretrial conferences.

- Present your position.

- Settle when possible—if not on the entire case, then on certain issues.

- Agree on stipulations when possible; reduce them to writing when necessary.

☐ Prepare exhibits.

☐ Prepare direct and cross examinations of witnesses.

☐ Prepare witnesses.

☐ Prepare the closing argument.

☐ Develop a permanency position.

At adjudication:

☐ Advocate your position, and always present the child's position, even when it is not your own position.

☐ Examine witnesses.

☐ Present evidence when necessary.

At disposition:

☐ Advocate your position, and always present the child's position, even when it is not your own position.

☐ Examine witnesses.

☐ Present evidence when necessary.

☐ Report to the court on compliance issues; seek appropriate orders.

☐ Report to the court and seek appropriate orders regarding the essential needs of the child: placement issues, food, clothing, shelter or health needs, educational status, sibling relationships, visitation issues.

After adjudication and disposition:

☐ Obtain copies of court orders and distribute to them to necessary people.

☐ Monitor compliance with court orders by the respondents and the Department of Social Services.

☐ Reassess your permanency position.

☐ Visit and counsel clients and explain the court's findings and orders. Determine the clients' positions for review and permanency hearings.

☐ Speak to the foster parents, therapists, and other service providers. Update them on court orders and gather information.

Preparing for review hearings/permanency hearings:

☐ Investigate facts, including observing visits when appropriate, speaking to child's caregivers and other collateral sources, and interviewing witnesses.

☐ Determine position.

☐ Determine whether children are in a potentially permanent placement: if not, advocate with the Department of Social Services for transfer.

☐ Subpoena witnesses.

☐ Obtain court reports from the Department of Social Services and other discovery.

☐ Investigate any new placement options.

☐ Obtain other parties' stipulations when appropriate.

☐ Make a home visit, if possible and appropriate.

☐ Interview the parents, if possible and appropriate.

At review/permanency hearings

☐ Advocate your position: always state the child's position, even when it is not your own position.

☐ Present evidence when necessary.

☐ Seek necessary orders consistent with your position (e.g., an order to file a TPR, or an order that a trial discharge plan be developed.

☐ Report to the court on compliance issues; seek appropriate orders.

☐ Report to the court and seek appropriate orders regarding the essential needs of the child: placement issues, food, clothing, shelter or health needs, educational status, sibling relationships, visitation issues.

☐ Seek orders for services for the child when necessary.

After review/permanency hearings

☐ Obtain copies of court orders and distribute them to necessary people.

☐ Monitor compliance with court orders by the respondents and the Department of Social Services.

☐ Reassess permanency position, if need be.

☐ Visit and counsel clients and explain the court's findings and orders. Determine their positions for a termination hearing, if appropriate.

☐ Speak to foster parents, therapists, and other service providers. Update them on court orders and gather information.

Before termination of parental rights trial

☐ Obtain a certified copy of the adjudication findings if necessary.

☐ Obtain the adjudication transcript/record if necessary.

☐ Order a certified copy of criminal or other collateral proceedings if necessary.

☐ Obtain and analyze discovery.

☐ Obtain independent evaluations if necessary.

☐ Develop a litigation strategy.

☐ Interview the respondents, if possible and appropriate.

☐ Interview witnesses.

☐ Conduct depositions or send out interrogatories when appropriate.

☐ Subpoena witnesses.

☐ Participate in pretrial conferences.

　　• Present your position.

　　• Settle when possible: if not on the entire case, then on certain issues such as visitation, suspended judgment, and placement with relatives.

　　• Agree on stipulations when possible; reduce them to writing when necessary.

☐ Prepare exhibits.

☐ Prepare stipulations when possible.

☐ Prepare direct and cross examinations.

☐ Prepare closing argument.

At termination of parental rights trial:

☐ Advocate your position: always state the child's wishes, even if that is not your position.

☐ Participate in the trial—conduct examinations of witnesses and present evidence.

☐ Seek appropriate orders, including sibling or parental visitation, placement, expedite adoption, or other orders, if appropriate and necessary.

After TPR trial:

- ☐ Obtain court orders and distribute them to the necessary people.

- ☐ Monitor compliance with court orders by the Department of Social Services, or the respondents, if TPR is not granted.

- ☐ Visit and counsel clients and explain the court's findings and orders.

- ☐ Speak to foster parents, therapists, and other service providers. Update them on court orders and gather information.

- ☐ If the children are in an adoptive home, work with the adoption attorney to see that the adoption is filed.

- ☐ If the children are not in an adoptive home, work with the agency to identify an adoptive home and to ensure a smooth transition to the new home. Then work with the adoption attorney.

- ☐ Prepare a court report if required.

Before post termination review:

- ☐ Investigate the facts, including speaking to the child's caregivers and other collateral sources, and interviewing witnesses.

- ☐ Determine your position.

- ☐ Determine whether the children are in an adoptive placement: if not, advocate with the Department of Social Services for transfer or file a motion.

- ☐ File motions for compliance with court orders when necessary.

- ☐ Subpoena witnesses if necessary.

- ☐ Obtain court reports from the Department of Social Services and other discovery.

- ☐ Investigate any new placement options.

Chapter 22   TRIAL ADVOCACY

Part 22A: Case Analysis*

by Steven Lubet[1]

§ 22A.1 The Idea of a Persuasive Story

§ 22A.1.1 Trials as Stories

The function of a trial is to resolve factual disputes. Trials are only held when the parties are in disagreement concerning historical facts. These disagreements commonly involve the existence or occurrence of events or actions, but they may also turn upon questions of sequence, interpretation, characterization, or intent. Thus, trials may be held to answer questions such as these: What happened? What happened first? Why did it happen? Who made it happen? Did it happen on purpose? Was it justified or fair? All of these questions are resolved by accumulating information about past events; if there is no dispute about past events the case should be resolved on summary judgment.

Trials, then, are held in order to allow the parties to persuade the judge or jury by recounting their versions of the historical facts. Another name for this process is storytelling. Each party to a trial has the opportunity to tell a story, albeit through the fairly stilted devices of jury address, direct and cross examination, and introduction of evidence. The framework for the stories—or their grammar—is set by the rules of procedure and evidence. The conclusion of the stories—the end to which they are directed—is controlled by the elements of the applicable substantive law. The content of the stories—their plot and mise-en-scène—is governed, of course, by the truth, or at least by so much of the truth as is available to the advocate. Thereafter, the party who succeeds in telling the most persuasive story should win.

But what is persuasive storytelling in the context of a trial? A persuasive story can establish an affirmative case if it has all, or most, of these characteristics:

---

* This material appears in *Modern Trial Advocacy: Analysis and Practice*, 3rd Edition, copyright © 2004, National Institute for Trial Advocacy (NITA). Reproduced with permission from the National Institute for Trial Advocacy. The NACC is grateful to NITA for permitting the use of these materials as a gift to the child advocacy community. The NACC highly recommends the full publication of *Modern Trial Advocacy* and additional NITA trial skill material available at www.NITA.org or 800-225-6482.

Editor's Note: Nonsubstantive changes have been made to the text and formatting to reflect the style of this publication. Section numbers have also been added to reflect the style of this publication.

[1] Steven Lubet, J.D., is Professor of Law at Northwestern University School of Law in Chicago, Illinois.

(1) it is told about people who have reasons for the way they act; (2) it accounts for or explains all of the known or undeniable facts; (3) it is told by credible witnesses; (4) it is supported by details; (5) it accords with common sense and contains no implausible elements; and (6) it is organized in a way that makes each succeeding fact increasingly more likely. On the other hand, defense lawyers must often tell "counter-stories" that negate the above aspects of the other side's case.

In addition to persuasiveness, a story presented at trial must consist of admissible evidence, and it must contain all of the elements of a legally cognizable claim or defense.

An advocate's task when preparing for trial is to conceive of and structure a true story—comprising only admissible evidence and containing all of the elements of a claim or defense—that is most likely to be believed or adopted by the trier of fact. This is a creative process, since seldom will the facts be undisputed or capable of but a single interpretation. To carry through this process the lawyer must "imagine" a series of alternative scenarios, assessing each for its clarity, simplicity, and believability, as well as for its legal consequences.

§ 22A.1.2 Planning a Sample Story

Assume, for example, that you represent a plaintiff who was injured in an automobile accident. You know from your law school torts class that in order to recover damages you will have to tell a story proving, at a minimum, that the defendant was negligent. You also know from your evidence class that the story will have to be built on admissible evidence, and you know from your ethics class that the story cannot be based on false or perjured testimony. Your client knows only that when traffic slowed down to allow a fire truck to pass, she was hit from behind by the driver of the other automobile.

How can these basic facts be assembled into a persuasive trial story? First, we know that the story must be about people who act for reasons. Your client slowed down for a fire truck, which explains her actions. But why didn't the defendant slow down as well? Your story will be more persuasive if you can establish his reason.

True, a reason is not absolutely essential. Perhaps the defendant was such a poor driver that he simply drove about banging into other automobiles. On the other hand, consider what the absence of a reason implies. The plaintiff claims that traffic slowed for a fire truck, but the defendant—also part of traffic—did not slow down. Could it be that there was no fire truck? Perhaps there was a fire truck, but it was not sounding its siren or alerting traffic to stop. Is it possible that the plaintiff didn't slow down, but rather slammed on her brakes? In other words, the very absence of a reason for the defendant's actions may make the plaintiff's own testimony less believable.

The skilled advocate will therefore look for a reason or cause for the defendant's actions. Was the defendant drunk? In a hurry? Homicidal? Distracted? You can begin to choose from among these potential reasons by "imagining" each one in the context of your story. Imagine how the story will be told if you claim that the defendant was drunk. Could such a story account for all of the known facts? If the police came to the scene, was the defendant arrested? Did any credible, disinterested witnesses see the defendant drinking or smell liquor on his breath? If not, drunkenness does not provide a persuasive reason for the defendant's actions.

Next, imagine telling your story about a homicidal defendant. Perhaps this wasn't an accident, but a murder attempt. Envision your impassioned plea for punitive damages. But wait, this story is too implausible. How would a murderer know that the plaintiff would be driving on that particular road? How would he know that a fire truck would be attempting to bypass traffic? How could he predict that the plaintiff would slow down enough, or that there would be no other cars in the way? Barring the discovery of additional facts that support such a theory, this story is unpersuasive.

Finally, imagine the story as told about a defendant who was in a hurry. This story accounts for the known facts, since it explains why traffic might slow while the defendant did not. Perhaps the defendant saw the fire truck but was driving just a little too fast to stop in time; or he might have been so preoccupied with the importance of getting somewhere on time that he simply failed to notice the fire truck until it was too late. Moreover, there is nothing implausible or unbelievable about this theory. It is in complete harmony with everyone's everyday observations. Furthermore, details that support the story should not be hard to come by. Was the defendant going to work in the morning? Did he have an important meeting to attend? Was he headed home after a long day? The trial lawyer can find details in virtually any destination that will support the theory of the hurried defendant. Note, however, that while such additional evidence of the defendant's haste will be helpful, the story does not rest upon any external witness's credibility. All of the major elements of the story may be inferred from the defendant's own actions.

How can this last story best be organized? Let us assume that the occurrence of the collision itself is not in issue, and recall that it is important that each fact make every succeeding element increasingly more likely. Which aspect should come first: the presence of the fire truck or the fact that the defendant was in a hurry? Since the presence of the fire truck does not make it more likely that the defendant was in a hurry, that probably is not the most effective starting point. On the other hand, the defendant's haste does make it more likely that he would fail to notice the fire truck.

A skeletal version of our story, with some easily obtained details supplied, might go like this: we know there was a collision, but why did it happen? The defendant was driving south on Sheridan Road at 8:20 in the morning. It was the end of rush hour, and he had to be at work downtown. In fact, he had an important meeting that was to begin at 8:30 a.m. sharp. The defendant's parking lot is two blocks from his office. As traffic slowed for a passing fire truck, the defendant did not notice it. Failing to stop in time, the defendant ran into the plaintiff's car.

Other details might also be available to support this story. Perhaps, immediately following the collision, the defendant pulled out a cellular phone to call his office. Similarly, there might be "counter-details" for the plaintiff to rebut. The point, however, is to organize your story on the principle of successive supporting detail.

§ 22A.2 The Ethics of Persuasive Storytelling

In the preceding section we discussed the way in which an advocate imagines a persuasive theory or story. We also noted that lawyers are bound to the truth—we are not free to pick stories simply on the basis of their persuasive value. Within this parameter, exactly how much room is there for creative theory choice?

§ 22A.2.1 Assuming That You "Know" the Truth

Let us begin with the proposition that in most cases neither the lawyer nor the client will know with certainty what we might call all of the "relevant truth." As in the scenario above, for example, the plaintiff knows her own actions but has no special knowledge about the defendant. The lawyer, of course, is not free to persuade or coach the plaintiff to alter her own story simply to make it more effective.

This is not to say, however, that legal ethics permit us to do nothing more than put the plaintiff on the witness stand. The lawyer's duty of zealous representation requires further inquiry into the existence of additional details, not to mention the artful use of sequencing and emphasis. For instance, let us assume that the plaintiff has informed her lawyer with certainty that the fire truck was flashing its lights but not sounding its siren or bell. There is no doubt that an attorney absolutely may not coach the plaintiff to testify that the siren and bell were sounding. Such testimony would be false, perjurious, and unethical.

On the other hand, there is no requirement that the absence of bell and siren be made the centerpiece of the plaintiff's direct examination. Sequencing and emphasis may be used to minimize the adverse impact of this information. Therefore, the direct examination could be developed as follows: "The fire truck was the largest vehicle on the road. It was the standard fire-engine red. All of its lights were flashing brightly—headlights, taillights, and red dome lights. It could be seen easily from all directions. All of the traffic, save the defendant, slowed down for the fire truck. It was not necessary to hear a siren in order to notice the fire truck." Thus, the lawyer has held closely to the truth, while establishing the irrelevance of the damaging information.

§ 22A.2.2 Assuming That You Do Not Know the Truth

A different situation arises when the advocate is not able to identify truth so closely, as in the example above concerning the defendant's reasons for failing to notice the fire truck in time. Recall that we considered a variety of possible reasons, including inattention, drunkenness, and aggression. Some reasons have clear forensic advantages over others. What are ethical limitations on the attorney's ability to choose the best one?

First, it should be clear that we are not bound to accept the defendant's story in the same way that we must give credence to our own client. The duty of zealous representation requires that we resolve doubts in our client's favor. Moreover, we speak to our client within a relationship of confidentiality, which not only protects her communication, but also gives her additional credibility. Without her consent, what our client tells us will go no further, and this knowledge gives her every reason to make a full disclosure. When our client gives us damaging facts (such as the absence of the fire truck's siren), it is even more likely to be true, since she obviously has no reason to inject such information falsely. Conversely, statements that we obtain from the defendant are not necessarily accompanied by comparable indicia of reliability, and we are entitled to mistrust them.

This is not to say that we must always accept information from our clients as revealed wisdom. Clients may mislead us as the result of misperception, forgetfulness, mistake, wishful thinking, reticence, or ignorance, and, unfortunately, they occasionally lie. Moreover, opposing parties in litigation usually tell what they perceive as the truth. As a tactical matter, trial lawyers must always examine every statement of every witness for potential error or falsehood. As an ethical matter, however, we should be more ready to assume that our client's words—both helpful and damaging—are likely to be true. It is, after all, the client's case.

Recognizing, then, that we must go beyond the opposite party's version of the facts, we next evaluate the entire universe of possible stories. In our example we determined that the "in a hurry" story would be the most persuasive. Simultaneously, we must also determine whether it is an ethical story to tell.

The key to determining the ethical value of any trial theory is whether it is supported by facts that we know, believe, or have a good faith basis to believe, are true. In other words, the story has to be based on facts that are "not false."

Returning to our fire truck case, assume that the defendant has denied that he was in a hurry. He has the right to make this denial, but as plaintiff's lawyers we have no duty to accept it. Assume also that we have not been able to locate a witness who can give direct evidence that the defendant was in a hurry. We do know where and when the collision occurred, and assume that we have also been able to learn numerous facts about the defendant's home, automobile, occupation, and place of employment. The following story emerges, based strictly on facts that we would have no reason to doubt.

The defendant lives sixteen miles from his office. He usually takes a commuter train to work, but on the day of the accident he drove. The accident occurred on a major thoroughfare approximately eleven miles from the defendant's office. The time of the accident was 8:20 a.m., and the defendant had scheduled an important, and potentially lucrative, meeting with a new client for

8:30 a.m. that day. The parking lot nearest to the defendant's office is over two blocks away. The first thing that the defendant did following the accident was telephone his office to say that he would be late.

Our conclusion is that the defendant was in a hurry. Driving on a familiar stretch of road, he was thinking about his appointment, maybe even starting to count the money, and he failed to pay sufficient attention to the traffic. We are entitled to ask the trier of fact to draw this inference because we reasonably believe its entire basis to be true. The known facts can also support numerous other stories, or no story at all, but that is not an ethical concern. Perhaps the defendant was being particularly careful that morning, knowing how important it was that he arrive on time for his appointment. Perhaps the appointment had nothing to do with the accident. Those arguments can be made, and they may turn out to be more persuasive stories than our own. Our ultimate stories might be ineffective, or even foolish, but they are ethical so long as they are not built on a false foundation.

§ 22A.2.3 The Special Case of the Criminal Law

The analysis above, regarding both persuasion and ethics, applies to civil and criminal cases alike. In the criminal law, however, the prosecutor has additional ethical obligations and the defense lawyer has somewhat greater latitude.

A criminal prosecutor is not only an advocate, but also a public official. It is the prosecutor's duty to punish the guilty, not merely to win on behalf of a client. Therefore, a public prosecutor may not rely upon the "not false" standard for determining the ethical value of a particular theory. Rather, the prosecutor must personally believe in the legal validity of each case and must refrain from bringing any prosecution that is not supported by probable cause.

Conversely, a criminal defendant is always entitled to plead not guilty, thereby putting the government to its burden of establishing guilt beyond a reasonable doubt. A plea of not guilty need not in any sense be "true," since its function is only to insist upon the constitutional right to trial. Of course, a criminal defendant has no right to introduce perjury or false evidence. However, a criminal defendant need not present any factual defense, and in most jurisdictions a conviction requires that the prosecution "exclude every reasonable hypothesis that is inconsistent with guilt." Thus, so long as she does not rely upon falsity or perjury, a criminal defense lawyer may argue for acquittal—that is, tell a story—based only upon "a reasonable hypothesis" of innocence.

§ 22A.3 Preparing a Persuasive Trial Story

Assume that you have decided upon the story that you want to tell. It is persuasive. It is about people who have reasons for the way they act. It accounts for all of the known facts. It is told by credible witnesses. It is supported by details. It accords with common sense. It can be organized in a way that makes each succeeding fact more likely. How do you put your story in the form of a trial?

§ 22A.3.1 Developing Your Theory and Your Theme

Your case must have both a theory and a theme.

Theory

Your theory is the adaptation of your story to the legal issues in the case. A theory of the case should be expressed in a single paragraph that combines an account of the facts and the law in such a way as to lead to the conclusion that your client must win. A successful theory contains these elements:

It is logical. A winning theory has internal logical force. It is based upon a foundation of undisputed or otherwise provable facts, all of which lead in a single direction. The facts upon which your theory is based should reinforce (and never contradict) each other. Indeed, they should lead to each other, each fact or premise implying the next, in an orderly and inevitable fashion.

It speaks to the legal elements of your case. All of your trial persuasion must be in aid of a "legal" conclusion. Your theory must not only establish that your client is good or worthy (or that the other side is bad and unworthy), but also that the law entitles you to relief. Your theory therefore must be directed to prove every legal element that is necessary both to justify a verdict on your behalf and to preserve it on appeal.

It is simple. A good theory makes maximum use of undisputed facts. It relies as little as possible on evidence that may be hotly controverted, implausible, inadmissible, or otherwise difficult to prove.

It is easy to believe. Even "true" theories may be difficult to believe because they contradict everyday experience, or because they require harsh judgments. You must strive to eliminate all implausible elements from your theory. Similarly, you should attempt to avoid arguments that depend upon proof of deception, falsification, ill motive, or personal attack. An airtight theory is able to encompass the entirety of the other side's case and still result in your victory by sheer logical force.

To develop and express your theory, ask these three questions: What happened? Why did it happen? Why does that mean that my client should win? If your answer is longer than one paragraph, your theory may be logical and true, but it is probably too complicated.

Theme

Just as your theory must appeal to logic, your theme must appeal to moral force. A logical theory tells the trier of fact the reason that your verdict must be entered. A moral theme shows why it should be entered. In other words, your theme—best presented in a single sentence—justifies the morality of your theory and appeals to the justice of the case.

A theme is a rhetorical or forensic device. It has no independent legal weight, but rather it gives persuasive force to your legal arguments. The most compelling themes appeal to shared values, civic virtues, or common motivations. They can be succinctly expressed and repeated at virtually every phase of the trial.

In a contracts case, for example, your theory will account for all of the facts surrounding the formation and breach of the contract, as well as the relevant law, say, of specific performance. Your theory will explain why a particular verdict is compelled by the law. Your theme will strengthen your theory by underscoring why entering that verdict is the right thing to do. Perhaps your theme will be, "The defendant would rather try to make money than live up to a promise." Or you might try, "This defendant tried to sell some property, and keep it too." Whatever the theme, you will want to introduce it during your opening statement, reinforce it during direct and cross examinations, and drive it home during your final argument.

§ 22A.3.2 Planning Your Final Argument

Good trial preparation begins at the end. It makes great sense to plan your final argument first, because that aspect of the trial is the most similar to storytelling; it is the single element of the trial where it is permissible for you to suggest conclusions, articulate inferences, and otherwise present your theory to the trier of fact as an uninterrupted whole.

In other words, during final argument you are most allowed to say exactly what you want to say, limited only by the requirement that all arguments be supported by evidence contained in the trial record. Thus, by planning your final argument at the beginning of your preparation, you will then be able to plan the balance of your case so as to ensure that the record contains every fact that you will need for summation.

Ask yourself these two questions: What do I want to say at the end of the case? What evidence must I introduce or elicit in order to be able to say it? The answers will give you the broad outline of your entire case.

§ 22A.3.3 Planning Your Case in Chief

Your goal during your case in chief is to persuade the trier of fact as to the correctness of your theory, constantly invoking the moral leverage of your theme. To accomplish this, you have four basic tools: (1) jury address, which consists of opening statement and final argument; (2) testimony on direct examination, and to a lesser extent on cross examination; (3) introduction of exhibits, including real and documentary evidence; and (4) absolutely everything else that you do in the courtroom, including the way you look, act, react, speak, move, stand, and sit. The skills involved in each of these aspects of a trial will be discussed at length in later chapters. What follows here is an outline of the general steps to take in planning for trial.

Consider Your Potential Witnesses and Exhibits

Your first step is to list the legal elements of every claim or defense that you hope to establish. If you represent the plaintiff in a personal injury case, then you must offer evidence on all of the elements of negligence: duty, foreseeability, cause-in-fact, proximate cause, and damages. Next, list the evidence that you have available to support each such element. Most likely the bulk of your evidence will be in the form of witness testimony, but some of it will consist of documents, tangible objects, and other real evidence. For each such exhibit, note the witness through whom you will seek its introduction.

You are now ready to make decisions concerning your potential witnesses by inverting the informational list that you just created.

Evaluate Each Witness Individually

Imagine what you would like to say in final argument about each witness you might call to the stand: What does this witness contribute to my theory? What positive facts may I introduce through this witness? Are other witnesses available for the same facts? Is this witness an effective vehicle for my theme? What can I say about this witness that will be logically and morally persuasive?

Once you have assembled all of the "positive" information about each witness, you must go on to consider all possible problems and weaknesses.

Factual Weaknesses. Are there likely to be inconsistencies or gaps in the witness's testimony? Does the witness have damaging information that is likely to be elicited on cross examination? If the answer to either question is affirmative, how can you minimize these problems? Can you resolve the inconsistencies by reevaluating your theory? Can another witness fill the gaps? Can you defuse the potentially damaging facts by bringing them out on direct examination?

Evidentiary Problems. Each witness's testimony must be evaluated for possible evidentiary problems. Do not assume that any item of evidence or testimony is automatically admissible. Instead, you must be able to state a positive theory of admissibility for everything that you intend to offer during your case in chief. To prepare for objections ask yourself, "How would I try to keep this information out of evidence?" Then plan your response. If you are not absolutely confident in your ability to counter any objections, you have to go back to the law library.

Credibility Problems. How is the witness likely to be attacked? Is the witness subject to challenge for bias or interest? Will perception be in issue? Is there potential for impeachment by prior inconsistent statements? Can you structure your direct examination so as to avoid or minimize these problems?

Decide Which Witness to Call

Having evaluated the contributions, strengths, and weaknesses of all of your potential witnesses, you are now in a position to decide which ones you will call to the stand. Your central concern will be to make sure that all of your necessary evidence is admitted. You must call any witness who is the sole source of a crucial piece of information. Except in rare or compelling circumstances, you will also want to call any witness whose credibility or appearance is central to the internal logic or moral weight of your case.

All nonessential witnesses must be evaluated according to their strengths and weaknesses. You will want to consider eliminating witnesses whose testimony will be cumulative or repetitive of each other, since this will increase the likelihood of eliciting a damaging contradiction. You must also be willing to dispense with calling witnesses whose credibility is seriously suspect, or whose testimony has the potential to do you more harm than good.

Once you have arrived at your final list of witnesses, arrange them in the order that will be most helpful to your case. While there are no hard and fast rules for determining witness order, the following three principles should help you decide:

Retention. You want your evidence not only to be heard, but also to be retained. Studies have consistently suggested that judges and juries tend to best remember the evidence that they hear at the beginning and the end of the trial. Following this principle, you will want to call your most important witness first and your next most important witness last. Start fast and end strong.

Progression. The "first and last" principle must occasionally give way to the need for logical progression. Some witnesses provide the foundation for the testimony of others. Thus, it may be necessary to call "predicate" witnesses early in the trial as a matter of both logical development and legal admissibility. To the extent possible, you may also wish to arrange your witnesses so that accounts of key events are given in chronological order.

Impact. You may also order your witnesses to maximize their dramatic impact. For example, you might wish to begin a wrongful death case by calling one of the grieving parents of the deceased child. Conversely, a necessary witness who is also somewhat unsavory or impeachable should probably be buried in the middle of your case in chief. A variant on the impact principle is the near-universal practice of calling a criminal defendant as the last witness for the defense. This practice has arisen for two reasons. First, it postpones until the last possible moment that time that the lawyer must decide whether to call the defendant to the stand for exposure to cross examination. Second, and far more cynically, calling defendants last allows them to hear all of the other testimony before testifying. (While all occurrence witnesses are routinely excluded from the courtroom, the defendant has a constitutional right to be present throughout the trial.)

§ 22A.3.4 Planning Your Cross Examinations

It is inherently more difficult to plan a cross examination than it is to prepare for direct. It is impossible to safeguard yourself against all surprises, but the following four steps will help keep them to a minimum.

First, compile a list of every potential adverse witness. Imagine why the witness is likely to be called. Ask yourself, "How can this witness most hurt my case?" Always prepare for the worst possible alternative.

Second, consider whether there is a basis for keeping the witness off the stand. Is the witness competent to testify? Is it possible to invoke a privilege? Then consider whether any part of the expected testimony might be excludable. For every statement that the witness might make, imagine all reasonable evidentiary objections. Do the same thing concerning all exhibits that might be offered through the witness. For each objection plan your argument and prepare for the likely counter-argument. You won't want to make every possible objection, but you will want to be prepared.

Third, consider the factual weaknesses of each opposing witness. Are there inconsistencies that can be exploited or enhanced? Is the witness's character subject to attack? Can the witness be impeached from prior statements? How can the witness be used to amplify your own theme?

Finally, catalog all of the favorable information that you will be able to obtain from each opposing witness.

§ 22A.3.5 Reevaluating Everything That You Have Done

Now that you have planned your case in chief and cross examinations, it is imperative that you go back and reevaluate every aspect of your case. Do your direct examinations fully support and establish your theory? Do they leave any logical gaps? Are you satisfied that all of your necessary evidence will be admissible? Will it be credible? Do the potential cross examinations raise issues with which you cannot cope? Will you be able to articulate your moral theme during most or all of the direct and cross examinations? If you are unable to answer these questions satisfactorily, you may need to readjust your theory or theme.

Assuming that you are satisfied with your theory, you should now have an excellent idea of what the evidence at trial will be. With this in mind, go back again and rework your final argument. Make sure that it is completely consistent with the expected evidence and that it makes maximum use of the uncontroverted facts. Consider eliminating any parts of the argument that rest too heavily on evidence that you anticipate will be severely contested. Be sure that you structure your argument so that you can begin and end with your theme, and invoke it throughout. Finally, outline your opening statement, again beginning and ending with your theme, and raising each of the points to which you will return on final argument.

§ 22A.4 Conclusion

The following chapters discuss all aspects of persuasion at trial, from the opening statement to the final argument. Trial lawyers must master numerous forensic skills, procedural rules, and examination techniques, but your starting point must always be your theory of the case—the story that you want to tell.

Part 22B: Evidentiary Foundations*

by Steven Lubet[2]

§ 22B.1 The Requirement of Foundation

Before any evidence can be considered at trial there must be some basis for believing it to be relevant and admissible. This basis is called the foundation for the evidence. Depending upon the nature of the evidence, the foundation may be painfully complex or strikingly simple. The law of evidence determines exactly which facts form the predicate for the admission of all testimony and exhibits. In any event, the question of foundation is directed to the judge, who must make a preliminary determination as to whether the particular evidence will be received.

Regarding much testimony, foundation is so obvious that it is almost overlooked as a formal aspect of the trial. For example, the basic foundation for eyewitness, or percipient, testimony is that the witness observed relevant events and is able to recall them. This foundation is typically established as a means of introducing the witness, virtually as a matter of course. For example:

QUESTION:

Where were you on the afternoon of December 19?

ANSWER:

I was at the corner of Central and Ridge.

QUESTION:

What did you see?

ANSWER:

I saw an automobile collision.

It has now been shown that the witness has personal knowledge of relevant facts. On the basis of this foundation, and in the absence of some objection that is not apparent from the example, the witness should be allowed to describe the colli-

---

* This material appears in *Modern Trial Advocacy: Analysis and Practice*, 3rd Edition, copyright © 2004, National Institute for Trial Advocacy (NITA). Reproduced with permission from the National Institute for Trial Advocacy. The NACC is grateful to NITA for permitting the use of these materials as a gift to the child advocacy community. The NACC highly recommends the full publication of *Modern Trial Advocacy* and additional NITA trial skill material available at www.NITA.org or 800-225-6482.

Editor's Note: Nonsubstantive changes have been made to the text and formatting to reflect the style of this publication. Section numbers have also been added to reflect the style of this publication.

[2] Steven Lubet, J.D., is Professor of Law at Northwestern University School of Law in Chicago, Illinois.

sion. Of course, not all foundations are so straightforward. Many require the proof of substantial predicate facts, as will be discussed below.

Foundations are required in the interest of both efficiency and fairness. In order to conserve the court's time, evidence will not be heard unless there is first a threshold showing of relevance and admissibility. In the above example, for instance, there would be no reason for a court to hear a narrative about the accident from a witness who was not qualified to describe it.

Similarly, fairness dictates that an adversary be given notice of the basis for offering evidence before it is actually received. Imagine this scenario at the very beginning of a direct examination:

QUESTION:

What is your name?

ANSWER:

Ari Madison.

QUESTION:

Please describe the automobile accident that occurred at the corner of Central and Ridge last December 19.

In the absence of some basis for the witness's testimony, opposing counsel has no way of knowing whether the proffered evidence will be competent or inadmissible. The witness may be about to testify on the basis of speculation or hearsay. Foundation is therefore required in order to prevent unfair prejudice.

§ 22B.2 Components of Foundation

There are three universal aspects to virtually all evidentiary foundations. To be received, evidence must be shown to be (1) relevant, (2) authentic, and (3) admissible under the applicable laws of evidence. While the discrete elements of foundation will differ according to the nature of the evidence and the purpose for which it is offered, these three considerations must always apply.

§ 22B.2.1 Relevance

Relevance defines the relationship between the proffered evidence and some fact that is at issue in the case. Evidence will not be admitted simply because it is interesting or imaginative. Rather, it must be shown to be probative in the sense that it makes some disputed fact either more or less likely. The relevance of most evidence is generally made apparent from the context of the case, but occasionally it must be demonstrated by the establishment of foundational facts.

In the intersection example above, the relevance of the testimony is made clear by the recitation of the date and place of the witness's observation. The witness is about to testify concerning the collision at issue, not just any accident.

Note, however, that this basic foundation might not always be adequate. Had there been more than one accident on December 19 at the corner of Central and Ridge, the witness would have to provide additional identifying facts before testifying to the events. What time was the witness there? What colors were the automobiles involved?

§ 22B.2.2 Authenticity

The concept of authenticity refers to the requirement of proof that the evidence actually is what the proponent claims it to be. In other words, evidence is not to be admitted until there has been a threshold showing that it is "the real thing." The judge decides whether an item of evidence has been sufficiently authenticated, and the criteria vary according to the nature of the evidence involved. In many jurisdictions the strict rules of evidence do not apply to the court's preliminary determination of admissibility.

We generally think of authentication as it applies to tangible evidence such as documents, physical objects, or photographs. Is that really the contract that the parties executed? Is this actually the machine part that caused the injury? Does the photograph fairly and accurately depict the scene of the accident? Before any exhibit can be received a foundation must be established that adequately supports the proponent's claim of authenticity. Note that the court's initial ruling on authenticity is preliminary. It bears only on admissibility and is not binding as a factual determination. Opposing counsel may continue to controvert the genuineness of the exhibit, and the trier of fact (either judge or jury) remains free ultimately to reject the exhibit.

The requirement of authenticity is not, however, limited to tangible objects. It also applies to certain testimonial evidence. For example, a witness generally may not testify to a telephone conversation without first establishing her basis for recognizing the voice of the person on the other end of the line. That is, the identity of the other speaker must be authenticated.

§ 22B.2.3 Specific Admissibility

While evidence will generally be received if it is relevant and authentic, the law of evidence contains a host of specific provisions that govern the admissibility of various sorts of proof. In many cases evidence can be admitted only following the establishment of foundational facts. Most exceptions to the hearsay rule, for example, require such a preliminary showing. Similarly, a foundation must be laid for the admission of evidence of habit or routine practice or for the admission of evidence of subsequent remedial measures. It is impossible to generalize about such prerequisites except to say that the advocate must be aware of the rule of evidence under which each item of evidence is proffered. As is discussed in detail below, a foundation can then be tailored to meet the rule's requirements.

§ 22B.3 Establishing Foundations

§ 22B.3.1 Using a Single Witness

The most common approach to the establishment of a foundation is simply to call a witness who can provide the necessary facts, and then to offer the evidence after that testimony has been elicited. Consider this example from the direct examination of the plaintiff in our fire engine case:

QUESTION:

Do you recognize the object that I am showing you, which has been marked as plaintiff's exhibit 12?

ANSWER:

Yes, it is the neck brace that I got from my doctor.

QUESTION:

When did you get it from your doctor?

ANSWER:

When I was discharged from the hospital following the accident.

QUESTION:

What is it made of?

ANSWER:

Stiff plastic.

QUESTION:

Do you still wear it?

ANSWER:

Yes, I have to wear it at least eight hours a day.

Counsel may now offer the neck brace into evidence. Its relevance to the issue of damages is apparent from the context of the case, its authenticity as the actual neck brace has been established by the witness, and there are no special evidentiary considerations that govern the admission of this real evidence.

§ 22B.3.2 Using Multiple Witnesses

Some foundations cannot be laid by a single witness. In such cases counsel must establish separate parts of the foundation from each of several witnesses before offering the evidence. In a purse-snatching case, for example, it may be necessary to call two witnesses in order to lay the foundation for the admission of the stolen purse. First, the arresting officer:

QUESTION:

Officer, do you recognize prosecution exhibit 1?

ANSWER:

Yes. It is a lady's purse that was in the possession of the defendant when I arrested him.

The officer has laid some of the foundation, but not all of it. The defendant's possession of a purse is not relevant until it is shown to have been stolen. It is therefore necessary to call the crime victim:

QUESTION:

Ma'am, do you recognize prosecution exhibit 1?

ANSWER:

Yes. It is my pocketbook.

QUESTION:

Before today, when was the last time that you saw it?

ANSWER:

The last time I saw it was when it was ripped off of my shoulder by a purse snatcher.

Now the purse is admissible. The victim provided the missing aspect of relevance, and she also authenticated the purse as the object that was stolen.

Note that it is possible to combine both direct and cross examinations to lay a single foundation. Thus, defense counsel can begin to lay a foundation during the cross examination of a plaintiff's witness and can conclude the foundation during the defendant's case in chief. Assume, for example, that the defendant wants to introduce a letter from the plaintiff. To be admissible it must be shown both that the plaintiff wrote the letter and that the defendant received it. Defense counsel can begin the foundation during the plaintiff's case by having the plaintiff authenticate his own signature on cross examination. The foundation can later be completed by having the defendant testify during her own case that the letter was actually received.

§ 22B.3.3 Conditional Admissibility

It is not always possible to complete a foundation during the testimony of a single witness. However, a witness who is responsible for part of the foundation will in many cases have other important information concerning the exhibit. In the absence of a special rule, this witness could not testify about the exhibit until a second witness had been called to complete the foundation. Only then could the first witness return to the stand to complete his testimony about the exhibit.

Fortunately, such an awkward and inefficient procedure is generally not necessary. The courts have developed the doctrine of conditional admissibility, which allows the temporary or conditional admission of the evidence based upon counsel's representation that the foundation will be completed through the testimony of a subsequent witness.

In the above purse-snatching case the prosecution might want to elicit further testimony about the purse from the arresting officer:

PROSECUTOR:

Officer, do you recognize prosecution exhibit 1?

ANSWER:

Yes. It is a lady's purse that the defendant was concealing under his jacket when I arrested him.

PROSECUTOR:

Officer, please show us how the defendant was concealing the purse when you arrested him.

DEFENSE:

Objection. There is no foundation for this demonstration.

PROSECUTOR:

Your Honor, we will complete the foundation when we call the victim, who will testify that exhibit 1 is the same purse that was stolen from her.

COURT:

On the basis of counsel's representation, the objection is overruled.

The further testimony of the officer has been conditionally allowed, subject to the perfection of the foundation. In the event that the victim does not identify the purse, all of the conditionally accepted testimony will be subject to a motion to strike.

§ 22B.3.4 Using Adverse Witnesses

Potentially complex foundations can often be simplified through the use of adverse examination. In a case where executed contracts have been exchanged through the mail, for example, it may be extremely difficult for one party to authenticate the other party's signature. This problem can be completely alleviated, however, simply by calling the opposing party as an adverse witness:

QUESTION:

Are you the defendant in this case?

ANSWER:

I am.

QUESTION:

Is this your signature at the bottom of plaintiff's exhibit 1?

ANSWER:

Yes, it is.

The signature has now been authenticated.

§ 22B.3.5 Cross Examination

Foundation requirements apply equally during cross and direct examinations. Testimonial foundations must be laid on cross examination for personal knowledge, voice identification, hearsay exceptions, and in every other circumstance where a foundation would be necessary on direct examination. In addition, there are special foundations for certain cross examination techniques such as impeachment by past omission or prior inconsistent statement.

It is also often necessary to use cross examination to lay the foundation for the admission of exhibits. Defense counsel in particular can avoid the need to call adverse witnesses by attempting to establish foundations for her own exhibits while cross examining a plaintiff's witness.

In some jurisdictions, however, exhibits cannot actually be offered other than in counsel's case in chief. In such jurisdictions you may proceed to elicit the appropriate foundational testimony during cross examination, but you must delay actually offering the exhibits until the other side has rested. Following this rule, a plaintiff's attorney who develops the foundation for exhibits while cross examining defense witnesses must wait until the defense has rested, and may then offer the exhibits on rebuttal.

The "case-in-chief" rule is very difficult to justify analytically. Counsel can develop affirmative testimonial evidence on cross examination, and there is no good reason to treat real or documentary evidence any differently. Moreover, delaying the offer of an exhibit until after cross examination also delays any objections to the exhibit. This may prove awkward in situations where an objection is sustained for some technical reason and the witness is no longer on the stand to cure the defect.

It is far preferable to be able to offer exhibits on cross examination. Nonetheless, the case-in-chief rule must be followed where it exists.

Part 22C: Direct Examination*

by Steven Lubet[3]

§ 22C.1 The Role of Direct Examination

Cases are won as a consequence of direct examination.

Direct examination is your opportunity to present the substance of your case. It is the time to offer the evidence available to establish the facts that you need to prevail. Having planned your persuasive story, you must now prove the facts upon which it rests by eliciting the testimony of witnesses.

Direct examination, then, is the heart of your case. It is the fulcrum of the trial—the aspect upon which all else turns. Every other aspect of the trial is derivative of direct examination. Opening statements and final arguments are simply the lawyer's opportunity to comment upon what the witnesses have to say; cross examination exists solely to allow the direct to be challenged or controverted. While we could easily imagine a reasonably fair trial system consisting solely of direct examinations, it is impossible to conceive of anything resembling accurate fact finding in their absence.

Direct examinations should be designed to accomplish one or more of the following basic goals.

§ 22C.1.1 Introduce Undisputed Facts

In most trials there will be many important facts that are not in dispute. Nonetheless, such facts cannot be considered by the judge or jury, and will not be part of the record on appeal, until and unless they have been placed in evidence through a witness's testimony. Undisputed facts will often be necessary to establish an element of your case. Thus, failing to include them in direct examination could lead to an unfavorable verdict or reversal on appeal.

Assume, for example, that you represent the plaintiff in a case involving damage to the exterior of a building, and that the defense in the case is consent. Even if the question of ownership of the premises is not in dispute, it is still an

---

* This material appears in *Modern Trial Advocacy: Analysis and Practice*, 3rd Edition, copyright © 2004, National Institute for Trial Advocacy (NITA). Reproduced with permission from the National Institute for Trial Advocacy. The NACC is grateful to NITA for permitting the use of these materials as a gift to the child advocacy community. The NACC highly recommends the full publication of *Modern Trial Advocacy* and additional NITA trial skill material available at www.NITA.org or 800-225-6482.

Editor's Note: Nonsubstantive changes have been made to the text and formatting to reflect the style of this publication. Section numbers have also been added to reflect the style of this publication.

[3] Steven Lubet, J.D., is Professor of Law at Northwestern University School of Law in Chicago, Illinois.

element of your cause of action. Thus, you must present proof that your client had a possessory or ownership interest in the building, or run the risk of a directed verdict in favor of the defendant.

§ 22C.1.2 Enhance the Likelihood of Disputed Facts

The most important facts in a trial will normally be those in dispute. Direct examination is your opportunity to put forward your client's version of the disputed facts. Furthermore, you must not only introduce evidence on disputed points, you must do so persuasively. The true art of direct examination consists in large part of establishing the certainty of facts that the other side claims are uncertain or untrue.

§ 22C.1.3 Lay Foundations for the Introduction of Exhibits

Documents, photographs, writings, tangible objects, and other forms of real evidence will often be central to your case. With some exceptions, it is necessary to lay the foundation for the admission of such an exhibit through the direct testimony of a witness. This is the case whether or not the reliability of the exhibit is in dispute.

It is not unusual for a witness to be called only for the purpose of introducing an exhibit. The "records custodian" at a hospital or bank may know absolutely nothing about the contents of a particular report, but nonetheless may be examined solely in order to qualify the document as a business record.

§ 22C.1.4 Reflect Upon the Credibility of Witnesses

The credibility of a witness is always in issue. Thus, every direct examination, whatever its ultimate purpose, must also attend to the credibility of the witness's own testimony. For this reason, most direct examinations begin with some background information about the witness. What does she do for a living? Where did she go to school? How long has she lived in the community? Even if the witness's credibility will not be challenged, this sort of information helps to humanize her and therefore adds weight to what she has to say.

You can expect the credibility of some witnesses to be attacked on cross examination. In these situations you can blunt the assault by bolstering the witness's believability during direct examination. You can strengthen a witness by eliciting the basis of her knowledge, her ability to observe, or her lack of bias or interest in the outcome of the case.

You may also call a witness to reflect adversely on the credibility of the testimony of another. Direct examination may be used, for example, to introduce negative character or reputation evidence concerning another witness. Alternatively, you may call a witness to provide direct evidence of bias or motive, to lay the foundation for an impeaching document, or simply to contradict other testimony.

§ 22C.1.5 Hold the Attention of the Trier of Fact

No matter which of the above purposes predominates in any particular direct examination, it must be conducted in a manner that holds the attention of the judge or jury. In addition to being the heart of your case, direct examination also has the highest potential for dissolving into boredom, inattention, and routine. Since it has none of the inherent drama or tension of cross examination, you must take extreme care to prepare your direct examination so as to maximize its impact.

§ 22C.2 The Law of Direct Examination

The rules of evidence govern the content of all direct examinations. Evidence offered on direct must be relevant, authentic, not hearsay, and otherwise admissible. In addition, there is a fairly specific "law of direct examination" that governs the manner and means in which testimony may be presented.

§ 22C.2.1 Competence of Witnesses

Every witness called to testify on direct examination must be legally "competent" to do so. This is generally taken to mean that the witness possesses personal knowledge of some matter at issue in the case, is able to perceive and relate information, is capable of recognizing the difference between truth and falsity, and understands the seriousness of testifying under oath or on affirmation.

In the absence of evidence or other indications to the contrary, all individuals called to the stand are presumed competent to testify. If the competence of a witness is reasonably disputed, it may be necessary to conduct a preliminary examination in order to "qualify" the witness. Such inquiries are usually conducted by the direct examiner but may also be conducted by the trial judge. In either case, the examination must be directed toward that aspect of competence that has been called into question.

In the case of a very young child, for example, the qualifying examination must establish that the witness is capable of distinguishing reality from fantasy, is able to perceive such relationships as time and distance, and appreciates that it is "wrong to tell a lie." Following the preliminary examination, the adverse party should be allowed an opportunity to conduct a "voir dire," which is a preliminary cross examination limited to a threshold issue such as competence.

Note that there are several exceptions to the general rules of competence. Expert witnesses, for example, are excused from the requirement of testifying exclusively from personal knowledge. Judges and jurors are generally disqualified from giving evidence in cases in which they are involved.

§ 22C.2.2 Non-leading Questions

The principal rule of direct examination is that the attorney may not "lead" the witness. A leading question is one that contains or suggests its own answer. Since the party calling a witness to the stand is presumed to have conducted an interview and to know what the testimony will be, leading questions are disallowed in order to insure that the testimony will come in the witness's own words.

Whether a certain question is leading is frequently an issue of tone or delivery, as much as one of form. The distinction, moreover, is often finely drawn. For example, there is no doubt that this question is leading:

QUESTION:

Of course, you crossed the street, didn't you?

Not only does the question contain its own answer, its format also virtually requires that it be answered in the affirmative.

On the other hand, this question is not leading:

QUESTION:

Did you cross the street?

Although the question is highly specific and calls for a "yes or no" answer, it does not control the witness's response.

Finally, this question falls in the middle:

QUESTION:

Didn't you cross the street?

If the examiner's tone of voice and inflection indicate that this is meant as a true query, the question probably will not be considered leading. If the question is stated more as an assertion, however, it will violate the leading question rule.

There are, in any event, numerous exceptions to the rule against leading questions on direct examination. A lawyer is generally permitted to lead a witness on preliminary matters, on issues that are not in dispute, in order to direct the witness's attention to a specific topic, in order to expedite the testimony on nonessential points, and, in some jurisdictions, to refresh a witness's recollection. In addition, it is usually permissible to lead witnesses who are very young, extremely old, infirm, confused, or frightened. Finally, it is always within the trial judge's discretion to permit leading questions in order to make the examination effective for the ascertainment of the truth, avoid needless consumption of time, protect the witness from undue embarrassment, or as is otherwise necessary to develop the testimony.

In the absence of extreme provocation or abuse, most lawyers will not object to the occasional use of leading questions on direct. It is most common to object to leading questions that are directed to the central issues of the case or that are being used to substitute the testimony of counsel for that of the witness.

§ 22C.2.3 Narratives

Another general rule is that witnesses on direct examination may not testify in "narrative" form. The term narrative has no precise definition, but it is usually taken to mean an answer that goes beyond responding to a single specific question. Questions that invite a lengthy or run-on reply are said to "call for a narrative answer."

An example of a non-narrative question is, "What did you do next?" The objectionable, narrative version would be, "Tell us everything that you did that day."

As with leading questions, the trial judge has wide discretion to permit narrative testimony. Narratives are often allowed, indeed encouraged, when the witness has been qualified as an expert.

§ 22C.2.4 The Non-opinion Rule

Witnesses are expected to testify as to their sensory observations. What did the witness see, hear, smell, touch, taste, or do? Witnesses other than experts generally are not allowed to offer opinions or to characterize events or testimony. A lay witness, however, is allowed to give opinions that are "rationally based upon the perception of the witness." Thus, witnesses will usually be permitted to draw conclusions on issues such as speed, distance, volume, time, weight, temperature, and weather conditions. Similarly, lay witnesses may characterize the behavior of others as angry, drunken, affectionate, busy, or even insane.

§ 22C.2.5 Refreshing Recollection

Although witnesses are expected to testify in their own words, they are not expected to have perfect recall. The courtroom can be an unfamiliar and intimidating place for all but the most "professional" witnesses, and witnesses can suffer memory lapses due to stress, fatigue, discomfort, or simple forgetfulness. Under these circumstances it is permissible for the direct examiner to "refresh" the witness's recollection. It is most common to rekindle a witness's memory through the use of a document such as her prior deposition or report. It may also be permissible to use a photograph, an object, or even a leading question.

In order to refresh recollection with a document, you must first establish that the witness's memory is exhausted concerning a specific issue or event. You must then determine that her memory might be refreshed by reference to a certain writing. Next, show the writing to the witness, allow her time to examine it, and inquire as to whether her memory has returned. If the answer is yes, remove the document and request the witness to continue her testimony. Note that in this situation the testimony must ultimately come from the witness's own restored memory; the document may not be offered as a substitute.

§ 22C.3 Planning Direct Examinations

There are three fundamental aspects to every direct examination plan: content, organization, and technique.

Your principal tool in presenting a persuasive direct examination is, of course, the knowledge of the witness. If the underlying content of the examination is not accurate and believable, the lawyer's technique is unlikely to make any notice-able difference. Your primary concern, then, must be content—the existence of the facts that you intend to prove.

The content of a direct examination can be enhanced through the use of organization, language, focus, pacing, and rapport. Effective organization requires sequencing an examination in a manner that provides for logical devel-opment, while emphasizing important points and minimizing damaging ones. Questions should be asked in language that directs the progress of the examina-tion without putting words in the witness's mouth. A direct examination uses focus to underscore and expand upon the most crucial issues, rather than allow them to be lost in a welter of meaningless details. Pacing varies the tone, speed, and intensity of the testimony to insure that it does not become boring. Finally, the positive rapport of the direct examiner with the witness is essential to estab-lish the witness's overall trustworthiness and believability.

§ 22C.3.1 Content

Content—what the witness has to say—must be the driving force of every direct examination. Recall that direct examination provides your best opportu-nity to prove your case. It is not meant merely as a showcase for the witness's attractiveness or for your own forensic skills. The examination must have a cen-tral purpose. It must either establish some aspect of your theory, or it must con-tribute to the persuasiveness of your theme. Preferably, it will do both.

Begin by asking yourself, "Why am I calling this witness?" Which elements of your claims or defenses will the witness address? How can the witness be used to controvert an element of the other side's case? What exhibits can be intro-duced through the witness? How can the witness bolster or detract from the credibility of others who will testify? How can the witness add moral strength to the presentation of the case, or appeal to the jury's sense of justice?

Since a witness might be called for any or all of the above reasons, you must exhaustively determine all of the possible useful information. List every conceiv-able thing that the witness might say to explain or help your case.

Now you must begin to prioritize and discard. This is a ruthless process. In direct examination, length is your enemy. You must work to eliminate all nonessential facts that are questionable, subject to impeachment, cumulative, distasteful, implausible, distracting, or just plain boring.

What to Include

First, go through a process of inclusion. List the witness's facts that are nec-essary to the establishment of your theory. What is the single most important thing that the witness has to say? What are the witness's collateral facts that will make the central information more plausible? What is the next most important part of the potential testimony? What secondary facts make that testimony more believable? Continue this process for every element of your case.

For example, assume that in our fire engine case you have located a witness who saw the defendant driver at an automobile repair shop just a few days before the accident. The witness told you that the defendant was advised that his brakes were in poor repair, but that he left without having them fixed. This is a fact of central importance, and you will no doubt present it in the direct examination. Collateral or supportive facts will include corroborative details such as the time of day, the witness's reason for being in the auto shop, the witness's location during the crucial conversation about the brakes, the reason that the witness can remember the exact language used, and why the witness can identify the defendant. These details, while not strictly relevant to your theory, give weight and believability to the crucial testimony.

You must also be sure to include those "thematic" facts that give your case moral appeal. Returning to the intersection case, perhaps you have an additional witness who will testify that at the time of the collision the defendant was already late for an important meeting. Your theme, then, might be that the defendant was "Too busy to be careful." How can this theme be developed in the testimony of the "auto shop" witness? The answer is to look for supportive details. Was the defendant curt or abrupt with the repairperson? Was he constantly looking at his watch? Was he trying to read "important-looking papers" while discussing the brakes? Did the defendant rush out of the shop? In other words, search for details that support your image of the defendant as busy, preoccupied, and unconcerned with safety.

In addition to central facts and supporting details, your "content checklist" should include consideration of the following sorts of information:

Reasons. Recall that stories are more persuasive when they include reasons for the way people act. A direct examination usually should include the reasons for the witness's own actions. Some witnesses can also provide reasons for the actions of another.

Explanations. When a witness's testimony is not self-explanatory, or where it raises obvious questions, simply ask the witness to explain. In the above "repair shop" scenario it may not be immediately apparent that a casual observer would recall the defendant's actions in such detail. Ask for an explanation:

QUESTION:

How is it that you can remember seeing and hearing what the defendant did that morning?

ANSWER:

I was at the shop to have my brakes fixed, and it really made an impression on me that he was leaving without taking care of his.

Credibility. The credibility of a witness is always in issue. Some part of every direct examination should be devoted to establishing the credibility of the witness. You can enhance credibility in numerous ways. Show that the witness is neutral and disinterested. Demonstrate that the witness had an adequate opportunity to observe. Allow the witness to deny any expected charges of bias or misconduct. Elicit the witness's personal background of probity and honesty.

What to Exclude

Having identified the facts that most support your theory and most strengthen your theme, you may now begin the process of elimination. It should go without saying that you must omit those facts that are "untrue." While you are not required to assure yourself beyond reasonable doubt of the probity of each witness, neither may you knowingly elicit testimony that you believe to be false. By the time you are preparing your direct examinations you certainly will have abandoned any legal or factual theory that rests upon evidence of this sort.

More realistically, unless you have an extraordinarily compelling reason to include them, you will need to consider discarding facts that fall into the following categories:

Clutter. This may be the single greatest vice in direct examination. Details are essential to the corroboration of important evidence, and they are worse than useless virtually everywhere else. Aimless detail will detract from your true corroboration. In the "auto shop" example, for instance, the witness's proximity to the service counter is an essential detail. The color of the paint in the waiting room is not.

How do you determine whether or not a certain fact is clutter? Ask what it contributes to the persuasiveness of your story. Does it supply a reason for the way that someone acted? Does it make an important fact more or less likely? Does it affect the credibility or authority of a witness? Does it enhance the moral value of your story? If all of the answers are negative, you're looking at clutter.

Unprovables. These are facts that can successfully be disputed. While not "false," they may be subjected to such vigorous and effective dispute as to make them unusable. Is the witness the only person who claims to have observed a certain event, while many other credible witnesses swear to the precise contrary? Is the witness herself less than certain? Is the testimony contradicted by credible documentary evidence? It is usually better to pass up a line of inquiry than to pursue it and ultimately have it rejected. This is not, however, a hard and fast rule. Many true facts will be disputed by the other side, and your case will virtually always turn upon your ability to persuade the trier of fact that your version is correct. Sometimes your case will depend entirely upon the testimony of a single witness who, though certain and truthful, will come under massive attack. Still, you must be willing to evaluate all of the potential testimony against the standards of provability and need. If you can't prove it, don't use it. Especially if you don't need it.

Implausibles. Some facts need not be disputed in order to collapse under their own weight. They might be true, they might be useful, they might be free from possible contradiction, but they still just won't fly. Return to the "auto shop" witness and assume that she informed you that she recognized the defendant because they had once ridden in the same elevator fifteen years previously.

You may have no reason to disbelieve the witness, and it is certainly unlikely that anyone could contradict or disprove her testimony. The testimony might even add some support to your theme, say, if the defendant rushed out of the elevator in an obvious hurry to get to work. Nonetheless, the testimony is simply too far-fetched. If offered, it will give the trier of fact something unnecessary to worry about; it will inject a reason to doubt the other testimony of the witness.

Note, however, that implausibility must be weighed against importance. If the case involved a disputed identification of the defendant, then proof of an earlier encounter might be of sufficient value to risk its introduction.

Impeachables. These are statements open to contradiction by the witness's own prior statements. By the time of trial many witnesses will have given oral and/or written statements in the form of interviews, reports, and depositions. Many also will have signed or authored documents, correspondence, and other writings. With some limitations, the witnesses' previous words may be used to cast doubt upon their credibility; this is called impeachment by a prior inconsistent statement. The demonstration that a witness has previously made statements that contradict her trial testimony is often one of the most dramatic, and damning, aspects of cross examination. Unless you can provide an extremely good explanation of why the witness has changed, or seems to have changed, her story, it is usually best to omit "impeachables" from direct testimony.

Door Openers. Some direct testimony is said to "open the door" for inquiries on cross examination that otherwise would not be allowed. The theory here is that fairness requires that the cross examiner be allowed to explore any topic that was deliberately introduced on direct. For example, in the intersection case the defendant almost certainly would not be allowed to introduce the fact that the plaintiff had been under the care of a psychiatrist. On the other hand, assume that the plaintiff testified on direct that the accident had forced her to miss an important appointment with her doctor, and that the appointment could not be rescheduled for a week due to the nature of the doctor's schedule. In these circumstances the door would be opened, at a minimum, to a cross examination that covered the nature of the appointment and the reason that it could not be rescheduled; in other words, that the plaintiff was on her way to see her psychiatrist.

Another common door opener is the misconceived "defensive" direct examination. It is considered a truism in many quarters that the direct examiner should defuse the cross by preemptively bringing out all of the bad facts. The danger, however, is that you will "defensively" bring out facts that would have been inadmissible on cross examination. Assume, for example, that your client has a prior juvenile conviction for theft. While you might ordinarily want to raise a prior crime yourself in order to explain it or otherwise soften the impact of the evidence, juvenile convictions are almost never admissible. Thus, a defensive direct examination would not only introduce otherwise excludable information, it could very well open the door to further exploitation of those facts on cross. You cannot always avoid door openers, but you must learn to recognize them.

§ 22C.3.2 Organization and Structure

Organization is the tool through which you translate the witness's memory of events into a coherent and persuasive story. This requires idiom, art, poetry. An artist does not paint everything that she sees. Rather, she organizes shapes, colors, light, and texture to present her own image of a landscape. In the same manner, a trial lawyer does not simply ask a witness to "tell everything you know," but instead uses the placement and sequence of the information to heighten and clarify its value.

The keys to this process are primacy and recency, apposition, duration, and repetition.

Primacy and recency refer to the widely accepted phenomenon that people tend best to remember those things that they hear first and last. Following this principle, the important parts of a direct examination should be brought out at its beginning and again at its end. Less important information should be "sand-wiched" in the middle. In our intersection case the presence of the fire truck may well be the most important part of the plaintiff's testimony. It should therefore be introduced early in her direct examination and perhaps alluded to again at the end.

Apposition is the placement or juxtaposition of important facts in a manner that emphasizes their relationship. Again looking at the intersection case, a strictly chronological direct examination might have the plaintiff begin by explaining where she was headed on the morning of the accident. Assume now that she was going to an art exhibit that would not open for another hour. The importance and value of this seemingly innocuous fact can be heightened tremendously by "apposing" it to the conduct of the defendant immediately fol-lowing the accident. Imagine the impact of contrasting the plaintiff's unhurried trip with the following information about the defendant:

QUESTION:

Where were you going on the morning of the accident?

ANSWER:

I was going to the Art Institute.

QUESTION:

Were you in any hurry to get there?

ANSWER:

It wasn't going to open for an hour, so I was in no hurry at all.

QUESTION:

What did you do immediately after the accident?

ANSWER:

I asked the defendant if he was all right.

QUESTION:

What did the defendant do immediately following the accident?

ANSWER:

He jumped out of his car and pulled out his cell phone. He shouted that he would talk to me later, but first he had to cancel an important appointment.

Duration refers to the relative amount of time that you spend on the various aspects of the direct examination. As a general rule you should dwell on the more important points, using the very length of coverage to emphasize the significance of the topic. Less important matters should consume less of the direct examination. In the fire truck example it should be obvious that the presence and noticeability of the fire engine is central to the plaintiff's case. Although the plaintiff's initial observation of the truck could be established in a single question and answer, the importance of the subject dictates greater duration for this part of the direct examination:

QUESTION:

What did you see as you drove south on Sheridan Road?

ANSWER:

I saw a fire truck.

QUESTION:

Describe it, please.

ANSWER:

It was your basic fire truck. It was red, and it had firefighters riding on it. It had lights and a bell.

QUESTION:

Were the lights flashing?

ANSWER:

Yes, and it was sounding its siren.

QUESTION:

How far away were you when you first noticed the fire truck?

ANSWER:

I would say almost a block away.

Repetition is a corollary of duration. Important points should be repeated, preferably throughout the direct examination, to increase the likelihood that they will be retained and relied upon by the trier of fact.

Even applying these principles, there is no set pattern for the structure of a direct examination, just as there is no correct way to paint a landscape. The following guidelines, however, will always be useful.

Start Strong and End Strong: The Overall Examination

Every direct examination, no matter how else it is organized, should strive to begin and end on strong points. The definition of a strong point will differ from trial to trial. It may be the most gripping and dramatic aspect of the entire examination; it may be the single matter on which the witness expresses the greatest certainty; it may be the case's most hotly disputed issue; or it may be a crucial predicate for other testimony. Whatever the specifics, the strong points of your overall examination should have some or all of these features:

Admissibility. There is little worse than having an objection sustained right at the beginning, or end, of a direct examination. You must be absolutely certain of the admissibility of your opening and closing points.

Theory Value. The very definition of a strong point is that it makes a significant contribution to your theory. What does the witness have to say that is most central to the proof of your case?

Thematic Value. Ideally, your strongest points will reinforce the moral weight of your case. Try to phrase them in the same language you use to invoke your theme.

Dramatic Impact. Dramatic impact at the beginning of an examination will keep the judge or jury listening. Dramatic impact at the end of the examination will help fix the testimony in their memories.

Undeniability. Choose strong points in the hope that they will be vividly remembered. It will do you little good if they are remembered as being questionable or controverted.

In most cases, of course, it will be necessary to use the opening part of the direct examination to introduce the witness and establish some of her background. Thus, the actual "beginning" of the examination should be understood as the beginning of the substantive testimony.

Start Strong and End Strong: The Sub-examinations

Each full direct examination is actually a combination of many smaller sub-examinations. As you move from topic to topic you are constantly concluding and reinitiating the sub-parts of the direct testimony. The "start strong/end strong" rule should not be applied only to the organization of the full direct; it should also be used to structure its individual components.

In our intersection case you might wish to begin and end the substantive part of the plaintiff's examination with evidence about the fire truck. In between, however, you will cover many other issues, including the plaintiff's background, the scene of the collision, and the plaintiff's damages. Each of these component parts of the direct should, if possible, begin and end on a strong point.

In something as simple as setting the scene, consider what elements of the description are most important to your case. Then begin with one and end with another. In the intersection case you might want to lead off with the clarity of the weather conditions in order to establish visibility. Perhaps you would then conclude the scene-setting portion of the examination with this description of the traffic:

QUESTION:

Of all of the cars that were present, how many stopped for the fire truck?

ANSWER:

All of them, except the defendant.

Use Topical Organization

Chronology is almost always the easiest form of organization. What could be more obvious than beginning at the beginning and ending at the end? In trial advocacy, however, easiest is not always best. In many cases it will be preferable to utilize a topical or thematic form of organization. In this way, you can arrange various components of the witness's testimony to reinforce each other, you can isolate weak points, and you can develop your theory in the most persuasive manner. The order in which events occurred is usually fortuitous. Your duty as an advocate is to rearrange the telling so that the story has maximum logical force.

Assume that you are the prosecutor in a burglary case. Your first witness is the police officer who conducted a stakeout and arrested the defendant on the basis of a description that she received from a superior officer. A strict chronology in such a case could be confusing and counterproductive. The witness would have to begin with the morning of the arrest, perhaps explaining the time that she came on duty, the other matters that she worked on that day, and her instructions in conducting the stakeout. She no doubt would have received the description somewhere in the middle of all this activity. Even if relevant, the importance of the surrounding details is not likely to be well understood at the outset of the examination. The officer, sticking to chronological order, would then describe the people she saw at the stakeout location whom she did not arrest. Finally, the witness would come to the defendant's arrival on the scene. Assume, however, that she did not immediately arrest him. Rather, she observed him for some time; perhaps he even left the scene (and returned) once or twice before the eventual arrest.

In plain chronological order, all of this can add up to a rather diffuse story. The officer's reasons for conducting the stakeout are separated from the activity itself; the receipt of the description has no immediate relationship to the apprehension of the suspect. The trier of fact is required to reflect both forward and back on the significance of the data.

A topical organization, however, could provide a framework that adds clarity and direction to the story. A structure based upon the description of the defendant, rather than chronology, would begin with a description of the arrest itself; then:

QUESTION:

Officer, why did you arrest the defendant?

ANSWER:

Because he fit a description that I had been given earlier of a wanted burglar.

QUESTION:

Did you arrest him as soon as you saw him?

ANSWER:

No. I wanted to make sure that he fit the description completely, so I waited until he was standing directly below a street light.

QUESTION:

Was there anyone else in the vicinity at that time?

ANSWER:

There had been a few people, but nobody who matched the description.

QUESTION:

Officer, please go back and tell us how you received the description that led to the arrest of the defendant.

Even in a matter as simple as our automobile collision case, a strictly chronological direct examination of the plaintiff could fail to be either dramatic or persuasive. Imagine beginning the examination with the time that the plaintiff left home that morning. State her destination and her estimated travel time. Describe the weather and traffic conditions. Trace her route from street to street until she arrives at the fateful intersection. Describe the appearance of the fire truck, the plaintiff's reaction, and finally the collision. After slogging through a series of details, some important and some not, the direct examination finally arrives at the most important event—the accident itself.

It would be more dramatic to (1) begin with the collision, (2) explain why the plaintiff had stopped her car, (3) describe the fire truck, (4) describe the response of the surrounding traffic, and (5) contrast that with the actions of the defendant.

Do Not Interrupt the Action

Every direct examination is likely to involve one, two, or more key events or occurrences. The witness may describe physical activity such as an automobile accident, an arrest, the failure of a piece of equipment, or a surgical procedure. Alternatively, the witness may testify about something less tangible, such as the formation of a contract, the effect of an insult, the making of a threat, the breach of a promise, or the existence of pain following an injury. Whatever the precise subject, it will always be possible to divide the testimony into "action" on the one hand and supporting details and descriptions on the other.

A cardinal rule for the organization of direct examination is never to interrupt the action. Do not disrupt the dramatic flow of your story, the description of the crucial events, in order to fill in minor details. There can be no more jarring or dissatisfying an experience during trial than when the witness, who has just testified to the sound of a gunshot or the screech of automobile tires, is then calmly asked the location of the nearest street light. The lighting conditions may be important, but they cannot possibly be important enough to justify the discontinuity created by fracturing the natural flow of occurrence testimony.

Many lawyers subscribe to the theory that you should "set the scene" before proceeding to the activity. Following this approach in our automobile case, you would first have the witness describe the intersection, the surrounding traffic, the condition of the streets, and the location of her car, all before proceeding to the events of the collision. This approach is based on the concept that the trier of fact can then place the activities within the framework that you have created.

An alternative approach is first to describe the events themselves and then to go back and redescribe them while filling in the details of the scene. Assume that the plaintiff in the automobile case has already testified about the events of the accident. You can now go back to set the scene, effectively telling the story a second time: What were the weather conditions when you entered the block where the collision occurred? How much traffic was there when you first saw the fire truck? What direction were you traveling when the defendant's car struck yours?

Give Separate Attention to the Details

We have seen that details add strength and veracity to a witness's testimony. Unfortunately, they can also detract from the flow of events. It is therefore often best to give separate attention to the details, an approach that also allows you to explain their importance.

Assume, for example, that you are presenting the testimony of a robbery victim and that the central issue in the case is the identification of the defendant. You know that you don't want to detract from the action, so you will present the events of the robbery without interruption. Then you will go back to supply the details that support the witness's ability to identify the defendant:

QUESTION:

How far was the defendant from you when you first noticed him?

ANSWER:

About twelve or fifteen feet.

QUESTION:

How much closer did he come?

ANSWER:

He came right up to me. His face wasn't more than a foot from mine.

QUESTION:

Did you look at his face?

ANSWER:

Yes, absolutely. He stared right at me.

QUESTION:

For how long?

ANSWER:

It was at least a minute.

QUESTION:

Was it still light out?

ANSWER:

Yes, it was.

QUESTION:

Could you see the color of his clothing?

There will be dozens of details available to support the witness's identification. Dispersing them throughout the description of events would both disrupt the testimony and diminish their cumulative importance. The remedy for this problem is to give the details separate attention.

Try Not to Scatter Circumstantial Evidence

Circumstantial evidence is usually defined as indirect proof of a proposition, event, or occurrence. The identity of a burglar, for example, could be proven directly through eyewitness testimony. It could also be proven indirectly through the accumulation of circumstantial evidence such as the following: The defendant was seen near the scene of the burglary on the evening of the crime; her scarf was found in the doorway of the burglarized house; she had been heard complaining about her need for a new radio; two days after the crime she was found in possession of a radio that had been taken in the burglary.

None of the above facts taken individually amount to direct proof that the defendant committed the crime. There could be a perfectly innocent explanation for each one. In combination, however, they raise an extremely compelling inference of guilt. In other words, the indirect circumstances accumulate to establish the likelihood of the prosecution's case.

Inferential evidence is at its strongest when a series of circumstances can be combined to lead to the desired conclusion. It is therefore effective to present all of the related circumstantial evidence at a single point in the direct examination, rather than scatter it throughout. This will not always be possible. The logic of a witness's testimony may require that items of circumstantial evidence be elicited at different points in the testimony. Chronological organization will dictate introducing the circumstances in the order that they occurred or were discovered. Even topical organization may require assigning individual circumstances to separate topics. In the burglary case, for example, a topical approach might divide the testimony into areas such as "condition of the premises" and "apprehension of the defendant." The discovery of the scarf and the recovery of the radio would consequently be separated in the testimony.

Nonetheless, it is a good idea to attempt to cluster your circumstantial evidence. Abandon this technique only when you have settled upon another that you believe will be more effective.

Defensive Direct Examination

From time to time it may be advisable to bring out potentially harmful or embarrassing facts on direct in order to blunt their impact on cross examination. The theory of such "defensive" direct examination is that the bad information will have less sting if the witness offers it herself and, conversely, that it will be all the more damning if the witness is seen as having tried to hide the bad facts. As we noted above, you should conduct a defensive direct examination only when you are sure that the information is known to the other side and will be admissible on cross examination.

Assuming that you have determined to bring out certain damaging information, be sure not to do it at either the beginning or end of the direct examination. Remember the principles of primacy and recency. By definition, bad facts cannot possibly be the strong points of your case, so you will always want to bury them in the middle of the direct examination.

An extremely useful technique is to allow the trier of fact to "make friends" with your witness before you introduce harmful information. It is a normal human tendency to want to believe the best of people whom you like. Thus, you should give the judge or jury every possible reason to like your witness before offering anything that might have a contrary effect. Recall the last time that you saw a television interview of the neighbors of an arrested crime suspect. They almost inevitably say something like, "He was such a nice man. I can't believe that he would do a thing like that."

If, for example, you have a witness who was previously convicted of a felony, you can reasonably assume that to be fair game for cross examination. You will therefore want to bring out the conviction, in sympathetic terms, during your direct examination. Do not elicit such a fact until you have spent some time "personalizing" the witness. Give the trier of fact a reason to discount the conviction before you ever mention it.

Affirmation Before Refutation

Witnesses are often called both to offer affirmative evidence of their own and to refute the testimony of others. In such cases it is usually best to offer the affirmative evidence before proceeding to refutation. In this manner you will accentuate the positive aspects of your case and avoid making the witness appear to be a scold.

As with all principles, this one should not be followed slavishly. Some witnesses are called solely for refutation. Others are far more important for what they negate than for their affirmative information. As a general organizing principle it is useful to think about building your own case before destroying the opposition's.

Get to the Point

A direct examination is not a treasure hunt or murder mystery; there is seldom a reason to keep the trier of fact in suspense. The best form of organization is often to explain exactly where the testimony is headed and then to go directly there.

End with a Clincher

Every examination should end with a clincher, a single fact that capsulizes your trial theory or theme. To qualify as a clincher a fact must be (1) absolutely admissible, (2) reasonably dramatic, (3) simple and memorable, and (4) stated with certainty. Depending upon the nature of the evidence and the theory on which you are proceeding, the final question to the plaintiff in our automobile case might be any of the following:

QUESTION:

How long was the fire engine visible before the defendant's car struck yours?

ANSWER:

It was visible for at least ten seconds because I had already seen it and stopped for a while when the defendant ran into me.

Or,

QUESTION:

Did the defendant start using his cell phone before or after he checked on your injuries?

ANSWER:

He began talking on his telephone without even looking at me.

Or,

QUESTION:

Do you know whether you will ever be able to walk again without pain?

ANSWER:

The doctors say that they can't do anything more for me, but I am still praying.

Ignore Any Rule When Necessary

By now you will no doubt have noticed that the above principles are not completely consistent with one another. In any given case you will probably be unable to start strong, organize topically, and separate the details, while still getting to the point without interrupting the action. Which rules should you follow? The answer lies in your own good judgment and can only be arrived at in the context of a specific case. If you need another principle to help interpret the others, it is this: Apply the rules that best advance your theory and theme.

§ 22C.4 Questioning Technique

Since content is the motive force behind every direct examination, you must use questioning technique to focus attention on the witness and the testimony. It is the witness's story that is central to the direct examination; the style and manner of your questioning should underscore and support the credibility and veracity of that story. The following questioning techniques can help you to achieve that goal.

§ 22C.4.1 Use Short, Open Questions

You want the witness to tell the story. You want the witness to be the center of attention. You want the witness to be appreciated and believed. None of these things can happen if you do all of the talking. Therefore, ask short questions.

Using short questions will help you to refrain from talking, but not every short question will get the witness talking. To do that, you will need open questions.

Don't ask a witness, "Did you go to the bank?" The answer to that short question will probably be an even shorter "Yes." Instead, as much of your direct examination as possible should consist of questions that invite the witness to describe, explain, and illuminate the events of her testimony. Ask questions such as these:

QUESTION:

Where did you go that day?

QUESTION:

What happened after that?

QUESTION:

Tell us who was there.

QUESTION:

What else happened?

QUESTION:

Describe where you were.

Your witness will almost always be more memorable and believable if you can obtain most of her information in her own words. Short, open questions will advance that goal.

§ 22C.4.2 Use Directive and Transitional Questions

You cannot use open questions to begin an examination or to move from one area of the examination to another. To do so you would have to start with

"When were you born?" and proceed to ask "What happened next?" in almost endless repetition.

A better approach is to use directive and transitional questions. Directive questions, quite simply, direct the witness's attention to the topic that you want to cover. Suppose that you want the witness to address the issue of damages. Ask,

QUESTION:

Were you in any pain after the accident?

Having directed the witness's attention, you can now revert to your short, open questions:

QUESTION:

Please describe how you felt.

QUESTION:

Where else did you hurt?

QUESTION:

How has this affected your life?

You may need to use more than one directive question during any particular line of testimony. To fill out the subject of damages, for example, you may need to ask additional questions such as,

QUESTION:

Do you currently suffer any physical disabilities?

Or,

QUESTION:

Did you ever have such pains before the accident?

Remember that the purpose of a directive question is to direct the witness's attention, not to divert the jury's.

Another problem with short, open questions is that they are not very good at underscoring the relationship between one fact and another. The best way to do this is through "transitional" questions that utilize one fact as the predicate, or introduction, to another. Here are some examples of transitional questions:

QUESTION:

After you saw the fire truck, what did you do?

QUESTION:

Do you know what the defendant did as the other traffic slowed to a stop?

QUESTION:

Once the defendant's car hit yours, did you see him do anything?

Note that directive and transitional questions will tend to be leading. As a technical matter, however, these questions are permissible so long as they are used to orient the witness, expedite the testimony, or introduce a new area of the examination. As a practical matter, objections to directive and transitional questions are not likely to be sustained so long as they are used relatively sparingly and are not asked in a tone that seems to insist upon a certain answer. It is unethical to abuse transitional or directive questions in a way that substitutes your testimony for that of the witness.

§ 22C.4.3 Reinitiate Primacy

The doctrine of primacy tells us that the trier of fact will pay maximum attention to the witness at the very beginning of the testimony. You can make further use of this principle by continuously "re-beginning" the examination. That is, every time you seem to start anew, you will refocus the attention of the judge or jury. This technique can be called reinitiating primacy, and there are several ways to achieve it:

Use General Headline Questions

Most direct examinations, including even those that are organized chronologically, will consist of a number of individual areas of inquiry. If you treat each such area as a separate examination you can reinitiate primacy every time you move to a new topic. You can divide the direct into a series of smaller examinations through the use of verbal headlines. Rather than simply move from area to area, insert a headline to alert the judge or jury to the fact that you are shifting gears or changing subjects.

The introduction should be overt. Don't ask,

QUESTION:

What happened as you were driving south on Sheridan Road?

Instead, announce the new subject by asking,

QUESTION:

Were you involved in an accident at the corner of Sheridan and Chase?

Similar headlines might include:

QUESTION:

Had you kept your own car in good repair?

Or,

QUESTION:

Were you hospitalized?

Or,

QUESTION:

Are you still disabled today?

None of these introductory questions would really be necessary to begin the particular segment of testimony. You could simply proceed to the detailed questioning, relying upon the witness to provide the necessary information. You could also write an entire novel without using chapter titles, paragraphs, or even punctuation. The headline question, however, serves the same function as a chapter heading in a book. It divides the "text" and reinitiates primacy.

Explain Where You Are Going

You can reinitiate primacy even more directly through the use of a few, well-chosen, declaratory statements. Everything that you say during a direct examination does not have to be in the form of a question. You may say to the witness, "Let's talk about the aftermath of the accident," or, "We need to move on to the subject of your injuries." Such statements are permissible so long as they are truly used to make the transition from one part of the testimony to another or to orient the witness in some other manner. You cannot, of course, use declaratory statements to instruct the witness how to testify.

Use Body Movement

Another way to segment your examination, and thereby reinitiate primacy, is through the use of body movement. Most jurisdictions, although not all, allow lawyers to move rather freely about the courtroom as they conduct their examinations. Unless you are in a court that requires you to remain seated at counsel table or standing at a lectern, you can effectively announce the beginning of a new topic by pausing for a moment and then moving purposefully to a different part of the room. You needn't stride dramatically—a few short steps will usually suffice.

The key to this technique is to stop talking as you move. The silence and movement will reinforce each other, making it clear that one topic has ended and another is about to begin.

§ 22C.4.4 Use Incremental Questions

Information usually can be obtained in either large or small pieces. Incremental questions break the "whole" into its component pieces so that the testimony can be delivered in greater, and therefore more persuasive, detail.

A large, nonincremental question might be,

QUESTION:

What did the robber look like?

Even a well-prepared witness will probably answer this question with a fairly general description. A common response might be,

ANSWER:

He was a white male, about twenty or twenty-five years old, maybe six feet tall.

You might be able to go back to supply any omitted information, but in doing so you will risk giving the unfortunate impression of doing just that—filling in gaps in the witness's testimony. Furthermore, at some point in the backtracking a judge might sustain an objection on the ground that the question—"Describe the robber"—had been asked and answered.

An incremental approach to the issue of identification, on the other hand, would be built upon a set of questions such as these:

QUESTION:

Were you able to get a good look at the robber?

ANSWER:

Yes, I was able to see him clearly.

QUESTION:

How tall was he?

ANSWER:

About six feet tall.

QUESTION:

How heavy was he?

ANSWER:

He was heavy, almost fat, over 200 pounds.

QUESTION:

What race was he?

ANSWER:

He was white.

QUESTION:

And his complexion?

ANSWER:

He was very fair, with freckles.

QUESTION:

What color was his hair?

ANSWER:

He was blond.

QUESTION:

How was his hair cut?

ANSWER:

It wasn't really cut at all—just sort of long and stringy.

QUESTION:

Did he have any facial hair?

ANSWER:

A small mustache.

QUESTION:

Could you see his eyes?

ANSWER:

Yes, he came right up to me.

QUESTION:

What color were they?

ANSWER:

Blue.

QUESTION:

Was he wearing glasses?

ANSWER:

Yes, he was.

QUESTION:

What sort of frames?

ANSWER:

Round wire rims.

QUESTION:

Did he have any scars or marks?

ANSWER:

Yes, he had a birthmark on his forehead.

QUESTION:

Was he wearing a jacket?

ANSWER:

He had on a Philadelphia Flyers jacket.

Depending upon the witness's knowledge, further questions could inquire into other facts. Could the witness see the robber's shirt? What color was it? His trousers? His shoes? Any jewelry? Tattoos?

As you can plainly see, the use of incremental questions, each seeking a single small bit of information, can drive home the accuracy of the identification without seeming to put words in the witness's mouth.

The incremental technique should be used sparingly. It will not work as an overall principle since the unrestrained use of details will quickly overwhelm the trier of fact. Use it only where the details are available, significant, and convincing.

First and foremost, the details must be available. It will only damage your case for you to ask a series of incremental questions that elicit negative or blank responses.

Second, the details must be significant. You will produce only boredom by providing every conceivable detail regarding every conceivable fact. No one will be interested in the location of the bell on the fire truck or the number of spots on the fire house dalmatian. Rather, you want the fine emphasis on small facts to come as a clear departure from the balance of the examination. What you are implying by the shift should be obvious: "Details weren't crucial before, but they are now. So pay close attention."

Finally, the incremental details have to be convincing; they have to lend verity to the larger point that you are trying to establish. Some details will be meaningless. It is unlikely to help an identification, for example, for the witness to testify that the robber was chewing gum. Other details may not be credible. Even if the witness claims absolute certainty, you probably won't want to offer testimony about the number of fillings in the assailant's teeth.

§ 22C.4.5 Reflect Time, Distance, Intensity

The very best direct examinations virtually re-create the incidents they describe, drawing verbal images that all but place the trier of fact at the scene of the events. Your pace and manner of questioning are essential to this process.

The timing or duration of an event, for example, is often crucial in a trial; one side claims that things happened quickly and the other asserts that they were drawn out. It is possible to use the pace of questioning to support your particular theory. Assume that you represent the defendant in our fire truck case. His defense is that the fire engine appeared only a moment before the collision and that he just didn't have enough time to stop his car. The goal of the defendant's direct examination must be to re-create that scene by collapsing the time available to react to the fire truck. Hence, you will ask only a few, fast-paced questions:

QUESTION:

When did the fire truck first become visible?

ANSWER:

It approached the intersection just as I did.

QUESTION:

What was the very first action that you took?

ANSWER:

I slammed on my brakes.

QUESTION:

How much time did that take?

ANSWER:

Less than a second.

Note that this direct examination proceeds quickly, emphasizing both short-ness of time and immediacy of response. This result will be enhanced if you fire off the questions, and if the witness doesn't pause before answering. Strive for the appearance of all but panting for breath.

In contrast, the plaintiff will claim that there was ample time for the defen-dant to stop. Her direct examination should therefore be drawn out in order to demonstrate exactly how much time there was:

QUESTION:

Where was the fire truck when you first saw it?

ANSWER:

It was about a quarter of a block away from the intersection.

QUESTION:

How far away from you was it?

ANSWER:

About one-hundred yards.

QUESTION:

How many other cars were between you and the fire truck?

ANSWER:

Three or four.

QUESTION:

What did they do in response?

ANSWER:

They all stopped.

QUESTION:

How long did it take those other cars to stop?

ANSWER:

Normal stopping time—a few seconds.

QUESTION:

What was the first thing that you did?

ANSWER:

I started to pull over to the side.

QUESTION:

How long did that take?

ANSWER:

Five seconds or so.

QUESTION:

What did you do after that?

ANSWER:

I brought my car to a stop.

QUESTION:

How long did that take?

ANSWER:

Well, I applied my brakes right away, and it took a few seconds for the car to stop.

QUESTION:

Then what happened?

ANSWER:

That's when the other car rear-ended me.

QUESTION:

How much time elapsed between the moment when you first saw the fire truck and the time that the defendant's car hit yours?

ANSWER:

At least ten or fifteen seconds.

There is every reason not to hurry through this part of the examination. The length, detail, and pace of your questions should be used to demonstrate the validity of your theory: The defendant had plenty of time to stop.

Similar techniques can be used to establish distance and intensity. Draw out your questions to maximize distance; move through them quickly to minimize it. Ask questions at a rapid pace to enhance the intensity of an encounter; slow down to make the situation more relaxed.

A word about ethics is important at this point. Lawyers are often accused of using verbal tricks to turn night into day. That is not what we are discussing here. Rather, the purpose of using "reflective" questioning is just the opposite—to insure that the witness conveys her intended meaning. The techniques and examination styles discussed above are not deceptive, but are useful to illuminate or underscore the content of a witness's testimony. If a witness says that an event took only moments, you can assist in the accurate presentation of that testimony by using a questioning style reflective of suddenness and speed. Use of the wrong style can actually inhibit the witness's communication and positively mislead the trier of fact.

§ 22C.4.6 Repeat Important Points

In every direct examination there will be several essential ideas that stand out as far more important than the rest. Do not be satisfied to elicit those points only once. Repeat them. Restate them. Then repeat them again. Then think of ways to restate them again. Since you are not allowed to ask the same question twice (Objection: asked and answered), you will need to employ your lawyer's creativity to fashion numerous slightly different questions, each stressing the same point. Repetition is the parent of retention, and your most important points should arise again and again throughout the testimony to insure that they are retained by the trier of fact.

The corollary to this principle is that less important points should not be repeated in like manner. Increased attention should be used to make key subjects stand out. If too many points are given this treatment they will all be made to seem equally unimportant. How do you decide which facts are sufficiently important to bear repetition? The answer is to consider your theory and theme. You will want to repeat those facts that are basic to your logical theory and those that best evoke your moral theme.

In our automobile accident case the gist of the plaintiff's theory is that she stopped for a passing fire truck while the defendant did not. Her single most important fact is definitely the observable presence of the fire truck. Thus, the words "fire truck" should be inserted at every reasonable point during the examination. At the close of her testimony you want to have created the image that the fire truck dominated the scenery. How many different ways can the witness describe the fire truck? In how many locations can she place it? How many ways can she use it as a reference point for other testimony?

Thematic repetition may be more elusive or subtle. If the plaintiff's theme is that the defendant was "too busy to be careful," you will want to use repetition to emphasize how unbusy the plaintiff was.

Bench and jury trials differ significantly regarding the use of repetition. Juries consist of six or twelve individuals whose attention may sometimes drift. You can never be certain that every juror will have heard and retained every point, so repetition is particularly important. You not only need to drive your key points home, you need to drive them home to everyone. Judges are usually aware of this problem, and they typically will allow a fair amount of latitude for repetition during jury trials.

Bench trials are a different matter. Judges usually expect bench trials to move along swiftly. They don't like to be battered with constant reiteration of the same points. Of course, judges may also be inattentive, but they don't like to be reminded of it. In short, many judges do not like to be treated like jurors, and they will cut off attempts at repetition. Use this technique sparingly in bench trials.

§ 22C.4.7 Use Visual Aids

Seeing is believing. In daily life we are accustomed to receiving as much as seventy percent of our information through the sense of sight. Ordinary witness testimony is received primarily through the sense of hearing. This makes it harder to follow and harder to retain. You can enhance the effectiveness of almost any witness by illustrating the testimony through the use of charts, photographs, maps, models, drawings, and other visual aids.

Always consider whether the witness's testimony can be illustrated. If the witness is going to testify about a pivotal document, determine whether it can be enlarged or projected on a screen in the courtroom. If the witness is going to testify about an event, create a map or produce an oversize photograph. If the witness will testify about a series of numbers or transactions, use a visual "time line" as your visual aid.

Demonstrations can also serve as visual aids. Ask the witness to re-enact crucial events or to re-create important sounds. "Please show the jury exactly how the defendant raised his hand before he struck you." "Please clap your hands together to show us how loud the sound was." "Please repeat the plaintiff's words in exactly her tone of voice."

Demonstrations must be carefully planned. They have an inevitable tendency to backfire when ill-prepared. Be certain that your expectations are realistic. A witness will not be able to illustrate the loudness of a rifle shot by clapping her hands. Nor will a witness be able to demonstrate the movement of a vehicle by walking about the courtroom. Finally, make sure that your demonstration doesn't look silly. Many lawyers have lost more ground than they gained by asking witnesses to roll around on the floor, climb up on chairs, or dash from one end of the courtroom to the other.

§ 22C.4.8 Avoid Negative, Lawyerly, and Complex Questions

For reasons unknown and unknowable, many lawyers think that it makes them sound more professional when they phrase questions in the negative:

QUESTION:

Did you not then go to the telephone?

No advocate, judge, juror, witness, English teacher, or speaker of our common language can possibly understand the meaning of that question. Even harder to understand are the two potential answers. What would "yes" mean? "Yes, I did not then go to the telephone?" Or, "Yes, I did." What would "no" mean? "No, I did then go to the telephone?" Or, "No, I didn't."

Furthermore, on direct examination your goal typically is to establish an affirmative case. It is therefore beneficial to phrase your questions so that your witnesses can answer them affirmatively. Do not use negative questions.

You must also avoid "lawyer talk." Many jurors and witnesses will not understand lawyerese and virtually all will resent it. On the other hand, everyone, including judges, will appreciate plain language. Do not ask,

QUESTION:

At what point in time did you alight from your vehicle?

Ask instead,

QUESTION:

When did you get out of your car?

Do not ask,

QUESTION:

What was your subsequent activity, conduct, or response with regard to the negotiation of an offer and acceptance?

Opt for,

QUESTION:

What did you agree to next?

Finally, do not pose questions that call for more than a single item or category of information. Although a witness may be able to sort through a fairly simple compound question—such as, "Where did you go and what did you do?"— many will become confused, and more will simply fail to answer the second part. Truly complex questions will almost certainly fail to elicit the answer that you seek.

Part 22D: Cross Examination*

by Steven Lubet[4]

§ 22D.1 The Role of Cross Examination

Cross examination is hard. It is frequently dramatic, often exciting, and in many ways it defines our adversarial system of justice. At bottom, however, cross examination is the ultimate challenge for the trial lawyer. Can you add to your case or detract from the opposition's case by extracting information from the other side's witnesses?

If direct examination is your best opportunity to win your case, cross examination may provide you with a chance to lose it. A poor direct can be aimless and boring, but the witnesses are generally helpful. Your worst fear on direct examination is usually that you have left something out. A poor cross examination, on the other hand, can be truly disastrous. The witnesses can range from uncooperative to hostile, and you constantly run the risk of actually adding weight or sympathy to the other side's case. Moreover, most cross examinations will inevitably be perceived by the trier of fact as a contest between the lawyer and witness. You can seldom afford to appear to lose.

In other words, cross examination is inherently risky. The witness may argue with you. The witness may fill in gaps that were left in the direct testimony. The witness may make you look bad. You may make yourself look bad. And whatever good you accomplish may be subject to immediate cure on redirect examination.

None of these problems can be avoided entirely, but they can be minimized. Although some cross examination is usually expected of every witness, and the temptation is difficult to resist, as a general rule you should cross examine carefully. You must always set realistic goals.

Brevity is an excellent discipline. Many trial lawyers suggest that cross examinations be limited to a maximum of three points. While there may often be reasons to depart from such a hard and fast rule, there is no doubt that short

---

* This material appears in *Modern Trial Advocacy: Analysis and Practice*, 3rd Edition, copyright © 2004, National Institute for Trial Advocacy (NITA). Reproduced with permission from the National Institute for Trial Advocacy. The NACC is grateful to NITA for permitting the use of these materials as a gift to the child advocacy community. The NACC highly recommends the full publication of *Modern Trial Advocacy* and additional NITA trial skill material available at www.NITA.org or 800-225-6482.

Editor's Note: Nonsubstantive changes have been made to the text and formatting to reflect the style of this publication. Section numbers have also been added to reflect the style of this publication.

[4] Steven Lubet, J.D., is Professor of Law at Northwestern University School of Law in Chicago, Illinois.

cross examinations have much to commend themselves. In terms of your own preparation, setting a mental limit for the length of the cross will help you to concentrate and to organize your thinking. Actually conducting a short examination will minimize risk, add panache, and usually make the result more memorable.

This chapter discusses the general law, content, organization, and basic technique of cross examination. Several more advanced aspects of cross examination—such as impeachment and the use of character evidence—are treated separately in later chapters.

§ 22D.2 The Law of Cross Examination

Cross examination is the hallmark of the Anglo-American system of adversary justice. Protected as a constitutional right in criminal cases, it is also understood as an aspect of due process in civil cases. The law of cross examination varies somewhat from jurisdiction to jurisdiction, but the following rules are nearly universal.

§ 22D.2.1 Leading Questions Permitted

The most obvious distinction between direct and cross examination is the permissible use of leading questions. It is assumed that your adversary's witnesses will have little incentive to cooperate with you, and that you may not have been able to interview them in advance. Consequently, virtually all courts allow the cross examiner to ask questions that contain their own answers. Moreover, the right to ask leading questions is usually understood to include the right to insist on a responsive answer.

As we will see below, the ability to use leading questions has enormous implications for the conduct of cross examination.

§ 22D.2.2 Limitations on Scope

The general rule in the United States is that cross examination is limited to the scope of the direct. Since the purpose of cross examination is to allow you to inquire of your adversary's witnesses, the scope of the inquiry is restricted to those subjects that were raised during the direct examination.

Note that the definition of scope will vary from jurisdiction to jurisdiction, and even from courtroom to courtroom. A narrow application of this rule can limit the cross examiner to the precise events and occurrences that the witness discussed on direct. A broader approach would allow questioning on related and similar events. For example, assume that the defendant in our collision case testified that his brakes had been inspected just a week before the accident. A strict approach to the "scope of direct" rule might limit the cross examination to questioning on that particular inspection. A broader interpretation would allow inquiries into earlier brake inspections and other aspects of automobile maintenance.

A more generous approach to the scope of cross examination is definitely the modern trend. Undue restriction of cross examination can result in reversal on appeal. Nonetheless, there is no way to predict how an individual judge will apply the scope limitation in any given case; much will depend on the nature of the evidence and the manner in which the lawyers have been conducting themselves.

A few American jurisdictions have adopted the "English rule," which allows wide-open cross examination concerning any issue relevant to the case. In the federal jurisdiction, and some others, the trial judge has discretion to allow inquiry beyond the scope of the direct examination, but the cross examiner is then limited to non-leading questions. Also, in most states a criminal defendant who takes the stand and waives the Fifth Amendment is thereafter subject to cross examination regarding all aspects of the alleged crime.

There are two general exceptions to the "scope of direct" rule. First, the credibility of the witness is always in issue. You may therefore always attempt to establish the bias, motive, interest, untruthfulness, or material prior inconsistency of a witness without regard to the matters that were covered on direct examination. Second, you may cross examine beyond the scope of the direct once the witness herself has "opened the door" to additional matters. In other words, a witness who voluntarily injects a subject into an answer on cross examination may thereafter be questioned as though the subject had been included in the direct.

§ 22D.2.3 Other Restrictions

Cross examination is also limited by a variety of other rules, most of which involve the manner or nature of questioning.

Argumentative Questions

You may ask a witness questions. You may suggest answers. You may assert propositions. But you may not argue with the witness. As you may have guessed, the definition of an argumentative question is elusive. Much will depend on your demeanor; perhaps an argumentative question is one that is asked in an argumentative tone. The following is a reasonable working definition: An argumentative question insists that the witness agree with an opinion or characterization, as opposed to a statement of fact.

Intimidating Behavior

You are entitled to elicit information on cross examination by asking questions of the witness and insisting upon answers. You are not allowed to loom over the witness, to shout, to make threatening gestures, or otherwise to intimidate, bully, or (yes, here it comes) badger the witness.

Unfair Characterizations

Your right to lead the witness does not include a right to mislead the witness. It is objectionable to attempt to mischaracterize a witness's testimony or to ask "trick" questions. If a witness has testified that it was dark outside, it would mischaracterize the testimony to begin a question, "So you admit that it was too dark to see anything …." Trick questions cannot be answered accurately. The most famous trick question is known as the "negative pregnant," as in Senator McCarthy's inquisitional, "Have you resigned from the Communist Party?"

Assuming Facts

A frequently heard objection is that "Counsel has assumed facts not in evidence." Of course, a cross examiner is frequently allowed to inquire as to facts that are not yet in evidence. This objection should only be sustained when the question uses the non-record fact as a premise rather than as a separate subject of inquiry, thus denying the witness the opportunity to deny its validity. Imagine a witness in the fire truck case who was standing on the sidewalk at the time of the accident. Assume that the witness testified on direct that the defendant never even slowed down before the impact, and that the witness said absolutely nothing about having been drinking that morning. At the outset of the cross examination, then, there would be no "facts in evidence" concerning use of alcohol. The cross examiner is certainly entitled to ask questions such as, "Hadn't you been drinking that morning?" The cross examiner should not be allowed, however, to use an assumption about drinking to serve as the predicate for a different question: "Since you had been drinking, you were on foot instead of in your car that morning?" The problem with this sort of bootstrapping is that it doesn't allow the witness a fair opportunity to deny having been drinking in the first place.

Compound and Other Defective Questions

Compound questions contain more than a single inquiry: "Are you related to the plaintiff, and were you wearing your glasses at the time of the accident?" The question is objectionable since any answer will necessarily be ambiguous. Cumulative or "Asked and Answered" questions are objectionable because they cover the same ground twice (or more). Vague questions are objectionable because they tend to elicit vague answers.

§ 22D.3 The Content of Cross Examination

The first question concerning any cross examination is whether it should be brief or extensive. Although it is standard advice in many quarters that you should refrain from cross examining a witness who hasn't hurt you, in practice almost every witness is subjected to at least a short cross examination. You will seldom wish to leave the testimony of an adverse witness appear to go entirely unchallenged. Moreover, as we will see below, there will often be opportunities to use cross examination to establish positive, constructive evidence. The most realistic decision, then, is not whether to cross examine, but how much. This evaluation must be made at least twice: once in your pretrial preparation and again at the end of the direct examination.

In preparation, you must consider the potential direct examination. What do you expect the witness to say, and how, if at all, will you need to challenge or add to the direct? At trial you must make a further determination. Did the actual direct examination proceed as you expected? Was it more or less damaging than you anticipated? You must always reevaluate your cross examination strategy in light of the direct testimony that was eventually produced. This process will often lead you to omit portions of your prepared cross because they have become unnecessary. It is considerably more dangerous to elaborate on or add to your plan, although this is occasionally unavoidable. In either situation always remember the risk inherent in cross examination and ask yourself, "Is this cross examination necessary?"

§ 22D.3.1 Consider the Purposes of Cross Examination

Though often an invigorating exercise, cross examination should be undertaken only to serve some greater purpose within your theory of the case. A useful cross examination should promise to fulfill at least one of the following objectives:

Repair or Minimize Damage. Did the direct examination hurt your case? If so, can the harm be rectified or minimized? Can the witness be made to retract or back away from certain testimony? Can additional facts be elicited that will minimize the witness's impact?

Enhance your Case. Can the cross examination be used to further one of your claims or defenses? Are there positive facts that can be brought out that will support or contribute to your version of events?

Detract from their Case. Conversely, can the cross examination be used to establish facts that are detrimental to your opponent's case? Can it be used to create inconsistencies among the other side's witnesses?

Establish Foundation. Is the witness necessary to the proper foundation for the introduction of a document or other exhibit, or for the offer of evidence by another witness?

Discredit Direct Testimony. Is it possible to discredit the witness's direct testimony through means such as highlighting internal inconsistencies, demonstrating the witness's own lack of certainty or confidence, underscoring lack of opportunity to observe, illustrating the inherent implausibility of the testimony, or showing that it conflicts with the testimony of other, more credible witnesses?

Discredit the Witness. Can the witness be shown to be biased or interested in the outcome of the case? Does the witness have a reason to stretch, misrepresent, or fabricate the testimony? Has the witness been untruthful in the past? Can it be shown that the witness is otherwise unworthy of belief?

Reflect on the Credibility of Another. Can the cross examination be used to reflect, favorably or unfavorably, on the credibility of a different witness?

The length of your cross examination will generally depend upon how many of the above goals you expect to be able to fulfill. It is not necessary, and it may not be possible, to attempt to achieve them all. You will often stand to lose more by over-reaching than you can possibly gain by seeking to cover all of the bases in cross examination. Be selective.

§ 22D.3.2 Arrive at the "Usable Universe" of Cross Examination

The Entire Universe

In preparing to cross examine any witness you must first determine the broadest possible scope, or universe, for the potential cross examination. From a review of all of the available materials and documents, construct a comprehensive list of the information available from the witness. In keeping with the purposes of cross examination, place each potential fact in one of the following categories:

- Does it make my case more likely?

- Does it make their case less likely?

- Is it a predicate to the admissibility of other evidence?

- Does it make some witness more believable?

- Does it make some witness less believable?

This process will give you the full universe of theoretically desirable information from which you will structure your cross examination.

The Usable Universe

You must now evaluate all of the potential facts in order to arrive at your "usable universe." Ask yourself the following questions:

Is a friendly witness available to present the same facts? There may be no point in attempting to extract answers from an unwilling source if a friendly witness can provide you with the same information. On cross examination you always run the risk that the witness will argue or hedge, or that the information will not be developed as clearly as you would like. Unless you stand to benefit specifically from repetition of the testimony, you may prefer to bypass cross examination that will be merely cumulative of your own evidence.

Can the information be obtained only on cross examination? You have no choice but to cross examine on important facts that are solely within the knowledge or control of the adverse witness. Such information will range from the foundation for the admission of a document to evidence of the witness's own prior actions.

Will the facts be uniquely persuasive on cross examination? Some information, though available from a variety of sources, will be particularly valuable when elicited on cross examination. For example, evidence of past wrongdoing may be more credible if it is presented as an admission by the witness herself rather than as an accusation coming from another. In the automobile accident case, consider the different ways in which evidence of the defendant's driving habits could be admitted. You could produce your own witness to testify that the defendant was a constant speeder. You would have to lay a foundation for this testimony, establishing both the witness's personal knowledge and the consistency of the defendant's "habit." Additionally, your witness would then be subject to cross examination not only on the foundation for the testimony but also regarding issues such as bias, accuracy, and opportunity to observe. On the other hand, the defendant's own testimony that he loved driving fast cars would be virtually uncontrovertible. It would also bolster the testimony of your own witnesses to the same effect. When possible, it is generally desirable to obtain negative or contested evidence from the mouths of the opposition witnesses.

How certain is it that the witness will agree with you? Certain information may be completely within the control of a witness for the other side, and it may be uniquely persuasive if elicited during the cross examination of that witness. You must nonetheless consider the contingency that the witness will deny you the answer that you want. You may need to abandon or modify a promising line of cross examination if you do not believe that you will be able to compel the answers that you anticipate. Can the information be confirmed by the witness's own prior statements? Can it be documented through the use of reports, photographs, tests, or other evidence? These and other devices for controlling a witness's testimony on cross examination are discussed in later sections.

The construction of your usable universe depends almost entirely on your mastery of the case as a whole. To prepare for cross examination you must know not only everything that the particular witness is liable to say but also every other fact that might be obtained from any other witness, document, or exhibit. Your effective choice of cross examination topics will be determined by your ability to choose those areas that will do you the most good, while risking the least harm.

§ 22D.3.3 Risk Averse Preparation

There are many ways to prepare for cross examination. The following is a "risk averse" method designed to result in a solid, if generally unflashy, cross that minimizes the potential for damage to your case.

Risk averse preparation for cross examination begins with consideration of your anticipated final argument. What do you want to be able to say about this particular witness when you address the jury at the end of the case? How much of that information do you expect to be included in the direct examination? The balance is what you will need to cover on cross.

Next, write out the portion of a final argument that you would devote to discussing the facts presented by this particular witness. This will at most serve as a draft for your actual closing, and you should limit this text to the facts contained in the witness's testimony. You need not include the characterizations, inferences, arguments, comments, and thematic references that will also be part of your real final argument. Depending upon the importance of the witness, the length of this argument segment can range from a short paragraph to a full page or more.

It is important that you write your text using short, single-thought, strictly factual sentences. You are not attempting to create literature. Do not worry about continuity, style, or transition. Simply arrange the declarative sentences one after another in the order that you believe will be the most persuasive, referring to the witness in the third person. For example, your argument concerning the defendant in the fire truck case might, assuming that all of these facts were readily available, include the following:

The defendant awoke on the morning of the accident at 7:00 a.m. He had to be downtown later that morning. He was meeting an important new client. He wanted to get that client's business. He stood to make a lot of money. The meeting was scheduled for 8:30 a.m. The defendant lived 16 miles from his office. He rented a monthly parking spot. That spot was in a garage located two blocks from his office. He left his home at 7:55 a.m. There was a lot of traffic that morning. The accident occurred at an intersection seven miles from downtown. It happened at 8:20 a.m.

An effective paragraph will include the facts that underlie your theory of the case. It should now be a simple matter to convert the text into a cross examination plan. You merely need to take each sentence and rephrase it into a second-person question. In fact, it is often best to leave the sentence in the form of a declaration, technically making it a question through voice inflection or by adding an interrogative phrase at the end. The above paragraph then becomes the following cross examination of the defendant:

QUESTION:

You awoke at 7:00 a.m. on the morning of the accident, isn't that right?

QUESTION:

You had to be downtown later that morning, correct?

QUESTION:

You were meeting an important new client?

QUESTION:

You wanted to get that client's business?

QUESTION:

You stood to make a lot of money?

QUESTION:

The meeting was scheduled for 8:30 a.m., correct?

QUESTION:

You lived 16 miles from your office?

QUESTION:

You rented a monthly parking spot?

QUESTION:

That spot was in a garage located two blocks from your office?

QUESTION:

You left your home at 7:55 a.m., right?

QUESTION:

There was a lot of traffic that morning?

QUESTION:

The accident occurred at an intersection seven miles from downtown?

QUESTION:

It happened at 8:20 a.m., isn't that right?

Note that the above questions also fit neatly into the "usable universe." Many of the facts are not likely to be available from friendly witnesses. Most others are of the sort that will be most valuable if conceded by the defendant himself. Finally, the facts are nearly all of the sort that can be independently documented or that the defendant is unlikely to deny.

This technique is useful for developing the content of your cross examination. The organization of the examination and the structure of your individual questions will depend upon additional analysis.

§ 22D.4 The Organization of Cross Examination

§ 22D.4.1 Organizing Principles

As with direct examination, the organization of a cross examination can be based on the four principles of primacy and recency, apposition, repetition, and duration. Unlike direct examination, however, on cross examination you will often have to deal with a recalcitrant witness. You may therefore have to temper your plan in recognition of this reality, occasionally sacrificing maximum clarity and persuasion in order to avoid "telegraphing" your strategy to the uncooperative witness. Thus, we must include the additional organizing principles of indirection and misdirection when planning cross examinations.

Three further concepts are basic to the organization, presentation, and technique of virtually every cross examination.

First, cross examination is your opportunity to tell part of your client's story in the middle of the other side's case. Your object is to focus attention away from the witness's direct testimony and onto matters that you believe are helpful. On cross examination, you want to tell the story. To do so, you must always be in control of the testimony and the witness.

Second, cross examination is never the time to attempt to gather new information. Never ask a witness a question simply because you want to find out the answer. Rather, cross examination must be used to establish or enhance the facts that you have already discovered.

Finally, an effective cross examination often succeeds through the use of implication and innuendo. It is not necessary, and it is often harmful, to ask a witness the "ultimate question." Final argument is your opportunity to point out the relationship between facts, make characterizations, and draw conclusions based upon the accumulation of details. Do not expect an opposing witness to do this for you.

Lay the groundwork for your eventual argument, then stop. This technique is premised on the assumption that many witnesses will be reluctant to concede facts that will later prove to be damaging or embarrassing. Thus, it may be necessary to avoid informing the witness of the ultimate import of the particular inquiry. This can be accomplished through indirect questioning, which seeks first to establish small and uncontrovertible factual components of a theory and only later addresses the theory itself.

For example, a witness may be loath to admit having read a certain document before signing it; perhaps the written statement contains damaging admissions that the witness would prefer to disclaim. Direct questioning, therefore, would be unlikely to produce the desired result. The witness, if asked, will deny having read the item in question. Indirect questioning, however, may be able to establish the point:

QUESTION:

You are a businessman?

QUESTION:

Many documents cross your desk each day?

QUESTION:

It is your job to read and respond to them?

QUESTION:

Your company relies upon you to be accurate?

QUESTION:

You often must send written replies?

QUESTION:

Large amounts of money can change hands on the basis of the replies that you send?

QUESTION:

You have an obligation to your company to be careful about its money?

QUESTION:

So you must be careful about what you write?

QUESTION:

Of course, that includes your signature?

By this point you should have obtained through indirection that which the witness would not have conceded directly. The final question should be superfluous.

Misdirection is an arch-relative of indirection, used when the witness is thought to be particularly deceptive or untruthful. Here the cross examiner not only conceals the object of the examination, but actually attempts to take advantage of the witness's own inclination to be uncooperative. Knowing that the witness will tend to fight the examination, the lawyer creates, and then exploits, a "misdirected" image. In our fire truck case, for example, the defendant is extremely unlikely to admit that he should have seen the fire engine; perhaps he would go so far as to deny the obvious. The lawyer may therefore misdirect the defendant's attention, as follows:

QUESTION:

Isn't it true that you expected to see a fire truck at that corner?

ANSWER:

Certainly not, I never expected a fire truck.

QUESTION:

You weren't looking for a fire truck?

ANSWER:

No.

QUESTION:

You didn't keep your eye out for one?

ANSWER:

No.

QUESTION:

And you never saw one?

ANSWER:

No.

QUESTION:

Until, of course, after it was too late?

To be effective in the use of this technique, the cross examination must be organized first to obtain the "misdirected" denial. Note that the above example would not work at all if the questions were asked in the opposite order. In other words, the principle of misdirection works best with an intentionally elusive witness who needs only to be given sufficient initial rope with which to hoist himself.

§ 22D.4.2 Guidelines for Organization

There are many ways in which you can employ the principles discussed above.

Do Not Worry About Starting Strong

It would be desirable to be able to begin every cross examination with a strong, memorable point that absolutely drives home your theory and theme. Unfortunately, this will not always be possible. Many cross examinations will have to begin with a shake-down period during which you acclimate yourself to the tenor of the witness's responses, and when you also attempt to put the witness in a cooperative frame of mind. Unless you are able to start off with a true bombshell, it will usually be preferable to take the time necessary to establish predicate facts through indirection.

Use Topical Organization

Topical organization is essential in cross examination. Your goal on cross examination is not to retell the witness's story, but rather to establish a small number of additional or discrediting points. A topical format will be the most effective in allowing you to move from area to area. Moreover, topical organization also allows you to take maximum advantage of apposition, indirection, and misdirection. You can use it to cluster facts in the same manner that you would on direct examination or to separate facts in order to avoid showing your hand to the witness.

Assume that you want to use the cross examination of the defendant in the automobile accident to show how busy he was on the day of the collision. You know that he had an important meeting to attend that morning, but he will be unlikely to admit that he might lose the client (and a lot of money) if he arrived late. You can solve this problem by using topical organization to separate your cross examination into two distinct segments: one dealing with the nature of the defendant's business and the other covering his appointment on the fateful morning.

In the first topical segment you will show that the defendant is an independent management consultant. It is a very competitive business in which client relations are extremely important. Part of his work involves seeking out potential new clients, whom he is always anxious to please. Since he is a sole proprietor, every client means more money. As a consultant, he must pride himself on professionalism, timeliness, and efficiency. He bills his clients by the hour. Time is money. In short, examine the witness on his business background without ever bringing up the subject of the accident. (The defendant's own lawyer almost certainly will have introduced his stable, business-like background; your examination on the same issue would then be within the scope of the direct.)

Later in the examination, after covering several other areas, you will shift topics to the defendant's agenda on the day of the accident. Now it is time to establish the details of his planned meeting and the fact that he was still miles from downtown shortly before it was scheduled to begin. You do not need to obtain an admission that he was running late or that he was preoccupied. Topical organization has allowed you to develop the predicate facts for that argument before the witness was aware of their implications.

There is another advantage to topical organization on cross examination. Assume, in the example above, that the witness was well-prepared and that he immediately recognized your reasons for inquiring into his business practices. Because your examination was segmented, however, he could scarcely deny the facts that you suggested. In a portion of the examination limited to the operation of his business it would be implausible for him to deny that his clients value "professionalism, efficiency, and timeliness." Denying your perfectly reasonable propositions would make him look either untrustworthy or defensive. Note that you would not obtain the same result without topical organization. In the middle of the discussion of the morning of the accident it would be quite plausible for the defendant to testify that this particular new client was not dominating his thoughts.

Give the Details First

Details are, if anything, more important on cross examination than they are on direct. On direct examination a witness will always be able to tell the gist of the story; details are used in a secondary manner to add strength and veracity to the basic testimony. On cross examination, however, the witness will frequently disagree with the gist of the story that you want to tell, and use of details therefore becomes the primary method of making your points. You may elicit details to lay the groundwork for future argument, to draw out internal inconsistencies in the witness's testimony, to point out inconsistencies between witnesses, to lead the witness into implausible assertions, or to create implications that the witness will be unable to deny later.

Within each segment of your cross examination it will usually be preferable to give the details first. No matter what your goal, the witness will be far more likely to agree with a series of small, incremental facts before the thrust of the examination has been made apparent. Once you have challenged, confronted, or closely questioned a witness it will be extremely difficult to go back and fill in the details necessary to make the challenge stick.

Assume that the weather conditions turn out to be of some value to you in the automobile accident case. If you begin your examination of the defendant with questions about the weather you will be likely to obtain cooperative answers. As a preliminary matter you may have no difficulty establishing that it was clear and sunny that day. Perhaps you will have additional details available—the defendant left home without an umbrella, he wasn't wearing overshoes, he didn't turn on his headlights. Conversely, imagine a first question such as, "Isn't it true that you never even tried to stop before the collision?" Now what is the witness likely to say when you ask whether the pavement was dry? Suddenly, the witness may remember all manner of fog and puddles; of course he tried to stop, but the street was just too wet.

There is an additional advantage to beginning a cross examination with details. It allows you to learn about the witness with a minimum of risk. We know that cross examination is not the time to try to gather new information about the case. You should only ask questions to which you know the answer, or where you at least have a good reason to expect a favorable answer. On the other hand, you frequently will not know how a particular witness will react to your questions. Will the witness be cooperative or compliant, or can you expect a struggle every inch of the way? Worse, is the witness slippery and evasive? Even worse, is the witness inclined to mislead and prevaricate? Worst of all, have you misinterpreted the information or made some other blunder in your own preparation? You must learn the answers to these questions before you proceed to the heart of your cross examination. While it may be mildly uncomfortable to receive an unexpectedly evasive answer to a question about a preliminary detail, it can be positively devastating to discover that you are unable to pin down a witness on a central issue. Beginning with details will allow you to take the witness's measure (and to evaluate your own preparation) at a time of minimum impact and risk.

Scatter the Circumstantial Evidence

Inferential or circumstantial evidence is most persuasive when a series of facts or events can be combined in such a way as to create a logical path to the desired conclusion. Unfortunately, facts arranged in this manner on cross examination will also be highly transparent to the witness. As you stack inference upon inference your direction will become increasingly clear. A hostile or unfriendly witness will then become increasingly uncooperative, perhaps to the point of thwarting your examination. A far safer approach is to scatter the circumstantial evidence throughout the examination, drawing it together only during final argument.

Save a Zinger for the End

The final moment of cross examination may well be the most important. No matter how low-key or friendly your style, almost every cross examination will in some sense be viewed as a contest between you and the witness. Were you able to shake the adverse testimony? Were you able to help your client? In short, did you do what you set out to do? In this regard the final impression that you leave is likely to be the most lasting. Were you able to finish on a high note, or did you simply give up?

It is therefore imperative that you plan carefully the very last point that you intend to make on cross examination. It must be a guaranteed winner, the point on which you are willing to make your exit. Indeed, you should write this point down at the very bottom of your note pad, underlined and in bold letters. It should stand alone with nothing to obscure it or distract you from it. Then if your entire examination seems to fail, if the witness denies every proposition, if the judge sustains every objection, if the heavens fall and doom impends, you can always skip to the bottom of the page and finish with a flourish. Satisfied that you have made this single, telling, case-sealing point, you may proudly announce, "No further questions of this witness," and sit down.

How do you identify your fail-safe zinger? The following guidelines should help:

It Must be Absolutely Admissible. There can be no doubt about the admissibility of your intended final point. Nothing smacks more of defeat than ending a cross examination on a sustained objection. If you suspect even for a moment that your zinger might not be allowed, abandon it and choose another. In fact, you should make an entry in the margin of your notes that reminds you of your theory of admissibility. Why is the point relevant? Why isn't it hearsay? How has the foundation been established? Why isn't it speculation?

It Should be Central to Your Theory. Since your closing point is likely to be the most memorable, you would be best served to make it one of the cornerstones of your theory. If there are eight facts that you must establish in order to prevail, you would like to end each cross examination on one of them. This may not always be possible. Not every opposing witness will testify about an essential matter, and it is important to insure admissibility by keeping your zinger well within the scope of the direct. Or it may be possible to undermine the witness's credibility by ending on a point that is collateral to your basic theory.

It Should Evoke Your Theme. The very purpose of a trial theme is to create a memorable phrase or invocation that captures the moral basis of your case. The closing moments of cross examination, therefore, constitute the perfect time to evoke your theme. Attention will never be more focused and memorability will never be higher. Imagine that the plaintiff in the fire truck case was taken directly to a hospital but that the unhurt defendant went on to his office after filling out a police report. If your theme is "Too busy to be careful," you can close your cross examination with these two questions: "You made it to your office later that morning, didn't you? Taking care of business, I suppose?" You know that the answer to the first question will be "Yes." You don't care about the answer to the second one.

It Must be Undeniable. It should be obvious by now that your final question must be undeniable. The end of your cross is not the time to argue or quibble with the witness. There are two good ways to insure undeniability.

First, choose a fact that you can document. Look for something that can be proven from a prior statement of the witness or some other tangible exhibit or writing. If evidence of that sort is unavailable, select a point that has already been made in the testimony of other opposition witnesses, thereby making a denial either implausible or inconsistent with the balance of the other side's case.

Second, phrase your question in terms of bedrock fact, making sure that it contains nothing that approaches a characterization. The more "factual" your question the less possible it is for the witness to deny you a simple answer. In the automobile accident case, for example, a purely factual closing question would be, "You arrived at your office later that morning?" The same point, but made with a characterization, would be, "You were so busy that you went straight to your office?" The witness can argue with you about the interpretation of the word "busy," but arrival at his office is a fact.

Remember that cross examination may be followed immediately by redirect examination. Your closing question on cross may provide the opening subject for redirect. Thus, another aspect of undeniability is that the point must not be capable of immediate explanation. For example, the fire truck defendant may have gone straight to his office, but only to retrieve medicine for his heart condition. After that he might not have worked for the next three days. You can omit those facts on cross examination, but you can be sure that they will be developed on redirect. Since that point can be explained, it is not sufficiently "undeniable" for use as a closing question.

It Must be Stated with Conviction. No matter what your closing question, you must be able to deliver it with an attitude of satisfied completion. If the subject makes you nervous, worried, or embarrassed, then you must choose another. It is neither necessary nor desirable to smirk, but you must exhibit confidence that your parting inquiry has done its work.

§ 22D.4.3 A Classic Format for Cross Examination

Because almost all cross examinations will be topical, there can be no standard or prescribed form of organization. The following "classic format" is designed to maximize witness cooperation. Of course, you may have a goal in mind for your cross examination other than witness cooperation; in that case, feel free to ignore or alter this approach. As a rule of thumb, however, you can best employ principles such as indirection and "detail scattering" by seeking information in this order.

Friendly Information

Be friendly first. Begin by asking all questions that the witness will regard as nonthreatening. These will often be background questions. For example, medical malpractice cases are often based upon errors of omission, and you may intend to argue in closing that the defendant physician, by virtue of her extraordinary training, should have known about certain available tests. You can start your cross examination, then, by asking friendly questions about the defendant's medical education, residency, fellowships, and awards. Most people, even defendants on trial, like to talk about their achievements. There is little doubt that a witness will be the most forthcoming when asked about aggrandizing information at the very outset of the cross examination.

Affirmative Information

After exhausting the friendly information, ask questions that build up the value of your case rather than tear down the opposition's. Much of this information will fill in gaps in the direct testimony. In fact, a good way to plan this portion of the cross is to list the information that you reasonably hope will be included in the direct. Whatever is omitted from the witness's actual testimony will form the core of your affirmative information section. Although adverse witnesses may not be enthusiastic about supplying you with helpful information, they will be unlikely to fight you over answers that might logically have been included in their own direct.

Uncontrovertible Information

You can now proceed to inquire about facts that damage the opposition's case or detract from the witness's testimony, so long as they are well-settled or documentable. On these questions a witness may be inclined to hedge or quibble, but you can minimize this possibility by sticking to the sort of information that ultimately must be conceded.

Challenging Information

It is unlikely that a witness will cooperate with you once you begin challenging her memory, perception, accuracy, conduct, or other aspects of her testimony. Therefore, it is usually desirable to proceed through friendly, affirmative, and uncontroverted information before you begin to take sharper issue with the witness. At some point, of course, you will have to ask most witnesses questions that they will recognize as challenges: "Mr. Defendant, the fact is that the first thing you did after the collision was to telephone your office?" Such questions are necessary. When used in their proper place they will not prevent you from first exploiting the other, more cooperative testimony from the witness.

Hostile Information

Hostile information involves confronting the witness directly. You may be able to extract the necessary answers to hostile questions, but certainly you can eliminate all hope of cooperation both then and thereafter. Hostile questions involve assaults on the witness's honesty, probity, peacefulness, character, or background. "Didn't you spend time in prison?" "You never intended to live up to the contract?" "That was a lie, wasn't it?"

Zinger

Always end with a zinger. You know why.

§ 22D.5 Questioning Technique

You know what you want to cover on cross examination and you know the order in which you want to cover it. How do you ask questions that will insure your success?

The essential goal of cross examination technique is witness control. As we noted above, your object on cross examination is to tell your client's story. This requires that you set the agenda for the examination, that you determine the flow of information, and that you require answers to your questions. In short, you must always be in control of the witness and the testimony. This does not, by the way, mean that you must appear to be in control, and it certainly does not mean that you must be domineering, rude, or overbearing toward the witness. In this context, control means only that the examination follow the course that you have selected and that the information produced be only that which you have determined helpful.

Control, therefore, can be either nonassertive or assertive. With a cooperative or tractable witness, control may mean nothing more than asking the right questions and getting the right answers. A hostile, evasive, or argumentative witness may require that you employ more assertive means.

There are numerous questioning techniques, to be discussed below, that you can employ to ensure witness control. At a minimum, however, every question on cross examination should have all of the following bedrock characteristics:

Short. Questions on cross examination must be short in both execution and concept. If a question is more than ten words long, it is not short in execution. Try to shorten it. If a question contains more than a single fact or implication, it is not short in concept. Divide it.

Leading. Every question on cross examination should be leading. Include the answers in the questions. Tell the witness exactly what to say. Cross examination is no time to seek the witness's interpretation of the facts. It is the time for you to tell a story by obtaining the witness's assent. A non-leading question invites the witness to wander away from your story.

Part 22E: Expert Testimony*

by Steven Lubet[5]

§ 22E.1 Introduction

Most witnesses are called to the stand because they have seen, heard, or done something relevant to the issues in the case. Such persons are often referred to as ordinary witnesses, lay witnesses, or percipient witnesses. Whatever the term used, the testimony of witnesses is generally limited to those things

---

* This material appears in *Modern Trial Advocacy: Analysis and Practice*, 3rd Edition, copyright © 2004, National Institute for Trial Advocacy (NITA). Reproduced with permission from the National Institute for Trial Advocacy. The NACC is grateful to NITA for permitting the use of these materials as a gift to the child advocacy community. The NACC highly recommends the full publication of *Modern Trial Advocacy* and additional NITA trial skill material available at www.NITA.org or 800-225-6482.

Editor's Note: Nonsubstantive changes have been made to the text and formatting to reflect the style of this publication. Section numbers have also been added to reflect the style of this publication.

[5] Steven Lubet, J.D., is Professor of Law at Northwestern University School of Law in Chicago, Illinois.

they have directly observed or experienced, as well as reasonable conclusions that can be drawn on the basis of their sensory perceptions. In short, lay witnesses must testify from personal knowledge, and they may not offer opinions.

Expert witnesses comprise an entirely different category. An expert witness is not limited to personal knowledge and may base her testimony on information that was gathered solely for the purpose of testifying in the litigation. Moreover, under the proper circumstances an expert witness may offer an opinion that goes well beyond her direct sensory impressions. An expert may opine on the cause or consequences of occurrences, interpret the actions of other persons, draw conclusions on the basis of circumstances, comment on the likelihood of events, and may even state her beliefs regarding such seemingly nonfactual issues as fault, damage, negligence, avoidability, and the like.

Expert witnesses may be helpful in a wide variety of cases. Experts can be used in commercial cases to interpret complex financial data, in tort cases to explain the nature of injuries, or in criminal cases to translate underworld slang into everyday language. Properly qualified, an expert can be asked to peer into the past, as when an accident reconstructionist re-creates the scene of an automobile collision. Other experts may predict the future, as when an economist projects the expected life earnings of the deceased in a wrongful death case. In some cases expert testimony is required as a matter of law. In legal or medical malpractice cases, for example, it is usually necessary to call an expert witness in order to establish the relevant standard of care; in narcotics cases the prosecution usually must call a chemist or other expert to prove that the substance in question is actually an illegal drug.

Given the extraordinarily broad scope of expert testimony, and its extreme potential for influencing the judgment of the trier of fact, certain rules have developed regarding the permissible use, extent, and nature of expert testimony.

§ 22E.2 Standards for Expert Testimony

§ 22E.2.1 Areas of Expertise

Rule 702 of the Federal Rules of Evidence provides that expert opinions may be admissible where the expert's "scientific, technical, or other specialized knowledge will assist the trier of fact to understand the evidence or to determine a fact in issue." Thus, there are two threshold questions: Does the witness possess sufficient scientific, technical, or other specialized knowledge? If so, will that knowledge be helpful to the trier of fact?

In a recent series of cases, the United States Supreme Court held that a trial judge must also make a preliminary assessment of the validity of the reasoning and methods that support proffered expert testimony. The Federal Rules of Evidence subsequently codified that requirement, specifying that opinion testimony is admissible only if: (1) the testimony is based upon sufficient facts or data; (2) the testimony is the product of reliable principles and methods; and (3) the witness has applied the principles and methods reliably to the facts of the case.

In the federal system, then, the trial judge has become a gatekeeper and makes an initial determination whenever the validity of opinion evidence is challenged. A number of states have also adopted this approach. In other jurisdictions, however, the soundness of an expert's methodology will still be a question for the jury. Needless to say, it is always essential to determine which test for admissibility will be used for scientific or other expert evidence.

§ 22E.2.2 Scope of Opinion

It was once considered improper for an expert to offer an opinion on the "ultimate issue" in the case, as this was regarded as "invading the province of the jury." This restrictive convention often led to extremely elliptical testimony, with the expert testifying to a series of inferences and opinions but not drawing the most obvious factual conclusions. This process was further complicated by the difficulty of determining exactly what were the ultimate issues in a case.

The Federal Rules of Evidence now provide that expert testimony, if otherwise admissible, "is not objectionable because it embraces an ultimate issue to be decided by the trier of fact." The only exception is that an expert in a criminal case may not state an opinion as to whether the defendant "did or did not have the mental state or condition constituting an element of the crime charged or a defense thereto."

Judges vary on their interpretations of the "ultimate issue" rule. Some courts will allow experts to opine on virtually any issue, including such casebreakers as whether the plaintiff in a personal injury case was contributorily negligent or whether the defendant in a tax evasion case had unreported income. Other judges draw the line at what they consider to be legal conclusions. So, for example, a medical expert in a malpractice case would no doubt be allowed to state that certain tests were indicated and that the defendant had not performed them. Many judges would also allow the expert to testify that the failure to order the tests fell below the standard of care generally exercised by practitioners in the relevant community, although this might be considered an "ultimate issue in the case." Most judges, though not all, would balk at permitting the expert to testify that the defendant's conduct constituted malpractice, on the theory that malpractice is a legal conclusion that is not within the specialized knowledge of a medical expert.

§ 22E.2.3 Bases for Opinion

Under the Federal Rules of Evidence an expert can testify to her opinion with or without explaining the facts or data on which the opinion is based. In theory, then, an expert, once qualified, could simply state her opinion on direct examination, leaving the cross examiner to search for its basis. In practice this approach is rarely followed since the expert's opinion could hardly be persuasive until its foundation is explained. The practical effect of the rule is to allow the witness to state her opinion at the beginning of the examination, followed by explication, rather than having to set forth all of the data at the outset.

A related issue is the nature of the information that an expert may rely upon in arriving at an opinion. At common law, experts could give opinions only on the basis of facts that were already in evidence. One way for an expert to comply with this requirement was to observe the actual testimony by sitting through the trial. The only alternative to this expensive and cumbersome routine was for the attorney offering the expert testimony to precede it with an elaborate "hypothetical question" that recited all of the facts—either admitted or eventually to be admitted—needed by the expert as the basis for an opinion.

The hypothetical question was usually the preferred option, if only because it was less costly, but it had numerous drawbacks. Because they had to include every relevant fact, the hypotheticals were often long, boring, and impossible to follow. Worse, the omission of a single fact could conceivably invalidate the entire hypothetical, as could the inclusion of a fact that was not eventually admitted into evidence. Trial lawyers spent countless hours, and appellate courts devoted untold pages, to discussion of the technical adequacy of expert hypotheticals.

The Federal Rules of Evidence have abolished the need for this highly stylized ritual. An expert witness may now testify on the basis of "facts made known to him at or before the hearing." Moreover, those facts or data need not be admissible in evidence so long as they are "of a type reasonably relied upon by experts in the particular field."

While it is certain that an expert may rely upon inadmissible date, it is less clear when the expert may recite that data as support for her testimony. For example, forensic pathologists regularly rely upon toxicology reports in determining the cause of death. A pathologist could presumably reach an opinion based upon such a written report even if it would be hearsay when offered at trial. The question, however, is whether the expert, having accepted the report, may also testify as to its contents.

According to Rule 703, otherwise inadmissible facts or data may not be disclosed to the jury by the proponent of the opinion "unless the court determines that their probative value in assisting the jury to evaluate the expert's opinion substantially outweighs their prejudicial effect." Thus, the pathologist in the above example could read the language of the toxicology report to the jury only if the court first determines that it is substantially more helpful than it is prejudicial. Otherwise, the witness would be limited to stating how and why she relied on the report, but would not be allowed to testify to its contents. Note, however, that there is no such limitation on the opponent of the proffered opinion, who may always require an expert "to disclose the underlying facts or date on cross examination."

§ 22E.3 The Expert's Overview

Just as a lawyer cannot succeed without developing a comprehensive theory of the case, neither will an expert be effective without a viable, articulated theory. An expert's theory is an overview or summary of the expert's entire position.

The theory must not only state a conclusion, but must also explain, in common-sense terms, why the expert is correct. Why did she settle upon a certain methodology? Why did she review particular data? Why is her approach reliable? Why is the opposing expert wrong? In other words, the expert witness must present a coherent narrative that provides the trier of fact with reasons for accepting, and, it is hoped, internalizing, the expert's point of view.

The need for a theory is especially true in cases involving "dueling experts." It is common for each of the opposing parties in litigation to retain their own expert witnesses. The trier of fact is then faced with the task of sorting through the opinion testimony and choosing which witness to believe. It is likely that both experts will be amply qualified, and it is unlikely that either will make a glaring error in her analysis or commit an unpardonable faux pas in her testimony. The trier of fact will therefore be inclined to credit the expert whose theory is most believable.

Consider the following case. The plaintiff operated a statewide chain of drive-in restaurants but was put out of business by the defendant's allegedly unfair competition. Assume that summary judgment was granted in favor of the plaintiff on the issue of liability and that the court set the case for trial on damages. Each side retained an expert witness who generated a damage model.

Not surprisingly, the plaintiff's expert opined that the restaurants, had they not been driven out of business, would have earned millions of dollars over the following five years. The defendant's witness, however, held the view that the stores would have been marginally profitable, with total profits amounting to no more than a few hundred thousand dollars. Each witness backed up her opinion with computer printouts, charts, and graphs. Both used reliable data, and all of their figures were rigorously accurate.

The rival experts reached different conclusions because they followed different routes. The plaintiff's expert calculated lost profits as a function of population growth and driving habits, opining that the revenues at drive-in restaurants would rise in proportion to expected increases in population and miles driven. The defendant's witness, on the other hand, estimated damages on a "profit-per-store" basis, taking the plaintiff's average profit for the existing restaurants and multiplying them by the number of outlets that the plaintiff planned to build.

Faced with this discrepancy, the task for counsel is to present the expert testimony in its most persuasive form. Whichever side you represent, it should be obvious that a simple recitation of your expert's methods will be unlikely to carry the day. After all, we have assumed that both experts were meticulously careful within the confines of their respective approaches. For the same reason, the trier of fact will probably be unimpressed by an expert who reviews in detail all of her calculations. Numbers are boring in any event, and both experts are sure to have been accurate in their arithmetic.

Instead, the key to this case is to persuade the trier of fact that your expert chose the correct approach. The plaintiff's expert must be asked to explain why lost profits can be determined on the basis of population growth; the defendant's expert has to support her reliance on profits-per-store. The prevailing expert will not be the one with the greatest mastery of the details, but rather the one who most successfully conveys the preferability of her theory. The most painstakingly prepared projection of population growth cannot succeed in persuading a jury if they ultimately decide that only profits-per-store can give them an accurate assessment of damages.

The importance of theory extends to all types of expert testimony. It is necessary, but not sufficient, for your expert to be thorough, exacting, highly regarded, incisive, honorable, and well-prepared. Her testimony will suffer if she cannot support her opinion with common-sense reasons.

§ 22E.4 Offering Expert Testimony

There is a certain logic to the direct examination of most experts. While the particulars and details will vary, there are a limited number of possible patterns for organizing the testimony. It is absolutely necessary, for example, to qualify the expert before proceeding to her opinion. The following is a broad outline that can accommodate the specifics of most expert testimony.

§ 22E.4.1 Introduction and Foreshadowing

The first step is to introduce the expert and explain her involvement in the case. Since expert testimony is qualitatively different from lay testimony, it is a good idea to clarify its purposes for the jury so that they will understand what they are about to hear. Ask the witness how she came to be retained and why she is present in court.

Moreover, the technical requirements of presenting expert testimony often result in a considerable time gap between the introduction of the witness and the substantive high points of her testimony. Thus, it is generally desirable to foreshadow the expert's opinion at the very outset of the examination.

The plaintiff's damages expert in the example from the preceding section might be introduced as follows:

QUESTION:

Please state your name.

ANSWER:

Dr. Andrea Longhini.

QUESTION:

Dr. Longhini, have you been retained to reach an expert opinion in this case?

ANSWER:

Yes.

QUESTION:

Did you reach an opinion concerning the plaintiff's lost profits?

ANSWER:

Yes, I have calculated the amount of money that the plaintiff would have earned.

QUESTION:

We'll talk about your opinion in detail in a few minutes, but right now we have to talk about your qualifications to testify as an expert in this case.

§ 22E.4.2 Qualification

To testify as an expert, a witness must be qualified by reason of knowledge, skill, experience, training or education. This is a threshold question for the judge, who must determine whether the witness is qualified before permitting her to give opinion testimony. The qualification of the witness, then, is a necessary predicate for all of the testimony to follow. Care must be taken to qualify the expert in a manner that is both technically adequate and persuasive.

Technical Requirements

The technical requirements for qualifying an expert witness are straightforward. It is usually adequate to show that the witness possesses some specialized skill or knowledge, acquired through appropriate experience or education, and that the witness is able to apply that skill or knowledge in a manner relevant to the issues in the case.

Thus, the minimal qualifications for the financial expert in the restaurant case could be established as follows:

QUESTION:

Dr. Longhini, could you please tell us something about your education?

ANSWER:

Certainly. I have an undergraduate degree in business from the University of Michigan and a Ph.D. in economics from the University of California.

QUESTION:

What work have you done since receiving your doctorate?

ANSWER:

I was a professor in the economics department at Washington University for six years. Then I left to start my own consulting firm, which is called Longhini & Associates.

QUESTION:

Do you have a specialty within the field of economics?

ANSWER:

Yes, my specialty is business valuation.

QUESTION:

Has business valuation been your specialty both at Washington University and at Longhini & Associates?

ANSWER:

Yes.

QUESTION:

What is the field of business valuation?

ANSWER:

It is the study of all of the components that contribute to the fair value of a business, including anticipated future profits, assets, receivables, good will, and investment potential.

The above examination confirms the expert's qualifications by reason of both education and experience. Dr. Longhini should now be able to give an opinion as to the projected profits for the restaurant chain.

There are, of course, many other areas of basic qualification beyond education and business experience. Examples include specialized training, continuing education courses, teaching and lecturing positions, licenses and certifications, publications, consulting experience, professional memberships, awards, and other professional honors.

The establishment of basic qualifications, however, should not be counsel's entire objective. It is equally if not more important to go on to qualify the witness as persuasively as possible.

Persuasive Qualification

The technical qualification of an expert merely allows the witness to testify in the form of an opinion. Counsel's ultimate goal is to ensure that the opinion is accepted by the trier of fact. Persuasive qualification is particularly important in cases involving competing experts, since their relative qualifications may be one basis on which the judge or jury will decide which expert to believe.

It is a mistake, however, to think that more qualifications are necessarily more persuasive. An endless repetition of degrees, publications, awards, and appointments may easily overload any judge or juror's ability, not to mention desire, to pay careful attention to the witness. It is often better to introduce the witness's detailed résumé or curriculum vitae and to use the qualification portion of the actual examination to focus in on several salient points.

It is usually more persuasive to concentrate on a witness's specific expertise, as opposed to her more generic or remote qualifications. Every economist, for example, is likely to hold a doctorate, so there is comparatively little advantage to be gained by spending valuable time expounding your expert's academic degrees. Similarly, there is usually scant reason to go into matters such as the subject of the witness's doctoral thesis, unless it bears directly on some issue in the case.

On the other hand, an expert's credibility can be greatly enhanced by singling out qualifications that relate specifically to the particular case. Thus, it would be important to point out that the witness has published several articles directly relevant to the issues in the case. It would be less useful to take the witness through a long list of extraneous articles, even if they appeared in prestigious journals. Other case-specific qualifications may include direct experience, consulting work, or teaching that is connected to an issue in the case.

Experience is often more impressive than academic background. So, for example, a medical expert may be more impressive if she has actually practiced in the applicable specialty, as opposed to possessing knowledge that is strictly theoretical. When presenting such a witness, then, counsel should typically dwell on her experience, pointing out details such as the number of procedures she has performed, the hospitals where she is on staff, and the numbers of other physicians who have consulted her.

Finally, it is frequently effective to emphasize areas of qualification where you know the opposing expert to be lacking. If your expert has a superior academic background, use the direct examination to point out why academic training is important. If your expert holds a certification that the opposing expert lacks, have her explain how difficult it is to become certified.

Tender of the Witness

In some jurisdictions it is necessary, once qualifications have been concluded, to tender the witness to the court as an expert in a specified field. The purpose of the tender is to inform the court that qualification has been completed and to give opposing counsel an opportunity either to conduct a voir dire examination of the witness or to object to the tender. In the restaurant example above, the financial expert would be tendered as follows:

COUNSEL:

Your Honor, we tender Dr. Andrea Longhini as an expert witness in the field of business valuation and the projection of profits.

It may be an effective tactic to tender an expert witness to the court even in jurisdictions where a formal tender is not required. First, tendering the witness signals that the qualification segment has been completed and requires opposing counsel either to object or accede to the witness's qualifications. By forcing the issue early in the examination, the direct examiner can avoid being interrupted by an objection to the witness's qualifications at some more delicate point in the testimony. Additionally, assuming that the judge rules favorably on the tender, counsel in effect has obtained the court's declaration that the witness is, indeed, an expert. This will give additional weight to the opinions that follow.

§ 22E.4.3 Opinion and Theory

Following qualification, the next step in the direct examination of an expert witness is to elicit firm statements of opinion and theory.

Statement of Opinion

The Federal Rules of Evidence provide that an expert "may testify in terms of opinion or inference and give reasons therefor without first testifying to the underlying facts or data, unless the court requires otherwise." Consequently, once the witness has been qualified (and accepted as an expert in jurisdictions requiring a formal tender and ruling), she may proceed to express her opinion without additional foundation. In other words, she may state her conclusions without first detailing the nature or extent of her background work or investigation.

Many attorneys believe strongly in taking advantage of the "opinion first" provision. Expert testimony tends to be long, arcane, and boring. The intricate details of an expert's preparation are unlikely to be interesting or even particularly understandable. They will be even less captivating if they are offered in a void, without any advance notice of where the details are leading or why they are being explained. On the other hand, a clear statement of the expert's conclusion can provide the context for the balance of the explanatory testimony. Compare the two following vignettes, each taken from the "fast food" example above:

QUESTION:

Dr. Longhini, what did you do to arrive at your opinion in this matter?

ANSWER:

My first step was to gather all of the available data regarding vehicle registrations and anticipated population growth in the state.

QUESTION:

Then what did you do?

ANSWER:

I correlated population growth with expected vehicle miles to arrive at a reasonable estimate of "miles per person" over each of the next five years.

QUESTION:

How was that calculation performed?

Even the most diligent and attentive juror would be baffled by this examination. What is the relevance of vehicle miles and population growth to fast food profits? The nature of the witness's computation is meaningless in the absence of some connection to his opinion in the case. Indeed, the more thoroughly the witness explains her calculations, the more incomprehensible they will become. In contrast, consider the following:

QUESTION:

Dr. Longhini, do you have an opinion as to the profits that the plaintiff's restaurant chain would have made, if they hadn't been forced out of business?

ANSWER:

Yes, I do.

QUESTION:

What is your opinion?

ANSWER:

I believe that the restaurant chain would have earned at least $3.2 million over the next five years, if they had been able to stay in business.

QUESTION:

How did you reach that opinion?

ANSWER:

I based my calculations on the state's projected population growth, combined with the probable demand for fast-food, drive-in restaurants.

This examination is far more understandable. By providing her opinion at the outset the expert allows the trier of fact to comprehend the significance of the following details. The jury will be much more able to understand the relationship between lost profits and the data on vehicle registration and population growth.

Statement of Theory

Once the expert's opinion has been stated, immediately provide the underlying theory. The theory should furnish the nexus between the expert's conclusion and the data used to support the conclusion. In other words, the examination should follow this pattern: (1) here is my opinion; (2) here are the principles that support my opinion; (3) here is what I did to reach my final conclusion.

In the fast food example, the expert's theory should explain why population growth and vehicle miles are reliable indicators of projected profits:

QUESTION:

Dr. Longhini, why did you base your calculations on the state's projected population growth?

ANSWER:

The demand for fast food will rise as population grows. This is particularly true because teenagers and parents of young children are the largest purchasers of fast food, and they are also two of the groups that increase most rapidly as population goes up.

QUESTION:

Why did you also consider growth in vehicle miles?

ANSWER:

Drive-in restaurants are especially sensitive to vehicle miles. As people drive more they are exposed to more drive-in restaurants, and they therefore buy more meals.

QUESTION:

What did you conclude from these relationships?

ANSWER:

I concluded that the profitability of a drive-in restaurant chain will rise in proportion to a combination of general population growth and increases in miles driven.

QUESTION:

Did you consider only population growth and vehicle miles?

ANSWER:

Of course not. I began by determining the chain's profits under current conditions, and I used those figures as a base. Then I projected them forward for five years, using the government's statistics for population and driving.

QUESTION:

Please tell us now exactly how you did that.

Note how this examination provides the context for the explanation to follow.

§ 22E.4.4 Explanation and Support

Having stated and supported her theory choice, the expert can now go on to detail the nature of her investigation and calculations. The trier of fact cannot be expected to take the expert at her word, so the validity and accuracy of her data and assumptions must be established.

Data

The expert should be asked how she chose and obtained her data. She should also explain why her information is reliable. In the scenario above, for example, the expert could point out that government statistics on population and vehicle miles are used to make many crucial decisions such as the configuration of traffic lights, the expansion of highways, and even the construction of schools.

The expert should also be asked to describe any tests or computations that she performed.

The treatment of underlying data is one of the trickiest aspects of expert testimony. Many experts will be in love with their data, and they will be anxious to lay them out in excruciating detail. Unfortunately, most judges and jurors will have little tolerance for lengthy descriptions of enigmatic scientific or technical processes. Counsel must therefore strike a balance, eliciting a sufficiently detailed treatment of the data to persuade the jury of its reliability but stopping well short of the point where their attention span is exhausted.

It is not sufficient for the expert simply to relate the nature of the data. Rather, the expert should go on to explain how and why the data support her conclusions.

Assumptions

Most experts rely upon assumptions. The financial expert in the fast food case, for example, would no doubt assume that the relationship between sales and population growth would continue at historical rates. The expert would also probably assume a certain financial "discount rate" for reducing the dollars in his projection to present value. There is obviously nothing wrong with using appropriate presumptions, but their validity should be explained:

QUESTION:

Dr. Longhini, did you make any assumptions in reaching your opinion that the plaintiff's restaurant chain would have earned $3.2 million in profits?

ANSWER:

Yes, I assumed that fast food sales would continue to increase in proportion to population at the same rate as they had in the past.

QUESTION:

Why did you make that assumption?

ANSWER:

The restaurant chain was put out of business, so there were no actual sales to look at. I therefore had to project their most likely sales, and for that I had to assume a base figure to project forward.

QUESTION:

What did you use as your base figure?

ANSWER:

I used the average growth for the entire industry.

QUESTION:

Why did you use the industry average?

ANSWER:

I used the industry average precisely because it is an average of all of the companies in that particular business. That way I could be sure that I wasn't using a figure that was abnormally high or abnormally low.

It is not necessary to explain or outline every hypothesis used by your expert, but the more important assumptions should be noted and supported.

§ 22E.4.5 Theory Differentiation

In cases involving dueling experts there will also be competing theories. Properly prepared and presented, each expert will attempt to explain to the trier of fact why her theory ought to be accepted. It can be particularly effective, therefore, to ask your expert to comment on the opposing expert's work. This technique can be called theory differentiation because it is most convincing when your expert discusses the shortcomings of the opposition theory.

In the previous sections we have seen illustrations taken from the testimony of the plaintiff's financial expert in a case involving lost profits. Now consider this example of theory differentiation, offered by the expert witness for the defendant:

QUESTION:

Please state your name.

ANSWER:

Benjamin Haruo.

QUESTION:

Dr. Haruo, have you had an opportunity to review the work done in this case by Dr. Andrea Longhini?

ANSWER:

Yes, I have.

QUESTION:

Do you agree with Dr. Longhini's damage projections?

ANSWER:

No, I do not.

QUESTION:

Why not?

ANSWER:

Dr. Longhini based her estimate on a combination of population growth and mileage assumptions, and this approach cannot yield a reliable result.

QUESTION:

Why is that?

ANSWER:

Because it assumes too much. Dr. Longhini's theory is that restaurant revenues will inevitably rise along with population and automobile miles. While this might possibly be true for the entire restaurant industry, there is no reason to think that it would be true for any particular chain of restaurants. To reach a dependable result for an individual chain you would have to consider many other factors.

QUESTION:

What factors are those?

ANSWER:

At a minimum you would have to consider location, market niche, product recognition, potential competition, specific demographics, and general economic climate.

QUESTION:

Did Dr. Longhini consider any of those factors?

ANSWER:

No, she did not.

QUESTION:

Could you please give us an example of how location could affect the profit projections?

ANSWER:

Certainly. Population always grows unevenly. Even if the overall population rises in a state or a city, it might stay constant or fall in certain areas. Therefore, a restaurant chain might not be able to take advantage of population increases if all of their outlets were placed in stagnant or declining locations.

The defense expert has deftly exposed the flaws in the plaintiff's theory. There are two advantages to such theory differentiation. First, it enables the expert to concentrate on major issues, as opposed to picking out petty mistakes. Second, it allows the expert to avoid personal attacks. In essence, the above example has Dr. Haruo saying: "I have no personal quarrel with Dr. Longhini; she simply chose an inadequate theory." This "high road" approach will contribute to the dignity and persuasiveness of the witness.

The timing of theory differentiation can be important. Plaintiff's counsel generally will want to establish her own theory first, before proceeding to criticize the defense expert. Depending upon the circumstances of the case, plaintiff's counsel might even want to forego theory differentiation entirely during her case in chief, and recall her expert for that purpose on rebuttal.

The defense, on the other hand, should address the plaintiff's expert's theory at some point during the direct examination of the defendant's own expert. This can be done early in the examination (in order to rebut the plaintiff's expert immediately and forcefully), or it can be done toward the end of the testimony (in order to allow the defense expert to build up the positive aspects of his own theory before turning his attention to the opposition).

§ 22E.4.6 Conclusion

An expert's direct examination should conclude with a powerful restatement of his most important conclusions.

Part 22F: Exhibits*

by Steven Lubet[6]

§ 22F.1 The Role of Exhibits

Exhibits are the tangible objects, documents, photographs, video and audio-tapes, and other items that are offered for the jury's consideration. Exhibits are the only form, apart from the testimony of witnesses, in which evidence can be received. Spoken testimony typically presents the jury with a recitation of the witness's memories and perceptions. As effective as testimony might be, it remains a secondhand account that is, at best, once removed from the jury's own experiences. Exhibits, on the other hand, allow the jurors to utilize their own senses and perceptions. It is one thing to hear somebody describe, for example, the texture of a piece of cloth; it is far more striking actually to run your hand over the material itself. Your direct experience will be infinitely more informative than listening to another person's description. Having touched the cloth you will remember it better, you will appreciate more of its nuances or details, and you will be much less likely to change your mind about it in the future.

Life is full of experiences that cannot truly be described, and exhibits bring reality into the courtroom in a way that spoken testimony will never approach. Imagine the melody of the last popular song that you heard on the radio. No matter how simple the tune, even the most gifted critic cannot recapture it in words. The use of an audiotape, however, can re-create the experience almost exactly. The same is true of visual exhibits. Think of a scene as commonplace as the street immediately outside the room in which you are sitting. It would take hours to describe everything that you could see there, and even then you would be unable to capture all of the colors, distances, spatial relationships, angles, and other particulars. A photograph can depict these details, and numerous others, all at once.

At trial, exhibits enhance or supplement the testimony of the witnesses. Exhibits can make information clearer, more concrete, more understandable,

---

*   This material appears in *Modern Trial Advocacy: Analysis and Practice*, 3rd Edition, copyright © 2004, National Institute for Trial Advocacy (NITA). Reproduced with permission from the National Institute for Trial Advocacy. The NACC is grateful to NITA for permitting the use of these materials as a gift to the child advocacy community. The NACC highly recommends the full publication of *Modern Trial Advocacy* and additional NITA trial skill material available at www.NITA.org or 800-225-6482.

    Editor's Note: Nonsubstantive changes have been made to the text and formatting to reflect the style of this publication. Section numbers have also been added to reflect the style of this publication.

[6]   Steven Lubet, J.D., is Professor of Law at Northwestern University School of Law in Chicago, Illinois.

and more reliable. The sections immediately following will discuss the general procedures for the introduction of exhibits.

§ 22F.2 Types of Exhibits

While the categories tend to overlap and the lines cannot be drawn with precision, it is often helpful to think of exhibits as falling into these three categories: (1) real or tangible evidence, (2) demonstrative evidence, and (3) documentary evidence.

§ 22F.2.1 Real Evidence

The term "real evidence" generally refers to tangible objects that played an actual role in the events at issue in the trial.

The proceeds or instrumentalities of the crime are often introduced in criminal cases. Typical examples might include the "marked money" recovered in a suspect's possession, the bullet casing found at the scene of the crime, an item of clothing that the defendant was wearing when arrested, or a quantity of narcotics seized by the police.

Real evidence is also used in all categories of civil cases. In personal injury cases it is common for plaintiff's counsel to introduce objects that allegedly caused or contributed to the injury. Such real evidence might include a frayed wire that led to a steering failure or a rusty canister that failed to contain a corrosive liquid. Similarly, defense counsel in a tort case would be expected to introduce the actual safety devices that were available to, but ignored by, the plaintiff. Real evidence in a commercial dispute might include samples of allegedly nonconforming goods.

Photographs, while obviously different from tangible objects, are so close to reality that they are also often treated as real evidence.

Documents such as contracts, memoranda, letters, and other primary writings can also be considered real evidence, although the special rules that apply to out-of-court writings generally make it more convenient to treat "documentary evidence" as a separate category.

§ 22F.2.2 Demonstrative Evidence

The term "demonstrative evidence" refers to exhibits that did not play an actual role in the events underlying the case but that are used to illustrate or clarify a witness's testimony. Demonstrative evidence can take the form of models, graphs, diagrams, charts, drawings, or any other objects that can explain or illustrate issues in the case.

A familiar form of demonstrative evidence is the simple intersection diagram on which a witness can indicate the locations of the automobiles involved in an accident. The intersection itself, not the diagram, would constitute real evidence of the configuration of the streets. The diagram, however, may be used to demonstrate the relative positions of the cars, traffic signals, and witnesses. It is easy to see why demonstrative evidence can be superior to real evidence—the intersection cannot be transported into the courtroom. And even if the jury were to be taken to the scene of the accident, it would still be extremely difficult for the lawyers to push real automobiles around at the instruction of the witnesses.

Another common type of demonstrative evidence is the "comparison" object. In many cases it is not possible to produce the original objects involved—they may have been destroyed, lost, or concealed. It is therefore permissible to use a similar object for the purpose of illustration. Imagine an automobile accident in which a young child was injured. If the child's safety seat was destroyed in the crash, either party could use an identical seat to demonstrate, for example, how the child fit into it and how it was fastened.

More complex displays are also possible. An anatomical model of a human shoulder can be used to show the effects of surgery on an individual's ability to move or work. "Day in the life" videotapes have been used with great impact to demonstrate the limitations and obstacles faced by accident victims and the extraordinary effort and expense that is necessary to cope with severe injuries. Computer simulations can rotate or enlarge objects; animations can virtually recreate past events or depict complex interactions.

The distinguishing feature of demonstrative evidence is that it is lawyer-generated. Real evidence exists by virtue of the activities of the parties and witnesses in the case. Counsel can search for it, discover it, preserve it, and utilize it, but a lawyer can never create real evidence. Demonstrative evidence is not intrinsic to the case. It is never handed to counsel, but must be developed by the attorneys as an aspect of the presentation of the case.

The production of demonstrative evidence is a creative task. It allows counsel, in effect, to dream about ways of presenting a case and then to fashion those dreams into a persuasive reality. The attorney must constantly ask, "How can I make this testimony more concrete?" Or, "How can I help the jury visualize this point?" Or, "Is there a way to accentuate the relationship between these two ideas?" The answer will often be found in the development of demonstrative exhibits.

§ 22F.2.3 Documentary Evidence

"Documentary evidence" is the term used to refer to virtually all writings, including letters, contracts, leases, memoranda, reports, ledgers, printouts, and business records. Written documents, almost by definition, contain out-of-court statements, and they are typically offered because their contents are relevant to the case. Thus, most documents face hearsay hurdles in a way that real and demonstrative exhibits do not. Tangible objects are admitted into evidence because of what they are; documentary exhibits are admitted because of what they say.

The value of documentary evidence cannot be overstated. Intrinsic writings can provide proof of past events in a way that mere testimony cannot. Imagine a criminal case in which the defendant has raised an alibi defense, claiming that on the day of the crime he was visiting relatives in a distant city. The testimony of the defendant and his family is relevant and admissible to establish the alibi, but it will be subject to vigorous attack on cross examination. A signed hotel receipt for the date in question stands to be far more persuasive than any witness as to the defendant's whereabouts.

Documentary evidence has the power to document past events. Barring fraud or forgery, contemporaneous writings often provide the best proof possible. For that reason counsel must always take pains to ensure that all potentially relevant documents are discovered. Thorough searches must be made not only of the client's files, but also of every conceivable third-party source. Many businesses, institutions, and even individuals keep copious records and notes. It is the lawyer's job to inquire into and investigate every conceivable source of favorable documentary evidence.

Perhaps more than any other form of evidence, however, documents have the potential to overwhelm the trier of fact. Only the most determined judge or juror will have the patience to wade through a foot-tall stack of reports in order to extract some evidentiary gem. Thus, while your search for documents should be exhaustive, your presentation of documents must be judicious. Truly important exhibits can be emphasized effectively only if trivial or repetitive ones are omitted. The final section of this chapter deals in greater depth with the persuasive use of documentary evidence and other exhibits.

§ 22F.3 Pretrial Procedures for the Admission of Exhibits

The foundations for various exhibits can be lengthy and cumbersome even though the eventual admissibility of the exhibit is not really in doubt. At trial, foundation testimony can be boring and repetitive; worse, it can distract attention from the truly contested issues in the case. For this reason the courts have developed a number of streamlined procedures that allow pretrial rulings on the admissibility of exhibits, including real, demonstrative, and documentary evidence.

§ 22F.3.1 Pretrial Conferences and Orders

Many jurisdictions now require pretrial conferences, especially in large or complex cases. Under the Federal Rules of Civil Procedure, for example, parties may be required to attend one or more pretrial conferences at which there may be "advance rulings from the court on the admissibility of evidence."

Many federal judges have adopted a routine practice of requiring the parties to submit written pretrial orders identifying every exhibit that they anticipate offering at trial. Counsel must also indicate whether or not they object to each other's proposed exhibits, giving the basis for the objection. Where there is no objection, the exhibit will automatically be received. Rulings on contested exhibits may be made at a pretrial conference or may be reserved until trial.

In jurisdictions utilizing extensive pretrial practice, every exhibit may be ruled upon in advance of the trial. Lawyers will therefore know exactly which exhibits have been admitted and which have been refused, thereby freeing counsel of the necessity of expending valuable trial time on unnecessary foundations.

§ 22F.3.2 Motions in Limine

Even in the absence of a formalized pretrial process it is possible to secure advance decisions on the admissibility of exhibits through the use of the motion in limine. Contrary to some opinion, the motion in limine is not merely the civil analog to the motion to suppress evidence in criminal cases. Although the motion in limine is most commonly used to obtain the exclusion of evidence, there is no reason that it cannot also be used affirmatively to seek a ruling that certain evidence is admissible. "In limine" means "at the threshold," and there is nothing about the motion that restricts its use to excluding evidence.

The reason to object to evidence before trial is obvious. An order barring the use of an exhibit will prevent opposing counsel from referring to it during the opening statement or from displaying it to the jury while ostensibly laying a foundation.

It can be equally useful to obtain a pretrial ruling allowing an exhibit into evidence. Advance knowledge of the admissibility of an exhibit will allow counsel to prepare an opening statement that takes full advantage of the exhibit but which does not risk a reprimand from the court or reversible error. By the same token, knowing that an exhibit has been admitted will permit the attorney to work it more easily into direct and cross examinations. It may even be worthwhile to lose an affirmative motion in limine, since the early exclusion of an exhibit will enable counsel to adapt her approach to the witnesses, or even to change her trial theory.

§ 22F.3.3 Stipulations

In situations where judicial involvement is unavailable, impractical, or unnecessary, pretrial admissibility of an exhibit may still be obtained by stipulation. A stipulation is an agreement between counsel as to some aspect of the case. Lawyers may stipulate, for example, to the filing of an amended pleading or to the existence of a certain set of facts. While judges are technically free to reject stipulations, this is seldom done other than in the case of over-reaching or abuse.

Stipulations to the admissibility of exhibits are almost uniformly honored by the courts since they really amount to nothing more than a pretrial agreement not to object to certain evidence. Since the stipulating attorney would be equally free to refrain from objecting at trial, the end result of the stipulation is to save time for all concerned.

There is no formal procedure for obtaining a stipulation. Any lawyer may request a stipulation from opposing counsel, who may either refuse or accede. This can be done by letter, telephone conversation, at a meeting, or in court.

Informal stipulations, however, and especially oral ones, have a maddening way of dissolving or becoming ambiguous at trial. It is therefore desirable to reduce stipulations to writing, preferably in the form of a signed document. Even when oral stipulations between counsel have been stenographically recorded, either in court or at a deposition, it is wise to review a transcript before relying too heavily on the stipulation during trial preparation.

Finally, it is important for all parties that stipulations be as precise as possible. If the stipulation is to the admissibility of an exhibit, the object or writing must be specifically identified, and the stipulation should also include any understood limitations on the exhibit's use.

§ 22F.3.4 Requests to Admit

Modern discovery practice allows counsel to obviate the need to lay many foundations at trial. Under the Federal Rules of Civil Procedure, and comparable provisions in most states, any party may serve "Requests for Admission" on any other party. The opposing party must then either admit or deny the request and may suffer sanctions for making false denials.

The Federal Rules specifically provide for a request to admit "the genuineness of documents." Once opposing counsel has admitted the genuineness of a document, no objection on that ground can be made to its admissibility at trial.

Additionally, counsel may serve requests to admit the "truth" of virtually any fact relevant to the case. Such facts definitely include all of the elements of the foundations for exhibits. A carefully drafted request to admit can result in the admissibility of even an otherwise contested exhibit.

Opposing counsel is free to deny any of the facts presented in a request for admission. Significant sanctions, however, may attend false or dilatory denials or other evasive replies. Moreover, failure to respond to such a request is, under the Federal Rules, treated as an admission.

§ 22F.4 Offering Exhibits at Trial

Whether they consist of real, demonstrative, or documentary evidence, there is one basic protocol for offering exhibits at trial. Although the details vary somewhat from jurisdiction to jurisdiction, the following steps form a nearly universal procedure.

§ 22F.4.1 Mark the Exhibit for Identification

Every exhibit should be marked for identification before it is offered into evidence or even referred to in the course of a trial. Marking the exhibit identifies it for the record so that it will be uniquely recognizable to anyone who later reads a transcript of the proceedings. References to "this letter" or "the first broken fastener" may be understood in the courtroom, but they will be meaningless to an appellate court. "Defendant's exhibit three," on the other hand, can mean only one thing, assuming that the exhibit was appropriately marked and identified.

Exhibits are generally marked sequentially and further identified according to the designation of the party who has first offered them. Thus, the exhibits in a two-party trial will be called plaintiff's exhibit one, plaintiff's exhibit two, defendant's exhibit one, defendant's exhibit two, and so forth. In multiple-party trials it is necessary to identify an exhibit by the name, and not merely the designation, of the party who offers it. Accordingly, you will see references to plaintiff Bennett exhibit one or Weber exhibit two. In some jurisdictions plaintiffs are expected to use sequential numbers for their exhibits, while defendants are requested to use letters. Hence, plaintiff's exhibit one and defendant's exhibit A. The details of the particular marking system are unimportant so long as it produces a clear and understandable indication of which exhibit is which.

The "mark" itself usually takes the form of a sticker placed directly on the object or document. Stickers are available in a variety of forms. Many attorneys use color-coded sets that already contain the words plaintiff or defendant, with a space left blank for the number assigned to each exhibit.

It was once the prevailing practice to have the court reporter or clerk mark each exhibit in open court. Often counsel was required to ask the judge's permission to have an exhibit marked. This time-consuming procedure has been widely replaced by the premarking of exhibits either at a pretrial conference or in the attorney's office.

The term "marked for identification" means that the exhibit has been marked and can be referred to in court but has not yet been admitted into evidence. Exhibits that have been marked for identification may be shown to witnesses and may be the subject of limited examinations for the purpose of establishing a foundation, but they usually may not be shown to the jury.

The distinction between exhibits that have and have not been admitted is crucial. Many jurisdictions, however, have abolished the "for identification" notation as redundant. All exhibits need to be marked, and the record will show which have been allowed into evidence even in the absence of a special inscription.

§ 22F.4.2 Identify the Exhibit for Opposing Counsel

Exhibits should be identified for opposing counsel before they are shown to the witness. This may be done by referring to the exhibit number or by indicating its designation in the pretrial order if one has been prepared. In some jurisdictions you may be expected actually to hand or display the exhibit to opposing counsel before proceeding.

In any event, these common courtesies allow opposing counsel to confirm that the exhibit is the same one that was produced during discovery or that was discussed and marked at the pretrial conference. Opposing counsel is also afforded an opportunity to make an early objection to the use of the exhibit.

§ 22F.4.3 Examine the Witness on the Foundation for the Exhibit

Having identified the exhibit, you may now proceed to lay the foundation for its admission.

Show the Exhibit to the Witness

The first step is to show the exhibit to the witness. This is typically done by handing it to the witness. If the exhibit is something as large as a life-sized model or an enlarged photograph, you may point to it and direct the witness's attention. In either case you should announce for the record what you are doing, using a shorthand description of the exhibit as well as its identification number:

COUNSEL:

Ms. Harris, I am handing you defendant's exhibit eleven, which is a letter dated July 26.

The description ensures clarity. The term "defendant's exhibit eleven" will mean nothing to the jury and even less to someone reading the transcript. Many lawyers prefer to have the witness give the initial description of the exhibit, but this approach unnecessarily cedes control of the examination. The witness, especially on cross examination, might give a misleading or inadmissible description. In any event, the witness will have plenty of opportunity to describe the exhibit during the identification phase of the testimony.

Your initial description of the exhibit must be scrupulously neutral. While you are allowed to ask a leading question on preliminary matters, you are not allowed to begin arguing your case under the pretext of laying a foundation. Thus, you cannot say:

COUNSEL:

Ms. Harris, I am handing you defendant's exhibit eleven, which is the letter in which the plaintiff agreed to provide repair service at no additional cost.

The date of the letter, and perhaps the name of its author, would be sufficient. If the very description of the exhibit is in issue, you may briefly describe what it "purports" to be.

Identify the Exhibit

The next step is to have the witness identify the exhibit. The witness should state the basis for her familiarity with the exhibit and then describe it in some detail:

QUESTION:

Have you ever seen plaintiff's exhibit seven before?

ANSWER:

Yes, I have seen it many times.

QUESTION:

What is plaintiff's exhibit seven?

ANSWER:

It is a piece of the stationery that I received when my order was delivered from Quickset Printing.

QUESTION:

How is it that you recognize it?

ANSWER:

I remember how it looked when I took it out of the box.

Numerous variations are possible once the witness has examined the exhibit: "Are you familiar with the exhibit? Do you recognize the exhibit? Are you able to identify the exhibit?" While it is technically necessary to establish initially that the witness has a basis for giving a description, it is often possible to elicit the description first: "What is it? How do you know?"

Complete the Foundation for the Exhibit

In some situations, particularly those involving real evidence, the identification of the exhibit will provide a sufficient foundation for admission. In other circumstances the foundation will be much more elaborate, perhaps calling for chain of custody or the establishment of a hearsay exception. These and other foundations for the introduction of real, demonstrative, and documentary evidence are discussed at length in subsequent sections of this chapter.

§ 22F.4.4 Offer the Exhibit Into Evidence

Once the foundation has been completed the exhibit can be offered into evidence. Jurisdictions vary as to the formality with which this must be done. In the simplest version:

COUNSEL:

Your Honor, we offer plaintiff's exhibit three.

Some courts, however, expect a more highly mannered presentation:

COUNSEL:

Your Honor, we move that the identifying mark be stricken and that plaintiff's exhibit three be received as plaintiff's exhibit three in evidence.

In any case, the exhibit must be shown to the judge who will then ask opposing counsel if there are any objections to its admission. At this point it is sufficient to recall that objecting counsel is entitled to request a limited cross examination of the witness (voir dire), which will be restricted to the subject of the admissibility of the exhibit.

§ 22F.4.5 Publish and Use the Exhibit

Once an exhibit has been received it can be "published" to the jury and also used as a basis for further testimony.

Publication

The term "publication" refers to the communication of the exhibit to the jury. Exhibits may be published in a variety of ways. Large objects and oversize graphics are usually turned toward the jury. Smaller objects typically are handed to the jurors and passed among them. Documents can be enlarged and displayed, passed among the jurors, or read aloud. The choice of publication method is customarily left to counsel, although the court may deny leave to use overly dramatic, prejudicial, or dangerous means.

While the right of publication follows inherently from the admission of the document, the court still exercises discretion over the timing and manner of publication. Consequently, it is necessary to obtain the judge's permission to communicate an exhibit to the jury:

COUNSEL:

Your Honor, may I show defendant's exhibit six to the jury?

Or,

COUNSEL:

May I have leave to publish plaintiff's exhibit three by passing it among the jurors?

Or,

COUNSEL:

Your Honor, may the witness read prosecution exhibit nine to the jury?

There is no requirement that the entire exhibit be published. In the case of a lengthy document or voluminous record, it is appropriate to ask a witness to read only the portions that you deem most important. The entire exhibit, however, must be made available to the jury for inspection, as well as to opposing counsel for use on cross examination.

Using the Exhibit

Once an exhibit has been admitted in evidence it can be used to illustrate or amplify a witness's testimony. In addition to publishing it to the jury, a witness can give further testimony that interprets or otherwise explains the significance of the exhibit.

Tangible objects can be used in demonstrations. A witness can show how a gun was aimed or how a tool was used. Maps, diagrams, and photographs can be used to illustrate the movement of persons and vehicles, the locations of incidents, or the relationship and distances between stationary objects. It is permissible to have a witness mark directly on the exhibit or to use velcro "stick-ons" to elaborate on her testimony. These techniques will be discussed further in the section below on demonstrative evidence.

Additionally, once an exhibit is in evidence, a witness can testify about its contents:

QUESTION:

Do the words in defendant's exhibit nine have a particular meaning in your profession?

QUESTION:

Why was the color of the stationery, plaintiff's exhibit one, so important to you?

QUESTION:

What did you do once you received plaintiff's exhibit twelve?

QUESTION:

What was your reaction when you saw Lynn Stromski holding defendant's exhibit four?

The right to testify about an exhibit is constrained by the applicable rules of evidence. Contrary to a frequently heard objection, however, an exhibit is not required to "speak for itself."

Finally, be aware that once an exhibit has been admitted it may be used, subject to the rules of evidence, in the examination of any witness, not only the witness who introduced it.

Part 22G: Making and Meeting Objections in Child Welfare Cases

by Marvin Ventrell[7]

§ 22G.1 Introduction

Objections are a critical piece of the trial process. The objections process is the means by which we ensure appropriate testimony and evidence, and as such it is one of our most important advocacy tools. Yet, objecting is a grossly under-utilized tool in many children's courts.

Lawyers struggle with the rules of evidence and the art of objecting, and that condition is compounded by the mistaken view that the rules of evidence in general, and objections in particular, are less important in children's cases. The culture of many children's courts is one of "relaxed" evidentiary standards. The theory is that because we must be vigilant in our effort to ensure children's interests, we want the court to have as much information as possible, and, therefore, we should let most everything into evidence. The problem with this theory is that it fails to recognize that the proper application of evidentiary standards promotes *reliable* evidence and keeps out unreliable evidence. When we "relax" the rules, we are actually defeating our purpose to protect children with the best possible information.

So the rules of evidence and the art of objecting should be honored in children's cases. While it is true that many courts have specific exceptions to traditional evidentiary standards, particularly at the disposition phase, attorneys who practice in children's court should recognize these as exceptions and not operate under a notion of relaxed evidentiary standards.

Competent use of objections requires an understanding of:

- Evidentiary foundations.

- The form of specific objections.

- The protocol for making and meeting an objection.

---

[7] Marvin Ventrell, J.D., is the President/CEO of the National Association of Counsel for Children (NACC). Portions of this chapter are adapted with permission from *Modern Trial Advocacy: Analysis and Practice*, 3rd Edition, copyright © 2004, National Institute for Trial Advocacy (NITA). The NACC is grateful to NITA for permitting the use of these materials as a gift to the child advocacy community. The NACC highly recommends the full publication of *Modern Trial Advocacy* and additional NITA trial skill material available at www.NITA.org or 800-225-6482.

Attorneys who practice in children's court should acquire these three pieces and use objections to promote the interest of their clients.

§ 22G.2 Whether to Object

The decision to object should be tied to the theory and theme of your case. As to substantive, evidentiary objections, you should object if excluding the evidence serves your theory and theme. As to form of the question objections, you should object in order to ensure understandable and reliable testimony.

The primary reasons to object are:

- To exclude prejudicial evidence.
- To protect the record.
- To protect your witness.

The primary reasons not to object are:

- Jurors' reactions.
- Judge's reaction.
- Opponent's reaction.

None of the reasons not to object should prevent you from making a well-founded objection based on the primary reasons to object. Rather, they are reminders to use objections wisely and appreciate how they are being received by judge, jury, and opposing counsel.

§ 22G.3 Protocol for Objecting

Effective objections are made *forcefully* and *concisely*. Tentative objections and rambling objections are ineffective.

§ 22G.3.1 Making the Objection

- Stand up completely.
- State the objection forcefully and concisely (no rambling objections): "Objection! – Hearsay."
- Listen to the opposing attorney's response.
- Be prepared to argue the objection once recognized by the court. If opposing counsel has given a response to which you would like to respond, ask the judge for permission to respond: "May I respond?" or "May I be heard?"
- Argue to the court, not to opposing counsel.
- Receive the court's ruling with professionalism.

§ 22G.3.2 Meeting the Objection

- Ask the judge for the opportunity to respond—tactfully, but quickly—before a ruling. Do not assume the court wants argument and just begin speaking.

- Argue to the court, not to opposing counsel, by explaining why the objection is not valid.

- With the exception of rephrasing leading, compound, or vague questions, do not abandon your question just because there is an objection.

- Consider voir dire. You may ask for limited voir dire for the purpose of determining the admissibility of the evidence. For example, where a witness lacks foundation for a statement, you may want to show that by asking the foundational questions.

- Remember that questions that show the bias or credibility of the witness are almost always admissible (FRE 607).

- If the objection is sustained, consider making a conditional offer or offer of proof as set forth below.[8]

§ 22G.3.3 Conditional Offers (FRE 104)

To the extent that the admissibility of testimony you are eliciting is tied to later testimony, you may need to make an offer of proof to get it in. Following the objection, ask the court for permission to make a conditional offer and either promise to "tie it up" later or state (outside the presence of the jury) the nature of the evidence that will be introduced later. This typically arises regarding relevance or foundation.

§ 22G.3.4 Offers of Proof (FRE 103)

It may be necessary to make an offer of proof when evidence is excluded by objection. For an appellate court to rule on whether the exclusion was reversible error, there must be record of the excluded evidence. Ask the court for an opportunity to make an offer of proof, and either have the witness testify or make a statement of what the evidence would have been. The offer may also educate the court into reversing its prior ruling.

§ 22G.4 Preservation of the Record for Appeal (FRE 103)

Failure to object waives any right to appellate consideration of the error in admission of the evidence. The only exception is "plain error," which has very

---

[8] See §§ 22G.3.3, 22G.3.4.

limited application. Objections must state the specific ground unless it is obvious. Objections must be timely, such that they are made as soon as the objectionable nature of the question becomes apparent.

§ 22G.5 Objecting Before Trial: Motion in Limine

A motion in limine is the tool to exclude evidence before trial. It is generally not granted unless the evidence is not only subject to a sustainable objection at trial, but is so damaging that once mentioned, its impact cannot be managed by a sustained objection.

§ 22G.6 Making and Meeting the Objections

§ 22G.6.1 The General Rule

Rule 611 of the Federal Rules of Evidence gives the court authority to control witness examination to insure the ascertainment of truth, avoid delay, and protect witnesses.

§ 22G.6.2 Objections as to Form

Objections as to the form of the question should be made timely, before the answer is given. The following is a list of eight "form of the question" objections.

- **Leading (FRE 611).**

  The question suggests the answer and is objectionable on direct examination.

  Example: Be alert to agency attorneys leading their caseworker.

  Response: Foundational / Special witness (young, old, infirm, hostile) / Rephrase.

- **Compound.**

  The question is two separate questions.

  Response: Show that the two questions have a relationship, or rephrase.

- **Vague.**

  The question is likely to get an ambiguous answer.

  Response: Rephrase.

- **Argumentative.**

  Asks the witness to accept the questioner's conclusion rather than provide a fact.

Response: Do not ask argumentative questions. If it's not argumentative, explain how it calls for a fact.

- **Narrative.**

Applies to questions and answers. Witnesses are required to answer questions, not give speeches.

Response: Break it up with questions. Some complex issues require longer answers, such as expert testimony.

- **Asked and Answered.**

You may not repeat a question to a witness.

Response: Explain how the question is a variation of the previous question or rephrase to get to the new information.

- **Facts Not in Evidence.**

You may not include, as a predicate to a question, a fact that is not proven. To do so is unfair because it requires the witness to admit an unproven assumption in order to answer the question.

Response: Establish the fact not in evidence by a question.

- **Nonresponsive.**

You may move to strike an answer that does not respond to the question.

Response: Explain how the answer was in fact responsive if you want the answer in or just move on.

§ 22G.6.3 Evidentiary Objections

Focus on the theme and theory of your case. Does making the objection promote the theme and theory? If not, don't make the objection. The following is a list of 12 common evidentiary objections.

PRACTICE TIP: Spend some time learning the big three and you will catch the majority of objectionable evidence:

- Relevance.
- Foundation (including foundation, lack of personal knowledge, improper lay opinion, and speculation).
- Hearsay.

PRACTICE TIP: To avoid asking objectionable questions, simply ask yourself, is this:

- A fact.
- That the witness has knowledge of.

Stay away from:

- Conclusions.
- Opinions (except for experts).

- **Relevance (FRE 401, 402).**

  The information sought does not make a fact at issue more or less likely.

  Example: Post-filing actions by parent, such as compliance with treatment plan, should not be admissible at adjudication.

  Response: The evidence is relevant because it makes _____ more/less likely.

- **Foundation.**

  The evidence lacks its required foundation.

  Response: Explain how the foundation exists or lay the foundation.

- **Lack of Personal Knowledge (FRE 602).**

  Lay witnesses must testify from their sensory perceptions.

  Response: Explain how the testimony has shown personal knowledge or show the knowledge with more questioning.

- **Improper Lay Opinion (FRE 701).**

  Lay witnesses generally cannot offer opinions or inferences. They may testify to opinions or inferences, however, if the opinion or inference is rationally based on the witness's perception.

  Example: Non-expert caseworker or other fact witnesses giving opinions as to mental health of the child or others.

  Response: Explain how the opinion is "rationally based on the witness's perception."

- **Speculation.**

  Witnesses may not speculate.

  Example: Witness testifying as to someone's feelings, state of mind, or motivation.

  Response: Explain how the answer is the witness's perceived knowledge.

- **Hearsay (FRE 801(c)).**

  Hearsay is inadmissible unless it falls within a specific exception. Hearsay is "a statement other than one made by the declarant while testifying at trial or hearing, offered in evidence to prove the truth of the matter asserted."[9] Be on the lookout for any question that asks the witness what he or she or anyone else said before. Remember that documents can be hearsay or hearsay in part.

Examples: Statements made by hotline reporters; statements made by teachers, neighbors, and doctors; therapist's report; statements by previous caseworkers.

Response:

○ Not Hearsay (FRE 801(c)). It is not offered for the truth of the matter asserted.

Example: Criminal defendant accused of killing wife's lover introduces a note from wife to lover. It is not hearsay if it is offered to prove defendant's state of mind, that he acted in the heat of passion, as opposed to being offered to show truth of matter asserted—that his wife had an affair.

A caseworker might be allowed to testify to statements that show he or she conducted a competent investigation in response to claim that caseworker was biased against parents.

○ Not Hearsay (FRE 801(d)(1)). Prior consistent and prior inconsistent statements.

○ Not Hearsay (FRE 801(D)(2)). Admission by party opponent.

Example: Parent's statement to a caseworker admitting abuse.

○ Falls within a hearsay exception:

– Present Sense Impression (FRE 803(1)).

– Excited Utterance (FRE 802(2)).

– State of Mind (FRE 803(3)).

– Statements Made for Medical Diagnosis (FRE 803(4)).

Example: Child or parents' statements to physician.

– Past Recollection Recorded (FRE 803(5)).

– Business Records (FRE 803(6)).

Example: Contents of caseworker's file.

– Reputation as to Character (FRE 803(21), 404, 405).

---

9 FRE 801(c).

- Prior Testimony (FRE 804(b)(1)).

- Dying Declaration 804(b)(2)).

- Statement Against Interest (FRE 804(b)(3)).

- Residual Exception (FRE 803(24)).

- Child Hearsay Exceptions (see state and local rules and JOHN E.B. MYERS, EVIDENCE IN CHILD ABUSE AND NEGLECT CASES (3rd Ed.) §7.53).

  Example: If your jurisdiction has the child hearsay exception, statements by the child may be admitted, even though otherwise hearsay. The Washington statute, on which many jurisdiction's statutes are modeled, requires the child be under 10 and if not present, that there must be corroborating evidence. Many jurisdictions also require a pretrial hearing. The exception may also be limited to certain types of proceedings.

- Special Dependency Court Exceptions (see state and local rules and JOHN E.B. MYERS, EVIDENCE IN CHILD ABUSE AND NEGLECT CASES (3rd Ed.) Chapter 7).

- **Unfair Prejudice.**

  Probative value of the information outweighs the danger that it will cause unfair prejudice.

  Example: Expert witness smashing or shaking doll to show force in shaken baby case.

  Response: Explain how significant the value of the testimony is relative to any prejudice. Remember, it's alright to introduce prejudicial evidence—that's your job. The objection is "unfair" prejudice.

- **Improper Character Evidence.**

  As a general rule, past activity (character) cannot be used to prove current activity.

  Response:

  ○ Generally. Exceptions are: motive, opportunity, intent, preparation, plan knowledge, identity, or absence of mistake under FRE 404(b).

  ○ Crimes. Prosecution in criminal case may offer character as rebuttal of good character of defendant under FRE 404(a)(1). Under FRE 609, you can impeach credibility using a conviction if it was a felony or it involved dishonesty within the last 10 years, except for juvenile adjudications.

- ○ Truthfulness. Under FRE 608(b), you can cross-examine regarding bad acts that reflect on truthfulness.
- ○ Reputation. Under FRE 608(a), reputation is admissible if it goes to truthfulness.

- **Authenticity (FRE 901).**

There must be a showing, by foundation, that an exhibit is what it purports to be.

Response: Lay further foundation.

- **Best Evidence (FRE 1001 through 1004).**

The modern rule is that duplicates are admissible.

Response: Show that the document is a duplicate of the original or that the original is unavailable.

- **Privilege (FRE 501).**

Statute and common law provide certain privileges, including psychotherapist-patient, attorney-client, physician-patient, marital, and clergy.

Example: Child's or parents' statements to therapists.

Response: Cite waiver or exception.

- **Settlement Offers (FRE 408).**

Settlement offers and offers made during settlement negotiations are not admissible.

Example: Parents' statements during mandatory mediation.

Response: Such statements may be admissible to show bias or to rebut a claim of delay.

Appendices

Appendix A-1: NACC Recommendations for Representation of Children in Abuse and Neglect Cases 647

Appendix A-2: American Bar Association Standards of Practice for Lawyers Who Represent Children in Abuse and Neglect Cases (NACC Revised Version) 667

Appendix B: Recommended Readings 711

Appendix C: Child Welfare Organizational Resources 717

APPENDIX A-1

NACC Recommendations for Representation of Children in Abuse and Neglect Cases

NATIONAL ASSOCIATION OF COUNSEL FOR CHILDREN

Funded by a Grant from The Anschutz Foundation

National Association of Counsel for Children (NACC)
1825 Marion Street, Suite 340
Denver, CO 80218
303/864-5320
1/888-828-NACC
Fax 303/864-5351
E-mail advocate@NACCchildlaw.org
Web NACCchildlaw.org

NACC Recommendations for Representation of Children in Abuse and Neglect Cases was produced as part of the NACC's objective to establish the practice of law for children as a legitamate profession and legal specialty. As part of that objective, the NACC periodically produces standards of practice or guidelines for the representation of children.

The document was drafted by the NACC Program Committee and the prinipal authors listed below.

The document was adopted by a unanimous vote of the NACC Board of Directors on April 28, 2001.

Principal Authors
David Katner
Philip (Jay) McCarthy, Jr.
Miriam Rollin
Marvin Ventrell

NACC Drafting Committee Members
Angela Adams
Donald Bross
Donald Duquette
Ann Haralambie
Katherine Holliday
Ellen Jones
Laoise King
Patricia Macias
Philip (Jay) McCarthy, Jr.
John Myers
Jacqueline Parker
Henry Plum
Miriam Rollin
John Stuemky
Marvin Ventrell
Christopher Wu

Funding for this project was provided by The Anschutz Foundation, Denver, Colorado.

For additional copies or reprint permission, contact the NACC 1-888-828-NACC or advocate@NACCchildlaw.org

CONTENTS

EXECUTIVE SUMMARY

NACC RECOMMENDATIONS FOR REPRESENTATION OF CHILDREN
IN ABUSE AND NEGLECT CASES

I.   Introduction

II.   Children's Legal Representation Policy
      A.   Overview
      B.   Child Welfare Cases
      C.   Private Custody and Adoption Cases

III. Needs Checklist for Children Involved in Abuse and Neglect Cases
      A.   Systemic Safeguards
      B.   Advocacy Duties
      C.   Advocacy Issues

IV.   Representation Models
      A.   Advocate Directed Representation
            1.   The Attorney Guardian *ad Litem* Hybrid
            2.   The Lay Guardian *ad Litem* Model
            3.   The "Two Distinct Lawyer Roles" Model
      B.   Client Directed Representation
            1.   Traditional Attorney
            2.   Child's Attorney (ABA Standards Model)
            3.   Child's Attorney (ABA / NACC Model)

V.   Resources

EXECUTIVE SUMMARY

The lack of standards of practice or guidelines for attorneys representing children in child protection proceedings has frequently been cited as a major cause of substandard and ineffective legal representation of children. Unlike more traditional areas of practice where the model of representation and the lawyer code of conduct are essentially uniform from state to state, the practice of law for children has no commonly accepted uniform model or code, and many states provide inadequate guidance for attorneys doing this work. This is the case in part because the practice of law for children is a unique and relatively recent development, and because the evolution has occurred on a state by state basis. Additionally, there has been significant disagreement as to whether representation for children should take a traditional client directed ("expressed wishes"), or an advocate directed ("best interests") form, making it difficult to adopt a model.

Important progress was made toward the creation of a uniform model of representation with the creation of the *ABA Standards of Practice for Lawyers Who Represent Children in Abuse and Neglect Cases* in 1996. Still, jurisdictions struggle to adopt clear and comprehensive guidelines for children's attorneys, frequently because of the long-standing debate over the form of representation.

The *NACC Recommendations for Representation of Children in Abuse and Neglect Cases* is a document designed to assist jurisdictions in the selection and implementation of a model of child representation. Rather than urging jurisdictions to choose a particular model, this document sets out a checklist of children's needs that should be met by whatever representation scheme is chosen. It is the NACC's hope that this approach will allow jurisdictions to focus on what matters, serving the child client, and avoid becoming mired in the debate over best interests and expressed wishes.

The NACC believes that children's legal service needs can be met by both client directed ("expressed wishes") and advocate directed ("best interest") models of representation. In an effort to help jurisdictions understand various models, this document includes a section describing the various models of representation.

Whatever form of representation jurisdictions choose, the NACC believes that every child subject to a child protection proceeding must be provided an independent, competent, and zealous attorney, trained in the law of child protection and the art of trial advocacy, with adequate time and resources to handle the case.

NACC RECOMMENDATIONS FOR REPRESENTATION
OF CHILDREN IN ABUSE AND NEGLECT CASES

I.   Introduction

This document is designed to assist children's attorneys, courts, and policy makers working to improve the legal representation of children. The focus is on the representation of children in abuse and neglect proceedings. The document also has application in private custody and adoption matters.

Rather than prescribing one specific model of representation, this document provides a policy framework for the legal representation of children, followed by a checklist of children's needs that representation should meet, whatever form of representation states choose. The document describes various models of representation in an effort to help the reader appreciate the strengths and weaknesses of each.

The NACC is aware of the debate in the child advocacy community over the two primary models of representing children - the attorney guardian *ad litem* (advocate directed "best interests" model) and the traditional attorney (client directed "expressed wishes" model). While this debate can be useful, the NACC suggests that rather than spending time and resources debating the merits of the various models, states should focus on ensuring that the model of representation used meets the children's needs checklist.

II.   Children's Legal Representation Policy

A.   Overview

The NACC believes that each child must be valued as a unique human being, regardless of race, ethnicity, religion, age, social class, physical or mental disability, gender, or sexual orientation. Each child is vested with certain fundamental rights, including a right to physical and emotional health and safety. In order to achieve the physical and emotional well being of children, we must promote legal rights and remedies for children. This includes empowering children by ensuring that courts hear and consider their views in proceedings that affect their lives.

Children's attorneys play a critical role in empowering children and ensuring that children's views are heard in legal proceedings. Outcomes in our adversarial process are directly tied to the quality of legal representation. Additionally, the presence of children's attorneys is critical to ensuring the timeliness of proceedings.

The NACC believes that attorneys representing children should have a combination of knowledge, training, experience, and ability which allows them to effectively discharge their duties to their clients. The NACC supports federal, state, and local programs to enhance the competence of these attorneys.

B.   Child Welfare Cases

The NACC believes that in order for justice to be done in child abuse and neglect related court proceedings, all parties, including children, must be represented by independent *legal* counsel[1]. The children who are the subjects of these proceedings are usually the most profoundly affected by the decisions made, and these children are usually the least able to voice their views effectively on their own. In many jurisdictions, however, courts do not appoint independent attorneys for all children in abuse and neglect related proceedings. NACC believes that federal, state, and local law must mandate that independent attorneys be appointed to represent the interests of children in all such proceedings.

C.   Private Custody and Adoption Cases

The NACC believes that while legal representation is not required for every child who is the subject of a child custody determination, the judge *should* appoint an attorney to represent the child in certain cases: when there are certain substantive allegations that make child representation necessary -- i.e., when there is an allegation of child neglect or abuse (physical, sexual, or emotional) by a parent or household member, when there is a culture of violence between the parents, when there is an allegation of substance abuse by a parent, when there are allegations of non-paternity, or when there is an allegation of or fear about child snatching -- as well as when there are certain procedural situations which make child representation necessary -- e.g., when a child will be a witness or when the case develops an extremely adversarial nature. In addition, the judge *should consider* appointing an attorney to represent the child in certain other cases: when there is an allegation of mental illness on the part of a parent, when a custodial parent is relocating geographically, when child representation can reduce undue harm to the child from the litigation itself, when the child has exceptional physical or mental health needs, when the child expresses a strong desire to make his or her opinions known to the judge, when there is a *pro se* parent, when there is a third-party custody action against a parent (e.g., by a grandparent), or when the failure to appoint a representative for the child would otherwise impede the judge's capacity to decide the case properly. (Attorneys can be instrumental in ensuring that judges have the necessary data upon which to make an informed decision.)

III.   Needs Checklist for Children Involved in Abuse and Neglect Cases

The NACC encourages jurisdictions to adopt a system of legal representation of children which satisfies the following checklist. The representation scheme should ensure that each of the following children's rights or needs are satisfied

---

[1] *The U.S. Department of Health and Human Services supports this principle.* Adoption 2002: The President's Initiative on Adoption and Foster Care. Guidelines for Public Policy and State Legislation Governing Permanence for Children, *U.S. Dept. of HHS ACF ACYF Children's Bureau, 1999.*

through a combination of systemic safeguards, advocacy duties, and basic advocacy issues.

A.   Systemic Safeguards

☐ 1.   Children need competent, independent, and zealous attorneys. The system of representation must require the appointment of competent, independent, zealous attorneys for every child at every stage of the proceedings. The same attorney should represent the child for as long as the child is subject to the court's jurisdiction.

Comment A: Competence is the foundation of all legal representation. The fundamental requirements of competency as defined in each jurisdiction, combined with the ability to function without constraint or obligation to any party other than the child client is of paramount importance. (See, ABA Model Rules of Professional Conduct (Model Rules): Preamble; 1.14(a); ABA Model Code of Professional Responsibility (Model Code): EC 7-1; EC 7-12; ABA Standards of Practice for Lawyers who Represent Children in Abuse and Neglect Cases (ABA Standards): Preface; A-1.)

Comment B: Competent representation includes knowledge, skill, thoroughness, and preparation. This includes knowledge of placements and services available for the child, and services available to the child's family. (See, Model Rule: 1.1; Model Code DR 6-101(A)(1)(2); ABA Standards B-1; C.) Jurisdictions should provide special initial and periodic training to all attorneys in child welfare proceedings covering substantive law (federal, state, statutory, regulatory, and case law), procedure, trial advocacy, child welfare and child development.

Comment C: Continuity of representation is important to the child. The same lawyer should represent the child for as long as the child is under the jurisdiction of the court. Temporary substitution of counsel, although often unavoidable, should be discouraged. Any substitute counsel must be familiar with the child and the child's case.

☐ 2.   Children need attorneys with adequate time and resources. The system of representation must include reasonable caseload limits and at the same time provide adequate compensation for attorneys representing children.

Comment A: The NACC recommends that a full time attorney represent no more than 100 individual clients at a time, assuming a caseload that includes clients at various stages of cases, and recognizing that some clients may be part of the same sibling group. This is the same cap recommended by the U.S. Dept. of HHS Children's Bureau and the American Bar Association[2]. One hundred cases averages to 20 hours per case in a 2000-hour year.

---

[2] *ABA Standards of Practice for Lawyers Who Represent Children in Abuse and Neglect Cases, §§L-1, L-2; The U.S. Department of Health and Human Services supports this principle.* Adoption 2002: The President's Initiative on Adoption and Foster Care. Guidelines for Public Policy and State Legislation Governing Permanence for Children, *U.S. Dept. of HHS ACF ACYF Children's Bureau, 1999, page VII-5.*

Comment B: For the sake of the child client and the interests of the system, attorneys must be provided appropriate and reasonable compensation. The NACC adopts the following position of the Dept. of HHS on this point: "Primary causes of inadequate legal representation of the parties in child welfare cases are low compensation and excessive caseloads. Reasonable compensation of attorneys for this important work is essential. Rather than a flat per case fee, compensate lawyers for time spent. This will help to increase their level of involvement in the case and should help improve the image of attorneys who are engaged in this type of work. When attorneys are paid a set fee for complicated and demanding cases, they cope either by providing less service than the child-client requires or by providing representation on a pro bono or minimum wage basis. Neither of these responses is appropriate. Rates should also reflect the level of seniority and level of experience of the attorneys. In some offices, lawyers handling child welfare cases receive lower pay than other attorneys. This is inappropriate. Compensation of attorneys handling children's cases should be on a par with other lawyers in the office handling legal matters of similar demand and complexity. The need for improved compensation is not for the purpose of benefiting the attorney, but rather to ensure that the child receives the intense and expert legal services required."[3]

❏ 3. **Children need attorneys who understand their role and duties.** The system of representation of children must be well defined by statute, bar standards, administrative guidelines, supreme court directive or other documents such that every attorney appointed for a child can understand his/her precise role and duties, and such that an attorney can be held accountable for performance of those duties.

Comment: It is helpful here to distinguish between role and duties. Role refers to whether, for example, the attorney is client directed (traditional attorney model or child's attorney models) while duties refer to those actions to be taken by the attorney (investigation, calling witnesses, etc.). Although duties are in part dependent on role, most commentators agree that certain fundamental duties should apply regardless of role. See ABA and ABA / NACC Revised Standards § C Actions to be Taken.

❏ 4. **Children need an opportunity to present their positions to the court through counsel.** The system of representation must provide the child with an opportunity for his/her needs and wishes to be expressed to the court.

Comment: Children have an independent perspective and may have information and positions to present to the court on a wide range of issues including but extending beyond the issue of placement. Other parties and the court may otherwise be unaware of the child's perspective or of how certain decisions subjectively affect the child.

❏ 5. **Children need confidential communication with their attorneys.** The attorney has a duty to explain the extent of confidentiality in developmentally appropriate language.

---

[3] *Adoption 2002: The President's Initiative on Adoption and Foster Care. Guidelines for Public Policy and State Legislation Governing Permanence for Children,* U.S. Dept. of HHS ACF ACYF Children's Bureau, 1999, page VII-4.

Comment A: Every child should have the right to communicate confidentially with the representative. (See, Model Rules: 1.6, 3.7; Model Code: DR 4-101; 5-102; ABA Standards: A-1; Comment B-2(2).)

Comment B: But see Alaska Ethics Op. 854. Some jurisdictions include attorneys as mandatory reporters, and pure confidentiality may be precluded with a GAL - advocate directed representation system.

❑ 6. Children need to be involved as litigants in the entire litigation process, including any post disposition, termination of parental rights, and adoption proceedings. The system of representation must recognize the child as a party to the litigation and must include the child in all phases of the litigation, including the opportunity to participate in arguments and jury selection where applicable, offer exhibits, call witnesses, examine and cross examine witnesses and engage in motions and discovery processes. The child must also be given notice of all proceedings and copies of all pleadings.

Comment: The child should be physically present early in the proceedings, so as to allow all parties and their representatives the opportunity to become acquainted with the child as an individual. Although the child's presence may not be required at every court hearing, it should not be waived by the representative, unless the child has already been introduced to the court and his/her presence is not required by law, custom, or practice in that jurisdiction. Every child should be notified through counsel of every court hearing, every agency meeting, and every case conference or negotiation among the various professionals involved in the case and the child's attorney should be notified concerning any change in the child's welfare, placement, education, or status. Every child should be considered a party to the litigation, and should therefore, be entitled to any and all benefits under the law granted to any other party. Every child should have access to sufficient information to allow his/her representative to provide competent representation including the child's representative having access to social services, psychiatric, psychological, drug and alcohol, medical, law enforcement, school and other records relevant to the case, and opportunity for interviewing child welfare caseworkers, foster parents and other caretakers, school personnel, health professionals, law enforcement, and other persons with relevant information. This access may require the representative to file motions for discovery, subpoenas, subpoenas duces tecum, depositions and interrogatories, according to the discovery mechanisms available in the jurisdiction. Every child should have the opportunity to present his/her witnesses in the court proceedings. This requires the representative to investigate facts, identify and communicate with witnesses, and issue subpoenas to ensure that witnesses appear in court.

❑ 7. Children need judicial review of adverse decisions. The system of representation must provide an opportunity to appeal an adverse ruling.

Comment: Children need to have access to the court after the adjudication occurs. This may require the representative to forego informal resolution of issues at the review stage of the litigation. See State ex rel. Jeanette H., 529 S.E. 2d 865 (2000).

❑ 8. Children need to be able to hold their attorneys accountable. The system of representation must provide recourse for ineffective assistance of counsel.

Comment: Every child should be able to hold the representative accountable for providing less than competent representation.

❑ 9. Children need an attorney with a fair opportunity to be effective in the court system. The system of representation must include a court system that devotes adequate time and resources to cases.

Comment: Courts cannot be "rubber stamp" agencies for social service agencies and must be equipped to handle caseloads responsibly. See, *Resource Guidelines, Improving Court Practice in Child Abuse and Neglect Cases*, National Council of Juvenile and Family Court Judges, © 1995 NCJFCJ, Reno, NV.

B. Advocacy Duties

❑ 1. Children need attorneys who fully understand their cases. The attorney must perform a full and independent case investigation.

Comment: The child's attorney has a duty of full investigation of the case. (See, Model Rule: 4.2; Model Code: DR 7-104 (A) (1); ABA Standards: C-2(4); C-6.)

❑ 2. Children need meaningful communication with their attorneys. The attorney must observe the child, and dependent upon the child's age and capabilities, interview the child. The attorney must engage in regular and meaningful communication with the child. Children need to participate in making decisions that affect their cases. The attorney has a duty to involve the child client in the process, whether under a client directed model or advocate directed model. The attorney has a duty to explain his/her role to the child in developmentally appropriate language.

Comment A: Under a client directed model, the scope of representation by the child's attorney includes the duty to abide by the client's decision concerning the objectives of the representation. (See, Model Rule: 1.2(a); Model Code: DR 7-101(A)(1); EC 7-7; EC 7-8; ABA Standards: B-4.)

Comment B: This is a universal need, and it applies whether or not the child is pre-verbal. Visual encounters with children who are represented, even with pre-verbal children, are crucial to the representation. Otherwise, the representative is limited by relying upon the mental impressions of third parties. The child's attorney has a duty of effective, thorough, and developmentally appropriate communication with the client, including the duty to meet with the client. (See, Model Rules: 1.4 (a), (b); Model Code: EC 7-8; 9-2; ABA Standards: C-1; A-3; B-1(5); D-2; E-2; F-4.)

Comment C: Children need education about the law and all options available under the legal system. This need is restricted to developmentally appropriate clients, capable of communication.

Comment D: The child client must be informed about the responsibilities and obligations of the representative, as well as the ability and requirements of the representative to accomplish these things.

❑ 3. Children need loyal attorneys. The child's attorney is prohibited from representation that would constitute a conflict of interest.

Comment: Attorneys must be aware of the potential for conflict while representing a sibling group. Additionally, the child's attorney must be sensitive to the age and maturity of the client where waiver is an issue. (See, Model Rules: 1.7; Model Code: DR 5-101 (A); 5-105(A), (C); 5-107 (B); ABA Standards: B-2(2).)

❑ 4. Children need the full benefit of legal counsel. The attorney must provide competent, independent and zealous representation for each client. The attorney must have adequate time and resources to devote to the child's case, and to understanding his/her role and duties, insuring confidentiality, and full active participation in all stages of the child's case.

C.   Advocacy Issues

❑ 1. Children need permanence. The attorney must advocate for timely resolution and permanent resolution (absent compelling reasons to the contrary) of the case.

Comment: The child's attorney has a duty of diligent and prompt representation, and a duty to expedite litigation, especially where placement of a young child is at issue. (See, Model Rule: 1.3; 3.2; Model Code: DR 6-101(A)(3); EC 6-4; ABA Standards: B-1(4); C-6.)

❑ 2. Children need their immediate and basic needs met. The attorney must advocate for food, shelter, clothing, and safety, including a safe temporary placement where necessary and for educational, medical, mental health, and dental needs.

Comment: The child's most immediate physical needs must be addressed and should be the highest priority for the child's representative. After the immediate needs of sustaining life have been addressed, the child's education, mental health, medical, and dental needs must be addressed. Children's attorneys should act as a kind of "watchdog" for the children's needs, insuring that services are provided.

❑ 3. Children need family relationships. The attorney must advocate for continuation of appropriate familial relationships and family preservation services where appropriate.

Comment: Without jeopardizing the child's physical or emotional safety, arrangements to maintain familial relationships (including siblings) which are not deemed to be harmful to the child should be established as soon as practicable. Family services may include visitation and services for family members: parenting education, medical and mental health care, drug and alcohol treatment, housing, etc. Such family services may also be appropriate to continue other meaningful relationships and ongoing activities where feasible.

❑ 4. Children need to be protected from unnecessary harm that can result from legal proceedings. The attorney must advocate for the utilization of court processes that minimize harm to the child, and make certain that the child is properly prepared and emotionally supported where the child is a witness.

IV.   Representation Models

The following representation models are presented to assist states in evaluating and formulating models of representation. States should consider the requirements of the federal Child Abuse Prevention and Treatment Act (CAPTA) regarding the appointment of representation for the child. The U.S. Department of Health and Human Services, Children's Bureau has indicated that although CAPTA requires a GAL best interests representative, that role may be filled by either an attorney GAL or more traditional client directed attorney.[4]

A.   Advocate Directed Representation

1.   The Attorney Guardian *ad Litem* Hybrid[5] Model.

This model provides an attorney to represent the child and instructs the attorney to represent the child's "best interests." The attorney GAL advocates for a result which he/she believes (not necessarily what the child believes) is in the child's "best interests." Rather than taking direction from the client, as is the case in traditional attorney representation of adults, the attorney GAL is charged with forming the client's position by using his/her own judgment. Under this model, the attorney GAL's judgment as to the child's "best interests" takes precedence over the client's wishes.

Pros: This model is favored by many as the traditional model of representing children, particularly young children who cannot meaningfully participate in their litigation. It is also thought to protect older children from the harm of their own bad choices.

Cons: Critics charge that this is an "old fashioned," paternalistic model of representation that treats children as chattel rather than empowering them in the system. Critics charge that advocate directed representation is wrong by definition because: 1) attorneys are not ethically allowed to disregard their clients directives; 2) attorneys are not qualified to make "best interests" determinations; and 3) the legal

---

[4] *Adoption 2002: The President's Initiative on Adoption and Foster Care. Guidelines for Public Policy and State Legislation Governing Permanence for Children,* U.S. Dept. of HHS ACF ACYF Children's Bureau, 1999, p. VII-21.

[5] *Ann M. Haralambie identifies and discusses the "hybrid' role in The Child's Attorney, A Guide to Representing Children in Custody, Adoption and Protection Cases,* ABA 1993 at p. 37.

system requires that attorneys be zealous advocates for a client's position, not agents of the court. Critics also charge that the system results in "relaxed advocacy" where attorneys appointed as GAL feel, and are treated, as relieved of their traditional lawyering responsibilities. Critics argue that this model has contributed to sub standard representation of children across the country.

Jurisdictions Using a Form of This Model: Approximately 60% of the U/S jurisdictions use a form of this model.[6]

Source: The Colorado version is comprised of the following sources: Colorado Revised Statutes §§ 19-1-103, 19-1-111, 19-3-203; The Colorado Rules of Professional Conduct at CRS, Volume 12 - pages 711-831; Supreme Court of Colorado Chief Justice Directive 97-02; Colorado GAL Standards of Practice.

2. **The Lay Guardian *ad Litem* Model**
    This advocate directed model provides for a non-attorney to "represent" the child's "best interests." This person, usually a non-professional volunteer, advocates for what he/she believes (not necessarily what the child believes) is in the child's "best interests." The lay GAL "stands" in the proceeding for the presumptively incompetent child. The focus is the protection of the child by an adult who attempts to know and then articulate the child's best interests.

    The NACC discourages the use of this as an exclusive model. Children, even more than adults, require trained legal representation and this model, by definition, is not legal representation. While the NACC recognizes the value of non-legal advocacy for children, whether in the form of lay GAL or CASA, we stress that it cannot be a substitute for trained professional attorneys for children. On this point, the NACC and National CASA have agreed. Non-legal advocates play an important role in the process, and jurisdictions should consider implementing such programs *in addition* to appointing attorneys.

    Due to the substantial shortcomings of this model, states which use this model of representation frequently appoint an attorney to represent the child or the lay GAL.

    Pros: The model has value when used in conjunction with legal counsel.

---

[6] *Child Abuse and Neglect Cases: Representation as a Critical Component of Effective Practice.*   NCJFCJ Permanency Planning for Children Project, Technical Assistance Bulletin, 1999, page 45.

Cons: Assuming this is the only "representation" provided, the child has no legal counsel. Lay GALs are unable to provide "legal" counsel and cannot, for example, present evidence, examine witnesses, appeal adverse decisions, or advise the client of the ramifications of legal matters. Lay GALs attempting to serve in the role of legal counsel are engaging in the unauthorized practice of law. Additionally, lay representatives are less accountable than professionals for their actions because their conduct is not governed by ethical and legal standards.

Jurisdictions Using a Form of this Model Include: Florida, Hawaii, Maine

Sources: Florida uses a lay volunteer Guardian *ad litem* model. Florida's Guardian *Ad Litem* Program includes an attorney who advises volunteers on the protection of children's rights and represents the program in contested court proceedings. Fla. Stat. § 39.820 (2000).

In Hawaii, children in dependency cases are generally represented by volunteer lay guardians *ad litem* and CASAs called Volunteer Guardians *Ad Litem* (VGAL). Children *may also* be represented by an Attorney Guardian *Ad Litem*. H.R.S § 587-40.

Maine law calls for a GAL who is usually an attorney but is not required to be by statute. The GAL is considered a party and has the right to call and cross examine witnesses and has access to discovery. Should the GAL be an attorney, he/she essentially functions in the hybrid role of Attorney GAL defined in IV. A. 1. above. It is not clear how such duties can be performed competently or without violating the law against unauthorized practice of law if the appointment is of a lay person. Maine Supreme Judicial Court Rules for Guardians *Ad Litem*; 22 M.R.S. § 4005; 4 M.R.S. §1501.

3. **The "Two Distinct Lawyer Roles" Model.**
   A single lawyer model, either advocate directed (best interests) or client directed, may not meet the needs of all children, given their developing and varied capacities from infants to mature and articulate teens. This model would require appointment of a best interest lawyer-guardian *ad litem* or a traditional attorney under certain circumstances as set out in law.

   In 1998, Michigan passed a version of this model that creates two separate and distinct roles for the lawyer representing children: attorney and lawyer-guardian *ad litem*. Michigan requires the appointment of a lawyer-GAL in every case and the lawyer-GAL is to represent the best interests of the child. The statute permits the court to appoint an attorney where the mature child and lawyer-GAL are in conflict about identification of the child's interests. The model prescribes aggressive duties for the lawyer-GAL and provides for attorney-client privilege. It requires the lawyer-GAL to tell the court the wishes and preferences of the child even if the lawyer-GAL advocates for a different view and requires the lawyer-GAL to weigh the child's wishes in making the best interests determination according to the age and maturity of the client. When a lawyer is appointed as "attorney," however, the attorney owes the same duties of undivided loyalty, confidentiality and zealous representation of the child's express wishes as the attorney would to an adult client. Some proponents of the Two Distinct Lawyer Role model urge that the law *require* appointment of an attorney instead of a lawyer-GAL at a certain age (unless the child is mentally handicapped), rather than leave attorney appointment to the discretion of the court.

Pros: Proponents argue that the pure forms of either advocate directed ("best interests") or client directed ("expressed wishes") models are deficient when applied to all children, so that a model which provides clear lawyer duties depending on the age and maturity of the child better serves the child client. This model is also well defined by statute and lessens the tendency toward "relaxed advocacy." This model also reduces the risk inherent in the ABA and NACC models that a lawyer appointed as "attorney" would find an exception to (or water down) the duty of aggressive and client-directed advocacy.

Cons: Critics argue that, at its foundation, this is just an attorney directed model with most of the shortcomings of model A. 1. above. The appointment of an attorney GAL is the rule, not the exception, and an attorney is appointed only in rare circumstances. Also, under rare circumstances the child could be represented by both an attorney and a lawyer-guardian *ad litem* which adds to the cost. The test for appointing one or the other lawyer roles remains unsettled.

Jurisdictions Using the Model: Michigan

Source: MCL 712A.13a(1)(b) (for definition of "attorney") and MCL 712A.17d (for duties of lawyer-guardian *ad litem*).

B.   **Client Directed Representation.**

1. **Traditional Attorney.**
    A traditional attorney functions as a client directed advocate. He/she advocates for the expressed wishes of the client and is bound by the client's directives concerning the objectives of representation. The model does not prohibit the attorney from acting in his/her capacity as counselor for the client, and state ethics codes include the counseling function. Attorneys are not required, without first counseling their client as to more appropriate options, to blindly follow directives that are clearly harmful to the client. Further, the model does not require attorneys to advocate positions not supported by facts and the law.

    Pros: The model is thought to give voice and autonomy to the client and to empower the child within the system. It allows attorneys to function in a familiar setting. Proponents believe it produces good outcomes for children because it encourages independent, zealous advocacy, and the attorney is not confused by the role or duties.

    Cons: Critics charge that the model does not work for young children who cannot meaningfully direct their litigation or for older children who may misdirect their litigation.

    Jurisdictions Using a Form of This Model Include: Oregon uses a traditional attorney, but not in all cases. Additionally, a CASA appointment is required in Oregon. Likewise, in many cases a traditional attorney is used in Massachusetts, but in conjunction with a Guardian *ad Litem.*

    Sources: Oregon Revised Statutes §§ 419A.170; 419A.012; 419B.195; Ethics provision 3.3. Mass. Gen. Laws ch. 119, § 29; Mass. Ethics Opinion 93-6. ABA Model Rules of Professional Conduct (Model Rules): Preamble; 1.14(a); ABA Model Code of Professional Responsibility (Model Code): EC 7-1; EC 7-12.

2. **Child's Attorney (ABA Standards Model)**
    The following selected provisions from the *ABA Standards of Practice for Lawyers Who Represent Children in Abuse and Neglect Cases* define the model. "The term 'child's attorney' means a lawyer who provides legal services for a child and who owes the same duties of undivided loyalty, confidentiality, and competent representation to the child as is due an adult client. The child's attorney should elicit the child's preferences in a developmentally appropriate manner, advise the child, and provide guidance. The child's attorney

should represent the child's expressed preferences and follow the child's direction throughout the course of litigation. To the extent that a child cannot express a preference, the child's attorney shall make a good faith effort to determine the child's wishes and advocate accordingly or request appointment of a guardian *ad litem*. To the extent that a child does not or will not express a preference about particular issues, the child's attorney should determine and advocate the child's legal interests. If the child's attorney determines that the child's expressed preference would be seriously injurious to the child (as opposed to merely being contrary to the lawyer's opinion of what would be in the child's interests), the lawyer may request appointment of a separate guardian *ad litem* and continue to represent the child's expressed preference, unless the child's position is prohibited by law or without any factual foundation."

Pros: Proponents see the model as the most significant advance in child representation in many years. They see the model as an evolution from the GAL model of the 1970s. The model is a detailed roadmap for representation taking role and duty confusion out of the picture. The model also discourages relaxed advocacy.

Cons: Critics argue the model still does not work well for young children and that the directive to resort to representation of the child's "legal interests" in some cases is not a meaningful directive. Critics complain that focusing on the child's so-called "legal interests" is unsatisfactory because the legal interests of the child may be unclear or contradictory. For example, a child has a legal interest in being protected from abusive or neglectful parents. The ABA Standards are also criticized for including broad exceptions to the client-directed ideal and thus giving the lawyer unfettered and unreviewed discretion identifying the goals of the child - the same sort of unbridled discretion that critics complain about in the best interests substituted judgment model.

Jurisdictions Using a Form of This Model Include: At the time of the preparation of this document, no jurisdiction had adopted the ABA Standards as the exclusive system of representation. A number of jurisdictions have adopted many of the "duties" requirements of the standards (e.g., case investigation, motion practice) as opposed to the "role" requirements. As to "role" of counsel, Oregon uses a traditional attorney similar to this model.

Source: *ABA Standards of Practice for Lawyers Who Represent Children in Abuse & Neglect Cases*, © 1996 American Bar Association, Chicago, IL.

3. **Child's Attorney (ABA / NACC Model)**
The *ABA Standards* were adopted by the ABA in 1996. The following year, the NACC adopted the standards with reservation as to Standard B-4. Standard B-4 is the critical client direction language of the standards and some members of the NACC board believed the *ABA Standards* gave too much autonomy to the child client and was unrealistic where young children were concerned. The *ABA Standards (NACC Revised Version)*, is the NACC's attempt to achieve a better balance of client autonomy and protection within standard B-4. This child's attorney model places the attorney in the role of traditional attorney and addresses the needs of the young child through the application of an objective best interests evaluation in limited situations. The model requires that the attorney assume the traditional role of zealous advocate and not GAL to avoid any propensity toward relaxed advocacy. At the same time, it recognizes that some children are not capable of directing their litigation. The model allows for a degree of advocate direction so long as it is the exception to the rule, and based on objective criteria.

The distinction between the *ABA Standards* and the *NACC Revised ABA Standards* is that where the ABA remained consistent with the client directed attorney throughout, the NACC carved out a significant exception where the client cannot meaningfully participate in the formulation of his or her position. In such cases, the NACC's version calls for a GAL type judgment using objective criteria. Additionally, the NACC's version *requires* the attorney to request the appointment of a separate GAL, after unsuccessful attempts at counseling the child, when the child's wishes are considered to be seriously injurious to the child.

Pros: Proponents believe this is the best blending of the traditional attorney and attorney / GAL, providing the best of both options.

Cons: One critic has suggested that, by blending the attorney and GAL roles, this model dilutes both. The NACC model is also criticized for giving the lawyer unfettered and unreviewed discretion identifying the goals of the child - the same sort of unbridled discretion that critics complain about in the best interests advocate directed model.

Jurisdictions Using a Form of This Model Include: At the time of the preparation of this document, no jurisdiction had adopted the ABA NACC Revised Standards as the exclusive system of representation. A number of jurisdictions have adopted many of the "duties" requirements of the model (e.g., case investigation, motion practice) as opposed to the "role" requirements. As to "role" of counsel, Oregon uses a traditional attorney similar to this model.

Source: *ABA Standards of Practice for Lawyers Who Represent Children in Abuse & Neglect Cases*, (NACC Revised Version) NACC Children's Law Manual Series, 1999 Edition, p. 177.

V.   Resources

ABA Standards of Practice for Lawyers Who Represent Children in Abuse & Neglect Cases, © 1996 American Bar Association, Chicago, IL. Available on line at http://www.abanet.org/child.

ABA Standards of Practice for Lawyers Who Represent Children in Abuse & Neglect Cases, (NACC Revised Version) NACC Children's Law Manual Series, 1999 Edition, p. 177. Available on line at http://naccchildlaw.org.

Adoption 2002: The President's Initiative on Adoption and Foster Care, Guidelines for Public Policy and State Legislation Governing Permanence for Children. US Dept. of HHS, Administration on Children, Youth and Families, June 1999. Available on line at http://www.acf.dhhs.gov/.

Advocating for the Child in Protection Proceedings: A Handbook for Lawyers and Court Appointed Special Advocates, by Donald Duquette, © Jossey-Bass, Inc., San Francisco, CA.

Child Abuse and Neglect Cases: Representation as a Critical Component of Effective Practice. Technical Assistance Bulletin, NCJFCJ / OJJDP, © 1998.

Coming to Praise, Not to Bury, The New ABA Standards of Practice for Lawyers Who Represent Children in Abuse and Neglect Cases, by David Katner, NACC Children's Law Manual, 1997 Edition, page 247.

The Courts and Child Maltreatment, by Howard A. Davidson, page 482 in *The Battered Child*, Fifth Edition, edited by Helfer, Kempe and Krugman, © 1997 University of Chicago Press, Chicago, IL.

The Child's Attorney, by Ann M. Haralambie, © 1993 American Bar Association, ABA Section of Family Law, Chicago, IL (Call 303/864-5320).

Ethical Issues in the Legal Representation of Children, Fordham Law Review, Vol. LXIV No. 4 March 1996.

Facts About Children and the Law, American Bar Association Division for Media Relations and Public Affairs.

Handling Child Custody, Abuse and Adoption Cases, by Ann M. Haralambie, Second Edition © 1993 Shepard's McGraw-Hill, Colorado Springs, CO, now published by Clark, Boardman, Callaghan, Deerfield, IL.

Independent Representation for the Abused and Neglected Child: The Guardian Ad Litem, by B. Fraser, 13 *California Western Law Review* 16 (1976).

A Judges Guide to Improving Legal Representation of Children, edited by Kathi Grasso, ABA Center on Children and the Law, © ABA May 1998.

Lawyers' Roles in Child Protection, by Donald N. Duquette, page 460 in *The Battered Child*, Fifth Edition, edited by Helfer, Kempe, and Krugman, © 1997 University of Chicago Press, Chicago, IL.

Legal Representation for Children in Protection Proceedings: Two Distinct Lawyer Roles are Required, by Donald N. Duquette, *FAMILY LAW QUARTERLY* , (Fall 2000).

Legal Representation of Children in Dependency Court: Toward A Better Model - The ABA (NACC Revised) Standards of Practice, by Marvin Ventrell, NACC Children's Law Manual Series, 1999 Edition.

Representing Children in Child Protective Proceedings: Ethical and Practical Dimensions, by Jean Koh Peters, © 1997, LEXIS Law Publishing, Charlottesville, VA.

Representing the Child Client, by Dale, Soler, Shotton, Bell, Jameson, Shauffer, Warboys, © 2000, Mathew Bender and Company, Inc., New York, NY.

Resource Guidelines, Improving Court Practice in Child Abuse and Neglect Cases, National Council of Juvenile and Family Court Judges, © 1995 NCJFCJ, Reno, NV.

Rights and Duties: An Overview of the Attorney-Child Client Relationship, by Marvin Ventrell, Loyola University of Chicago Law Journal, Vol. 26 No. 2 Winter 1995.

APPENDIX A-2

AMERICAN BAR ASSOCIATION

STANDARDS OF PRACTICE FOR LAWYERS WHO REPRESENT

CHILDREN IN ABUSE AND NEGLECT CASES

(NACC Revised Version)

Printed with permission from the American Bar Association Center on Children and the Law.

The *Abuse & Neglect Standards* were drafted by the American Bar Association Representing Children Standards of Practice Committee.

Adopted, The American Bar Association February 5, 1996.

Adopted, with reservation as to Standard B-4, National Association of Counsel for Children, October 13th, 1996.

Amended, Section B-4 and B-5, National Association of Counsel for Children, April 21, 1999.

PREFACE

All children subject to court proceedings involving allegations of child abuse and neglect should have legal representation as long as the court jurisdiction continues. These Abuse and Neglect Standards are meant to apply when a lawyer is appointed for a child in any legal action based on: (a) a petition filed for protection of the child; (b) a request to a court to change legal custody, visitation, or guardianship based on allegations of child abuse or neglect based on sufficient cause; or (c) an action to terminate parental rights.

These Standards apply only to lawyers and take the position that although a lawyer *may* accept appointment in the dual capacity of a "lawyer/guardian ad litem," the lawyer's primary duty must still be focused on the protection of the legal rights of the child client. The lawyer/guardian ad litem should therefore perform all the functions of a "child's attorney," except as otherwise noted.

These Standards build upon the ABA-approved JUVENILE JUSTICE STANDARDS RELATING TO COUNSEL FOR PRIVATE PARTIES (1979) which include important directions for lawyers representing children in juvenile court matters generally, but do not contain sufficient guidance to aid lawyers representing children in abuse and neglect cases. These Abuse and Neglect Standards are also intended to help implement a series of ABA-approved policy resolutions (in Appendix) on the importance of legal representation and the improvement of lawyer practice in child protection cases.

In support of having lawyers play an active role in child abuse and neglect cases, in August 1995 the ABA endorsed a set of RESOURCE GUIDELINES: IMPROVING COURT PRACTICE IN CHILD ABUSE & NEGLECT CASES produced by the National Council of Juvenile and Family Court Judges. The RESOURCE GUIDELINES stress the importance of quality representation provided by competent and diligent lawyers by supporting: 1) the approach of vigorous representation of child clients; and 2) the actions that courts should take to help assure such representation.

These Standards contain two parts. Part I addresses the specific roles and responsibilities of a lawyer appointed to represent a child in an abuse and neglect case. Part II provides a set of standards for judicial administrators and trial judges to assure high quality legal representation.

PART I—STANDARDS FOR THE CHILD'S ATTORNEY

A. DEFINITIONS

A-1. The Child's Attorney. The term "child's attorney" means a lawyer who provides legal services for a child and who owes the same duties of undivided

**loyalty, confidentiality, and competent representation to the child as is due an
adult client.**

Commentary —

These Standards explicitly recognize that the child is a separate
individual with potentially discrete and independent views. To ensure
that the child's independent voice is heard, the child's attorney must
advocate the child's articulated position. Consequently, the child's
attorney owes traditional duties to the child as client consistent with ER
1.14(a) of the Model Rules of Professional Conduct. In all but the
exceptional case, such as with a preverbal child, the child's attorney will
maintain this traditional relationship with the child/client. As with any
client, the child's attorney may counsel against the pursuit of a particular
position sought by the child. The child's attorney should recognize that
the child may be more susceptible to intimidation and manipulation than
some adult clients. Therefore, the child's attorney should ensure that the
decision the child ultimately makes reflects his or her actual position.

**A-2. Lawyer Appointed as Guardian Ad Litem.   A lawyer appointed as
"guardian ad litem" for a child is an officer of the court appointed to protect the
child's interests without being bound by the child's expressed preferences.**

Commentary —

In some jurisdictions the lawyer may be appointed as guardian ad
litem. These Standards, however, express a clear preference for the
appointment as the "child's attorney." These Standards address the
lawyer's obligations to the child as client.

A lawyer appointed as guardian ad litem is almost inevitably
expected to perform legal functions on behalf of the child. Where the
local law permits, the lawyer is expected to act in the dual role of
guardian ad litem and lawyer of record. The chief distinguishing factor
between the roles is the manner and method to be followed in
determining the legal position to be advocated. While a guardian ad
litem should take the child's point of view into account, the child's
preferences are not binding, irrespective of the child's age and the ability
or willingness of the child to express preferences. Moreover, in many
states, a guardian ad litem may be required by statute or custom to
perform specific tasks, such as submitting a report or testifying as a fact
or expert witness. These tasks are not part of functioning as a "lawyer."

These Standards do not apply to nonlawyers when such persons are
appointed as guardians ad litem or as "court appointed special
advocates" (CASA). The nonlawyer guardian ad litem cannot and

should not be expected to perform any legal functions on behalf of a child.

A-3. Developmentally Appropriate. "Developmentally appropriate" means that the child's attorney should ensure the child's ability to provide client-based directions by structuring all communications to account for the individual child's age, level of education, cultural context, and degree of language acquisition.

Commentary —

The lawyer has an obligation to explain clearly, precisely, and in terms the client can understand the meaning and consequences of action. See DAVID A. BINDER & SUSAN C. PRICE, LEGAL INTERVIEWING AND COUNSELING: A CLIENT-CENTERED APPROACH (1977). A child client may not understand the legal terminology and for a variety of reasons may choose a particular course of action without fully appreciating the implications. With a child the potential for not understanding may be even greater. Therefore, the child's attorney has additional obligations based on the child's age, level of education, and degree of language acquisition. There is also the possibility that because of a particular child's developmental limitations, the lawyer may not completely understand the child's responses. Therefore, the child's attorney must learn how to ask developmentally appropriate questions and how to interpret the child's responses. See ANNE GRAFFAM WALKER, HANDBOOK ON QUESTIONING CHILDREN: A LINGUISTIC PERSPECTIVE (ABA Center on Children and the Law 1994). The child's attorney may work with social workers or other professionals to assess a child's developmental abilities and to facilitate communication.

B. GENERAL AUTHORITY AND DUTIES

B-1. Basic Obligations. The child's attorney should:

(1)   Obtain copies of all pleadings and relevant notices;

(2)   Participate in depositions, negotiations, discovery, pretrial conferences, and hearings;

(3)   Inform other parties and their representatives that he or she is representing the child and expects reasonable notification prior to case conferences, changes of placement, and other changes of circumstances affecting the child and the child's family;

(4)   **Attempt to reduce case delays and ensure that the court recognizes the need to speedily promote permanency for the child;**

(5)   **Counsel the child concerning the subject matter of the litigation, the child's rights, the court system, the proceedings, the lawyer's role, and what to expect in the legal process;**

(6)   **Develop a theory and strategy of the case to implement at hearings, including factual and legal issues; and**

(7)   **Identify appropriate family and professional resources for the child.**

Commentary —

The child's attorney should not be merely a fact-finder, but rather, should zealously advocate a position on behalf of the child. (The same is true for the guardian ad litem, although the position to be advocated may be different). In furtherance of that advocacy, the child's attorney must be adequately prepared prior to hearings. The lawyer's presence at and active participation in all hearings is absolutely critical. See, RESOURCE GUIDELINES, at 23.

Although the child's position may overlap with the position of one or both parents, third-party caretakers, or a state agency, the child's attorney should be prepared to participate fully in any proceedings and not merely defer to the other parties. Any identity of position should be based on the merits of the position, and not a mere endorsement of another party's position.

While subsection (4) recognizes that delays are usually harmful, there may be some circumstances when delay may be beneficial. Section (7) contemplates that the child's attorney will identify counseling, educational and health services, substance abuse programs for the child and other family members, housing and other forms of material assistance for which the child may qualify under law. The lawyer can also identify family members, friends, neighbors, or teachers with whom the child feels it is important to maintain contact; mentoring programs, such as Big Brother/Big Sister; recreational opportunities that develop social skills and self-esteem; educational support programs; and volunteer opportunities which can enhance a child's self-esteem.

B-2. Conflict Situations.

(1) If a lawyer appointed as guardian ad litem determines that there is a conflict caused by performing both roles of guardian ad litem and child's attorney, the lawyer should continue to perform as the child's attorney and withdraw as guardian ad litem. The lawyer should request appointment of a guardian ad

litem without revealing the basis for the request.

(2) If a lawyer is appointed as a "child's attorney" for siblings, there may also be a conflict which could require that the lawyer decline representation or withdraw from representing all of the children.

Commentary —

The primary conflict that arises between the two roles is when the child's expressed preferences differ from what the lawyer deems to be in the child's best interests. As a practical matter, when the lawyer has established a trusting relationship with the child, most conflicts can be avoided. While the lawyer should be careful not to apply undue pressure to a child, the lawyer's advice and guidance can often persuade the child to change an imprudent position or to identify alternative choices if the child's first choice is denied by the court.

The lawyer-client role involves a confidential relationship with privileged communications, while a guardian ad litem-client role may not be confidential. Compare Alaska Bar Assoc. Ethics Op. #854 (1985) (lawyer-client privilege does not apply when the lawyer is appointed to be child's guardian ad litem) with Bentley v. Bentley, 448 N.Y.S.2d 559 (App. Div. 1982) (communication between minor children and guardian ad litem in divorce custody case is entitled to lawyer-client privilege). Because the child has a right to confidentiality and advocacy of his or her position, the child's attorney can never abandon this role. Once a lawyer has a lawyer-client relationship with a minor, he or she cannot and should not assume any other role for the child, especially as guardian ad litem. When the roles cannot be reconciled, another person must assume the guardian ad litem role. See Arizona State Bar Committee on Rules of Professional Conduct, Opinion No. 86-13 (1986).

B-3. Client Under Disability. The child's attorney should determine whether the child is "under a disability" pursuant to the Model Rules of Professional Conduct or the Model Code of Professional Responsibility with respect to each issue in which the child is called upon to direct the representation.

Commentary —

These Standards do not accept the idea that children of certain ages are "impaired," "disabled," "incompetent," or lack capacity to determine their position in litigation. Further, these Standards reject the concept that any disability must be globally determined. Rather, disability is contextual, incremental, and may be intermittent. The child's ability to contribute to a determination of his or her position is functional, depending upon the particular position and the circumstances prevailing at the time the position must be determined. Therefore, a child may be able to determine some positions in the case but not others. Similarly, a child may be able to direct the lawyer with respect to a particular issue at one time but not at another. This Standard relies on empirical knowledge about competencies with respect to both adults and children. See, e.g., ALLEN E. BUCHANAN & DAN W. BROCK, DECIDING FOR OTHERS: THE ETHICS OF SURROGATE DECISION MAKING 217 (1989).

<table>
<tr><td>NOTE ON Section B-4</td><td>Two versions of Standard B-4 are presented below. The first version is the "ABA Version" which is the version drafted and adopted by the ABA. The second version is the "NACC Version" adopted by the NACC as a recommended replacement to the "ABA Version." The NACC had originally adopted the ABA Standards with reservation as to Standard B-4 because of "concerns about the availability to the court of information about the interests of the child." The NACC Board of Directors subsequently adopted the "NACC Version." The NACC version is not approved or adopted by the ABA.</td></tr>
</table>

B-4. ABA Version

Client Preferences. The child's attorney should elicit the child's preferences in a developmentally appropriate manner, advise the child, and provide guidance. The child's attorney should represent the child's expressed preferences and follow the child's direction throughout the course of litigation.

Commentary —

The lawyer has a duty to explain to the child in a developmentally appropriate way such information as will assist the child in having maximum input in determination of the particular position at issue. The lawyer should inform the child of the relevant facts and applicable laws and the ramifications of taking various positions, which may include the impact of such decisions on other family members or on future legal proceedings. The lawyer may express an opinion concerning the likelihood of the court or other parties accepting particular positions. The lawyer may inform the child of an expert's recommendations germane to the issue.

As in any other lawyer/client relationship, the lawyer may express his or her assessment of the case, the best position for the child to take, and the reasons underlying such recommendation. A child, however, may agree with the lawyer for inappropriate reasons. A lawyer must remain aware of the power dynamics inherent in adult/child relationships. Therefore, the lawyer needs to understand what the child knows and what factors are influencing the child's decision. The lawyer should attempt to determine from the child's opinion and reasoning what factors have been most influential or have been confusing or glided over by the child when deciding the best time to express his or her assessment of the case.

Consistent with the rules of confidentiality and with sensitivity to the child's privacy, the lawyer should consult with the child's therapist and other experts and obtain appropriate records. For example, a child's therapist may help the child to understand why an expressed position is dangerous, foolish, or not in the child's best interests. The therapist might also assist the lawyer in understanding the child's perspective, priorities, and individual needs. Similarly, significant persons in the child's life may educate the lawyer about the child's needs, priorities, and previous experiences.

The lawyer for the child has dual fiduciary duties to the child which must be balanced. On one hand, the lawyer has a duty to ensure that the child client is given the information necessary to make an informed decision, including advice and guidance. On the other hand, the lawyer has a duty not to overbear the will of the child. While the lawyer may attempt to persuade the child to accept a particular position, the lawyer may not advocate a position contrary to the child's expressed position except as provided by these Abuse and Neglect Standards or the Code of Professional Responsibility.

While the child is entitled to determine the overall objectives to be pursued, the child's attorney, as any adult's lawyer, may make certain decisions with respect to the manner of achieving those objectives, particularly with respect to procedural matters. These Abuse and Neglect Standards do not require the lawyer to consult with the child on matters which would not require consultation with an adult client. Further, the Standards do not require the child's attorney to discuss with the child issues for which it is not feasible to obtain the child's direction because of the child's developmental limitations, as with an infant or preverbal child.

(1)   **To the extent that a child cannot express a preference, the child's attorney shall make a good faith effort to determine the child's wishes and advocate accordingly or request appointment of a guardian ad litem.**

Commentary —

There are circumstances in which a child is unable to express a position, as in the case of a preverbal child, or may not be capable of understanding the legal or factual issues involved. Under such circumstances, the child's attorney should continue to represent the child's legal interests and request appointment of a guardian ad litem. This limitation distinguishes the scope of independent decision-making of the child's attorney and a person acting as guardian ad litem.

(2) **To the extent that a child does not or will not express a preference about particular issues, the child's attorney should determine and advocate the child's legal interests.**

Commentary —

The child's failure to express a position is distinguishable from a directive that the lawyer not take a position with respect to certain issues. The child may have no opinion with respect to a particular issue, or may delegate the decision-making authority. For example, the child may not want to assume the responsibility of expressing a position because of loyalty conflicts or the desire not to hurt one of the other parties. The lawyer should clarify with the child whether the child wants the lawyer to take a position or remain silent with respect to that issue or wants the preference expressed only if the parent or other party is out of the courtroom. The lawyer is then bound by the child's directive. The position taken by the lawyer should not contradict or undermine other issues about which the child has expressed a preference.

(3) **If the child's attorney determines that the child's expressed preference would be seriously injurious to the child (as opposed to merely being contrary to the lawyer's opinion of what would be in the child's interests), the lawyer may request appointment of a separate guardian ad litem and continue to represent the child's expressed preference, unless the child's position is prohibited by law or without any factual foundation. The child's attorney shall not reveal the basis of the request for appointment of a guardian ad litem which would compromise the child's position.**

Commentary —

One of the most difficult ethical issues for lawyers representing children occurs when the child is able to express a position and does so, but the lawyer believes that the position chosen is wholly inappropriate or could result in serious injury to the child. This is particularly likely to happen with respect to an abused child whose home is unsafe, but who desires to remain or return home. A child may desire to live in a dangerous situation because it is all he or she knows, because of a feeling of blame or of responsibility to take care of the parents, or because of threats. The child may choose to deal with a known situation rather than risk the unknown world of a foster home or other out-of-home placement.

In most cases the ethical conflict involved in asserting a position which would seriously endanger the child, especially by disclosure of privileged information, can be resolved through the lawyer's counseling function. If the lawyer has taken the time to establish rapport with the child and gain that child's trust, it is likely that the lawyer will be able to persuade the child to abandon a dangerous position or at least identify an alternate course.

If the child cannot be persuaded, the lawyer has a duty to safeguard the child's interests by requesting appointment of a guardian ad litem, who will be charged with advocating the child's best interests without being bound by the child's direction. As a practical matter, this may not adequately protect the child if the danger to the child was revealed only in a confidential disclosure to the lawyer, because the guardian ad litem may never learn of the disclosed danger.

Confidentiality is abrogated for various professionals by mandatory child abuse reporting laws. Some states abrogate lawyer-client privilege by mandating reports. States which do not abrogate the privilege may permit reports notwithstanding professional privileges. The policy considerations underlying abrogation apply to lawyers where there is a substantial danger of serious injury or death. Under such circumstances, the lawyer must take the minimum steps which would be necessary to ensure the child's safety, respecting and following the child's direction to the greatest extent possible consistent with the child's safety and ethical rules.

The lawyer may never counsel a client or assist a client in conduct the lawyer knows is criminal or fraudulent. See ER 1.2(d), Model Rules of Professional Conduct, DR 7-102(A)(7), Model Code of Professional Responsibility. Further, existing ethical rules requires the lawyer to disclose confidential information to the extent necessary to prevent the client from committing a criminal act likely to result in death or substantial bodily harm, see ER 1.6(b), Model Rules of Professional Conduct, and permits the lawyer to reveal the intention of the client to commit a crime. See ER 1.6(c), Model Rules of Professional Conduct, DR 4-101(C)(3), Model Code of Professional Responsibility. While child abuse, including sexual abuse, are crimes, the child is presumably the victim, rather than the perpetrator of those crimes. Therefore, disclosure of confidences is designed to protect the client, rather than to protect a third party from the client. Where the child is in grave danger of serious injury or death, the child's safety must be the paramount concern.

The lawyer is not bound to pursue the client's objectives through means not permitted by law and ethical rules. See DR-7-101(A)(1), Model Code of Professional Responsibility. Further, lawyers may be subject personally to sanctions for taking positions that are not well grounded in fact and warranted by existing law or a good faith argument for the extension, modification, or reversal of existing law.

B-4.   NACC Version.

Client Preferences. The child's attorney should elicit the child's preferences in a developmentally appropriate manner, advise the child, and provide guidance. The child's attorney should represent the child's expressed preferences and follow the child's direction throughout the course of litigation. except as specifically provided herein. Client directed representation does not include "robotic allegiance" to each directive of the client. Client directed representation involves the attorney's counseling function and requires good communication between attorney and client. The goal of the relationship is an outcome which serves the client, mutually arrived upon by attorney and client, following exploration of all available options.

Commentary —

The lawyer has a duty to explain to the child in a developmentally appropriate way such information as will assist the child in having maximum input in determination of the particular position at issue. The lawyer should inform the child of the relevant facts and applicable laws and the ramifications of taking various positions, which may include the impact of such decisions on other family members or on future legal proceedings. The lawyer may express an opinion concerning the likelihood of the court or other parties accepting particular positions. The lawyer may inform the child of an expert's recommendations germane to the issue.

As in any other lawyer/client relationship, the lawyer may express his or her assessment of the case, the best position for the child to take, and the reasons underlying such recommendation. A child, however, may agree with the lawyer for inappropriate reasons. A lawyer must remain aware of the power dynamics inherent in adult/child relationships. Therefore, the lawyer needs to understand what the child knows and what factors are influencing the child's decision. The lawyer should attempt to determine from the child's opinion and reasoning what factors have been most influential or have been confusing or glided over by the child when deciding the best time to express his or her assessment of the case.

Consistent with the rules of confidentiality and with sensitivity to the child's privacy, the lawyer should consult with the child's therapist and other experts and obtain appropriate records. For example, a child's therapist may help the child to understand why an expressed position is dangerous, foolish, or not in the child's best interests. The therapist might also assist the lawyer in understanding the child's perspective, priorities, and individual needs. Similarly, significant persons in the child's life may educate the lawyer about the child's needs, priorities, and previous experiences.

The lawyer for the child has dual fiduciary duties to the child which must be balanced. On one hand, the lawyer has a duty to ensure that the child client is given the information necessary to make an informed decision, including advice and guidance. On the other hand, the lawyer has a duty not to overbear the will of the child. While the lawyer may attempt to persuade the child to accept a particular position, the lawyer may not advocate a position contrary to the child's expressed position except as provided by these Abuse and Neglect Standards or the Code of Professional Responsibility.

While the child is entitled to determine the overall objectives to be pursued, the child's attorney, as any adult's lawyer, may make certain decisions with respect to the manner of achieving those objectives, particularly with respect to procedural matters. These Abuse and Neglect Standards do not require the lawyer to consult with the child on matters which would not require consultation with an adult client. Further, the Standards do not require the child's attorney to discuss with the child issues for which it is not feasible to obtain the child's direction because of the child's developmental limitations, as with an infant or preverbal child.

(1) **While the default position for attorneys representing children under these standards is a client directed model, there will be occasions when the client directed model cannot serve the client and exceptions must be made. In such cases, the attorney may rely upon a substituted judgment process (similar to the role played by an attorney guardian ad litem), or call for the appointment of a guardian ad litem, depending upon the particular circumstances, as provided herein.** ~~To the extent that a child cannot express a preference, the child's attorney shall make a good faith effort to determine the child's wishes and advocate accordingly or request appointment of a guardian ad litem.~~

~~*Commentary*~~ —
~~There are circumstances in which a child is unable to express a position, as in the case of a preverbal child, or may not be capable of~~

understanding the legal or factual issues involved. Under such circumstances, the child's attorney should continue to represent the child's legal interests and request appointment of a guardian ad litem. This limitation distinguishes the scope of independent decision-making of the child's attorney and a person acting as guardian ad litem.

(2) **To the extent that a child** ~~does not or will not express a preference about particular issues, the child's attorney should determine and advocate the child's legal interests.~~ **cannot meaningfully participate in the formulation of the client's position (either because the child is preverbal, very young or for some other reason is incapable of judgment and meaningful communication), the attorney shall substitute his/her judgment for the child's and formulate and present a position which serves the child's interests. Such formulation must be accomplished through the use of objective criteria, rather than solely the life experience or instinct of the attorney. The criteria shall include but not be limited to:**

   a.   **Determine the child's circumstances through a full and efficient investigation;**

   b.   **Assess the child at the moment of the determination;**

   c.   **Examine each option in light of the two child welfare paradigms; psychological parent and family network; and**

   d.   **Utilize medical, mental health, educational, social work and other experts.**

Commentary —

The following resources are recommended reading regarding assessing children's best interests:

1.   *The Best Interests of the Child, The Least Detrimental Alternative*, **the landmark trilogy of Beyond the Best Interests of the Child, Before the Best Interests of the Child, and In the Best Interests of the Child, by Goldstein, Solnit, Goldstein and Freud, Copyright © 1996 The Free Press, New York, NY.**

2.   *Representing Children in Child Protective Proceedings: Ethical and Practical Dimensions*, **by Jean K. Peters, Copyright © 1997, LEXIS Law Publishing, Charlottesville, VA.**

3.   *Advocating for the Child in Protection Proceedings: A Handbook for Lawyers and Court Appointed Special Advocates*, **by Donald Duquette, Copyright © Jossey-Bass, Inc., San Francisco, CA.**

<u>**4.**</u>   <u>***The Child's Attorney*, by Ann M. Haralambie, Copyright © 1993 American Bar Association, ABA Section of Family Law, Chicago, IL (Call 303/864-5320).**</u>

<u>**5.**</u>   <u>***Handling Child Custody, Abuse and Adoption Cases*, by Ann M. Haralambie, Second Edition Copyright © 1993 Shepard's McGraw-Hill, Colorado Springs, CO, now published by Clark, Boardman, Callaghan, Deerfield, IL.**</u>

<u>**6.**</u>   <u>**Department of Justice, National Institute of Justice, *Research Preview*, Jeremy Travis, February 1996.**</u>

~~The child's failure to express a position is distinguishable from a directive that the lawyer not take a position with respect to certain issues. The child may have no opinion with respect to a particular issue, or may delegate the decision-making authority. For example, the child may not want to assume the responsibility of expressing a position because of loyalty conflicts or the desire not to hurt one of the other parties. The lawyer should clarify with the child whether the child wants the lawyer to take a position or remain silent with respect to that issue or wants the preference expressed only if the parent or other party is out of the courtroom. The lawyer is then bound by the child's directive. The position taken by the lawyer should not contradict or undermine other issues about which the child has expressed a preference.~~

<u>**(3)**</u>   <u>**It is possible for the child client to develop from a child incapable of meaningful participation in the litigation as set forth in section B-4 (2), to a child capable of such participation during the course of the attorney client relationship. In such cases, the attorney shall move from the substituted judgment exception of B-4 (2) to the default position of client directed representation described in section B-4 "Client Preferences."**</u>

(4)   **If the child's attorney determines that the child's expressed preference would be seriously injurious to the child (as opposed to merely being contrary to the lawyer's opinion of what would be in the child's interests), the lawyer ~~may~~ <u>shall, after unsuccessful use of the attorney's counseling role,</u> request appointment of a separate guardian ad litem and continue to represent the child's expressed preference, unless the child's position is prohibited by law or without any factual foundation. The child's attorney shall not reveal the basis of the request for appointment of a guardian ad litem which would compromise the child's position.**

Commentary —

    One of the most difficult ethical issues for lawyers representing children occurs when the child is able to express a position and does so, but the lawyer believes that the position chosen is wholly inappropriate or could result in serious injury to the child. This is particularly likely to happen with respect to an abused child whose home is unsafe, but who desires to remain or return home. A child may desire to live in a dangerous situation because it is all he or she knows, because of a feeling of blame or of responsibility to take care of the parents, or because of threats. The child may choose to deal with a known situation rather than risk the unknown world of a foster home or other out-of-home placement.

In most cases the ethical conflict involved in asserting a position which would seriously endanger the child, especially by disclosure of privileged information, can be resolved through the lawyer's counseling function. If the lawyer has taken the time to establish rapport with the child and gain that child's trust, it is likely that the lawyer will be able to persuade the child to abandon a dangerous position or at least identify an alternate course.

If the child cannot be persuaded, the lawyer has a duty to safeguard the child's interests by requesting appointment of a guardian ad litem, who will be charged with advocating the child's best interests without being bound by the child's direction. As a practical matter, this may not adequately protect the child if the danger to the child was revealed only in a confidential disclosure to the lawyer, because the guardian ad litem may never learn of the disclosed danger.

Confidentiality is abrogated for various professionals by mandatory child abuse reporting laws. Some states abrogate lawyer-client privilege by mandating reports. States which do not abrogate the privilege may permit reports notwithstanding professional privileges. The policy considerations underlying abrogation apply to lawyers where there is a substantial danger of serious injury or death. Under such circumstances, the lawyer must take the minimum steps which would be necessary to ensure the child's safety, respecting and following the child's direction to the greatest extent possible consistent with the child's safety and ethical rules.

The lawyer may never counsel a client or assist a client in conduct the lawyer knows is criminal or fraudulent. See ER 1.2(d), Model Rules of Professional Conduct, DR 7-102(A)(7), Model Code of Professional Responsibility. Further, existing ethical rules requires the lawyer to disclose confidential information to the extent necessary to prevent the client from committing a criminal act likely to result in death or substantial bodily harm, see ER 1.6(b), Model Rules of Professional Conduct, and permits the lawyer to reveal the intention of the client to commit a crime. See ER 1.6(c), Model Rules of Professional Conduct, DR 4-101(C)(3), Model Code of Professional Responsibility. While child abuse, including sexual abuse, are crimes, the child is presumably the victim, rather than the perpetrator of those crimes. Therefore, disclosure of confidences is designed to protect the client, rather than to protect a third party from the client. Where the child is in grave danger of serious injury or death, the child's safety must be the paramount concern.

The lawyer is not bound to pursue the client's objectives through means not permitted by law and ethical rules. See DR-7-101(A)(1), Model Code of Professional Responsibility. Further, lawyers may be subject personally to sanctions for taking positions that are not well grounded in fact and warranted by existing law or a good faith argument for the extension, modification, or reversal of existing law.

NOTE ON Section B-5:	Section B-5 below describes the determination of the child's "legal interests" as used in Section B-4 (2) (ABA Version) which reads: "to the extent that a child does not or will not express a preference about particular issues, the child's attorney should determine and advocate the child's legal interests." Under the NACC version of B-4, however, the ABA's Section B-4 (2) has been deleted. Because the NACC version of B-4 does not use the term "legal interests," B-5 is irrelevant and has been deleted.

B-5. Child's Interests. The determination of the child's legal interests should be based on objective criteria as set forth in the law that are related to the purposes of the proceedings. The criteria should address the child's specific needs and preferences, the goal of expeditious resolution of the case so the child can remain or return home or be placed in a safe, nurturing, and permanent environment, and the use of the least restrictive or detrimental alternatives available.

Commentary —

A lawyer who is required to determine the child's interests is functioning in a nontraditional role by determining the position to be advocated independently of the client. The lawyer should base the position, however, on objective criteria concerning the child's needs and interests, and not merely on the lawyer's personal values, philosophies, and experiences. The child's various needs and interests may be in conflict and must be weighed against each other. Even nonverbal children can communicate their needs and interests through their behaviors and developmental levels. See generally JAMES GARBARINO & FRANCES M. STOTT, WHAT CHILDREN CAN TELL US: ELICITING, INTERPRETING, AND EVALUATING CRITICAL INFORMATION FROM CHILDREN (1992). The lawyer may seek the advice and consultation of experts and other knowledgeable people in both determining and weighing such needs and interests.

A child's legal interests may include basic physical and emotional needs, such as safety, shelter, food, and clothing. Such needs should be assessed in light of the child's vulnerability, dependence upon others, available external resources, and the degree of risk. A child needs family affiliation and stability of placement. The child's developmental level, including his or her sense of time, is relevant to an assessment of need. For example, a very young child may be less able to tolerate separation from a primary caretaker than an older child, and if separation is necessary, more frequent visitation than is ordinarily provided may be necessary.

In general, a child prefers to live with known people, to continue normal activities, and to avoid moving. To that end, the child's attorney should determine whether relatives, friends, neighbors, or other people known to the child are appropriate and available as placement resources. The lawyer must determine the child's feelings about the proposed caretaker, however, because familiarity does not automatically confer positive regard. Further, the lawyer may need to balance competing stability interests, such as living with a relative in another town versus living in a foster home in the same neighborhood. The individual child's needs will influence this balancing task.

In general, a child needs decisions about the custodial environment to be made quickly. Therefore, if the child must be removed from the home, it is generally in the child's best interests to have rehabilitative or reunification services offered to the family quickly. On the other hand, if it appears that reunification will be unlikely, it is generally in the child's best interests to move quickly toward an alternative permanent plan. Delay and indecision are rarely in a child's best interests.

In addition to the general needs and interests of children, individual children have particular needs, and the lawyer must determine the child client's individual needs. There are few rules which apply across the board to all children under all circumstances.

C. ACTIONS TO BE TAKEN

C-1. Meet With Child. Establishing and maintaining a relationship with a child is the foundation of representation. Therefore, irrespective of the child's age, the

child's attorney should visit with the child prior to court hearings and when apprised of emergencies or significant events impacting on the child.

Commentary —

Meeting with the child is important before court hearings and case reviews. In addition, changes in placement, school suspensions, in-patient hospitalizations, and other similar changes warrant meeting again with the child. Such in-person meetings allow the lawyer to explain to the child what is happening, what alternatives might be available, and what will happen next. This also allows the lawyer to assess the child's circumstances, often leading to a greater understanding of the case, which may lead to more creative solutions in the child's interest. A lawyer can learn a great deal from meeting with child clients, including a preverbal child. See, e.g., JAMES GARBARINO, ET AL, WHAT CHILDREN CAN TELL US: ELICITING, INTERPRETING, AND EVALUATING CRITICAL INFORMATION FROM CHILDREN (1992).

C-2. Investigate. To support the client's position, the child's attorney should conduct thorough, continuing, and independent investigations and discovery which may include, but should not be limited to:

(1)   Reviewing the child's social services, psychiatric, psychological, drug and alcohol, medical, law enforcement, school, and other records relevant to the case;

Commentary —

Thorough, independent investigation of cases, at every stage of the proceedings, is a key aspect of providing competent representation to children. See, RESOURCE GUIDELINES, AT 23. The lawyer may need to use subpoenas or other discovery or motion procedures to obtain the relevant records, especially those records which pertain to the other parties. In some jurisdictions the statute or the order appointing the lawyer for the child includes provision for obtaining certain records.

(2)   Reviewing the court files of the child and siblings, case-related records of the social service agency and other service providers;

Commentary —

Another key aspect of representing children is the review of all documents submitted to the court as well as relevant agency case files and law enforcement reports. See, RESOURCE GUIDELINES, at 23. Other relevant files that should be reviewed include those concerning child protective services, developmental disabilities, juvenile delinquency, mental health, and educational agencies. These records can provide a more complete context for the current problems of the child and family. Information in the files may suggest additional professionals and lay witnesses who should be contacted and may reveal alternate potential placements and services.

(3)   Contacting lawyers for other parties and nonlawyer guardians ad litem or court-appointed special advocates (CASA) for background information;

Commentary —

The other parties' lawyers may have information not included in any of the available records. Further, they can provide information on their respective clients' perspectives. The CASA is typically charged with performing an independent factual investigation, getting to know the child, and speaking up to the court on the child's "best interests." Volunteer CASAs may have more time to perform their functions than the child's attorney and can often provide a great deal of information to assist the child's attorney. Where there appears to be role conflict or confusion over the involvement of both a child's attorney and CASA in the same case, there should be joint efforts to clarify and define mutual responsibilities. See, RESOURCE GUIDELINES, at 24.

(4)   Contacting and meeting with the parents/legal guardians/caretakers of the child, with permission of their lawyer;

Commentary —

Such contact generally should include visiting the home, which will give the lawyer additional information about the child's custodial circumstances.

(5)   Obtaining necessary authorizations for the release of information;

Commentary —

If the relevant statute or order appointing the lawyer for the child does not provide explicit authorization for the lawyer's obtaining necessary records, the lawyer should attempt to obtain authorizations for release of information from the agency and from the parents, with their lawyer's consent. Even if it is not required, an older child should be asked to sign authorizations for release of his or her own records, because such a request demonstrates the lawyer's respect for the client's authority over information.

(6)   Interviewing individuals involved with the child, including school personnel, child welfare case workers, foster parents and other

caretakers, neighbors, relatives, school personnel, coaches, clergy, mental health professionals, physicians, law enforcement officers, and other potential witnesses;

Commentary —

In some jurisdictions the child's attorney is permitted free access to agency case workers. In others, contact with the case worker must be arranged through the agency's lawyer.

(7) **Reviewing relevant photographs, video or audio tapes and other evidence; and**

Commentary —

It is essential that the lawyer review the evidence personally, rather than relying on other parties' or counsel's descriptions and characterizations of the evidence.

(8) **Attending treatment, placement, administrative hearings, other proceedings involving legal issues, and school case conferences or staffings concerning the child as needed.**

Commentary —

While some courts will not authorize compensation for the child's attorney to attend such collateral meetings, such attendance is often very important. The child's attorney can present the child's perspective at such meetings, as well as gather information necessary to proper representation. In some cases the child's attorney can be pivotal in achieving a negotiated settlement of all or some issues. The child's attorney may not need to attend collateral meetings if another person involved in the case, such as a social worker who works the lawyer, can get the information or present the child's perspective.

C-3. File Pleadings. The child's attorney should file petitions, motions, responses or objections as necessary to represent the child. Relief requested may include, but is not limited to:

(1) **A mental or physical examination of a party or the child;**

(2) **A parenting, custody or visitation evaluation;**

(3) **An increase, decrease, or termination of contact or visitation;**

(4) **Restraining or enjoining a change of placement;**

(5) **Contempt for non-compliance with a court order;**

(6)   **Termination of the parent-child relationship;**

(7)   **Child support;**

(8)   **A protective order concerning the child's privileged communications or tangible or intangible property;**

(9)   **Request services for child or family; and**

(10)   **Dismissal of petitions or motions.**

> *Commentary —*
>   Filing and arguing necessary motions is an essential part of the role of a child's attorney. See, RESOURCE GUIDELINES, at 23. Unless the lawyer is serving in a role which explicitly precludes the filing of pleadings, the lawyer should file any appropriate pleadings on behalf of the child, including responses to the pleadings of the other parties. The filing of such pleadings can ensure that appropriate issues are properly before the court and can expedite the court's consideration of issues important to the child's interests. In some jurisdictions, guardians ad litem are not permitted to file pleadings, in which case it should be clear to the lawyer that he or she is not the "child's attorney" as defined in these Standards.

C-4. Request Services. Consistent with the child's wishes, the child's attorney should seek appropriate services (by court order if necessary) to access entitlements, to protect the child's interests and to implement a service plan. These services may include, but not be limited to:

(1)   **Family preservation-related prevention or reunification services;**

(2)   **Sibling and family visitation;**

(3)   **Child support;**

(4)   **Domestic violence prevention, intervention, and treatment;**

(5)   **Medical and mental health care;**

(6)   **Drug and alcohol treatment;**

(7)   **Parenting education;**

(8)   **Semi-independent and independent living services;**

(9)   **Long-term foster care;**

(10)   **Termination of parental rights action;**

(11)   **Adoption services;**

(12)   **Education;**

(13)   **Recreational or social services; and**

(14)   **Housing.**

Commentary —
The lawyer should request appropriate services even if there is no hearing scheduled. Such requests may be made to the agency or treatment providers, or if such informal methods are unsuccessful, the lawyer should file a motion to bring the matter before the court. In some cases the child's attorney should file collateral actions, such as petitions for termination of parental rights, if such an action would advance the child's interest and is legally permitted and justified. Different resources are available in different localities.

C-5. Child With Special Needs. Consistent with the child's wishes, the child's attorney should assure that a child with special needs receives appropriate services to address the physical, mental, or developmental disabilities. These services may include, but should not be limited to:

(1)   **Special education and related services;**

(2)   **Supplemental security income (SSI) to help support needed services;**

(3)   **Therapeutic foster or group home care; and**

(4)   **Residential/in-patient and out-patient psychiatric treatment.**

Commentary —
There are many services available from extra-judicial, as well as judicial, sources for children with special needs. The child's attorney should be familiar with these other services and how to assure their availability for the client. See generally, THOMAS A. JACOBS, CHILDREN & THE LAW: RIGHTS & OBLIGATIONS (1995); LEGAL RIGHTS OF CHILDREN (2d ed. Donald T. Kramer, ed., 1994).

C-6. Negotiate Settlements. The child's attorney should participate in settlement negotiations to seek expeditious resolution of the case, keeping in mind the

effect of continuances and delays on the child. The child's attorney should use suitable mediation resources.

> *Commentary* —
>
> Particularly in contentious cases, the child's attorney may effectively assist negotiations of the parties and their lawyers by focusing on the needs of the child. If a parent is legally represented, it is unethical for the child's attorney to negotiate with a parent directly without the consent of the parent's lawyer. Because the court is likely to resolve at least some parts of the dispute in question based on the best interests of the child, the child's attorney is in a pivotal position in negotiation.
>
> Settlement frequently obtains at least short term relief for all parties involved and is often the best resolution of a case. The child's attorney, however, should not become merely a facilitator to the parties' reaching a negotiated settlement. As developmentally appropriate, the child's attorney should consult the child prior to any settlement becoming binding.

D. HEARINGS

D-1. Court Appearances. The child's attorney should attend all hearings and participate in all telephone or other conferences with the court unless a particular hearing involves issues completely unrelated to the child.

D-2. Client Explanation. The child's attorney should explain to the client, in a developmentally appropriate manner, what is expected to happen before, during and after each hearing.

D-3. Motions and Objections. The child's attorney should make appropriate motions, including motions *in limine* and evidentiary objections, to advance the child's position at trial or during other hearings. If necessary, the child's attorney should file briefs in support of evidentiary issues. Further, during all hearings, the child's attorney should preserve legal issues for appeal, as appropriate.

D-4. Presentation of Evidence. The child's attorney should present and cross examine witnesses, offer exhibits, and provide independent evidence as necessary.

> *Commentary* —
>
> The child's position may overlap with the positions of one or both parents, third-party caretakers, or a child protection agency. Nevertheless, the child's attorney should be prepared to participate fully in every hearing and not merely defer to the other parties. Any identity

of position should be based on the merits of the position (consistent with Standard B-6), and not a mere endorsement of another party's position.

D-5. Child at Hearing. In most circumstances, the child should be present at significant court hearings, regardless of whether the child will testify.

Commentary —

A child has the right to meaningful participation in the case, which generally includes the child's presence at significant court hearings. Further, the child's presence underscores for the judge that the child is a real party in interest in the case. It may be necessary to obtain a court order or writ of habeas corpus ad testificandum to secure the child's attendance at the hearing.

A decision to exclude the child from the hearing should be made based on a particularized determination that the child does not want to attend, is too young to sit through the hearing, would be severely traumatized by such attendance, or for other good reason would be better served by nonattendance. There may be other extraordinary reasons for the child's non-attendance. The lawyer should consult the child, therapist, caretaker, or any other knowledgeable person in determining the effect on the child of being present at the hearing. In some jurisdictions the court requires an affirmative waiver of the child's presence if the child will not attend. Even a child who is too young to sit through the hearing may benefit from seeing the courtroom and meeting, or at least seeing, the judge who will be making the decisions. The lawyer should provide the court with any required notice that the child will be present. Concerns about the child being exposed to certain parts of the evidence may be addressed by the child's temporary exclusion from the court room during the taking of that evidence, rather than by excluding the child from the entire hearing.

The lawyer should ensure that the state/ custodian meets its obligation to transport the child to and from the hearing. Similarly, the lawyer should ensure the presence of someone to accompany the child any time the child is temporarily absent from the hearing.

D-6. Whether Child Should Testify. The child's attorney should decide whether to call the child as a witness. The decision should include consideration of the child's need or desire to testify, any repercussions of testifying, the necessity of the child's direct testimony, the availability of other evidence or hearsay exceptions which may substitute for direct testimony by the child, and the child's developmental ability to provide direct testimony and withstand possible cross-examination. Ultimately, the child's attorney is bound by the child's direction concerning testifying.

Commentary —

There are no blanket rules regarding a child's testimony. While testifying is undoubtedly traumatic for many children, it is therapeutic and empowering for others. Therefore, the decision about the child's testifying should be made individually, based on the circumstances of the individual child and the individual case. The child's therapist, if any, should be consulted both with respect to the decision itself and assistance with preparation. In the absence of compelling reasons, a child who has a strong desire to testify should be called to do so. See ANN M. HARALAMBIE, THE CHILD'S LAWYER: A GUIDE TO REPRESENTING CHILDREN IN CUSTODY, ADOPTION, AND PROTECTION CASES ch. 4 (1993). If the child should not wish to testify or would be harmed by being forced to testify, the lawyer should seek a stipulation of the parties not to call the child as a witness or seek a protective order from the court. If the child is compelled to testify, the lawyer should seek to minimize the adverse consequences by seeking any appropriate accommodations permitted by local law, such as having the testimony taken informally, in chambers, without presence of the parents. See JOHN E.B. MYERS, 2 EVIDENCE IN CHILD ABUSE AND NEGLECT CASES ch. 8 (1992). The child should know whether the in-chambers testimony will be shared with others, such as parents who might be excluded from chambers, before agreeing to this forum. The lawyer should also prepare the child for the possibility that the judge may render a decision against the child's wishes which will not be the child's fault.

D-7. Child Witness. The child's attorney should prepare the child to testify. This should include familiarizing the child with the courtroom, court procedures, and what to expect during direct and cross-examination and ensuring that testifying will cause minimum harm to the child.

Commentary —

The lawyer's preparation of the child to testify should include attention to the child's developmental needs and abilities as well as to accommodations which should be made by the court and other lawyers. The lawyer should seek any necessary assistance from the court, including location of the testimony (in chambers, at a small table etc.), determination of who will be present, and restrictions on the manner and phrasing of questions posed to the child.

The accuracy of children's testimony is enhanced when they feel comfortable. See, generally, Karen Saywitz, Children in Court: Principles of Child Development for Judicial Application, in A JUDICIAL PRIMER ON CHILD SEXUAL ABUSE 15 (Josephine Bulkley &

Claire Sandt, eds., 1994). Courts have permitted support persons to be present in the courtroom, sometimes even with the child sitting on the person's lap to testify. Because child abuse and neglect cases are often closed to the public, special permission may be necessary to enable such persons to be present during hearings. Further, where the rule sequestering witnesses has been invoked, the order of witnesses may need to be changed or an exemption granted where the support person also will be a witness. The child should be asked whether he or she would like someone to be present, and if so, whom the child prefers. Typical support persons include parents, relatives, therapists, Court Appointed Special Advocates (CASA), social workers, victim-witness advocates, and members of the clergy. For some, presence of the child's attorney provides sufficient support.

D-8. Questioning the Child. The child's attorney should seek to ensure that questions to the child are phrased in a syntactically and linguistically appropriate manner.

Commentary —

The phrasing of questions should take into consideration the law and research regarding children's testimony, memory, and suggestibility. See generally, Karen Saywitz, supra D -7; CHILD VICTIMS, CHILD WITNESSES: UNDERSTANDING AND IMPROVING TESTIMONY (Gail S. Goodman & Bette L. Bottoms, eds. 1993); ANN HARALAMBIE, 2 HANDLING CHILD CUSTODY, ABUSE, AND ADOPTION CASES §§ 24.09_24.22 (2nd ed. 1993); MYERS, supra D-6, at Vol. 1, ch 2; Ellen Matthews & Karen Saywitz, Child Victim Witness Manual, 12/1 C.J.E.R.J. 40 (1992).

The information a child gives in interviews and during testimony is often misleading because the adults have not understood how to ask children developmentally appropriate questions and how to interpret their answers properly. See WALKER, SUPRA, A-3 Commentary. The child's attorney must become skilled at recognizing the child's developmental limitations. It may be appropriate to present expert testimony on the issue and even to have an expert present during a young child's testimony to point out any developmentally inappropriate phrasing.

D-9. Challenges to Child's Testimony/Statements. The child's competency to testify, or the reliability of the child's testimony or out-of-court statements, may be called into question. The child's attorney should be familiar with the current law and empirical knowledge about children's competency, memory, and suggestibility and, where appropriate, attempt to establish the competency and

reliability of the child.

> *Commentary —*
> Many jurisdictions have abolished presumptive ages of competency. See HARALAMBIE, SUPRA D-8 AT §24.17. The jurisdictions which have rejected presumptive ages for testimonial competency have applied more flexible, case-by-case analyses. See Louis I. Parley, Representing Children in Custody Litigation, 11 J. AM. ACAD. MATRIM. LAW. 45, 48 (Winter 1993). Competency to testify involves the abilities to perceive and relate.
> If necessary, the child's attorney should present expert testimony to establish competency or reliability or to rehabilitate any impeachment of the child on those bases. See generally, Karen Saywitz, supra D-8 at 15; CHILD VICTIMS, SUPRA D-8; Haralambie, supra D-8; J. MYERS, SUPRA D-8; Matthews & Saywitz, supra D-8.

D-10. Jury Selection. In those states in which a jury trial is possible, the child's attorney should participate in jury selection and drafting jury instructions.

D-11. Conclusion of Hearing. If appropriate, the child's attorney should make a closing argument, and provide proposed findings of fact and conclusions of law. The child's attorney should ensure that a written order is entered.

> *Commentary —*
> One of the values of having a trained child's attorney is such a lawyer can often present creative alternative solutions to the court. Further, the child's attorney is able to argue the child's interests from the child's perspective, keeping the case focused on the child's needs and the effect of various dispositions on the child.

D-12. Expanded Scope of Representation. The child's attorney may request authority from the court to pursue issues on behalf of the child, administratively or judicially, even if those issues do not specifically arise from the court appointment. For example:

(1)   Child support;

(2)   Delinquency or status offender matters;

(3)   SSI and other public benefits;

(4)   Custody;

(5)   Guardianship;

(6)   **Paternity;**

(7)   **Personal injury;**

(8)   **School/education issues, especially for a child with disabilities;**

(9)   **Mental health proceedings;**

(10)   **Termination of parental rights; and**

(11)   **Adoption.**

Commentary —
       The child's interests may be served through proceedings not connected with the case in which the child's attorney is participating. In such cases the lawyer may be able to secure assistance for the child by filing or participating in other actions. See, e.g., In re Appeal in Pima County Juvenile Action No. S-113432, 872 P.2d 1240 (Ariz. Ct. App. 1994). With an older child or a child with involved parents, the child's attorney may not need court authority to pursue other services. For instance, federal law allows the parent to control special education. A Unified Child and Family Court Model would allow for consistency of representation between related court proceedings, such as mental health or juvenile justice.

D-13. Obligations after Disposition. The child's attorney should seek to ensure continued representation of the child at all further hearings, including at administrative or judicial actions that result in changes to the child's placement or services, so long as the court maintains its jurisdiction.

Commentary —
       Representing a child should reflect the passage of time and the changing needs of the child. The bulk of the child's attorney's work often comes after the initial hearing, including ongoing permanency planning issues, six month reviews, case plan reviews, issues of termination, and so forth. The average length of stay in foster care is over five years in some jurisdictions. Often a child's case workers, therapists, other service providers or even placements change while the case is still pending. Different judges may hear various phases of the case. The child's attorney may be the only source of continuity for the child. Such continuity not only provides the child with a stable point of contact, but also may represent the institutional memory of case facts and procedural history for the agency and court. The child's attorney should stay in touch with the child, third party caretakers, case workers, and service

providers throughout the term of appointment to ensure that the child's
needs are met and that the case moves quickly to an appropriate
resolution.

Generally it is preferable for the lawyer to remain involved so long
as the case is pending to enable the child's interest to be addressed from
the child's perspective at all stages. Like the JUVENILE JUSTICE
STANDARDS, these ABUSE AND NEGLECT STANDARDS require ongoing
appointment and active representation as long as the court retains
jurisdiction over the child. To the extent that these are separate
proceedings in some jurisdictions, the child's attorney should seek
reappointment. Where reappointment is not feasible, the child's attorney
should provide records and information about the case and cooperate
with the successor to ensure continuity of representation.

E. POST-HEARING

**E-1. Review of Court's Order. The child's attorney should review all written
orders to ensure that they conform with the court's verbal orders and statutorily
required findings and notices.**

**E-2. Communicate Order to Child. The child's attorney should discuss the
order and its consequences with the child.**

Commentary —

The child is entitled to understand what the court has done and
what that means to the child, at least with respect to those portions of the
order that directly affect the child. Children may assume that orders are
final and not subject to change. Therefore, the lawyer should explain
whether the order may be modified at another hearing, or whether the
actions of the parties may affect how the order is carried out. For
example, an order may permit the agency to return the child to the parent
if certain goals are accomplished.

**E-3. Implementation. The child's attorney should monitor the implementation
of the court's orders and communicate to the responsible agency and, if
necessary, the court, any non-compliance.**

Commentary —

The lawyer should ensure that services are provided and that the
court's orders are implemented in a complete and timely fashion. In
order to address problems with implementation, the lawyer should stay
in touch with the child, case worker, third party caretakers, and service
providers between review hearings. The lawyer should consider filing
any necessary motions, including those for civil or criminal contempt, to

compel implementation. See, RESOURCE GUIDELINES, at 23.

F. APPEAL

F-1. Decision to Appeal. The child's attorney should consider and discuss with the child, as developmentally appropriate, the possibility of an appeal. If after such consultation, the child wishes to appeal the order, and the appeal has merit, the lawyer should take all steps necessary to perfect the appeal and seek appropriate temporary orders or extraordinary writs necessary to protect the interests of the child during the pendency of the appeal.

> *Commentary —*
>
> The lawyer should explain to the child not only the legal possibility of an appeal, but also the ramifications of filing an appeal, including the potential for delaying implementation of services or placement options. The lawyer should also explain whether the trial court's orders will be stayed pending appeal and what the agency and trial court may do pending a final decision.

F-2. Withdrawal. If the child's attorney determines that an appeal would be frivolous or that he or she lacks the necessary experience or expertise to handle the appeal, the lawyer should notify the court and seek to be discharged or replaced.

F-3. Participation in Appeal. The child's attorney should participate in an appeal filed by another party unless discharged.

> *Commentary —*
>
> The child's attorney should take a position in any appeal filed by the parent, agency, or other party. In some jurisdictions, the lawyer's appointment does not include representation on appeal. If the child's interests are affected by the issues raised in the appeal, the lawyer should seek an appointment on appeal or seek appointment of appellate counsel to represent the child's position in the appeal.

F-4. Conclusion of Appeal. When the decision is received, the child's attorney should explain the outcome of the case to the child.

> *Commentary —*
>
> As with other court decisions, the lawyer should explain in terms the child can understand the nature and consequences of the appellate decision. In addition, the lawyer should explain whether there are further appellate remedies and what more, if anything, will be done in the trial court following the decision.

F-5. Cessation of Representation. The child's attorney should discuss the end of the legal representation and determine what contacts, if any, the child's attorney and the child will continue to have.

> *Commentary —*
>
> When the representation ends, the child's lawyer should explain in a developmentally appropriate manner why the representation is ending and how the child can obtain assistance in the future should it become necessary. It is important for there to be closure between the child and the lawyer.

PART II—ENHANCING THE JUDICIAL ROLE IN CHILD REPRESENTATION

PREFACE

Enhancing the legal representation provided by court-appointed lawyers for children has long been a special concern of the American Bar Association [*see, e.g.,* JUVENILE JUSTICE STANDARDS RELATING TO *COUNSEL FOR PRIVATE PARTIES* (1979); ABA Policy Resolutions on Representation of Children (Appendix). Yet, no matter how carefully a bar association, legislature, or court defines the duties of lawyers representing children, practice will only improve if judicial administrators and trial judges play a stronger role in the selection, training, oversight, and prompt payment of court-appointed lawyers in child abuse/neglect and child custody/visitation cases.

The importance of the court's role in helping assure competent representation of children is noted in the JUVENILE JUSTICE STANDARDS RELATING TO COURT ORGANIZATION AND ADMINISTRATION (1980) which state in the Commentary to 3.4D that effective representation of parties is "essential" and that the presiding judge of a court "might need to use his or her position to achieve" it. In its RESOURCE GUIDELINES: IMPROVING COURT PRACTICE IN CHILD ABUSE & NEGLECT CASES (1995), the National Council of Juvenile and Family Court Judges stated, "Juvenile and family courts should take active steps to ensure that the parties in child abuse and neglect cases have access to competent representation. . . ." In jurisdictions which engage nonlawyers to represent a child's interests, the court should ensure they have access to legal representation.

These Abuse and Neglect Standards, like the RESOURCE GUIDELINES, recognize that the courts have a great ability to influence positively the quality of counsel through setting judicial prerequisites for lawyer appointments including requirements for experience and training, imposing sanctions for violation of standards (such as terminating a lawyer's appointment to represent a specific child, denying further appointments, or even fines or referrals to the state bar committee for professional responsibility). The following Standards are intended to assist the judiciary in using its authority to accomplish the goal of quality representation for all children before the court in abuse/neglect related proceedings.

G. THE COURT'S ROLE IN STRUCTURING CHILD REPRESENTATION

G-1. Assuring Independence of the Child's Attorney. The child's attorney should be independent from the court, court services, the parties, and the state.

Commentary —

To help assure that the child's attorney is not compromised in his or her independent action, these Standards propose that the child's lawyer be independent from other participants in the litigation. "Independence" does not mean that a lawyer may not receive payment from a court, a government entity (e.g., program funding from social services or justice agencies), or even from a parent, relative, or other adult so long as the lawyer retains the full authority for independent action. For ethical conflict reasons, however, lawyers should never accept compensation as retained counsel for the child from a parent accused of abusing or neglecting the child. The child's attorney should not prejudge the case. The concept of independence includes being free from prejudice and other limitations to uncompromised representation.

JUVENILE JUSTICE STANDARD § 2.1(d) states that plans for providing counsel for children "must be designed to guarantee the professional independence of counsel and the integrity of the lawyer-client relationship." The Commentary strongly asserts there is "no justification for . . . judicial preference" to compromise a lawyer's relationship with the child client and notes the "willingness of some judges to direct lawyers' performance and thereby compromise their independence."

G-2. Establishing Uniform Representation Rules. The administrative office for the state trial, family, or juvenile court system should cause to be published and disseminated to all relevant courts a set of uniform, written rules and procedures for court-appointed lawyers for minor children.

Commentary —

Although uniform rules of court to govern the processing of various types of child-related judicial proceedings have become common, it is still rare for those rules to address comprehensively the manner and scope of representation for children. Many lawyers representing children are unclear as to the court's expectations. Courts in different communities, or even judges within the same court, may have differing views regarding the manner of child representation. These Standards promote statewide uniformity by calling for written publication and distribution of state rules and procedures for the child's attorney.

G-3. Enhancing Lawyer Relationships with Other Court Connected Personnel. Courts that operate or utilize Court Appointed Special Advocate (CASA) and other nonlawyer guardians ad litem, and courts that administer nonjudicial foster care review bodies, should assure that these programs and the individuals performing those roles are trained to understand the role of the child's attorney. There needs to be effective coordination of their efforts with the activities of the child's attorney, and they need to involve the child's attorney in their work. The court should require that reports from agencies be prepared and presented to the parties in a timely fashion.

Commentary —

Many courts now regularly involve nonlawyer advocates for children in various capacities. Some courts also operate programs that, outside of the courtroom, review the status of children in foster care or other out-of-home placements. It is critical that these activities are appropriately linked to the work of the child's attorney, and that the court through training, policies, and protocols helps assure that those performing the nonlegal tasks (1) understand the importance and elements of the role of the child's attorney, and (2) work cooperatively with such lawyers. The court should keep abreast of all the different representatives involved with the child, the attorney, social worker for government or private agency, CASA volunteer, guardian ad litem, school intermediator, counselors, etc.

H. THE COURT'S ROLE IN APPOINTING THE CHILD'S ATTORNEY

H-1. Timing of Appointments. The child's attorney should be appointed immediately after the earliest of:

(1)   **The involuntary removal of the child for placement due to allegations of neglect, abuse or abandonment;**

(2)   **The filing of a petition alleging child abuse and neglect, for review of foster care placement, or for termination of parental rights; or**

(3) **Allegations of child maltreatment, based upon sufficient cause, are made by a party in the context of proceedings that were not originally initiated by a petition alleging child maltreatment.**

Commentary —

These ABUSE AND NEGLECT STANDARDS take the position that courts must assure the appointment of a lawyer for a child as soon as practical (ideally, on the day the court first has jurisdiction over the case, and hopefully, no later than the next business day). The three situations are described separately because:

(1) A court may authorize, or otherwise learn of, a child's removal from home prior to the time a formal petition is instituted. Lawyer representation of (and, ideally, contact with) the child prior to the initial court hearing following removal (which in some cases may be several days) is important to protect the child's interests;

(2) Once a petition has been filed by a government agency (or, where authorized, by a hospital or other agency with child protection responsibilities), for any reason related to a child's need for protection, the child should have prompt access to a lawyer; and

(3) There are cases (such as custody, visitation, and guardianship disputes and family-related abductions of children) where allegations, with sufficient cause, of serious physical abuse, sexual molestation, or severe neglect of a child are presented to the court not by a government agency (i.e., child protective services) but by a parent, guardian, or other relative. The need of a child for competent, independent representation by a lawyer is just as great in situation (3) as with cases in areas (1) and (2).

H-2. Entry of Compensation Orders. At the time the court appoints a child's attorney, it should enter a written order addressing compensation and expense costs for that lawyer, unless these are otherwise formally provided for by agreement or contract with the court, or through another government agency.

Commentary —

Compensation and expense reimbursement of individual lawyers should be addressed in a specific written court order is based on a need for all lawyers representing maltreated children to have a uniform understanding of how they will be paid. Commentary to Section 2.1(b) of the JUVENILE JUSTICE STANDARDS observes that it is common for court-appointed lawyers to be confused about the availability of reimbursement of expenses for case-related work.

H-3. Immediate Provision of Access. **Unless otherwise provided for, the court should upon appointment of a child's attorney, enter an order authorizing that lawyer access between the child and the lawyer and to all privileged information regarding the child, without the necessity of a further release. The authorization should include, but not be limited to: social services, psychiatric, psychological treatment, drug and alcohol treatment, medical, evaluation, law enforcement, and school records.**

Commentary —

Because many service providers do not understand or recognize the nature of the role of the lawyer for the child or that person's importance in the court proceeding, these Standards call for the routine use of a written court order that clarifies the lawyers right to contact with their child client and perusal of child-related records. Parents, other caretakers, or government social service agencies should not unreasonably interfere with a lawyer's ability to have face-to-face contact with the child client nor to obtain relevant information about the child's social services, education, mental health, etc. Such interference disrupts the lawyer's ability to control the representation and undermines his or her independence as the child's legal representative.

H-4. Lawyer Eligibility for and Method of Appointment. **Where the court makes individual appointment of counsel, unless impractical, before making the appointment, the court should determine that the lawyer has been trained in representation of children and skilled in litigation (or is working under the supervision of an lawyer who is skilled in litigation). Whenever possible, the trial judge should ensure that the child's attorney has had sufficient training in child advocacy and is familiar with these Standards. The trial judge should also ensure that (unless there is specific reason to appoint a specific lawyer because of their special qualifications related to the case, or where a lawyer's current caseload would prevent them from adequately handling the case) individual lawyers are appointed from the ranks of eligible members of the bar under a fair, systematic, and sequential appointment plan.**

Commentary —

The JUVENILE JUSTICE STANDARDS § 2.2(c) provides that where counsel is assigned by the court, this lawyer should be drawn from "an adequate pool of competent attorneys." In general, such competency can only be gained through relevant continuing legal education and practice-related experience. Those Standards also promote the use of a rational court appointment process drawing from the ranks of qualified lawyers. The Abuse and Neglect Standards reject the concept of ad hoc appointments of counsel that are made without regard to prior training or practice.

H-5. Permitting Child to Retain a Lawyer. The court should permit the child to be represented by a retained private lawyer if it determines that this lawyer is the child's independent choice, and such counsel should be substituted for the appointed lawyer. A person with a legitimate interest in the child's welfare may retain private counsel for the child and/or pay for such representation, and that person should be permitted to serve as the child's attorney, subject to approval of the court. Such approval should not be given if the child opposes the lawyer's representation or if the court determines that there will be a conflict of interest. The court should make it clear that the person paying for the retained lawyer does not have the right to direct the representation of the child or to receive privileged information about the case from the lawyer.

Commentary —

Although such representation is rare, there are situations where a child, or someone acting on a child's behalf, seeks out legal representation and wishes that this lawyer, rather than one appointed by the court under the normal appointment process, be recognized as the sole legal representative of the child. Sometimes, judges have refused to accept the formal appearances filed by such retained lawyers. These Standards propose to permit, under carefully scrutinized conditions, the substitution of a court-appointed lawyer with the retained counsel for a child.

I. THE COURT'S ROLE IN LAWYER TRAINING

I-1. Judicial Involvement in Lawyer Training. Trial judges who are regularly involved in child-related matters should participate in training for the child's attorney conducted by the courts, the bar, or any other group.

Commentary —

JUVENILE JUSTICE STANDARDS § 2.1 indicates that it is the responsibility of the courts (among others) to ensure that competent counsel are available to represent children before the courts. That Standard further suggests that lawyers should "be encouraged" to qualify themselves for participation in child-related cases "through formal training." The Abuse and Neglect Standards go further by suggesting that judges should personally take part in educational programs, whether or not the court conducts them. The National Council of Juvenile and Family Court Judges has suggested that courts can play in important role in training lawyers in child abuse and neglect cases, and that judges and judicial officers can volunteer to provide training and publications for

continuing legal education seminars. See, RESOURCE GUIDELINES, at
22.

**I-2. Content of Lawyer Training. The appropriate state administrative office of
the trial, family, or juvenile courts should provide educational programs, live or
on tape, on the role of a child's attorney. At a minimum, the requisite training
should include:**

(1)   **Information about relevant federal and state laws and agency regulations;**

(2)   **Information about relevant court decisions and court rules;**

(3)   **Overview of the court process and key personnel in child-related
litigation;**

(4)   **Description of applicable guidelines and standards for representation;**

(5)   **Focus on child development, needs, and abilities;**

(6)   **Information on the multidisciplinary input required in child-related
cases, including information on local experts who can provide
consultation and testimony on the reasonableness and appropriateness
of efforts made to safely maintain the child in his or her home;**

(7)   **Information concerning family dynamics and dysfunction including
substance abuse, and the use of kinship care;**

(8)   **Information on accessible child welfare, family preservation, medical,
educational, and mental health resources for child clients and their
families, including placement, evaluation/diagnostic, and treatment
services; the structure of agencies providing such services as well as
provisions and constraints related to agency payment for services; and**

(9)   **Provision of written material (e.g., representation manuals, checklists,
sample forms), including listings of useful material available from other
sources.**

Commentary —

The ABUSE AND NEGLECT STANDARDS take the position that it is
not enough that judges mandate the training of lawyers, or that judges
participate in such training. Rather, they call upon the courts to play a
key role in training by actually sponsoring (e.g., funding) training
opportunities. The pivotal nature of the judiciary's role in educating
lawyers means that courts may, on appropriate occasions, stop the
hearing of cases on days when training is held so that both lawyers and

judges may freely attend without docket conflicts. The required elements of training are based on a review of well-regarded lawyer training offered throughout the country, RESOURCE GUIDELINES, and many existing manuals that help guide lawyers in representing children.

I-3. Continuing Training for Lawyers. The court system should also assure that there are periodic opportunities for lawyers who have taken the "basic" training to receive continuing and "new developments" training.

Commentary —

Many courts and judicial organizations recognize that rapid changes occur because of new federal and state legislation, appellate court decisions, systemic reforms, and responses to professional literature. Continuing education opportunities are critical to maintain a high level of performance. These Standards call for courts to afford these "advanced" or "periodic" training to lawyers who represent children in abuse and neglect related cases.

I-4. Provision of Mentorship Opportunities. Courts should provide individual court-appointed lawyers who are new to child representation the opportunity to practice under the guidance of a senior lawyer mentor.

Commentary —

In addition to training, particularly for lawyers who work as sole practitioners or in firms that do not specialize in child representation, courts can provide a useful mechanism to help educate new lawyers for children by pairing them with more experienced advocates. One specific thing courts can do is to provide lawyers new to representing children with the opportunity to be assisted by more experienced lawyers in their jurisdiction. Some courts actually require lawyers to "second chair" cases before taking an appointment to a child abuse or neglect case. See, RESOURCE GUIDELINES, at 22.

J. THE COURT'S ROLE IN LAWYER COMPENSATION

J-1. Assuring Adequate Compensation. A child's attorney should receive adequate and timely compensation throughout the term of appointment that reflects the complexity of the case and includes both in court and out-of-court preparation, participation in case reviews and postdispositional hearings, and involvement in appeals. To the extent that the court arranges for child representation through contract or agreement with a program in which lawyers represent children, the court should assure that the rate of payment for these legal services is commensurate with the fees paid to equivalently experienced individual court-appointed lawyers who have similar qualifications and

responsibilities.

Commentary —

JUVENILE JUSTICE STANDARDS § 2.1(b) recognize that lawyers for children should be entitled to reasonable compensation for both time and services performed "according to prevailing professional standards," which takes into account the "skill required to perform...properly," and which considers the need for the lawyer to perform both counseling and resource identification/evaluation activities. The RESOURCE GUIDELINES, at 22, state that it is "necessary to provide reasonable compensation" for improved lawyer representation of children and that where necessary judges should "urge state legislatures and local governing bodies to provide sufficient funding" for quality legal representation. Because some courts currently compensate lawyers only for time spent in court at the adjudicative or initial disposition stage of cases, these Standards clarify that compensation is to be provided for out-of-court preparation time, as well as for the lawyer's involvement in case reviews and appeals. "Out-of-court preparation" may include, for example, a lawyer's participation in social services or school case conferences relating to the client.

These Standards also call for the level of compensation where lawyers are working under contract with the court to provide child representation to be comparable with what experienced individual counsel would receive from the court. Although courts may, and are encouraged to, seek high quality child representation through enlistment of special children's law offices, law firms, and other programs, the motive should not be a significantly different (i.e., lower) level of financial compensation for the lawyers who provide the representation.

J-2. Supporting Associated Costs. The child's attorney should have access to (or be provided with reimbursement for experts, investigative services, paralegals, research costs, and other services, such as copying medical records, long distance phone calls, service of process, and transcripts of hearings as requested.

Commentary —

The ABUSE AND NEGLECT STANDARDS expand upon JUVENILE JUSTICE STANDARDS § 2.1(c) which recognizes that a child's attorney should have access to "investigatory, expert and other nonlegal services" as a fundamental part of providing competent representation.

J-3. Reviewing Payment Requests. The trial judge should review requests for compensation for reasonableness based upon the complexity of the case and the hours expended.

Commentary —

These Standards implicitly reject the practice of judges arbitrarily "cutting down" the size of lawyer requests for compensation and would limit a judge's ability to reduce the amount of a per/case payment request from a child's attorney unless the request is deemed unreasonable based upon two factors: case complexity and time spent.

J-4. Keeping Compensation Levels Uniform. Each state should set a uniform level of compensation for lawyers appointed by the courts to represent children. Any per/hour level of compensation should be the same for all representation of children in all types of child abuse and neglect-related proceedings.

Commentary —

These Standards implicitly reject the concept (and practice) of different courts within a state paying different levels of compensation for lawyers representing children. They call for a uniform approach, established on a statewide basis, towards the setting of payment guidelines.

K. THE COURT'S ROLE IN RECORD ACCESS BY LAWYERS

K-1. Authorizing Lawyer Access. The court should enter an order in child abuse and neglect cases authorizing the child's attorney access to all privileged information regarding the child, without the necessity for a further release.

Commentary —

This Standard requires uniform judicial assistance to remove a common barrier to effective representation, i.e., administrative denial of access to significant records concerning the child. The language supports the universal issuance of broadly-worded court orders that grant a child's attorney full access to information (from individuals) or records (from agencies) concerning the child.

K-2. Providing Broad Scope Orders. The authorization order granting the child's attorney access to records should include social services, psychiatric, psychological treatment, drug and alcohol treatment, medical, evaluation, law enforcement, school, and other records relevant to the case.

Commentary —

This Standard further elaborates upon the universal application that the court's access order should be given, by listing examples of the most common agency records that should be covered by the court order.

L. THE COURT'S ROLE IN ASSURING REASONABLE LAWYER CASELOADS

L-1. Controlling Lawyer Caseloads. Trial court judges should control the size of court-appointed caseloads of individual lawyers representing children, the caseloads of government agency-funded lawyers for children, or court contracts/agreements with lawyers for such representation. Courts should take steps to assure that lawyers appointed to represent children, or lawyers otherwise providing such representation, do not have such a large open number of cases that they are unable to abide by Part I of these Standards.

> *Commentary —*
> THE ABUSE AND NEGLECT STANDARDS go further than JUVENILE JUSTICE STANDARD § 2.2(b) which recognize the "responsibility of every defender office to ensure that its personnel can offer prompt, full, and effective counseling and representation to each (child) client" and that it "should not accept more assignments than its staff can adequately discharge" by specifically calling upon the courts to to help keep lawyer caseloads from getting out of control. The Commentary to § 2.2.(b) indicates that: Caseloads must not be exceeded where to do so would "compel lawyers to forego the extensive fact investigation required in both contested and uncontested cases, or to be less than scrupulously careful in preparation for trial, or to forego legal research necessary to develop a theory of representation." We would add: "...or to monitor the implementation of court orders and agency case plans in order to help assure permanency for the child."

L-2. Taking Supportive Caseload Actions. If judges or court administrators become aware that individual lawyers are close to, or exceeding, the levels suggested in these Standards, they should take one or more of the following steps:

(1) Expand, with the aid of the bar and children's advocacy groups, the size of the list from which appointments are made;

(2) Alert relevant government or private agency administrators that their lawyers have an excessive caseload problem;

(3) Recruit law firms or special child advocacy law programs to engage in child representation;

(4) Review any court contracts/agreements for child representation and amend them accordingly, so that additional lawyers can be compensated for case representation time; and

(5)   Alert state judicial, executive, and legislative branch leaders that excessive caseloads jeopardize the ability of lawyers to competently represent children pursuant to state-approved guidelines, and seek funds for increasing the number of lawyers available to represent children.

APPENDIX

Previous American Bar Association Policies Related to Legal Representation of Abused and Neglected Children

GUARDIANS AD LITEM
FEBRUARY 1992

BE IT RESOLVED, that the American Bar Association urges:

(1)   Every state and territory to meet the full intent of the Federal Child Abuse Prevention and Treatment Act, whereby every child in the United States who is the subject of a civil child protection related judicial proceedings will be represented at all stages of these proceedings by a fully-trained, monitored, and evaluated guardian ad litem in addition to appointed legal counsel.

(2)   That state, territory and local bar associations and law schools become involved in setting standards of practice for such guardians ad litem, clarify the ethical responsibilities of these individuals and establish minimum ethical performance requirements for their work, and provide comprehensive multidisciplinary training for all who serve as such guardians ad litem.

(3)   That in every state and territory, where judges are given discretion to appoint a guardian ad litem in private child custody and visitation related proceedings, the bench and bar jointly develop guidelines to aid judges in determining when such an appointment is necessary to protect the best interests of the child.

COURT-APPOINTED SPECIAL ADVOCATES
AUGUST 1989

BE IT RESOLVED, that the American Bar Association endorses the concept of utilizing carefully selected, well trained lay volunteers, Court Appointed Special Advocates, in addition to providing attorney representation, in dependency proceedings to assist the court in determining what is in the best interests of abused and neglected children.

BE IT FURTHER RESOLVED, that the American Bar Association encourages its members to support the development of CASA programs in their communities.

COUNSEL FOR CHILDREN ENHANCEMENT
FEBRUARY 1987

BE IT RESOLVED, that the American Bar Association requests State and local bar associations to determine the extent to which statutory law and court rules in their States guarantee the right to counsel for children in juvenile court proceedings; and

BE IT FURTHER RESOLVED, that State and local bar associations are urged to actively participate and support amendments to the statutory law and court rules in their State to bring them in to compliance with the Institute of Judicial Administration/American Bar Association Standards Relating to Counsel for Private Parties; and

BE IT FURTHER RESOLVED, that State and local bar associations are requested to ascertain the extent to which, irrespective of the language in their State statutory laws and court rules, counsel is in fact provided for children in juvenile court proceedings and the extent to which the quality of representation is consistent with the standards and policies of the American Bar Association; and

BE IT FURTHER RESOLVED, that State and local bar associations are urged to actively support programs of training and education to ensure that lawyers practicing in juvenile court are aware of the American Bar Association's standards relating to representation of children and provide advocacy which meets those standards.

BAR ASSOCIATION AND ATTORNEY ACTION
FEBRUARY 1984

BE IT RESOLVED, that the American Bar Association urges the members of the legal profession, as well as state and local bar associations, to respond to the needs of children by directing attention to issues affecting children including, but not limited to: ... (7) establishment of guardian ad litem programs.

BAR AND ATTORNEY INVOLVEMENT IN
CHILD PROTECTION CASES
AUGUST 1981

BE IT RESOLVED, that the American Bar Association encourages individual attorneys and state and local bar organizations to work more actively to improve the handling of cases involving abused and neglected children as well as children in foster care. Specifically, attorneys should form appropriate committees and groups within the bar to ... work to assure quality legal representation for children....

JUVENILE JUSTICE STANDARDS
FEBRUARY 1979

BE IT RESOLVED, that the American Bar Association adopt (the volume of the) Standards for Juvenile Justice (entitled) Counsel for Private Parties...

Appendix B RECOMMENDED READING

BOOKS

Adoption Law & Practice, by Joan Heifetz Hollinger, et al. (New York, NY: Mathew Bender & Co., Inc., 1995).

The Backlash: Child Protection Under Fire, edited by John E.B. Myers (Thousand Oaks, CA: Sage Publications, 1994).

The Battered Child, 5th Ed., edited by Helfer, Kempe & Krugman (Chicago, IL: University of Chicago Press, 1997).

The Best Interests of the Child: The Least Detrimental Alternative, The Landmark Trilogy of **Beyond the Best Interests of the Child, Before the Best Interests of the Child,** *and* **In the Best Interests of the Child**, by Goldstein, Solnit, Goldstein & Freud (New York, NY: The Free Press, 1996).

Cases and Materials in Juvenile Law, by J. Eric Smithburn (Cincinnati, OH: Anderson Publishing Co., 2002).

Child Abuse and the Legal System, by Inger J. Sagatun and Leonard P. Edwards (Chicago, IL: Nelson-Hall, Inc., 1995).

Child Abuse and Neglect: Cases and Materials, by Robert D. Goldstein (St. Paul, MN: West Group, American Casebook Series, 1999).

The Child Abuse-Delinquency Connection, by David N. Sandberg (Lexington, MA: Lexington Books, 1989).

Child Maltreatment: A Clinical Guide and Reference, edited by James A. Monteleone & Armand E. Brodeur (St. Louis, MO: G.W. Medical Publishing, Inc, 1994).

Child Rights and Remedies: How the U.S. Legal System Affects Children, by Robert C. Fellmeth (Atlanta, GA: Clarity Press, 2002).

Children and the Law: Rights and Obligations, by Thomas A. Jacobs (Deerfield, IL: Clark Boardman Callaghan, 1995).

The Child's Attorney: A Guide to Representing Children in Custody, Adoption, and Protection Cases, by Ann M. Haralambie (Chicago, IL: American Bar Association, ABA Section of Family Law, 1993).

Classic Papers in Child Abuse, edited by Anne Cohn Donnelly & Kim Oates (Thousand Oaks, CA: Sage Publications, 2000).

Desk Reference to the Diagnostic Criteria From DSM-IV-TR, 4th Ed., Text Revision, by American Psychiatric Association (Washington, D.C.: American Psychiatric Association, 2000).

Diagnostic and Statistical Manual of Mental Disorders DSM-IV-TR, 4th Ed., Text Revision, by American Psychiatric Association (Washington, DC: American Psychiatric Association, 2000).

Diagnostic Imaging of Child Abuse, 2nd Ed., by Paul K. Kleinman (St. Louis, MO: C.V. Mosby, 1998).

A Digest of Cases of the United States Supreme Court as to Juvenile and Family Law, edited by National Council of Juvenile and Family Court Judges (Reno, NV: National Council of Juvenile and Family Court Judges, 2001).

Evidence in Child Abuse and Neglect Cases, 3rd Ed., by John E.B. Myers (New York, NY: Wiley Law Publications, 1997).

Expert Witnesses in Child Abuse Cases, edited by Stephen J. Ceci & Helene Hembrooke (Washington, D.C.: American Psychological Association, 1998).

Facts About Children and the Law, by American Bar Association, Division for Media Relations and Public Affairs (Chicago, IL: American Bar Association), *available at* http://www.abanet.org/media/factbooks/chtoc.html.

Families By Law: An Adoption Reader, edited by Naomi R. Cahn & Joan Heifetz Hollinger (New York, NY: New York University Press, 2004).

Glass Walls: Confidentiality Provisions and InterAgency Collaborations, by Mark I. Soler, Alice C. Shotton & James R. Bell (San Francisco, CA: Youth Law Center, 1993).

Handbook on Questioning Children: A Linguistic Perspective, 2nd Ed., by Anne Graffam Walker, Ph.D. (Chicago, IL: American Bar Association, 1999).

Handling Child Custody, Abuse and Adoption Cases, 2nd Ed., by Ann M. Haralambie (Deerfield, IL: Clark, Boardman, Callaghan, 1993).

A History of Child Protection in America, John E.B. Myers (Philadelphia, PA: Xlibris Corporation, 2004).

Juvenile Sexual Offending: Causes, Consequences, and Correction, by Gail D. Ryan & Sandy L. Lane (Lexington, MA: Lexington Books, 1991).

Legal Ethics in Child Welfare Cases, by Jennifer Renne (Washington, D.C.: ABA Center on Children and the Law, 2004).

Legal Issues in Child Abuse and Neglect Practice, 2nd Ed., by John E. B. Myers (Thousand Oaks, CA: Sage Publications, 1998).

Legal Rights of Children, 2nd Ed., by Donald T. Kramer (Deerfield, IL: Clark, Boardman, Callaghan, 1994).

Modern Trial Advocacy: Analysis and Practice, 3rd Ed., by Steven Lubet (South Bend, IN: National Institute for Trial Advocacy, 2004).

Recognizing Child Abuse: A Guide for the Concerned, by Douglas J. Besharov (New York, NY: The Free Press, 1990).

Representing Children in Child Protective Proceedings: Ethical and Practical Dimensions, 2nd Edition, by Jean Koh Peters (New York, NY: Mathew Bender and Co., Inc., A Member of LexisNexis Group, 2001).

Representing the Child Client, by Michael J. Dale, et al. (New York, NY: Lexis Publishing, 2000).

The Spectrum of Child Abuse: Assessment, Treatment, and Prevention, by R. Kim Oates, M.D. (New York, NY: Brunner/Mazel, Inc., 1996).

Trial Manual for Defense Attorneys in Juvenile Court, by Hertz, Guggenheim & Amsterdam, (Philadelphia, PA: ALI-ABA, 1991).

What Are My Rights?: 95 Questions and Answers About Teens and the Law, by Thomas A. Jacobs (Minneapolis, MN: Free Spirit Publishing, 1997).

REPORTS

ABA Standards of Practice for Lawyers Who Represent Children in Abuse and Neglect Cases, by American Bar Association (Chicago, IL: American Bar Association, 1996).

ABA (NACC Revised) Standards of Practice for Lawyers Who Represent Children in Abuse and Neglect Cases (1999).

Adoption 2002: Guidelines For Public Policy and State Legislation Governing Permanence For Children, by Donald N. Duquette & Mark Hardin (Washington, D.C.: U.S. Department of Health and Human Services, 1999).

Advocacy For Children by Foster Parents: A Manual on the Legal Rights of Foster Parents in Colorado, by Shari Shink & Seth Grob (Denver, CO: Rocky Mountain Children's Law Center, 1997).

America's Children at Risk: A National Agenda for Legal Action, by American Bar Association Presidential Working Group on the Unmet Legal Needs of Children and Their Families (Chicago, IL: American Bar Association, 1993).

America's Children Still at Risk, by American Bar Association Steering Committee on the Unmet Legal Needs of Children (Chicago, IL: American Bar Association, 2001).

Building a Better Court: Measuring and Improving Court Performance and Judicial Workload in Child Abuse and Neglect Cases, by The National Council of Juvenile and Family Court Judges, The American Bar Association Center on Children and the Law, and The National Center for State Courts (Washington, D.C.: American Bar Association, 2004).

Child Abuse and Neglect State Statutes Series, by U.S. Department of Health and Human Services, (Washington, D.C.: U.S. Department of Health and Human Services, 1997).

Child Development: A Judge's Reference Guide, by Cassady, Durst, Greydnus, Russ, Schonberg, Sikorski, & Stein, (Reno, NV: National Counsel of Juvenile and Family Court Judges, 1993).

Child Maltreatment: Reports from the States to the National Center on Child Abuse and Neglect, published annually by U.S. Department of Health and Human Services, National Center on Child Abuse and Neglect, Washington, D.C.

Children in the States 2000, by the Children's Defense Fund (Washington, D.C.: 2000).

The Children's Law Manual Series, by the National Association of Counsel for Children, produced annually from 1989 to present (Denver, CO: National Association of Counsel for Children).

Defending Child Abuse and Neglect Cases: Representing Parents in Civil Proceedings, by Douglas J. Besharov (Washington, D.C.: The District of Columbia Bar, 1987).

Foundations For Success: Strengthening Your Agency Attorney Office, edited by Mimi Laver & Claire Sandt (American Bar Association, 1999).

The National Directory of Children, Youth & Families Services 2004-2005, 20th Ed., by The National Directory of Children, Youth, and Families Services (Englewood, CO: The National Directory of CYS Services, 2004).

Preparing Children for Court: A Practitioner's Guide, by Lynn M. Copen (Thousand Oaks, CA: Sage Publications, 2000).

Prosecuting Attorneys in Dependency Proceeding in Juvenile Court: Defining and Assessing a Critical Role in Child Abuse and Neglect Cases, by Meghan Scahill, Esq. (Pittsburgh, PA: National Center for Juvenile Justice, 1999).

Resource Guidelines: Improving Court Practice in Child Abuse and Neglect Cases, National Council of Juvenile and Family Court Judges (Reno, NV: National Counsel of Juvenile and Family Court Judges, 1995).

A Sourcebook on Child Sexual Abuse, by David Finkelhor (Newbury Park, CA: Sage Publications, 1986).

The State of America's Children Yearbook, published annually by the Children's Defense Fund (CDF), Washington, DC.

JOURNALS

Child Abuse & Neglect: The International Journal, Official Monthly Publication of the International Society for Prevention of Child Abuse and Neglect, Denver, CO.

Child Law Practice, Monthly Publication of the ABA Center on Children and the Law, Washington, DC.

Child Maltreatment, Quarterly Publication of American Professional Society on the Abuse of Children, Chicago, IL.

Children's Legal Rights Journal, Quarterly Publication of the American Bar Association on Children & the Law and Loyola University Chicago School of Law in cooperation with the National Association of Counsel for Children, Buffalo, NY.

Family Law Quarterly, Quarterly Publication of the ABA Section of Family Law, Chicago, IL.

The Guardian, Quarterly Newsletter of the National Association of Counsel for Children, Denver, CO.

Juvenile and Family Court Journal, Quarterly Publication of the National Council of Juvenile and Family Court Judges, Reno, NV.

Juvenile and Family Law Digest, Monthly Publication of the National Council of Juvenile and Family Court Judges, Reno, NV.

The Quarterly Update: Reviews of Current Child Abuse Medical Research, Quarterly Publication, Norwich, VT.

Appendix C   Child Welfare Organizational Resources

National Association of Counsel for Children (NACC)
Denver, CO
888/828-NACC
http://www.NACCchildlaw.org

American Academy of Pediatrics
Elk Grove Village, IL
847/434-4000
http://www.aap.org/

ABA Center on Children and the Law
Washington, DC
202/662-1720
http://www.abanet.org/child/home.html

ABA Section of Litigation, Children's Rights Committee
Washington, DC
202/547-3060
http://www.abanet.org/litigation/committee/childrens_l/home.html

ABA Steering Committee on the Unmet Legal Needs of Children
Washington, DC
202/662-1675
http://www.abanet.org/unmet/home.html

American Humane, Children's Services
Denver, CO
303/792-9900
http://www.americanhumane.org/site/PageServer?pagename=pc_home

American Professional Society on the Abuse of Children
Charleston, SC
877-40A-PSAC
http://www.apsac.org/

American Psychological Association
Washington, DC
800-374-2721
http://www.apa.org/

Association of Family and Conciliation Courts
Madison, WI
608/664-3750
http://www.afccnet.org/

Children's Defense Fund
Washington, DC
202/628-8787
http://www.childrensdefense.org/

Child Welfare League of America
Washington, DC
202/638-2952
http://www.cwla.org/

First Star
Washington, DC
202/293-3703
http://www.firststar.org/

Immigrant Legal Resource Center
San Francisco, CA
415/255-9499
http://www.ilrc.org

Kempe Children's Center
Denver, CO
303/864-5300
http://www.kempecenter.org/

National Center for Juvenile Justice
Pittsburgh, PA
412/227-6950
http://ncjj.servehttp.com/NCJJWebsite/main.htm

National Center for Prosecution of Child Abuse
Alexandria, VA
703/549-9222
http://www.ndaa-apri.org/apri/programs/ncpca/ncpca_home.html

National Center for State Courts
Williamsburg, VA
800/616-6164
http://www.ncsconline.org/

National Council of Juvenile and Family Court Judges
Reno, NV
775/784-6012
http://www.ncjfcj.org/

National Institute for Trial Advocacy
South Bend, IN
800/225-6482
http://www.nita.org/

U.S. Department of Health and Human Services
Children's Bureau/Administration for Children and Families
National Clearinghouse on Child Abuse and Neglect Information
Washington, DC
202/619-0257
http://nccanch.acf.hhs.gov/

INDEX

References are to pages.

A

Abandoned Infants Assistance, 148
ABA Standards of Practice
    agency counsel. *See* Agency counsel
    child's attorney. *See* Child's attorney
Abdominal injuries, 21-22
Abduction of children
    Hague Convention on Child
        Abduction, 242-244
    International Child Abduction
        Database, 244
    International Child Abduction
        Remedies Act, 242
    Parental Kidnapping Prevention Act,
        167-168
    United Nations Protocol to Prevent,
        Suppress and Punish Trafficking in
        Persons, 245-246
    Victims of Trafficking and Violence
        Protection Act, 180
Abuse
    generally. *See* Maltreated children
    emotional abuse. *See* Emotional abuse
    physical abuse. *See* Physical abuse
    sexual abuse. *See* Sexual abuse
Achenbach Child Behavior Checklist, 48
Achievement tests, 47-48
Acute Distress Disorder, 317
Adjudication, 225-226
    parents' counsel's role, 456-457
Adoption, 365
    Adoption Awareness, 148
    Adoption Incentives, 148
    Adoption Opportunities, 148
    assistance reimbursement to states, 147
    Hague Convention on Intercountry
        Adoption, 244-245
    Interstate Compact on Adoption and
        Medical Assistance, 237
    post-adoption contact, 367
        advantages/disadvantages, 368-369
        agreements, 369, 370-371
        appropriateness, 369-370
        enforcing agreements, 370-371
        state laws, 367-368
    subsidies, 365-366

Adoption and Safe Families Act (ASFA),
    146
    parents' counsel's responsibilities,
        446-456
    statutory requirements, 153-157
    summary of, 146
Adoption Assistance and Child Welfare
    Act (AACWA)
    statutory requirements, 152-154
    summary of, 145
Adoption Awareness, 148
Adoption Incentives, 148
Adoption Opportunities, 148
Agency counsel
    ABA standards, 403-404
        administrative responsibilities,
            421-428
        advise and counsel obligation,
            410-411
        agency representation model, 405
        agency's credibility, protection of,
            409
        appellate practice, 417-418
        continuances, reduction of, 409
        cooperation and communication
            standards, 409-410
        court preparation, 411-414
        definitions, 404-405
        ethical and practice considera-
            tions, 419-421, 433
        fulfillment of obligations, 408-418
        hearings, 414-416
        legal requirements, compliance
            with, 408-409
        manager obligations, 421-428
        models of representation, 405-408
        post-hearing obligations, 416-417
        prosecutorial model of represen-
            tation, 405-408
        role of counsel, 405-408
        timely hearings, promotion of, 409
    administrative responsibilities, 421-428
    advise and counsel obligation, 410-411
    agency's credibility, protection of, 409
    appellate practice, 417-418
    caseworker-counsel relationship, 431
        collaboration, 434-436
        communication, 435

decision making, 434
informal sessions, 436-438
interdisciplinary training, 438-439
multidisciplinary teams, 439
mutual respect, 435
protocol for dispute resolution
between agency attorney and
caseworker, 441
protocol for termination petitions,
440
respective roles, 432-436
strengthening, 436-439
teamwork, 436
trust, 435
"client," who is, 432-433
continuances, reduction of, 409
cooperation and communication standards, 409-410
court preparation, 411-414
ethical and practice considerations,
419-421, 433
fulfillment of obligations, 408-418
hearings, 409, 414-416
incarcerated parents, practice tips
agency efforts for parental reunification, 472-473, 475
parents' right to participate, 470
termination of parental rights, 478
legal requirements, compliance with,
408-409
manager obligations, 421-428
models of representation, 405-408
post-hearing obligations, 416-417
responsibilities, defining, 433-434, 442
role of, 405-408
social workers. caseworker-counsel
relationship, *above*
timely hearings, promotion of, 409
Aid to Families With Dependent Children
(AFDC), 145
Alternate permanent planned living
arrangement (APPLA), 376-378
cultural/subcultural context, 108-110
Alternative dispute resolution. *See* Case
resolution, subheading non-adversarial
Americans With Disabilities Act (ADA),
170-171
Appellate practice, 381-382
additional evidence, request for, 396
agency counsel, 417-418

appealable orders, 382-383
appeals of right
appellant's opening brief, 392-393
appellant's reply, 393
appellate record, 391-392
appellee's brief, 393
notice of appeal, 391
oral argument, 393-394
child's attorney, 510
collateral final orders, 382
discretionary appeals, 394
extraordinary writs. *See* Extraordinary
writs
final judgment rule, 382
interlocutory orders
appealable by statute, 382-383
reviewable as a matter of discretion, 383
judicial notice, 395-396
notice of appeal, 384
appeals as of right, 397
parents' counsel, 466
post-judgment event problem, 394-395
prejudicial error, 388-389
preservation of error, 385, 638-639
procedural sequence, 391-396
standard of review, 386-388
standing, 384-385
stay requests
effect of filing an appeal, 389
request for stay, 390
ruling on request, 390
time limits, 384
Attachment to parents, 70-72
Attorneys
agency counsel. *See* Agency counsel
child's attorney. *See* Child's attorney
cultural/subcultural context, 97
parents' counsel. *See* Parents' counsel

B

Battered Child Syndrome, 308, 309-310
Battering Parent Syndrome, 311
Bayley Scales of Infant Development-II,
46
Beck Depression Inventory, 48
Bender Visual-Motor Gestalt Test
(Bender-Gestalt II), 47
"Best interests," *versus* expressed wishes,
498-500

Bibliography, 711-715
Biology, 84
Block grants to states and localities, 179-180
"Body touch" testimony, 326
Bruises, 17-19
Burden of proof. *See* Evidence
Burns, 19-21

C

Case checklist, 538-544
Case plans, 228-229
Case resolution
    cultural/subcultural context, 104-108
    Family Group Conferencing, 354
        philosophy and principles, 354
        structure of, 354-355
        uses of, 356-357
    mediation. *See* Mediation
    non-adversarial, 349-350
        agency counsel-caseworker disputes, protocol for, 441
        compromising child safety or well-being, 361-362
        effectiveness, 359-361
        Family Group Conferencing, *above*
        mediation. *See* Mediation
        parents' counsel's role, 454-456
        uses, 356-359
        voluntary relinquishment counseling, 355-356
    voluntary relinquishment counseling, 355-356
Caseworkers
    agency counsel relationship. *See* Agency counsel
    social workers, 38. *See also* Mental health professionals
Causes of action, 235-236, 535
Certiorari, writ of, 399
Chafee Foster Care Independence Program, 147
    statutory requirements, 164-166
Chicago Legal Advocacy for Incarcerated Mothers (CLAIM), 479
Child Abuse Potential Inventory, 48
Child Abuse Prevention and Treatment Act (CAPTA)
    child's attorney's role, 494

programs, 148
    statutory requirements, 149-150
    summary of, 145
Child/Adult Care Food program, 178
Child Care and Development Block Grant (CCDBG), 178
Child development, 53-56
    abuse/neglect issues, developmental level and, 74-75
    cognitive development, 57-60
    communicating with children, 75-76
    emotional development. *See* Social and emotional development
    language development, 60-61
    and lawyering. *See* Child's attorney, *subheading* developmentally appropriate lawyering
    maltreatment, impact of, 53-77
    physical development, 56-57
    psychological tests, 46-47
    psychopathology, 84
    social development. *See* Social and emotional development
Child maltreatment. *See* Maltreated children
Child population, 1-2
Child protective services
    agency counsel. *See* Agency counsel
    constitutional duties of state agencies, 201-204
    emergency protective custody, 222-223
    "founded" agency reports, 222
    investigating maltreatment. *See* Investigating maltreatment
    records, access to, 204-205
    "unfounded" agency reports, 222
Children's Apperception Test (CAT), 46
Children's Health Act of 2000, 173
Children's Justice Act (CJA), 148, 249
Child's attorney
    ABA Standards of Practice, 501
        NACC Revised Standards, 501-502, 505-511, 667-710
    appellate practice, 510
    asking questions, 517
    attorney-client privilege, 526-527
    awareness of own responses, 517
    "best interests" *versus* expressed wishes, 498-500
    bias, 536

case checklist, 538-544
causes of action, 535
child's capacity, determining, 518-519
child's preferences
     versus "best interests," 498-500
     determining, 533-534
     importance of, 511-513
child's safety and well-being, 535
"client-directed" representation
     model, 500-501
comfortable, helping child feel, 517
communicating with child, 515-516
conflicts of interest, 521
     fees paid by a third party, 524-525
     siblings, representation of, 521-524
criminal cases, 251
developmentally appropriate lawyer-
     ing, 514
     child's capacity, determining,
          518-519
     duties to child, 519-521
     meeting with child, *below*
"duties" representation model, 502
     ABA/NACC Revised ABA
          Standards, 505-511
     actions to be taken, 506-508
     advocacy duties, 504
     advocacy issues, 504-505
     appellate practice, 510
     hearings, 508-510
     NACC Recommendations, 502-505
     post-hearing actions, 510
     systemic safeguards, 503-504
duties to child, 519-521
educational advocacy. *See* Special edu-
     cation services
Ethics Code/Rules, 496-498
fact analysis, 535-536
focus questions, 532-536
hearings, 508-510
identifying permanency needs, 519-520
incarcerated parents, practice tips
     agency efforts for parental reunifi-
          cation, 473, 475
     parents' right to participate,
          470-471
     termination of parental rights,
          478-479
individual child's characteristics, 535
informing child about case, 518

investigation of facts, 531
litigation
     stage of, 534
     strategy, 537
meeting with child, 514-515
     asking questions, 517
     awareness of own responses, 517
     comfortable, helping child feel,
          517
     communicating with child, 515-
          516
     informing child about case, 518
     location of, 515
     rapport, establishing, 517
     role as attorney, explaining, 518
mental health commitment proceed-
     ings. *See* Mental health commitment
     proceedings
Model Code/Rules, 496-498
NACC recommendations, 647-666
NACC Revised ABA Standards of
     Practice, 501-502, 505-511, 667-710
permanency
     goal of, 534
     identifying needs, 519-520
preliminary facts, 532
property of child, maintaining, 520
protecting important affiliations, 520
rapport, establishing, 517
records of child, maintaining, 520
role and responsibilities, 493-495, 518,
     532-533
siblings
     association, maintenance of,
          529-530
     confidentiality concerns, 523-524
     representation of, 521-523
     waiver of conflict, 524
social history of child, maintaining, 520
termination of parental rights, advo-
     cating closure after, 521
theory of case, development of,
     531-536
"two distinct roles" representation
     model, 502
waiver of rights, 527-529
Child Sexual Abuse Accommodation
     Syndrome (CSAAS), 308-309, 318
Child Sexual Behavior Inventory, 48
Child's journey through system, 215

Child's preferences
    versus "best interests," 498-500
    determining, 533-534
    importance of, 511-513
Child Support Enforcement Program, 180
Child welfare agency
    attorney for. *See* Agency counsel
    child protective services. *See* Child
        protective services
Child Welfare Services Program, 147
Child Welfare Training grants, 148
Child well-being
    child's attorney's role, 535
    indicators of, 2-4
    and non-adversarial case resolution,
        361-362
Child witnesses
    accusatory atmosphere, 326-328
    age, and suggestibility, 323-324
    aids/props, 335
    authority figures, questioning by, 325
    "body touch" testimony, 326
    comfort items, bringing, 335
    competency to testify, 329
        burden of proof, 332
        communicate, capacity to, 330
        intelligence, 330
        memory, 330
        oath or affirmation, 332-333
        observe, capacity to, 330
        truth and truthfulness, 330-332
    constitutional case law, 206-210
    criminal cases, 251
    emotional support, 334
    hearsay. *See* Hearsay
    leading on direct, 334
    negative stereotypes, interviewer's use
        of, 326-328
    oath or affirmation, 332-333
    participants *versus* bystanders, 326
    peripheral *versus* central details, 325
    preparation of, 334
    presence in courtroom, 345-347
    psychological effects of testifying, 333
    recesses during testimony, 335
    scheduling testimony, 334
    social demands of interviews, 325
    suggestibility, 323-329
    Uniform Child Witness Testimony by
      Alternative Methods Act, 240-242

Circumstantial evidence
    cross examination, 606
    direct examination, 578-579
Clinical Social Workers, 38. *See also*
    Mental health professionals
    agency counsel relationship. *See*
      Agency counsel
Cognitive development, 57-60
Colonial America, 120-123
Commencement of case
    cultural/subcultural context, 99
    initiating court action, 223
Communicating with children, 75-76
Community Prisoner Mother Program,
    The, 479
Confidentiality
    child's attorney's representation of
      siblings, 523-524
    juvenile court proceedings and
      records, 299-304
    mental health professionals, 38
    open court proceedings. *See* Open
      court proceedings
    parents with diminished capacity,
      counsel for, 489
Conflicts of interest. *See* Child's attorney
Constitutional case law
    child protective services records,
      access to, 204-205
    children born out of wedlock, 192-196
    children's statements and testimony,
      206-210
    child's/youth rights, 188-192
        children born out of wedlock,
          192-196
        foster care children's social securi-
          ty benefits, 205
        right against self-incrimination,
          210-211
    foster care children's social security
      benefits, 205
    foster parent relationships, 199-200
    Indian Child Welfare Act, 205-206
    open court proceedings, 299-300
    parent's rights, 185-188
        foster parent relationships, 199-200
        freedom of religion *versus* com-
          pulsory education law, 191-192
        putative fathers/children born out
          of wedlock, 192-196

termination of parental rights, 197-199
state agency duties, 201-204
termination of parental rights, 197-199
Criminal offenses
maltreated children and, 12-13
status offenses, 247-248
Criminal proceedings, 248-251
child's attorney, 251
child witnesses, 251
guardians ad litem, 251
persuasive storytelling at trial, 550
Cross examination
affirmative information, 608-609
argumentative questions, 595
assuming facts not in evidence, 596
attention to details, 605-606
challenging information, 609
circumstantial evidence, 606
classic format, 608-609
compound questions, 596
content of, 596-601
defective questions, 596
ending, 606-608, 609
foundation evidence, 562
friendly information, 608
hostile information, 609
intimidating behavior, 595
law of, 594-595
leading questions, 594
objections. *See* Objections
organization of
guidelines, 603-608
principles, 601-602
planning for, 554-555
purpose, content for, 597-598
questioning technique, 609-610
risk averse question, 599-601
role of, 593-594
scope limitations, 594-595
starting, 604
uncontrovertible information, 609
unfair characterizations, 595-596
"usable universe," 598-599
Cultural/subcultural context, 95-96, 110-111
APPLA option, 108-110
players, 97-98
process, 98-108
Custody proceedings. *See* Divorce, child
custody, and visitation proceedings

D

Delinquency proceedings, 247-248
Demonstrative evidence, 626-627
Denver Development Screening Test, 46
Dependency court
early 21st century, 139
"best interests" and family preservation, 140-141
criticism and improvement, 141-142
incidents of maltreatment, 139-140
jurisdiction, 113-115, 235
Development. *See* Child development
Developmental psychopathology, 84
Developmental tests, 46-47
Direct examination
affirmation before refutation, 579-580
attention to details, 577-578
body movement during, 584
child witnesses, 334
circumstantial evidence, 578-579
competence of witnesses, 565
complex questions, 591
content of, 568
what to exclude, 570-571
what to include, 568-570
credibility of witnesses, 564
defensive direct, 579
directive questions, 581-583
disputed facts, enhancing likelihood
of, 564
distance, establishing, 589
ending, 574-575, 580
exhibits, introduction of, 564
explaining where you're going, 584
getting to the point, 580
headline questions, 583-584
ignoring rules, 580-581
incremental questions, 584-587
intensity, establishing, 589
law of, 565-567
lawyerly questions, 592
narratives, 566-567
negative questions, 591
non-interruption of action, 576-577
non-leading questions, 565-566
non-opinion rule, 567
objections. *See* Objections
organization and structure, 572-581
overall examination, 574
planning, 567-581

primacy, doctrine of, 583-584
questioning technique, 581-592
refreshing recollection, 567
repeating important points, 590
role of, 563-565
short, open questions, 581
starting, 574-575
sub-examinations, 574-575
timing of events, establishing, 587-589
transitional questions, 581-583
trier-of-fact's attention, holding, 565
undisputed facts, introducing, 563-564
visual aids, use of, 591
what to exclude, 570-571
what to include, 568-570
Disabled persons
    Americans With Disabilities Act, 170-171
    Individuals With Disabilities Education Act, 171-172. *See also* Special education services
Discovery
    pretrial discovery, 225
    protective orders, 252
Disposition, 226-228
    cultural/subcultural context, 102-104
    parents' counsel's role, 457-460
Divorce, child custody, and visitation proceedings
    child welfare/family court interaction, 255-256
    coordinating legal proceedings, 256-257
    staying together *versus* divorcing, 252-255
Documentary evidence, 627-628
Domestic violence, 257-259
    maltreatment circumstances, 81-82
    protection orders, 252
Draw-a-Person Test, 46

E

Education
    child neglect, 33
    Education for Homeless Children and Youths Act, 172
    Education for the Disadvantaged, Title I, 180
    Family Education Rights and Privacy Act, 173-174
    foster youth, 10

freedom of religion *versus* compulsory education law, 191-192
    Individuals With Disabilities Education Act, 171-172
    parents' education, child well-being and, 3
    special education. *See* Special education services
Education for Homeless Children and Youths Act, 172
Education for the Disadvantaged, Title I, 180
Emancipated foster children, challenges facing, 9-10
Emergency removal/detention, 224-225
    emergency protective custody, 222-223
    parents' counsel's role, 452-454
Emotional abuse, 28-30
    as cause of action, 236
    definition, 114
    during various stages of development, 63, 64, 66, 69
Emotional development. *See* Social and emotional development
Emotional neglect, 30
    during various stages of development, 62, 64
Evaluations, 38-39, 51
    evaluating evaluations, 39-40
    mental health, 40-41
    parent-child relationship, 41-43
    psychological tests. *See* Psychological tests
    sexual abuse, 49-51
    special education services, children in need of, 284-286
Evidence
    additional evidence on appeal, request for, 396
    adjudicatory hearing, 226
    child testimonial competence, 332
    demonstrative evidence, 626-627
    documentary evidence, 627-628
    exhibits. *See* Exhibits at trial
    foundation. *See* Foundation evidence
    hearsay. *See* Hearsay; Hearsay exceptions
    Indian Child Welfare Act cases, 159
    investigating maltreatment evidence, 221-222

objections. *See* Objections
privileges. *See* Privileges
real evidence, 626
syndromes. *See* Syndrome evidence
testimony. *See* Witnesses and testimony
Excited utterances, 340
Exhibits at trial
    admission of exhibits, 628-630
    demonstrative evidence, 626-627
    documentary evidence, 627-628
    foundation evidence, 564
    foundation witnesses, 632-633
    identifying
        by foundation witnesses, 632-633
        marking exhibits, 630-631
        for opposing counsel, 631
    marking for identification, 630-631
    motions *in limine*, 629
    offering at trial, 630-635
    offering into evidence, 633
    potential exhibits, considering, 552-553
    pretrial conferences and orders, 628-629
    publication of, 634
    real evidence, 626
    requests to admit, 630
    role of, 625-626
    showing to witness, 632
    stipulations, 629-630
    types of, 626-628
    using, 634-635
Expert testimony, 38-39, 305, 610-611
    areas of expertise, 611-612
    assumptions, 622
    bases for opinion, 306-307, 612-613
    data, establishment of, 621
    ending, 624
    expert's overview, 613-615
    foreshadowing, 615-616
    introduction of, 615-616
    offering, 615-624
    opinion, statement of, 619-620
    persuasive qualification, 617-618
    qualifications of experts, 305-306, 616
    scope of opinion, 612
    standards for, 611-613
    syndrome evidence. *See* Syndrome evidence
    technical requirements, 616-617

tender of witness, 618
theory, statement of, 620-621
theory differentiation, 622-625
Extraordinary writs
    abolition of, 400
    jurisdiction, 397
    nature of relief, 397
    parties, 398-399
    petition, 401
    review, 398
    reviewing court's alternatives, 401-402
    statutory writs, distinguished, 400
    types of, 399-400

F

Failure to thrive syndrome (FTT), 32
Family and Corrections Network, 479
Family Education Rights and Privacy Act (FERPA), 173-174
Family Foundations Program, 479
Family Group Conferencing (FGC), 354
    philosophy and principles, 354
    structure of, 354-355
    uses of, 356-357
Family Preservation and Support Services program, 146
Federal funding legislation, 143-145. *See also specific legislation*
    application of (Sally's case), 181-183
    current programs, 174-180
    1960s-2002, 145-146
Federal funding sources
    Abandoned Infants Assistance, 148
    adoption assistance reimbursements to states, 147
    Adoption Awareness, 148
    Adoption Incentives, 148
    Adoption Opportunities, 148
    Chafee Foster Care Independence Program, 147, 164-166
    Child Abuse Prevention and Treatment Act Programs. *See* Child Abuse Prevention and Treatment Act (CAPTA)
    Children's Justice Act, 148
    Child Welfare Services Program, 147
    Child Welfare Training grants, 148
    foster care reimbursements to states, 146-147

Promoting Safe and Stable Families
Program (PSSF), 146, 147
"Safe Haven," 148
Victims of Child Abuse Act, 148
Food Stamps, 178
Foster care
Chafee Foster Care Independence
Program, 146, 147
children. *See* Foster care children
parents. *See* Foster care parents
purpose of, 214
reimbursements to states, 146-147
Foster care children, 7-8
current system, 8-9
decisions affecting, 214
emancipated children, challenges facing,
9-10
improving the system, 11-12
mental health commitment proceedings, 270-271
social security benefits, 205
special education services, 287-289
Foster Care Independence Act, 146
Foster care parents
constitutional case law, 199-200
educational decision makers, 287-289
Foundation evidence
authenticity, 558
components of, 557
authenticity, 558
relevance, 557-558
specific admissibility, 558
conditional admissibility, 560-561
cross examination, 562
establishing foundations
adverse witnesses, using, 561
conditional admissibility, 560-561
cross examination, 562
multiple witnesses, using, 559-560
single witness, using, 559
exhibits, 632-633
exhibits at trial, 564
objection to, 641
relevance, 557-558
requirement of foundation, 556-557
specific admissibility, 558
Fractures, 16-17

G

Grounds for cases, 235-236
Guardians ad litem
criminal proceedings, 251
cultural/subcultural context, 97-98
role and responsibilities, 494-495
Guardianships, 259-260
parents with diminished capacity,
488-489
permanent guardianships, 371-375
standby guardianships, 375-376

H

Habeas corpus, writ of, 399-400
Hague Convention on Child Abduction,
242-244
Hague Convention on Intercountry
Adoption, 244-245
Head Start, 178-179
Head trauma, abusive, 22-23
Health insurance
and child well-being, 4
State Children's Health Insurance
Program, 176-177
Health Insurance Portability and
Accountability Act (HIPAA), 169
Hearings
adjudicatory hearing, 225-226
agency counsel, 409, 414-416
child's attorney, 508-510
initial hearing, cultural/subcultural
context, 100-101
permanency hearings. *See* Permanency
review hearings, 229-230
parents' counsel's role, 460-462
post-termination, 233
Hearsay
Confrontation Clause issues, 344-345
defined, 336
exceptions. *See* Hearsay exceptions
importance in litigation, 335
objections, 641-643
Hearsay exceptions, 336
catch-all exception, 342-344
diagnosis, statements made for, 342
excited utterances, 340
fabrication, charge of, 338
fresh complaint of rape or sexual
abuse, 341

impeachment evidence
    contradictory testimony, 338
    memory, lapse of, 339
    prior inconsistent statements, 339
    untruthful character, evidence of,
      338-339
  present sense impressions, 339-340
  prior consistent statements, 337-338
  prior inconsistent statements, 337
  impeachment evidence, 339
  residual exception, 342-344
  treatment, statements made for, 342
Higher Education Act, post-secondary
  education loans, grants, and work-study,
  179
Historical antecedents, 115-116. *See also*
  Parens patriae system
  pre-16th century efforts, 116-117
  16th/17th century England, 117-118
    poor persons, 118-120
    wealthy persons, 118
  Colonial America, 120-123
  19th century America, 123
    Ex parte Crouse, 126-127
    Ferrier case, 127-128
    Hewellette case, 128-129
    House of Refuge Movement,
      124-126
    Mary Ellen case, 129-132
    Tardieu's findings, 132
  early 21st century dependency court,
    139-142
  evolving dependency philosophy,
    challenge of, 142
House of Refuge Movement, 124-126
Housing Assistance, Section 8, 178

I

Immigrant status. *See* Special Immigrant
  Juvenile Status (SIJS)
Immunity for reporting maltreatment,
  218-219
Impeachment evidence
  contradictory testimony, 338
  memory, lapse of, 339
  prior inconsistent statements, 339
  untruthful character, evidence of,
    338-339
Imprisoned parents. *See* Incarcerated
  parents

Incarcerated Mothers Law Project, The,
  480
Incarcerated parents
  agency efforts for parental reunifica-
    tion, 471-475
  practice tips
    agency's reasonable efforts toward
      parental reunification, 472-473
    parents' right to participate, 469-
      471
  programs, 479-480
  right to participate, 467-471
  termination of parental rights. *See*
    Termination of parental rights
Incompetent persons. *See* Mental health
Independent Living Program, Title IV-E,
  145
Indian Child Welfare Act (ICWA), 157
  constitutional case law, 205-206
  coverage, 158, 160-161
  evidentiary standards, 159
  jurisdiction, 157-158
  noncompliance with, 160
  notice, 158-159
  placement of children, 160
  standing to intervene, 158
  summary of, 145
Individualized Education Programs (IEPs),
  171-172, 292-294
  implementation of, 296
Individuals with Disabilities Education Act
  (IDEA), 171-172. *See also* Special edu-
  cation services
Intelligence tests, 46-47
Intercountry Adoption Act (IAA), 244
Interethnic Adoption Provisions of the
  Small Business Job Protection Act
  (IEP). *See* MEPA-IEP
Interlocutory orders
  appealable by statute, 382-383
  reviewable as a matter of discretion,
    383
International Child Abduction Database
  (INCADAT), 244
International Child Abduction Remedies
  Act (ICARA), 242
International proceedings, 242-246
Interstate Compact on Adoption and
  Medical Assistance (ICAMA), 237

Interstate Compact on Mental Health
(ICMH), 237
Interstate Compact on the Placement of
Children (ICPC), 237
Interstate proceedings, 237-242
Investigating maltreatment, 219
  by child's attorney, 531
  evidence of maltreatment, 221-222
  parents' counsel, 451-452
  risk assessments, 220-221
  safety assessments, 221
  time for, 219-220
IQ scores, 47

J

Judges
  incarcerated parents, practice tips
    agency efforts for parental reunifi-
    cation, 472, 474
    parents' right to participate, 469-
    470
    termination of parental rights, 478
  judicial notice, 395-396
Judicial notice, 395-396
Jurisdiction
  collateral courts, 235
  dependency court, 113-115, 235
  extraordinary writs, 397
  Indian Child Welfare Act, 157-158
Juvenile court
  confidentiality of proceedings and
    records, 299-304
  dependency's evolution
    delinquency component's trans-
    formation, 135
    within *parens patriae,* 135-138
    founding philosophy, 132-133
    19th century dependency philosophy,
    133-134
Juvenile Justice and Delinquency
  Prevention programs, 180

K

Kidnapping
  Hague Convention on Child
    Abduction, 242-244
  International Child Abduction
    Database, 244
  International Child Abduction
    Remedies Act, 242

Parental Kidnapping Prevention Act,
  167-168
United Nations Protocol to Prevent,
  Suppress and Punish Trafficking in
  Persons, 245-246
Victims of Trafficking and Violence
  Protection Act, 180

L

Lacerations, 19
Language development, 60-61
Leading questions
  child witnesses, 334
  cross examination, 594
  objections, 639
Legal Services for Prisoners with Children
  (LSPC), 480
Living arrangements
  alternate planned permanent living
    arrangement, 108-110, 376-378
  and child well-being, 2-3
Loss, 71

M

Maltreated children
  advocate's role in promoting improve-
    ment, 13
  biology, 84
  circumstances in which maltreatment
    occurs, 79-80
    domestic violence, 81-82
    empathy, lack of, 80-81
    isolation, 82-83
    mental conditions, 82
    postnatal depression, 82
    substance abuse, 82
    "trigger" behaviors, 81
  consequences of maltreatment, 12-13,
    73-74, 85-86
  criminal offenses, 12-13
  developmental level, importance of,
    74-75
  developmental psychopathology, 84
  economic impact, 13
  emotional abuse. *See* Emotional abuse
  foster care children. *See* Foster care
    children
  impact on America, 12-13
  investigating maltreatment. *See*
    Investigating maltreatment

long-term effects, 73-74
minority children, 6-7
neglect. *See* Neglect
parental treatment
  change in parenting capacity,
    measuring, 90-91
  difficult-to-treat parents, 91-92
  effectiveness of, 88-90
  goals, 88
parents' counsel
  emergency removal hearings, 452-
    454
  independent investigation, pretrial,
    451-452
physical abuse. *See* Physical abuse
poor children, 6-7
psychodynamic theory and practice, 83
reporting maltreatment, 216-217
  by nonprofessionals, 218-219
  by professionals, 217-218
sexual abuse. *See* Sexual abuse
social and economic ecology, 83
statistics, 4-6
treatment for, 86-88
Mandamus, writ of, 399
Maternal and Child Health Block Grant,
  179
McKinney-Vento Homeless Assistance Act
  program, 180
Mediation
  agenda setting, 353
  agreement
    building, 353
    writing, 353
  closing, 353
  defined, 350-351
  exchanges, 353
  opening statement, 352
  parents' counsel's role, 454-456
  philosophy, 351
  principles, 351-352
  process of, 352-353
  separate meetings, 353
  uninterrupted time, 352-353
  uses of, 356-357
Medicaid, 175
  benefits, 186
  eligibility, 186

Medical experts
  mental health. *See* Mental health pro-
    fessionals
  testimony. *See* Expert testimony
Medical neglect, 31-32
Mental health, 35-36
  commitment proceedings. *See* Mental
    health commitment proceedings
  evaluations, 40-41
  Interstate Compact on Mental Health,
    237
  parents with diminished capacity. *See*
    Parents' counsel
  professionals. *See* Mental health pro-
    fessionals
  tests. *See* Psychological tests
Mental health commitment proceedings,
  263-264
  child's attorney, 274-275
    advocating child's legal entitlements
      and needed services, 280-282
    as counselor, 275-276
    as negotiator and mediator, 276-
      277
    protecting children's rights within
      commitment facilities, 278-280
    as zealous advocate, 277-278
  Due Process issues, 265-270
  erroneous placement concerns, 264-
    265
  foster care children, 270-271
  state laws, 269-270
  therapeutic jurisprudence considera-
    tions, 271-273
Mental health professionals, 36
  confidentiality, 38
  evaluations, 40-41
  evidentiary privileges, 38
  psychiatrists, 37
  psychologists, 37
  social workers, 38
  testimony. *See* Expert testimony
Mental health tests. *See* Psychological tests
MEPA-IEP, 96, 146
  coverage, 161-162
  enforcement of, 162-163
Millon Adolescent Clinical Inventory
  (MACI), 45
Millon Clinical Multiaxial Inventory, 45

Minnesota Multiphasic Personality Inventory (MMPI), 45
Minority children, 6-7
Motion practice, 225
    exhibits at trial, 629
    objections, 639
Multi-Ethnic Placement Act. *See* MEPA-IEP
Munchausen Syndrome by Proxy, 23, 311-313

N

NACC recommendations
    open court proceedings, 303-304
    representation of children, 647-666
Neglect, 30
    definition, 114
    educational, 33
    emotional. *See* Emotional neglect
    failure to thrive syndrome, 32
    medical, 31-32
    physical. *See* Physical neglect
Neuropsychological tests, 47
Non-adversarial case resolution. *See* Case resolution
Notice of appeal, 384
    appeals as of right, 397

O

Objections, 636-637
    argumentative questions, 639-640
    asked and answered, 640
    authenticity, 644
    best evidence, 644
    character evidence, improper, 643-644
    compound questions, 639
    conditional offers, 638
    decision to object, 637
    evidentiary objections, 640-644
    facts not in evidence, 640
    form, objections as to, 639-640
    foundation, lack of, 641
    hearsay, 641-643
    lack of personal knowledge, 641
    lay opinion, improper, 641
    leading questions, 639
    making and meeting, 637-638
        evidentiary objections, 640-644
        form, objections as to, 639-640
        general rule, 639

motions *in limine,* 639
narrative questions, 640
nonresponsive questions, 640
offers of proof, 638
preservation of error, 638-639
pretrial, 639
privileges, 644
protocol for objecting, 637-638
relevance, 641
settlement offers, 644
speculation, 641
unfair prejudice, 643
vague questions, 639
Offenses. *See* Criminal offenses
Offers of proof, 638
Open court proceedings
    arguments against, 302-303
    benefits of, 300-302
    constitutional case law, 299-300
    NACC's position, 303-304
Organizational resources, 717-719

P

Parens patriae system
    delinquency, transformation of, 135
    dependency's evolution within, 135-138
    19th century America, 123
        Ex parte Crouse, 126-127
        Ferrier case, 127-128
        Hewellette case, 128-129
        House of Refuge Movement, 124-126
        Mary Ellen case, 129-132
        Tardieu's findings, 132
Parental Alienation Syndrome (PAS), 318-320
Parental Kidnapping Prevention Act (PKPA), 167-168
Parent-child relationship
    attachment, 70-72
    evaluations, 41-43
    loss, 71
    reunification with parents
        considerations, 93
        incarcerated parents, 271-275
    separation, 71-72
    termination of. *See* Termination of parental rights
Parent-Child Relationship Inventory, 48
Parenting Stress Index, 48

Parents
attorney for. *See* Parents' counsel
child relationship. *See* Parent-child
relationship
diminished capacity, representing. *See*
Parents' counsel
educational attainment, child well-
being and, 3
foster care. *See* Foster care parents
incarcerated. *See* Incarcerated parents
self-incrimination, right against, 210-
211
termination of rights. *See* Termination
of parental rights
treatment of
change in parenting capacity,
measuring, 90-91
difficult-to-treat parents, 91-92
effectiveness of, 88-90
goals, 88
Parents' counsel, 443-444
adjudications, 456-457
Adoption and Safe Families Act,
effect of, 446-451
alternative dispute resolution, 454-456
appellate practice, 466
cultural/subcultural context, 97
dispositions, 457-460
incarcerated parents, practice tips
agency efforts for parental reunification, 472, 474-475
parents' right to participate, 470
termination of parental rights, 478
mediation, role in, 454-456
parents with diminished capacity,
representing, 481
advocating in and out of court,
490-491
assessing client capacity, 484-486
capacity as a continuum, 480
client confidentiality, maintaining,
489
eliciting the client's position, 489-
490
guardians, appointing, 488-489
Mason case, 481-483
Model Rule 1.14, 483-491
normal client-lawyer relationship,
maintaining, 483-484
protective action, taking, 487-488

permanency hearings, 462-463
responsibilities, 444-446
review hearings, 460-462
termination of parental rights proceedings, 463-466
Parties, 236
extraordinary writs, 398-399
standing. *See* Standing
Peabody Individual Achievement Test-R,
48
Pedophilia, 25-26
Permanency, 363-364
adoption. *See* Adoption
alternate planned permanent living
arrangement, 108-110, 376-378
child's attorney
goal of permanency, 534
identifying needs, 519-520
guardianships
permanent guardianships, 371-375
standby guardianships, 375-376
hearings, 230-232
cultural/subcultural context, 104-
108
parents' counsel's role, 462-463
options, principles for, 364-365
parental rights
re-establishing after termination,
378-379
termination of. *See* Termination of
parental rights
Personality tests, 45
Persuasive storytelling. *See* Trial(s)
Physical abuse, 15-16
abdominal injuries, 21-22
bruises, 17-19
burns, 19-21
definition, 114
during various stages of development,
62-64, 66-70
fractures, 16-17
head trauma, 22-23
lacerations, 19
medical ramifications, 24
Munchausen by proxy syndrome, 23
thoracic injuries, 21-22
Physical development, 56-57
Physical neglect, 30-31
during various stages of development,
62-65

Placement of children
  adoption. *See* Adoption
  alternate permanent planned living
    arrangement (APPLA), 376-378
  considerations, 93
  disposition order, 226-228
  foster care. *See* Foster care
  Indian Child Welfare Act, 160
  Interstate Compact on the Placement
    of Children, 237
  mental health commitment. *See* Mental
    health commitment proceedings
  permanent guardianships, 371-375
  standby guardianships, 375-376
Poor persons
  16th/17th century England, 118-120
  maltreatment children, 6-7
  well-being of child, 4
Population statistics, 1-2
Posttraumatic Stress Disorder (PTSD),
  314-315
  in litigation, 315-317
Preferences of child
  versus "best interests," 498-500
  determining, 533-534
  importance of, 511-513
Prejudicial error, 388-389
Present sense impressions, 339-340
Preservation of error, 385, 638-639
Pretrial discovery, 225
Prior consistent statements, 337-338
Prior inconsistent statements, 337
  impeachment evidence, 339
Prisoner-parents. *See* Incarcerated parents
Privileges, 320-321
  child's attorney-client privilege, 526-
    527
  mental health professional-client, 38
  objections, 644
Professionals
  evaluations. *See* Evaluations
  maltreatment reporting, 217-218
  mental health. *See* Mental health pro-
    fessionals
  testimony. *See* Expert testimony
Prohibition, writ of, 399
Projective tests, 45-46
Promoting Safe and Stable Families
  Program (PSSF), 146, 147
Protective orders, 252

Psychiatrists, 37. *See also* Mental health
  professionals
Psychodynamic theory and practice, 83
Psychological tests, 43-44
  achievement tests, 47-48
  checklists and inventories, 48
  developmental tests, 46-47
  intelligence tests, 46-47
  interpreting results, 48-49
  neuropsychological tests, 47
  personality tests, 45
  projective tests, 45-46
  psychometric tests, 44-45
  scoring, 48-49
Psychologists, 37. *See also* Mental health
  professionals
Psychometric tests, 44-45
Putative fathers, 192-196

R

Rape Trauma Syndrome, 308
Real evidence, 626
Refreshing recollection, 567
Removal of child
  emergency removal. *See* Emergency
    removal/detention
  foster care. *See* Foster care
Reporting maltreatment, 216-217
  false or malicious reports, 219
  by nonprofessionals, 218-219
  by professionals, 217-218
Respondents' counsel. *See* Parents' counsel
Reunification with parents
  considerations, 93
  incarcerated parents, 271-275
Review hearings, 229-230
  parents' counsel's role, 460-462
  post-termination, 233
Risk assessments, 220-221
Rorschach Inkblot Technique, 45-46

S

"Safe Haven," 148
Safety assessments, 221
Safety/well-being of child
  child's attorney's role, 535
  indicators of, 2-4
  and non-adversarial case resolution,
    361-362
School Breakfast program, 178

School Lunch program, 178

Section 8 Housing Assistance, 178

Self-incrimination, parent's right against, 210-211

Sentence Completion Tests, 46

Separation from parents, 71-72

Sexual abuse, 24
  Child Sexual Abuse Accommodation Syndrome, 308-309, 318
  definition, 114
  diagnosing, 27-28
  during various stages of development, 66, 68
  evaluations, 49-51
  "fresh complaint" evidence, 341
  intrafamilial, 24-25
  pedophilia, 25-26

Shaken Baby Syndrome, 313-314

Siblings
  association, maintenance of, 529-530
  child's attorney representation of, 521-523
    confidentiality concerns, 523-524
    sibling association, maintenance of, 529-530
    waiver of conflict, 524

Social and economic ecology, 83

Social and emotional development, 61-62
  attachment, 70-72
  autonomy *versus* shame and guilt, 63-65
  identity *versus* role confusion, 68-70
  industry *versus* inferiority, 66-68
  initiative *versus* self-doubt, 65-67
  loss, 71-72
  separation, 71-72
  trust *versus* mistrust, 62-63

Social Security Act, Titles IV-B and IV-E, 151

Social Services Block Grants (SSBG), 145, 175, 179

Social workers, 38. *See also* Mental health professionals
  agency counsel relationship. *See* Agency counsel

Special education services
  decision makers
    surrogate parents, *below*
    who can act as a parent, 286-287
  eligibility meeting, 289-291

identifying exceptional children
  evaluations, 284-286
  long disability, child identified with, 295
  signs to look for, 284

IEP meeting, 294-295

IEPs, 171-172, 292-294
  implementation of, 296

IEP team, 291-292
  disagreements with decisions of, handling, 296-297

long disability, child identified with, 295

monitoring student's progress, 296

surrogate parents
  foster care children, appointment for, 287-288
  foster parents, 287-289
  who can act as, 286-287

Special Immigrant Juvenile Status (SIJS), 163-164, 260-261
  applications
    benefits and risks, 261
    denial, risk of, 262
    procedure, 261-262
    time limits, 262
  denial, risk of, 262
  requirements for, 261
  technical assistance, 262
  what is, 261

Special Milk program, 178

Special Supplemental Nutrition Program for Women, Infants, and Children (WIC), 178

Spousal privileges, 321

Standby guardianships, 375-376

Standing, 236
  appellate practice, 384-385
  Indian Child Welfare Act, 158

Stanford Achievement Test (SAT-10), 48

State agencies' constitutional duties, 201-204

State Children's Health Insurance Program (SCHIP), 176-177

Status offenses, 247-248

Stay requests. *See* Appellate practice

Subcultural context. *See* Cultural/subcultural context

Substance abuse
  maltreatment circumstances, 82
  treatment records, access to, 168-169

Substance Abuse and Mental Health Services Grants, 179
Summer Food program, 178
Supplemental Security Income (SSI), 177
Syndrome evidence, 307-309
    Acute Distress Disorder, 317
    Battered Child Syndrome, 308, 309-310
    Battering Parent Syndrome, 311
    Child Sexual Abuse Accommodation Syndrome, 308-309, 318
    Munchausen Syndrome by Proxy, 23, 311-313
    Parental Alienation Syndrome, 318-320
    Posttraumatic Stress Disorder, 314-315
        in litigation, 315-317
    Rape Trauma Syndrome, 308
    Shaken Baby Syndrome, 313-314

T

Temporary Assistance for Needy Families (TANF), 146
    statutory requirements, 163-164
    summary of, 146, 175
Termination of parental rights, 232-233
    agency counsel-caseworker protocol, 440
    child's attorney's role, 521
    considerations, 93
    constitutional case law, 197-199
    incarcerated parents
        crime, nature of, 477
        incarceration as a ground or factor, 475-476
        length of incarceration, 476-477
        practice tips, 478-479
        right to participate, 468-469
    parents' counsel's role, 463-465
    post-termination review hearings, 233
    re-establishing parental rights, 378-379
Testimony. *See* Witnesses and testimony
Thematic Apperception Test (TAT), 46
Thoracic injuries, 21-22
Trafficking Victims Protection Act (TVPA), 245
Trial(s)
    cross examination. *See* Cross examination

direct examination. *See* Direct examination
ethics of persuasive storytelling, 548
    assuming you do not know the truth, 548-550
    assuming you "know" the truth, 548
    criminal cases, 550
evidence. *See* Evidence
exhibits. *See* Exhibits at trial
expert witnesses. *See* Expert testimony
persuasive trial story
    assuming you do not know the truth, 548-550
    assuming you "know" the truth, 548
    case-in-chief, planning, 552-554
    criminal cases, 550
    ethics of, 548-550
    final argument, planning, 552
    preparation of, 550-555
    reevaluating, importance of, 555
    sample story, planning, 546-548
    theme development, 551-552
    theory development, 551
storytelling
    persuasive. persuasive trial story, *above*
    trials as stories, 545-546
witnesses. *See* Witnesses and testimony

U

Uniform Child Custody Jurisdiction and Enforcement Act (UCCJEA), 166-167, 238-240
Uniform Child Witness Testimony by Alternative Methods Act (UCWTA-MA), 240-242
United Nations Protocol to Prevent, Suppress and Punish Trafficking in Persons, 245-246

V

Victims of Child Abuse Act (VOCA), 148
Victims of Trafficking and Violence Protection Act, 180
Violence Against Women Act (VAWA), 180

Visitation proceedings. *See* Divorce, child custody, and visitation proceedings
Voluntary relinquishment counseling, 355-356

W

Wechsler Adult Intelligence Scale-III (WAIS-III), 47
Wechsler Intelligence Scale for Children-IV (WISC-IV), 47
Wechsler Preschool and Primary Scale of Intelligence-III (WPPSI-III), 47
Well-being of child
    child's attorney's role, 535
    indicators of, 2-4
    and non-adversarial case resolution, 361-362
Whiplash Shaken Infant Syndrome, 313-314
Wide Range Achievement Test-III (WRAT-III), 48

Witnesses and testimony
    child witnesses. *See* Child witnesses
    competency to testify
        child witnesses. *See* Child witnesses
        direct examination, 565
    cross examination. *See* Cross examination
    deciding whom to call, 553-554
    direct examination. *See* Direct examination
    evaluation of witnesses, 553
    experts. *See* Expert testimony
    foundation, establishing. *See* Foundation evidence
    hearsay. *See* Hearsay
    objections. *See* Objections
    potential witnesses, considering, 552-553
    privileges. *See* Privileges
Woodcock-Johnson III Complete Battery, 48
Workforce Investment Act, 180